GUTS AND GLORY
The Rise and Fall of Oliver North

Also by Ben Bradlee, Jr.

The Ambush Murders

Prophet of Blood
(with Dale Van Atta)

GUTS AND

GLORY The Rise and Fall of Oliver North

By BEN BRADLEE, JR.

DONALD I. FINE, INC.   New York

For Martha and Greta

COPYRIGHT ©1988 BY BEN BRADLEE, JR.

ALL RIGHTS RESERVED, INCLUDING THE RIGHT OF REPRODUCTION IN WHOLE OR IN PART IN ANY FORM. PUBLISHED IN THE UNITED STATES OF AMERICA BY DONALD I. FINE, INC. AND IN CANADA BY GENERAL PUBLISHING COMPANY LIMITED.

LIBRARY OF CONGRESS CATALOGING-IN-PUBLICATION DATA

BRADLEE, BEN.
  GUTS AND GLORY .
  INCLUDES INDEX.
  1. NORTH, OLIVER. 2. MARINES—UNITED STATES—
BIOGRAPHY. 3. UNITED STATES. MARINE CORPS—BIOGRAPHY.
4. IRAN-CONTRA AFFAIR, 1985–   . I. TITLE.
VE25.N67B76 1988   359.9'6'0924 [B] 87-46034
ISBN 1-55611-053-7 (ALK. PAPER)

MANUFACTURED IN THE UNITED STATES OF AMERICA

10 9 8 7 6 5 4 3 2 1

CONTENTS

ACKNOWLEDGMENTS

I AM grateful to many people who helped and encouraged me to write this book.

Boston *Globe* editor Jack Driscoll enthusiastically and generously granted me a leave of absence from the newspaper to undertake the project starting in March of 1987. Executive Editor Ben Taylor indulged me and graciously extended the leave a month or two when I was running a little late. My dear friend Steve Kurkjian, the dean of all Washington bureau chiefs, cheerfully provided me with a desk and every conceivable kind of support whenever I came to Washington, though he was a little slow in reading the galleys. Cynthia Taylor, who really runs the bureau, was extraordinarily helpful and patient with Xeroxing and other logistical help. Thanks also to the other members of the bureau for their hospitality.

The great Diletta LaCortiglia also indulged me back at The *Globe* in Boston. Thanks also to Rose Devine, Barbara McDonough and the other ladies of the message center; to Charley Liftman for not logging me off; to Donna Buonopane and Shirley Jobe in the library and a special thanks to Richard Pennington, who provided me with the world's definitive Ollie North clip file.

I discovered the wonders of research help on this book through the efforts of Ellen Mahoney, Eve Porter, and John Maddock. But indispensable to me for six months was Sharon Felzer who worked cheerfully, long and hard, and conducted scores of substantive interviews—particularly with North's friends and associates at Annapolis and the Marine Corps.

The National Security Archive in Washington is almost like having another researcher. Thanks to Scott Armstrong, Tom Blanton, Jeff Nason, and especially to Peter Kornbluh for his insights into Spitz Channell and the Contra fundraising network. All these people are experts at what they do and are an invaluable resource to all reporters.

The final report of the congressional Iran-Contra committees was a great help to me, as were the numerous depositions of witnesses which the committees obtained, along with other primary source documents— much of which would likely have been unavailable to a reporter working alone.

I would like to give special thanks to Robert McFarlane, Richard Secord and Fawn Hall—three of the key Iran-Contra players who generously spent many hours with me under trying circumstances. Still, they willingly contributed their insights and thereby enhanced the book.

A special thanks also to Art Harris of the Washington *Post*, who wrote the definitive early profile of North, and willingly shared his thoughts and work product with me.

For their time, their insights, their views, their generousity and/or their friendship, I would also like to thank: Richard Armitage, Hugh Aynesworth, Michael Barnes, Sidney Blumenthal, Peter Braestrup, Joel Brinkley, Representative Jack Brooks, Plato Cacheris, Kurt Campbell, Lynore Carnes, Richard Cohen, George Coleman, Charles Cooper, Arnaud deBorchgrave, Jim Dickenson, Tony Dolan, Representative Bob Dornan, John Dowd, Bob Dutton, Audrey Eisman, Joe Elbert, David Evans, Mark Feldstein, Donald Fine, Roger Fontaine, Fred Francis, Leonard Garment, Denzil Garrison, David Greenway, Keith Haines, David Halberstam, David Halevy, Sandy Hawes, Michael Hedges, Randy Herrod, Sy Hersh, David Ignatius, Representative Ed Jenkins, General P. X. Kelley, Charlie Kenney, Senator John Kerry, Janet Knott, Mike Kranish, Arthur Liman, Neil Livingstone, Peter Maas, Karen McKay, Andy Messing, Senator George Mitchell, Don Moore, Greg Mowry, John Nields, David Nyhan, Stan Ostazeski, Tom Palmer, Robert Parry, Patricia Peck, Ross Perot, Adam Pertman, Mike Pilgrim, Walter Pincus, John Premack, David Rogers, Senator Warren Rudman, William Safire, Richard Sandza, Daniel Schorr, Peter Dale Scott, Tom Shales, Jay Sharbutt, Uri Simhoni, John Sinclair, Emerson Smith, Bill Snead, Jim Thistle, Roger Vergnes, Jack Wheeler, Tom Winship, Bob Woodward, Susan Wornick and Lance Zellers. My apologies to anyone I've forgotten.

I'd also like to thank my mother and stepfather, Jean and Bill Haussermann, for their love, support and encouragement over the past year or so. Likewise to my father, Ben Bradlee, Sr., and to Sally Quinn for their generous hospitality, help, encouragement and constructive criticism.

My wife Martha also supported and encouraged me throughout the year, and read the manuscript carefully, thoughtfully and skillfully—for all of which I am grateful. Working at home most of the time, I got to see more of my fabulous daughter Greta than I ever have, and we had lots of moments together that I'll always remember.

FOREWORD

THIS book is based on three-hundred-and-twelve interviews and the wealth of documents that have attended the Iran-contra case, including: the Tower Commission report; the treasure trove of internal National Security Council messages which a Tower panel computer wizard was able to coax from the White House computer system; the transcripts of the congressional hearings in the summer of 1987; the final report of the Iran-contra committees and the numerous supporting documents that the committees released during and after the hearings.

The three-hundred-and-twelve interviews represent conversations with almost all the key people who crossed Oliver North's path at various stages of his life, from childhood, to Annapolis, to Vietnam, through the Marine Corps and the White House. Many of the most important sources were interviewed several times. All but a handful spoke on the record.

North himself declined several requests for interviews, and members of his immediate family, acting at North's request, also declined to be interviewed. I did meet with North informally for about ten minutes outside a restaurant in suburban Virginia on July 26, 1987, to introduce myself and to press my case for a formal interview. North was polite and friendly, but nothing of substance was exchanged.

All the quotes in the book come either from the interviews which I and my researchers conducted; from various documents; from transcripts of testimony at the hearings; or from sections of the Tower report or the final report of the congressional Iran-Contra committees.

In my account of the trip to Tehran by North and former National Security Advisor Robert McFarlane, the dialogue at the meetings between the Americans and the Iranians was taken from notes taken by some of the American principals and from transcripts of the sessions reproduced in the Tower Commission report. The Iran-contra committees had access to the tapes of meetings between the American and the Iranian delegations in Europe and Washington, and they published excerpts of the transcripts in their final report. In my accounts of those meetings, I drew from the report to recreate dialogue as well.

In Chapter One, my account of North's end of the telephone conversation between himself and President Ronald Reagan on November 25, 1986, comes from Richard Secord, who was in the room with North at the time. The President's comments come from accounts of the conversation that North gave several people, some of which were published in the press.

All the names in the book are real, except for the two agents of the federal Drug Enforcement Administration in the "Ransom" chapter, to whom I gave pseudonyms.

—*BEN BRADLEE, JR.*
April, 1988

"NATIONAL HERO"

J UST before seven o'clock on the morning of November 25, 1986, a sleek black limousine carrying the attorney general of the United States, Edwin Meese, pulled up in front of the home of CIA Director William Casey in a fashionable section of northwest Washington. It was two days before Thanksgiving and the dawn of what would become perhaps the most momentous day of the Reagan Administration.

Three weeks earlier on November 4, Ronald Reagan's six-year stranglehold on the soul of the body politic had ended in a general election that saw the Republicans lose control of the Senate to the Democrats. The administration's dramatic eleventh-hour effort to salvage the election through the November 2 release of David Jacobsen, one of the American hostages being held in Beirut, had been more than negated the following day when a Lebanese magazine revealed that the United States had been selling arms and ammunition to Iran, and that former National Security Advisor Robert McFarlane had led a high-level White House delegation on a secret trip to Tehran.

The American press, beaten on a seismic story by an obscure Middle East weekly and until then largely smitten by Reagan's aura of invincibility, smelled blood and got on the case in earnest. Another American president had been tripped up by the Ayatollah, but this president—Ronald Reagan, who had placed Iran on an arms-embargo list, launched a major effort to persuade western allies not to sell arms to Iran, called Iran a leading sponsor of terrorism, pledged never to make concessions to terrorists and saved some of his most cutting rhetoric for Tehran, including calling it "Murder Incorporated"? It couldn't be.

From the White House there had been great confusion on how to react in the days after the story broke.

Reagan himself stonewalled, bobbed and weaved. At first he refused to disclose any details of U.S. dealings with Iran, saying no laws had been broken. Then he tried to couch the initiative as part of a strategic effort to reach alleged moderates in a post-Khomeini Iran, but conceded Tehran was also to have used its influence with radical Lebanese Shiites to release the American citizens they had kidnapped in Beirut. He said that no more than one plane load of defensive weaponry had been sent to Tehran, but actually there had been several planeloads of weapons and spare parts that could be used for offense or defense. Then, at a nationally televised press conference Reagan had denied that Israel participated in the arms shipments, but the White House was forced to put out a hasty correction, conceding that "there was a third country involved in our secret project with Iran."

Within the administration there had also been much finger-pointing and little agreement on how to handle the mounting crisis. Part of the problem was that beyond knowing that the operation had been run by the National Security Council—first under McFarlane and then by his successor, Adm. John Poindexter—even people at the most senior levels of the White House were not sure who had done what in the Iran initiative. So on November 21 Meese had resolved to conduct a "fact-finding inquiry."

This three-day investigation, while less than exhaustive, did uncover an explosive piece of evidence that added a major new dimension to the Iran affair. Some of Meese's aides, while searching through a safe belonging to Marine Lt. Col. Oliver North, a top aide to Poindexter, had discovered a memorandum indicating that millions of dollars from the profits of the Iran arms sales had been diverted to the Contras—the rebels fighting to topple the Sandinistas in Nicaragua.

Meese had informed the president of this development late the afternoon of November 24 in a meeting also attended by White House Chief of Staff Donald Regan. Meese told the president that the diversion had been carried out by North, but that Poindexter had admitted knowing of it and allowing it to happen. Poindexter was offering to resign.

Regan immediately began thinking about damage control. First of all, they couldn't sit on this long. The president would have to hold a press conference to make the general announcement, then quickly turn the proceedings over to Meese, who could handle the details. They should appoint an independent commission to conduct an investigation. And Poindexter would have to go. The president, reportedly stunned and crestfallen, suggested they all sleep on it overnight and take action the next day.

Now, Meese had come to Casey's house after receiving a 6:30 A.M. call from the CIA director asking if he could stop by on his way to work. Casey, who was involved up to his eyeballs in both the Iran and Contra operations, had delivered one of his typically opaque briefings to the congressional intelligence committees on the Iran arms sales four days earlier. But now the diversion had been uncovered and he wanted to know what Meese's plan was. Poindexter would resign, the attorney general responded, and the president was scheduled to have a press conference that day.

Regan called Meese at Casey's house to make sure the attorney general was prepared for the press conference scheduled for later that morning. Regan also said he planned to meet first thing with Poindexter to take him up on his offer to resign. Meese decided he should inform the admiral first. So he called Poindexter, who answered the phone in his chauffeur-driven car just as it was pulling into the southwest gate of the White House. Meese asked if Poindexter could stop by and see him at the Justice Department.

In his office, Meese said the time had come for the admiral to resign. He was sorry but it had to be. Stoical, Poindexter said he understood and would be prepared to tell the president personally at the regular 9:30 national security briefing that morning. Meese mentioned that he didn't think North had done anything illegal, and they talked briefly about North's being transferred back to the Marine Corps.

Poindexter returned to his office at the White House and ordered some breakfast. As he sat eating from a tray at a conference table, Regan walked in, steaming.

"What's going on, John?" the chief of staff demanded. "What the hell happened here?"

Poindexter, deliberate and seemingly unruffled, adjusted his glasses, then dabbed at his mouth with a napkin. "Well," he said, "I guess I should have looked into it more, but I didn't. I knew that Ollie was up to something, but I didn't know what. I just didn't look into it."

"Why not? What the hell, you're a vice-admiral. What's going on?"

"That damn Tip O'Neill," Poindexter replied. "The way he's jerking the Contras around, I was just so disgusted . . ."

"Well, John," said Regan, "I think when you go in to see the president at 9:30 you better make sure you have your resignation with you."

"I will," said Poindexter.

Regan left without asking Poindexter if he had ever told the president of the diversion.

At the appointed hour the admiral walked into the Oval Office where the president was waiting for him, along with Vice-President George Bush, Meese and Regan. It was an awkward but dramatic moment, and the room fell silent in anticipation of Poindexter doing his duty and walking the plank. Reagan, who hated to fire anyone and who had no stomach for confrontation, waited for Poindexter to convene the proceedings and hang himself.

"Mr. President," the National Security Advisor obliged, "I assume that you are aware of the paper that Ed Meese has found that reveals a plan to transfer funds to the Contras. I was generally aware of that plan, and I would like to submit my resignation to give you the necessary latitude to do whatever you need to do." Poindexter decided not to acknowledge that he had approved the diversion.

"Well, John," the president responded, "it's really a shame that it had to end this way, and what you're doing is in the great tradition of a naval officer accepting responsibility."

Poindexter stood up and shook hands with everyone in the room, then walked out. When he returned to his office he let it be known that he had resigned and that an announcement would be forthcoming in a few hours. He called North and they discussed the likely ramifications of the diversion disclosure. North's notes of the conversation contain a suggestion to "put it off on Ghorbanifar"—a reference to Manucher Ghorbanifar, the Iranian arms dealer who had acted as the middleman between Washington and Tehran in the arms sales.

Back in the Oval Office, the president, Bush, Meese and Regan discussed North's fate. It was agreed that he should be immediately reassigned to the Marine Corps. Unlike Poindexter, North wasn't a presidential appointee, so a resignation would not be necessary. He could just be given his orders.

Reagan informed other key members of his cabinet of the morning's developments and of his pending press conference. Then, from 11:00 until noon, congressional leaders were called in for a briefing. Secretary of State George Shultz, Casey, Meese and

Regan flanked the president as he met with the senators and congressmen. Meese did most of the talking on behalf of the administration.

The attorney general depicted North as the driving force behind the diversion but said Poindexter had known of the general outlines of the plan and had therefore volunteered to resign. House Speaker Jim Wright asked Casey if he had known of the diversion. The CIA director lied and replied that he had not.

Outside Washington in suburban Tyson's Corner, Richard Secord was beside himself. A retired air-force major general with extensive experience in covert operations, Secord had been recruited by North and Casey to be the private-sector commercial cutout that disguised the administration's hand in end-running congressional prohibitions on official support for the Contras from 1984 to 1986, and in implementing the Iran initiative during the past year. Secord and his Iranian-born business partner, Albert Hakim, had created an elaborate international network of corporate shells to hide Washington's role, and all the money to support both initiatives had flowed through them. Millions of dollars in commissions remained in their Swiss bank account.

Now Secord saw it all unraveling and was powerless to do anything about it. He had become involved, he says, to help his country and to make a profit. But after a while, he said he decided to forswear the millions of dollars that were coming his way from the Iran-Contra affair because he had wanted to return to government. He feared that the specter of his making a huge profit out of the deals would cause perception problems, conflict-of-interest problems. He already had enough worries about his image, having resigned from the air force in 1983 under a cloud because of his association with Edwin Wilson, the renegade former CIA agent convicted of running guns and explosives to Libya.

The job Secord wanted was deputy director of the CIA, in charge of covert operations. Being head of the clandestine services would be a natural for him. He was a can-do superpatriot who had contempt for bureaucrats and the post-Watergate obsession with process that had, he and others felt, demoralized the agency and reduced it largely to shuffling paper. A veteran combat pilot, Secord had helped run the CIA's secret war in Laos during the agency's salad days from 1966 to 1968. He wanted to finish the job Casey had started in unleashing the company, restoring its esprit de corps, its sense of mission and greatness. He had hoped the Iran-

Contra affair would be his ticket back to a prime spot in government. Now he could see it all going down the tubes.

There was no need for this. The White House was handling it all
wrong. They were panicking. It was that gutless Ed Meese who
was chiefly to blame, he thought. And Reagan didn't have the
strength of his convictions to stand up and do the right thing either.
On Iran, at least, Secord had been telling North since the summer
that the administration should stage a preemptive strike and announce what it had been doing before everything leaked. Take the
high road and put the proper spin on it. It was only responsible to
contact moderates in a government that would soon be in turmoil
after the death of Khomeini. Iran was one of the most strategically
important countries in the world, a country where the U.S. had
absolutely nothing going, and where the Soviets were primed to
make a move . . . But they hadn't taken his advice, and now look
what was happening.

"When you've got a dolt like Meese over there rumbling around
breaking china, what are you gonna do?" Secord recalls. "Here is
the real tragedy of it all. You've got this fool, Meese. He jumps into
the pool for an over-the-weekend inquiry, comes up with a piece of
paper, panics, says 'Oh my God, it's the son of Watergate. They'll
impeach the president.' Doesn't even talk to the principals."

In a last-ditch effort to head off Meese, Secord had had his lawyer, Tom Green, contact William Bradford Reynolds, the assistant
attorney general in charge of the Justice Department's Civil Rights
Division. Green and Reynolds were old friends. On November 24,
the previous day, Green had met with Reynolds and another Meese
aide, Charles Cooper. Green, who at Secord's urging was also informally representing North at the time, had tried to disclose
enough of what North and Secord had been doing to make it clear
to the men from Justice that Meese should not do anything hasty.
Green cast Hakim as the heavy, erroneously telling Reynolds and
Cooper that it had been the Iranian who had come up with the
diversion idea, but that in any case no laws had been broken because the money in question did not belong to the United States.
To go public with this now would risk the lives of the hostages and
of the Iranian intermediaries, Green warned. He characterized
North as "your ultimate Marine [who] wants to step forward and
take the spears in his own chest."

Late the morning of November 25, Secord called North. He had
heard that both North and Poindexter were resigning. North confirmed that Poindexter had resigned, and said he felt that was a

mistake. He agreed with Secord that the admiral should have hung in there and resisted any attempt to oust him. North said he had submitted his own resignation and was prepared to take the fall. Secord said no one should resign. They should all fight.

Then Secord called Poindexter. "They wouldn't put me through at first but I raised Cain with a few aides," he remembers. "John finally came on the line. We had a short conversation. I said, 'What in the name of God is going on down there? Have you idiots lost your goddamn mind? You don't desert and face the enemy. Let's stand in there and fight!' He said, 'Dick, it's too late. I've already talked to the old man. It has to be this way. The real tragedy is that people like you will suffer.'

"He was giving me a lot of platitudes... I told Poindexter I demanded to see the president. He said it was too late. They'd built a wall around him... I tried to argue and was unsuccessful."

At noon, a grim-faced Reagan appeared before the White House press corps.

"Last Friday," he began, "after becoming concerned whether my national security apparatus had provided me with... a complete factual record with respect to the implementation of my policy toward Iran, I directed the attorney general to undertake a review of this matter over the weekend and report to me on Monday. And yesterday, Secretary Meese provided me and the White House chief of staff with a report on his preliminary findings. And this report led me to conclude that I was not fully informed on the nature of one of the activities undertaken in connection with this initiative. This action raises serious questions of propriety."

The president said he had briefed congressional leaders and was appointing a commission to review the role and procedures of the National Security Council. Meanwhile, the Justice Department was continuing its investigation.

"Although not directly involved, Vice-Admiral John Poindexter has asked to be relieved of his assignment as assistant to the president for national security affairs and to return to another assignment in the navy," Reagan continued. "Lieutenant Colonel Oliver North has been relieved of his duties on the National Security Council staff."

In his office next door at the old Executive Office Building, North sat in disbelief as he watched his commander-in-chief on television utter that last sentence. *Relieved of his duties?* No one had told him anything about being fired. Nobody had given him a heads-up. He had done the honorable thing and offered to resign, fully expecting that he would be taken up on that offer. He had long ago told Poindexter, Casey and others that he was ready to take the fall. He had known this day would come. But being fired was never part of the deal.

North began to reorient his frame of reference away from knee-jerk loyalty to the administration as he continued to watch the press conference and tried to fathom what was happening to him. His fate was really a matter of semantics. He was going back to the Marine Corps in any case. He was being reassigned. Yet Reagan had chosen to say he was being "relieved of his duties." They needed a pound of flesh, and he was it. Poindexter had offered to resign, but that apparently wasn't enough. They needed to say they had fired somebody.

He heard Reagan continue: "I am deeply troubled that the implementation of a policy aimed at resolving a truly tragic situation in the Middle East has resulted in such controversy. As I've stated previously, I believe our policy goals toward Iran were well founded. However, the information brought to my attention yesterday convinced me that in one aspect, implementation of that policy was seriously flawed. While I cannot reverse what has happened, I am initiating steps, including those I've announced today, to insure that the implementation of all future foreign and national security policy initiatives will proceed only in accordance with my authorization. Over the past six years, we've realized many foreign-policy goals. I believe we can yet achieve, and I intend to pursue, the objectives on which we all agree—a safer, more secure and stable world."

Reagan tried to turn the floor over to Meese but was immediately bombarded by questions from the assembled press.

"What was the flaw?"

"Do you still maintain you didn't make a mistake, Mr. President?"

"Hold it," said Reagan to no avail.

"Did you make a mistake in sending arms to Tehran, sir?"

"Is anyone else going to be let go, sir?"

"What about Secretary Shultz, Mr. President?

"Is Shultz going to stay, sir?"

"And who is going to run national security?"

"Why don't you say what the flaw is?"

North looked at this spectacle in disgust. The reporters were swarming around Reagan like vultures. They had no respect. They had accumulated an inordinate amount of power in this country now, and they couldn't be trusted with it. Most of them had a blatant liberal bias. Most of them had never fought for their country. They were cynical elitists who seemed to scorn most of the things he held dear: God, the flag, the armed services, the role of the United States in making the world more free.

Meese finally gained control of the proceedings and quickly got to the point: "What is involved is that in the course of the arms transfers—which involved the United States providing the arms to Israel, and Israel in turn transferring the arms, in effect selling the arms to representatives of Iran—certain monies which were received in the transaction between representatives of Israel and representatives of Iran were taken and made available to the forces in Central America, which are opposing the Sandinista government there."

That was it. The diversion. Now it was public. A few of the people who had gathered in the office to watch the press conference with North glanced over at him to gauge his reaction. There was Fawn Hall, his striking blonde secretary, fiercely loyal and mercurial, who had been sobbing off and on since learning that her boss had been fired; Robert Earl, another Marine lieutenant colonel who had a desk upstairs in North's office suite and assisted Ollie on terrorism issues; and Bill Kernan, a retired Marine buddy of North who had happened to drop in.

Craig Coy, a Coast Guard commander who also worked on terrorism and had a desk next to Earl's, was watching the press conference on his TV upstairs. Fascinated by what Meese had just said about the diversion, Coy bounded downstairs and burst into North's office and put it right on Ollie: "What was that all about?" he asked.

But North was now in his own world. He shrugged his shoulders and said nothing, making it clear he didn't want to talk. Coy ran back upstairs to see what the next bombshell was going to be.

Meese put the amount of money diverted to the Contras as between $10 million and $30 million. He said "the only person in the United States government that knew precisely about this, the only person, was Lieutenant Colonel North." Then, asked by one reporter if North had committed a crime, Meese replied: "We are presently looking into the legal aspects of it as to whether there's any criminality involved. We're also looking precisely at his involvement and what he did, so that the conclusion as to whether there's any criminal acts involved is still under inquiry by us."

North absorbed that with even more difficulty than he did the news about being fired. First he was unceremoniously sacked, not merely reassigned, and now he was to be the target of a criminal investigation? Could this really be happening? Did anyone seriously believe that a Marine lieutenant colonel, hotshot or not, would even consider making the sort of moves he had made over the last three years without keeping his superiors informed every step of the way? Did Meese seriously mean to say that he might be prosecuted for conducting top-secret operations in the name of national security?

North had been ready to take the fall, but he would not be a criminal scapegoat. He would draw the line there. Whereas just days before he had been shredding quantities of documents in order to keep the operations from being revealed, now he looked around his office and began to gather up whatever documents he could find to take home with him, including the daily notebooks he had kept. Things were different now. He was going to have to protect himself.

Even before the Meese press conference was over, Tom Green, Secord's lawyer, who had been informally advising Ollie as well, appeared. North shooed the others out of his office so he could confer privately with Green.

Soon Secord called, demanding that he, North and Green get together immediately to confer. Secord said they couldn't meet at his office. Reporters were already starting to call. He would rent a room at the Sheraton Hotel in Tyson's Corner.

Secord and Green were already there when North arrived a few hours later. "Ollie always portrayed an enthusiasm and fighting spirit," Secord recalls. "He wasn't as dejected as I was...I was attacking Meese because I could see it better than Ollie did. I was more experienced...I could see the forest for the trees better. I can recall very few days when I felt worse. North said he'd seen a lot of darker days. But I can't recall a darker day. To me the sense of crushing defeat and the blizzard of details being revealed in statements by the attorney general...was just a crushing blow. And the fact that the president didn't step up to this thing was another crushing blow...Where did this guy Meese ride in from, for God's sake? Where's the president? They built a Chinese wall around the president...

"Ollie knew Green was my lawyer all along. Technically, he became Ollie's lawyer then, but the first thing Green said to North was, 'We gotta get you a lawyer.' But you just don't run to the street and flag down a lawyer. He knew Ollie didn't have any money. The next day he introduced Ollie to Brendan Sullivan...That afternoon...Green was trying to get the story, like any lawyer would do. He was starting to think like a defense lawyer. He recognized the seriousness. Most of our time was spent trying to fill his computer."

Around mid-afternoon the phone rang. Secord answered. It was Vice-President Bush calling for North. Bush liked North. They had worked together on terrorism and he wanted to say how sorry he was. "Well, sir, it's very kind of you to call," North said. "I appreciate that. Sorry it had to end this way."

Not long afterward Fawn Hall called saying that now President Reagan wanted to speak with North too. Should she give the Oval Office the number of the hotel? North may just have been fired, but he wasn't about to say no to the president of the United States. He was still the commander-in-chief. Any thoughts of anger and resentment toward Reagan that North may have developed in the last few hours immediately evaporated as he waited for the phone call to come through.

When it did, he was actually standing at attention.

"Ollie?"

"Yes, Mr. President!" North's chest was puffed forward.

"I just wanted to say I'm sorry the way things turned out."

"I understand, sir. I have nothing but the highest regard for you."

"This whole affair"—Reagan paused, speaking of the diversion—"I...I just didn't know."

"I'm sorry this has brought you under a cloud," said North. "I just wanted to serve you, Mr. President."

"You have. You've served the country remarkably, Ollie. You're a national hero."

Secord, finally realizing that the president of the United States was on the line, wanted to seize the opportunity to give Reagan a piece of his mind. "Let me have the phone!" he said to North.

But Ollie was breathing rarified air and wasn't about to be disturbed. He held up his hand, as if to tell Secord not even to think about doing anything rash or disrespectful. The presidency was still the presidency.

"That's good of you to say, sir," North continued.

Reagan, ever the son of Hollywood, couldn't resist adding: "I'd say this is going to make a great movie one day."

North laughed politely.

"Well, good to talk to you," said the president, wrapping it up.

"And you too, sir. An honor."

"Goodbye."

"Goodbye, sir."

North hung up the phone, starry-eyed. "He called me a national hero."

"Yeah, some hero, for Chrissakes," snapped Secord, still seething. "Look at what Meese did."

But in the flush of the call, North didn't seem as bitter. Despite everything that had happened that day, he still spoke of Reagan respectfully.

Back at North's office, meanwhile, Fawn Hall was in a panic. Brenda Reger, an NSC security officer, was moving to seal the office and gather up all the documents inside to protect evidence for the ensuing investigations. As she glanced over some of the files stacked on her desk, Hall noticed that they included several incriminating memoranda that North had asked her to alter, computer messages that she thought she had shredded, and minutes from North and McFarlane's top-secret meeting with Iranian leaders in Tehran that May. The memos demonstrated that North had been involved in providing military aid to the Contras in 1985 while such aid was barred by Congress. Four days earlier he had ordered her to edit out the incriminating references and shred numerous other documents.

Trying to maintain her composure as Reger and an aide milled about, Hall called North, who was still in the hotel room with Secord and Green. As revealed in her testimony and in an interview with the author, the conversation went like this:

"Brenda Reger is here closing up the office," she whispered into the phone. "I think you'd better come over."

North saw no need. He had enough troubles. "No, I don't think so."

"Ollie, I found some important documents that didn't get thrown out," Fawn insisted. "You've got to come back here. Now."

North heard the urgency in her voice and agreed to return. He told her to have Green cleared through security.

Hall scooped up the incriminating files, along with some innocuous documents to try not to arouse any suspicion, and walked upstairs to the suite's second floor. She walked into Robert Earl's office and asked him to help her separate the computer messages from the pile of documents. As he did that, Fawn began stuffing some of the papers into her boots.

Assessing what needed to be done, Earl began putting some of the documents inside his jacket, which was hanging up on the wall. Fawn walked out of the room but soon returned and asked him to give her back the documents he had hidden. "You shouldn't have to do this," she said. "I'll do it."

Earl walked out of the room as Hall lifted her blouse and placed the documents against her back. After finishing she pirouetted and asked Earl if he could detect anything. He couldn't.

Finally North and Green appeared. Ollie walked into his office and took a phone call. Fawn followed him in and executed another pirouette like the part-time model she was. North also said he couldn't notice anything.

Fawn put on her overcoat, then she, North and Green walked out of the office, but not before Brenda Reger stopped them and inspected the briefcases the two men were carrying. Reger, embarrassed even to subject North to that, was hardly about to insist on a pat-down body search. So they continued on their way.

Once they were out of immediate danger, Hall told North she wanted to pass him the documents.

"No, just wait until we get outside," Ollie responded coolly.

They rode down the elevator and exited the Old Executive Office Building onto Seventeenth Street. Fawn again said she wanted to unload the documents that were inside her boots and blouse. But now Ollie said to wait until they got to Green's car. They kept walking over to G Street, where the lawyer's car was parked, and climbed inside. He began driving them to the parking lot where their cars were parked as Fawn started removing the papers from her person and handing them to North.

As they pulled up at the parking lot and Fawn got out to leave, Green asked her: "If you're asked about the shredding, what are you going to say?"

"We shred every day," Fawn replied, not missing a beat.

"Good," said Green.

Six days after being called a national hero by the president of the United States, North was on Capitol Hill, in full Marine dress with six rows of ribbons—taking the Fifth Amendment before the Senate Intelligence Committee.

Eight days after that, in a preview of the kind of bravura performance that would captivate the nation the following summer at the

Iran-Contra hearings, North told the House Foreign Affairs Committee, his voice choked with emotion: "I don't think there's another person in America who wants to tell the story as much as I
do." But again he took the Fifth.

There was little or no outrage at his refusal to tell that story at a
time when Washington was thirsting for answers. Rather, several
members of the committee openly fawned over Ollie as a patriotic
prince.

Representative Gerald Solomon, a Republican from upstate New
York in the district where North had grown up, staked out hometown turf and called him a "great American." Ollie flashed Solomon
a wink and a brave smile.

Dan Mica, Democrat of Florida, said he'd never seen a more
anguished face and wished Ollie the best. Tom Lantos, a California
Democrat, allowed as to how it gave him "a great deal of pleasure,
publicly, here and now, to express my respect, affection and admiration" for North. And Bob Dornan, Republican of California and a
hawk's hawk, went so far as to read Ollie a Kipling poem in praise
of the English foot soldier. Dornan substituted North's name for
that of the title character:

> It's 'Ollie this and Ollie that,
> an' chuck 'im out, the brute!'
> But it's saviour of his country
> when the guns begin to shoot.

Lantos and Solomon announced they would make contributions
to North's legal defense fund.

Why national heroes are fired and why they invoke the Fifth
became the logic-defying stuff of North's quickly emerging legend.
This was a forty-three-year-old Marine lieutenant colonel who until
November 25 had been toiling away in near obscurity. True, there
had been a handful of newspaper stories spotlighting him as a key
NSC operative who had been instrumental in sustaining the Contras when official U.S. assistance was banned. But the stories had
lacked staying power.

Now all of a sudden, all roads led North. The press quickly
dubbed him "the most powerful lieutenant colonel in the world,"
and gave him personal credit for a string of Reagan successes, pre-
Iran-Contra, including the invasion of Grenada, the interception
of the plane carrying the hijackers of the Achille Lauro in 1985
and the 1986 raid on Libya. He was quickly romanticized as a "cow-

boy," a good and loyal soldier probably taking the fall for Reagan himself.

If most of the country would tune out the day-to-day minutiae of the complex Iran-Contra story, they couldn't get enough of North, and the press was quick to oblige them, for he was irresistible copy.

He had dash and panache, rugged good looks and a quintessentially American face. He had been a bona fide war hero in Vietnam. He embraced traditional God, country and family values. He had a pleasant and attractive wife and four children, and they lived out in the Virginia suburbs on a two-acre tract with horses and dogs. He was deeply religious—raised a Catholic but now born-again and given to dropping references to the Lord into everyday conversation at work.

But lest that be perceived as too milquetoasty, North also remained a Marine who liked bourbon, a good cigar and an occasional pinch of snuff. He worked killer hours, supported by a drop-dead good-looking secretary who had inevitably enhanced his image at the White House as a boy wonder, and caused, also inevitably, the wiseguys to ask: were they or weren't they?

Now, as a flood of scrutinizing profiles began appearing in the press, as the longest-running stakeout in TV history continued in front of his house, the philosophical and political fault-lines on North were drawn. Hero, villain or fallguy—everybody had an opinion, and there wasn't much middle ground.

To the hard right, for whom he was already supplanting Ronald Reagan as a jingoistic icon, North was a thoroughly likable, bureaucracy-busting superpatriot who pushed the limits of the law without breaking it as he took necessary action to fight communism and further the aims of the Reagan Revolution. With hard blue eyes, a gapped-toothed grin and turned-out ears, North, to his adulators, was an appealing blend of Chuck Yeager, Dirty Harry and Dobie Gillis.

To the left, on the other hand, he was a reckless, romantic ideologue who had probably broken laws in an effort to implement the Reagan gospel in defiance of Congress and other constitutional checks and balances. His demise represented the shattering of Reagan's blue-smoke-and-mirrors presidency, whose wing-and-a-prayer brand of cowboy diplomacy had finally, and deservingly, crashed and burned.

In many ways North was Reagan in miniature—a nostalgic throwback who evoked the same sort of insouciant, feel-good brand of patriotism that was the president's stock-in-trade. They both struck deep and responsive chords within the American people. They both couched their hard-right zealotry in a friendly, aw-shucks package. But being in the military, North had a slightly harder edge; he was a sort of steel-coated Huck Finn whose actions seemed an ongoing quest for guts and glory. That quest was his constant frame of reference, the prism through which he viewed his life.

Much of his work had been off-lines—too sensitive for the average bureaucrat even to know or talk about. He worked in the National Security Council, not the CIA, but rumor had it that he reported directly to Casey and that all lines of authority inside the NSC had been rewritten to accommodate North and his mysterious mission. Indeed it was the mystery surrounding North's work that was the source of much of the country's curiosity of and fascination with him.

But as the implications and dimensions of the Iran-Contra affair grew, as it became clear that this was a scandal that would at least shake the administration to its foundations, as Washington slipped hard into its Watergate crouch, more fundamental questions about North began to emerge.

Just how was it that a Marine lieutenant colonel on the staff of the NSC had attained such astonishing influence? How had he evolved from a functionary in 1981 to assuming direct control over two of this administration's most important, and some said illegal, covert operations in 1986—by which time he also had the clout to reposition National Security Agency satellites? Who was this North who had received back-to-back calls from the president and vice-president the day he was fired, and what were the elements of his background, personality and skills that had propelled him to such heights?

Was North dangerous? Was his power real, illusory or some of both? How had he effectively gained control of the national security and intelligence establishment? Was there a de facto North-Casey alliance that amounted to a government within a government? Were they a buccaneering cabal that reflected this administration's not-so-latent passion for secrecy and disdain for process—due or otherwise—if that got in the way of what they thought to be in the national interest?

Was there an effort to use the national security instruments of power to implement secretly policies which the White House knew the Congress or the public would reject if done openly? By trying to promote democracy abroad had democracy at home been subverted? And what did it say about the Reagan administration that a Marine lieutenant colonel with more *chutzpah* than covert-operations experience would be entrusted with such power and influence?

The press, the Congress and a newly appointed special prosecutor all began their investigations.

PHILMONT

O N a scorching hot Saturday morning on August 15, 1987, more than two thousand people assembled on Main Street in Philmont, New York, to honor Oliver Laurence North, the village's adoptive first son and most famous former resident.

Since the population of Philmont, a small burg in the Hudson Valley thirty-five miles south of Albany, is only about sixteen hundred, organizers of the event were congratulating themselves on the turnout. The crowd was swelled by a few hundred protesters who had come to stage a counterdemonstration against North, but they were mostly out-of-towners.

The vast majority of the Philmont townfolk and those from surrounding communities were solidly in North's corner. Ollie himself —or Larry, as he was called as a boy to distinguish him from his father and grandfather, also named Oliver—was not present to hear his praises sung. He had been instructed by his lawyer to send regrets since an indictment was then pending; and there were security concerns too. Even Philip Mossman, the fifty-seven-year-old first-term village mayor who had proposed and organized Oliver North Day, had had his life threatened, and was being shadowed by a deputy sheriff as he marched down Main Street in the parade.

Strolling along behind a vintage Thunderbird, followed by other local politicos, policemen, firemen, Legionnaires and members of the VFW, the short and stout Mossman seemed unfazed by the three threats against him which had been telephoned in, evidently long-distance, to the sheriff's department. In fact, he was ebullient as he greeted his constituents by name and pronounced himself incredulous at the big turnout.

"Larry was a local boy and he went higher than anybody we ever had in this town," Mossman said later in discussing his reasons for wanting to honor North. "I think he's a wonderful man. I think he deserves a lot of credit. I like the way he had the guts to stand up there and take all those questions from those congressmen. Looked 'em right in the eye and answered 'em. He didn't go, 'Uh, uh, uh.' He's a hero in my book."

If the afterglow from North's bravura July performance on Capitol Hill had somewhat faded around the nation by mid-August, it hadn't in Philmont. "Welcome to Larry North Day . . . Philmont, New York . . . Boyhood home of Larry North," read the sign at the entrance to town. "Oliver North, Our Hometown Hero," proclaimed another banner atop Nick's Restaurant further down Main Street. A car parked along the parade route had a sign in its rear window saying, "I'm a North American."

But there was opposition as well as adulation in action. The protesters, knowing the parade was scheduled to start at eleven A.M., had rallied in front of the post office an hour earlier to stage a press conference. Most of the anti-Ollies were members of the antinuclear group PREVENT. They carried placards saying: "Honesty is the Best Foreign Policy" or calling North an "All-American Fascist."

But the pro-Ollies weren't about to see their day desecrated, so confrontations ensued. "Hey, folks, all you patriots, what do you say? God Bless America!" shouted out one man wearing a dark green VFW hat. The North supporters quickly obliged him by breaking into song.

There were a few insults exchanged, but no fisticuffs. Then, as the parade stepped off and wound its way down Main Street to Maple Avenue and the sprawling lawn next door to North's old house, the anti-Ollies receded and let the pro-Ollies carry the rest of the day. A band struck up the "Star-Spangled Banner," "You're a Grand Old Flag," and "God Bless America" while the villagers sang along and snapped up "Give 'em Hell, Ollie" T-shirts and other pro-Ollie paraphernalia from an array of hawkers.

Philmont had not seen such excitement since 1977 when its last textile mill was leveled in a fire. Now there were no functioning mills anymore; they had long since fallen victim to polyester and the more favorable labor climate of the Sun Belt, leaving Philmont to fray away at the edges, since the mills had always been its *raison d'être*. Half the shops along Main Street were now boarded up, and the village itself had no self-sustaining economy. Today it is basically a bedroom community for people commuting to jobs in Albany, Schenectady, or Pittsfield across the state line in Massachusetts. Nestled between the Catskills and the Berkshires amid pastoral, rolling hills, surrounding Columbia County remains pleasant and attractive but even the locals acknowledge that time seems to have passed Philmont by.

Still, they retain their memories. Mildred Johnson, an elderly lady with white hair and a sing-song voice who has lived in Philmont all her life, recalls the village's prosperity:
"The Harlem division of the old New York Central railroad used to run through town, and we had our own high school, four churches and a youth club. But when the textile mills closed down, the town fell into disrepair. It's gotten kind of seedy around the edges," says Mrs. Johnson, a retired teacher who used to teach social studies and history to young Ollie North, and who still lives just down the street from the Norths' old house on Maple Avenue.

But it was in the textile heydays in the forties when the North family began making their mark in town. Oliver North, grandfather to Ollie of Iran-Contra fame, ran a mill on Main Street then, and in the fifties started up his own wool-processing plant in neighboring Ghent.

The elder North had been a struggling door-to-door yarn salesman facing what he considered to be a dead end in his native England when he decided to seek his fortune in America, landing in Philadelphia around the turn of the century. A small man—about five feet two and no more than 125 pounds—Mr. North nonetheless married well, and convinced his wife Mabel's well-to-do parents to invest in the textile business he started up in Philadelphia. The couple settled in suburban Upper Darby, and raised two children: a daughter, Elizabeth, and a son, Oliver Clay, who was called Clay in honor of his mother's maiden name.

Clay graduated from the Upper Darby schools and went on to the University of Pennsylvania, where he obtained a bachelor's degree in economics from the Wharton School of Finance in 1937. Like his father, Clay was a slight, small man, about five feet, six inches tall. He was the coxswain on the Penn crew for four years, president of the Theta Chi fraternity, and majored in transportation studies, producing a thesis on transportation and city planning.

After graduation Clay opted to follow his father to Philmont and enter the textile business, serving for the next four years as plant superintendent at the same mill where Mr. North was office manager—the Philmont Yarn Company. In November 1941, just weeks before Pearl Harbor, Clay entered the army and was a transportation officer stationed at Fort Ontario, New York, not far from Philmont. He married Ann Clancy, a teacher from Oswego, north of Syracuse on the shores of Lake Ontario. Ann was one of five children, the daughter of a dry-goods proprietor.

Clay rose quickly through the ranks during the next two years, serving as a battalion training officer in Arkansas, then winning a promotion to major after being transferred to Fort Sam Houston in San Antonio. There, on October 7, 1943, Ann North gave birth to the couple's first child, a boy they named Oliver Laurence North. He was the third generation of North boys to carry the name Oliver, but it seemed more a bow to tradition than anything else. As with his father, the boy's middle name for all intents and purposes quickly became his first name. They called him Larry.

In 1944 Clay was sent to Europe with the 95th Infantry Division and served as a supply officer in Gen. George Patton's famed Third Army. He was awarded the Silver Star and the Bronze Star for heroism, returning home in 1945 in time to lead the Veteran's Day parade down Main Street in Philmont. Ann North looked on proudly, holding two-year-old Larry and a second infant son, John, who had arrived earlier that year.

Clay resumed his textile career, and after several more years he and his father started ther own wool-combing mill, which they built on the elder North's farm in neighboring Ghent. By this time Oliver North, Sr., who had white hair and a mustache and retained his British accent, was firmly established as one of the leading textile men in the area.

"He was a mill man and a businessman and very good at both," recalls Joe Haag, a retired millworker, now sixty-three, who was seventeen when he first went to work for North at the Philmont Yarn Company in 1941 along with his twin brother and father. He said the workers used to call North "the old man. Those were tough days after the Depression . . . I was just thankful for the chance to work.

"Some folks in town didn't always get paid on time in the mills they worked at. But all of us who worked for the old man, we always had a check at the end of the week. Other people in town at that time, why I think they resented it just a little bit. Or maybe they envied us. In those days the Depression didn't care if you were hard up for money, but the old man cared."

After a stint in the service Haag returned to work for the Norths at their Ghent plant. "He and Clay were both good men to work for. Not demanding, but they both had everyone's respect. I think it was the way they approached you. Either one of 'em, when they started walking towards you in the mill, they'd be looking you right in the eye from clear across the place. When they did get over and started to talk to you, they did the same, looked you right in the eye. I always admired the old man . . . He was a professional wool man. They didn't come any better in wools and in blending wools. He could work the shoddy end real good. That's where you take rags and old pieces of cloth and reweave them without dye into a new fabric that looked like new. Like recycling.

"In those days at Ghent, Clay was more active in the mill; the old man became strictly a pencil man with Clay running the place physically. But they both looked after the business and they worked very well together. I remember Clay used to bring the kids around the mill. You know how kids are. They want to see where the old man works. Well, they would stand outside the office door, almost at attention, while their father finished up inside."

At first, Clay, Ann and their two boys lived with his parents in their grand, white-picket-fenced colonial farmhouse across the street from the mill. But before long they moved into Philmont and bought their own house. Two other children were added to the household: a daughter, Patricia, and later another son, Timothy.

As Clay assumed more and more control over the family business during the fifties he and Ann also began making their presence felt in Philmont town affairs. Clay was president of the Rotary Club and a member of the school board. Ann, who had graduated in 1939 from Oswego State Teachers College, was a library trustee, a substitute teacher, a Sunday school teacher and was active in the PTA. They were also both strong backers of scouting.

The Norths were pillars of the community with decided views about how they and their children should lead their lives. Clay was a stern disciplinarian, intensely patriotic, quiet and rigid. Ann, who stood at least two inches taller than Clay, was Irish, prematurely gray, with a more outgoing, gregarious personality. Where Clay was a relatively indifferent Episcopalian, Ann was a deeply religious

Catholic. At her urging he agreed to convert to Catholicism and have their children raised as Catholics, though not in parochial schools.

"Clay had an air of being a military man, and was a man of a few words, but she ran the house," says Jean Carl, the postmaster of Philmont, who spent seven years as a summer nanny for the North children and did additional babysitting for the family as needed. "He never crossed her. She was a strong person...They were a refined family, a wonderful family. They were polished. They did the right thing at the right time. They were well-connected."

Though a prominent family, the Norths lived modestly, first on Summit Street in Philmont, then in a better neighborhood on Maple Avenue, a lovely tree-lined roadway with stately old Victorian houses. But the North house was perhaps the smallest on the block—a tiny white wood-frame structure with a roof that swooped down less than ten feet from the ground, curling up slightly at the end. It was the former guest cottage of the huge stone mansion that still stands next door behind the sprawling lawn that served as the destination for the parade on Ollie North Day. The mansion, currently a nursing home, had been owned by the Harter family, which at one time had also owned most of the textile mills in Philmont.

Inside the North home there was no mistaking the patriotic fervor of the household. A pair of crossed swords hung over the mantelpiece, standing as the dominant article of decor in the living room. A flag flew outside the house on Flag Day or other patriotic occasions, and Clay would never miss a chance to march in full uniform in the Memorial Day and Armistice Day parades. As his wife tells it, he also stayed active in the army reserves, retiring in 1953 as a colonel. "They were very patriotic, no question about it," says postmaster Carl.

If Clay let Ann run the household, he was not afraid to assert himself outside the home, either on the job or in community activities, remembers Harold Rhoades, a neighbor of the Norths who served with Clay in Rotary and who would become young Larry's guidance counselor in high school.

"Clay was directive, a take-charge fellow on committees and what have you," says Rhoades. "This is a small town. Without a few people like that we wouldn't get anything done. He gave leadership to the town."

So the Norths and their four children cut a formidable swath in Philmont, especially on Sundays when all six of them would appear at the Sacred Heart Church en masse, freshly scrubbed and in formal dress. Young Larry was an altar boy. They looked and acted every bit the model American family.

But Clay and Ann did not seem to have any close friends. They were self-reliant and inward-turning, rarely socializing with other couples, according to Jean Carl and others. For them life revolved around the family unit.

Carl remembers the infant Ollie: "Larry was two and a half when I went to take care of him. I changed Larry North's diapers. He called me 'Neenie.' Anybody would have loved to own him. He was a beautiful kid... Not a mean bone in his body. I read to him by the hour. We knew the stories by heart, we read them so often."

Friends, schoolmates, teachers and mentors of young Larry North say their earliest memories of him are of an unfailingly courteous and polite boy who was given a very short leash by his parents.

Peter Post, one of thirty-five other students who would graduate with North from tiny Ockawamick High School in 1961, remembers a time when he and Larry were about six and at a little girl's birthday party. While all the rest of the kids were gobbling up cake and ice cream Larry was away from the pack profusely thanking the girl's parents for the party favors he'd gotten.

"He didn't hang around much growing up," recalls another classmate, Dale Rowe. "His parents were very strict. There was this soda fountain in town—Palens, it was called. A lot of the kids would hang out there after school or at night, but not Larry. His folks wouldn't allow it. In a strange way he was a loner because of his parents being so strict. But I don't think he wanted to be a loner. He didn't seem the type. He mixed really well with all kinds of people.

"I remember some kids—and you know how kids treat each other—would tease Larry. See, his mother used to blow a whistle for him when it was time to come home. Sometimes, one or two of the other kids would bring along their own whistle and ditch it somewhere, then start blowing the whistle. Of course, the minute Larry heard it he'd start running home and we'd all laugh. It wasn't meant in a cruel way. Just teasing. But he was a good kid.

"I remember my parents liked him. They used to say, 'Why can't you be more like Larry? By that I think they meant they were impressed with how courteous he was. Always more so than the rest of us. And he was more apt to dress neater than we did. But I never resented him for it because he was such a good guy."

Once when North was about ten his parents dropped him and a friend off at a movie. But somehow there was a mixup and they ended up at a Brigitte Bardot film. Ollie's eyes fairly bugged out as Brigitte steamed across the screen. "There's no way we oughta be seeing this," Ollie reportedly told his pal. "It's not right at all. It's against our religion." So they got up and went to an ice-cream parlor instead.

When he got to high school North dated infrequently. "Clay preferred that Larry not bother with girls," recalls Alma Shutts, whose daughter Annette used to go roller skating with North and went to a prom with him. "His father would have him cancel dates that he had. He sure was rough on him. We felt sorry for Larry . . . His father was very ambitious for him. Girls got in the way."

Peter Reiss, a pilot for Northwest Airlines who was perhaps North's closest childhood friend, agrees that Clay and Ann "were quite strict. They ran a tight ship . . . I never heard Larry speak in a disrespectful manner of his parents. Sure, he'd sometimes question them, sometimes to me, but in a wondering sort of way, not with contempt . . . His dad taught him many of the basic values of life, apart from the church. He was also greatly influenced by his mother. She was around more. . . . But I think the loyalty he has now, he got from his dad."

Thomas Gibbons, who taught young North English and knew the family, says Clay was "a disciplinarian because he realized that without discipline, responsibility and a strong family background, school was nothing."

By the end of Ollie's eighth-grade year the Norths evidently concluded that he was not, in fact, getting enough from school. Neither was younger brother John. So both boys were pulled out and sent to Christian Brothers Academy, a private Catholic military school in Albany where the students wear army uniforms and are called cadets.

The goals of the school, according to a current catalogue, are to "instill Christian values while providing a solid academic program . . . To assist in the transition from immature boyhood to the duties and responsibilities of young manhood; to impress upon the student a proper attitude toward legitimate authority as expressed by the family, the Church and the State; and to establish among the students a firm conviction of the importance of the family and of the community as a source of temporal and eternal happiness."

But as it turned out, Ollie and John spent only one year at Chris-

tian Brothers, perhaps worn out by the three-and-a-half hour
round-trip school bus ride to Albany each day. Or maybe Ann and
Clay had merely intended it as a year of shock therapy. In any case,
they decided to let the boys finish off school in a lay-civilian environment.

Not that his friends recall young Larry ever needing any of the
straightening out that a military school might provide. They all say
he was a model child. Yet if he was something of a goody-two-
shoes, he never flaunted it, and he remained popular with his more
rowdy classmates.

"In high school I was into six-packs and chasing women," remembers Peter Hermance, a North classmate who today is a dentist in the Philmont area. "Larry wasn't like that... He was just a
normal all-American kid. He wasn't a hellion." While Hermance
and the rest of his pals cut a high-teen profile on street corners
smoking cigarettes, North would cheerfully pass them by, resisting
with a wave and a smile invitations to join in. He was a fifties
precursor to an eighties Say-No-to-Drugs campaign, fending off
peer pressure firmly but deftly enough to avoid alienating his
friends. "He was just a good guy," says Hermance. "You couldn't
hate him."

North could also resist the entreaties of the opposite sex. One
summer he landed a much-sought-after summer job cutting grass
and doing yard work at Mrs. Burleigh's, an exclusive girls' private
school in nearby Harlemville that the local studs viewed as a prime
hunting ground.

According to Thomas Gibbons, the school was a "glorified babysitting service," and one of its missions was to protect the girls'
virtue against the encroachments of the townies. "Larry was the
envy of every stud in Philmont," Gibbons recalls. "The girls were
cloistered and they idolized him. But Larry was no Don Juan. He
was respectful to girls. He was no ladykiller."

Too shy or too disinterested to ask the girls out, Ollie was jeered
by his more aggressive buddies. When he did have a date he took
care to mind his p's and q's. "Larry was especially polite and nice
and proper around girls," recalls Barbara (Daldrich) Schackenberg,
a classmate who went out with Ollie a few times. "He had a degree
of humility, you know? To me, that meant an ability to stand but a
willingness to kneel, as the situation warranted."

So if the image that North would later project to the nation was
that of a dashing, macho warrior *cum* diplomat who as a youth was
undoubtedly a straight-A student and three-sport varsity star the

reality was that he was considerably less than a phenom. He was too small to make the football team, not, apparently, talented enough to make the basketball team, so he settled for being its manager and water boy. He ran track, but as former teammate and classmate Eric Van Deusen says: "You didn't make the track team. You joined it. We were pretty mediocre. We sort of ran whatever was available. Those of us who were not that good—and that included me and Larry—would sometimes end up doing the broad jump just to earn a couple of extra points."

"He wasn't an all-American, I'll tell ya," agrees the track coach and athletic director at the time, Russell Robertson, who had a policy not to cut anyone. "But he pushed himself to better his times. He was a darn good team player." In other words Ollie was no burner, but he exuded the sort of Boy Scout persona that could make Robertson reflect back and say, in what would become the first in a rash of similar testaments, "He was the type of kid you'd be proud to have as your own son."

On the scholastic front North was a better-than-average student but not a distinguished one. He showed a particular interest in history. His teacher, Robert Bowes, remembered that he was no slouch "but he was not the smartest kid in school either." Still, North tried so hard that "he was the type of kid, if he had an eighty-nine average, you'd give him the ninety," says Bowes.

In a debate staged in Bowes's class in 1960 just before the presidential election, which many of North's classmates remember, Ollie argued passionately for Richard Nixon and helped win the judgment for his team. "I remember thinking that Larry was very convincing," says Jane (Minkler) Freedman, a classmate who led the pro-JFK opposition.

Voted "nicest looking and most courteous" in his class, Ollie was always impeccably dressed and often wore a jacket and tie to school, Freedman says. As for extracurricular activities, North was a student-council alternate and an active member of the science club, the drama club and the chess club.

He also went in for spelunking. During their junior and senior years, Ollie, Eric Van Deusen and Peter Reiss would go off and explore caves in the Helderberg Mountains west of Schenectady, about a ninety-minute drive from Philmont. Sometimes Kenneth Sommers, the high school physics teacher and faculty advisor to the science club, would join them. Actually the caves were considered a hazard and were no longer open to the public, but an elderly lady who owned the land where some of the best caves were situated

gave the boys permission to go in. She liked their enthusiasm and
their sincerity. They were very careful and had even joined a national spelunkers' society.

"Before we went we'd drop by and talk to the lady for a while,
and then after we were done we would go back and see her again,"
recalls Reiss. "She'd offer us milk and cookies, and she liked the
company, I think... The lady knew we wouldn't go in there breaking off stalagmites and stalactites. She knew we'd respect the integrity of the cave. She knew we were there with strictly good
intentions...

"There was a section of the caves that we called the 'Gun Barrel.'
This particular part used to take a long while to get across. You had
to go along inch-by-inch, like a worm. I suppose it was dangerous
but not for us because we were real careful. I think each of us had
no qualms about relying on the other. I mean, you couldn't have
dragged someone back through the gun barrel if any of us got hurt.
We had complete trust in one another. No screwing around. It was
serious business. In a way, that caving taught us teamwork. We had
no near-misses or accidents that I can recall... We decided to have
controlled practices of falls and things of that nature. It was very
group-oriented. We wanted to be ready for any problems that
might arise along the way."

The boys wore miners' hats with lights on top to illuminate the
darkness ahead of them. Behind them—shades of Tom Sawyer and
Becky—they unfurled string to help find their way out. Sommers
recalls it was claustrophobic and dangerous inching along on their
stomachs inside the 'Gun Barrel.' Years later, he said, a boy trying
to negotiate the same passage got stuck and died of exposure.

If chess, drama, science and caving did not seem the stuff of
which American legends were cut, a more charitable interpretation
was that those activities were perhaps indicative of a free-thinker—
someone who could resist peer pressure and find pleasure in more
esoteric pursuits.

"That's what drew us together—we had our own sense of values,
a sense of honor," says Reiss, who was a year behind North in
school. "It's something that has very much stuck with him... He
has a sense of honor.

"I really enjoyed being with him. He was a true friend, someone
I could call up at any time, and if I needed someone for moral
support, by God he'd be there... He was someone I knew I could

count on. He's a man of the utmost loyalty, even if it's an unpopular cause. He's a man of integrity...

"Larry was, and still is, an individual thinker. He could take responsibility for things... and he had a very strong feeling for justice. I recall a particular case, where in eighth or ninth grade one of the bigger kids was bullying a smaller kid outside of class. We were talking nearby and Larry said something to the effect that this has got to stop. He walked over and stepped abruptly in between them. 'If you push him, you gotta push me too,' he said. That incident personifies him. Larry had, and probably still has, an aversion to bullies...

"He was not the macho tough guy in high school. In fact, that's what turned me to him. He was beyond that shit before he was ever out of high school. He never needed to be macho... People who are macho have to use that to buoy up an insecurity. He never had that... If I had a daughter, I'd be very comfortable with him taking her out. He would not have violated a trust. He was never someone to brag or boast about exploits... He wasn't out to score. He was just damn decent... He was very, very courteous. He was an officer and a gentleman, that's what he was."

Reiss, whose father was an architect, remembers that when he was a teenager his parents always wanted to know where he was at all times. In part so that they would worry less, the Reisses would insist on having dinner-dances for Peter and his friends at the family farm outside Philmont. They'd have a roaring fire going and five or six couples would come over—usually including North and a date. It was good clean fun, and Reiss says he does the same thing today with his kids.

Reiss would also go over to Ollie's house. "At the North home they talked about current events around the dinner table," he remembers. "It was a small town but the family was very much aware of what was going on in the world. It was from them that he got interested in the welfare of the U.S. He was very constant and consistent. Even in the seventh and eighth grade we'd talk about what was going on. I enjoyed talking with him about events beyond Columbia County."

Looking back, with a broader perspective, Reiss admits that he and North were "too good to be true." When they ventured out on a double-date in Peter's 1952 black Chevy coupe, they were not exactly a threat to society. Sometimes they'd go to the movies, or occasionally to the stock-car races near Albany. They were expected to set their own curfews, but neither was inclined to stay out late anyway. And though the drinking age in New York was eighteen, Reiss and North had a firm agreement that whoever was the designated driver would not touch a drop... "The other, if he wanted, could then have a beer," Reiss says. "But we weren't very into that, and as for drugs, I don't recall even really hearing the word while we were growing up in Philmont."

In hindsight, friends caution that North's actions and *modus vivendi* tend to make him out to be more of a conservative cartoon figure than he perhaps was. Actually, they note, no one was terribly wild in Philmont during the fifties. The times, after all, were conservative. It was don't-rock-the-boat, I-Like-Ike, sock hops, Elvis, malts, shakes and "Leave it to Beaver"—an unflinchingly patriotic life in the slow lane, particularly in rural America.

"Back then we were all pretty straight," says Eric Van Deusen, now a librarian at a community college in nearby Hudson. "We were products of the late fifties... I think everyone has missed the point about Larry growing up. They're all trying to make him out to be this superpatriot as a kid. But we were *all* patriotic... in the traditional sense. Now, if he had been unpatriotic, then that would have been out of the ordinary."

Still, classmate James Grasso remembers one unvarnished outburst from young North that seemed to make even the flag-waving locals stand up and take notice: "One of the guys in school said something about how stupid the Army was. Then he said that we, meaning the U.S., shouldn't get involved in any wars overseas. Well, Larry got pretty mad. He told the guy, 'If you don't like living in America, you can just get the hell out.' Then he said to the guy, 'You'll be back in six months kissing American soil again.'"

For the average student graduating in Ockawamick's class of 1961, college was by no means a given, but for Larry North it was. That was the direction his parents had pointed him in all along. The problem was where to go. His grades were not exceptional, though he did take and pass the state Regents exam, which qualified him to win a scholarship to a state college or university. But more fundamentally, he seemed unsure about a career direction. At that point, entering the military was not a foregone conclusion. Though clearly influenced by Clay's war record and continued service in the army reserves, Ollie wasn't pushed into the military by his father. In fact, at the time he seemed just as drawn to his mother's background as a teacher. And after traveling to have a look at several colleges around New York State, North settled on a small teacher's college just west of Rochester, then called Brockport State College, where he would major in English and train to become a teacher.

Away from home for the first time, Ollie settled into college life at the remote campus chilled by a cold wind that blew in off the shores of Lake Ontario. There were about fifteen hundred students at Brockport then—and rigid rules. Men's and women's dorms were located on opposite ends of the campus, and students were not permitted to drive until their junior year. If caught, they could be expelled.

North's was not a spectacular presence at Brockport. He posted a B average, including a D in calculus and geometry. He ran cross-country, where his teammates and coach were characteristically more impressed by his grit and determination than by his talent. On a team of about fifteen runners, North ranked in the middle, which meant he ran in home competitions, sometimes traveled with the team but did not participate in championship meets that involved several colleges. At practices, coach Harold Emmerson had the team run five to seven miles one day, then sprints the next. North was always willing to do whatever was asked of him. "He was the kind of guy who if you said, 'We're gonna run two hundred miles,' he'd say, 'Okay,'" recalls Emmerson.

Once the fall cross-country season ended, North, as he had in high school, opted to be manager of the basketball team, tending to the uniforms and equipment and keeping the statistics. Records show that Ollie had a meticulous way of scoring the games, using three different-colored pens to neatly record every conceivable stat. Despite such attention to detail, Ollie apparently did not get too much respect from the Brockport team. Once, after an away-game, the team bus took off without him, leaving him stranded. The coach, Curtis Gaylord, later explained to a perplexed North that he merely had been testing his manager's "mental health."

North looked forward to coming back to Philmont on vacations. It was a break from a college he didn't seem exactly enamored with, and he now also had a girlfriend back home. The summer before he entered Brockport North had begun a relationship with a girl who was to become his first serious flame: Lynore White, the daughter of a prominent Philmont doctor who was a year behind him in school. She looked up to Ollie, who was a year older, and was determinedly polite and respectful of her.

"We got along very well together," Lynore recalls. "We hit it off.

We were good friends. We liked the same things—movies, reading, skiing. We ended up discussing books—but please don't ask
me what. I liked him better than anybody else I'd ever dated."

On their first date Ollie took her to see *Ben Hur*, followed by
pizza, then *Gone With the Wind* on their second date. But, they
didn't just go to the movies. He would take her swimming at the
Columbia Country Club, where the Norths belonged, or they
would drive across the state line to Massachusetts to see a play in
Stockbridge, or maybe take in the Boston Symphony Orchestra at
Tanglewood, followed by dinner at the Red Lion Inn. Ollie, it
seemed, didn't mind showing he had some culture, and he was
willing to spend a buck on a girl he liked.

Sometimes they would just go to Kozel's, a teen hangout in Philmont, where they'd talk and dance to music from the jukebox. The
hits of the day included Chubby Checker doing "The Twist," Dion's
"Run-Around Sue" and "Please, Mr. Postman" by the Marvelettes.
But Ollie usually ducked the fast songs and waited for the slow
tunes, Lynore remembers. Songs like "Moon River," "Georgia
On My Mind" or Elvis' "Are You Lonesome Tonight?" In Ollie's
case, it didn't seem a ploy to get her cheek-to-cheek. He moved
well, she says, and was easy to follow—no Fred Astaire to be
sure, but certainly smoother than your basic Ockawamick graduate.

While North was at Brockport, he and Lynore wrote letters,
and they continued to see each other over holidays. Around
Christmas in 1962, she remembers, they got into a car accident
while on their way to ski in the Berkshires. They were on a dirt
road, and though Lynore says Ollie was only going about fifteen
miles an hour, the car slipped on a patch of ice going around a
curve and veered into a tree. Clay North's Rambler station wagon
was totaled. Lynore got a few bumps on her head and chin. Ollie
emerged without a scratch.

North's life changed in the summer of 1962 after his first year at
Brockport. He was evidently unsatisfied at the prospect of spending the rest of his life as a teacher. Teaching was a noble calling, to
be sure, but in many respects it seemed faceless, anonymous work
the rewards of which were too often intangible and the visibility too
low. Teachers could toil away forever in obscurity. He began to feel
the need to do something that could have more impact, something
where the missions and goals were clearer, more defined, something with a greater sense of immediacy, urgency and importance.

All of which seemed to point to the military, which had been looming in his life via his father all along. Now he decided to get a good
taste of it by enlisting in a Marine Corps officer's training program
at Camp Lejeune, North Carolina.

It was a summer of bootcamp in which North got to match his
mettle against dozens of others. Where others flagged under the
grueling regimen—the running, conditioning, negotiating obstacle
courses, rappelling, cleaning and breaking down an M–16 and the
classwork—North thrived on it. According to friends, he thought it
was the hardest but most rewarding thing he had ever done. He
loved the discipline and the regimentation, and he revelled in the
mystique of the Corps. The Marines were the toughest, the bravest
and the best, North thought.

He decided that was what he wanted to be. Returning to Brockport for his second year in the fall of 1962, North found life tame
and dull compared to the Camp Lejeune fast track. Brockport students at the time remember Ollie coming back with a much higher
intensity level than he had shown his freshman year. He seemed
increasingly gung-ho and out of step with civilian life.

Gary Dross, who was on the Brockport cross-country team with
North, says, "It was evident all fall that he was a military man. He
wasn't a Rambo type . . . He was into it in terms of how it can protect our democracy."

North seemed eager to talk of his summer in North Carolina and
to show off what he had learned. Once, Dross recalls, when they
were warming up for cross-country practice, North suddenly bolted
up and ran across the field to confront a hunter he had seen point
his gun in a careless manner. Dross said North gave the hunter
"holy hell. He was upset about it because, as he said, he had seen
movies all summer about how dangerous guns were." A good Marine knew when to point his gun and where.

Ollie now began looking for the right vehicle to channel his new-
found zeal. When it became increasingly apparent he was not going
to stay four years at Brockport, he began thinking of transferring to
the Naval Academy at Annapolis. The Marines, after all, were part
of the navy, and what better way for an aspiring young Marine to
get his start than by being commissioned an officer from Annapolis?

As Ollie talked of his dream to whomever would listen, another
Brockport student, Glenn Warner, Jr., happened to mention that
his father coached swimming and soccer at Annapolis. Would North
like to meet him?

Ollie hardly needed a second invitation. The elder Warner recalls that he was impressed by North's gung-ho attitude, by his
better-than-average grades, by his leadership qualities and by the
fact that he had already spent a summer at Camp Lejeune. "He was
a pretty spunky kid...He impressed me as a kid who really
wanted to be a Marine...He exhibited real leadership qualities,
and that's what you're looking for," the now-retired coach says.

Warner took North to meet Edgar Miller, the head of recruiting
for the Academy. Miller also found Ollie appealing and agreed that
they could not afford to pass up a prospect who spent his vacations
training for the military and who so desperately wanted to be a
Marine. Miller proceeded to get J. Ernest Wharton, then the Republican congressman from New York's 28th District, to give North
an official appointment.

Ollie was launched.

ANNAPOLIS

NORTH was awed by the Naval Academy.

There was no other word to describe his feelings that hot June morning in 1963 when he first arrived on the campus and began strolling its storied grounds along the Severn River in Annapolis, Maryland, soaking up the beauty, tradition and mystique all around him.

Many of the buildings and monuments carried the names of men who had been vital players in United States naval history. There was Rickover Hall—the center for engineering studies—named after Admiral Hyman Rickover, father of the nuclear navy. Nimitz Library was named for Fleet Admiral Chester Nimitz, commander-in-chief of the Pacific fleet during World War II.

Anchoring the Yard, as the campus was known, was Bancroft Hall, named in honor of former Secretary of the Navy George Bancroft. It was home for the entire brigade of some 4,500 midshipmen and contained 1,873 rooms, almost five miles of corridors and about thirty-three acres of floor space. Inside Bancroft were Memorial Hall and the Rotunda—a high ceilinged shrine containing tributes to navy men killed in action, and murals of sea battles. Then, in the basement of the huge building, was the mess hall where the entire brigade sat together for meals.

Just outside Bancroft was Tecumseh, the statue of a Delaware Indian which the midshipmen traditionally showered with pennies to bring them luck before exams and big sports events. The statue was known as the "Lord of Football Games and God of 2.0." The area around the statue—Tecumseh Court—was where the brigade gathered for noon formations. Then there was Herndon Monument, a phallic granite projectile that is the site of one of the oldest rites of passage at the Academy. Every June, during Commissioning Week, plebes signify the end of their first year by massing around Herndon to have one of their classmates scale the monument to retrieve a cap placed at the summit. The monument is always greased for the occasion.

The most imposing building in the Yard is the Naval Academy Chapel, whose copper-covered dome is 192 feet tall. Then there is the 80,000–square foot Hasley Field House, the 30,000–seat Navy-Marine Corps Memorial Stadium and MacDonough Hall, which houses facilities for soccer, lacrosse, gymnastics and boxing, among other things.

Hard by the quaint and narrow cobblestoned streets of Annapolis, the Academy might be light years away for all the contact midshipmen have with the capital of Maryland. They live in a world of their own—literally and figuratively a world of austerity and deprivation governed by power, precision, pride and patriotism. They live tribally and harshly, anchored by the concepts of duty, honor, country.

But North fairly tingled to be a part of it all. He couldn't imagine he'd wasted two years in a wishy-washy outpost like Brockport before coming to Annapolis. Now, for the first time, his life seemed to have purpose and direction.

North looked around him at the other freshly scrubbed, wide-eyed innocents from every state in the union who comprised the Academy's class of 1967, and felt like he was part of the cream of American youth. They had all come early for Plebe Summer, a two-month period of indoctrination wherein they would learn the facts of Academy life and be subjected to an unending array of hardships and indignities—all in the name of developing physical stamina, motivation, leadership ability and character.

By tradition, the first thing members of any plebe class are told is to look to their left and then to their right—one of those people would not be there by the time they graduated. Many would drop out that summer, concluding that the sort of thing they were doing was simply insane. In many respects, plebe year was like one long fraternity hazing session in which a midshipman's civilian value system is systematically scraped away and replaced by a new military ethos.

Basically, plebes had to do anything upperclassmen ordered them to do. The plebe bible was a little booklet called "Reef Points"—a manual of naval history, trivia and nautical do's-and-dont's which they had to have memorized cold. If an upperclassman asked a plebe something from the book and he did not know the answer to it, he could be "fried," or penalized. The penalty might consist of anything from doing scores of pushups to drinking cups of olive oil, to "shoving out": standing at a three-quarters squat with back rigid until you dropped.

Another favorite indulgence of upperclassmen was to send erring plebes off to service Bill the Goat—a large bronzed statue which was the symbol of Navy's fighting tradition. The statue, which stood in front of MacDonough Hall, depicted a raging goat in an attack mode down to every last detail—including his testicles. Though the Academy officially frowned on it, upperclassmen persisted in frying plebes by sending them sprinting out on a moment's notice to brass-polish Bill the Goat's privates. With the regular polishing that the balls received, they were far shinier than any other part of his anatomy.

The questioning of plebes was usually less than polite. It was not as if an upperclassman excused himself and asked a plebe if he happened to know whom Dewey Field was named for. More likely the questions were screamed in his ear in mock rage, ostensibly to test his reactions under fire.

Plebes had to sit at rigid attention at all times during meals. They got last pick of the food, and had to remain vigilant at all times to do upperclassmen's bidding in the mess hall. A common demand on plebes at meals was "rigging pitchers," holding pitchers of water outstretched until their arms dropped.

Every time plebes turned a corner on their way from one point to another, they had to pivot smartly at ninety-degree angles and shout out to no one in particular: "Beat Army!" If an upperclassmen caught them cutting a corner at an obtuse angle or failing to exhort the Academy over West Point, it was a reportable offense. Plebes also were responsible for telling any upperclassman who might want to know what the three most important stories from the morning newspaper were, what the day's menu was, who the watch officers were, what movies were in town, and how many days were left until such milestones as the Army game or spring leave.

The plebes also spent hours trying to keep themselves and their rooms in a permanently sparkling state. But for every hour spent by his classmates in the spit-and-polish department, North would spend two. He was always immaculately turned out, his uniform an extension of himself, and his room was hospital-clean. He was always, as the middies liked to say, squared away.

At the noon meal inspection—the main reviewing session of the day—North would have buffed his black shoes and swabbed them with wet cotton balls to remove every speck of lint and get a mirror shine. The white plastic cover on his cap would be freshly Cloroxed and the visor shined with Pledge. His belt buckle would be freshly Brassoed, his uniform brushed down with a damp whisk broom, and his necktie tied off with a sharp Windsor knot, and dimpled at the center. His shirt was tucked in so tightly to eliminate wrinkles that it tugged at the back of his neck. At the least hint that his shirttail might be coming out, North would quickly stuff it back in.

John Sinclair, a short-term roommate of North's who has left the service and now lives outside Pittsburgh, remembers that he once tried to humor North by scuffing his shoes and separating the cleaning fluid in his Brasso bottle, but Ollie went berserk.

"He was very neat," recalls Shelby Guilbert, another classmate. "He took more outward pride in his uniform than anyone else. When he came out of his room, his uniform was immaculate and stayed that way. His shirt was always tucked in . . . It looked like he never moved."

Nor did North have any problems with white-glove room inspections, which were held on Saturdays. His bedding had the proper hospital tucks at forty-five-degree angles. His wall locker had perfectly folded socks, underpants, shirts and sweat clothes all stacked in neat rows. His shoes gleamed, the windows were always Windexed, the desks Pledged, the floor Glo-Coated.

North's summer with the Marine reserves when he was still at Brockport might have given him a leg up on the other plebes in mastering military inspections. He seemed to know all the tricks and didn't mind helping his classmates if they asked.

Classmate Gary McBride stressed that North knew exactly how to do everything demanded of him as a plebe, and didn't seem to mind the demands in the least. "He loved it," says McBride. "It was right down his alley. He ate it up because it was something he could excel in. North did great with all those physical and military demands . . . [He] was the Right Stuff. He was the type of guy they were looking for."

Where others constantly complained about the rigors of hazing, North took it in stride and readily accepted it as a necessary part of military discipline—especially Marine discipline. "Another beautiful day at Navy," he'd quip to a classmate while snapping off a trademark wink. Or he would tell his fellow plebes that they simply had to suck it up and get with the program. It was part of paying the price.

"North was very committed," says Ray Roberts, another classmate. "He complained less than anyone. He knew what he was getting into."

But Ollie couldn't escape being fried, even if he knew the answers to all the navy trivia questions—and even if he was perfectly squared away. Discerning upperclassmen could always find a flaw, and some found it in what they felt was North's smugness.

"He seemed to draw the wrath of the upperclassmen," recalls Walter Teichgraber, a member of the class of 1965 who was assigned to Plebe Summer detail in 1963. "A little of it was cockiness. It could've been his military background that gave him an attitude problem. You'd be yelling at him, and he'd get a smirk on his face and then I'd just yell at him more. You got the impression that he thought it was all a big game. Ollie always measured up. He was always squared away. The only thing that got him into trouble was that cockiness."

For many of the first-year midshipmen, Plebe Summer was filled with conflicting pulls. On the one hand they were still attracted to their original concept of a naval career, highlighted as it was by visions of being part of a starched elite doing vital work on behalf of their country. On the other hand, the indoctrination system seemed so harsh and the deprivation so total that they envied their old high school friends who were freshmen at normal colleges— dating whenever they pleased, being able to drive a car, watch TV, listen to a radio, drink, go out with girls, come and go as they liked. These were all basic freedoms taken for granted by every American but denied a Naval Academy plebe. One of the famous sayings at Annapolis was that they took away all your God-given rights, then gave them back to you one at a time and called them privileges. So there were times when many of the plebes would call home in tears, threatening to pack it in and resume a normal life.

One of North's classmates, James Webb, who went on to become a best-selling novelist and Secretary of the Navy, recalls that he lay in bed his first night at the Academy crying bitterly over the loss of his youth.

Once, Webb said, four upperclassmen took turns beating him with cricket bats as hard as they could, telling him if he told them it hurt, they would stop. But Webb was too proud to say he felt any pain. "Finally, they got embarrassed, and finally the bat broke,"

Webb told the Baltimore *Sun* in 1983. "I went back to my room and went into my closet and put my head in my laundry bag and cried for fifteen minutes. That's bad. But if I had to choose that abuse or a total abrogation of the concept, I'd choose that. In any harsh military system you need harsh indoctrination."

There were small ways in which plebes could get back at the upperclassmen. One was the ritual of "getting the brick." The purpose was to give a brick—and a cold shower—to the upperclassman in the company who, by consensus, had gone out with the ugliest girl that weekend. Only those who had steady girls and those who had not dated were exempt. After evening meal a company's plebes would line up in a long column, two across, and the two men in front would hold a brick between them. Then they all would begin to chant: "Who gets the brick (Uh!) Who gets the brick (Uh!)!" They would do an Indian dance in stutter step to the rhythm of the chant. Slowly they would comb the corridors looking for likely candidates as the upperclassmen watched nervously. Actually, only the two plebes holding the brick knew who it was going to be awarded to, and they delighted in making fake tosses at some terrified middie as the procession snaked its way along the corridors. Finally they would arrive at the room of the intended victim and toss the brick inside. Then the plebes would swarm in the room like a pack of wolves and happily do their duty.

If every plebe had periods when his enthusiasm flagged and he yearned to become a civilian again, then North had the absolute minimum of such pulls. If anyone was firm and resolute about the direction his life was taking, it was North. All the abuse they could dish out, he would gladly accept. He would do all the pushups they told him to do, plus one to Beat Army. He would never complain or try and get out of hazing on some technicality, as some plebes tried to do. He was no sea lawyer. He would gladly do everything that was asked of him, and more, because it was the system. Everyone had to do it. It was tradition. And actually, he enjoyed it. When the upperclassmen screamed at him, Walt Teichgraber was right, traces of a smirk did creep across his face, because he knew it was all part of the game. Part of the way fighting men were molded and turned out.

Though the attrition rate in his class would ultimately be more than one third, for North, the stigma associated with quitting would have been unthinkable. He couldn't understand those who had scrawled the initials IHTFP—which stood for "I hate this fucking place"—all over the Academy. North *loved* the "fucking place." It might be tough and harsh, but it was, after all, a military academy, not a normal college or university. The deprivations they endured were part of what made them special. A breed apart, and all that. No one liked the Academy—until they had to leave it, he thought. The midshipmen were all part of something far bigger than themselves. He could feel it that summer when the plebes marched through the Yard whistling the theme song from "The Bridge Over the River Kwai," or when they came into Bancroft Hall and heard "Anchors Aweigh" and the "Marine Hymn" being piped in over the loudspeakers. It was enough to blow him away.

"From day one, duty, honor and country are drilled into you in that order," remembers Rick Bayer, one of North's classmates. "Those three things are the ultimate and nothing but death relieves you. They told us, 'If your country ever needs you, you will be put into the cannon and fired. If you come back, fine. If you don't, that's fine too.' You had to give up something to make it through . . . They stripped us right down to the core of our existence. But we could have walked any time. We wanted it. We were a very elite group. The forefront of the baby-boom generation. Every day we were told how special we were."

Yet within this naval elite, North knew he would join a group still more elite: the Marine Corps. *Semper Fi*, do or die. North got caught up in the zeal exuded by the Academy. He liked that it stood for something. No subtleties or shades of gray. Absolutes. For North, the Academy personified patriotism and upholding the American way. He loved his country and wanted to help keep it great. He could think of no finer or more noble calling. It was not a particularly difficult progression for him to decide he was ready to die for his country. Nothing was more important.

North quickly picked up the other elements of Academy life. He was assigned to the Ninth Company. There were thirty-six companies comprising the brigade of midshipmen, and a hundred-odd men in each company, made up of members of each class. Six companies made a battalion, three battalions made a regiment, and two regiments made the brigade. North's class, though known universally as plebes, was technically called the fourth class. The sophomores were the third class, juniors second class and seniors first class.

The midshipmen's lives were largely controlled by bells. The first sounded at 6:15 A.M. for reveille and rang regularly thereafter throughout the day. Being late to anything was a reportable offense, so most of the midshipmen—especially the plebes—moved briskly all the time in a gait between walking and jogging known as a "chopping." Punctuality and precision were ingrained concepts.

Attending all meals was mandatory—except for breakfast Sunday morning, which would interfere with mandatory church services. Catholic formation was at 7:15, while the Protestants got a break, not having to gather until 9:15. Midshipmen belonging to other faiths had to attend services on their own in town.

They were awarded bachelor of science degrees when they graduated, signifying their mastery of such engineering esoterica as fluid dynamics and electronic systems. For those like North who wanted combat infantry careers in the Marine Corps, these courses were irrelevant and hard to take, but the rules were the rules. Still, academics were far from everything at Annapolis or any other military academy where education seemed schizophrenic: class standing was based not just on proficiency in course work but on intangibles like leadership ability and other skills needed to shine in the military realm.

The plebe year is devoted largely to indoctrination into the naval system. Between plebe and third-class years, the midshipmen get their first exposure to life at sea by taking their "youngster cruise." They meet the enlisted men they will later command as commissioned officers and they stand deck, operations, engineering and gunnery watches.

Returning for their second year they begin work in their academic majors and begin to accept more military responsibility. In the summer after their second year the middies go on a tour to get an introduction to the four warfare specialties from which they will choose their careers: the submarine service at New London, Connecticut; surface warfare at Norfolk, Virginia; naval aviation at Pensacola, Florida and the Marine Corps Basic School at Quantico, Virginia.

The second classmen, or juniors, take on much of the responsibility for indoctrinating plebes and further specialize in their majors, while the first classmen look forward to completing their academic requirements, assume more and more military responsibilities and select their areas of service.

All midshipmen were required to take sports at either the intercollegiate or intramural level, and for plebes boxing was mandatory during the summer introductory period. The *mano à mano* combat of boxing was thought to help instill the toughness and resiliency prized by the Academy, so it was one of the most prestigious sports at Annapolis. North would take up boxing and sailing—once going on a cruise from Newport to Bermuda.

All the midshipmen were instructed closely in the Academy's concept of honor, which they swore to uphold at all times. Honor was defined as a "quality which renders a person unable to say anything less than absolute truth in any situation, regardless of the outcome, and it leaves him incapable of any action which would bring reproach upon his integrity."

Rather than promulgating specific rules and regulations, the Academy had an Honor Concept which provided that:

1. Midshipmen will not lie, cheat or steal, nor will they mislead or deceive anyone as to known facts. A midshipman will be truthful, trustworthy, honest and forthright at all times and under all circumstances.
2. Midshipmen are presumed to be honorable at all times and to possess moral integrity in the fullest sense and will be treated accordingly, unless they prove otherwise by their words or actions.
3. Midshipmen should neither permit nor accept anything which is not just, right and true. They should do the right thing because it is right, not because of fear of punishment.

The Honor Concept was administered through a Midshipmen Honor Organization consisting of elected representatives from each class. Honor violations could be reported by midshipmen, faculty or other officers who could also exercise discretion and simply warn the offender. This was different than the West Point honor code which gave cadets no discretion in reporting honor violations.

Dewey Beliech, Jr., North's roommate for two years, recalls that Ollie took the Honor Concept seriously. Roommates had to trust each other at Annapolis, and if North promised the room would be clean for inspection, Beliech could take it to the bank. "I'd say that Ollie was dependable and honest to the point that if he told me anything, I'd stake my reputation on that being true..." Beliech says. "You could trust him at his word. He would put his life on the line. I'd go anywhere with him and do anything with him."

Any plebe who needed a morale boost received one the evening of August 1, when President John F. Kennedy appeared in the courtyard of Bancroft Hall at a ceremony honoring the new class. Kennedy, himself a Navy veteran, had spoken at the 1961 Annapo-

lis commencement during his first year in office. Another appearance, especially one in honor of the plebes, was unusual, but JFK
made no secret of his special affection for the Academy. Though he
did not note it, it was twenty years to the day since Kennedy's PT
boat 109 was sunk by a Japanese destroyer in the South Pacific. He
had been decorated for heroism for swimming many hours to find
rescue craft.

At the lectern Kennedy told the members of the brigade: "I hope
you will stand at ease." When none of the midshipmen moved a
muscle, Kennedy drew laughter when he said: "Perhaps the plebes
will."

Then, speaking without notes, the president thanked the plebes
for having entered the navy, and said he sometimes thought the
American people did not appreciate that the security and peace
they enjoyed was made possible by the devotion and sacrifices of
young men such as themselves.

"I want to express our strong hope that all of you who have come
to the Academy as plebes will stay with the navy," Kennedy said. "I
can think of no more rewarding a career. You will have a chance in
the next ten, twenty and thirty years to serve the cause of freedom
and your country all over the globe, to hold positions of the highest
responsibility, to recognize that upon your good judgment in many
cases may well rest not only the well-being of the men with whom
you serve but also in a very real sense the security of your country...

"And any man who may be asked in this century what he did to
make his life worthwhile, I think can respond with a good deal of
pride and satisfaction: 'I served in the United States Navy.' So I
congratulate you all. This is a hard job, particularly now as you
make the change, but I think it develops in you those qualities
which we like to see in our country, which we take pride in. I am
sure you are going to stay with it. I am sure you are going to be
able, by what you are now going through, to find the means to
command others.

"So I express our very best wishes to you, and tell you that
though you will be serving in the Navy in the days when most of
those who hold public office have long gone from it, I can assure
you in 1963 that your services are needed, that your opportunities
are unlimited, and that if I were a young man in 1963 I can imagine
no place to be better than right here at this Academy..."

At the end of the president's remarks, which lasted less than five
minutes, the plebes gave him three 'hip-hip-hurrahs,' then broke

into prolonged cheering. North and the plebes were thrilled to be addressed by the young, dashing president, whose own navy background swelled them with new pride. How many freshmen of other colleges were addressed by an incumbent president? His words had been inspirational and helped to give meaning to the weeks of pain and anguish they had been going through.

Reacting to the ovation, Kennedy quipped: "In view of that warm cheer, I'd like to—using the full powers of the office—grant amnesty to whomever needs it, whomever deserves it!" There were laughs all around and more cheering, as the plebes, their sense of esprit de corps reinvigorated, filed off to resume their mission.

Just three months later, Kennedy was dead in Dallas. The country and the world were shocked, but the Academy—notably the class of 1967 which the president had so inspired in August—was especially shaken. For North and the rest of the plebes, the assassination marked their induction into the turbulent sixties—a cosmic event that even the isolation of Annapolis could not shield them from.

Three months later North was involved in a serious car accident that threatened his dream of a commission in the Marine Corps. It was Washington's Birthday weekend, 1964, and he and four other plebes had decided to rent a car and drive to upstate New York for the brief holiday.

Tom Parker, a classmate of North's and one of the other passengers, remembers the midshipmen got off to a late start, leaving the Academy at 4 P.M. and heading to nearby Washington to pick up their new Chevy II.

Snow was falling heavily as they started their trip. After several hours on the road, everyone in the car was asleep when the driver, nineteen-year-old Edward R. Wagner, also dozed off as they sped along Route 15 near Corning, New York. Their car veered over into the path of an oncoming tractor trailer truck and struck it head on. Wagner was killed and the other four plebes sustained injuries of varying severity. North, who had been sitting in the back seat directly behind Wagner, was the least seriously hurt, according to Dr. Paul Darling, general surgeon at Corning Hospital, where the midshipmen were initially taken. He sustained a broken nose, injuries to his back, and had cartilage damage in his right knee that would require two operations.

North's injuries were serious enough that after the corrective surgery on his knee was performed at the Bethesda Naval Hospital outside Washington he was put on a rehabilitation program and was forced to drop out of Annapolis for a time to round himself back into shape. He returned home to Philmont to recuperate over the summer.

Friends, classmates, neighbors and family who saw North during this period remain struck by the memory of his dogged determination to rehabilitate his knee so that no one could deny him the Marine commission he so badly wanted. Howard Rhoades, a Philmont neighbor, recalls that while he was home North went so far as to jump off the roof of his house to build up the strength in his knee.

"He told me during the recuperative period he was going to overcome this injury and get back in the swing of things," says Rhoades. "He didn't want this to beat him."

Though North had completed more than half a year before the accident occurred, Academy officials ruled that he would have to repeat his plebe year—but he would not have to be subjected to hazing again. So he returned to Annapolis in the fall of 1964, now twenty-one—three years older than the average incoming plebe— and a member of the class of 1968.

Some of North's classmates speculate that having to repeat his plebe year must have had a traumatic effect on him. Now a "turn-back," as those who had to repeat a year were called, North was left behind by members of the class of 1967 with whom he had sweated out so much. The sense of accomplishment he had felt in weathering most of his plebe year was negated now that he had to repeat it. But others remember that he took the setback with equanimity and grace, seeming just glad to be back at the Academy and on track for his commission again.

"I think Ollie was appreciative that they were letting him in for another try," says classmate Jack Holly, still on active duty in the navy. "He looks at the glass half-full."

Still, North was caught betwixt-and-between that second plebe year. His original class was ahead of him, he was considerably older than his new classmates, and being exempt from hazing he was very much the outsider, not having to share in the pain of other plebes.

"He seemed almost guilty," remembers John Sinclair, "He probably would have preferred to be run just for the camaraderie."

One thing is clear: if North had been gung-ho before the accident, he became even more so afterward. His knee evidently caused him pain and he was forced to wear a brace on it when exercising. But he seemed extremely conscious of proving to all concerned that the injury would not prevent him from keeping pace physically with any other midshipman.

So by the time reveille sounded, North had already taken a long run, regardless of the weather. Like most Marines in training he ran in combat boots, and he ran the ominous sea wall along Chesapeake Bay. Negotiating the wall's large, smooth, slippery rocks on the dead run was hard enough under any conditions. It must have been doubly so for North on a gimpy knee, skimming along in the predawn darkness. Still, North would usually take another run around the Yard when evening rolled around, or hop through the Academy's obstacle course.

Against doctor's orders he would draw pads to play in the annual Turkey Bowl intramural tackle football game, and in still another effort to prove he was fit enough to be a Marine, North took up boxing in earnest. "Ollie probably didn't belong in my boxing program," recalls Emerson Smith, the navy's longtime boxing coach, now retired. "He just wasn't physically qualified. But because of his personality and his insistence on being in the program, I accepted him."

There was more. During holidays, when other plebes would go home, North would travel to military bases for extra training in such things as parachuting and survival tactics—programs the navy did not offer. He went to jump school at Fort Benning, Georgia and survival school in Nevada.

No pain, no gain, as they say. "He drove himself to anguish just to get his knee back in shape," says Sinclair.

As he honed his body, North took care not to neglect his spiritual dimension. The Catholic chaplain, the Reverend John Laboon, remembers North not only attending mass every Sunday but also the early morning mass in Saint Andrews Chapel during the week. Laboon said it took a dedicated midshipman to walk across the Yard for the 6 A.M. call to prayer.

As for academe, that proved more problematic for North. Though he was pleased that the Academy had just instituted academic reforms that allowed the midshipmen to branch out to take electives and choose their own majors (rather then force them to take just engineering), North still had to study harder than many of his company-mates to maintain an acceptable grade-point average. He took a correspondence course to help get him through thermodynamics and fluid mechanics.

"Ollie did everything on blood, sweat and tears," says Jack Holly.

"He was not a wing-it sort of guy. He was not one of those people with a gift for doing things easily. Whatever Ollie did, he researched it and developed it and worked hard at it." Adds former roommate Sinclair: "He wasn't too sharp in sciences and math. He was frightened that he'd fail, because if you failed you were out of the Academy."

But North did much better in the humanities like history, political science and English, subjects referred to as "bull" courses at the Academy. He was most interested in geopolitical issues and military strategy. North chose to major in international relations and was particularly involved in a course on Communist China taught by William Corson. The course was full of midshipmen who knew that U.S. involvement in Vietnam was escalating, and it offered important insights into Southeast Asia.

Another of North's instructors, Robert Hennemeyer, who would later become the United States ambassador to Gambia, recalls that North was one of his better students in a course on contemporary African problems. "I remember him as one who did the readings, got papers in on time and spoke in class," Hennemeyer says. "He had decided views."

Indeed North did. Sinclair remembers that he and his roommate used to talk about communism in Central America. "He said to me, 'Johnny, that's where communism is going to be in the late seventies or eighties...' He held strong anticommunist opinions. It was an on-going threat, it was there, ever prevalent, and we—being in the front lines of the military—we had to fight it." North boned up on his enemies, studying insurgency, and the writings of Mao and Ché.

The Academy basically preached action over reflection, and North gravitated to the philosophy. Above all else he was a doer. He was someone who if assigned a job would get it done. He wouldn't ask how or why—he would just do it, and this was a quality that superiors at the Academy and in later life would always find attractive in him. This ethos of getting the job done was extolled in a small pamphlet entitled "A Message to Garcia" given to all midshipmen at the time.

According to the pamphlet, written in 1899 by a man named Elbert Hubbard, when the Spanish-American War broke out in 1898, President William McKinley needed to get a message to an insurgent leader named Garcia who was somewhere in the mountainous jungles of Cuba—out of reach of the mail or telegraph.

How to transmit the message? Someone suggested to McKinley that if anyone could get the message to Garcia, it was a man named Rowan. Rowan took the letter, sealed it in an oilskin pouch, strapped it over his heart, sailed to Cuba in an open boat and landed there four days later. He plunged into the jungle, traversed hostile territory, found Garcia, gave him the message from McKinley and emerged on the other side of the island three weeks later.

"The point I wish to make is this," writes Hubbard. "McKinley gave Rowan a letter to be delivered to Garcia; Rowan took the letter and did not ask, 'Where is he at?' By the Eternal! There is a man whose form should be cast in deathless bronze and the statue placed in every college of the land. It is not book-learning young men need, nor instruction about this and that, but a stiffening of the vertebrae which will cause them to be loyal to a trust, to act promptly, concentrate their energies: to do the thing—'Carry a message to Garcia!'

". . . My heart goes out to the man who does his work when the 'boss' is away, as well as when he is at home. And the man, who, when given a letter for Garcia, quietly takes the missive, without asking any idiotic questions, and with no lurking intention of chucking it into the nearest sewer, or of doing aught else but deliver it, never gets 'laid off,' nor has to go on strike for higher wages. Civilization is one long anxious search for just such individuals. Anything such a man asks will be granted; his kind is so rare that no employer can afford to let him go. He is wanted in every city, town and village—in every office, shop, store and factory. The world cries out for such: he is needed and needed badly—the man who can carry a message to Garcia."

North thought he was up to that.

He finally completed his seemingly interminable plebe year in the spring of 1965, then went off on his youngster cruise, sailing from California to Hawaii on a destroyer. He got a good taste of life at sea, swabbing the decks, cleaning the bottom of the ship and standing watch. North evidently was not overly taken with being a sailor, taking care to stress to anyone who would listen that he intended to be a Marine. One classmate on board the same destroyer remembers that Ollie would often take the Marine enlisted uniform he had gotten while at summer camp at Brockport out of his seabag and show everyone how to fold it perfectly. It was a way to set himself apart from the rest of the mids.

But the cruise wasn't all drudgery. North got to try surfing at

Waikiki, and unlike his younger classmates, made use of the night-clubs and bars on liberty—along with John Sinclair, who was on a different destroyer in the same squadron, and who also was twenty-one.

The cruise lasted nearly two months, and they made their way back to the Academy in August. As tradition had it, they officially became upperclassmen when they first sighted the chapel dome on entering the Yard.

When it came time for North to run the plebes, he didn't haze them as zealously as might have been expected. It was common for some upperclassmen who had gotten a thorough going-over as plebes to take it out on a new plebe class to see that they endured the same hardship.

North seemed to have no appetite for that. Others remember his approach as tough but fair. Dewey Beliech says Ollie had a hard exterior but always retained a degree of sympathy for plebes who were having a hard time getting through the trials of their first year. North would look for a plebe's strengths and weaknesses and try to develop him, not break him, said Beliech.

Actually, by the fall of 1965 hazing had been restricted as a result of congressional investigations and other outside pressure. North's second plebe year in 1964 was the last time a class had been officially subjected to hazing, though midshipmen concede it continued behind closed doors. Still, North showed restraint.

"He wasn't a guy who would yell at them to do pushups—he'd do pushups with them," recalls Chris Glutting, another classmate. "He wasn't someone who ran around putting people on report. He'd give them personal counseling."

The commanding officer of North's new company (the Seventh), Reid Olson, was morally opposed to humiliation and other kinds of abuse. Olson, who had just returned from Vietnam, said North had the right approach. "He was an example of how I wanted someone to treat plebes or subordinates," Olson says. "He was more mature. He treated them with fairness and dignity. He did not abuse power."

Occasionally North allowed his mind to wander to women, specifically Lynore White, the hometown girl whom he had been dating off and on since 1961. After his car accident, Lynore had written to him every day and gone to visit him in June of 1964 at the hospital down at Annapolis.

"It was beautiful but quiet," she remembers. "None of the other midshipmen were there at the time. He showed me around the campus, and he showed me Washington. He was given leave from the hospital. He was wearing a knee brace, and walked with a limp and was in pain. He didn't know if he was going to be allowed to continue. But he was very determined. Repeating his freshman year didn't bother him ... He was very proud of the school. I remember being struck by how much it meant to him, and how determined he was to recover and start over again."

They saw each other that summer of 1964 when he was home recuperating. She was home from Smith, getting ready for her junior year. She thought they were forging a relationship. They went back to a few of their old high school haunts like Kozel's, and he spent time at her family's house.

North was especially popular with her grandfather, Frank White, a Lithuanian immigrant. North and the elder White would sit out on the front porch on hot summer nights and talk about the evils of communism. Mr. White, whose country had been swallowed up by the Soviet Union, felt very strongly about the Red Menace, and North wasn't about to disagree. He was fascinated to hear firsthand about what it was like to be victimized by the Russians. They discussed the growing American involvement in Vietnam and both agreed that the U.S. role there was proper. Communism had to be quashed, or at the least contained, wherever it reared its ugly head, they thought. "My grandfather thought Larry was a fine young man," Lynore remembers.

So did she. They had a casual, easy relationship that seemed to blossom when they were in the relatively mundane setting of Philmont rather than away at college, when they saw each other infrequently and only in the context of a big weekend where there was never enough time and the situations were often artificial, she thought. They just laughed and had fun together. Nothing heavy. No searing or particularly illuminating talks about life. They never seemed to fight, though Lynore remembers North getting mildly irritated with her when she smoked, or when the rabbit hair from her coat shed onto his navy blues. She liked his traditional, courtly view of women, and she knew he would never pressure her to do anything she didn't want to do. "He had a very Catholic attitude about sex," Lynore says. "He didn't think you should be promiscuous ... He was a romantic who thought sex should properly take its course."

When North returned to Annapolis for his second plebe year he was all business. He was so obsessed with getting back on track and proving himself physically fit that he felt he had no time for distractions like women. He called Lynore and told her so.

"He said he had to devote himself to preparing for his career," she remembers. "It was very abrupt. I thought our attraction had been mutual. I said I didn't understand. Then he called again in the summer of 1965 after his second plebe year. He was in San Francisco. I don't know if he was on a cruise, or what. He said he wanted to see me again. I said, 'When you're home, call.' I was happy, but I didn't know how serious he was about this. He'd been with friends who'd said, 'Why don't you call her if you're thinking about her?' So he did call when he got home and we started dating again.

"We'd known each other so long it wasn't like getting to know each other all over again. He invited me down for the Army-Navy game that fall. I went down with his brother and sister. It was an important date. But we didn't sit together because all the midshipmen sit together. There was a party after the game. I stayed over Saturday night and went back the next day."

They wrote and telephoned each other that year, and in the spring of 1966, just before Lynore's graduation from Smith, she asked him to come to a party a girlfriend was having outside Princeton. North agreed, which was something of a rarity, since it was the first college function of hers he had attended since her freshman year. The girls at Smith had thought North was a mystery because while Lynore talked about him a lot, he never came to see her.

But that was in the past, and North had big plans for a future with Lynore. After the party, when they were alone in the kitchen of her host's house, North presented her with his Annapolis pin. Would she accept it?

"I was thrilled," she remembers. "It wasn't like being engaged, but it was the step before that, and the assumption was that we would be. We had never discussed it before. He was still only a sophomore. I didn't expect him to talk about marriage because a midshipman had to be single, and if it was discovered that he was married, he could be thrown out . . . Anyway, we had a nice hug. Back at my college, I got thrown in the shower, which was tradition for people who had just gotten pinned."

North did not attend her graduation from Smith, but as soon as Lynore got her diploma she hurried down to attend June Week at Annapolis, which included commencement and formal dances. They were still on something of a postpinning high, but again, the event seemed to dominate their time together. She stayed in a

house with a bunch of other girls as Ollie whirled around the Yard
going from one function to the next. She remembers feeling a little
neglected: "I guess I felt like I gave him more than he gave me."

Lynore went off to Europe to spend the summer traveling, then
returned in the fall of 1966 to enroll in a graduate English program
at the University of Indiana. "There I started thinking I didn't want
to be pinned anymore," she recalls. "He was very serious then, and
I was just not ready to commit myself. I guess I started thinking.
First, I didn't want to settle down. We had pretty much had a
long-distance relationship, and I wasn't sure I wanted to be married
and be left for long periods of time. I had had a taste of that from
the way our romance had gone.

"The military life was so important to him, I suppose I finally
decided I didn't want to be number two. It wasn't something I did
lightly. Also, back in the sixties, girls were pretty shy, but I was
starting to become more assertive. I felt I was just as important as
he was . . . He thought men were action-oriented, and women were
there for support . . . But I was less willing to wait by the phone. I
guess I felt getting a masters in English was just as important as
what he was doing. He thought what he was doing was very, very
important. I thought he'd consider his career to be much more
important than me.

"This was the Vietnam War and Larry thought that a lot of graduate students were flaky intellectuals—nonpatriotic, you know. He
might have had the general impression that people going to graduate school in English were not as committed to the United States as
he was . . . I think I had changed from being pretty shy and sort of
completely agreeing with him to having my own opinions. I'd met
some people in graduate school who were still very patriotic, even
though they didn't support the Vietnam War. But Larry always
thought we were doing absolutely the right thing over there. He
was experiencing one kind of education, and I was experiencing
another.

"I wrote him and told him I'd send the pin back. He was angry.
He told me not to bother because he'd throw it in the Severn if I
did. So I kept it."

Back at Annapolis, North took out his frustrations in the boxing
ring. Boxing was one of the biggest sports at the Academy and the
boxers were widely respected among the midshipmen. North liked
to box for predictable reasons. It was basic and primal, it was individual, and it was subtle reinforcement for any who still doubted

his physical capacities after the accident, that he was all the way
back. He decided to give himself the ultimate test by entering the
brigade championships in his 147-pound weight class.

Boxing was noted for turning out combat leaders. The boxing
teams had already had several of its members from the classes of
1966 and 1967 either killed or wounded in Vietnam. "Everyone
boxes because it teaches the kids how to get hit in the head," says
Gary McBride. "Boxing prepares you for combat in the sense that if
a concussion goes off and you get knocked off your tank and you're
in command, you can say to yourself, 'Well, I've been hit before
and I can take a hit to the head. They teach boxing to everyone.
Therefore everyone respects it. The brigade championship is a big
deal."

North had had no boxing experience prior to the Academy. He
was a plodding southpaw, short on style and finesse. But he was
aggressive, could take a punch and he had guts. He was also in
better condition than most of his opponents and could often overwhelm them with a flurry of punches.

Emerson Smith, the Academy's legendary boxing coach, called
North a "Friday night fighter," meaning that he often looked like a
bum sparring in practice but come fight night, he invariably put on
a quality performance.

North won his five preliminary bouts in the brigade championships to reach the finals against Jim Webb. Webb and North were
two of the leading members of their class, rivals for leadership positions outside the ring, and neither was particularly fond of the
other; so the fight was a natural.

Four or five days before the bout North was sparring with another lefthander to prep for Webb, who was also a southpaw, when
the sparring partner, Dennis Dilly, decked North. Smith was concerned that North's head might have been scrambled just days before the big fight.

Actually, Smith had been worried about North as a boxer ever
since the car accident. At first he had planned to deny Ollie permission to enter the brigade championships, but after he won all
his fights the previous year the coach had had no choice. Still,
Smith had insisted that North get medical clearance before being
allowed to participate in the tournament.

Smith, who was like a father to all the boxers, remained concerned that North might get hurt in the finals because of the Dilly
incident and because of the quality of North's opponent: Webb. If
truth be told, Smith thought, North was simply not in Webb's class.

Webb was a stylish, accomplished boxer who figured to dominate Ollie the way Apollo Creed figured to lick Rocky Balboa.

"Ollie's work in the gym ten days before the fight was unsatisfactory as far as I was concerned," Smith remembers. So the coach spent hours after practice in one-on-one sessions with Ollie, teaching him how to circle against another left-hander and how best to counter Webb's moves. Webb felt this private attention was unprecedented and amounted to the coach favoring his opponent. "What about me, coach?" he asked as he watched Smith tutor North.

Smith told Webb he was more than ready for the fight. It was North who needed help. "My main concern was that he had gotten hurt in the [car] wreck," Smith says. "I told Jimmy that Oliver was hurt from the wreck. I said, 'I'm concerned, and you should know what my concern is, and I don't want anyone to get hurt, and that's the reason I'm trying to prepare Oliver so he can go three rounds with you.' I didn't feel I'd overdone the work with Oliver. I just felt he would be completely dominated in the bout."

Smith's attention to North may have psyched Webb out. It certainly demoralized him, while the fears being voiced about North's physical condition confused him. And since the NCAA had dropped intercollegiate boxing in 1960 after a University of Wisconsin fighter had died of brain damage sustained in a fight, there were widespread fears at the time about other serious injuries. Webb later told friends he'd heard the talk about North's injuries and wondered if he should go all out.

Come fight night, MacDonough Hall was packed to the rafters with 2,500 midshipmen screaming and stomping their feet. Officers and their wives were at ringside. A band played the old Gillette fight song to get the crowd even more aroused. When North and Webb entered the arena and strode to the ring, the crowd—about equally divided with boosters for each fighter—stood as one, screaming for blood. It was the third fight on a four-fight card. There were even celebrities around: the first fight had been refereed by Rocky Marciano.

According to many who witnessed it, the North-Webb three-round match was one for the books. North eked out an upset win by two points. Ollie was awarded the first round, 20–19. The second round was scored evenly, 20–20, while North again won the third round, 20–19.

"I was there the night of the fight," boasts Gary McBride. "It was one of the greatest matches ever." Many of the old grads remember, and there are still Webb and North factions with strong views on the subject. The Webb partisans continue to maintain their man was in a funk and a fog that night—definitely not himself because of Smith's apparent tilt toward North and the hype about North's physical condition. Ollie's boosters say the bout was classic testament to his lust for guts and glory. "Ollie was the original Rocky," says Keith Haines, a classmate who would later raise money for North's legal defense fund. "The difference was that he won the championship. He didn't tie."

In any case, the fight has attained legendary status today not only because of the fame that both the combatants later went on to attain, but because many believe at least parts of the bout are recounted in *A Sense of Honor*, Webb's bestselling novel about life at the Academy. North has bragged to some people he is the character named Chervanek, who in the book beats Fogarty, the protagonist and presumably Webb. But Webb, who remains irritated to this day by North's crowing, scoffs at Chervanek being Ollie, noting that the book has Fogarty losing on a TKO, while North beat him on points.

North was awarded his varsity letter for winning the championship, and wore it proudly around the Yard—some say too proudly. "You couldn't go near North without him patting his letter sweater," says one classmate, a Webb partisan.

But Coach Smith said North had reason to be proud. "It was an honor to get a varsity *N* in boxing," he says. "It was a symbol. You were a macho man in your weight class at the Academy." Smith, who retired after 1986 after twenty-seven years as head coach, retains a deep affection for North, and the feeling is mutual. At Smith's retirement dinner North showed up with a letter in tribute to the coach signed by President Ronald Reagan.

"I'd say that of all the young people at the Naval Academy, this person was as dedicated to service of country as any other—ever," says Smith of North. "He was dedicated to following orders... I can't say enough good things about him. He's truly an American. He is a very determined young man. A fierce competitor. A young man who knows what he wants to do, sets out to achieve things and gets them done."

Occasionally North could take the fierce competitor trait too far, some thought. His senior year, North opted to quit boxing at the top of the heap and help Smith coach instead. Each battalion

fielded an intramural team and Ollie coached his team. In trying to
get his squad up for bouts with rival battalions, North would sometimes resort to a Knute Rockne number.

A classmate who coached another battalion getting ready to box
North's remembers that just before the bout both squads were on
either side of a big room getting last minute instructions from their
coaches.

"I can hear [North] talking right before the match, there was no
partition," the classmate says. "He was over there . . . haranguing
them: 'When you look across the ring, think to yourself that guy has
been fucking your mother and called your sister the worst name he
could possibly call her,' and on and on trying to get these guys
excited about killing someone. Using names. 'A guy called you a
motherfucker and a sonuvabitch. Think of the worst names this guy
called you and that's what he called you.'

"My guys were looking that way and I wondered what was going
on. I said, 'Don't bother. I don't want your psyche to be broken.
Just concentrate on what I tell you on breaks and take it from
there.' As it turned out, my battalion lost not one fight. We cleaned
him out . . . It showed something about his attitude. What a
schmuck. When we were talking amateur boxing, he'd think we
were going out to swing chains at each other or have knives in our
boots."

Another classmate who boxed with North says he recalls seeing
North taunt opponents he had beaten. "I observed a couple of situations where he was overzealous when it came to a fight, and he
didn't keep in mind the right amount of respect for an opponent
. . . You don't degrade an opponent if you're victorious . . . You
maintain a level of respect. In getting pumped up for the fight he
would lose respect for the opponent. He'd be so charged up he'd
want to kill the guy."

Adds David Evans, a member of the class of 1966: "He was
known, after fights, to call his opponent, behind his back, a turkey."

Competition seemed to permeate life at Annapolis, more so than
at the average college or university. The quest for class standing,
for leadership positions, for dominance in sports, for general excel-
lence everywhere seemed all-consuming. The navy officially spoke
of building "competitive spirit and desire to win" as key attributes
in a midshipman.

No area seemed too mundane to compete in—not even the presidency of the foreign-affairs club. North was going up against Keith

Haines and sought every edge he could get, convincing Professor William Corson to nominate him in front of the club members. But the ploy backfired: Haines won by three votes.

Constant competition eventually broke up North's friendship with his former roommate, Sinclair. North and Sinclair were alike in many ways. They were both three years older than the rest of their classmates, having entered the Academy later in life. Sinclair had flunked out of Kent State in 1962, then gone to the Naval Academy prep school for a year before entering the class of 1968. North was slightly shorter than Sinclair, they both had substantial egos and loved to lead men. They aspired to be flag officers: Ollie had confided to Sinclair and others he wanted to be commandant of the Marine Corps. They had even discussed the kind of woman it would take to complement their budding careers—what it took to be a good military wife.

"Ollie and I were very similar—we were in competition from the start because we were so similar," Sinclair says. "It was a good thing we were inseparable because it drove us to do a better job. It drove me to be a better football player and him to be a better boxer."

But in subtle ways, which Sinclair has difficulty expressing, the competition between them tore at the fabric of their friendship. The fierce rivalry went too far—perhaps played out in North's besting of Sinclair for the prestigious position of commander of the Seventh Company in two of their final three semesters senior year. North had the job in the fall and spring, Sinclair the winter.

As company commander Ollie would lead the company in parades and processions, and he would run formations. Shelby Guilbert says the Seventh Company was in the top ten in every parade competition during their first class year. "We were the best marching company in the battalion, and that probably had to do with the pride Ollie had for the processions."

Neither North nor Sinclair seemed to care to grapple with the root cause of their friendship's erosion. "The split affected me deeply, but Ollie seemed to get over it a lot easier." Sinclair said.

North was busy looking onward and upward, and the company commander slot would help propel him on his way. The position was largely a popularity contest, but company officer Reid Olson, with whom North had grown close, had had the final say. Olson remembers why he chose North: "He was one of the outstanding members of the company. He was one of the five or six best members of the class. People looked up to him because he wouldn't tell them to do something if he couldn't do it himself... He was not cocky. He was self-assured. I knew when I asked him to carry out something he'd do it without abuse . . . He motivated people rather than directed them . . . I wouldn't mind having North as my son."

Reverend Laboon said North seemed like a son to whomever was his boss. "That was the relationship he had with those in a leadership capacity. He loves to follow. Fierce loyalty is one of the traits of the graduates of the Naval Academy. At times it goes unquestioned."

If North was searching for a father figure, some who know him speculate it was because he was disenchanted with his own. Professor Corson, who would remain in close contact with North after the Academy, said he has told his former pupil that he is searching for a surrogate father. "Ollie did not get along with his father . . ." says Corson. "If he brought home a ninety-nine, his father wanted to know why it wasn't a hundred."

According to a Chicago *Tribune* profile, a Marine officer and former classmate agrees that North's father was "aloof, demanding, never satisfied with anything he did," and that therefore Ollie might have sought some sort of paternal guidance elsewhere. But he added: "Others make the argument he was an ass-kisser who wanted to be close to his seniors. It's a tried-and-true way to get ahead, and Ollie was always ambitious, always determined to get ahead."

His ability to get along with superiors or authority figures also saved him from getting into trouble. Professor William H. Russell a former history professor at the Academy now living outside Philadelphia, recalls that once North drove into Washington to do some research for a paper and borrowed a navy car. On the way home he got into an accident. But according to the police the accident was unavoidable as far as North was concerned, and there could have been serious loss of life if he hadn't handled the car the way he did. Police gave North a letter to that effect which he could show to his bosses back at Annapolis. North was not disciplined. "It showed me—well, to get a letter of praise for being in an accident—that's a man that lands on his feet," says Russell.

North had continued to date casually here and there—as casually as one could date at Annapolis. Most of the midshipmen had strict curfews. Any public display of affection, including hand-holding, was a punishable offense, and drinking was not permitted within a seven-mile radius of the Yard.

Coach Smith used to fix up his daughter, Debbie, with some of the midshipmen, and though she never dated North she remembers going on double-dates with him. He would "keep the other couples laughing," she says. "He talked the most and entertained everybody." She adds she wished her father had set her up with Ollie instead of his buddies.

But some of North's classmates who went along on those double and triple dates were less impressed with his behavior around women. One says he was courtly and chivalrous "to the point of me and my friends rolling our eyes." And the classmate interpreted North's garrulousness and hilarity as a rather obvious quest for attention. When a group photo was taken, they said, North would almost invariably wave his hands or make a face so that he would stand out.

"He can't just be one of the guys," the classmate continues. "He always has to do something to attract attention to himself. It's a cultivated charm purely on the face of it... This guy gives me a headache just thinking about him... He had so much potential. He was very articulate and bright, but he had this overwhelming desire to be recognized, always, always, always. He was so obsessed with it."

With cultivated charm or not, North was still looking to settle down with someone, and he still had not given up on Lynore White. Passing through Indiana in the summer of 1967 while driving a commanding officer's Cadillac crosscountry, back to the East Coast, North called his old flame to say hello and asked if they could get together. Lynore declined. Later that fall when the navy football team played Notre Dame at South Bend, North called her again to see if she would come to the game with him. But again Lynore said no.

"I guess I was a bit hostile," she recalls. "I just decided it wasn't right to see him again."

Finally getting the message, North began dating Kathy Cunningham, a speech therapist in the Annapolis public schools. She met North through a teacher at her school whose husband had known North before the Academy. Their first date was dinner at her colleague's apartment.

"He was more mature than the other midshipmen," Kathy recalls. "I was twenty-four years old... He was special and different. Some guys would rent a motel room and have a keg of beer. Ollie never participated in that... We just went out to dinner. We'd sit and talk. It was a more mature level of dating.

"I remember him being extremely patriotic... We talked about his future as a career in the service. I didn't feel I could live that kind of life. I knew what it entailed—going to admirals' teas and parties. He was a gung-ho Marine, which I thought was the most dangerous branch of the service. I could envision myself being a widow at a young age, and I didn't want that... I knew he was going to Vietnam. He made that quite clear. He wanted to go to the front lines. That scared me. But also I had someone whom I had been involved with that was on the back burner. So I knew I could go back to him. I know Ollie cared about me. He didn't actually propose. We were both forthright and honest."

Kathy says North talked candidly about how he had been jilted by Lynore White, and she thought that had put him on the defensive with women. But North had impeccable manners and was very solicitous of her during their six-month courtship. Their last date was the Army-Navy football game of 1967.

"We had a long talk before the game, sitting in the car... I was honest with him. He'd known I was dating someone seriously at home and I'd told him that Gary asked me to stop dating... Larry was just really a gentleman. He didn't put any pressure on me. I don't even know if it would have gotten to marriage talk... But Larry said: 'If you decide to take this proposition, this will be our last date.' I cried. He put his arm around me. He didn't try to use sexual advances to change my mind—just very sensitive and loving...

"I saw *An Officer and a Gentleman*, and it made me think of him."

Perhaps it didn't even occur to North that two women whom he had been serious about had now, it seemed, jilted him because he was so gung-ho. They cared for him but they didn't want to be military wives—or widows. North may or may not have made the causal connection, but it's doubtful he would have let a woman stand between him and the Marine Corps in any case.

The Marines remained his *raison d'être*. All his classmates knew it and kidded him about it. "No matter where his career may lead, we know his thoughts will always be of the Corps, the Corps and the Corps," the yearbook noted of North.

Another classmate, commenting on the Academy pecking order, said: "The hard-core Marine types were different. They traveled in totally different circles. There was a certain segment of us who liked to go out and enjoy ourselves—others ate, slept and drank the Marine Corps and their whole goal was to get down to Quantico as fast as they could. When everyone else was relaxing, they'd be off running. Ollie was in that group."

Adds Shelby Guilbert: "He was the kind of guy who if you'd told him to march off the Empire State Building with a platoon of Marines, he would have done it... His zeal came from always trying to prove he could come back from the auto accident."

Indeed, North seemed obsessed with the possibility, however remote, that he would be prevented from getting a Marine commission because of his bad knee. He had passed various physicals for boxing and other purposes, but the one for acceptance into the Corps was more stringent, and he had been warned since just after the accident that there was a chance he could be surveyed out. After all the work he had done, all the dreams he had invested in, North couldn't even bear the thought.

So strong was this fear that in the early part of 1968 North apparently decided to go into administration offices after hours and alter his records so that they would not reflect the injuries he had sustained from the car crash. Richard A. Petrino, a classmate who was then the brigade commander, remembers being on duty one night in Bancroft Hall when he ran into North—apparently on such a mission.

"I was surprised to encounter Ollie," Petrino recalled, writing of the incident in December of 1986 for the Los Angeles *Times*. "It was well after light out, and although I was on duty it was unusual to see anyone else up and about. Not as a challenge but out of curiosity I asked why he was up at that time. He replied that he had been looking for his medical records, which contained information about serious injuries that he had received in an automobile accident. He said that he wanted to get the information out of his file because it might prevent him being accepted by the Marine Corps.

"I don't know if he succeeded in his mission. I do recall admiring his determination to do whatever he had to do to be a Marine and to serve his country, even if it meant altering his medical records. There was no question that this would be wrong, but I said nothing about it at the time; I was more concerned about the risk he was taking. There was little doubt in my mind that he considered the higher ideal of serving our country worth the risk, and that as long as he was doing it for our country, it couldn't be wrong."

Petrino, who today is a psychologist outside Philadelphia, was vague about just where and precisely under what circumstances he encountered North. But the fact that the then brigade commander did not turn North in was perhaps a commentary on North's popularity.

"Everybody liked Ollie, from the Academy's top scholars to the lowest midshipmen muddling through," Petrino continued. "He was flamboyant and a little wild, a gung-ho patriot but a dedicated midshipman who would do whatever had to be done if he thought it was in the best interests of what he believed in . . . The Ollie I knew eighteen years ago was the personification of patriotism. So were the vast majority of us at the Naval Academy. Most of us were shielded from the complicated and sometimes disorienting political and social arguments of that time. Right and wrong were defined in terms of patriotism and loyalty, and it was rare that a midshipman would run into problems with the law . . . There is no question that something about [Ollie's] sincerity, loyalty, commitment and unswerving belief in the American way was endearing and disarming. Yet I can also see the dangers of such blinding commitment and the potential for rationalization to justify breaking the rules."

Ultimately a burglary was unnecessary, but North opted for almost as dramatic a stratagem to ensure his admission to the Marines. He went to Emerson Smith and asked for the film of his boxing triumph over Jim Webb. Then, according to Smith, he screened the fight for the medical board of inquiry. Webb was going into the Marine Corps, and he had beaten Webb in boxing, North told the board. Therefore he should be given his commission. The board could not disagree with North's logic, and waved him in.

It was also true that the Marines were in need of volunteers in 1968. It was the first time ever that the Academy had not made its quota for Marines. The problem was Vietnam. The Tet Offensive in January of that year had come screaming into American living rooms on television, and everyone could see that the leathernecks were the first to fall.

The class of 1968 was a group that had known it was going to war for a long time. They had entered the Academy the week of the Gulf of Tonkin incident in August of 1964 and were preparing to graduate when Tet occurred. The character and nature of the war had changed during those four years, and domestically it had evolved from tolerable to increasingly unpopular. Society seemed to be growing antimilitary.

Though the midshipmen had labored in splendid isolation inside the walls of the Academy—sheltered even from television until their final year—they could not remain totally oblivious to what was happening in the real world. Even on excursions into Annapolis proper, students at the civilian college, Saint John's ("Johnnies," as the midshipmen called them), would taunt the middies and call them warmongers.

"The country was completely antimilitary," says Ken Kolarcik, a North classmate. "There was nothing to bolster us or give us confidence... That kind of made you angry."

"We lead a very regimented existence," remembers Tom Hayes, a graduate of the class of 1968 and a Vietnam veteran. "Our high school classmates had long hair, smoked pot and filled up Haight-Ashbury. There was a real split between us and our contemporaries. That drove us together at the Academy and fostered a sense of community—over and above the normal socialization process there that pushes you together."

But many were confused and uncertain about what lay ahead. One class member, Jeffrey Dumas, felt "stranded and more than a little frightened... unable to comprehend the drastic shift in the American psyche. Treated more as villains than heroes, and more confused than certain about our own values, we set out to explore a terrain both alien and more hostile than what we had left behind in June of 1964."

Vietnam loomed large for North and his classmates, not only because most were going there in one branch of the navy or another, but because virtually all of them knew someone who had gone there and not returned.

At the bottom of the marble steps leading up to Memorial Hall was a solemn display entitled "To Those Who Went Before Us." It consisted of three six-by-eight-foot posters containing the names and pictures of those who had been killed or were missing in Vietnam.

"It had a great impact on us," remembers Kolarcik. "We related to those guys a lot. We felt for them... They had really sacrificed something."

The Academy tried to counter that slightly macabre exhibit and boost morale by bringing in graduates who had not only made it back from Vietnam alive, but had done so with distinction. They would be introduced to the brigade at noon mess and given a hero's welcome. Usually they were winners of at least the Silver Star, more likely the Navy Cross. The mess hall would burst into applause, and then a dozen or so plebes would sprint forward and carry the men aloft on their shoulders and parade them past every table in the dining room.

If some of North's classmates were beginning to contemplate the social tumult around them that spring of 1968—the assassination of Martin Luther King, Jr., the resulting rioting in the ghettos, and the mounting opposition to the war—Ollie himself was certainly not in the vanguard of that group. He remained singleminded in focusing on his Marine Corps career. Where others may have dreaded the prospect of going to Vietnam, North could not wait to get there: war, after all, was where careers were made.

He beat the bushes trying to recruit more members of his class to opt for the Marine Corps. Using his new 427–horsepower Marine Corps green Ford Shelby Cobra muscle car he had bought with the newly received insurance money from the 1964 car accident, North led a caravan of midshipmen down to Quantico, and he debriefed company officer Reid Olson thoroughly on his Vietnam experience, questioning him about the terrain, the enemy, survival skills, battlefield tactics and what sort of leadership styles worked best in combat.

The happiness of graduation exercises on June 5, 1968, was marred by the assassination of Robert Kennedy earlier that morning in Los Angeles, and by people yelling "Cannon fodder" at the Marines as they were commissioned.

But North, who graduated 468th out of 835 (483 others had dropped out since 1964), did not really care. By now he had near-tunnel vision: Vietnam or bust. Worried that the war might somehow end before he could complete the five-month basic training program and get over to Southeast Asia, North opted to forego his traditional sixty-day leave and head directly for Quantico—the only member of his class to do so.

"People in the Academy were saying, 'Hey did you hear about North? He's going straight in,'" recalls one classmate. Professor Corson thought North was too eager. "One of the things you should do is take leave whenever you can," he says. "You should pause. Impatience in a warrior is deadly."

At Quantico, North's peers going through the Marine basic school course picked up immediately on his zeal.

"I noticed he was so intense about everything..." remembers

Doyle Newson, a classmate at the time who has since left the Marine Corps and is a seminary student in Oklahoma. "Quantico is a huge military training base. Even though you know it's make-believe I remember noticing how he treated it like it was real. Back then I was amazed at how intense he was. I think we all started taking it really seriously because of him. He had that kind of impact on us . . . He was really into what they were teaching us: tactics and strategy. He was good at all of it. A real natural."

At first they spent most of their time in classrooms taught by one teacher or a team of teachers—all veterans of Vietnam who were regarded as the Corps' up-and-comers. There was rigorous physical training. As time went on they spent more and more time out in the field working on practical problems and simulating combat. There were mock Vietnamese villages erected, and the trainees might discuss, for example, what kind of strategy to use against Vietcong hiding inside the huts.

Newson says that out in the field North seemed more concerned about what would happen to his men than what would happen to him. When a problem was posed to the platoon, North asked how many men he would lose.

"He was very open and personable once he got to know someone. He wasn't the type of person to go up and introduce himself around to everyone. His tendency was to sit back and watch and let relationships develop. Our friendship was the product of working on problems together out in the field."

The Marines spent virtually all their free time talking about their work and the upcoming war. Newson, who had gone through OCS, remembers feeling that the commissioned officers from the Academy were the elite. But they would all hang out together at the officers' club, rarely drinking too much because they had to get up early and the physical demands were so strenuous. There was a sense of excitement about going off to war.

Newson was married and lived off base, and recalls that the rigors of Quantico and the specter of Vietnam put considerable strain on many marriages.

It seemed an odd time even to contemplate getting involved with a woman, but since March, North had been seeing Frances Elizabeth Stuart, a sales manager for a department store in suburban Virginia. North's cousin, Kathy Finneran, who also worked at the store, had introduced him to Betsy, as she was called.

A graduate of Penn State, where she studied consumer services in business and belonged to the Alpha Sigma Alpha sorority, Betsy had grown up in Somerset, Pennsylvania, southeast of Pittsburgh, the youngest of three girls. Her father, James Roy Stuart, a southerner, was called Jeb, after Jeb Stuart, the Civil War Confederate general from whom he was descended. Mr. Stuart, who has since died, ran a small canning factory in Somerset.

When Finneran told Betsy she should meet her cousin, Larry North, Betsy initially said she wasn't interested. She had never had a decent blind date. Plus if he was going to the Naval Academy he was probably too young. But when Stenerin showed her North's picture she changed her mind. "He's good-looking," Betsy said. "You can give him my number."

They finally made a date, and Betsy took note of North's car. "He had a fancy car—a real pretty dark green Shelby Cobra," she would later tell *Life* magazine. "I acted impressed. We had a lovely, elegant dinner. I don't believe in love at first sight. I really thought he was nice, and I suppose he thought I was. We went back to my apartment and my roommate said, 'That's the one, Betsy...'

"You want an idea of what kind of person he was? Larry was like he is now: very solid. He was young, but he seemed to have definite goals established. He was unbelievably dedicated, unbelievably patriotic—which was a revelation to me. It's not like I had been antipatriotic. I just hadn't appreciated it like he does."

If Betsy did not believe in love at first sight, apparently neither did North. Although his involvement with Betsy began in March, he still invited Lynore White to his Academy graduation in June (she declined again). But North cared for Betsy and grew more attached to her. Finally, he asked her to marry him.

"I remember when he gave me my engagement ring," says Betsy. "I had always wanted a Naval Academy miniature—an exact replica of his ring. One night he arrived for a date with one rose. He just handed it to me without saying anything, and I just happened to notice the miniature on one of the leaves. I was very excited."

Back at Quantico, the boys were surprised to hear of North's plans. According to Newson, North had never mentioned that he planned to get married, and the wedding plans were hastily arranged. North quickly rounded up a few of his friends, including Newson, to be in the wedding. Time was short. There was graduation, then they'd be off to war.

On November 13, 1968, they were married in a military ceremony at Quantico. North wore his full-dress blues and Betsy wore a long, flowing white gown with veil. Passing through an arch of swords held aloft by North's ushers, the couple left the church, entered a car and sped away.

They had a short honeymoon in Puerto Rico. On arriving back in the States, North called home from Amarillo, Texas. His father told him his orders for Vietnam had arrived: he was due in San Diego in two days.

North and Betsy drove day and night to get there on time, arriving on Thanksgiving Day, when the only restaurant open was a Denny's.

"We were very sad," Betsy remembers, but "he was strong, mature, prepared for going into battle."

VIETNAM

SECOND Lieutenant North arrived in Vietnam in camouflage fatigues, ready to do battle. He wore a flak jacket and black greasepaint under his eyes to cut the glare, and in the field he always kept his helmet buckled. He was squared away. In addition to the .45–caliber revolver issued each officer, Ollie opted to carry a 12–gauge shotgun for extra firepower. And if that wasn't enough protection, he also wore a crucifix.

North was given command of the Second Platoon in K Company, Third Battalion, Third Regiment, Third Marine Division—headquartered at the Dong Ha Combat Base in Quang Tri Province, in the northern part of South Vietnam, along the DMZ. The mission of the Third Division's 21,000 men was to stop NVA regulars from penetrating down across the 17th parallel.

It was December 3, 1968. By the end of 1968, a threshold seemed to have been crossed in the American involvement in Vietnam, and it was evident that the war would be settled politically, not militarily. While some generals continued to argue that the U.S. was making significant inroads against the enemy, and that the war could be won if the White House would only up the ante with still more men and materiel, it was clear that was no longer politically palatable. Vietnam had already destroyed Lyndon Johnson, and Richard Nixon, who had just been elected the thirty-seventh president of the United States, was determined to learn from history.

By the turn of the year, some 31,000 American servicemen had died in Vietnam since 1961—14,314 in 1968 alone—and it was apparent that domestic public opinion would not tolerate an indefinite U.S. commitment in Indochina. So the focus of the war turned to "Vietnamization." By June of 1969, Nixon would announce the first phased withdrawal of American troops, and there came to be a greater emphasis on beefing up and improving the quality of the South Vietnamese forces so that they could eventually replace the Americans. Even at that, there were continued political convulsions from Vietnam on the home front in 1969, culminating in November when 250,000 people descended on Washington for the largest antiwar demonstration in U.S. history.

But North, at least initially, was oblivious to the politics of the war at home. He was a professional warrior in Vietnam to do a job, and he would get on with it.

He got oriented and learned what was what. Things like the brevity codes: blue was north, red was south, green east and yellow west. Over the radio they would talk of going "four clicks blue and three clicks red." Troops were "sheep" and the enemy were "rats." In honor of the code word for north, Ollie soon picked up the name "Blue," and his platoon became known as Blue's Bastards. North reveled in the name, thinking it combined both macho-endearment and respect.

The four main platoons of K Company would rotate out on missions, taking point duty, rear, flank security and ambush. The platoon leaders would usually gather together once or twice a day and meet with the company captain, Paul B. Goodwin, who was known as PB.

Goodwin was a cigar-smoking southerner with a thin, angular face and deep-set eyes. He was a tough, intense, driven man who was a stickler for detail. He stressed to his platoon leaders that for any mission or operation to be successful they had to take care of the small things first—like making sure the troops' weapons were clean and their feet dry. If they took care of the little things, the big things would take care of themselves. But when the bullets started flying, the natural inclination was for everyone to look out for himself and forget about the mission. That's when the platoon leaders earned their money, Goodwin would say. They couldn't forget the battle plan and the greater good. They had to be alert at all times. Often in the bush, battles would erupt instantly. Whoever got out the most firepower quickest would likely emerge with the least casualties.

If the platoon leaders screwed up, Goodwin would let them know. He was not long on compassion. They were responsible for the actions of their men and shouldn't blame failure on anyone else. Those who didn't accept responsibility, he didn't want with him. But those lieutenants whom Goodwin deemed had done well on any given day were invited over to his foxhole at night for ceremonial swigs from his bottle of whiskey. North was awarded regular tugs. They'd pass the bottle and talk of war.

Goodwin and North became close. The captain liked that North was sharp and correct, like him. He liked that Ollie was a doer, not a naysayer, who followed orders to the letter, accepted responsibility and had guts. Goodwin and North would have long conversations that were obviously personal, and it became well-known throughout K Company that they had a relationship that transcended the formal ties between captain and lieutenant. Later, Goodwin would ask North to be the godfather of his son.

North made his presence felt quickly with his troops, but there were those who were less than impressed at first.

Radio operator Mike Smith, then eighteen, from Fort Worth, had been in-country about three months when North arrived: "He told us up front he was gonna be a lifer. War was where you got the rank at, and he told us he'd volunteer us for patrols," Smith remembers. "He was gonna do what he had to do . . . A lot of us we're thinkin, 'What did we get into here?' I thought we'd got the green weenie. The first impression was he was gonna get a lotta people killed. He was volunteering us for things we had no business going to. He was the most gung-ho guy I'd ever seen."

Others were intimidated by North. "I was a little scared of him," recalls Randy Herrod, another eighteen-year-old grunt, from Oklahoma. "There was an aura of command about him. You find leaders that you know instinctively you'll follow. Some guys don't have it. North does. He looks bigger than life. I thought I could look eye-to-eye with him, and I'm six-four. I didn't realize until about four months ago that he was five-ten."

But if Smith and Herrod had doubts about North at first brush, their doubts were soon dispelled. Whatever else would later be said about North, in Vietnam he was by all accounts a first-rate platoon leader who never asked his men to take on a task he wasn't ready to lead them in himself.

"He didn't have us do anything he wouldn't do," says Smith, who today works as a car salesman. "That's why he gained everyone's respect. He wasn't out back giving orders. He was up in front."

"Some officers just hang back and tell you to do it," agrees Herrod, a karate instructor. "North led you into it. We all respected him. He was the kind of officer who when he told you to do something, you knew he meant for you to do it. He led by example, instead of by order."

North was also attentive to his troops' needs and wants.

Occasionally, he'd see to it that they got beer by using his privileges at the makeshift officers' club. And once, according to Smith, North persuaded some sailors to give him a pallet of beer—enough to service the entire company—in return for some souvenir enemy AK–47 assault rifles that U.S. forces were prohibited from taking home.

In the bush, Ollie was swarthy and had a heavy beard. But in the rear, he was always freshly shaved and well scrubbed. He had his own set of clippers and insisted that his men have gleaming new high-and-tight haircuts before going back into the field. There, North went strictly by the book. He insisted his charges wear their flak jackets and helmets, with chin straps fastened at all times. The helmets were weighty and cumbersome and the chin straps sometimes caused bad rashes in the tropical humidity, but North was adamant. He also made them use water purification tablets, clean their rifles regularly and keep their boots dry.

"It was things like that that kept a lot of us alive," says Herrod. "I never saw the man make a mistake in the field. Even when the gooks hit us, we were prepared... In Nam it was kind of an unwritten rule that when you were a short-timer getting ready to go home, you would rotate out and go to the rear. But in our platoon, we didn't want to leave 'cause we figured we had a better chance with Ollie than we did at the rear.

"He was more of a sensitive man than a lot of people think. You didn't hear anyone in his platoon popping off against him. Other officers maybe—but that's just jealousy... Ollie North was a doer. He wouldn't sit back and wait for others to do things. He went and did it. He was that way before Vietnam, in Vietnam, and he's that way now."

North's platoon didn't seem to have the morale problems that some other platoons did. For example, his unit wasn't often visited by the "phantom can-opener," a term used to refer to the sudden appearance of a rat bite on the eve of a major combat operation. Some grunts would take a can opener and puncture two marks on their hand and claim that a rat had bitten them, hoping they then could get medivac shots that would keep them out of action for three weeks. And there were no drugs—not in the bush at least. "We'd buy some pot from the Mamazan when we got back to the rear," says Smith. "But Ollie never went in for that stuff."

Lloyd Banta, the company gunnery sergeant, remembers that North seemed to anticipate dangerous situations. "He had eyes in the back of his head," Banta recalls. "Whenever anything tough came up, the captain always sent North." And North took care to warrant Goodwin's confidence in him. Banta said on one mission in which they were trying to flush out NVA regulars from their bunkers, North tossed a grenade that struck the branch of a tree and bounced back at him. Shrapnel from the explosion caused a wound to his hand. North asked Banta, who witnessed the incident, not to tell the captain. "He didn't want Goodwin thinking he was careless."

Mike Smith recalls perhaps the only instance when Goodwin got even mildly upset with Ollie. "Every night they'd send a few guys out to a listening post ahead of the company to keep an eye out for the gooks. One night, they called in on the radio that a tiger was creepin' around out there. They asked what to do. The company commander got on the radio and told 'em to throw a grenade at the tiger. North heard about the tiger, got on the air and tried to work a deal with the guys that if they killed it, he wanted the skin to send to his wife to make a coat. The company commander had to tell him to get off the radio because they had to take care of business... Finally the tiger just wandered off."

But that was an aberration. In the final analysis, North's troops seemed most impressed simply by his leadership. "We were all sort of in awe of him," recalls Ernie Tuten, a machine gunner in North's platoon. "He was warm when the time called for it... He could communicate with us nonverbally. He'd put his heart and soul into leading the platoon. He was like a mother hen too. . . . He'd make sure we were squared away. He made us keep our weapons cleaner than any other lieutenant did. He made sure we stayed awake on the lines... He'd give you a little nudge. He'd stay up with you. He never got down. None of us did. After you see a bunch of people get killed, you build up an immunity. He had to especially, because he was the leader."

Tuten remembers that North's anticommunism burned for everyone to see. "Seeing our people get killed made North very angry and we'd talk a lot about how little we liked Communists. He helped form some of my opinions about Communists. We would talk about it a lot. He would talk about how terrible their lifestyle was. We had formed our anger at NVA soldiers."

North preached discipline too. Once, Tuten recalls, the platoon went about five days without eating. They were out of food and waiting to be resupplied, but it was the rainy season and the choppers couldn't find them through the monsoon clouds. "We were eating bamboo roots. Then finally we shot a pig. Weighed about four hundred pounds... Yeah, North ate it with us."

When they did eat in the bush they would have to be careful not to heat their food with campfires that could send up smoke revealing their position. Herrod remembers that his favorite C-ration was hot dogs and beans. He would usually eat it cold, but when he wanted to heat it North taught him an inconspicuous way: by using C-4 plastic explosives. The grunts each carried about twenty pounds of C-4, but Herrod would rip off a quarter-size block that wouldn't explode—it would only burn and it could heat food quickly. Sometimes they'd take the cap off a hand grenade and burn that. When they heated the food they'd stuff it in a hole inside the wall of a bunker to cut down on smoke.

The responsibility of command had matured North, thought John F. (Jake) Laboon, then the chaplain for the Third Marine Division in Vietnam who also had served as the Naval Academy Chaplain during North's years at Annapolis. Sometimes Laboon would go out to the bush and drop in on Ollie to offer spiritual services and counseling.

"I saw a man who had matured overnight because he was in combat," Laboon remembers. "Ollie was like a big kid when he graduated the Academy. Most of that is because of the Academy's structure. Growth is retarded, but they grow up in a hurry. He was a very mature second lieutenant in Vietnam. He took his responsibilities with great care and cause. He felt personally responsible. He was like a father to all of them. He would meet all their needs —physical and emotional—by counseling. He was very open with these kids... He's a very emotional person. I didn't see the emotion at the Academy but I did in Vietnam... If things didn't go well, it could throw him for a loop for a while. I'd see him down and out, but he could always bounce back. I don't think Ollie suppressed any feelings. He let it all out. We'd talk about the morality of war, what we were doing there... We all questioned the way we were fighting the war. We were all angry that there was little support from the U.S. government and from the American people."

Maybe Laboon's counseling prompted North to talk about his fears. Mike Smith remembers North "used to speak about how proud he was of his wife. His wife had just had a baby, as I recall. Even though he was volunteering for everything, he was real conscious of not getting hurt. He didn't want to get hurt." So he would take small precautions, like not wearing his lieutenant bars in combat, Smith said. No sense sending the gooks a message.

Fellow officers had a more detached, often critical view of North.

Don Moore was the commander of the First, and then the Fourth Platoon in K Company. Moore, who arrived at the end of May, 1969, had been a philosophy major at George Mason University outside Washington, DC, when he got drafted and decided to go into Officers Candidate School. Though his father had been a career navy man, Moore was not about to become a lifer, and in Vietnam he remembers immediately feeling the social distinction between those who were and those who weren't. His brother was a war protester, and Moore was wrestling to sort out the cross-generational conflicts that so permeated the Vietnam era.

"I remember that time as being like a long hockey game that was tension-filled," Moore says. "Both sides were Americans and the gooks were the referees. Death to me was like going in the penalty box. It didn't bother me. My family would send me letters. My brother would tell me about a peace march he'd been in. Dad would write to say give 'em hell. Mother would say, 'Take care, loving son.' I read all the letters in the bush and said, 'What the hell's going on?' The world changed for me in nineteen sixty-nine."

Moore met North the first night he arrived in Quang Tri. They were assigned to the same officers' tent. Moore walked in and found it dark except for a lantern turned low. North was sitting at his bunk and Moore introduced himself. Shaking hands, he noticed North's hand was bandaged under the fleshy part of his thumb. He also noted North's eyes, and in the soft light he thought they gleamed lighter and bluer than any other eyes he'd ever seen. They were piercing, staring.

North's fresh hand wound brought home for Moore the realities of the situation he was about to enter. In many ways he felt woefully unprepared, so he began pumping North for details about the war, and for advice. North invited Moore for a drink at what was grandiosely called the officers' club—a tin-roofed hut which the commissioned officers shared with the noncoms. On their way over, North picked up a rock and threw it over the tin roof and it made a loud noise as it landed. As North led Moore inside the club they found the dozen or so men inside lying on the floor with their arms over their heads, thinking the rock had been the opening salvo of a fragging. North roared with laughter at his practical joke.

Fragging—the maiming or killing of fellow troops—was an increasing occurrence, often because of racial tension, Moore learned. In combat there were usually no problems, but in the rear base camps tensions often seethed. Blacks and whites began declaring certain tents off limits to each other. Not long after Moore arrived, he remembered an instance in Dong Ha where a black Marine riding in the back of a pickup truck was shouting out black power slogans when he was suddenly shot dead. Army CID investigated but never determined who was responsible. No one said he had seen anything.

North was filled with helpful suggestions for Moore. He said, for example, that Moore could immediately be a hit with the Hispanic members of his platoon if he brought a case of Tabasco sauce and a crate of onions out into the bush to liven up the bland C-rations.

Moore, who today works as a sheriff's investigator in Virginia, liked North and was grateful for the advice, but the more they talked, the more uneasy he became about Ollie. "When I asked him what happened to his hand, he said it was a gook grenade—a Chinese Communist grenade that they called Chicoms," Moore recalls. "I learned later that he had thrown the grenade himself and it hit a tree or something and blew up on him.

"He was never one to admit a mistake or to be philosophical about anything. Philosophy was not his orientation. He was mission-oriented. I'd use the term zealot. He was very proud. Very proud of himself. Very good at everything he did, and pride motivated him more than anything.

"I remember he was especially proud of his Academy ring. He wore the ring in combat. It glowed in the dark and was practically the size of a golf ball. It was the first thing you noticed when you met him. The ring was one man's foible, since it was unusual to wear jewelry in combat. No one wore their rings—not even married guys. Watches yes, but not jewelry.

"He made no bones about loving the Academy. We used to kid him about being a ring knocker—when an Academy grad thinks he's not being paid enough attention to he knocks his ring. He took the kidding well, but sometimes he might take it serious. He had a sense of humor, but it was very gruff and very linear—locker room, to a certain extent. There were certain things you didn't kid about —generally with Ollie it was mom, apple pie and the flag.

"He was thin. He reminded you of cable strung together. He was wiry, had high cheekbones, a grin with teeth spaced and very deep-set eyes. Ollie looks better when he doesn't smile. When he smiles he reminds you of an alligator.

"He used to wear his army jump wings. Marines don't have parachute troops so he had gone to army jump school. But the Marines treated the army with disdain. So who was he trying to impress—

the gooks? Ollie was kind of a hotdog. He had a chin strap for his helmet that looked like a strap for a football helmet rather than the simple conventional band that went across. The guys in his platoon all wore the same strap.

"But his troops adored him, no question. They were proud of being Blue's Bastards. Certain people can create good morale by being the kind of persons they are. I'm short and stubby... Ollie was the type who could physically command respect. Even though he wasn't that big, he always appeared larger than life. There was a demeanor, a personality, an intensity—don't ever fuck with the little guy with mean eyes. That was Ollie.

"I do recall on several occasions that if someone screwed up, as far as Ollie was concerned he screwed up forever... If he viewed someone as worthless, he was always gonna be worthless. He wasn't a man to forget anything. That was one of the reasons he was so intent that he not screw up himself. He was one of the most careful men I've ever met... He would spend more time covering his tracks than a lot of guys.

"But the man knew what the hell he was doing in combat. He was very good on the radio. Very calm... He was a motivator—he scared the shit out of people. He was well spoken and given to very graphic and very cutting language. He could give a talk and impress the dogshit out of them. It was a John Wayne speech... He used to say that after all they taught us about the techniques of war—tank and air support and what have you—a battle could often turn on pure leadership, on some lieutenant standing up and saying, 'Let's go, boys.'... When he got excited speaking I remember his eyes. I swear to God you were looking down gun barrels at that point.

"I had a different relationship with my troops—they called me by my first name. In his case it was always Lieutenant or Blue. PB wrote in my jacket that I listened to enlisted men too much. I always took that as a compliment. I'm not sure Ollie would.

"Three or four times a month the officers would get together to drink and bullshit about life in general. Ollie wasn't shy on drinking... hard liquor and beer. Basically you drank whatever was there. We're not talking a stocked bar where you can come in and order a Bloody Mary. Sometimes we'd kid Ollie by singing 'Good old Blue... you're a good dog too'—from the Peter, Paul and Mary song out at the time. We mostly talked about work... I had several philosophical talks with other officers, but with Ollie it was always the battle. When they landed on the moon that year, I said, 'We

got a man on the moon and here we are in the trenches.' He looked
at me like I was weird. That just did not compute. When you're in
combat you're in combat. Politics and the external influences on
Vietnam were off-limits. The other officers all had feelings about
the war and how we got into it. But I got nothing from Ollie on
that. His view was just that he was there, and he was going to
prosecute the war to the fullest extent. He was bitter about the
perception back home of what we were doing. His view was that
we were winning the war but the press was portraying our victories
as defeats.

"There were a lot of battles at the end that were what was called
ticket punching—in order to get promoted you have to have combat. New guys were coming in and ordering up missions to say they
had combat. Ollie never questioned that. To him an order was an
order was an order. There was a division between those saying,
'Hey let's cool it, we're going home,' and others who were gung-ho.
Ollie was always gung-ho. To him it was always, 'Let's sweep this
ridge, take this hill.'"

Eric Bowen of Orchard Park, New York, outside Buffalo, was
commander of K Company's First Platoon. He had gone to Boston
University on a football scholarship. But a broken leg cast a cloud
over his athletic career, so Bowen, a six-foot-four-inch tight end,
decided to drop out and become a Marine. After graduating from
OCS and the Marine basic school in Quantico, he ended up in
Vietnam. Bowen would only be in-country a total of three months.
In September of 1969 he was leading his platoon on a search-and-
destroy mission when they came under heavy fire and he was riddled from head to toe by grenades and ricochet rounds. His chest
was blown open, and he had to be medivaced home.

"Ollie was one of those fortunate ones who only got a scratch,"
Bowen remembers. "Some of the rest of us took it right through the
flesh and out the other side... We used to say it was either us or
them and if it moved it had to be them. We had very little exposure
to any villagers or natives. We were dealing in areas of supply
routes, bunker positions—all hostile territory.

"Ollie's platoon was out on search-and-destroy when I arrived. I
met him the next day. What I remember most was his face—the
dark eyes and the crewcut. The Annapolis Marine look about him.
He was very friendly. We'd periodically talk about war and what we
were doing over there... We looked at it as the United States stopping communism and expanding its world realm. Unfortunately it

became a political war and you cannot fight a war that way. And we used to talk about that. We used to clear out an area knowing two weeks later the North Vietnamese would be right back in there. Higher-ups would move you out of an area you'd just cleared. We weren't privy to why.

"If Ollie found himself in a situation where he might embellish something to take advantage of an opportunity to get something done, he would do that—for the greater good, not necessarily his own good. He did what had to be done the same as many of us would do, but I never knew him to be reckless or endanger his people. Ollie and I used to talk about some officers who were John Wayne hotdogs and had greater numbers of casualties than they ever should have. Some people who got heroic medals probably should have been shot for allowing the heroic situation to develop in the first place.

"When I knew Ollie his total loyalty was to God, country and his commanding officer. He was destined to stay in and move up. I used to say he'd be the next commandant of the Corps . . . He was a super-great guy, but he bordered on the fanatic."

North was not averse to mentioning to anyone who would listen that he had won the brigade middleweight boxing championship at Annapolis. He didn't look that imposing so there were plenty of skeptics. But after two celebrated incidents, news of Ollie's fighting prowess had spread to Nam as well.

One time, North's platoon was selected to represent the Marines in a change-of-command ceremony at a nearby base. Mike Smith recalls:

"We had to march and stand at attention and all that. It was primarily an army base. They had the ceremony on an airstrip. We went to a flick that night and got real rowdy with the army guys. We were fighting with them. We got real drunk and slept in a gym. Everybody was about to crash out. North was trying to get everybody settled down. But two of the guys in our platoon wouldn't go to sleep. Finally North told 'em if they didn't lie down by the time he counted to ten he was gonna deck 'em. The one guy—pretty big ol' boy, too—said, 'Let me count for you.' He stuck out his jaw and said to Ollie: 'Why don't you just knock me out.' So Ollie decked the guy. Then the other guy said 'I'm going, I'm going.' That made a believer out of me."

Another time, when K Company and the entire Third Battalion were taking a few days off inside a secured defensive perimeter, there was an informal boxing tournament where the combatants wore gloves.

Eric Bowen, at six-four, 220 pounds, had just knocked down three challengers in a row when Ollie got up for a go at him.

"We danced around a few times and then—slam, bam, wham— he knocked me right on my ass," says Bowen, still incredulous at the memory. "I blacked out for about twenty or thirty seconds. That's when he told me he was the Academy boxing champion. Later we both went out and had a beer. I remember my pride was hurt. I'm thinking, 'God, this little shit just knocked the shit out of me.'"

On the battlefield, North fought courageously and well, and was highly decorated as a result. He was awarded a Bronze Star with Combat "V," a Silver Star, two Purple Hearts and a Navy Commendation Medal, which reported that he had carried out "more than seventy day-and-night ambushes, and devised tactical innovations that resulted in heavy enemy casualties."

North was given the Bronze Star for a battle that occurred February 22, 1969. According to the medal citation, he was aboard the lead tank in his platoon's reconnaissance patrol near Con Thion when the platoon came under a machine-gun and grenade attack from NVA regulars dug in behind dense woods.

Staying in a dangerously exposed position aboard the top of the tank, North assessed the situation, delivered a burst of return fire, then began deploying his troops in an effort to establish a defensive perimeter. As he was directing traffic, North evidently forgot about the tank's revolving turret, which slammed into him with such force that he was sent flying to the ground with broken ribs and a punctured lung. But he waved off medical attention, got back on the tank, picked up an M-79 grenade launcher and led a volley of return fire that eventually silenced the attackers and resulted in seven enemy killed, the citation reported.

He got the Silver Star for a May 25, 1969, battle during Operation Virginia Ridge, an effort to flush out the NVA around the DMZ. The point platoon on the mission had radioed for help after walking into an ambush and suffering heavy casualties. North responded, leading his men up a hill, past their fallen buddies, in a charge that pushed the enemy back. That gave helicopters a chance to come in and fly out the wounded. Then North led another advance, forcing the NVA to beat another retreat to a previously entrenched ridgeline. When the enemy regrouped North led a third assault, but then his platoon ran low on ammunition. According to Mike Smith, who participated in the battle, North then called for an F–111 air strike on the enemy position. The F–111s made three passes at their target and a fourth dummy run which North coat-tailed on by leading a fourth and final charge that forced the NVA to abandon what was designated as Hill 410 and turn it over to the U.S. The entire battle lasted several hours.

The grunts thought North had been inspirational. "In Boot Camp, they tell you if the enemy's on top of the hill you charge up the hill," says Smith. "Same thing with an ambush—you don't run from it, you go into it. That's the way North was. When he got the Silver Star, he was running up the hill, screaming and hollering."

One of the great frustrations of fighting the war in Vietnam was the transient nature of real estate seized.

"All of us were totally frustrated," recalls Ernie Tuten. "We'd leave Hill 410 and the NVA would come right back in. We were frustrated we couldn't do more . . . North thought we should have been there to win the war. He thought going over there and fight-ing it the way we did was a pile of bullshit."

Don Moore also considered many of their efforts futile: "For a lot of us it was, 'Jesus, this is just a hill we're giving back tomorrow . . .' We did it several times—chopper in, clean gooks off, wait a few days, climb back on the chopper and do the same thing a week later, losing men each time."

But North wouldn't let himself get down for long. There were always new battles, new challenges and certainly no time to rest on his laurels at Hill 410. The following day he got an order to try and capture an NVA prisoner in the DMZ. The U.S. wanted proof for the Paris peace talks that there was enemy movement there. No one seemed to question that the Americans would have to go into the DMZ themselves to get the proof. But that was nothing out of the ordinary.

"We worked the DMZ all the time," says Herrod, who volun-teered to go with North on the mission to capture the prisoner. He recalls there were about a dozen Marines in blackface and camou-flage who set out around midnight.

Herrod said it took them four to five hours to reach their destina-tion. The terrain was mountainous. Ridges were no more than three to four feet across, and helicopters couldn't land. They walked up a ridge in single file, then descended down into the DMZ, which was like a densely foliated canyon. There was a point man ahead, followed by North. On the way down, the point man came back and said he'd seen an enemy soldier. North and the point man then went off while the rest of the patrol team stayed put. "They were gone about thirty minutes," says Herrod. "When they got back, North was carrying a North Vietnamese prisoner— over his shoulder like a sack of potatoes."

Herrod figured North had coldcocked the gook, but Smith, who was bringing up the rear as the radio man, said the point man had shot the prisoner in the face. In any case, it wasn't kosher to ask such detailed questions.

"You didn't talk about things like that," Herrod says. "Especially after North said we shouldn't tell anyone about it . . . There was just kind of an unwritten code. No one talked about anything to do with combat. You just did your job. You went back to the rear—drank a little whiskey, partied and went back to the front. Any time you got back you just tried to forget about everything. . . . If someone got killed, you didn't talk about it. You didn't even mention the name anymore. If you did, maybe you wouldn't make it . . . You had to wipe things out of your mind to keep your sanity."

Smith radioed back to company headquarters that they had their prisoner, but they received orders to keep on going and try to seek out enemy contact.

"When we got down to the basin, we walked into a battalion-sized bunker-complex," Smith recalls. "We could smell the NVA. They were everywhere. They must have just left. It was really eerie. I get goosebumps just talking about it. There were maybe fifteen of us and maybe one thousand of these little dudes around someplace. The company told us to go up the hill and set up an ambush. I said, 'Oh shit.' We set it up. It rained all night long. We heard rumbling, like footsteps, and that oriental-type talking. They were walking in a ravine—the prisoner we captured later told us they were doing a rehearsal for an assault on our company. We stayed quiet . . . They were about one-hundred meters away. We could hear twigs breaking. We were in bushes and stuff. We couldn't see 'em, we just heard 'em. The foliage was so dense it was like they knew we were there. We had mines set out filled with C-4. We had 'em on the front and rear of the ambush. But we went and collected 'em in the morning because the NVA didn't show."

So the patrol went back to South Vietnam, the prisoner mission at least accomplished. Smith remains struck by the beauty of the DMZ. "South Vietnam was riddled with bomb craters. The DMZ was a pretty forest that was like virgin country. At the top of the ridge you could look across at the north and see the red flag with a star on it."

The only known instance in which Oliver North himself is on record discussing Vietnam is a thirty-minute tape-recording he made on September 21, 1969, at Dong Ha. The tape is North's debriefing of Operation Virginia Ridge—the effort by the Third Battalion to flush out NVA regulars around the DMZ in the ten weeks spanning May 4 to July 16. In the tape North speaks for posterity in a cool, even monotone and delivers a technical account of his platoon's activities in that period. Though one can hear helicopters flying in the background, North's remarks are antiseptic and decidedly unemotional as he tells in commandspeak of "interdicting" the enemy, "retrograding" off a hill, and the importance of keeping the North Vietnamese from "ascertaining" the U.S. position at any given time.

North delivered a critique in which he questioned the tactics of his own battalion during the operation while praising the enemy's. He said U.S. intelligence on NVA doings was sorely lacking, artillery support was too slow and resupply inadequate. He spoke of the toll that "fevers of undetermined origin" had taken on his men, and how important it was to wear flak jackets at all times and to maintain "water discipline" in the ranks. He praised his troops for maintaining good morale throughout. In perhaps the most revealing part of the tape, at the very end, North said his company had never lost a battle or been forced to retreat, and he spoke of the "reassurance" of driving through the enemy and counting the dead by standing on their bodies.

In his criticism of U.S. troop deployment North said: "The operation continued sweeping toward the north with the battalion abreast for the most part . . . The companies were rarely within four to five clicks of each other. This, to me, left the company rather exposed and unsupportable by the battalion . . . We often found ourselves on our own . . . I don't think we could have been supported in any way by the companies on either of our flanks and I'm sure they felt the same way . . . It was often too far to go to support a company when they were in contact . . . Once we made an attempt to go to the assistance of India Company. Although we moved at a maximum rate of speed, it was still impossible for us to catch up and close in on time to be of any assistance."

North was more charitable in assessing enemy operations. For example, he found NVA bunkers "all well built, well prepared and readily defensible, built on commanding terrain... Most of the bunkers open to the north or to the west... and therefore allow him to stay in during incoming [rounds] and move about freely as soon as the incoming has stopped... He has a readily available source of water and his resupply routes for the southern half of the DMZ allow him ready access to a good source of supply."

North also seemed impressed that the enemy looked squared away. "All of the enemy that we met from about twenty-one May through the beginning of June were well armed... Apparently they all had recent haircuts, fresh uniforms... Most of them appeared to be fresh troops... You can tell just by looking at the soles of their boots that most of them were fresher than we were... They appeared to be extremely well led and well motivated. Certainly had no hesitancy to stand and fight... They were by far the best of the NVA troops I have seen in my ten months over here."

The enemy, he continued, seemed bent on staging hit-and-run, probing attacks, "to ascertain how strong we were... and exactly where we were." The North Vietnamese would never return immediately to pick up their dead, North noted, but they always came back eventually. "We could've made a lot of money by staying on top of those bodies and ambushing them" when they returned to get their comrades.

North worried about resupply logistics and wished the U.S. could come up with more helicopters to make more supply runs, thereby letting the troops carry lesser loads.

"Throughout the whole Mutters Ridge area and the LZ Sierra complex... there is a great deal of difficulty in maintaining an adequate supply. Water throughout that area is a daily need. The troops do come up—especially the replacements—with a good number of heat casualties. The hotter it gets the more water you need... And we never seem to get quite enough of it. We'd be resupplied with water once a day if possible, once every two days practically all the time. To say that water discipline was a problem is an understatement. It's not really possible to take a brand-new troop into the field and expect him to be water disciplined... As a consequence we did suffer heat casualties and they had to be medivaced. And medivacs of a noncombat nature are cause for a great deal of tactical concern... The company often had to slow down a great deal in order to minimize our heat casualties... You lose speed and maneuverability by doing this."

Assessing the entire operation, North said that in his company, twenty-one troops had been killed and about seventy wounded,

including himself. He gave no figures for enemy casualties. He had
been impressed by morale, especially after he was medivaced June
6, and the platoon was well below strength. "There were about
thirty people left in my platoon. Those thirty were probably the
most effective combat Marines that I have ever had the fortune to
serve with. They were lean and mean . . . And I think they learned
a lot."

Still, North wished there could have been more troops available
for the operation. "I think the problems we encountered . . . were
simply due to the fact that we have too few people to cover too
large an area . . . On the occasions we were fortunate enough to be
able to exploit a contact and successfully prosecute it, the enemy
always was defeated. There was never any doubt on this issue . . .
[but] if we could've had more troops available, perhaps enemy
units that moved off in one direction or another could've been
flanked by friendlies operating on our flanks. It always made you
feel that you were kind of stuck on a limb. Despite the fact that we
were extremely successful in our contacts . . . it always seemed that
we could've been more successful. There was never a time when
the enemy forced us back . . . There were always times when he
held us up long enough to pull out his own needy. You know you've
hit him . . . and you know you've hit him hard . . . when you can
drive right on through the contact and count his bodies by standing
on them."

North's closest brush with The Reaper, as the grunts called
death, came on July 28, 1969, when his life was saved by Randy
Herrod. K Company had set up a night defensive perimeter about
three miles northwest of Cam Lo in Quang Tri Province. Around
3:00 A.M. North Vietnamese regulars suddenly opened up on the
Marines with a chorus of mortars, machine guns and rocket-pro-
pelled grenades.

"We had a company of tanks with us," remembers Herrod. "Our
holes were dug two between each tank. The NV came in and
knocked out three or four of the tanks—they were battalion-size.
They were running over our lines. It was practically hand-to-hand
. . . I guess it lasted about three hours."

A rocket grenade exploded near Herrod, wounding him and
North and another man. North was knocked out for a few minutes,
apparently suffering a concussion from the force of the explosion.
Leaving himself exposed to incoming rounds, Herrod draped his
body over both his buddy and the fallen North, grabbed his M–60

machine gun and began firing away at enemy positions and helped
to repel the attack.

"Ollie came back to and started bringing up reinforcements to
bring up our side of the line," adds Herrod, down-playing his own
role. "He'd also gotten hit with shrapnel in his rear and the back of
his legs. But he never reported it. No one knew about it until we
saw him have a corpsman take care of it three days later when we
got back to base. He didn't put in for anything. He's tough."

But North put Herrod in for a medal. He was awarded the Silver
Star.

North remained in Quang Tri on combat duty until August 21,
1969, when he received orders for a G–3 operations billet in the
relatively tame confines of the Third Marine Division's headquarters battalion in Dong Ha. Before he left the field Ollie was
presented with a plaque by the members of his platoon. The plaque
said: "To the Big Blue Bastard from the Little Blue Bastards."
North was touched, and he showed it to Captain Goodwin. Goodwin turned around, dropped his tiger-striped shorts and mooned
North. Ollie quipped to the troops that they'd just seen their captain's best side, and there were laughs all around. It was the kind of
military, macho camaraderie North loved.

In recognition of his combat duty, North was quickly promoted to
first lieutenant on September 5, 1969. He was pleased with the
promotion, but not with the overall U.S. war effort in Vietnam,
which he had more and more time to ponder as he took on essentially administrative duties in Dong Ha.

As the year wound down, the United States was basically in a
retreat mode in Vietnam, North thought. We were beginning to cut
and run. U.S. fighting forces by December would number 479,000,
down from a high of 549,000 in June. The South Vietnamese were
now doing most of the fighting, and huge quantities of American
weapons—planes, ships, helicopters, tanks and more than a million M–16 rifles—were simply being turned over to Saigon.

The number of Americans killed in 1969 dropped about 5,000
from the year before to 9,414, but morale in the ranks was down as
protests on the home front mounted and as a growing realization
set in that Hanoi had weathered America's best shot. Drug use
among the troops and fraggings were up, as were outright acts of
mutiny and refusal to obey orders. In the army alone, there had
been 117 convictions for such acts in 1969, as against eighty-two in
1968.

North attributed much of this malaise simply to a lack of moral fiber and toughness. If America was to be the greatest country in the world, she could not fall prey to the political exigencies of the moment. He believed in the Domino Theory. If Washington quit in Vietnam, there went Southeast Asia. But more fundamentally, North believed in America and the sanctity of its commitments. If we had promised South Vietnam we would stand by it, then we had to do so, since in the final analysis what did a country have but its word? Especially a great power. This is what upset North most as he sat in a catbird seat watching his country slowly renege on an ally.

As he left for home on November 23, 1969, preparing to see his baby daughter for the first time, North looked beyond the prospect of that happy event and promised himself that if he ever had anything to say about it, the United States would never again turn its back on a friend in need.

North had been home less than three months when he heard shocking news from Vietnam: Randy Herrod, who had saved his life the previous July, had been charged with the first-degree murder of sixteen Vietnamese civilians: five women and eleven children.

Herrod was a strapping, six-foot-four-inch man-child from Calvin, Oklahoma, who was part good 'ol boy, part Creek Indian. A basketball player with a thirty-nine-inch vertical leap, Herrod had been awarded an athletic scholarship to Southeastern Oklahoma State but opted to enlist in the Marines instead. He had been tired of school and ready for war. "It was just the thing to do," Herrod remembers. "We still wave the flag down here in Oklahoma. In that era, you either went into the service or ended up being a draft dodger and burning your card. There was no middle way. You either went for the gusto or you didn't."

Now the gusto had landed Herrod in a serious jam. By then a corporal, Herrod had been leading a five-man patrol in the village of Sonthang twenty-seven miles southwest of Danang the night of February 19, 1970, when the shootings occurred. The other four Marines in the patrol had also been charged. The alleged massacre quickly became known as the Marine Corps My Lai, coming as it did just three months after journalist Seymour Hersh broke the story of the army My Lai massacre, which had occurred in March of 1968. Unlike the army, which covered up My Lai for twenty months until confronted by the Hersh revelations, the Marine Corps itself disclosed the Sonthang incident a week after it took

place. The five men were quickly charged and separate trials were
begun, even before the My Lai accused had come to trial.

But if the Marines scored points for candor and decisiveness,
Herrod's lawyers, at least, were determined not to let them
steamroll their client in a political show-trial designed to prove that
the Corps would tolerate no My Lais. Dissatisfied with just a Marine defense lawyer, Alvin Self, Herrod's grandfather, contacted an
Oklahoma state senator and noted criminal lawyer named Gene
Stipe and asked him if he would represent Herrod. Stipe agreed.

"I was kind of touched by the story," recalls Stipe. "A local boy
half-a-world away from home being tried for murder. At that time
everybody was beginning to have second thoughts about the war
and they felt one way to purge their conscience was to prosecute
these kids. I felt they were picking on some people who didn't have
a helluva lot to say about their destiny."

Stipe mounted an aggressive defense, taking two trips to Vietnam to meet with Herrod and conduct his own investigation. He
also persuaded three other Oklahoma lawyers to help him.

Soon after agreeing to take the case, Stipe got a letter from
North. In the letter, North wrote that he had commanded Herrod
in Vietnam; that Herrod had once saved his life and that in North's
opinion, Herrod was an excellent Marine with sound judgment
who would not have shot anyone unless provoked. He volunteered
to come to Vietnam on his own time and at his own expense to
testify on Randy's behalf at trial. Stipe was impressed and decided
to take North up on his offer.

By the time Stipe made his third trip to Vietnam in August for
the trial, things were not looking especially bright for Herrod. One
of the other four accused, Michael S. Krichten of Hanover, Pennsylvania, had been granted immunity from prosecution in return
for his agreement to become a state's witness and testify against
Herrod and the three remaining Marines: Thomas R. Boyd of
Evansville, Indiana, Samuel G. Green of Cleveland and Michael A.
Schwarz of Weirton, West Virginia.

Herrod was the last of the four to be tried. Schwarz, the first,
had been convicted of murdering twelve of the sixteen women and
children and sentenced to life in prison at hard labor. He was found
not guilty on four of the counts. The conviction came on the
strength of testimony from Krichten that he had watched Schwarz,
along with Boyd, Green and Herrod, shoot the sixteen women and
children under orders from Herrod, the patrol leader. Krichten
claimed he himself had shot over the people's heads. Testifying on

his own behalf, Schwarz admitted to shooting at some of the civilians, but denied he had intentionally hit any of them. He too said
he had been acting on Herrod's orders to "shoot 'em, kill 'em all."

Next, Boyd was acquitted, but the third Marine to stand trial,
Green, was convicted of fifteen counts of murder; he was acquitted
on one count. In a change of testimony Krichten said at Green's
trial that all sixteen killings had actually been committed by
Schwarz and Herrod, and that Green had only fired his rifle in the
air three times. Still, Green was convicted, though only sentenced
to five years in prison.

North took a commercial flight to San Francisco, then hopped a
military flight to Vietnam. The wisdom of this trip was questioned
by many, not the least of whom was his wife Betsy, who was pregnant with their second child. On the career front North was only
several months into his new assignment as an instructor at Quantico, and there were a few eyebrows raised at his taking leave after
such a short time at his new post. And for an up-and-coming young
officer as ambitious as North, there seemed better ways to gain
favor with his superiors than to testify on behalf of a man whom the
Marine Corps badly wanted to convict in a highly visible massacre
trial. But North was adamant. Herrod had been there for him, and
now he would be there for Herrod.

Lawyers on the Herrod defense team took one look at North and
immediately concluded they'd struck gold. He was gung-ho, looked
sharp, had that ramrod military bearing and generally looked like
he'd leaped off a Marine recruiting poster. His distinguished record
in Vietnam wouldn't hurt either.

"You'd have to have seen him to have known what a great young
officer he was," recalls Denzil Garrison, one of Herrod's lawyers.
"He came over there with a traveling iron and before he could be
seen, he'd have ironed his fatigue uniforms. He wasn't a fop, just a
superb soldier . . . He told me, 'A man can look like a Marine under
any circumstances and that's what I try to do.'"

As they were awaiting trial, Stipe and Garrison decided they
could use North to help buttress their motion for a change of venue
on the grounds that Herrod couldn't get a fair trial in Danang. They
wanted the trial moved either to the Philippines or the U.S. So
they sent North out to conduct a survey among the officers of the
First Marine Division from which a jury would be chosen to sit in
judgment of Herrod. North went down to the officers' club, and
without making it clear he was on the defense team questioned
about thirty officers about whether they thought Herrod could get a

fair trial in Danang. One lieutenant colonel took exception to being polled by a first lieutenant, and North had to beat a hasty retreat before getting into an altercation with a superior. But he had accomplished his mission: all but one of the thirty officers reportedly said they thought Herrod could not get a fair trial there. The results of the survey were duly incorporated into Stipe's change of venue motion as a "scientific poll." But the motion was denied.

There was other down-time for North as he waited for the trial to begin, so if the lawyers had nothing special for him to do, he thought he might as well make the most of his time back in Vietnam. Maybe show the boys a thing or two. He began going down to the Marine intelligence unit and volunteering to go out on patrols.

Stipe says he saw North fly out on a helicopter with a patrol at least twice. Adds Garrison: "He would leave in the morning and come back late in the afternoon, extremely fatigued. We'd ask him what he'd done and he'd smile and say, 'That's classified.' We were worried that our star witness was gonna get killed in combat before he got a chance to testify, so we tried to get him not to go out on those damn patrols. But Ollie just said 'When you need me, I'll be there.'

"This intelligence unit he went to was an elite, super-secret unit. On the gate at the entrance to their headquarters they had a patch with a skull-and-crossbones on it and the words 'Swift, silent death.' The other officers were all talking about what Ollie was doing. It was common knowledge. They'd say, 'That damn Ollie North is going out there in Indian country.' That's what they called it... They were all laughing about it... They said, 'Well hell, they just go out and lay behind a tree, be quiet and wait 'til some VC comes by and slit his throat'.... When we brought it up, he just shrugged it off but he didn't deny it. We said, 'You're going to get your butt knocked off,' and he laughed and said, 'I'll guarantee you I'll be here to testify'... Ollie was the kind of fella who is of-service wherever he is."

At night North and the defense team bunked together in a hooch at the officers' quarters in Danang. It was about twenty by forty feet with a tin roof and screen-wire sides. The base was set against a hill that looked out over the South China Sea. Every night the base was shelled, but most of the rockets flew harmlessly overhead and landed on the beach. "It was kinda like watching the fireworks," recalls Stipe.

During his two weeks back in Vietnam, North made the unlikely acquaintance of an Associated Press reporter named Jay Sharbutt. Sharbutt, who was there to cover the Herrod court-martial, had been chatting with North one day as he was waiting to testify. Interested that a Marine officer was appearing as a character witness for Herrod, Sharbutt learned that North had come to Vietnam on his own time and at his own expense. North explained that Herrod had served under him in a different division and a different rifle platoon stationed up near the DMZ.

That jogged Sharbutt's memory. In June of 1969 he had been at Dong Ha to do a story about the first withdrawal of U.S. troops from Vietnam. Two scruffy Marine grunts just in from the bush had urged him to interview their platoon leader. "Blue, that's his call sign," one of the grunts had said. "You really should do a story on him. Man definitely has his Sierra together." But it turned out that Blue, recovering from shrapnel wounds in his legs, had gone on R&R, so Sharbutt never got to interview him.

It was a long shot, but now Sharbutt asked North if his call sign had happened to be Blue. North beamed and said that as a matter of fact it had. Whereas North, displaying typical military distrust of the press, had initially seemed to regard Sharbutt as something of a pinko, he now warmed to the reporter and they fell into easy conversation. Sharbutt asked North if he'd read *Catch-22*, and North replied it was one of his favorite books.

The trial began August 22 inside a twenty-by-thirty foot Quonset hut with a window air-conditioner that only partially cooled the room from the oppressive heat outside. There was a five-man jury of officers selected by the commander of the First Marine Division. The defense used its one peremptory challenge to dismiss the lieutenant colonel who had jousted with North during his polling operation. Herrod's lawyers were satisfied with the other jurors, though they fretted that one, who was in the habit of reading the *Atlantic Monthly*, might be too liberal.

Stipe and Garrison made sure the jury understood the context of the event in question—at least as they and their client saw it. Herrod and the other members of his patrol, ranging in age from nineteen to twenty-two, were members of Company B of the First Battalion, Seventh Regiment, First Marine Division—a unit Herrod had been transferred to after North left the country. The company had been involved in a clearing operation in the heavily mined Queson Valley, where after dark the rule of thumb was "If it moves, shoot it." Snipers and booby traps were everywhere. Caves and bunkers peppered the hills surrounding the valley, and North

Vietnamese and Vietcong regiments used them as sanctuaries from which to observe Marine doings from a distance and to plot attacks. At night enemy soldiers would come down from the hills to villages like Sonthang to get food and other supplies from the villagers who sympathized with their cause. The hooches in these villages contained trapdoors leading to underground bunkers that shielded the villagers from artillery shells lobbed from Landing Zone Ross, the Marine battalion headquarters in the center of the valley.

The night of February 19 Herrod and the four other Marines had volunteered to go out on what the grunts called a "killer team," designed to ambush Charlie as he came down from the hills to get resupplied. Sonthang village was in a so-called free-fire zone, meaning that the area could be shelled at will. The area was part of a gateway to the coastal plain and the cities of Danang and Hoian, where allied forces had been fighting enemy troops off and on for the last five years in what was basically a stalemate.

Herrod's story, as recalled in an interview, was that "we walked into this village. We heard men's voices coming out of the hooches. We pulled women and kids out. The point man went inside to look for tunnels. About that time an American M–60 machine gun opened up on us. I learned later the gooks had knocked down a chopper and took the guns out of it. We opened up on the hill where the fire was coming from. Some of the women reached for what we thought were weapons. We killed some of them, and they got killed in crossfire from the M–60. We took off."

At trial, Herrod testified: "I do not now, and I did not then, feel that I had killed anyone it wasn't necessary to kill."

Stipe, trying to prove "command influence" in the case, introduced into evidence some internal Marine Corps memoranda. One said that South Vietnamese officials were not bothered by the incident since the victims were considered to be Vietcong. Another, from Marine headquarters in Washington, urged that murder charges be brought because the Marine Corps did not want to be charged with a My Lai-type cover-up the way the army had been.

The defense also called a psychiatrist expert on combat fatigue who testified that the Marine Corps could not reasonably teach its men to move and shoot by reflex in wartime, then prosecute them when they do just that.

North, finally getting his chance, took the witness stand and sang Herrod's praises. The prosecution had successfully objected to having Herrod's Silver Star included in the record, so the defense used North as a means to tell the jury how Herrod had won it—by

saving North's life. North recounted the details vividly in a manner
that was far more compelling than if the Silver Star had simply
been stipulated to for the record. For almost thirty minutes North
sat erect on a steel folding chair, his back never touching the back
of the seat. "He was an outstanding witness," recalls Garrison.

The prosecution again relied mainly on the testimony of Kritchen
and argued that Herrod had shot the sixteen civilians with "no
provocation whatsoever." But Stipe, in his summation, countered
that Sonthang had been populated by Vietcong or their sympathizer, and that to bring criminal charges in such cases could ruin
the armed forces.

The jury went out late Saturday afternoon, August 29, deliberated for a few hours and recessed for the day without reaching a
verdict. That night Herrod, North and the defense team partied.
Win or lose, they had done all they could, and it was time to let
their hair down a little. There were jokes about fragging the jurors
unless they came back with an acquittal. North arm-wrestled Garrison and lost. He was incredulous that a gray-haired lawyer could
whip him. Garrison charitably attributed his victory to North's war
wounds or the injuries from his 1964 car accident.

The jury deliberated for about another hour Sunday morning,
then announced it had reached a verdict: not guilty on all counts.

North was not there for the verdict. He had already left for the
airbase where he hoped to hop a military charter bound for California. But several planes had left without him—he was having difficulty getting a seat. Either space was genuinely hard to come by, or
perhaps the Marine brass was none too pleased at the role North
had played in Herrod's acquittal and wasn't about to go overboard
to facilitate his trip home.

North decided to give his new reporter friend Sharbutt a call at
the press center in Danang. Sharbutt says he doesn't think North
was calling for help, just to shoot the breeze. But the reporter
mentioned North's predicament to Dale Dye, a Marine sergeant
and ex-grunt who was assigned to the press center. Dye expressed
outrage at the delay North was being subjected to and concluded
the Marines were "messing with him." He arranged to send North
a bottle of fine wine to ease the pain of waiting, then consulted with
a friend who was an air force dispatcher at the Danang airbase.

Late that night Dye got word from the dispatcher there was a
slot for North on a flight leaving in an hour for Okinawa. Dye woke
up Sharbutt, who got his jeep, and they sped off to pick up North,
getting him to the plane with about ten minutes to spare. Sharbutt,

writing later about the incident for the Los Angeles *Times*, where he now works, recalled watching North, still wearing his camouflage fatigues, walk off toward the waiting C–130. He was toting a seabag and limping noticeably, presumably from his shrapnel wounds.

"Sir!" shouted Dye as he whipped North a high ball—a picture-perfect salute.

North turned around and snapped off a salute in return.

Sharbutt, perhaps more cynical than the average Marine, watched this closing scene unfold before him and thought it "too Hollywood." So to break the spell, he called out to North: "Wait, do you need any after-crash mints?"

North laughed. "You guys are nuts," he yelled before entering the plane.

The Herrod defense team was effusive in its praise of North after the verdict, regarding his testimony as pivotal to the result. The lawyers later sought North out and told him, as many others around that time apparently did, that in their humble opinion he was destined to become the next commandant of the Marine Corps. "He was so head-over-heels above the rest," said Garrison. "He was in a class by himself."

As for Herrod, he remains eternally grateful to Ollie.

"If it hadn't been for him I'd still be in the brig," he said. "We're talkin' over five hundred years.

"I agree that Ollie North, if he hadn't gone to the White House, would have been commandant of the Marine Corps. It makes me mad that they call him a zealot. If they're gonna call him a zealot they might as well call Washington and Jefferson zealots. The man's a patriot. We don't have enough of 'em. When we're in a war, we want people like Ollie North. But when we're at peace, we try to get rid of guys like that and punish 'em. They're the part of the United States—the professional soldier—that everyone wants to forget about.

"I'd follow him anywhere. If he wanted to go to hell, I think we could make it back . . . Ollie's all guns, guts and glory."

THE CORPS

BACK in Quantico, a warrior without a war, North concentrated on the business of making rank and advancing his career.

On rainy days or sometimes at lunch, the officers would gather for basketball games. The colonel in command of the Basic School would usually play, together with eight or ten underlings. In basketball, as in the rest of Marine society, there seemed a clear distinction between the lifers and those who were biding their time until their tours finished and they could become civilians again.

"Those officers who were staying in the service would go on the colonel's team," recalls Bob Pfeiffer, a nonlifer who served as an officer with North at Quantico. "The guys who were leaving would form their own team against the colonel. Ollie would spend his whole time getting the ball and then passing it to the colonel. He'd say, 'Hey, that's the game. I want rank . . . I want to be a general.'

"I wasn't interested in going to teas and pushing rank . . . [But] Ollie was really into it. He ate it up . . . Ollie would go to receptions and Betsy would have to go. Poor Betsy. She hated it but she went anyway. The women sit according to the rank of their husbands. It's terrible. But Ollie always went to receptions for generals. He loved it. Those guys were his heroes."

When North heard there was going to be a visiting dignitary, like Louis "Chesty" Puller, the Marine Corps' most decorated general, he would, it seemed, shift into overdrive: "Ollie mowed the whole neighborhood—all the lawns," Pfeiffer recalls. "When Chesty came for an event, Ollie thought the place was a mess. He made sure everything was spruced up. He'd take everyone's laundry off the lines."

But if North sucked up to the brass, no one could accuse him of
not cutting it in the field with the "studs," as the second lieuten-
ants-in-training were known. He taught patrolling and counterinsurgency tactics for platoons or small infantry units.

"The lieutenants ate him up," recalls Mark Treanor, another fellow instructor at Quantico, now a Maryland lawyer who would become active in raising money for North's legal defense. "They
thought he was the greatest thing since sliced bread. He's a show-
man and he taught by entertainment, but he never let people forget that war is a deadly game. He was a hotdog—there's no
question about it. But when it came to leading troops in combat, he
definitely was not a hotdog. Having that kind of an attitude was
something he would tear a lieutenant apart for. It's okay to be a
hotdog in class, but when you're out there patrolling, there's no
room for it."

While having a beer with the boys, Treanor said he would
overhear the second lieutenants say that North was their favorite
instructor. "They'd love to shoot the breeze with Ollie. He was
the kind of guy who was difficult to dislike because he's such a
great conversationalist. He can [tell] the most outrageous story
and keep a straight face... Ollie has kind of an athletic personality. He's strung like a bow, but that's a natural state for him. He's
kind of taut, but it's not nervous energy... He can sit around
with his feet up on the desk, chew on tobacco and shoot the
breeze with the rest of us... But when something needs to get
done, he's always ready to do what he has to do. Ollie always
seemed to be working... To see Ollie there at night and on Saturdays was not unusual. Among a group of hardworking people,
he was a workaholic."

John Lieno, a Notre Dame football player who went through the
Basic School under North from September 1972 to March 1973,
still raves about his former instructor. "He simply was the best at
what he was about," says Lieno, now a lawyer in Virginia. "It wasn't
a popular time to be in the military, and he was teaching a very
difficult subject—how to kill the enemy. I considered him to be a
varsity player... He'd barge in sometimes wearing camouflage and
firing blanks to get our attention, or he'd go up against the green
blackboard to show how difficult it was to see him while in camouflage."

During one such Ollie-show, North charged into a classroom carrying a rifle loaded with blanks and jumped on top of a desk, stomach first. The rifle went off, apparently accidentally, spraying some

students with gas and powder emissions. Fortunately no one was seriously hurt.

But that incident didn't cramp his style much. Another one of North's favorite antics was the game known as "Carrier Quals," a human simulation of the qualifying landings fighter pilots make aboard aircraft carriers. After Mess Night, a formal dinner held when a Quantico class graduates, some of the graduates and the other officers would repair to a local bar for a couple of beers. They would hook up a few tables and take running dives on the surface, trying to stop short at the end, like jets landing on carriers. Ollie once slid off and went flying into a wall, coming up bloodied. He drew a big hand from the studs.

Lieno said performing such dramatic stunts was not unusual at Quantico—other instructors did it too. Many of the courses—like supply and logistics—were dull, so the good teachers were the ones who could make the subject matter come alive. And, some felt, theatrics could help illustrate the madness and unpredictability of war.

Still, there were those who thought North's theatrics went beyond the bounds of legitimate creativity in teaching. "He played the role to the hilt," says a former Quantico instructor who worked with North and disliked him. "You can just see Ollie there with his camouflage utilities with his bush hat . . . camo on his face as if it had been put on in Hollywood, two bandoliers of ammo strapped across and three pouches, four weapons and three knives. It was as if he had walked into Sunday Surplus, bought all he could find and strapped it on at one time . . . Ollie was popular with the studs because he was their image of what the Marine Corps was about . . . He invented Rambo before Rambo made the movie. He was the creator of his own myth . . . We always felt he was overrated, but his superiors always seemed to like him. He was a pretty good apple-polisher . . . I only worked with him for two years and we used to follow him around and say, 'Hey, did you hear the latest Ollie story?' . . . Everyone who knows him calls this thing [the Iran-Contra affair] Ollie's Follies."

But Lieno insisted North was also pragmatic, thorough and meticulous. He taught them such things as how to bring helicopters in for a night landing, how to open a can of C-rations at night—how not to get killed. "North would hang his head down and say, 'What are you gonna tell your dead troops? I'm so terribly sorry?' When he taught, he taught through example," Lieno says. "You knew that he fully understood what he was doing. He had a great knowledge of how to deal with certain situations, certain terrains. He didn't want his men to die for no reason.

"You learn your stuff inside out and you learn every nut and screw, because something will go wrong in a combat situation. Something always goes wrong. So when the shit hits the fan you rely on your instincts . . . And that's why it was hammered into us. North was preparing us for the fact that war really is hell. Actual combat is a motherfucker. He was a varsity player. He had been there, and he knew what he was doing. He was the consummate professional. You know when a guy is teaching you from a manual, and you know when a guy is teaching you from experience. North was teaching from experience.

"He didn't view the enemy with the attitude of blood-lust-kill-a-commie-for-Christ. He approached it with a clinical discussion of how to stay alive. 'This is how you do it. It's worked for me.' The enemy was merely the opponent."

North would not publicly embarrass a second lieutenant who had made a mistake. "He would stress that mistakes in real life could be deadly," says Treanor. "If a guy made a mistake, Ollie would point it out, but he'd do it in such a way so as not to make the guy feel incompetent."

George Kresovich, another student under North at the Basic School, recalls that North took care to know the students in his class before he lectured to them. "I was struck by the way he presented an issue and played on the audience in front of him. He knew his audience. It was a perfect pitch for his audience . . . I think that's what happened on TV at the hearings."

North wouldn't mince words on what their agenda was, continued Kresovich, now a lawyer in Seattle. "One lecture on ambushes started this way: 'The purpose is to kill the enemy, so you have to have killing zones.' Apparently instructors were not supposed to use the phrase 'killing zones.' Instead they were supposed to use some euphemism. Well, North's attitude was: 'Screw them. It's vital that it be made clear that the enemy must be killed. I don't care what they say. We're Marine officers, and this is what we're going out there to do.' North was clearly confident. He was a prima donna. He knew he was real good at what he was doing . . . He clearly liked to be on stage. He told jokes. He was a funny guy. And he was highly ambitious. He also had a high opinion of himself."

North and Pfeiffer rewrote the handbooks for the lieutenants, feeling that the existing books were written in antiquated World War II language that was inappropriate for modern jungle warfare.

They also taught as a team, with Pfeiffer often playing off North's personality.

Pfeiffer, today an assistant professor of education at Colby College, would get North to barge into his classes to liven things up. Ollie, ever obliging, would burst in and say, "It's too late for your shoes, roll up your pants, and don't believe anything this guy says!"

The next day Pfeiffer would be teaching another group how to set up an ambush when North would explode into the room again, this time with a machine gun, firing blanks. "It always got me energized," Pfeiffer recalls. "It was pretty exciting. I'd get a good chuckle out of it . . . Ollie loves attention. He loved running into my class and running around with camouflage and face black with paint. He'd have run around with a machine gun for an hour if I'd let him. He really likes being at the center . . . Washington is his place."

Often, if they had taught ambushing in the classroom during the day, they would practice what they had learned in the field at night. North would lead one group while Pfeiffer's squad tried to trap them, or vice versa. "We'd teach them how to camouflage. He'd really get into that. He'd come in painted blue, black and green with bushes all over his head. He'd demonstrate how he could disappear in any background."

After an evening patrol, North and Pfeiffer would get together and critique the lieutenants. The two men liked each other even though they had sharply different political views. Pfeiffer thought the Vietnam War was America's stupidest military venture, and he was angry at how the country was treating veterans. He would later place candles on the steps of the White House and become a Quaker. North, on the other hand, thought the U.S. had lost the war because of the politicians. "He felt that the country was going through a stupid phase with all the peaceniks running around . . ."

Still, they both had a lot in common, Pfeiffer felt. They both were the sort who woke up in the morning and began looking for something to do. "Ollie's the kind of guy that if you needed to put up a fence or something, he'd be a perfect neighbor to have. He gets things *done*."

North could also be loyal to his friends. Pfeiffer, a lacrosse player, was in a league at the time and was looking for someone to come watch him play a big game at Johns Hopkins University. "It was really important to me . . . I asked North. He said sure, he'd come. I sat on the bench half the time . . . But when I was on the field he was screaming and yelling for me. He's very loyal and devoted."

But such breezy excursions into the world of civilian fun-and-games were rare. For the most part North remained deadly serious about his Marine mission and rarely strayed off base. Late at night North and Mark Treanor would sometimes sit and talk about the future of the country and of the Corps. "Ollie got philosophical," recalls Treanor. "Ollie has always been a patriot in the best sense of the word. We'd talk for hours about where the country was going, about the lieutenants who would be leading eighteen- and nine-teen-year-olds through the fields. We took our responsibility to the country very seriously."

North lived with his family on the sprawling Quantico base located about thirty-five miles south of Washington. It was damp, windy and cold in the winter and hot and humid in summer. Spiders, ticks and chiggers abounded. There was a big dorm with double rooms for the students, classroom facilities, workout areas, parade grounds, rifle and pistol ranges.

Ollie, Betsy, daughter Tait and a new infant son, Stuart, lived in Unit F, which was half of a brick duplex comprising building number 2905. The living area consisted of two stories, two bedrooms, and a living room/dining room. While Ollie was running around the base Betsy did not lead the most exciting life in the world. She and a neighbor would push the kids on the swings, take them down to the commissary, maybe do some sewing or play with the family Siamese cat. There wasn't much partying or socializing —Ollie would often be out on night maneuvers and not get home until two A.M. or later.

Pfeiffer remembers that North still had his Shelby Cobra muscle car and was very proud of it. People would often mistakenly call it a Mustang and he would lecture them on the differences between the two cars.

He didn't much like talking about his experiences in Vietnam. "Larry said, 'I lost too many good friends and too many good men, and I don't want to talk about it,'" remembers his sister, Patricia Balthazor.

But he did complain about so-called medal inflation in Vietnam, telling Pfeiffer that his father Clay North had won a Silver Star in World War II "when they didn't give them away." Pfeiffer said he gathered Ollie felt his Silver Star and Bronze Star weren't worth as much.

Lieno, Kresovich and others recall how hard it was to be a ser-viceman in those days, particularly a Marine. "We used to go to

Georgetown and have girls spit on us and then have the bartender ask us to leave," says Lieno. Living at Quantico "was a lot like being in a monastery. Your whole world is dedication to the Corps and its purpose. Mainly, North affirmed in us a belief that what we were doing was right."

Where others often found their spirits flagging in the face of mega-events like the November 1969 peace march on Washington, which attracted 250,000 protesters; the Kent State shootings in the spring of 1970 and the March 1971 conviction of William Calley on twenty-two counts of murder in the My Lai massacre—North, perhaps comforted by the Quantico womb, seemed to never waver in his zeal or commitment to the Corps. He was privately contemptuous of the peace activists, and angered by what he felt was a growing perception—created in large part by the liberal media establishment—among the public that My Lai, and to a lesser extent, the Herrod case, had been standard operating procedure in Vietnam. He had neither witnessed, nor been party to, anything of the sort during his tour there.

In July 1971, just after he was promoted to captain, North and two other Marine captains stationed at Quantico—Donald B. Carpenter and John F. Bender—decided they would do their bit to try and change public opinion about the American serviceman. They wrote a letter to the three major television networks and to William F. Buckley, Jr., the conservative columnist and host of Public Broadcasting's "Firing Line."

"For the past several months," the letter began, "we, as well as the rest of the American public, have been subjected to intense media coverage from a variety of sources regarding atrocities and war crimes allegedly committed in the Republic of Vietnam. We have been confronted with numerous confessions and accusations from those who feel an overwhelming guilt about their participation in our involvement in Southeast Asia. Several of these individuals claim to speak for all who have served on the grounds that the guilt is shared by all... Yet none of us have ever witnessed, participated in, or been cognizant of, a single instance wherein any Vietnamese noncombatant, North or South, was treated in anything less than a humane fashion. We believe that the American public should know this..."

(Bender and Carpenter were getting ready to quit the service and return to civilian life. Bender had graduated from Exeter Academy and Princeton before serving in Vietnam and was about to begin graduate studies at the Fletcher School of Law and Diplomacy. Carpenter had graduated from Andover and Brown University and was preparing to enter Harvard Business School.)

The networks showed no interest in the letter, but Buckley invited the three to come on his program. The show aired July 21, 1971. In reading North's biographical sketch, Buckley said among other things that he had graduated as an honor student from Annapolis. Actually Ollie had ranked toward the lower portion of his class, but they weren't there to discuss biographical sketches.

Buckley, intrigued that three spit-polished Marines would stand up publicly to deny any knowledge of atrocities occurring in Vietnam, began by asking the group if anyone had put them up to writing the letter. They assured him no one had.

North, quickly asserting himself as the group's most articulate and principal spokesman, told Buckley that what motivated him was concern for the reputation of the 216 enlisted men he said had served in his platoon in Vietnam during the nine and a half months he had commanded it. "I felt, personally, that I didn't want the families of any of those people to feel that their sons or their husbands were coming home as, quote, 'war criminals,'" Ollie said. "My original motivation was just that: that I thought it was becoming a known fact, almost, throughout our country, that anyone who had participated in the war was, by the nature of the fact that there was participation, a war criminal.

"What we say in the letter is that, through our experience over the three-plus years of commanding or observing troops in combat, we never knew of a single instance of an atrocity. Since we have come home, we certainly have been made aware of a number of them. We don't dispute a single one of these instances; we're not questioning the veracity of any one of those who have confessed or accused. We're simply saying that within our experience, this did not happen."

It was a carefully worded, nondenial denial.

North quoted from an order he said he read to his men prior to a February 22, 1969 assault on Con Thien. "'Despite . . . the declaration of this being a so-called free-fire zone, we will continue our policy of firing only at known armed enemy on the conduct of this patrol.'"

Far from committing atrocities, Marines had shown restraint, North said. ". . . There are times when American Marines probably have died and certainly have been put into extreme situations to avoid inflicting casualties on civilians or noncombatants in the area."

North complimented his superiors in taking issue with a statement by journalist Seymour Hersh, who had broken the My Lai story and had recently been on the Buckley program. Hersh had asserted that most lieutenant colonels who want to be colonels will hush up crimes. On the contrary, North said, the four battalion commanders he had served under while in Vietnam "placed tremendous direct emphasis on the treatment of civilians within our area... I don't think it's a matter of hushing up, because I've never seen that. These men were sincerely concerned with the welfare of the civilian in that area..."

When a student in the audience asked if perhaps the army was more prone to committing atrocities than the Marines, North diplomatically declined to criticize the My Lai-implicated army but said: "We certainly believe as Marine officers that we're just tremendous; we wouldn't be Marine officers if we didn't think so."

Winning the hearts and minds of the Vietnamese civilians was a concept that was constantly stressed to the Marines, so it was only natural that they accorded civilians respect, North indicated. He spoke of the "tremendous drive" and the "tremendous emphasis" that the Corps placed on such civic programs as medical and dental care for Vietnamese villagers. "The idea behind the whole thing," said North, "is to make the South Vietnamese feel that this is not the great and glorious Uncle Sam that's giving the stuff away, but it's the district or province chief, the local authorized government of Vietnam. And we don't go running around showing the flag, if you will."

Another student asked North if prisoners had been mistreated.

"I was fortunate enough to take several prisoners while I was in Vietnam, once on a specific mission to take a prisoner," North replied. "I think it's a wonderful tribute to the Marine, the young fellow up there who is actually doing the capturing, or involved in this face-to-face confrontation, that he made every effort to take a prisoner without even hurting the guy. And once this prisoner had been wounded—because that's what the resultant action was—this prisoner was afforded every facility, medically, that we had available to our own resources—the attempt being to make sure that this guy made it and made it alive."

"But did you ever yourself witness the mistreatment of Vietcong prisoners by either American or South Vietnamese troops?" pressed the student.

"I never witnessed a single ear being cut off, a single round being fired at a man without a rifle, a single piece of ordnance dropped at,

on or near a village of any type, or a single civilian being maltreated
by either South Vietnamese or American personnel. Is that specific, sir?"

North was displaying the same cool, cocksure demeanor that
he would show the nation sixteen years later on Capitol Hill. He
looked every bit the poster Marine with his high-and-tight haircut and his summer khaki uniform studded with combat decora-
tions. He was articulate and had a relaxed yet earnest tone to his
voice. But where Buckley, Carpenter and Bender decorously kept
their legs crossed for the studio and television audience, North's
legs were splayed out, spread-eagled. It was the only flaw in an
otherwise impressive performance, which did not go unnoticed at
Marine headquarters. If the brass had been perturbed by North's
testimony on behalf of Randy Herrod in Vietnam the year before,
the consensus was that he recouped on the Buckley show.

North finished his stint at Quantico in September of 1973. He
then received orders to join Battalion Landing Team ¾, 3rd Marine
Division, in the Northern Training Area of Okinawa, Japan.

He assumed his post on December 16, 1973, leaving his family at
home just ten days before Christmas. The tour of duty was for one
year, and according to Pfeiffer and others it was becoming apparent
that North's military career was putting an increasing strain on his
marriage. Betsy, it was suggested, was growing frustrated with raising children by herself and not having a husband around for such
long stretches at a time—and when he was around, he worked
ridiculously long hours, to the point where it seemed he was rarely
home. It was not exactly "quality time," as they would say in the
eighties.

Ollie headed out for Okinawa, and Betsy was not, according to
Pfeiffer, happy about it. By the end of the Okinawa tour, North
would have been away two of the six years they had been married.

But orders were orders, so North flew ahead to Japan. Okinawa
was considered good but not great duty for an up-and-comer like
Ollie. According to Col. Pat Collins, who is in charge of the Special
Operations-Marine Amphibious Force at Camp Lejeune, some
people felt North was avoiding command billets when he went to
Okinawa as a captain. "He ran afoul of the system by not serving as
a rifle commander," says Collins. "Back in those days, serving in
the line units was very unpleasant—the racial and the drug problems were out of control. The guys who went to Okinawa were the

best of a bad lot... In one battalion I had 537 court martials for rape, robbery and murder."

Retired Maj. Gen. Fred Haynes, who commanded the 3rd Marine Division in Okinawa while North was there, agreed that the Corps was then having difficulty keeping up the quality of its enlisted men. U.S. involvement in Vietnam was winding down, the draft had been abolished, the military was perhaps as unpopular as it had ever been, so the Marines were no longer attracting the *crème de la crème*. The general admitted that often the only difference between those sent to Okinawa and those who were not was that the former "just weren't under indictment."

North was assigned to head up a training facility on the remote northern part of the island amid jungle, ravines, mountains and poisonous snakes. He and a staff of about a dozen subordinate officers processed eight hundred to a thousand Marines a month through a training course that included rappelling down cliffs, night infiltration, swimming, fording streams, map reading, small-units tactics and surviving on wild vegetation, animals and insects. It was sort of a jungle-warfare Outward Bound.

The only proper place for training was in the north because most of the rest of Okinawa was used for farming. Yet even the north seemed an incongruous area to train since troops couldn't fire guns on any part of the island because of an endangered species of woodpeckers—a fact that the Corps didn't play up in its recruiting pitches; leathernecks weren't known to lie down for woodpeckers. There were areas where they couldn't even shoot blanks because of the birds.

North and his men lived in Quonset huts and used pit latrines. There was partial electricity. It was hot and humid in the dry season, rainy and chilly in the winter. The base camp was a ten-square-mile area. A couple of huts were used as barracks, a first-aid station and as offices. Some of the area was covered with tall elephant grass and bamboo-tree ferns. As the commanding officer of the training area, Ollie had his own hooch. In his office, he kept a "Lead, Follow, or Get the Hell Out of the Way" plaque on his desk. Communication was by radio.

Stan Ostazeski, the medical corpsman who worked under North at the time, recalls that their typical daily routine consisted of getting up at 5 A.M. to go for a three-mile run, followed by physical training such as pullups, pushups and the like. Then breakfast, field training or lectures, lunch, more field training, dinner and sometimes more physical training.

North still had the same penchant for the dramatic that he had displayed at Quantico. He called one obstacle course "Disneyland East," and liked to trip a booby trap that spewed red dye all over the grunts to drive home his bloody point that combat was life or death.

As usual, no one outworked North, and he seemed to revel in the physical intensity of the assignment. He ran with his troops, could outrun virtually all of them—doing three miles in eighteen minutes. He always participated in every exercise; he never just observed.

"I liked him very much," says General Haynes. "He was an attractive, cheerful and energetic captain. He was very good at briefings and describing the training in detail and what we were about to accomplish. I had no problem bringing VIPs to the area to visit because I was impressed with the way he was running things . . . He had characteristics which were somewhat captivating. He had a very honest approach. He wasn't sycophantic. If he felt there were problems he'd discuss them honestly. Some people have a knack for handling everyone. North handled senior officers as well as he handled junior officers or subordinates. He seemed to be able to do it both ways."

As he had in Vietnam, North made all his charges wear their helmets and flak jackets in the field and preached that a Marine's best friend was a corpsman and a flak jacket.

North didn't brag about his experiences in Vietnam, but if he thought a particular experience he had had would help someone, he'd mention it in an instructive way. He was firm but compassionate with the troops.

Paul McHale, then a platoon leader in Okinawa, remembers North working with one grunt for twenty minutes trying to coax him to rappel down a hundred-foot rope dangling from a CH-53 helicopter. "The way he communicated to you was cool and professional," recalls McHale, now out of the service and a Democratic state representative in Pennsylvania. "He'd turn to you and say, 'See you on deck, busher.'"

"I think he instilled a sense of teamwork in us while we were training," says Ostazeski, to whom North seemed more a coach than a commanding officer. "While I was in the navy we had a lot of problems with race . . . But in North's company it was different. Everyone got along."

North once took a radio operator who had gotten into trouble with drugs in southern Okinawa under his wing, got him trans-

ferred to the north and went out of his way to keep the guy clean.
Another time, Ostazeski says, a lieutenant was getting ready to
rotate back to the States when North had to tell him word had just
arrived that his girlfriend had been killed in a car crash. The lieutenant started crying; so did North and they hugged each other.

During monsoon season the Marines would fly out and there
would be no training, but North and his instructors would stay
behind. They'd play Monopoly to pass the time, and there was also
a ping-pong table, a pool table and a dart board. It was the only
base on the island without pawnshops and whores surrounding it.
The isolation grated on some, but North and most of the others got
into the mood and spirit of the place. They let themselves go a little
wild—for Ollie that meant he could leave his chaw of tobacco in a
little longer than when he was at home. On Okinawa, after all,
there was no one to come home to, though Betsy did come over for
one visit.

"Some people did think we were kind of crazy in Okinawa," says
Ostazeski. "We had no flushing toilets. We lived in huts. So if they
wanted to believe it, we'd lead them on a little bit. When they'd
visit, we'd sort of hotdog it up a little bit to show how much we
were roughing it."

In the isolation of northern Okinawa North seemed more relaxed
and less concerned about rank–up and down–than he was state-
side. There was an all-for-one, one-for-all feeling, a sense that they
were a hardship outpost unto themselves and could live pretty
much by their own rules. Ostazeski recalls that on an occasion
when they were having problems with a malingering Marine who
refused to do his exercises, "Ollie said if we have a problem like
that we'll just take him out back." Another time, North uncharac-
teristically issued a threat to a commanding officer, warning that he
would steal the officer's personal air-conditioner unless North's out-
fit was supplied with one for common use.

On December 16, 1974, shortly after returning home from Okinawa, North's clear-eyed, all-American world suddenly cracked. He
voluntarily entered Bethesda Naval Hospital where he remained
for twenty-two days suffering from what was officially diagnosed as
"emotional distress."

According to several sources it was a marital crisis that triggered
North's "breakdown." Apparently growing more dissatisfied with
her role, Betsy North had written her husband in Okinawa to say
that she was leaving him.

News of the hospitalization was first reported in the Miami *Herald* on December 23, 1986, approximately a month after North became a household name when he was fired from the National Security Council. The New York *Times* and the Washington *Times,* particularly the latter, followed the next day with more details.

The Washington *Times* had had a story on North's hospitalization ready to run for about two weeks, but the paper, in a decision that caused considerable internal controversy, did not publish the story until it was effectively forced to do so by the *Herald.* The cynical rank-and-file view at the *Times* was that the ultraconservative powers-that-be at the newspaper had been reluctant to tarnish North, the new hero of the Right.

The Washington *Times* story said that before he was hospitalized, North had threatened to commit suicide. It quoted a high-ranking administration official who has known North well as saying that Ollie "called his old Vietnam battalion commander and told him he didn't have anything to live for, that he was going to shoot himself."

The paper cited three sources who identified the recipient of the call as Col. Richard C. Schulze, who had in fact been North's battalion commander in Vietnam and was then commander of the Basic School in Quantico. After receiving the call, the *Times* said Schulze went directly to North's home, where he found the young officer "babbling incoherently and running around naked, waving a .45 pistol."

The New York *Times*, citing Pentagon sources, reported the same day, December 24, that North had told Marine officials in 1986 that the hospitalization records had been removed from his files by Schulze, who had gone on to become a major general and director of Marine personnel policy. Schulze retired in 1981 and died of a heart attack in 1983.

Schulze's widow, Sally, says he never told her about receiving a distress call from North and she thinks he would have. But others confirm the essence of the Washington *Times* report. They include Dwayne Gray, a retired Marine lieutenant-general and close friend of Schulze, who says: "Dick knew Ollie and thought well of him, took care of him and worried about him. He was a headstrong youngster. Dick counseled him and tried to keep him headed in the right direction . . . Schulze was the type of guy that was respected by younger people. Ollie wasn't famous at that time. He was one of the energetic, ambitious and hardworking officers. We all knew officers like him . . . I can confirm that Ollie had some sort of mental disturbance or nervous problem and his head wasn't working right.

Dick learned about it and at the time of the occurrence, Dick was
one of the people, if not the only person, who did see Ollie, talked
to him and encouraged him to seek psychiatric help. Dick was concerned about Ollie's mental state, and it was in conversation later
that Dick told me he was worried about suicidal tendencies—attempt is too strong a word, but he was worried that Ollie would try
to harm himself."

A close friend of North says the marital crisis in 1974 "changed
the way he [North] felt about his family and his priorities, and he
realized that he had put his work so far ahead of his wife, and that
he could easily have lost his family . . . He talked about how it
helped him prioritize; he is often brought to tears talking about it."

If the crisis ultimately had a salutary effect on his marriage,
North was still worried about the effect of the hospitalization on his
career and, evidently and understandably, wanted no trace of it on
his records. So it would seem he prevailed on Schulze to sanitize
his files, and Schulze, according to the New York *Times* story,
agreed. The Washington *Times* article quoted a Marine who served
in Vietnam and Okinawa with North as saying that Ollie had
"bragged" that he had been able to get all references to the hospitalization purged from his records.

The Washington *Times* story, by reporter Hugh Aynesworth, was
notable for one other piece of information: it said North had been
hospitalized at Bethesda in September 1974, not December, while
in Washington on emergency leave from Okinawa. The Marine
Corps, reacting to the Miami *Herald* story, issued a statement on
December 24, 1986—the day the Washington *Times* story appeared—confirming only that North had been voluntarily hospitalized during the twenty-two-day period from December 16, 1974 to
January 7, 1975.

However, the first official biography of North issued by the Marine Corps shortly after he was fired from the NSC has an unex-
plained five-week gap in North's service record in Okinawa during
which time, some sources say, he was in fact back in the United
States.

The biography says North headed up the Northern Training Area
until July 31, 1974. The next five weeks are unaccounted for, then
the biography goes on to say North served as the officer in charge of
Headquarters and Service Company, 3rd Motor Transport Battalion, 3rd Marine Division, from September 5 to November 9. It also
says he served as a company commander from November 10 to
December 10 before ending his tour and coming home.

Two military sources say they saw North at Norton Air Force Base outside Los Angeles in August 1974 en route back to Washington. One of the sources says North was actually hospitalized twice —once in August and again in December, after the Okinawa tour ended. Aynesworth says his account that North was hospitalized in September was based on two sources who said they saw North in Washington then, and an unidentified military officer who was hospitalized in Bethesda himself in September and said he saw North there at that time.

In a section of his story that was not published, Aynesworth quoted the officer as saying that when North mingled with others from the ward in the recreation room he would insist that his uniform be brought out. "He'd set it up in a chair beside him so that everybody could see all his medals," the officer said. "He always had to prove that he was better than everybody else. He said he needed the uniform with him because it might get wrinkled."

Gen. Walter Boomer, chief spokesman for the Marine Corps, told Aynesworth that North denied ever leaving Okinawa before his duty assignment ended on December 10, 1974, and had "no explanation for any accounts that he was elsewhere."

In later North resumés issued by the Marine Corps the five-week gap noted in the first version is absent. The revised version simply extends North's assignment at the training area to November 8 and eliminates all reference to a second job with the 3rd Motor Transport Battalion from September 5 to November 9, as it initially reported. Asked by the author to account for the discrepancy, Boomer had an aide issue a statement attributing the five-week gap on the first biography to "an administrative goof." He said the first biography was hurriedly put together and that there was no gap.

In any case, after the twenty-two-day stay at Bethesda ending in January, North was given a clean bill of health and allowed to resume active duty.

Returning in February 1975, North landed well—he was assigned to work in the Manpower Division at Marine Headquarters in Washington.

Manpower was considered a plum assignment; it brought North into close contact with what fellow Marines called the "Board of Directors"—the generals who ran the corps day-to-day and did all the promoting. Though this assignment was North's first stint as a desk jockey, if he had to sit behind a desk this was the place to do it.

Some four hundred officers worked in the Manpower Division, making it the biggest unit at headquarters. At a time when the draft had ended and the quality of the enlisted ranks was considered relatively poor, Manpower was in charge of assigning and deploying Marines around the country and the world. It was a powerful department where movers and shakers were concentrated.

During this period North helped implement a new program that changed the way Marine units were deployed worldwide. Under the so-called unit deployment program, rotation policies were changed so that units stayed together as a group for thirteen months before being rotated en masse rather than incrementally. It was felt this approach would save money, facilitate training and create more organizational cohesion and *esprit de corps*.

Marine headquarters is near the Pentagon in the Navy Annex, a dingy old World War II warehouse. Manpower was on the top floor. Everyone sat in close quarters at gray metal desks whose chairs were often missing a leg or a wheel. The lighting was terrible. Just before North arrived, workers had finally placed dry-wall over exposed rafters where pigeons roosted and regularly sent droppings flying down into the Marines' in-baskets.

North was an effective salesman for the unit-deployment program, but in the course of his salesmanship his peers began noticing a character trait that others would later remark on at the NSC: in making a point or arguing his case, North would often invoke the name of a superior or even the commandant of the Marine Corps —even if the superior hadn't explicitly authorized whatever it was Ollie was selling.

"It was obvious to me that Ollie was quite capable of getting things done in the name of the commandant of the Marine Corps without the commandant necessarily having approved the details," said retired Major Lance Zellers. "Ollie was not averse to dropping names, saying, 'Gentlemen, the commandant would like...' He spoke in the name of the commandant. For all practical purposes he had four stars." Since North was a captain and most of the people doing the sort of work he was doing were majors, perhaps he felt the need to invoke rank to get things done, but that often seemed to alienate his peers.

Co-workers thought he worked longer than necessary, spending two days on a job that could have been finished in less than one, and adding dramatic flourishes along the way.

"Everyone put in about ten or twelve hours a day, but Ollie tended to burn the evening oil more than others," recalls David Evans, a retired Marine lieutenant-colonel who served in Manpower with North and now covers military affairs for the Chicago *Tribune*. "I thought a lot of it was unnecessary. Ollie's physical capacity for work was amply demonstrated."

Evans says that while North was bright, articulate and aggressive, he was "a mile wide and an inch deep... Ollie liked the limelight—he liked briefing [generals]. But his briefings were very superficial... Ollie was a can-do kind of guy, while the rest of us would react to a problem realistically, knowing there were no easy options."

But superior officers, perhaps predictably, had a far more favorable opinion of North:

"When I knew him at headquarters he was a captain, a relatively junior officer to be doing the kind of staff work he was doing," recalls a general who asked not to be identified. "Oliver came to my attention because he sat in on briefings for the commandant on Manpower—I noticed that he was doing the main briefings. He was looked to by staff officers for the answers. He answered eloquently and well. He's a young man who did good staff work and was well prepared for any work he did. He was a superb staff officer.

"North was analytical in his approach to problems at Marine headquarters. I think anyone would be happy to have Oliver North on staff simply because he performed well. He was conscientous about work and delivered rather complicated products in a timely and comprehensive fashion."

Lance Zellers says he watched North time and again deftly reduce complex issues to what some might consider patriotic oversimplifications and successfully argue the position he was advancing.

"He's clearly the little guy who's suddenly given a position of power—Jack-the-giant-killer..." Zellers says. "The people who saw Ollie North on TV in July saw him at his best, and I saw the same Ollie North in the Manpower division. He was very patriotic—very red-white-and-blue. North was able to make any issue an apple-pie issue and then sell it."

In Manpower it was the responsibility of the "action officer" on a given project to do research for his boss and offer an objective analysis of an issue and present recommendations. But according to Zellers, North would adjust his analyses to present only one side of an issue. "I believe he picked his favorite side and sold it strongly. I think Ollie liked to play up his side of the issue and not discuss the serious payoffs. He could package things well and sell them with a sincere conviction... He didn't know there were twenty-four hours in a day. He had an incredible capacity for work...

"They don't come much more American than Ollie North. He was the antithesis of communism. I'd have to say I know few people as obviously patriotic. He wore his flag on his sleeve... Ollie enjoyed being in the halls of power. He loved to complete the mission of the red, white and blue over the communist enemy. To him, the end justified the means.

"Ollie was upbeat and optimistic and saw only the good side of things. Ollie was not a philosopher. He was not one who would dwell long enough on the negative side of a course of action. Generals like to hear positive can-do approaches. They don't like to hear bad news... Therefore the system aided and abetted Ollie in the way he was approaching issues. He fed them what they wanted ... My view was that Ollie was manipulative... That bothered me as a contemporary because I felt an officer had the responsibility to show both sides of an issue."

Briefing generals and the Marine commandant as a captain on a regular basis and having his recommendations respected was heady, and Ollie clearly enjoyed it. It was a pattern that would continue on the NSC—a junior officer assuming far more responsibility than someone of his rank and position customarily did and relating to his superiors as an equal.

"I believe I sensed a long time ago that Ollie had the potential to be a general because of the way he was accepted by his superiors," adds Zellers. "But I sensed conversely that same capacity to get himself into deep trouble by overextending himself, by getting so wrapped up in things that he lost proper balance. There's a bit of a Superman syndrome buried in there. You start thinking that everything you do will be successful."

North was promoted to major on July 1, 1978, soon after being transferred to Camp Lejeune, North Carolina as the operations officer for the 3rd Battalion, 8th Marines, 2nd Marine Division. David Evans recalls that North's promotion stirred considerable controversy—even resentment—among his peers since it was common knowledge that he had been hospitalized for emotional problems in early 1975. Rightly or wrongly, at that time there was more of a career-damaging stigma in the Marine Corps associated with hospitalization for emotional difficulty than there is today. So Evans says the prevailing view among North's peers was that even though he had been declared fit to return to duty, the hospitalization would have retarded the career of the average Marine officer. That it did not affect North was widely viewed among mid-level officers—sour grapes or not—as an example of cronyism and favoritism at work.

At Camp Lejeune, the Marine Corps' Amphibious Warfare Training center, North threw himself into his new job with his customary energy and zeal, continuing to draw favorable reviews from his superiors. As the S–3 officer, or the number-three man in the battalion, he was a key staff aide commanding officers turned to for advice on what tactics and organizational structure to use in the field. North quickly gained added visibility through his role in helping to get a battalion ready to go to the Mediterranean.

"I was highly impressed with his preparations and his involvement and his knowledge," says a general who knew North at Lejeune. "As I discussed with other senior officers, I wasn't the only one impressed. He was creating a good reputation, and it's difficult to do that as a junior officer... He's the type of professional who, when assigned a job, works at it until such time that he becomes an expert at it... I'd say that Ollie performed well in everything he did—field and staff work. When you find a guy who is so talented, you identify talent and you put that capable person in responsible positions. That's why his name always came up."

The general said he considered it inevitable that a doer like North alienated people, because to get things done you often had to rub others the wrong way. He noted the pattern of superiors and underlings liking Ollie while many of his peers disliked and even despised him, but he attributed the latter mostly to jealousy.

In addition to keeping his career moving on a steadily upward track, North's two years at Camp Lejeune were perhaps most notable for a personal religous experience that transformed his life.

Ollie's commanding officer at Lejeune was Lt. Col. John S. Grinalds, who then and now was regarded as one of the brightest lights in the military. Grinalds, a West Point graduate, former Rhodes Scholar and Harvard MBA, is a born-again Christian. One day in 1978, during a field-training exercise at Lejeune, Grinalds noticed

that North still walked with a slight limp and had pain in his back
—the residue of the 1964 car accident, aggravated by war wounds.

Grinalds, who also had worked with North at Marine headquarters
in Washington, fell to talking with Ollie about the power of prayer.
According to Marine Maj. Michael Lundblad, one of many to whom
Grinalds has told the story, the general then asked North to sit down
on a chair and extend his legs: one was shorter than the other. So
Grinalds, who today is a brigadier-general, began to pray and knelt
down, placing his hands on North. After a few minutes, Ollie got up,
his legs seemingly the same length. He walked around without a limp
and the pain in his back seemed to be gone.

"Gee, colonel, you've got power!" said an amazed North.

"No, God has the power to do all things, and he's using me to get
to you," replied a solemn Grinalds, who has also told others that he
once healed his wife of painful back spasms in similar fashion.

Stunned by his experience, North began drifting from his relatively tame Catholicism and, at Grinalds's urging, eventually joined
a charismatic branch of the Episcopal Church. He would also join
and become active in Officers Christian Fellowship, an organization
that offers bible study and spiritual solace for military officers who
are born-again Christians.

In the summer of 1980 North was selected to be one of twenty
Marine officers to attend the Naval War College in Newport, Rhode
Island.

The War College, which overlooks Narragansett Bay, offers a
ten-month, nondegree, graduate-level program for officers from
every branch of the armed services. It is a military finishing school
for the best and the brightest considered likely to become flag officers. Students are divided into the college of naval warfare for
higher-ranking officers, and the college of naval command and staff
for lower-ranking officers. North, then a major, attended the latter.

The required core curriculum consists of defense-economics decision-making, strategy and policy, and operations. After these the
officers can take several electives. Ollie took "Soviet Union: Domestic and Foreign Policy"; "The Soviet Navy"; and "Military Justice and Administrative Law for the Commander."

Prof. Jerome Holloway, a retired foreign service officer who
taught North and still teaches at the War College, thought Ollie
was "extremely bright. He got very high marks. He was conservative, but not the right-wing kook he came across as in the hearings.
He was right-of-center but certainly within the American political

tradition... He was articulate. He had good ideas and he wasn't afraid of ideas. Many officers tended to be restrictive in class participation because they were embarrassed if they were wrong. Ollie was always ready to try out ideas and argue them out... He was witty and very charming. His sense of humor came out in class... He was brighter than the others. He stood out academically."

Richard Carlson taught North defense-economics decision-making. They would postulate how to generate funds for the defense budget and then how to spend them—on a carrier, a destroyer, another division for a service, and why. Carlson, now an evangelical minister in California, says one of his goals was to get students to think in broader terms than the battalion or other organizational structure they had been a part of to that point. He found North very much up to that.

"He always had very strong opinions," says Carlson. "They were very well thought out. He articulated his positions well and he never turned down a good argument... Ollie was forceful in deciding what was the right course. He was one of the fellows who could look at an issue with a broader perspective. He didn't just ask himself, 'Is it good for the Marine Corps?'"

Carlson recalls that reactions to North's strong personality were mixed. Some people were intimidated by him. Others couldn't believe his presentation and thought he was being theatrical to look good for the professor. But Carlson believed one needed a little arrogance to get anywhere in the military, and that Ollie had that proper arrogance.

Bruce Valley, an Annapolis graduate who went through the War College with North, was one of those whom Carlson said were incredulous of North's classroom style.

Valley, an articulate arch-conservative who made an unsuccessful run for the U.S. Senate from New Hampshire in 1986, said he told Carlson in 1981 before the class graduation: "North has the talent to be commandant or a contender, based on honest work. I think he's a man of enormous talent. He's likable, smart, good-looking and hard-working. But I think I've never met a person so intensely self-promoting. My feeling is he spent half his time working on his image, trying to make himself look harassed, hardworking and overworked."

At the Naval War College there was a large lecture hall known as "the Bedroom." It was used for the most prominent speakers. Valley recalls that North would sit in the first row and ask the first, second or third question following a speaker's presentation. "He would do it in a sycophantic way. He had a pattern. As the person would finish the lecture North would stand up and introduce himself and comment on how great the lecture was and then he'd say how he agreed with points a, b and c. 'However,' North would say, 'I have this question in light of that,' and then he would throw up a softball question for the lecturer . . . I saw it happening every time. I saw a person who was sycophantic and self-promoting . . . I found he liked to be around people he could instruct and who didn't know enough to call him on his ideas . . . He wanted to show how smart he is, how broadly informed — but liked to play to audiences where no one could go very deep into what he knows . . . He hides behind the mask of patriotism and warriorism."

Pro and con. North rarely inspired neutrality.

North and 161 of his classmates graduated from the Naval War College in June 1981.

One of the more coveted duty assignments for any graduate of the War College is a stint at the National Security Council, which regularly takes on military aides for one- or two-year tours, after which they rotate back to their service branch. It is a valuable chance for a serviceman to broaden his horizons and work at the vortex of power. It was considered a particularly plum assignment for a gung-ho military man in 1981 at the dawn of the Reagan Administration, which was promising a reassertion of military strength, indeed a reassertion of American strength around the world.

But according to friends, North had no interest in going to the NSC. The reasons had to do with traditional Marine goals and with what was considered proper Marine behavior. Marines are generally apolitical, action-oriented anti-intellectuals who are far more comfortable leading men in the field than they are sitting behind a desk. In fact, unless they are in a command billet at headquarters or the like, there is something of a stigma associated with desk jobs, and there is perhaps nothing worse than to be known as a "political Marine" who has gone "white shoe."

Says ex-Marine and ex-National Security Advisor Robert McFarlane: "The Marine mentality . . . is to believe that your obligations as a Marine are to always be in the field, a leader and a field Marine. 'Shoot, move, communicate.' And if you don't do that, especially if you do the other end of that, which is to be a politician, it's awful. And if you ever talk to the press, and if you are ever involved in non-Marine things, it's a little bit aberrant."

North was still only a major. He could not command a battalion until he was a lieutenant-colonel—the next step up the promotional ladder. But the most logical next move would have been to take an upper-staff-level job at headquarters, a recruiting office or a training base.

"He would have preferred working at headquarters or Quantico or in Personnel rather than wearing civilian clothes and working directly for the President," says Donald Frahler, a navy commander and a friend of North.

Still, one does not always get one's choice of assignments in the Marine Corps, so North's name was advanced as a candidate for the NSC. Gen. Ed Bronars, who was deputy chief-of-staff for Manpower at the time and had known and liked North at Camp Lejeune, approved a short list of about three other names in addition to North's. The list went to then-Marine Commandant Robert Barrow, and ultimately to the new Secretary of the Navy, John Lehman.

Secretary Lehman recalls that besides the Marines, the faculty at the War College also recommended North to him and mentioned that he had written some incisive papers while he was there. One of them was on the recommissioning of World War II battleships, a subject of interest to Lehman. Lehman said he signed off on North without having met him and notified the NSC, which made the final selections based on recommendations from the service branches and interviews with the men themselves.

Robert L. Schweitzer, now a retired army major-general but then in charge of the Defense Group at the NSC, was the man who winnowed the lists and effectively chose the candidates after presenting his choices for formal approval by the new National Security Advisor, Richard Allen. Schweitzer recalls that the main reason he picked North was that North did not want the job.

"I was the one that could have turned Ollie down," he says. "I didn't want an Ollie North. I made an argument for policy-oriented guys, veterans who were experienced and who had advanced degrees in international relations—people who understood the give and the take of policy-making. What endeared Ollie to me was, I asked him did he want to be here. 'No, absolutely not,' he responded. I'd rather have someone who wanted to be a soldier or lead troops, than someone who wanted to get into the White House. He was a very humble guy. His honesty and fundamental approach drew me to take him in."

As a nominee for the NSC post North would have been required to disclose his hospitalization at Bethesda less than seven years before. Though the NSC would later refuse to say whether the disclosure was made or not, it evidently was not, since the White House would acknowledge it had not known of the hospitalization. The FBI, Secretary Service and the Office of White House Counsel would have been the three agencies empowered to conduct background checks on NSC nominees, but apparently none turned up the hospitalization. Allen would later say that had he known about the stint at Bethesda, he probably would not have approved North.

Officials often do not investigate a person's medical background unless he discloses that he has a history of a medical or nervous disorder. Every Marine seeking a top-secret or higher clearance must complete a DD–398 Statement of Personal History form, which asks if he has been "hospitalized or treated by a doctor for nervous disorders." Failure to fill out the form accurately constitutes perjury.

In selecting North for largely a negative reason—that he didn't want the job—General Schweitzer perhaps misjudged the whirlwind energy that Ollie would nonetheless bring to the position. Nor did he give particular thought to who would contain such zeal.

Says Richard Carlson: "I believe Ollie has a characteristic we'd all like to have, and that is, if we believe something, our actions are then driven by those beliefs... When you have a man with that much initiative, you as his boss have to understand you have a tiger by the tail. All military guys like that need control. He's not any different than other military men who want to get the job done. He was not the kind of guy who was just going to sit around the NSC."

Adds Secretary Lehman: "I regret the whole disaster, but I don't think the cause of it was Ollie. When you send Marine [majors] who are trained to take hills over to the NSC, you need to control them."

WHITE HOUSE

NORTH reported for duty at the National Security Council on August 4, 1981, along with two Army officers, Richard Childress and Allan Myer.

Richard Allen, was anxious for the military detail to help staff the White House effort to get its $8.5 billion sale of sophisticated Airborne Warning and Control System (AWAC) electronic surveillance planes to Saudi Arabia approved by the Senate.

Until then the new Reagan Administration had been almost totally preoccupied with the economy and other domestic issues, and the AWACS sale was seen as its first major foreign-policy initiative.

North, Childress and Myer set up shop in an old Executive Office Building office that Allen had used during the transition before moving next door to the White House. The three military officers were charged with coordinating briefings for senators and keeping close track of the head-count as the lobbying progressed and the vote drew near.

The administration fielded three briefing teams, which in the patriotic glow of the day were christened the red, white and blue teams. Heading up one of the teams was Maj. Gen. Richard Secord, then deputy assistant secretary of defense for the Near East and South Asia, who would later become North's private-sector point man in the Iran-Contra affair. But North, still something of a factotum had little or no contact with Secord during the AWACs lobbying drive.

The work was largely clerical, tedious and boring, and North and his confreres couldn't wait to move on to tasks they considered more substantive and meaningful. Childress and Myer, after all, had graduate degrees and were specialists in East Asian affairs and Soviet-European affairs respectively. Ollie was the generalist, said to be the only person on the NSC staff at the time who did not have an advanced degree. But the three officers dutifully did their part and won praise for their grunt work in helping the administration win approval of the AWACs sale by a 52–48 vote in the Senate on October 28.

Perhaps the most exciting thing to happen to North, Childress and Myer during their three-month AWACs stint had nothing whatever to do with high tech spy planes or the Saudis. Rather, it was the discovery of ten crisp $100 bills and several other gifts in the office safe which had been used by Allen. They had wanted a place to store some of their briefing material and so asked an administrator for the combination. Myer and the secretary the three men shared had opened the safe and discovered the cash and gifts.

The three took the contents and handed it over to NSC Security Officer Jerry Jennings, who informed then presidential counselor Edwin Meese. Shortly thereafter the FBI began an investigation. The $1000 turned out to be money Allen had accepted from two Japanese journalists who had interviewed Nancy Reagan at the White House in January, and the other gifts were three watches Allen had received from Japanese friends.

Allen went on a paid leave after Thanksgiving while the inquiry was conducted, and the Justice Department later cleared him of any wrongdoing. Reagan elected to replace Allen in January of 1982 with a trusted friend and political associate from California, William Clark, who was then deputy secretary of state.

The move also signaled a change in the way the NSC was to function. Reagan had taken office with a stated commitment to cabinet-government, which meant a reduced role for the National Security Advisor. The idea was to avoid the tensions that had arisen when stars like Henry Kissinger and Zbigniew Brzezinski had transcended their positions as security advisor to become de facto secretaries of state.

Allen, who had been a deputy to Kissinger, says he approved of the reduced role and symbolically opted to take an office in the White House basement rather than the old Kissinger office next to the president in the West Wing. The administration wanted to restore the NSC to its traditional role of policy-coordinator rather than implementer—a largely neutral agency that would sift through the enormous paper flow from various agencies of the executive branch all competing for the president's attention, synthesize it and present policy options for decision. It was to be a referee, not a player.

"When we started," says Allen, "I told my staff, 'I hope you haven't come to the wrong place. If you want day-to-day action, you really are in the wrong place. Your job is to affect long-range policy.'"

While that was all well and good in principle, in practice Allen saw his access to Reagan sharply restricted and was forced to report through Meese. Allen says that was not his original understanding when he took the job—the idea of "coordinating" through Meese came up during the transition. Still, Allen initially thought Meese would serve as a bureaucratic blocking back to preserve his access to Reagan, but concedes that Meese later became "an enormous impediment." The other two prongs in the White House staff troika—James Baker and Michael Deaver—were not particularly interested in enhancing Allen's influence either, nor, certainly, was the self-styled vicar of foreign policy, Secretary of State Alexander Haig.

All of which apparently served to lower morale among NSC staffers as they watched most of their handiwork disappear into Meese's briefcase. "The NSC was the pimple on the ass of an enormous elephant," recalls Myer. "It didn't amount to a lot back then."

But NSC clout began to increase with the arrival of Clark, the presidential confidante and former California supreme court justice who had served as chief-of-staff for Reagan in Sacramento during the president's first term as governor. He had also recruited Deaver and Meese to the governor's team and was a close friend of Defense Secretary Caspar Weinberger. With those allies, and with the work he had done in 1981 mediating personality disputes between Haig and the White House, Clark was well positioned to elevate the stature of the NSC—despite his reputation as a less-than-intellectual heavyweight who had displayed an embarrassing lack of foreign-policy expertise during his confirmation hearings as deputy secretary of state. He couldn't, for example, name the leaders of South Africa or Zimbabwe and had been unable or unwilling to state his views on certain foreign-policy issues. But in mitigation, NSC staffers at the time say Judge Clark showed a refreshingly small ego by readily conceding his deficiencies and delegating broad authority to regional experts on the council.

Meese, Baker and Deaver had recognized the weakness of the old system of preventing direct presidential access by the National Security Advisor, and institutionalized such access for Clark through a daily half-hour briefing beginning at 9:30 A.M. The morning briefings were made all the more valuable to the NSC because of Reagan and Clark's obviously close personal relationship, and because Clark regularly brought into the Oval Office NSC staffers who could give the president a more detailed brief on the issue of the day. To the several dozen professionals on the NSC staff who had been toiling away in obscurity under Allen, the opportunity occasionally to explain their work to the commander-in-chief was a great morale-booster that restored their faith that they could each make a mark and a difference in furthering the Reagan agenda.

After the AWACs vote, and with Allen on leave at the end of the year during the FBI investigation, the NSC was rudderless, and North had nothing particularly to do, no one giving him specific direction or assignments. In fact, there seemed to be some confusion as to how long he was supposed to have stayed at the NSC in the first place. Allen insists that North, Childress and Myer were only to have come over on temporary duty to help with the AWACs drive and were to return to their respective services by January at the latest; also according to Allen, during the vacuum that existed during his leave, North and the others were able to convince their superiors to make their assignments permanent. But the Marine Corps says it was always clear that North was going to stay at least three years, and that he had merely been sent over earlier than scheduled to help with AWACs.

In any case, it was Allen who was gone by January, not North. Another void had been the firing, just before the AWACs vote, of Gen. Robert Schweitzer—the chief military officer on the NSC who had selected North—for making a rambling speech in which he warned that the United States was in the greatest danger ever from a Soviet Union that was "on the move. They are going to strike." Allen sacked him for speaking out without clearance.

So in an NSC increasingly devoid of leadership, Ollie began the process of gaining a toehold in a new organization, learning how the system worked, how others accumulated power and influence. Among the professional staff there were essentially three categories of people: the career government types from the State Department, Pentagon or CIA on detail to the NSC; the academics who were specialists in certain areas of the world; and the military officers who were both area specialists and generalists.

Most striking about the Reagan NSC in those early years—Allen being on leave or not—was the vacuum. The organization was de-

cidedly unmilitary. There was no one around telling you what to do
and when to do it. People seemed to do what they wanted, at their
own pace. It seemed a natural place for self-starters willing to work
hard.

"I think it's fair to say that when you start at the NSC you're a
flunky, period," recalls Roger Fontaine, who headed up the Latin
America section of the NSC from 1981–1983. "Roles are not terribly clearly defined. Unless you have a very specific job to do . . .
you're left in a vacuum. If you think you're going to have a program
all laid out for you to do at the staff level of the NSC, you better
find yourself another job. It's a job for self-starters."

Under Allen, Fontaine says the NSC was badly understaffed.
There was an overwhelming amount of work to do in spartan conditions. They had no word-processors, cranky typewriters and not
enough secretaries. In mid–1981 there was no money for secretarial overtime, so the secretaries all went home at six o'clock unless
they could be convinced to stay on their own time. The cable machine dated from World War II and cables had to be sorted one by
one. There were not enough secure telephones, and even replacing
lightbulbs was a major bureaucratic undertaking that could stretch
out over a month. All this improved greatly under Clark, who,
according to Fontaine, strolled the third floor of the Executive Office Building and was appalled by the conditions.

Positioned at the throat of the executive branch, the NSC
seemed always to be drowning in paperwork. Everything needing
White House approval or attention came through the Council. The
core unit of work was a long brown folder known as an "action"—an
initiative from one department or another, channeled by the NSC
secretariat to one staffer or another, who was "tasked" with reviewing the proposal and making a recommendation, after obtaining the
"concurrence" of several other staff members.

But the issues dealt with were often less than weighty. Perhaps
the Ivory Coast had designated a new ambassador to Washington
and the envoy wished to come to the White House to present his
credentials to President Reagan.

"The president and the ambassador exchange letters, so number
one you've got to read the letter that the president is going to give
to make sure that you agree with the letter," says Fontaine. "Then
you've got to prepare a memo to the National Security Advisor
saying, here's the letter, here's the ambassador, this is who he is.
Attached, a memo to the president saying he is coming, talking

points for the president regarding anything he wants to say to the ambassador, also a memo regarding anticipated things the ambassador may say so there are no surprises for the president. You've got to do all that stuff. For what? A five-minute ceremony.

"It's endless. The first five you do are interesting. The next two hundred fifty you do are not very interesting. So there are two kinds of guys. One wants to avoid that kind of thing and spend his time on the big picture. Everyone wants to work on the big picture. And the other kind of guy will take the scut work on. Ollie was the second kind of guy.

"Some people who come to the NSC get instant White Houseitis. I've seen it. The first thing they say when they see all the routine work that needs to be done is: 'I'm not going to do that, that's mundane, that's second rate.' But nobody else is going to do it. Secretaries aren't going to do it. There's no one it's been delegated to and somebody's got to do it. And it's guys like Ollie North who take on those jobs. I remember one time Ollie said: 'Look, you've got some work to do. If the latrines need to be cleaned, I'll do it. If the job has to be done, I'll do it.'"

The willingness to do work that others consider beneath them is a quality grateful superiors find endearing and will often reward by giving the willing underling more work—and then more significant work. This is a natural tendency that North exploited—all the more so by his willingness to outwork all his peers.

"If some guys want to take a month off in the summer and a winter vacation, and go to Georgetown dinner parties at six o'clock, then the rest of the staff has got to pick up the slack," notes Fontaine.

The first time Fontaine met North, Ollie had been walking down the hall with Childress and Myer during the AWACs period and stopped to introduce himself. "Hi, I'm Ollie North—the jarhead Marine around here," he had said to Fontaine, flashing his trademark gap-toothed smile.

"I thought, 'Christ, who's this chump?' and I took an immediate dislike to him," recalls Fontaine. But he says he has learned that half of his initial impressions of people prove wrong, and that he later grew to like and admire North greatly.

Looking for something to do, North volunteered to help Fontaine on Central America. "I think Ollie told me that he had nothing literally to do after the AWACs was over . . . There was no chain of command. We just went to the EOB and sat down in an office somewhere and decided what we were going to work on that day. It was very informal."

Things got rather more formal and organized under Judge Clark, whose military aide was John Poindexter, and whose deputy was Robert McFarlane. Poindexter, the consummate organization man, lent greater structure and stricter accountability to the NSC operation.

McFarlane was far better known in Washington than Clark. Most recently he had served as Haig's counselor and troubleshooter at the State Department. Known as "Bud," McFarlane's face seemed permanently cast in melancholy, though he was said on occasion to display a wry sense of humor in private. McFarlane was the son of a New Deal Democratic congressman from Texas and a graduate of Annapolis who had gone on to become a Marine and serve in Vietnam. He retired from the Marine Corps in 1979 as a lieutenant colonel after serving the previous several years as a staff member on the National Security Council.

He had been Kissinger's military assistant from 1973 to 1975, then worked under Brent Scowcroft from 1976 to the end of the Ford administration in January of 1977. Returning to active duty, McFarlane was sent to Okinawa but was passed over for a battalion command, a snub that annoys him to this day. He had been away so long in the rarified air of the White House that many in the Corps concluded he had gone political. So McFarlane retired and spent the last two years of the Carter Administration on the staff of the Senate Armed Services Committee. He was well regarded on Capitol Hill as a conciliator with good political instincts.

With Annapolis, Vietnam and the Marine Corps in common, it seemed natural that McFarlane would gravitate toward North, and vice versa. McFarlane found himself spending more time with Ollie than the average NSC staffer, taking an active interest in his career and, though he was only six years older, developing something of a father-son relationship with North. The paternal instinct was something Ollie had successfully brought out in numerous other superiors on the road to the NSC, and the White House was proving no exception. There, McFarlane was as good a rabbi to have as any.

Reflecting on the early Ollie, McFarlane remembers being amazed by the number of hours North worked:

"North is truly an extreme example of workaholicism," he says. "Because it wasn't fourteen hours a day, it was almost sixteen, on average, except Sundays. Sundays he might knock off with about eight hours. Every day of every year. Which is unwise. But that's what Ollie did. And by dint of that, he just always had the draft memo written before anybody else ever did, and to be fair, before anybody else ever *would*. But he used to always take the initiative, saying, 'Here's a memo to the boss.' And people always gravitate to someone who'll do the work.

"Ollie was perhaps at a bit of an advantage because I was a Marine, and George Shultz was a Marine, but I think he kind of personified what we thought a young officer ought to be. A very resourceful person who would take a task and go perform the mission without asking a lot of questions. He personified the 'Message to Garcia' mission that they preached at the Academy... He didn't ask, 'Where is he?' or 'Who's going to pay my per diem' or 'What kind of support will I have?' He just turned around and did the job. And Ollie's that kind of person. And it impressed people from Jim Baker, to the judge, to Shultz, to the president. He's a can-do person.

"I've never had the illusion that the average Marine or even superior Marine is superior in intellect. That's not historically what Marines have been. So it seemed to me that Ollie's advantage was in the sense of energy he communicated, along with above-average intelligence and judgment. There were officers on the staff that I thought were more analytically sound and more experienced—arms-control people, strategic planners, that sort of thing. Specialists. But as a generalist, Ollie was without peer, I think, because with the grasp of substance went enormous energy.

"He was darn near the only Marine that I ever met that was really a Marine. I was very bitter about my Marine Corps experience and in many ways still am. The Marine Corps by and large does its job, but with enormous inefficiency, clumsiness, lack of breadth and brainpower and poor leadership. But Ollie is the archetype Marine: brave, courageous, self-disciplined, a good leader, an inspiring figure. But there aren't many of them around."

McFarlane also recalls talking frequently with North about the concepts of duty, honor and country which had been ingrained in them at Annapolis.

"We talked about how fundamental it was—honoring our country... The core of it was that both he and I had been raised with the same kind of values and priorities about service and obligations... The attachment to Annapolis is very special, especially the sense of success, instilled with appreciation for sacrifice by others. And it requires of you a real grappling with questions about whether you are really prepared to make those same sacrifices. That's a question that's posed for you directly many times by many people, so it becomes a value that isn't trivial at all. By the time you leave there, it is not the *yes* or the *no* that's firm. It's the *yes*. It becomes a matter of accountability to all those people involved. You are in an elite community of people: public servants. It is what sustains you in the nuclear age—a profession that if you do it perfectly well, you will never do anything. There will be peace and nothing will happen. But that's quite different from the dentist or the heart surgeon, or somebody who can say, 'I did this or that.' You've got to be somebody who can say, 'Nothing happened.'

"Annapolis was a trashy education when I went through it, and I imagine when Ollie went through it, but these other tests of values and superficial macho qualities were strong... They lived with a more palpable consciousness of the risks they were about to accept. And while a lot of the best people didn't stay, a lot of the smartest people did and went ahead and knocked it out. And Ollie stayed. He feels very strongly, and should, about the rightness of whatever he does, because he falls back on his experience at the Academy, which is quite different from what other people of his age went through to test and confirm their sense of right and wrong. It wasn't just a move from adolescence to early manhood. It was part religious and part moral."

Vietnam seared the soul, taught North firsthand the meaning of sacrifice, and was also a seminal experience in terms of how he would later approach his dealings with the Nicaraguan Contras, McFarlane thought.

"I know for a fact that Ollie came to terms with having been there at a very human level that had nothing to do with politics or strategic analysis about our larger purpose. He told me why he felt comfortable with having been there and taking part in great violence... He felt his effect and the aggregate effect of the Americans in the military was justified from the testimony, both visible and verbal, of the Vietnamese with whom he came into contact every day. There were enough clear signs of appreciation for him by both the South Vietnamese military and nonmilitary people. Whether as a consequence of patrols with them, or civic action programs building roads, hospitals or whatever else, he could come back and say, 'Those people were glad I was there.'

"And yet, apart from that very human level, to accept the reality that we were losing, and to think through why, was very difficult. Like me, he believed it was largely because our leadership couldn't define the problem for the American people—why we should care, what strategy would succeed, evoke support and get on with it . . . If you are unable to rally a democracy to conflict in support of a legitimate purpose, then you must not do it in the first place. You must not say to [the South Vietnamese] 'Let's join together and win this thing, and if you want to do that, you can count on us never running out on you.' Because for them it was a matter of lives. Of human beings. And there were enough people that Ollie held in his arms and watched die, Vietnamese that he saw blown apart. This was a very graphic personal experience that he knew would happen in Nicaragua if we broke faith . . . If he ever got into a position where the stakes were the same as in Vietnam, then he was not going to be a party to selling out or breaking faith. This is speculation, but I think it is reasonable . . .

"All in all, Ollie was kind of a son-figure for me. That is, someone that I treated as a man but always remembered was a boy. I would counsel him fairly often about his assignment—going back to the Marine Corps, what he ought to be doing, family life and things that went beyond his portfolio. And he would come to me often for career advice and for advice on bureaucratic problems . . . 'How do I deal with this personality, this kind of person, Bill Casey or George Shultz?' I was terribly fond of him and still am. And terribly sorry for my contribution to the fix he's in now."

Besides Central America, informally acquired through a willingless to be Roger Fontaine's gopher, North set about picking up other "accounts," as assignments or areas of responsibility on the NSC were known. Aided by the Allen-Schweitzer vacuum and the predictable early caution of the new Clark regime, North began working on terrorism, crisis management and "continuity of government." That last-named meant being the NSC's liaison with the Federal Emergency Manpower Agency (FEMA), the group charged with drawing up contingency plans for government operations in the event of a nuclear disaster or some other calamity.

With the exception of Central America, which in the early Reagan years had a much lower profile than the Middle East, North's other assignments had an action-oriented cast to them—the kind of work which could be highly visible in a crisis but largely invisible otherwise, the kind of operational work that a military generalist with no advanced degree might turn to. He was the snow-plow operator waiting for a blizzard. The more cerebral specialists on the NSC shunned such duty.

"Crisis management by and large is a routine job—first guy in in the morning and last guy to leave," says Geoffrey Kemp, a senior associate at the Carnegie Endowment for International Peace who served as a special assistant to the president during the first Reagan term working in the NSC's Middle East section. "It wasn't the sort of thing any brilliant academic would want to do. If there's no crisis, you don't do anything. If there is, you work your butt off— mostly being responsible for bringing people together."

But action tended to follow North around. In 1982 there was a dramatic increase in terrorism against U.S. citizens or property overseas—401 incidents as opposed to 257 in 1981. in January of eighty-two North had a hand in trying to resolve one of the most celebrated kidnappings of the year—that of American Brig. Gen. James Dozier, who had been abducted in Italy by Red Brigade terrorists on December 17, 1981.

Though it was a stated violation of U.S. policy to pay ransom to terrorists, as continued efforts to free the general failed, in January North secretly contacted Texas billionaire H. Ross Perot and asked if Perot, acting on his own behalf—not the government's—would be willing to ransom Dozier. The adventurous Perot, who in 1979 had hired a commando team to rescue two of his employees taken hostage in Iran, quickly agreed, and later wired $500,000 to an Italian bank, where it was converted to lira and taken to the U.S. embassy in Rome. But the logistics for the exchange could never be worked out and the money was eventually returned to Perot. Meanwhile in late January Italian police found and rescued Dozier.

Though the Perot effort failed, North met a kindred spirit and an important contact in the can-do electronics magnate. North would make frequent use of Perot in future efforts to free American hostages, and the overture represented a significant early example of his reaching out to the private sector to skirt government bureaucracy—and official policy—in pursuit of his goals.

On the crisis-management front, North began working closely with Richard Smith Beal, a young systems analyst and special assistant to the president who became the technical driving force behind a somewhat controversial proposal to convert Room 208 of the EOB into a state-of-the-art high-tech command center that would integrate communications and intelligence gathering and serve as the NSC's Crisis Management Center. The spiritual driving force behind the project was Poindexter, who convinced Judge Clark and others that bigger was better. The project was a dramatic expansion under Clark of a modest initiative begun under Richard Allen.

Allen recalls that domestic affairs advisor Martin Anderson had approached him with an idea to create a briefing room which could be used by both the domestic affairs and national security staffs. Anderson and Allen would each kick in $75,000 from their budgets for the room, which would include projection facilities and the like. But under Clark the concept mushroomed, and by the time it was finished in 1983—at a cost of $14 million—it was bursting with all manner of communications hardware, powerful computers and walls of electronic panels.

Critics of the center say it is a monument to waste and duplication of facilities that exist in some form or other in the White House Situation Room, the Pentagon, CIA and State Department. "With apologies to Hemingway," scoffs Allen, "that room should have been called 'A Farewell to Cash.'"

Kemp said the center was "an attempt to create what everybody who has seen movies and read about the Situation Room thinks the Situation Room is. It was an attempt to bring the electronic age to the White House, but while I was there it was always seen as a great white elephant."

The Situation Room remained the Situation Room in title and in function, and the new NSC center was never really used to manage any crisis, to the best of any staffer's recollection. Still, North began to have access to all the most sensitive, top-secret intelligence information that flowed into the center, and he would route messages on to various officials in the intelligence community. When Beal took ill, and in 1984 died at age thirty-eight of complications from open-heart surgery, North's responsibilities in the crisis center expanded. And as a traffic cop directing the flow of highly classified intelligence throughout the government, North used the knowledge-is-power maxim to meet, court and develop a broad array of contacts in the national security nexus.

"Ollie had a real mafia in town that he was on a first-name basis with," recalls McFarlane. "People are always flattered if someone at the White House wants to know what they think. In 'eighty-one he just started going around the government and meeting people. He'd go out to the NSA and spend all day, and be admiring—truly

admiring—and then he might send them a card on their birthday
signed by the president. It's easy to do and handled routinely in the
correspondence office. And he'd do that. It'd mean a lot to people.
Or he'd send a picture-o-graph if somebody had done a briefing,
and a signed picture of the president. It's just a nice thing to do.
He's got a lot of fans all over the place."

North's work for FEMA—from 1982 to the spring of 1984—was
highly classified and, some would say, bizarre. During that period,
the Miami *Herald* reported that he was involved in helping to draft a
sweeping contingency plan to impose martial law in the event of a
nuclear war, or less serious national crises such as widespread internal
dissent, or opposition to an American military invasion abroad.

The plan—which also gave FEMA itself broad authority to report directly to the president, appoint military commanders and
run state and local governments—ruffled many administration
feathers. Then Attorney General William French Smith considered
it such a bold power grab and so dubious legally that in the summer
of 1984 he asked Bud McFarlane, who by then had succeeded
Clark as National Security Advisor, not to forward the proposed
executive order containing the FEMA initiative to the president for
his signature. Smith's opposition effectively killed the plan, which
had been spearheaded by then FEMA Director Louis Guiffrida.

In his letter Smith criticized what he said was FEMA's unilateral
assumption of the role of "emergency czar." He added: "FEMA has
promulgated numerous plans and proposals that are in sharp contrast to the concept of utilizing the existing decision-making structure of the executive branch for emergency planning and response.
Recent FEMA continuity-of-government plans feature layers of
FEMA operational personnel inserted between the president and
all other federal civil agencies. Its mobilization-exercise scenarios
continue to assign FEMA the responsibility of representing the
Department of Justice and other cabinet agencies at meetings with
the president and the National Security Council during national
security emergencies."

The draft executive order was also said to have contained provisions for "alien control," the "detention of enemy aliens" and the
seizure of their property. This fear of an alien threat was evidently
an underreported factor in motivating the administration to support
the Nicaraguan Contras. CIA Director William Casey told *U.S.
News and World Report* that the U.S. feared uncontrolled immigration as a result of conflict in Central America.

Another North-FEMA collaboration was the proposed Defense Resources Act, according to the Miami *Herald*, The act was designed to serve as "standby" legislation in case "conflict contingencies" arose. If enacted, the Defense Resources Act would give the president powers to impose censorship, seize the means of production and ban strikes.

North would also play a role in helping FEMA stage a national emergency simulation exercise April 5–18, 1984—code-named "Rex–84 Bravo"—which Guiffrida, in a memo to Meese, described as "the largest civil mobilization exercise ever undertaken."

Rex–84 Bravo, authorized by President Reagan's signature of National Security Decision Directive 52, was predicated on his declaration of a state of national emergency concurrent with a mythical U.S. military invasion (code-named "Operation Night Train") of an unspecified Central American country, presumably Nicaragua. While the FEMA exercise was in progress the Pentagon staged its first annual military exercise involving U.S. troops in Honduras—blurring, for some, the distinction between exercise and the real thing.

An affidavit by Daniel Sheehan—the lawyer for plaintiffs in a multi-million-dollar federal lawsuit pending in Miami against twenty-nine defendants, including Richard Secord and Contra leader Adolfo Calero—makes several other significant allegations about FEMA and Rex–84 Bravo. The suit, filed in May of 1986, six months before the Iran-Contra affair became public, alleges a broad conspiracy to use drug money to buy weapons for the contras. Sheehan, chief counsel for the Christic Institute, a liberal, church-funded law group based in Washington, says his information on FEMA comes from private investigators, former federal agents and a member of FEMA's legal division during the time in question.

The affidavit says Rex–84 Bravo was designed to test FEMA's readiness to assume authority over Department of Defense personnel, all fifty-state National Guard forces and a number of "State Defense Force" units which were to be created by state legislative enactments. FEMA would "deputize" all DOD and state National Guard personnel so as to avoid violating the federal Posse Comitatus Act, which forbids using any military forces for domestic law enforcement. Then, the affidavit continued, the exercise was also designed to test FEMA's ability to carry out a twofold mission:

The first was to find and take into custody some 400,000 undocumented Central American aliens throughout the United States and to intern them in ten military bases around the nation. The second was the distribution by FEMA to the state-created Defense Forces of hundreds of tons of small arms and ammunition, ostensibly for use by the law enforcement "deputies" in keeping the peace during the president's declared state of national emergency.

The FEMA informant told Sheehan there had been considerable anxiety within the agency about the legality of the Rex–84 exercise. The official said he had never seen such security around any other activity inside FEMA, and that agency General Counsel George Jett had ordered the installation of a special metal security door into the hallway of the fifth floor of the FEMA building in Washington where all planning for Rex–84 was conducted. The official told Sheehan that FEMA officials with the highest security clearances had been prevented from going into the restricted area. He said only Guiffrida, Jett and FEMA Deputy Director Frank Salcedo—all of whom were inexplicably reported to have been wearing red Christian crosses or crucifix pins on their lapels—were allowed in.

Though very little has ever been publicized about Rex–84, the rest of Guiffrida's tenure at FEMA was scrutinized closely enough that he resigned in 1985 following a House committee report that charged him with contract favoritism, making home renovations and taking personal travel at government expense, and accepting gratuities from a government contractor. Guiffrida now runs a Washington consulting firm—Guiffrida International Associates—that specializes in "security issues."

Though Rex–84's dark plans to impose martial law and funnel arms and ammunition to murky "State Defense Forces" were staggering in their constitutional implications, Guiffrida, Edwin Meese, and Ronald Reagan all had had experience planning for martial law in California.

As governor of California from 1968 to 1972 Reagan organized a series of military exercises called Operation Cable Splicer involving state and local police, the California National Guard and parts of the Sixth Army. In a virtually unnoticed article published by now-defunct *New Times* magazine in 1975, journalist Ron Reidenhour, using the Freedom of Information Act, first disclosed that the military units were training for the imposition of martial law in California. Governor Reagan told about five hundred military and law enforcement officials assembled for the second phase of Operation Cable Splicer: "You know, there are people in the state who, if they could see this gathering right now and my presence here, would decide their worst fears and convictions had been realized—I was planning a military takeover."

The man Reagan appointed to head Cable Splicer was his executive secretary, Edwin Meese, who would become presidential counselor and later, attorney general of the United States. In an "after action" report following phase two of the exercises, Meese remarked: "We have to improve our ability in the investigation, identification and prosecution of those, particularly the leaders, who are responsible for the revolutionary activity in our state. We have to [have] even more of maximum photography, maximum evidence gathering by officers who are not involved in actual control activity, so that they can be free, utilizing detectives and others that normally do not get suited up for the conflict, and utilizing them as much as possible in gathering evidence so that we can successfully prosecute those who are raging the conflict on the campuses and on the streets."

Meese was referring to the unrest at Berkeley during the Free Speech movement and at other college campuses in California during the turbulent late sixties and early seventies. He also told the assembled Cable Splicer "combatants" that "despite the activities of some who state this is an overreaction [to the campus unrest], this is an operation, this is an exercise, this is an objective which is going forward because in the long run . . . it is the only way that we will be able to prevail."

The third key figure in Operation Cable Splicer was Guiffrida, then head of the California Specialized Training Institute, a National Guard school. Guiffrida was the operation's theoretician, articulating the concept of martial law for Cable Splicer in a manual entitled "Legal Aspects of Managing Civil Disorders."

That wasn't the only controversial piece of writing Guiffrida indulged in at the time. In 1970, while a student at the Army War College in Carlisle, Pennsylvania, he wrote a paper entitled "National Survival—Racial Imperative," in which he advocated martial law if there were a revolt by black militants. He discussed the most efficient way to remove an estimated 500,000 militant "American Negroes" by placing them in internment camps, as Japanese Americans were during World War II.

It was after the completion of Rex–84 that McFarlane would relieve North of his FEMA duties and charge him with keeping the Contras together "body and soul" while congressional funding was restricted. But North's two years on the FEMA beat, his exposure to the "continuity of government" ethos and to Guiffrida's clearly radical ideas on how government can be conducted, could well have planted a provocative. Or perhaps engendered in him a greater willingness to shortcut democratic channels in pursuit of whatever goal he and his superiors would later conclude to be in the national interest.

CENTRAL AMERICA

As 1982 progressed, North began spending most of his time on Central America. He immersed himself in the politics of the region, studied the key players—particularly in El Salvador, Nicaragua and Honduras—and aggressively signed on as a booster and implementer of Reagan Administration policy in the area.

That policy had taken on little shape or voice through 1981, as the White House remained focused on domestic affairs and the economy. But in 1982 and 1983 it became increasingly apparent that Central America was the area of the world where the administration wanted to draw a clear line against what it saw as Soviet expansionism—a place where the U.S. would finally stand tall again and declare to the world that it had shaken off its post-Vietnam malaise, as well as the impotence and humiliation of the Carter misadventures in Iran.

A strong faction of the administration had taken office almost spoiling to fight a quick little war somewhere to demonstrate that America was *back*—reading Reagan's landslide over Carter as a macho mandate. If Carter had "lost" Iran and Nicaragua, Reagan would see to it that no country within the American sphere of influence, particularly in the western hemisphere, would go communist on his watch.

Nicaragua's passage to the Sandinistas in 1979 was actually considerably more complicated than a strict won-and-lost equation for the United States. The rule of Anastosio Somoza Debayle had become increasingly corrupt through the 1970s, and as the civil war against the National Liberation Front—commonly called the Sandinistas—intensified, Somoza had employed his National Guard to wage harsher and harsher reprisals, including mass executions of peasants allegedly collaborating to overthrow the regime.

Carter's human rights crusade obliged him at first to cut back on military and economic aid to Somoza. Finally, in February of 1979, when Somoza refused to accept a negotiated settlement with his opponents—who by that time clearly enjoyed broad popular support—Washington suspended all new economic and military aid, thereby effectively ending the last vestiges of support for the regime. By July, Somoza had to flee the country.

The Sandinistas assumed power with broad international support as well. The Carter Administration immediately donated $39 million in emergency food aid to Nicaragua, and in 1980 Congress voted an additional $75 million in economic assistance. In the glow of victory the Sandinistas—who had established a Provisional Government of National Reconstruction controlled by a five-person directorate—promised free elections, free enterprise, a free press, an end to political oppression and an independent judiciary. Yet they quickly reneged on those pledges by continuing to detain political prisoners, seizing land, forcing the two moderate members of the ruling directorate to resign and censoring the newspaper *La Prensa* while taking over television and radio stations. And while continuing to receive aid from the West, the Sandinistas began reaching out to eastern bloc nations, signing accords with the Soviet Union, Bulgaria and East Germany for military and intelligence aid.

Carter thus hedged his bets in the fall of 1979 by signing an intelligence "finding" authorizing covert aid to democratic elements inside Nicaragua. But by January of 1981 before leaving office, Carter decided to suspend all aid to the Sandinistas. In April Reagan, who as a candidate had declared his opposition to any further U.S. support of the Sandinistas, continued the Carter policy by withholding the remaining $15 million in unspent U.S. aid to Nicaragua. Reagan said he would not request new aid until the Sandinistas democratized their revolution and stopped supporting leftist insurgents in neighboring El Salvador.

If Nicaragua was "gone," El Salvador was the next line the Reaganites had drawn in the dirt beyond which communism could not dare cross. A reform-minded civilian-military government had presided in Salvador since 1979, making vague promises about elections while trying to stave off the insurgency. The Salvadoran rebels had immediately presented Reagan with a challenge in January of

1981 by launching what it called its "final offensive." The attack was easily beaten back and the leftists retreated into the mountains, humiliated. But captured documents and materiel clearly established that the Sandinistas and the Cubans were helping supply the rebels.

This was a windfall for those in the new administration who wanted to cast the Salvadoran conflict not as a local civil war but as yet another struggle in the East-West imperative. According to this view, what was happening in Salvador and Nicaragua had to be integrated and seen as essentially the same war. The issues were not local: Soviet proxies were now making bold moves in our very backyard, four hundred-odd miles from Miami, and the U.S. had to take a stand.

Defending the Salvadoran government, particularly against terrorist right-wing death squads and atrocities like the 1980 slayings of Archbishop Oscar Arnulfo Romero and four American churchwomen, was not always easy, but when the conflict was portrayed as the Sandinistas trying to export Marxist revolution to El Salvador, Honduras, Guatemala and, ultimately, Mexico, then U.S. activism in the region was easily justified, the White House thought. In this light, what was needed was not just a containment of the status quo in Salvador, but a "rollback" of communism in Nicaragua so as to certify, as the electorate had wanted in 1980, that Washington again meant aggressively to guard its interests around the world.

The victorious Republican party platform that year had stated as much, noting that the GOP would put a high priority on improving intelligence-gathering capabilities and undertaking covert action. "We will provide our government with the capability to help influence international events vital to our national security interests, a capability which only the United States among the major powers has denied itself," the platform said.

The document also provided a clue to the administration's intentions in Central America. The Carter Administration, it said, had "often undermined the very governments under attack. As a result, a clear and present danger threatens the energy and raw-material lifelines of the Western World...We deplore the Marxist Sandinista takeover of Nicaragua and the Marxist attempts to destabilize El Salvador, Guatemala and Honduras. We will return to the fundamental principle of treating a friend as a friend and self-proclaimed enemies as enemies, without apology." It added that

Republicans not only opposed further assistance to the Sandinistas, but would "support the efforts of the Nicaraguan people to establish a free and independent government."

To that end, just six weeks after taking office, Reagan had signed a generalized finding authorizing increased covert action in Central America aimed at gathering more intelligence on the sources of support for the Salvadoran rebels and at "interdicting" supplies being sent to them.

Beefing up intelligence in the region meant beefing up the CIA itself. To do that, Reagan had selected William Casey to head the embattled agency which had been decimated by a post-Watergate morality and the hearings in 1975 and 1976 held by the late Sen. Frank Church. The hearings resulted in the curbing of the CIA's covert operations mission worldwide and the purging of hundreds of agents who worked in the clandestine services. Casey's mandate: deneuter the agency, unleash it, rebuild it, restore its covert operations capability—give it some snap, crackle and pop.

The consummate rich Wall Street Republican who had been chairman of the Securities and Exchange Commission, Casey hardly looked like a former swashbuckling OSS officer who had served under Wild Bill Donovan during World War II. But he was and he did. Still, Casey was now an old man who looked much older than his sixty-eight years, and didn't appear physically up to becoming director of Central Intelligence. He slouched when he walked, wisps of gray hair blew wildly over his balding head giving him an absentminded-professor air, and he mumbled so indistinctly it sounded like he had marbles in his mouth. But appearances deceived. Though he had wanted to be secretary of state or defense, Casey, who had been Reagan's campaign manager in 1980, turned to his new task at the CIA with great zest. "It was like he was hydroplaning on the way to the nursing home," one of his agency colleagues had said.

Casey would ultimately more than triple the intelligence budget, but by December of 1981 he was already set to offer two major initiatives.

One was Executive Order 12333, a sweeping fourteen-page reorganization and laying-out of goals for the intelligence community and the "national intelligence effort," signed by Reagan on December 4.

In a little-noticed section of 12333, which would later come to

have great significance for North and the National Security Council
at the height of the Iran-Contra affair, the NSC was charged with
being the lead intelligence agency in government. "The NSC shall
act as the highest executive branch entity that provides review of,
guidance for and direction to the conduct of all national foreign
intelligence, counter-intelligence, and special activities and attendant policies and programs...," the order said. "The NSC, or a
committee established by it, shall consider and submit to the President a policy recommendation, including all dissents, on each special activity and shall review proposals for other sensitive
intelligence operations." This proviso would boomerang on later
administration arguments that the NSC—since its charter had
nothing to do with intelligence activities—was not covered by congressional restrictions prohibiting assistance to the Nicaraguan
rebels.

The second initiative, presented by Casey to congressional intelligence committees in December as a fait accompli, was National
Security Decision Directive 17, signed by Reagan on December 1.
It provided for spending up to $20 million to build a five-hundred-
man force composed of Central Americans that would conduct
paramilitary operations inside Nicaragua.

The U.S. would work with "foreign governments as appropriate
... against the Cuban presence and Cuban Sandinista support infrastructure in Nicaragua and elsewhere in Central America," the
NSDD said, adding that while the intent was to use non-American
personnel for these forays, "in some circumstances CIA might (possibly using U.S. personnel) take unilateral paramilitary action
against special Cuban targets." The purpose was to "build popular
support in Central America and Nicaragua for an opposition front
that would be nationalistic, anti-Cuban and anti-Somoza."

The public dimension of the project included open economic and
military aid to friendly countries in the region, U.S. military maneuvers and American contingency planning in the event of "unacceptable military actions" taken by Cuba.

As Casey described this initiative at a secret session of the intelligence committees, he faced pointed questions about the operation
and its goals. But he shrugged off most of them, speaking on behalf
of a president who had been given a resounding victory and had
still not even finished his first year in office. The honeymoon was
over, but few on the Hill were picking many fights with the White
House. Besides, there was really nothing the congressmen could

do to stop the operation anyway. The law required only that they be informed of it, and they did not really control the purse strings in this case. The president had up to $50 million available to him in contingency funds for covert operations. In any case, Casey presented it as a done deal. Argentina had organized bands of Nicaraguan exiles in camps along the Honduran border, and Washington was merely signing on to a going concern, the director indicated.

The Argentine military government had presided over its own dirty war since seizing power in 1976, and had killed off thousands of dissidents whom it deemed threats to the security of the state. By 1980 the junta thought itself ready to lend a hand rolling back communist insurgencies beyond its borders in a "war without frontiers." It would be a sort of Latin American gendarme, more than willing to douse communist brush fires wherever they flared up, helping to fill the void left by a timid Carter Administration. As for its involvement in Nicaragua, if any justification were needed, the junta could always say it was worried about the Montonero guerillas who opposed the Argentine dictatorship and used Nicaragua as a base.

The generals were enchanted with Ronald Reagan's election. Where Carter had condemned them for atrocities and gotten Congress to halt U.S. arms sales to Argentina, Reagan treated them as an important regional ally in the holy war against communism. Just two months after his inauguration, Reagan had received Argentine President Roberto Viola. Then the Argentine Chief of Staff, Gen. Leopoldo Galtieri, had made reciprocal visits with his American counterpart, Gen. Edwin Meyer, during which they hatched a strategy to deal with the Sandinista threat. Galtieri had met with Casey on November 1. Also, United Nations Ambassador Jeane Kirkpatrick had visited Buenos Aires, and there was even discussion about a NATO counterpoint—a South Atlantic Treaty Alliance, of which Argentina would be a leading member.

But that was way down the road, if ever. For now Buenos Aires took satisfaction and pride in coming to the assistance of its new friend in Washington. Argentina ordered its Battalion 601 to help organize, train and support about one thousand members of the incipient Nicaraguan resistance force headquartered in several camps along the border just inside a cooperative Honduras. Honduras was again willing to allow itself to be used as a base for one of Washington's adventures. In 1954 the CIA had used Honduran soil as a base for its program that toppled the reformist government in

Guatemala. Honduras, of course, had reason to cooperate again now. In 1981 and 1982 it received $187 million worth of assistance from the United States.

The anti-Sandinistas—called Contras—were essentially three different kinds of people: the remnants of Somoza's National Guard; those who had fought against Somoza but felt betrayed by the Sandinistas; and a third group that had been neutral about Somoza but were finding life under the Sandinistas increasingly repressive. There were also the Miskito Indians and, after 1981, a Contra faction led by the former Sandinista guerrilla leader Eden Pastora, the legendary *Commandante Cero* (Commander Zero), based in southern Nicaragua along the border with Costa Rica.

But by the end of 1981, in the two-and-a-half years that the Sandinistas had been in power, the resistance had not really gelled. It had inflicted precious little punishment, and there hadn't even been much action. So, armed with the new secret finding authorizing covert action and $19 million plus, Casey meant to generate some heat and at least let Managua know it was in a new ballgame.

The director wanted to shake up his personnel and hand-pick the man who would run the Central American project. He was not pleased with Nestor Sanchez, the Latin American division chief in the CIA's Directorate of Operations. Theoretically, Sanchez was perfect for the job. He spoke fluent Spanish, had spent virtually his entire thirty-year career at the agency working in Latin America and was well plugged into a cross-section of the region's leaders. But he also struck Casey as a naysayer who was less than comfortable with Langley's bold new approach to the Central American isthmus. He seemed to Casey to be the kind of guy who always raised roadblocks to an idea rather than look for a way to implement it. In his heart of hearts Casey wanted more of a can-do cowboy for the job.

In the summer of 1981 at a meeting in Paris of the CIA's European station chiefs Casey found his perfect choice in Duane (Dewey) Clarridge, then the agency's man in Rome. Clarridge, forty-nine, looked like he still lifted weights and was a flashy dresser who stood out amid his more conservative, gray-flanneled peers. Dewey was an unabashed adventurer who liked silk shirts, cigars and fine food. He had served in India, Nepal, Turkey and Rome. While he had zero Latin American experience, Casey liked his brass. Besides, no experience in the region meant Clarridge

would not be burdened by the mistakes of the past and could bring
a fresh new approach to the job.

So Casey appointed Clarridge the Latin American division chief,
and pointedly told him he should bypass the chain of command and
report directly to the top—Casey himself. That was the measure of
the director's interest in Central America, and Nicaragua in particular. As for Sanchez, he retired from the agency and moved over to
the Pentagon where he took a job as deputy assistant secretary for
international security affairs.

Clarridge went to work with the Argentines trying to mold a
force of Contras that could conduct paramilitary operations inside
Nicaragua and make life tough on the Sandinistas. The CIA station
in Honduras doubled to about fifty agents. By February of 1982
Clarridge told Casey that the cross-border forays could soon begin.

But then word of the secret operation was leaked. On February
14 the Washington *Post* disclosed the CIA's $19 million plan,
though it said it had been unable to learn whether the proposal had
been approved or implemented. The story provoked a great hue
and cry in Congress and elsewhere about the administration's true
intentions.

The White House denied any intent to overthrow the Nicaraguan government, saying it was only helping the effort to interdict
supplies the Sandinistas were sending to the rebels in El Salvador.
But many critics began concluding that this rationale was a mere fig
leaf disguising the more ambitious goal of toppling the Sandinistas.

The administration thus began a concerted effort to build public
support for its presence in the region, and on March 9 held a rare
press briefing featuring declassified aerial photographs showing
what it said was evidence that Nicaragua was engaged in a massive
defense buildup that posed a threat to its neighbors. The briefing
was conducted by the deputy CIA director, Adm. Bobby Ray
Inman, and John Hughes, deputy director of the Defense Intelligence Agency. Inman noted that it had been Hughes who had conducted similar briefings during the 1962 Cuban missile crisis—as if
to suggest that the U.S. could be on its way to facing a problem of
similar import.

Hughes said the photos showed Cuban-style military installations, some with Soviet tanks and artillery in place, as well as airfields with runways lengthened to accommodate Soviet MIG
fighter jets, which Washington was now asserting were destined for
Nicaragua. Inman and Hughes said the Sandinistas, with Cuban

and Soviet help, were engaged in a military boom totally disproportionate to legitimate self-defense needs. The briefing was conducted with dramatic flair and stirring East-West rhetoric, clearly
signaling a White House public relations offensive aimed at depriving its critics of the upper hand in the battle for American public
opinion.

The next day, accompanying its account of the Inman-Hughes
briefing, the Washington *Post* gave more ammunition to administration critics by expanding on its article of February 14, reporting
flatly now that Reagan had approved covert action and that the
five-hundred-man paramilitary force of Contras would soon attempt
to destroy vital Nicaraguan targets such as power plants and bridges
in an effort to disrupt the economy and the government.

The story proved right. Just four days later two bridges inside
Nicaragua from Honduras were blown up by CIA-trained Contra
saboteurs. The Sandinistas quickly charged the Reagan Administration with being ultimately responsible and proclaimed a state of
emergency.

Explaining the bridge operations to Congress, the CIA again hid
behind the defensive cloak of interdicting supplies bound for the
Salvadoran exiles. Since the bridges were plausibly en route to El
Salvador to the northwest, the intelligence committees made no
fuss. The committees were also generally pleased to hear that summer that the CIA had decided to move the Contra camps from
Honduras across the border into Nicaragua itself. Though this
could be construed as an offensive step, it alleviated concern that
Honduras, by harboring the Contras, was increasingly vulnerable
to being drawn into the war itself.

Still, debate continued in Congress over the administration's true
intentions. Asked by officials of the intelligence committees to justify the premise of the operation and report how much arms and
ammunition bound for the Salvadoran rebels the Contras had "in-
terdicted," representatives of the CIA admitted that none had
been. But they asserted that this was because the paramilitary
operations of the Contras had greatly curbed the arms flow. Asked
if the Contras had encountered Cuban patrols in the Nicaraguan
countryside, which the CIA had said existed, the agency conceded
none had been seen.

Another crisis of confidence for Congress had been the sudden
resignation of Admiral Inman, the deputy CIA director, in March
—less than two weeks after he presided over the press briefing
stating that Nicaragua was engaging in its huge defense buildup.

Publicly it looked as if Inman had had doubts about what he had said at the briefing.

Actually, there were a combination of factors. Inman was fifty and had been considering a mid-career switch for some time. He had served as director of the National Security Agency—the super-secret electronic intelligence-gathering agency that was now supplying the most important intelligence information in government via satellite—for four years under Carter. Widely admired on Capitol Hill for his candor and his professionalism, Inman had been reluctant to join the Reagan Administration in the first place and had done so only after being personally contacted by Reagan. But for all of that, there was no question that the direction of the Nicaraguan policy was also a factor in Inman's departure.

He disapproved of the special waiver Clarridge had been given to report directly to Casey and, according to Bob Woodward's *Veil*, just before his resignation, Inman barged in on a private meeting the two were having to plot their secret war. He had questioned them closely about their real plans and said it was clear to him that the aim of the operation was to topple the Sandinista government. That wasn't what the original presidential finding had authorized, he reminded them.

By then Casey and Clarridge seemed to regard Inman as a meddlesome, timid goody-two-shoes too concerned with the niceties of the law. They, on the other hand, were living in the real world, combating communism, certain of their convictions, and carrying out Ronald Reagan's mandate. Inman, who viewed intelligence as only part of the larger mosaic in fashioning a coherent foreign policy, saw that increasingly in this administration secrecy was becoming a foreign policy in and of itself. The war against the Sandinistas was staying covert because the White House apparently believed if it was brought out in the open, Congress would refuse to go along. Inman felt out of step.

There were still other factors giving Congress pause about the contra operation. One was the CIA's channeling of aid to Eden Pastora, the former Sandinista operating out of Costa Rica on Nicaragua's southern border. It was hard to swallow that Pastora's forces operating in the south could have much to do with the stated mission of stopping the flow of arms to the rebels in El Salvador— north of Nicaragua.

Then the CIA admitted it was having command and control problems with the Contras. Argentina had left a void when it pulled out of the project following its spring invasion of the British-held Falkland Islands (after Washington's tilt toward London during the war, Buenos Aires was hardly going to do the Reagan Administration any more favors). And the agency also acknowledged that it was using more members of *Somoza's* old National Guard than had originally been planned because they were the ones who most wanted to fight. Predictably, some of the Somocistas themselves were soon quoted as saying their objective was to overthrow the Sandinista government.

Hopping in bed with the ex-Guardsmen could hardly have been expected to produce a public relations windfall for the White House, and it did not. In fact, there was a spate of negative press that fall on the administration's doings in Nicaragua, highlighted by a *Newsweek* cover story on November 8. Finally in December the CIA stirred some of the greatest fears yet when it told Congress in a briefing that the Contra forces now numbered four thousand men. This represented an eightfold increase in the size of the Contras during the year that Casey had first disclosed the existence of a five hundred-man paramilitary unit. Trying to turn a potential negative into a positive, the director explained that the Contras were recruiting more and more people themselves to join the fight against the unpopular Sandinistas.

Amid a growing sense on Capitol Hill that U.S. policy in Nicaragua was getting out of hand, the House in December voted 411–0 to approve the first of several amendments which would be offered by the chairman of the House Intelligence Committee, Rep. Edward Boland, the Massachusetts Democrat and confidante of House Speaker Thomas (Tip) O'Neill. The first Boland Amendment sought only to hold the Administration to its word that its intent was defensively to stop the flow of arms from Nicaragua to leftist insurgents in El Salvador. Attached as an amendment to the Defense Appropriations Act of 1983, the measure barred spending "for the purpose of overthrowing the government of Nicaragua or provoking a military exchange between Nicaragua and Honduras."

Casey and the rest of the Administration, while not pleased with the amendment, could live with it since it had no practical effect. A "purpose," after all, was readily deniable and had enough holes to drive a truck through. Theoretically the Contras could fight all the way to Managua while insisting they meant only to cut off munitions bound for El Salvador. Reagan signed the measure into law.

Despite the big loophole for the White House, Casey and Clarridge were increasingly unhappy dealing with Congress. They were sick of having to disguise their true intentions. Of course the Con-

tras were fighting to overthrow the Sandinistas. Who was kidding
who? How could the CIA be expected to ask them to risk their lives
for the modest, defensive effort of stopping the arms flow to leftists
in El Salvador, which wasn't even their native land? The CIA was
out there in the trenches in an imperfect world doing the best it
could to promote democracies. Wasn't that what they all wanted?
Did Congress want a communist Nicaragua? No, but it wasn't willing to support efforts to get rid of them for fear of violating due
process. The congressmen and senators were hypocrites who
wanted it both ways. So the CIA men felt.

The details of waging and managing the White House's increasingly not-so-secret war with Nicaragua were left to a group of four
men representing different sections of the executive branch. They
called themselves the RIG (for Restricted Interagency Group) or
the Core Group. The members were Thomas Enders, the assistant
secretary of state for Inter-American affairs; Nestor Sanchez, representing his new position at the Pentagon; Clarridge, as the CIA's
point man for Latin America, and Roger Fontaine, the National
Security Council's man for the region—as well as North's Central
American mentor.

Others sat in occasionally, but those four were the principals, the
men who represented the pressure points at their respective agencies and who were in a position to cut through the bureaucracy and
get things done. That was the group's raison d'être.

They met at the State Department as often as was necessary—on
average at least several times a week. Presiding was the six-foot-
eight-inch Enders, a tweedy career diplomat and eastern establishment aristocrat who had earned his stripes as the number-two man
at the embassy in Phnom Penh during the secret U.S. bombing of
Cambodia in the early seventies. The Left distrusted him for that,
but so did the Right, since he was seen as a Kissinger protegé.

After Cambodia Enders had gone on to become assistant secretary of state for economic and business affairs, and then ambassador
to Canada during the Carter Administration.

Now, Enders was charged with overseeing the implementation of
a hawkish Central American policy that was viewed with suspicion
by Congress—and the public, if polls were any indication. There
was lots of talk about Vietnam and the making of another quagmire.
It was left to the RIG to negotiate the political minefields that were
scattered about the Washington landscape—some within the administration itself—before the policy could actually be imple-

mented. The Baker-Deaver-Meese White House staff troika which had kept the agenda focused at home in 1981—and with great success—was still reluctant to get involved in any foreign policy adventures that posed high risks.

Secretary of State Haig, on the other hand, was chafing at being sent to the back of the bus, unable to seize the president's attention during the first year to develop a coherent foreign-policy strategy. Haig was far more doctrinaire than Caspar Weinberger, the secretary of defense. The former NATO commander was dreaming great dreams. If Cuba was fanning the flames in Managua, Haig argued, the U.S. should look beyond Nicaragua, which was, after all, a two-bit banana republic. If Reagan really wanted to make his mark, why not go to the source? Why not cordon off the export of arms from Cuba with a blockade?

But the White House pragmatists hardly wanted to pick a fight with Cuba or risk resurrecting Bay of Pigs or Cuban missile-crisis imagery at the dawn of a new administration. Haig was isolated. In his effort to become vicar of foreign policy, he had tried to grab for too much, too soon, and was seemingly alienating everyone.

There was still strong support for making a mark in a place that counted—like Nicaragua. Yet no one was leading. Weinberger wasn't. Clark was still too new at NSC. So, almost by default, the RIG began driving Central American policy. And in an administration whose secretary of state was seriously advocating a blockade of Cuba, a covert action strategy for Nicaragua had the ring of moderation and compromise.

Covert action had also been given more legitimacy as a result of Enders' August, 1981, visit to Nicaragua—a confrontational mission in which he had reiterated Washington's objections to the drift of the Sandinista revolution—the out-of-whack military buildup, the curbing of free enterprise, the restrictions on the press, etc. While some of this could be tolerated, the U.S. could not tolerate the export of arms to the Salvadoran leftists, Enders said.

When it soon became apparent that the token Enders trip had been futile, and that there remained an enormous ideological gulf between the two sides, the administration could still say it had tried to make peace but the Sandinistas would have none of it. Now, the covert-action hammer could be applied with impunity.

By 1982, the new secret operations ethos had reached into the U.S. Army as well. In the aftermath of the failed 1980 hostage rescue attempt in Iran, it was decided that the United States needed a much better, more reliable special operations capability.

Shortly after the Reagan Administration took office, Chief of Staff
Meyer named army Colonel James Longhofer, a Vietnam veteran,
to head up a top-secret Special Operations Division which would
have the capability to undertake various types of unconventional
missions in hotspots around the globe. Congress secretly put up
$90 million to fund the new unit, which operated out of the office of
the army's deputy chief of staff for operations.

But Congress was apparently not told that $20 million of its ap-
propriation would go to fund an intelligence group called the Intelligence Support Activity (ISA), which was put under the command
of another army colonel, supposedly working on a parallel track
with Longhofer's unit. Though the Pentagon had its own intelligence arm—the Defense Intelligence Agency—officials of the
fledgling secret army argued that DIA was oriented toward gathering tactical military information of little use to special operations.
So, ISA was to be a scout for the Special Operations Division, as
well as fill in gaps in the CIA's menu of offerings. Within five years
ISA would have hundreds of agents all over the world, including
ten Latin American countries.

Though the Special Operations Division was born of a desire to
combat terrorism and cope with hostage situations, it soon was
spreading its wings and working shoulder-to-shoulder with the CIA
in Central America. In 1982, according to Time magazine, one
special-ops unit known as Seaspray began working with ISA in
Honduras on a mission to pinpoint the location of rebels in El Salvador by intercepting their radio transmissions. The mission—
code-named Queens Hunter—was originally only meant to last a
month but was considered so successful that it lasted three years.

The army operatives and the army spies were uneasy allies, getting into constant squabbles over lines of authority. When Seaspray
agents carelessly covered the satellite dish outside their Honduran
safe house with just a plastic garbage bag, their ISA brethren
lodged a formal complaint against them for lax security. Longhofer
sent down a security team (dubbed Yellow Fruit) to install a large
commercial satellite dish, changing the group's cover to fat-cat *Yan-
qui* tourists. Now the boys could pick up all the ballgames from the
States on their down time.

The very existence of both the Special Operations Division and
ISA were closely held secrets in the army and the Pentagon, where
there were many generals and top civilians who had never heard of
either group. But Casey knew all about them and planned to rely

increasingly on them as another weapon at his disposal in the secret war against the Sandinistas.

The first six months of 1983 were marked by more sniping between Congress and the White House over the direction of Nicaraguan policy. By February lawmakers were told that the Contra forces had swelled to fifty-five hundred and were rising still higher.

Leaders on both sides of the issue seemed to be growing more polarized and less inclined to compromise. Within the administration the hard-right ideologues were flexing their muscles and driving the agenda. In February Jeane Kirkpatrick, who maintained an avid interest in Central America from her perch at the United Nations, was dispatched on a ten-day tour of the area to review administration policy, and she returned with a gloomy report about spreading Sandinista tentacles and a region "in crisis." Kirkpatrick, a hawk's hawk, began fashioning an ever closer bureaucratic alliance with Casey.

There was fervent anticommunism in the air.

On March 8, in a Florida speech to a group of evangelical ministers, Reagan delivered his famous remark calling the Soviet Union "an evil empire." Later that month the president unveiled his exotic Strategic Defense Initiative to deploy weapons in space against the Russians—the so-called Star Wars plan. Moscow called Reagan a lunatic.

Congress kept the pressure on against the Nicaraguan policy, threatening to cut off funding for the no-longer covert operation. Reagan himself summoned House leaders to the Oval Office on April 26 to plead with them to continue the covert operation. Then the following day he appeared before an unusual joint session of Congress on national television to appeal for $600 million in general assistance to Central America. Reagan did not mention covert aid to the Contras but obliquely noted: "We should not, and we will not, protect the Nicaraguan government from the anger of its own people."

On April 28 the president sent a less than conciliatory signal to the Sandinistas by appointing Richard Stone, the former Democratic senator from Florida who had been defeated running for reelection in 1980, as special ambassador to Central America. Stone, who had been representing the administration in its dealings with Capitol Hill on Central America, was a registered lobbyist for the rightist government of Guatemala from 1981 to 1982.

The Stone appointment was perhaps the official death-knell for Thomas Enders, who had been losing ground steadily the previous several months in the face of the conservative blitz. Enders, though certainly right of center, was a pragmatist. But the ascendant hard-right was coming to view pragmatists as turncoat wimps. Enders supported the covert policy against the Sandinistas, but knew it was on a collision course with Congress if Casey, Kirkpatrick, William Clark and Reagan himself insisted on adopting such a confronta-tional posture. So he sought to lower the profile of the secret war and bury it in the larger Central American strategy. Congress could not be allowed to think that the administration's sole purpose was to overthrow the Sandinistas: it had to believe that at least part of the policy was intended to achieve peace and settlement through negotiations. Even if negotiation was not the real goal, it should be stated as an aim so as to take the hard edge off the covert war and win the administration some breathing room with moderates, where it now had precious little.

Enders had put these thoughts to paper earlier in the year in a memorandum that codified his "two-track" approach. Clark and other hard-liners in the administration thought the memo amounted to treasonous appeasement, and in February someone had leaked it to the press—the first signal that Enders' days were numbered. By May he had been reassigned as ambassador to Spain. It was a measure of the growing, confident extremist ap-proach of the administration that Enders, whose conservative cre-dentials were, after all, in order as a result of his stint in Cambodia, was having his patriotism called into question because of the sup-posed lack of zeal he was displaying in advancing the Right's cur-rent *cause célèbre*, Nicaragua.

As if to validate Enders's concerns, on May 3 the House Intelli-gence Committee voted 9–5 on partisan lines to cut off further covert funding for the Contras. Three days later Casey appeared before the Senate Intelligence Committee in a more conciliatory mood and readily signed on to a suggestion from Senate Chairman Barry Goldwater, the Arizona Republican, that Reagan draft a new finding that would change the goals of the program along the lines that Enders had suggested: continued covert pressure, but with a view to democratizing the Sandinistas and getting them to negoti-ate. Casey conceded that the goals of the program had clearly grown beyond arms interdiction to the rebels in El Salvador, as the 1981 finding specified.

Goldwater suggested a compromise whereby covert funding

would be continued for another five months, and another $19 million provided for the following fiscal year, *if* Reagan drafted a new finding that was approved by a majority vote of the committee. Republican congressional leaders saw this as a significant erosion of the president's foreign policy prerogatives, but Casey and the other point men on Nicaragua thought they were getting off easy. Funding for the operation could continue, and the president would simply offer up another broader finding—with plenty of maneuvering room—that would officially change the rules of the game.

The Contras did not seem concerned either. Reacting to news of the five-month extension by Congress, a Contra leader in Honduras told United Press International: "There's no problem. We'll be in Managua in five months."

In early 1983 there began to be more discussion within the administration of putting the Nicaraguan effort in a larger anticommunist context. In the scheme of things a great power like the United States seemed to be devoting a totally disproportionate share of its time, energy, money and prestige toward the tiny backwater of Nicaragua—even if it was in the Western Hemisphere. But what if the drive against the Sandinistas was packaged and presented to the world as merely the cornerstone of a larger effort to assist anticommunist insurgencies around the world? Wouldn't such a policy lend more logic, credibility and coherence to the obsession with Nicaragua? What was needed was a better spin on the struggle.

One day in March a thirty-nine-year-old professional adventurer from California named Jack Wheeler stopped in at the White House to see Dana Rohrabacher, an old friend who was working as one of the president's speechwriters. The two had been pals since the sixties when they worked together in California on Youth for Reagan while the president was governor.

"I was looking at this map," Wheeler recalls, "and all of a sudden I realized there were a number of anti-Soviet guerrilla wars going on throughout the Third World. These were no series of isolated phenomena, but a wholesale rejection of the entire concept of Soviet imperialism. But no one had gone into the field to talk with these people who were fighting the communists."

Wheeler saw a changed world. If Radical Chic had exalted Mao, Fidel and Che in the sixties, the tide had now turned back to the Right and the heroes of the eighties could be anticommunist guerrillas like Angola's Jonas Savimbi, and the Afghan *mujaheddin*, he thought. Or the Contras, or the resistance in Cambodia and Ethiopia. No one had really integrated these disparate causes.

Rohrabacher urged him to go visit the new freedom frontiers and report back on what he found. So Wheeler got some conservative seed money, formed something called the Freedom Research Foundation and set out on a five-month trek that took him first to Nicaragua, and then to Angola, Afghanistan, Cambodia, Mozambique and Ethiopia. He saw action, and at each stop, like a visiting statesman, told the rebels they were not alone—others, on different fronts around the world, were fighting the same kind of fight. He thought this message gave them hope and inspiration.

Though Wheeler knew that Nicaragua would remain the Reagan Administration's priority, for him, of all the hotspots he had visited, nothing compared with Afghanistan. There, after all, the *mujaheddin* weren't up against any surrogates; it was the Red Army itself.

In November Wheeler returned to Washington, and Rohrabacher arranged for him to give a slide show and lecture to the president's speechwriters—a group that carried the purest ideological pedigree in the White House.

In a profile of Wheeler, Washington *Post* reporter Sidney Blumenthal, who chronicles the Right, described what happened next: "Wheeler's message leaped beyond intractable budgets and congressional deadlocks, 'the humdrum of government'... This was not some mundane realignment of the Republican Party; it was, rather, a cosmic realignment of the planet. Now conservative ideology began at the barrel of a gun. 'Jack,' says a White House source, 'was the one who brought it all together. He took random struggles and crystallized the concept that they were part of the same historic movement.'"

The speechwriters loved Wheeler because he put meat on the bones of the Reagan rhetoric and brought it to life. He had been to the bush and returned with the good news that the Reagan fantasy of beating back communism around the world not only existed, but was alive and well on at least five major fronts.

Wheeler was promptly mainstreamed into the conservative establishment and before long was reverently being called "the Indiana Jones of the Right." And he was introduced to North, who by then was becoming more and more involved with the Contras. The two hit it off immediately—a couple of can-do guys who wanted to make a contribution. Wheeler also gave well-received briefings on his unifying anticommunist theory to the administration's two foremost conservatives—Kirkpatrick and Casey—both of whom

adopted the idea enthusiastically and gave it intellectual cohesive-
ness and clout.

Soon Reagan's speeches were being sprinkled with tributes to
"freedom fighters" around the globe, a characterization which ele-
vated their stature and their cause. By 1985 in his State of the
Union address Reagan would be expounding the thesis clearly: "We
must not break faith with those who are risking their lives on every
continent, from Afghanistan to Nicaragua, to defy Soviet-supported
aggression." The press would give the theme an appropriately gran-
diose title—"the Reagan Doctrine," and the concept would serve to
unify an often fractious conservative movement.

Finally Wheeler would be given a conservative's ultimate badge
of honor: being attacked by the communist press. *Izvetsia*, the Soviet newspaper, called him an "ideological gangster," while *Barri-
cada*, the official Sandinista paper, warned ominously of "Wheeler's
shadow" and then gave credit where credit was due: "The concept
of 'freedom fighters' as an organizational principle emerged basically from the work of Jack Wheeler," it said.

But the Reagan Doctrine did not just mean providing enough
assistance for anticommunist insurgents to fight stalemated wars.
The goal was to "rollback" Soviet gains in the Third World by ousting the pro-Moscow regimes and installing pro-Western governments. It was about time America had a clear-cut foreign-policy
win. As the White House surveyed the list of likely possibilities,
Nicaragua was still number one.

In the Pentagon parlance of the day these guerrilla wars were
called "low intensity conflicts." About two dozen of them were
raging around the world, and there was a developing consensus
that the United States, preoccupied with the threat of nuclear
war or conventional war in Europe, was preparing for battles it
would never fight. There was a need to get greater bang for the
defense buck, and develop a better special-operations capability
that could have an impact on the wars that were being fought.
But how could the U.S. play an effective special-ops role in an
era of tight congressional oversight and constraints by American
public opinion?

Those were some of the provocative issues on the agenda at a
conference on "Special Operations in U.S. Strategy" in Washington, March 4 and 5, 1983. Many of the ideas advanced at the conference—particularly with regard to secrecy, tailoring operations to
domestic political realities, use of the private sector, short-circuit-

ing the bureaucracy and the pivotal role of the NSC—would later be incorporated by North in the Contra supply operation and in selling arms to Iran.

The conference was sponsored by Georgetown University, the National Defense University and the National Strategy Information Center—a right wing think tank. About 125 people attended— mostly military officers, Pentagon consultants, intelligence officials and various other members of the Reagan Administration. The session was not secret, and the government later published an edited version of the proceedings. Though that publication lists North as a "participant" in the conference, one of the organizers of the session said years later that North did not actually attend.

Many of those who did attend probably did not know of the existence of the army's secret Special Operations Division and the Intelligence Support Activity, which by then were already doing some of the things being advocated. But both units had been founded on the more narrow premise of countering terrorism, while the missions discussed at the conference were broader in scope. Speakers at the conference were pleased that the Reagan Administration had doubled spending on the Green Berets, the army group with the traditional mandate to carry out special operations, but complained that there was still no broad, coherent view on how such activities could be integrated into American foreign policy.

The conference organizers, in an introduction to the book later published, displayed thinly disguised contempt for what they assumed was a largely ignorant body politic unaware of what was really in its national interest. "An untutored American public," they complained, had "little enthusiasm for recourse to unconventional acts in a time of 'formal peace.'" So the U.S. had to "develop diverse and even novel ways to defend its economic and geopolitical interests when these are affected by unconventional conflicts, particularly in the Third World."

That attitude went to the core of the Father Knows Best approach that North, Casey, Poindexter and others would later use in conducting an off-lines foreign policy. It would be predicated on the notion that a military-intelligence nucleus was more equipped to decide what was in the national interest than the Congress of the United States or, by extension, the people. It would be pursuing "democratic revolutions" abroad while shunning democracy at home for fear that if the policies were put to an open test of the political process, they would be rejected. Indeed, in the case of

Central America and support for the Contras, polls showed that the public consistently disagreed with administration policy.

So, significantly, the conference spent less time debating the classic problem of how to win the hearts and minds of the people in whose land an unconventional war is being waged than in trying to figure out how to win the hearts and minds of *Americans* so that the operations could be launched in the first place.

"I think the most critical special operations mission we have in the United States today is to persuade the American people that the communists are out to get us, and that we have to help other countries to do the things that have to be done in order to keep the communists away from our doorsteps..." said John Michael Kelly, deputy assistant secretary of the Air Force. "By engaging in low-intensity conflict we avoid high-intensity warfare."

America was seen as cast in the role of "heroic wimp"—imagining itself crusading and fighting for a noble ideal against an evil adversary, but not wanting to do anything risky to attain its objectives. A guts-and-glory ethos permeated the conference. "Let's dare," said Secretary of the Army John Marsh in concluding his keynote address. "We will win."

George Tanham, a Rand Corporation scholar, saw a world in "total conflict. Special operations involve psychological, political and economic activities. It adds up to total conflict for political power... But what I cannot overemphasize is that we are engaged in a struggle for the minds of people, including our own citizens. That is the most important thing there is. If we lose our citizens, we will not have much going for us."

But Theodore Shackley, a legendary former CIA official who ran the agency's secret war in Laos in the mid-sixties, was skeptical of gaining support for covert operations. "An innate dislike for special operations by the mainstream of American political life will perforce limit Washington to a defensive mode in considering irregular warfare operations," he said.

If the masses could not be persuaded to sign on, perhaps the elite could, it was suggested. Or if public disapproval would kill an operation, it could be taken underground and carried out anyway if it had a good chance of succeeding. Then the public, presented with a success, would surely approve since "it is a hard, true fact of life that success overcomes a lot of moral, legal, political and cultural scruples." That lesson in *realpolitik* was offered by William O'Brien, professor of government at Georgetown.

Foreshadowing the role that would be played by Gen. Richard

Secord in the Iran-Contra affair, Marsh, citing the "limitations on military or government involvement," proposed that many special operations be transferred to the private sector. Pointing to "economic, political and psychological warfare" in particular, Marsh said: "This is an enormous area in which private-sector resources can be used... We live in a nation that has been the global pioneer in industrial development, marketing, advertising and communication. We must harness those resources in a common security endeavor." Coming from a man who oversaw one of the largest and most powerful armies on earth, Marsh's suggestion was a startling abdication of power and an admission of military failure, among other things. But others, too, spoke of the need for "private efforts to arouse a lethargic public" to the need for a democracy to more aggressively counter the Soviet menace.

Most conference participants agreed that in order for special operations to be effective they should be managed by one central authority that could integrate counterinsurgency, antiterrorist operations and guerrilla warfare. To avoid service rivalries and to be able to speak with the central authority of the White House that governing body should probably be the National Security Council. To accommodate this new role the NSC could be expanded and given new resources and powers, if necessary, but not so as to attract undue attention. "To do so would not only arouse false expectations but would also immediately attract the opposition of those in Congress and the media whose philosophy consists of repetition of the slogan 'No more Vietnams,'" said Douglas Blaufarb, a former CIA station chief.

Tanham concluded: "It seems to me this is a critical issue— developing the capability on the part of some element of the government, probably the NSC, which can seize these opportunities, take action to exploit them, and begin to head off some of the attacks on democracies."

Starting in the winter of 1983, North, as he developed more experience and familiarity with Central America, had begun sitting in occasionally at RIG meetings representing the NSC in place of Roger Fontaine. "He was the person we saw afterwards—vigorous and helpful in every detail," Enders recalls about North. "He was sort of a Mr. Fixit. The role he played in diplomatic discussion was small at that time. He was an operational, can-do guy. His role developed after I left."

By then, Enders could testify first-hand to the White House's clear preference for action over diplomacy in Central America, and he could see an atmosphere being created in which a man of North's boldness, fervor and operational orientation could emerge and have great impact. "I think it was an atmosphere in which it was quite clear that the president wanted action, but did not have a precise action plan to propose," Enders said. "A guy who could pick up the ball and run with it, with implicit, if not explicit, presidential encouragement, could run quite far."

North began taking trips to Central America with Richard Stone.

In late February Stone, who then was still the administration's liaison to Congress on Central America, flew down to El Salvador with North and another NSC staffer, Alfonso Sapia-Bosch. Their mission was to try and persuade the Salvadoran leadership to hold an election. The civil war in Salvador, often eclipsed by the attention given the White House policy toward Nicaragua, was going badly for the American-backed government. The leftist rebels were in the ascendancy again. The Salvadoran army was growing short on arms, ammunition and other supplies; it had abandoned special operations and was fighting only at battalion-size strength—and leadership was spotty. Congress—angered by the government's refusal to hold an election or negotiate with the rebels, and by reports of rampant killing by right-wing death squads—was only authorizing funding at minimal levels. The situation was generally thought to be deteriorating.

But after a few days of discussions in San Salvador the Stone-led delegation was able to get the government to agree to conduct an early election. That agreement was considered a key element in the push to democratize the regime and broaden its support in Washington and elsewhere.

Returning home on a commercial flight to Miami en route to Washington, Stone, North and Sapia-Bosch were elated at their successful mission and started celebrating—a little louder than is considered normal diplomatic behavior. The conversation was loud enough that it could easily be heard in an adjoining row where a reporter for a Tampa, Florida, television station quietly began taking notes on an air-sickness bag.

Mark Feldstein, then of WTSP–TV, was returning home from a vacation in Central America and had been just getting ready to go to sleep when he heard a man with a loud voice brag about his connections to Alexander Haig. Haig had resigned as secretary of state the previous year and been replaced by George Shultz. Feldstein, writing about the incident four years later in the Washington *Monthly,* identified the man with the loud voice as North.

"On the flight the men were laughing and celebrating. They had just convinced El Salvador's president to hold new elections, and now believed that this would force a reluctant Congress to approve more aid to the Salvadoran government," Feldstein wrote.

"North chortled that he had arranged things so that it would appear that the Salvadorans had thought up the idea. He read aloud a statement that the White House planned to release, praising the Salvadoran government for its courageous decision. North boasted that he had carefully worded it for 'domestic political consumption.' The result: Congress would now send an additional $60 million to El Salvador. Meanwhile, I had inadvertantly stumbled across a global power-play in the coach section of the plane."

After taking an air-bag full of notes, Feldstein confronted Stone, who was forced to confirm that what he and North had just been talking about was true.

"When I broke the story the next day it upset and embarrassed officials both in Washington and San Salvador," Feldstein recalls. "But somehow Oliver North remained unscathed. Richard Stone, the White House envoy, got most of the blame; he was reportedly chewed out by President Reagan for allowing the story to leak out, and his career as a diplomat soon came to an end. Yet it was North who had done most of the blabbing. Despite it all, it was the beginning of North's ascent to power."

Not long after the trip with Stone, North was reportedly involved in an incident that easily could have cost him his life or his career —not to mention creating a major international incident.

One day that spring Andy Messing, Jr., a conservative activist who was then executive director of the Conservative Caucus, stopped in to visit North in his office. Messing, a former Special Forces soldier and Vietnam veteran, had a keen interest in the war in El Salvador and wanted to chat with North, with whom he was developing a close friendship. As Messing sat down, he said he noticed North had cuts all over his face, including a three-quarter-inch gash on his forehead. It looked like he had been shattered with broken glass.

"I asked him how he got the cuts and he tried to brush it off," Messing recalls. "I kept pressing him on what happened, then he related the incident and told me not to tell anyone. I had to drag it out of him."

North told Messing he had just returned from another trip to El Salvador, where he had conferred with U.S. military advisors and received an update on the civil war. At one point North and Navy Lieutenant Commander Albert Schaufelberger, deputy chief of the fifty-five-member American military contingent in Salvador, decided to fly around the small country to get an aerial view of the theater of operations.

They rented a plane from the civilian side of the Ilopango Air Base so as not to attract any attention from the leftist insurgents. North, explaining that over the years he had learned to fly, told Messing he was piloting the plane. As they flew they heard over the radio that a Salvadoran army unit was coming under heavy fire and was taking a number of casualties. The unit's calls for an air medevac were going unanswered, evidently because all available Salvadoran military aircraft were being used elsewhere.

North and Schaufelberger were not far away from where the battle had taken place and decided they would respond. North told Messing he put the small plane down on a dirt airstrip and taxied the plane to where the army unit was waiting. The soldiers at first tried to load on some of their dead, but North said they would take the wounded out first. Schaufelberger took one of the soldiers into the back seat with him and began administering CPR to him. The other man was strapped into the front seat next to North.

"North started taxiing back down the runway," Messing says. "He didn't have the right fuel-air mixture and he wasn't getting full power. He started adjusting some instruments trying to get more power when a Salvadoran guerrilla came out on the airstrip with a light machinegun and hosed down the airplane with gunfire. He blew out the windshield and punctured the fuel tanks. North took off and barely cleared the trees at the end of the runway because he still wasn't getting full power. The whole way back to Ilopango, which was about thirty miles away, he was getting fuel blown in his eyes, the wind was buffeting the plane and he was just trying to maintain control. Finally he glided it in, making a dead-stick landing at Ilopango. One of the Salvadorans died as they landed, and the other one died on the way to the hospital."

Messing says that in a later trip to El Salvador he confirmed North's story from members of the Salvadoran air force who wit-

nessed the landing and saw the soldiers being taken off the plane in
an ambulance. "One said it made a very good impression that there
were some Americans who were willing to risk their lives for El
Salvador," Messing says. "Until that time they had just been advising but taking no risks. The Salvadorans regarded the Americans
with disdain because of that." But after the Sky King exploit,
North, at least, was seen as a golden gringo, and anything he asked
for he got, Messing relates. Schaufelberger, too—but not for long.
Just a few months later, in May, Schaufelberger was shot to death
by leftists as he sat in a car in front of the university in San Salvador
waiting to pick up his girlfriend. He was the first U.S. military
advisor to be killed in Central America.

North's air caper was the kind of spectacular story which, as
Messing circulated it years later, served to build Ollie's legend. But
the story—examined several years later—may have been apocry-
phal. Schaufelberger was dead, and thus not in a position to verify
anything. (As the years passed, several other people in a position to
corroborate key elements of other, more significant North assertions would also have died). North himself would be in a permanent no-comment mode.

But others who might have been expected to have known of the
incident if it happened—such as John Waghelstein, Schaufelberger's immediate superior and commander of the U.S. military
group, or Deane Hinton, the American ambassador to El Salvador
at the time—said they had never heard anything of the sort and
doubted that it occurred. Further, it developed that no one had
ever heard of North being able to fly before.

Messing, for his part, says he still believes the story. North, after
all, had not volunteered it and had been reluctant to say anything.
And he did have those cuts on his face.

That spring, North began helping to lead another administration
public-relations drive on Central America. With Congress raising
an ever increasing fuss about U.S. policy in the region, and with
polls showing the people to be even more skeptical of the policy
than were their representatives in Washington, White House strat-
egists determined that the populace was simply not getting the
message about the threat to American interests in the area.

So to get the word out, and to try and build public support for
the administration's policy, the White House created the Outreach
Working Group on Central America under the direction of Faith
Ryan Whittlesey, who would go on to be named the U.S. ambassa-

dor to Switzerland. Over the succeeding months the group published a series of White Papers under the title "White House Digest," and aggressively arranged hundreds of briefings on the president's policy for a broad array of organizations and interest groups.

While there was still substantial question about whether the government of El Salvador could stave off the leftist threat, the Outreach group made a conscious decision to focus the debate on Nicaragua, the issue of its arming the Salvadoran rebels, and generally exporting revolution. A catalogue of Sandinista human-rights abuses were laid out, and victims brought up to testify and tell their stories. The administration had many briefers, but based on audience feedback, a consensus soon emerged that the best, most dynamic and popular speaker was Ollie North.

"He was universally viewed as our star briefer on the subject," recalls Morton Blackwell, then a project officer for the Outreach group. "He really knew his stuff. He'd bring in declassified photographs and put on a fantastic slide show. The slides would show things like Soviet troops in Nicaraguan harbors unloading major munitions, or he'd show the building of expanded airfields . . . The guy has a great grasp of the world situation. He's very smart. He was patriotic. He was anticommunist . . . He was extraordinarily persuasive and passionate. But if it was just pure passion it would have turned people off. It was informed argumentation with great force of personality . . . He was just very good."

Most of the groups who requested or agreed to a briefing were of the conservative stripe, so in many cases North found himself preaching to the choir. But those on the receiving end of the pitch didn't just like his views on Central America. They liked *him*, his persona and the traditional American values he exuded. As Blackwell put it: "Ollie hit it off with these people because he was committed to beliefs that ranged across the Reagan coalition: moral values, traditional religious faith, and not being bashful about expressing either. And so Ollie was taken into people's hearts."

It was during the dozens of briefings that he conducted on behalf of the Central American Outreach group that North made numerous contacts within the conservative community—contacts he would tap later as his profile rose, as his responsibilities increased and as the lines he drew between the public and private sectors became increasingly blurred.

In June, not satisfied with just the Outreach project, the administration decided to expand its public relations blitz in support of the president's Central America policy by creating a parallel group whose mandate would be to try and influence international public opinion—particularly in Latin America and Europe—though it ended up working mostly domestically. The group was called the Office of Public Diplomacy, and though it was headquartered in the State Department, it was established and effectively run by the National Security Council—a bit of bureaucratic sleight of hand that signaled the rising influence of the NSC.

In a May 25 memo to Reagan, Secretary of State Shultz complained about the arrangement, asking that the president designate him the "sole delegate" in carrying out Central America policy. But Reagan replied in a memo of his own that the order would stand. "No single agency can do it alone," he told Shultz. It was National Security Advisor William Clark who chose the man to head the public diplomacy office, Otto Reich. And though the group was staffed by some interagency personnel, the principal staff was from the NSC, under the direction of Walter Raymond, a former senior CIA official sent over with the approval of Casey to head up the public diplomacy unit.

But the NSC's concept of public diplomacy turned out, more precisely, to mean public relations lobbying at taxpayers' expense. In its effort to persuade the public and Congress to support aid to the Contras, Reich's office would hire outside consultants and contractors, and award more than $400,000 in no-bid contracts to International Business Communications, a public relations firm North would come to use extensively in service of the Contra cause.

In what Jonathan Miller, a Reich deputy, called a "White Propaganda Operation," the office sought to place pro-Contra op-ed pieces in major newspapers. Reich wrote in a memo to Raymond that he wanted the office to adopt "a very aggressive posture vis-à-vis a sometimes hostile press" and "not give the critics of the policy any quarter in the debate." In a Nixonian afterthought Reich added that "attacking the president was no longer cost-free."

Later the comptroller general would conclude that some of the public diplomacy unit's activities, especially Miller's program, were "prohibited covert propaganda activities . . . beyond the range of acceptable agency public information activities." The comptroller general concluded that the office had therefore violated "a restriction on the State Department's annual appropriations prohibiting the use of federal funds for publicity or propaganda purposes not authorized by Congress."

White Propaganda was a term Miller used in writing a "confidential/eyes only" memorandum to White House Communications Director Patrick Buchanan by way of updating him on the public diplomacy unit's activities. The memo described how the unit had placed an article in the *Wall Street Journal*, influenced a television report on the "NBC Nightly News" and was preparing to submit pieces to the New York *Times* and Washington *Post*.

But for all the White House efforts to integrate public relations and public policy, it was clear that the Reagan Administration stance on Central America remained out-of-step with an American public wary of getting more deeply involved in the region. With "education" and public relations having fallen short of their intended goals, the administration retreated one step and adopted the more conciliatory approach of trying to fashion a broad consensus on what Central American policy should be. It would appoint a bipartisan, blue-ribbon commission to study the problem.

In July Reagan announced that the twelve-member panel would be chaired by Henry Kissinger. There was enough bipartisanship and diversity on the commission to give it credibility, though the backgrounds and political views of a majority of the members made it clear from the outset that the panel would not produce a final report straying too far from the current administration line. The presence of Kissinger gave the group cachet and star quality.

North was appointed by Clark to be the NSC's liaison with the commission—another in a flurry of moves during recent months that attested to North's rising influence.

In June North had been promoted to the position of deputy director of the NSC's political-military affairs division—at the same time taking over the NSC seat on the Central American RIG that had been held by Roger Fontaine. This put him at the core of day-to-day policy-making for the region. Thomas Enders was now gone, and there were new opportunities for influence to be asserted while Langhorne Motley, Enders' replacement as assistant secretary of state for inter-American affairs, got his feet wet. Motley was a forty-five-year-old real estate developer and Republican activist from Alaska who had been serving as the U.S. ambassador to Brazil.

The political-military affairs unit was created as part of a reorganization plan under Judge Clark and consisted of four or five military officers charged with "interfacing" with their counterparts at the State Department and the Pentagon. They provided the military component—arms sales and the like—for political work. The unit was headed by Don Fortier, who had just come over to the NSC from the State Department and successfully persuaded Clark to create the group.

North was charged with reviewing military systems programs for all of Latin America, but he also retained—and expanded—his responsibilities for planning against terrorism. Poindexter had taken charge of the terrorism portfolio and, at North's suggestion, formed another interagency group to cope with the problem. That group was known as TIWG (Terrorist Incident Working Group) and included representatives from State, Defense, CIA and FBI, who engaged in long-range planning on how to improve counterterrorist policies. They also served as a specific task force to deal with incidents as they arose. North's bosses liked that he was always coming up with ideas. "It certainly was an imagination that was very fertile," recalls McFarlane.

The mandate of political-military affairs was rather broad and ill-defined, which suited North fine, and there existed considerable opportunity for cutting across bureaucratic jurisdictions. "It was just such a vague charter that you could legitimately get involved in any issue because most everything has a political-military dimension to it," recalls Geoffrey Kemp, the Middle East expert. "There was an enormous capacity to meddle in other people's turf."

North's first encounter with Kissinger was amusing. The commission had gathered for its first briefing by the NSC. The session was held in Room 208 of the Executive Office Building—the new crisis-management center North had had a hand in setting up.

Roger Fontaine gave a presentation, and then North gave his usual slide show, expanded slightly to deal with the threat of Soviet-sponsored insurgencies around the world. Nicaragua had to be put in the proper context. As he discussed Soviet proxy wars around the globe, North flashed up a slide that he thought showed the countries in which these battles were taking place.

But then a slow, thickly accented baritone voice spoke up from the rear of the room. It was Kissinger, puzzled as to why the slide showed three red dots on Norway. "Major North," he said, "I was not aware of the Soviet-sponsored insurgency in northern Norway."

"Wrong slide, sir," smiled North sheepishly as the commission members laughed.

Representative Michael Barnes, the Maryland Democrat who was then chairman of the House Subcommittee on Western Hemisphere Affairs, served as a congressional adviser to the Kissinger

Commission and was struck by the ease and confidence with which North related to members of the panel. North was a lowly major, yet seemed to be chatting with Kissinger and the others as equals.

"He hung out with Henry," recalls Barnes, laughing. "Ollie has a rather remarkable facility for ingratiating himself with important people. He was a major. I'm a former Marine, and I never saw anyone like this guy. Here he was hobnobbing with Supreme Court justices (one of the commission members was retired Supreme Court Justice Potter Stewart) generals and senators, and very relaxed about the whole thing. Military guys around Congress tend to be incredibly stiff and deferential. But Ollie was more a peer. He arrived with the imprimatur of the White House, and more often than not he was at Henry's elbow."

Members of the commission were impressed by North. "He was a very dynamic, vigorous young man of excellent disposition," says John Silber, the conservative president of Boston University. "He was a friendly, boyish kind of man who conveyed a sense of commitment, not fanaticism. He was a man of great flexibility . . . Some people are so utterly lacking in commitment that they can't believe a flexible man could have the kind of commitment and integrity that Ollie North has. But he does, and that's a fact."

In early October, North accompanied the commission on its trip to Central America, where it visited six countries in six days. The last stop was Nicaragua, where thousands of Sandinista supporters —released from work for the afternoon—turned out to meet the panel by staging a raucous protest against U.S. policy supporting the Contras. Signs and slogans called Kissinger a "Nazi" and an "insect."

The Sandinistas thought Washington was on an all-out war footing. In August the U.S. had sent several thousand of its troops to nearby Honduras for military exercises code-named "Big Pine II." The exercises had also involved warships, fighter planes and the construction of radar sites, airstrips and other military facilities. In September a twin-engine Cessna carrying a 500-pound bomb under each wing had been shot down and crash-landed at the Managua airport. The plane had been on a Contra mission apparently approved by the CIA. And just four days before the commission's arrival the CIA had pulled off its splashiest operation yet: agency-trained operatives using speedboats had staged a pre-dawn raid against the Sandinista fuel-storage depot at the port of Corinto and exploded five oil-storage tanks, forcing the evacuation of twenty thousand people. The operation was carried out using rapid-firing cannons supplied to the CIA by one of the units in the army's newly established Special Operations Division.

North, annoyed by the fervid anti-American sentiment he saw on display in Managua, could not, it is said, resist delivering a quip to a Sandinista in the official greeting party at the airport. The commission, North deadpanned, was really not there on a fact-finding mission; it was actually the advance team for an American invasion.

In its final report, the Kissinger Commission said a "real and acute" crisis existed in Central America. It called for an $8.4 billion infusion of U.S. economic and military assistance to democracies and would-be democracies in the region. As the administration had hoped, the commission framed the issue in an East-West context, saying that while tensions may have originated with local poverty and repression, Soviet and Cuban intervention had changed the strategic equation. "Our credibility worldwide is engaged," the report warned. "The triumph of hostile forces in what the Soviet Union calls the 'strategic rear' of the United States would be read as a sign of U.S. impotence."

In September of 1983, the Congress had approved the new finding by President Reagan in which he made clear that his aims in Nicaragua were broader than stopping the flow of weapons from the Sandinistas to the rebels in El Salvador. The new finding authorized "materiel support and guidance to the Nicaraguan resistance groups," and said that the U.S. intended to induce the Sandinistas to negotiate with their neighbors while continuing to pressure them to stop supplying the Salvadoran rebels. It also called for the expansion of the Contra army to twelve to fifteen thousand men.

Armed with the new finding, Casey was anxious for the Contras to get more aggressive. He wanted more high-profile operations like the explosion of the oil depots. Casey pressured Motley, Clarridge and the RIG to come up with new, more dynamic ideas to keep pressure on the Sandinistas.

Planning for one operation that amounted to little more than creative—albeit legally questionable—bookkeeping was nearing completion. In June Reagan had authorized "Operation Elephant Herd," a joint CIA-military plan to skirt congressional restrictions on Contra aid. Under the program the Pentagon declared three small planes worth $12 million to be "surplus to requirements" of the military. As surplus materiel the planes were no longer considered to have any value and thus could be transferred to the Contras without counting as part of the $24 million cap on military aid to the Contras then being imposed by Congress. The plans called for the three Cessna 0-2 observation planes to be modified so that they could carry rockets, and then given to the Contras.

Motley had restricted membership in the RIG so that the effective core group now consisted of himself, Clarridge and North. There was some concern that Motley's boss, Shultz, might object to the restricted nature and increasingly operational role of the RIG. But North, gaining more confidence daily in his ability to work at the highest levels of government, according to Woodward's *Veil* said: "Fuck the secretary of state."

One day, in the Casey-mandated spirit of coming up with bold new initiatives, Clarridge suggested that they plant mines in the Nicaraguan harbors.

Clarridge, who was nothing if not a character, told several colleagues that he had been sitting around the previous night having a martini and thinking about the Russo-Japanese War of 1904. "Do you know what the most important element of that war was?" he asked. "It was mining!"

Mining, he said, would also be a good way to strangle the Sandinistas. Clarridge quickly sold North on the idea and introduced it formally at the RIG. When someone raised an objection and asked what would happen if a Soviet ship visiting Nicaragua hit a mine and sank, Clarridge reportedly said: "Good!"

Actually, Clarridge said he envisioned a defensive mining program—if such a thing were possible—whereby the main goal would be not to sink ships but to scare vessels, particularly oil suppliers, from coming into the ports, thereby depriving the Sandinistas of critical supplies. The mines would have a low explosive yield that would cause more noise than damage. But as word got around that a harbor was mined, insurance carriers would refuse to provide insurance for boats, and that would further reduce traffic, Clarridge said, seemingly oblivious to the potential political fallout in Washington.

The RIG approved the plan and sent it up the line for review. Casey presented it to the president as consistent with the new finding, and Reagan gave his approval. The CIA began the logistical chore of contracting out to have the mines manufactured and arranging for a mother ship that would sit in international waters and serve as a home base for the operation. Operatives on speedboats would then fan out from the ship and plant the mines when the time came.

That same month Clarridge commissioned a CIA contract agent

who went by the name of John Kirkpatrick to write a manual for the
Contras that was entitled "Psychological Operations in Guerrilla
Warfare." This document, whose cover showed rows of heads with
large holes through them, would become known as the "assassination manual" when disclosed a year later. In direct violation of CIA
policy, the booklet recommended "neutralizing" government officials as a means of attaining political ends. A presidential directive
specifies that "no person employed by or acting on behalf of the
U.S. government shall engage in or conspire to engage in assassinations."

But Clarridge thought he had a semantic out—what constituted
an assassination? Two months later, testifying in secret session before the congressional intelligence committees, Dewey would
freely admit that the Contras had killed "civilians and Sandinista
officials in the provinces, as well as heads of cooperatives, nurses,
doctors and judges." But he said that didn't contradict the presidential directive because as far as the CIA was concerned, the term
assassination applied only to heads of state. "I leave definitions to
the politicians," Clarridge added, according to Christopher
Dickey's *With the Contras*. War was hell. People got killed. He
wished the go-slow crowd would stop quibbling with abstractions
and stop meddling in his war.

On October 13 Reagan made a surprise announcement: Judge
Clark was resigning as National Security Advisor and would become Secretary of the Interior. It seemed Clark had grown wary of
bickering with Jim Baker and Mike Deaver, the far more moderate
senior White House staffers. Clark had seen his chief role on the
NSC as helping to hold the president's feet to the conservative fire,
particularly on Central America, while leaving most of the day-to-
day administration of the National Security Council to McFarlane
and Poindexter.

Initially, the president wanted to name Baker to replace Clark at
NSC, but when Clark, Casey and other leading conservatives
strongly objected, Reagan backed down and approved a compromise candidate: McFarlane.

McFarlane, who would name Poindexter his deputy, had won
praise for rescuing several Reagan initiatives from defeat in Congress, notably the MX missile program. And in July he had gained
attention when Reagan named him to be his personal representative in the Middle East, replacing Philip Habib. Reagan had
charged McFarlane with trying to promote a settlement between

Israel and her Arab enemies while trying to get all foreign nations to withdraw from Lebanon. In this, McFarlane had been unsuccessful. Instead he had become one of the leading voices behind the controversial policy of having a Marine detachment and offshore U.S. naval forces begin active support for the Lebanese government of President Amin Gemayel.

But all that was past. Whatever the merits or demerits of the positions he had taken, McFarlane had been given the job of National Security Advisor. It was the culmination of a dream. And to cap it off, he was able to get Reagan to agree to move him up from the White House basement and give him Kissinger's old office, adjacent to the president's. He had finally arrived.

For North, who had just been promoted to lieutenant colonel a few weeks before, the prospects under a McFarlane regime looked bright. He had remained close to his fellow Marine over the previous two years and was delighted with the appointment.

GRENADA

O N October 19, 1983, two days after his appointment as National Security Advisor, McFarlane faced his first crisis.

Maurice Bishop, the young Marxist leader of the tiny Caribbean island of Grenada, was assassinated in the aftermath of a bungled coup that had begun six days earlier when a group of even more militant, pro-Cuban Grenadians had placed Bishop under house arrest. The new leftists had placed the island under 24-hour-a-day curfew, but no one had actually emerged to take control. When the State Department tried to make official contact with a new government, there was no government to make contact with.

An immediate U.S. concern was the safety of about one thousand Americans who lived on Grenada—most of them students at the St. George University School of Medicine. The overlying worry, however, was the political direction the island had been taking for the last four years.

Grenada, until then known primarily for producing about a third of the world's nutmeg, had been granted its independence from Great Britain in 1974, and for the next five years remained essentially out of sight and out of mind under the strong, if repressive, leadership of Prime Minister Eric Gairy, an anticommunist stalwart. In March of 1979 Gairy was toppled in a bloodless coup led by Bishop, then thirty-four, the charismatic leader of the New Jewel Movement. Bishop allied himself closely with Fidel Castro, who soon dispatched a number of troops and Soviet weapons to Grenada.

In November Bishop announced that Castro would help Grenada build a new airport with a 10,000–foot runway, ostensibly to boost the island's fledgling tourist trade. Washington's fears about the true purpose of the expanded airport seemed confirmed in May of 1980 when Deputy Prime Minister Bernard Coard traveled to Moscow to sign a treaty giving the Soviets permission to land their TU–95 reconnaissance planes at the airport when it was finished.

President Reagan had monitored the situation in Grenada closely and in a 1982 meeting in Barbados with Caribbean allies took note of their concerns about spreading communism in neighboring Grenada. Strategically, the administration feared it was now looking at a "Red Triangle" in the hemisphere, consisting of Cuba to the north, Nicaragua to the west and Grenada to the east.

In March of 1983 Reagan had responded with irritation to critics who had questioned his concern about the tranquil, 133-square-mile island populated by just over one hundred thousand people. "It isn't nutmeg that's at stake in the Caribbean and Central America," Reagan said. "It's U.S. national security." In a television speech thirteen days later Reagan displayed a classified photograph of the continuing airport construction, along with Cuban military barracks, and asked: "Grenada doesn't even have an air force. Who is this intended for? The Soviet-Cuban militarization of Grenada can only be seen as power projection into the region."

In June, Bishop had traveled to Washington without invitation and met with Judge Clark at the NSC in an effort to cool tensions and perhaps reach a rapprochement of sorts with the administration. What followed that initiative was the October coup, led by Coard, and the subsequent murder of Bishop. The new government, when it organized, was likely to be even more anti-American and pro-Cuban/Soviet.

It was against this backdrop that the morning after Bishop's killing the administration's crisis-management structure began swinging into action. McFarlane's deputy, Poindexter, convened the so-called Crisis Preplanning Group, or CPPG, which in this case included North, Motley, Clarridge, several key Pentagon people and Constantine Menges, an ultraconservative who had just transferred to the NSC two weeks earlier from the CIA and quickly seized on the Grenada issue.

Menges, a former Hudson Institute scholar who had worked on the Reagan campaign, had been recruited by Director Casey to be his national intelligence officer for Latin America. Though Menges made his mark at the agency as a formidable intellect, his ideological fervor and tendency to see a Soviet hand behind every world event that was adverse to Washington's interests soon alienated many of his CIA colleagues, who began calling him "Constant Menace."

So Casey arranged to have him transferred to the NSC, where he could have more influence under Clark. Menges had been enthusiastic over the prospect of working for a smaller, more flexible organization like the NSC, and for Clark, whom he regarded as an energetic implementer of the president's conservative agenda. But then Clark had promptly resigned, leaving Menges working for McFarlane, whom he regarded as a pragmatic wimp unduly influenced by the State Department.

Still, it was Menges who initially took the bull by the horns on Grenada. He drafted a quick rescue plan to get the Americans off the island. But while the U.S. was at it, Menges argued, it should not lose this opportunity to topple the fledgling new communist regime and restore democracy to Grenada. Safety of the students would be the ideal pretext for a major administration statement of its resolve to roll back communism around the world, and particularly in his hemisphere. It could be round one of the Reagan Doctrine. Opportunity was knocking.

That evening Vice-President George Bush convened a meeting of the Special Situations Group, the administration's highest-ranking crisis management unit, which included senior White House staff, cabinet officials and representatives of the Joint Chiefs of Staff. The specter of the American students being taken hostage in an Iran redux was discussed. The group agreed to divert a twenty-one-ship navy flotilla headed by the aircraft carrier *Independence*, then bound for Lebanon, to the Caribbean in case it was needed. Sentiment began building for an all-out invasion. Gen. John Vessey, chairman of the Joint Chiefs of Staff, said that a surgical strike just to rescue the Americans would be difficult without securing the whole island. It seemed a case of in for a nickel, in for a dime.

"Hey, fuck it," Casey reportedly said at one point. "Let's dump these bastards."

A few of the less bold dared to point out that the administration needed further legal justification for a full-scale invasion. Fear for the students' safety and the questionable purposes of the elongated airport runway were not enough. North was one of those who pressed an idea that filled in the last legal blank.

The solution lay with the six-nation Organization of Eastern Caribbean States (OECS)—Antigua, Dominica, St. Vincent, St. Lucia, St. Kitts-Nevis and Montserrat—which were meeting in

Barbados the next day, October 21, to discuss the implications of the coup in Grenada. Leaders of the countries, worried that they too might be vulnerable to Havana-induced revolutionary movements, were sent word by Washington that the chances of the United States intervening militarily in Grenada would be enhanced if the U.S. received an official request from OECS to do so. The leaders voted unanimously to make the request and, with Jamaica and Barbados, offered to provide a token three-hundred-man landing force to accompany an American invasion.

However transparent a justification, some felt the OECS' formal request for assistance and offer to participate in an invasion improved the administration's legal position with regard to international law while bettering its public relations position.

That night North and Menges spent several hours drafting a National Security Decision Directive ordering an invasion under the president's name. Reagan, not known to let a minicrisis stand in the way of a minivacation, had proceeded with plans to take a long golfing weekend in Augusta, Georgia, along with Shultz and McFarlane. The NSDD was sent down to Augusta for the president's signature, but he decided to sleep on it overnight before signing.

Roger Fontaine, whose title as head of the NSC's Latin American section had been assumed by Menges, was nonetheless still active on Latin American issues and played a role in the Grenada crisis, working closely with North. That Friday all three men took an informal poll among themselves on whether the president would actually order the invasion or not. They put three pieces of paper in a sealed envelope. Fontaine said Reagan would go ahead. North said he would not. Menges hedged his bets and said the chances were fifty-fifty.

The next morning, Saturday, October 22, Bush, Poindexter, North, Menges, Motley and John McMahon—who had replaced Admiral Inman as deputy director of the CIA— met in Room 208, the new command post in the Executive Office Building. Using secure telephone speaker hookups they conferred with Reagan, Shultz and McFarlane in Georgia and thrashed through their options again. Within a few hours a consensus was reached on going ahead with a full-scale invasion of Grenada that would not only rescue the Americans on the island but topple the new government and restore democracy.

As North sat down to the nitty-gritty work of facilitating the Joint Chiefs of Staff's interaction with the White House in mapping out the actual plan of attack, he continued a series of contacts he had begun eight days before with one Kevin Kattke, a thirty-five-year-old maintenance engineer for Macy's department store on Long Island. After hours, Kattke was a right-wing ideologue and adventurer who made a hobby of getting involved in any cause or caper he could to damage the interests of the Soviet Union and help what he considered to be the interests of Uncle Sam.

Kattke had begun dabbling in Caribbean politics several years earlier when a stockbroker friend with a similar taste for adventure, George Hebert, had gotten him involved with right-wing Jamaican dissidents plotting, some said, to overthrow Socialist Prime Minister Michael Manley. Kattke and another friend went to Jamaica, met others of their philosophical stripe and just generally hung out. Then they called the CIA and reported on what they had learned. To their astonishment, the agents actually listened, prompting Kattke and company to speculate about the quality of U.S. intelligence in general.

When Edward Seaga, a conservative, was elected prime minister of Jamaica in 1980, Kattke moved on to other causes. He organized an anti-Iran demonstration on Long Island at the height of the hostage crisis, and sold IRAN SUCKS T-shirts on Wall Street. Then, in late 1981, Hebert introduced Kattke to Michael Sylvester, the former assistant attorney general of Grenada. Sylvester had left his homeland just before Maurice Bishop came to power in 1979 and was a leader of a group of several thousand Grenadian exiles who had come to the United States to flee communism and settled mostly in New York City. Now, with a few other exiles, Sylvester was trying to mount a coup against Bishop, so Hebert asked Kattke if he would take Sylvester down to Washington, introduce him around to some powers that be, and see if they couldn't generate a little interest in the anti-Bishop cause. To give Sylvester more legitimacy, Kattke helped create a group called the Grenadian Movement for Freedom and Democracy, with Sylvester as its leader.

One of the people Kattke and Sylvester met with on that trip was Constantine Menges, then still the CIA's national intelligence officer for Latin America. Menges had lunch with the two men and basically just listened, filing the information away for future use.

Meanwhile Kattke kept immersing himself in Grenada, adopting the exiles' anticommunist cause as his own. He said he also made contacts on the NSC, including Alfonso Sapia-Bosch, the staffer who had accompanied North on a trip to El Salvador with Special

Envoy Richard Stone. Kattke had submitted a long and prescient memo predicting that Bernard Coard would lead an attempt to oust Bishop as the latter become more moderate. The memo elaborated on Kattke's thoughts about how the United States might mount a countercoup, warned that the students on the island were increasingly unsafe, and also supplied some detailed intelligence information such as the activities of Russian and East German military advisors on Grenada.

Kattke said Sapia-Bosch invited him to the White House, listened to him further, then warned him that his schemes were a violation of the Neutrality Act forbidding private citizens from destabilizing governments at peace with the United States. Kattke knew about the Neutrality Act; he had been spending time the past several years working to circumvent it. But there was a greater good, he thought. "It may have been an awful act, but not an evil deed . . ." he said of his would-be coup. "It's a very trying situation when you feel a country so close to the United States that had democratic values the same as we do losing their personal freedoms. It gets you very upset."

Later Kattke and friends made a more substantive Grenadian contact when they were introduced to Lucky Bernard, the island's acting police commissioner who had come to the United States for medical treatment. Bishop had stripped Bernard of much of his authority, so Bernard was willing to supply Kattke some information on Cuban troop movements, detailed maps and photos of the airport runway Cuban soldiers were helping to build. Kattke passed on the intelligence to contacts in the Pentagon, but no one wanted to meet with Bernard. Still, all the information Kattke had been supplying may have been having its effect; President Reagan, in the spring of 1983, began talking publicly about Grenada more and more.

Then the night of October 13, night of the same day Maurice Bishop was placed under house arrest at the beginning of the coup led by Coard, Kattke received a phone call at home from Menges. Menges wanted to contact Sylvester and other Grenadian exiles. Kattke gave him the phone numbers, then Menges asked him to call Oliver North at the White House in the morning. North would be waiting for Kattke's call, Menges added.

Having finally attained the White House imprimatur, Kattke was bursting with excitement the next morning when he called North's office at 8:30 sharp. In fact, he didn't want his buddies thinking he'd gone off the deep end, so he asked a few of them to listen in on the conversation on extension phones. He wanted witnesses. "It's very hard to go through something like this when you're a working-class individual," says Kattke. "You feel you need support. Can you understand that?"

North got right to the point. The administrative office of the St. George University School of Medicine on Grenada was in Bay Shore, Long Island, where Kattke worked. North needed a complete list of the students who were on the island, along with their parents' names and phone numbers, and he asked if Kattke could persuade the school's board of directors to order the students home. It was getting too dangerous down there. Will do, Kattke said immediately, apparently thrilled by the notion of participating in a national security mission

He and Hebert arranged to see the chancellor of the medical school, Charles Modica. They had to admit it seemed odd that North, with the full weight of the White House behind him, didn't simply call Modica himself, but he must have had his reasons, they concluded. North had explained the U.S. wanted the school to quit the island voluntarily, without being officially requested to do so by Washington.

Modica was skeptical of Kattke's bonafides and resisted repeated suggestions that he call North's White House office if he had doubts. He had been dealing with the State Department, he said, and they had not told him an evacuation was necessary. Modica asked Kattke and Hebert to leave.

Kattke reported back to North that he had failed, but the two nonetheless stayed in close touch over the next several days. Events were moving swiftly on Grenada, and Kattke now seemed to be North's best source of information into the Grenadian exile community.

On Saturday, after the decision to launch an invasion had been finalized, North called Kattke again and asked if he could persuade the Grenadian expatriates to set up a government-in-exile. The White House had to begin thinking about how the island would be governed after the invasion was completed. Kattke, for whom no request or assignment was unmanageable, assured North he would see to it.

Kattke got on the phone and primed his contacts, but at a rally in Brooklyn on Sunday attended by a few hundred exiles, no one was willing to go nearly so far as to proclaim a new government. Rather, fearing further bloodshed, they voted merely to send telegrams to the United Nations condemning the violence. Kattke had to call North back and say that he had failed again.

That same day, October 23, half a world away from Washington and Grenada, a terrorist on a suicide mission drove a truck loaded with dynamite into the American Marine headquarters in Beirut, killing 241 Marines. It was an incomprehensible tragedy that immediately triggered a round of recriminating national debate about the purpose of the Marines being there in the first place, the rules of engagement governing their assignment and the exposure of their position at the Beirut airport. As the White House and the nation mourned, planning for Grenada was frozen.

North, shaken by the bombing, thought the president should nevertheless go ahead with Grenada but feared he would not. Some argued that the invasion should be scrapped because it would look as if the U.S. were picking on a tiny Caribbean backwater to win an easy victory that would deflect attention from the Beirut debacle. But Reagan held firm and ordered the Grenada operation to proceed.

North worked nearly around the clock, helping to plan the final details of the invasion. His recommendation that the Pentagon use only Marines in the operation had been overruled. Each service wanted a piece of the action and would be given some. It was better for morale that way. Undaunted, North continued in his role as general facilitator for the invasion's planning.

"He had as large a role as anyone in the White House did," recalls McFarlane. "The uniformed military, before it comes over and briefs the president on the options in any crisis, wants to know the lay of the land at the White House. They don't want to tell the old man something he doesn't want to hear, or at least be able to answer his questions. Ollie filled that role and he was kind of an in-house plans officer the Pentagon could call before they went into their own deliberations to get a very clear sense of what the president's sentiments were.

"Also, we didn't have anyone in the embassy in Grenada at the time, and our interests were maintained in Barbados, which is quite a ways away. Ollie made sure our ambassador there worked with the military. Plus he made the intelligence community work well with the military. And when the military came up with a problem that they were too embarrassed to admit they didn't know the answer to—like specifics on the beach in Grenada, what is the beach gradient, where are some beaches we can get a track vehicle over—Ollie would get the answer from the CIA and put two guys together in the same room, whereas it wouldn't have happened if he didn't do it."

Though he had failed in most everything he had been asked to do so far, Kattke still had North's attention. Maybe North saw a bit of himself in Kattke—a can-do, action-oriented guy with plenty of moxie. In a later interview with the FBI, North characterized Kattke as "a right-wing ideologue... like a rogue CIA agent who has no identifiable ties with the U.S. government."

Kattke, of course, swelled with pride to be dealing with North. Imagine someone like himself, a mere maintenance man, finding a way to ingratiate himself with the highest reaches of the White House and then to play a role in a national security crisis. That he was being listened to at all was a startling commentary on the quality of U.S. intelligence. North knew that, but using Kattke might point up the deficiencies and force someone to do something about them. North was coming to view the CIA with increasing disdain. He thought the agency was overrated and too timid. He would take help and information wherever he could get it. If someone on the outside was willing to take on a risky job, and the slow, ponderous government bureaucracy was not, then North would go outside. On Grenada, Kattke seemed like the only game in town.

When Kattke called North at the White House late Sunday night to report that the Grenadian exiles had been unwilling to proclaim a government, North was deeply disappointed. Kattke blamed himself, saying he had had to work that day. If he had been at the rally, he thought he could have persuaded some of the leaders to act more forcefully. North couldn't understand their reluctance. There had been reporters at the rally, and it would have been a public relations coup if they had seized the opportunity and sent a message to their Marxist brethren back home.

Suddenly North asked Kattke if he could arrange "Sky Red" for Monday night. In the first memo that Kattke had submitted to the NSC, which North had apparently seen, one of the things that he had said should be done the night before an invasion was to set fires all over the island which would occupy authorities and divert attention from a military landing in the early morning. He called the nighttime setting of the fires Sky Red, a term that had once been used by Grenadian slaves.

Kattke, now beside himself with excitement and knowing that an invasion must be imminent, told North he would get back to him. Kattke then called Charlie Maitlin, an exiled Grenadian auto mechanic from an old-line family who was reputed to have the best contacts on the island. Maitlin assured Kattke that Sky Red for Monday night would be no problem. Kattke called North back at his White House office about two A.M. Monday and relayed the word.

But the twenty-four-hour curfew and shoot-to-kill order on Grenada were evidently having an effect. Maitlin was unable to muster anyone out of their houses Monday night.

So the sky was black, not red, when a team of Navy SEALS first hit the beaches in Grenada in a predawn landing Tuesday, October 25, kicking off the invasion code-named Operation Urgent Fury. North, who spent the entire previous night at the White House, monitored the action in the Situation Room. Some two thousand U.S. troops took part in the operation and met stiffer-than-expected resistance. Three American helicopters, unaware that the Cuban troops had antiaircraft weapons, were shot down. In all, 19 U.S. servicemen were killed and 115 wounded.

It took about twenty-four hours for the island to be secured so that the medical students could be evacuated. North, not to mention the White House public relations men, were very concerned about how the students would react when they returned to American soil, what they would say to reporters. The administrators at the medical school back in Long Island, after all, had played down the danger and said there was no need for any evacuation.

So a key element of the plan was that intelligence briefers would accompany the transport planes that left Miami for Grenada to fly the students home. The briefers would then talk to the students in advance of their return, perhaps share with them some information that showed they had in fact been at risk, and generally put the U.S. landing in the proper context.

But North was shocked to learn that there had been a snafu in Miami and the transport planes had gone off to Grenada without the intelligence briefers. Now the students were about to land in Charleston, South Carolina, without having been told a thing. This was a wild card. What if the students got off the plane and accused the president of mounting a pointless military operation? That would play directly into the hands of administration critics who were already making that very argument.

Months later, at a Washington bar, North would give conserva-

tive adventurer and Reagan Doctrine guru Jack Wheeler—along
with several others who were also present—the following account
of what happened next:

A worried North immediately sought out President Reagan in
the living quarters of the White House to warn him that the students about to deplane had not been briefed, and to apologize in
advance for what might be a public relations nightmare.

Reagan, who was getting dressed, flipped on the TV to watch the
landing of the students in South Carolina as North worked the
phones. Reagan could not hear the television announcer and told
North to keep quiet. Then they watched as the first student got off
the plane, kissed the ground and said there was no more beautiful
sight than the United States.

Reagan walked over to North, put his arms around him and said:
"You see Ollie, I told you not to worry. You can trust Americans."

Wheeler said he was so moved that he and some of the others
present at the bar, including Conservative Caucus Chairman Howard Phillips, had tears welling in their eyes as North finished the
story, it was told with such feeling. "Ollie hugged me as he told the
story, as if he were Reagan," recalls Wheeler. "He told it so con-
vincingly. When he told the story, you were in the president's living quarters with him. You were there!"

Years later, after North attained celebrity status and the press
began churning out profiles of him, this story was widely circulated
as fact, with Wheeler the original, though always unnamed, source.
The anecdote served to add to North's stature as a man with walk-in
access to Reagan.

But on reflection, Wheeler says he now is not sure the story is
true: "Ollie can be prone to extreme exaggeration..." Wheeler
admits, laughing. "The point is, I don't know if it happened. I want
to believe it... I want that story to be true, but I'm not sure."

Marlin Fitzwater, President Reagan's press secretary, says that
North never set foot in the White House living quarters, and that
no such incident ever occurred there or anywhere else. North
never saw Reagan at all that day, Fitzwater added.

BODY & SOUL

MORE than anything else he had done to that time, North's role in the Grenada success established him as a man of rising influence within the National Security Council. He had been at the confluence of events in the epicenter of government—a key player in the crisis rubric. He had been one of the select few in the Situation Room, playing an important role in helping to bring about the most significant foreign policy victory of the Reagan administration.

To be sure there had been flaws in the Grenada operation. The preinvasion intelligence was inadequate and the performance of the military was open to question on a number of accounts. But the important thing was that a crisis had been solved, the grateful students had been rescued, Grenada had been purged of the godless communists and democracy had been restored to the island. The good guys had finally won one, and in the process the attention of the country had been at least diverted from the disaster in Beirut. Never mind the handwringing liberal criticism that the U.S. intervention in Grenada was akin to a giant swatting a gnat. A win was a win. It sent a clear message to Moscow and Havana and was an important redemption of Reagan's heretofore hollow rhetorical refrain that America was Back.

For a while North allowed himself to bask in the afterglow of Grenada. He even invited Kevin Kattke and a few of his fellow Long Island adventurers—George Hebert and Sal Imburgio—down to Washington to thank them for their efforts. Though virtually everything the Kattke team had tried failed, North was nevertheless grateful for their efforts and wanted to thank them personally. Until then he and Kattke had only been phone buddies.

Kattke and friends were now ushered into North's office, where they sat and chatted for about an hour. The office looked suitably used and disheveled, befitting a man who worked as hard as North did, the men thought. Ollie gave them a warm welcome, taking some satellite photographs off his couch so they could sit down.

Hebert presented North with a Grenadian flag that he had stolen from the country's mission at the United Nations when he and Kattke were staging a sit-in of sorts around the time of the invasion. That was a story in and of itself.

According to Kattke, the night of the invasion he had received a call at 11:00 from a man who identified himself as "Bill Casey, director of Central Intelligence." Later, comparing the voice he heard on the phone with Casey's true voice, Kattke says he thinks the caller was in fact Casey, but he cannot be sure. He said Casey first asked for the home number of Michael Sylvester, the Grenadian exile leader. Then Casey asked if Kattke could arrange to have exiles of the Sylvester stripe take over the Grenadian U.N. mission the following morning. No problem, Kattke quickly answered, per usual.

He called Sylvester and others to spread the word. He says he was assured they would show up in the morning to stage a symbolic takeover and show the world that there was a new day dawning in Grenada. Kattke and Hebert arrived at the mission at 7:45 the next morning. No Grenadians in evidence. They also noticed that there were no police around, as there had been the past few days while the sit-ins were in progress. Kattke began jimmying the lock on the front door of the mission, figuring he'd get a head start and have the place ready for the Grenadians when they showed up. Suddenly a policeman happened by and handcuffed Kattke, caught in the act of breaking and entering. Hebert, who had wandered away, freaked out when he saw his friend in handcuffs. "CIA!" he declared, invoking the agency's name as a protector, and telling anyone who would listen that they were authorized to undertake a mission in the name of national security. One of Kattke's FBI contacts came along and convinced the cops to let Kattke loose.

Sylvester, hardly cutting a committed-revolutionary swath, finally showed up around eleven A.M. apologizing that he had been partying late into the night in celebration of the liberation and had overslept.

North chuckled now, along with Kattke and the others as the story was rehashed. The boys had gotten a little carried away, was all. They talked about what lay ahead for Grenada. You couldn't just land and leave. They discussed long-range political strategies and economic development.

North made one remark that Kattke & Company found revealing. "He said he had never experienced that great moment that the soldiers going into Grenada must have felt when they were welcomed as liberators," Imburgio recalls. "He said you could be in a war and be successful at what you do, and not get any love from the local population at all. He was wistful about it."

The three men told North they were going to fly down to Grenada to see how the natives were taking to freedom. Sort of a victory tour. North smiled, wished them well and said that they were all ideologically sympatico. Kattke noted that they would be happy to be of service again in the future.

Though some questioned McFarlane's role in bringing the Marines to Beirut, negative feelings about that were mitigated by the positive fallout of the Grenada success and the role the NSC had played.

McFarlane had taken particular note of North's efforts on Grenada and appreciated them. It was widely known around the NSC that the two men were close. Plus, the secretary who had come to work for North earlier in 1983, Fawn Hall, had her own entré with the National Security Advisor's office. Her mother, Wilma Hall, was McFarlane's secretary. Some of North's more insecure colleagues were already complaining that whenever Ollie wanted access to McFarlane, all he had to do was have Fawn call mom.

Actually, North didn't need his secretary to help him gain access to McFarlane; he was already becoming the exception to the bureaucratic rule. He was being allowed to send his paperwork directly to McFarlane rather than through NSC executive secretary, Robert Kimmitt, like other staffers.

When Kimmitt called North on the end-run tactics, North would pleasantly explain that he was merely following McFarlane's instructions. "And I'd say, 'Look, I can get the paperwork in just as quickly,'" Kimmitt recalls. "And he'd say, 'Okay.' And Ollie really did try to do it, but the next day he'd get a call from Bud saying, 'Bring it over, or come and see me.' I don't think Ollie was taking it around me just to be difficult. But he basically thought he was working for the boss... Even when the electronic mail system was set up, North still had a separate bypass arrangement."

North's special deal did cause some friction and jealousy. "I didn't like it on the part of North or anyone else," Kimmitt says. "It wasn't so much resentment as the fact that I was supposed to be there and the work was supposed to go through me. I think it caused resentment on the part of staff officers who couldn't get that kind of time with McFarlane . . . I also thought Ollie was overextended. I thought he needed to pare his accounts back."

In December, continuing to raise his profile within the administration, North was chosen to accompany Vice-President Bush on a trip to El Salvador. The purpose of the trip was for Bush to convey the president's concern about the killings in Salvador that had been attributed to right-wing death squads. Thousands of Salvadorans had been killed in the previous four years by the roving teams, which were linked to the army and security forces. The murders had provoked a worldwide human-rights crusade that was causing Congress to balk at continuing to provide U.S. military aid to the Salvadoran regime. Already under siege for its Nicaraguan policy, the last thing the administration needed was for Congress to waver on Salvador, a key cog in the Central American wheel.

So Bush came to deliver the message loud and clear: unless the killings stopped, future U.S. aid was in jeopardy. Bush and some members of his party got off *Air Force 2* after it arrived at the airport in San Salvador and then flew off in several Black Hawk helicopters. A few minutes later North emerged from the plane and was greeted warmly by several Salvadoran military leaders whom he had come to know. They then boarded their own Black Hawk and took off—the working group in the official delegation.

North, like most other conservatives, initially had doubts about the death-squad issue. He thought it was largely a creation of human-rights bleeding hearts and the liberal press. But then he had taken a closer look and concluded that there were in fact rampant killings, and that the issue had to be dealt with—from a practical political standpoint if nothing else. Congressional support for U.S. aid to El Salvador now turned on the death-squad question.

So North became one of the first to begin lobbying the American conservative establishment, convincing its leaders that the death-squad problem was not just a liberal fabrication and that to continue backing the likes of Salvadoran ultrarightist Roberto D'Aubuisson was folly. New Right stalwarts like Paul Weyrich, president of the Free Congress Research and Education Foundation, and Andy Messing, then executive director of the Conservative Caucus, were convinced by North.

"I thought the death-squad stuff was communist propaganda at first," says Messing. "But when North told me about it, it was like getting hit over the head with a baseball bat. I knew North was at the information hub, and that he wouldn't lie to me. So I said it must be so."

North also briefed congressional leaders about what the administration was doing about the problem. Bush had linked continued U.S. aid to stopping the killings and had demanded that those involved in the murders be exiled. Also the U.S. was bringing some of its own investigative and intelligence-gathering resources to bear on identifying the actual killers, as well as whom they were working for. Suspects were placed under surveillance, phones were tapped, intelligence collection was generally stepped up.

The campaign worked. Given the increased investigative resources and the political ultimatums from Washington, the Salvadoran government finally cracked down, and the number of killings began to fall off dramatically. Reassured, Congress voted stepped-up military and economic aid, and the civil war began to turn in the government's favor.

North gained plaudits for leadership in cutting against the conservative grain on the issue.

By early 1984 perhaps the most complex and emotional problem facing the administration was another one of North's beats: terrorism. In the previous year there had been 393 terrorist incidents directed at Americans or American property overseas, and the number of casualties had soared off the charts: 274 persons had been killed and 118 wounded.

The suicide mission on the Marine barracks in Beirut had been the chief culprit, but there had been other spectacular attacks in 1983: in April a bomb exploded at the American embassy in Beirut killing 33 and wounding 80; then in December bombs exploded at the U.S. embassy in Kuwait.

The sad fact was that terrorism worked. It enabled obscure or often unheard-of groups to wreak havoc on great powers like the United States and reap enormous amounts of publicity for their causes. Those causes were usually esoteric, but they invariably served the interests of one country or another—like Libya, Iran or Syria, all of which were thought to aid and abet various terrorist groups. Every time the U.S. fell victim to a terrorist attack the perception grew that a darting mosquito was successfully biting a muscle-bound giant unable to do anything to counter the attacks.

American intelligence on terrorist groups was bad to nonexistent.

Terrorism was one area where the tilt toward electronic eavesdropping via satellite had left the country vulnerable. The U.S. had precious few informants inside any terrorist cells. Infiltration—someone on the ground inside the terror networks—was really the only way to know who or what you were dealing with. How could you retaliate if you didn't know whom to retaliate against? Washington could hardly take out Damascus, Tehran or Tripoli if it determined that a given attack was supported by one of those states. And hitting the elusive terrorists themselves through conventional means such as an air strike was impossible without risking the loss of many innocent civilian lives.

The Marine massacre in Beirut had caused great angst within the administration. There was much frustration and a great desire to do something to strike a blow against terrorism in both the short and long term. There was broad agreement that there had to be far better security at all U.S. installations abroad, particularly in the hotspots of the Middle East, and that there had to be much improved intelligence on the various terror networks and their operations.

But improving those two areas alone seemed too passive. There was a strong faction within the administration—surprisingly led by Secretary of State Shultz, a former Marine who had been devastated by the Beirut attack—that argued that the U.S. had to adopt a more aggressive military posture, including preemptive strikes when necessary, that could deter terrorists from attacking American targets.

The difficulty with the aggressive tack was that it invariably raised the question of assassinations. Some, including North and elements at the Pentagon, argued strongly that "surgical strikes" against known terrorists who had been identified as the culprits of one attack and perhaps the planners of another was the most effective and efficient way of dealing with the terrorist cancer. It went to the root of the problem and eliminated unnecessary civilian loss of life. This was essentially the Israeli policy.

But assassinations were against American law. Executive Order 12333, signed by Reagan during his first year in office, specified that "no person employed by or acting on behalf of the U.S. government shall engage in, or conspire to engage in, assassination." The order also prohibited the U.S. from using any surrogates to carry out such missions.

The order could be modified if Reagan wished, but more fundamentally, the assassination debate raised questions about American values and the role of a democracy that were almost theological.

Should a nation that holds democratic principles and human rights most dear engage in assassination as a matter of policy? Was not the U.S. a world power with responsibilities that prevented it from acting like, say, Israel?

Secretary of Defense Weinberger was strongly opposed to assassinations, as was the career CIA element that had gone down that road before and adapted to the post-Church Committee reformist order.

But North, positioned at the funnel to the Oval Office with terrorism in his portfolio, was well positioned to do something about the problem and to try to implement his own beliefs. So he drafted a National Security Decision Directive that authorized CIA-backed teams of foreigners to "neutralize" terrorists known to have attacked Americans or known to be planning such attacks. As North's draft directive circulated around the upper reaches of government, no one had any doubts what the euphemism "neutralize" meant.

The strongest reaction came from John McMahon, deputy director of the CIA, who read the draft at home late at night and decided not to wait until morning to express his views. He called North at home and began screaming into the phone: Hadn't North read Executive Order 12333? Was he that reckless that he would have the United States deputize a bunch of foreign cowboys to run around the world doing its dirty work? Did he care nothing for the reputation of the CIA, which had already been seared by the whole issue of assassination?

North let McMahon rant and said little before hanging up. But he considered McMahon a timid naysayer, stuck behind the curve of the emerging action—orthodoxy that was reshaping the administration. Casey agreed with North and sided against McMahon and the agency's careerists, whom the director concurred were too inclined not to take risks. Casey had the CIA's chief counsel, Stanley Sporkin, investigate the question, and Sporkin concluded that taking action against terrorists would not constitute assassination. He took the Dewey Clarridge view that the prohibition against assassinations was a political one applying to heads of state. If the president signed a finding, and if there was hard intelligence that terrorists were about to strike, then the principle of self-defense would apply, and the administration was on solid legal ground.

One of North's confidants and boosters on the terrorism issue was Noel Koch, deputy assistant secretary for international security affairs at the Department of Defense, and also director of special planning for the Pentagon—a portfolio which included terrorism.

According to Koch, it had not actually been the Marine bombing that generated the momentum on terrorism, but a July, 1983, incident in which Armenian gunmen stormed the residence of the Turkish ambassador in Lisbon, killing seven people.

"It was one of those things—an ugly bombing—that gets right down where the president lives," says Koch of Reagan. "A mother and a child were involved and the president just didn't like it. So he said, 'That's it. We're going to work with other governments and put a stop to this once and for all.' So I called Ollie and said, 'Let's do something with this—let's start to push it.' And he said, 'I'm already on it.' And he had begun drafting this thing that became NSDD 138. And now it's famous because he kept using the word 'neutralize,' and that got John McMahon to call him at home.

"Ollie was a smart guy. He had a tendency to talk like Spiro Agnew. Like he had just learned the language and he was pretty good at it. The syntax wasn't always right, and he wouldn't ever use a two-syllable word when a five-syllable one was available. And so I found him verbose. He had a funny manner about him. But he was earnest, and I thought he was honest, and he was a voice at the other end of the telephone. He reported back what was going on and could slide things under the door for you. You need a guy like that. At least I do. And so since McFarlane was just kind of a space cadet, and Poindexter was covering up that he was totally at sea, who could you deal with? . . . If Ollie was there, and he was steady, of course you dealt with Ollie, and pretty soon, lots of people did."

Meanwhile, as North's antiterrorism manifesto lay in the rewrite stage, events seemed to keep dictating a stronger U.S. position. On March 16, 1984, the CIA station chief in Beirut, William Buckley, was kidnapped by a pro-Iranian terrorist group calling itself Islamic Jihad. Casey and the White House immediately regarded the kidnapping as a serious threat to American interests. Buckley had extensive knowledge of CIA operations throughout the Middle East and had been sent to Beirut the previous summer to rebuild Washington's regional intelligence network, which had been severely damaged when several CIA agents were killed in the bombing of the embassy in Beirut.

The Buckley kidnapping was a watershed. It set into motion a series of events that would lead Washington to violate its own policy against shipping arms to Iran, and it was one in rash of more than a dozen kidnappings of American citizens in Beirut that would take place over the next three years. The man who would be given day-to-day responsibility for trying to free those hostages was North.

The following month, when the draft directive on terrorism surfaced again, North's term "neutralize" had been deleted, despite the legal opinion from CIA that assassinating terrorists could be finessed. In search of greater consensus, McFarlane proposed further study on the terrorism question from various government agencies. This call for more planning was incorporated into National Security Decision Directive 138, which Reagan signed on April 3, 1984. The directive nonetheless approved the principle of retaliatory and preemptive strikes, and Shultz began speaking publicly about the need for taking such steps in fighting terrorism—generating many headlines in the process. North thought his point had been made, with or without the word "neutralize."

Administration hopes that the expanded, more general finding on covert action in Nicaragua, which President Reagan had signed in September of 1983, would quiet debate over the Central American policy were short-lived. In October, 1983, the House voted to cut off all aid to paramilitary groups fighting in Nicaragua, but since the Senate wanted the aid continued, a compromise was reached. In December, Congress agreed to place a ceiling of $24 million on funding for the Contras in fiscal year 1984, also barring the CIA from using its contingency reserves to sweeten the pot.

While it still had money in hand, the White House decided to step up paramilitary attacks against Nicaragua in early 1984. The harbor mining operations planned earlier were implemented, and an air attack was launched against a Sandinista communications and naval arms depot.

North, in a series of memorandums written between October 1983 and March of 1984, outlined in detail the operations of the CIA in the Central American region. North on one occasion advised McFarlane to have the president increase by 3,000 the number of weapons supplied to the Contras. Reagan agreed. North also reported the results of paramilitary operations, including the February attack on the naval arms depot. "Well done," scrawled Poindexter in a note back to North.

North continued to propose significant military actions against the Sandinistas, careful to offer his superiors assurances that the measures lay within the ambiguous scope of the presidential finding, which allowed such actions if they were intended to promote a diplomatic solution. But the various operations cost a good deal of money, and the $24 million was being rapidly depleted. On February 13 North wished, in a memo to McFarlane, for "relief from the $24M ceiling" but was realistic enough to admit that "we may have to reassess our prospects and decide whether prudence requires that we somehow stretch our FY–84 effort to avoid running out of funds." He concluded that unless Congress appropriated additional money, Contra activities would have to be sharply cut back by May or June.

The administration requested $21 million in supplemental aid, but in April the harbor mining operations were disclosed, causing a furor in Congress and effectively killing any chances that more money would be appropriated. Casey went up to Capitol Hill to concede that Congress had been inadequately briefed and to "apologize profoundly," but the damage had been done. The purse strings were cut.

Still, the White House was determined to continue supporting the Contras—with or without the blessing of Congress. McFarlane would later testify that the president directed him to have the NSC keep the Contras together "body and soul" until Congress could be convinced to authorize more money. McFarlane assigned the task to North.

"I was given the job of holding them together body and soul," North would later testify before Congress. "To keep them together as a viable political opposition, to keep them alive in the field, to bridge the time when we would have no money and the time when the Congress would vote again, to keep the effort alive, because the president committed publicly to go back, in his words, again and again and again, to support the Nicaraguan resistance."

The body-and-soul charge from the president, via McFarlane, was pivotal—perhaps the most significant commitment to be made during North's tenure at the NSC, since it formed the basis for most of the actions he would undertake on behalf of the Contras over the next two and a half years—in the United States, Central America and Iran. Given this broad mandate, North ran a long way with it. To carry out the mission, he would essentially be allowed to fill in all operational details as he saw fit.

* * *

The immediate problem was where and how to get more money to fund the Contras if Congress was not going to provide it. The administration decided to ask other countries for support.

As early as February, North had suggested tapping allies for assistance. McFarlane, while officially rejecting the idea, unofficially began exploring it. McFarlane made an initial feeler to Israel but was rebuffed. On March 27, McFarlane met with Casey to discuss foreign support in greater detail. Casey enthusiastically supported the notion of asking allies for help, and in a memorandum written to McFarlane the same day suggested Israel and South Africa as likely targets. He said South African officials had already been approached and the initial reaction was positive. Casey also suggested in the memo that rich American benefactors might be solicited, and a foundation established to receive their private contributions.

McFarlane sent an aide to Israel to make a formal request for assistance, but again the request was denied. In April, Casey dispatched Dewey Clarridge to South Africa to try and nail down a commitment from Pretoria, but the visit was made at the height of the furor over the harbor mining, so Clarridge was directed to come home. The timing was bad; seeing the tumult in Washington, South Africa would be nervous about what it was getting into.

By May, with the $24 million just about to run out, McFarlane turned to someone he felt might come through for Washington: Prince Bandar, Saudi Arabia's ambassador to the United States. The two men knew each other well, having traveled together on secret diplomatic missions in the Middle East, and they met periodically to discuss subjects of mutual interest. Bandar had been happy to see McFarlane elevated to National Security Advisor. Though McFarlane was no Kissinger, Bandar thought he could still be a decent conduit to Reagan of Saudi concerns.

McFarlane went to see Bandar at his estate in suburban McLean, Virginia. Over a drink, McFarlane laid his cards on the table. Funds for the Contras were running out. The U.S. had invested its prestige in their cause and could not let them go down the chute, not without seriously damaging its credibility in Central America and beyond. McFarlane never actually asked, but Bandar knew he was being solicited. Before long the ambassador had pledged $1 million per month as a "humanitarian gesture" to sustain the Contras through the end of the year. There was no stated quid pro quo. But Bandar knew that helping the U.S. out of a jam could pay large dividends down the road in any manner of unspoken quids.

Bandar flew home to Saudi Arabia, obtained formal approval of
the deal from King Fahd, then drew a government check for $8
million. McFarlane assigned North to arrange the transfer of the
money to the Contras. Before long, North handed his boss a note-
card with the number of a Contra bank account in the Cayman
Islands. McFarlane met Bandar at the White House on June 22 and
handed him the card. Bandar then went to Geneva and personally
arranged the transfer of the funds through a Swiss bank.

McFarlane informed Reagan of the Saudi contribution shortly
after it was made. At the regular morning briefing, the National
Security Advisor slipped a note into the briefing book with a message on it for the president to read. McFarlane testified later he
chose to communicate with Reagan in this way so as to retain maximum secrecy and avoid telling anyone else present in the Oval
Office at the time. McFarlane also withheld news of the Saudi contribution from the secretaries of state and defense.

On June 25, three days after the McFarlane-Bandar meeting, the
National Security Planning Group—containing the highest ranking
officials in government—gathered to discuss the question of third-
country aid to the Contras. On hand were the president, Bush,
Shultz, Weinberger, Meese, Casey and McFarlane. Casey made a
strong pitch for seeking foreign assistance to skirt Congress, but
Shultz responded that White House Chief of Staff James Baker had
warned him that it would be an "impeachable offense" for the U.S.
to act as a conduit for third-country funding of the Contras—
thereby thwarting the intent of the Boland Amendment and the
$24 million cap. But Casey said foreign contributions were permis-
sible as long as they were made directly, not through the United
States government. McFarlane advised that no one should do anything, pending an opinion from the Department of Justice.

Neither McFarlane nor anyone else mentioned that the Saudi
contribution had already been arranged. And although McFarlane
had asked members of the Planning Group to do nothing further on
the foreign assistance issue for the moment, that did not stop North
from arranging the transfer of the Saudi funds to Contra leader
Adolfo Calero that very day. North instructed Calero that he was
not to tell anyone in his organization or the CIA about the amount,
the source or even the availability of the new funds.

North went ahead with the transfer arrangements and the instructions to Calero despite being told by Dewey Clarridge about
the Planning Group discussion in which Shultz had raised the

specter of impeachment if the U.S. were found to have been funneling money to the Contras via a third country.

Though the question of soliciting foreign aid was not explicitly
addressed in Congress during debate leading up to the $24 million
cap, there could be no mistaking congressional intent. Representative Boland said the $24 million represented a "cap on funding from
whatever source." And Representative J. Kenneth Robinson of Virginia, then the senior Republican on the House Intelligence Committee, said the cap meant that "no additional funding could be
made available . . . unless additional authorization and/or appropriations are approved by both Houses."

But in April, when press accounts speculated that the administration was secretly turning to its allies to fund the Contras, Congress called for an explanation. Casey led the stonewalling. On May
2, appearing before the House Intelligence Committee, the director denied that the U.S. was seeking outside help. This was five
weeks after Casey's memo to McFarlane calling for efforts to approach Israel and South Africa, and just a week after his "profound
apology" to Congress for his lack of candor over the harbor mining.
Casey's most recent statement was another indication of the depth
of White House resolve to aid the Contras. Congress would not be
informed of the Saudi donation until 1987.

As it became increasingly apparent that the CIA would be
phased out of the Contra operation and North phased in, Ollie
began dealing directly with the Contra leadership. In May, at a
meeting in Tegucigalpa, Honduras, Dewey Clarridge had introduced North to the hierarchy. The Contras, who knew Clarridge by
the alias of "Moroni," always treated him with the respect they felt
he deserved. Clarridge had, after all, been their lifeline for three
years. Still, they seemed rather bemused by Dewey's flashy silk
shirts and his blustery manner. He often told them that he had
access to President Reagan twice a week, and that Reagan loved to
hear how the war was going. Clarridge always addressed them in
English, speaking slowly so that he could be readily translated into
Spanish. Then he talked about North: "If something happens in
Congress, we will have an alternative way, and to assure that, here
is Colonel North. You will never be abandoned."

With the windfall from the Saudis, North set about the task of
establishing a more organized system for channeling weapons,
equipment, combat gear and other materiel support to the Contras.

Until now, despite official U.S. assistance, it had largely been a catch-as-catch-can operation. To create this necessary support-infrastructure, North needed an experienced combat veteran, preferably someone with covert-operations experience who could keep his mouth shut. And if, as seemed likely, Congress soon banned all CIA and Pentagon assistance to the Contras, there would have to be private-sector support. As long as a private organization was giving aid to the Contras, North and his superiors could argue that the law was being complied with. North would later testify that it was Casey who suggested to him the ideal man for the job: retired Air Force Maj. Gen. Richard Secord.

Secord was a legendary, if controversial, figure in military circles who moved easily with soldiers, senators, sultans and spies. A graduate of West Point, Secord had taken his commission in the air force and gone on to become one of the earliest participants in the war in Vietnam, where in 1962 he logged more than two hundred combat missions as a fighter pilot. He returned to Southeast Asia in 1966 and until 1968 was assigned to the CIA in Laos, where he helped run the agency's secret war.

Secord's other area of interest was Iran. He served as an advisor to the Iranian air force from 1963 to 1965, and from 1975 to 1978 was head of the U.S. Air Force's advisory group in Tehran. Back in Washington, Secord rose quickly through Pentagon ranks and was picked for numerous sensitive assignments.

In 1980 he was involved in setting up a secret U.S. air base in the Egyptian desert that was used as a staging area in the failed attempt to rescue the American hostages in Iran, and he was deputy to a second planned rescue mission of the hostages that was never carried out. When Reagan took office in 1981 Secord became the first noncivilian to be named deputy assistant secretary of defense for international security affairs, in charge of the Near East, Africa and South Asia. It was from this position that he had served as one of the administration's point men in the successful effort to win Senate confirmation of the 1981 AWACs sale to Saudi Arabia.

But after that, Secord fell on hard times as a result of his association with Edwin Wilson, the renegade ex-CIA agent now serving a fifty-two-year federal prison sentence for shipping weaponry to Libya in the 1970s.

In 1982 Secord was suspended in connection with an investigation into his role in the awarding of a $71 million contract to the now-defunct Egyptian American Transport and Services Corporation (EATSCO), a company formed in 1979 to ship arms to Egypt in the aftermath of the Camp David accords between Israel and Cairo.

Fifty-one percent of EATSCO was owned by an Egyptian concern, while the owner of record of the remaining forty-nine percent was Thomas Clines, a former CIA executive and longtime associate of both Wilson and Secord. Actually, according to Wilson, he, Clines, Theodore Shackley (another former CIA executive who had been deputy director of the operations diversion), Secord and one of Secord's colleagues at the Pentagon all had silent one-fifth shares in the minority interest. Wilson said he provided the start-up capital as part of a scheme that called for Secord—who in 1979 was director of military assistance and sales for the air force—and his colleague to use their influence to steer the lucrative military sales contract to EATSCO, the company in which by then they all had an interest.

EATSCO later pleaded guilty to inflating its bills to the Pentagon by $8 million. Secord, who strongly denies Wilson's conflict-of-interest allegations, was investigated by the Justice Department, which opted not to bring any charges against him. He was ordered reinstated to his job at the Pentagon, but apparently concluded that e had no future in the air force as a result of the EATSCO affair and his brush with Wilson, and in 1983 retired.

He took a job as a partner in Stanford Technology Trading Group International, a Vienna, Virginia, electronic-and-security-systems export firm. Secord's partner at Stanford Technology was Albert Hakim, an Iranian expatriate that Wilson had introduced him to in Tehran during the 1970s. In traditional Washington revolving-door fashion, Secord had, it seemed, been parlaying his political, military, diplomatic and intelligence contacts into a profitable business when the call came from North in July of 1984.

North asked if Secord would come meet with him at the Executive Office Building, and Secord agreed. After minimal small talk, North asked if the general would meet with Adolfo Calero, the Contra leader, and explore the possibility of private assistance for the Contras while the government was out of the business.

Secord again agreed and met with Calero later that month in North's office. North introduced Secord as a retired general experienced in special operations. Calero, who prior to the revolution in Nicaragua had worked as a Coca-Cola bottler, was in no mood to turn down any bona-fide offer of assistance. After this initial meeting Secord met again with Calero about a week later at a hotel near National Airport in Washington. This time Secord brought along a few of his experts to talk with Calero—Tom Clines and Raphael "Chi Chi" Quintero, a Cuban who was a longtime friend of both

Clines and Ed Wilson. Quintero had been a contract agent for the CIA dating back to the Bay of Pigs days.

Calero said that his arsenal of arms was in bad shape, and the prices he had been quoted by the CIA for new weapons were too high. He said the Contras were carrying three types of assault rifles. Secord advised him to standardize his arsenal as much as possible to avoid maintenance and logistics problems. Calero agreed to give Secord a list of the weapons and ammunition he had, along with the prices quoted him by the CIA.

Later Calero brought the list to Secord, who gave it to a Canadian arms dealer for analysis. Calero was right. The prices did seem exorbitant—over $300 per rifle. Secord, after consulting with his partner, Hakim, agreed to provide the weapons Calero wanted for less than $150 each. He ordered AK–47s from Poland and Romania, G–3s from Portugal and ammunition from China.

"The CIA had been with these people several years, yet formed no infrastructure with which they could sustain themselves," Secord recalls. "They dealt only with the *commandantes*. The other half of the job is viewed as mundane by the Rambo-types, but believe me, it's the sinews of war." Secord assigned Quintero to work with the Contra leadership and report back to him. Secord would then keep North apprised.

In striking an arrangement to work together, North and Secord did not discuss in detail the question of how much Secord would be paid, other than agreeing that the general was entitled to fair compensation. For the moment Secord would essentially be acting as a broker for the Contras to obtain arms and materiel. He was undertaking a foreign-policy initiative on behalf of the United States but being paid with the Saudi funds. The line between the public and private sectors was blurred, but the participants liked it that way. The general called his Contra-support operation "The Enterprise."

Though the tapping of Secord and, by extension, the equally Wilson-tainted Clines and Quintero, would years later be assailed as an incomprehensible return to a discredited old-boy network and an irresponsible privatizing of foreign policy, to North and Casey it seemed only logical. They, after all, were the true 1-1 believers on the frontlines being asked to keep the Contras patched together while, a spineless Congress shackled them. The operation had to go private to continue, and Secord was a pro. It was as simple as that.

North liked Secord. The general was a no-nonsense, action-or-

iented patriot who had disdain for timid bureaucrats and was prepared to go over them to get things done. He and Ollie were cut
from the same cloth. And if North had had any doubts, they were
dispelled by Casey, who had recommended Secord by saying that
he was a doer who had been unfairly tarred by his ties with Wilson.

If there was anyone North had come to admire, it was Casey.
Indeed, he seemed in awe of the director.

"I respected him as a man of incredible experience," North
would later testify. "Probably the most well-read man I have ever
met and dealt with on a direct, face-to-face basis. I watched Director Casey, on trips when I'd travel with him, read an entire book in
one plane flight... As I recall it was Paul Johnson's book, *Modern
Times*... And then I noticed he was working on the yellow legal
pad as we were flying along. And I said, 'What'd you do with the
book?' He said, 'I'm tired of reading. I've decided to write my
own...'."

To North, Casey was not just a man of action, a former OSS
stalwart trying to rebuild the CIA. He was also a man who gave
intellectual breadth, a unifying *raison d'être* and a coherent world
view of the administration. He had stature.

Casey, for his part, was always quick to spot and make use of an
ally. From the outset North had struck him as a dynamic go-getter
who craved the action—sort of a younger Dewey Clarridge—
and who was well-positioned at the NSC to do the things that too
many at the CIA were either unwilling or lacked the *chutzpah* to
do.

Casey kept an office down the hall from North's at the EOB and
began seeing more and more of the young Marine officer. North
would seek him out for counseling on this problem or that, and
Casey would always give him advice, such as tipping him off about
Secord, telling him to go private with the entire Contra operation,
or warning him that his calls to Central America were likely being
intercepted by the KGB from a Cuban monitoring station.

Occasionally, North and Casey would walk across Pennsylvania
Avenue from the White House and meet with Contra leaders at a
government-owned townhouse that was officially a residence for
former presidents. There was a secure conference room there, and
unlike the EOB, visitors were not required to sign in.

Some of Casey's top subordinates began to take notice of the
director's close relationship with North. "I remember sitting in the
office and hearing Ollie North call Casey, and talk to him, and
Casey would talk to him," Clair George, who would replace John

McMahon as deputy director for operations, later told the congressional Iran-Contra committees. "Oliver North... had guts in approaching anybody, anywhere, any time, in any conditions, without any concern about their title, rank—you know, we all grew up that you don't just storm into the CEO's office the third day with the company, and Ollie did it. Bill Casey liked Ollie North... He liked action people. Bill Casey was the last great buccaneer from OSS. He was dropping agents into Germany and France and saving lives when most of us were doing nothing. This was a great guy, Bill Casey, and he saw in Ollie North a part of that."

George said North would sometimes exploit his close relationship with Casey. If George refused a North entreaty on some subject or other, Ollie would call and make a pitch directly to the Director, often getting Casey's okay and "end-running" George.

Casey would become yet another father figure in North's life. In fact, when North's own father died on June 20, 1984, Casey was one of the only three government officials who expressed condolences (Vice-President Bush and Admiral Pointdexter were the others). In the coming months, as North's activities became more and more secret, Casey would become one of the few persons he would confide in and evidently take direction from. Casey could negotiate the bureaucratic tightrope of effectively using North for his own ends while not arousing any undue suspicion from McFarlane or Poindexter. Gradually, North would become, in effect, Casey's Washington station chief.

"Bill Casey was someone who became very intimate with Ollie— I didn't think that at the time, but I think it's true today," says McFarlane. "I thought we [the NSC] were as covered by Boland as the CIA and Defense were, and I think probably Casey did too. But Bill had nothing but contempt for the Congress and looked at things rather like Ollie did—that there is a moral issue and we should do the right thing here.

"And if North was good at it, it didn't matter if he was in the Pentagon or the White House or the CIA. North ought to be helped... I think Casey saw in North someone who was first of all tireless, discreet enough and a good operative and who had a passion for this like he did...

"I have a theory about Bill. He learned about his terminal state about two years before he died, and I think it's likely he thought that through and determined that he would try to make sure that the president, his friend Ronald Reagan, didn't lose this one, this Nicaraguan issue. And he thought beyond that that he didn't want to implicate the president. He never said so, he never told me, and I don't think he told the president what he was doing. But I think he wanted the president's policy to succeed. He worked very closely with Ollie in fundraising and operationally, to make it easy where he could."

Before linking up with Secord, North had made another reach into the private sector, this time for a thirty-year-old accolyte who would serve as his liaison and man Friday with the Contras.

Robert Owen was a preppie version of Kevin Kattke. He was the youngest of three sons born well to Dwight Owen—a Providence, Rhode Island, textile executive—and his wife Kathryn, a kind and genial woman who worked selflessly as a community activist and who, in the best traditions of *noblesse oblige*, instilled the same values in her boys.

Young Rob was only thirteen when his oldest brother Dwight was killed in Vietnam during a battle between the Vietcong and South Vietnamese district officials. But Dwight was not a combatant soldier; he was a State Department official. The killing had a telling effect on Rob, who vowed to carry on his brother's ideals and avenge his death by opposing communism in any way he could.

After prep school, where at six foot four and about two hundred twenty-five pounds he was more interested in football and lacrosse than academe, Rob matriculated to Stanford, where he majored in political science. He defied the anti-Vietnam spirit of the day and tried to enlist in the Marine Corps but was rejected because of a bad knee.

After college Owen applied some of his anticommunist zeal by helping Cambodian refugees through the International Rescue Committee in Thailand. In 1982 he came to Washington and went to work as a legislative aide to Sen. Dan Quayle, the arch-conservative Republican from Indiana.

One summer afternoon in 1983 two men showed up at Quayle's office trying to drum up support for the Contra cause: John Hull, an Evansville, Indiana, native who had moved to Costa Rica where he raised cattle, and Luis Rivas, a Contra fighting in southern Nicaragua under Eden Pastora. It was late afternoon, around quitting time, and no one was exactly eager to talk to Hull and Rivas. But Owen met with them, and before long, as he listened to the men speak passionately about the Contras and what they were trying to do, young Rob, it seemed, had found himself a new cause.

He took Hull and Rivas under his wing and squired them around to meet various officials whom he thought could help them. Even then, as Owen inquired as to whom they should see, Ollie North's name kept coming up. Owen called North and arranged an appointment for him to meet Hull and Rivas at the NSC. The meeting lasted about forty-five minutes. Owen and the others came away deeply impressed by North's dedication and sense of mission. So taken by North's zeal were Owen and Hull that they nicknamed him "Blood and Guts," or "BG" for short.

Hull and Owen stayed in touch. In November of 1983, following McFarlane's appointment as National Security Advisor, Hull wrote Owen saying he hoped that the move would make BG "more powerful, as we need more like him."

Owen left Quayle to take a job for Gray & Company, the Washington public relations firm. As luck would have it, in the spring of 1984 the Contras, in dire need of having their image boosted on Capitol Hill, approached Gray for help. When Owen's boss assigned him the account, Rob paid a call on North and asked if the administration would have any objections to Gray & Company taking on the Contras. North was enthusiastic about the idea. But when a top Gray executive, former Kennedy aide Frank Mankiewicz, threatened to resign if his company represented the Contras, Gray pulled out of the deal.

But by this time Owen had decided that the Contra cause was too important for him to ignore, Gray or no Gray. He went to North and told him about some ideas he had for helping the Contras, such as establishing front companies that could be used to purchase arms and other supplies overseas, or establishing a nonprofit corporation in the U.S. to raise money for nonlethal assistance. North, impressed by Owen's resolve, dispatched him on a trip to Central America to meet with the Contra leadership and help determine precisely what their long-range needs would be.

Taking a leave from his job, Owen made the trip in late May and early June, visiting Costa Rica and Honduras. He stayed nearly two weeks, then returned and produced a report for North saying that to sustain their present strength, the Contras would need $1 million a month and $1.5 million if they intended to increase their ranks.

Shortly afterward North had Adolfo Calero hire Owen at $2,500 per month to be the unofficial link between the Contras and the White House. Owen quit his job at Gray, and over the next two years would serve as North's personal aide-de-camp, shuttling back and forth from Washington to Central America, helping the NSC avoid the congressional ban on providing military aid and intelligence information to the Contras.

Owen soon learned that any secret agent worth his salt had to have a code name. He called himself "The Courier," or "TC" for short. He saw himself as a soldier in the cause for freedom, battling the Red tide. He was not stuck in some office up in Washington; he was down there in the jungles on the cutting edge. He seemed to loved the cloak-and-dagger aspect of it all.

In "eyes only" dispatches to North, Owen referred to Calero as "Sparkplug," and when he was not calling North "Blood and Guts," he would use "Steelhammer," or just "The Hammer." Young Rob's feelings toward Ollie North bordered on idolatry. Anything North wanted, all he needed to do was ask, because to Owen, Ollie was larger than life.

"Your commitment to this country, to truth and justice, and to man's freedom is an example that so many can and should learn from," Owen said to North in one of his first missives from the field, dated July 2, 1984. "Your dedication is an inspiration to me and many others. Somewhere these ideas were instilled in you; I wouldn't be surprised if at least some of them came from your family... May I just say it is a pleasure and an honor working with you. I hope something positive comes out of all this, but if nothing does, we will have at least tried, although in this case that will not be good enough. You and your family are in my prayers."

While Owen was in Central America, there occurred an important event that he did not mention in any of his memos to North—an event that startled the region and Washington alike, creating ripples that are still being felt in the courts at this writing.

For many months the CIA, North and the leading Contra faction known as the Nicaraguan Democratic Force (FDN) had been trying to get Eden Pastora to unify his Contra forces fighting on the southern front with the FDN. But Pastora was adamantly opposed to merging his ARDE (*Alianza Revolucionaria Democratica*) group because the FDN was dominated by the remnants of Somoza's dreaded National Guard, whom Pastora had originally fought against alongside the Sandinistas. Pastora's intransigence was irritating Washington. The Contras were a hard enough sell to Congress and the nation as it was without having to deal with a divided rebel front whose leading elements were ex-*Somocistas*, whom many thought still had blood on their hands. Pastora was a dashing, attractive figure who could add some much-needed panache and credibility to the Contra cause—a fellow one could allow to be interviewed on network television and not fear the worst.

The CIA had been giving Pastora assistance, and so concluded it had leverage over him. Around May 1 it had informed Commander Zero that unless he unified with the FDN within thirty days, his U.S. aid would be cut off. On May 30, the day the deadline arrived, Pastora called a news conference in La Penca, a rural outpost just across the Costa Rican border in southern Nicaragua. He intended to announce that he would refuse to accede to the CIA pressure and unify with the FDN; moreover he would split with ARDE leaders who did want to unify.

Then, as the journalists waited, and Pastora prepared to make his remarks, a powerful bomb suddenly exploded, killing three of the reporters and wounding eighteen other people. Pastora, the man for whom the bomb had rather clearly been intended, escaped with injuries to his legs.

Other attempts had been made on Pastora's life prior to this and many still had a reason to want him dead—including the Sandinistas, the FDN, possibly even the CIA. The authorities never charged anyone in connection with the bombing. But Tony Avirgan, an ABC television stringer who was wounded in the bombing, and his wife Martha Honey, began their own investigation into who was responsible. The probe took weeks, months and then years, finally turning into a still-pending federal lawsuit that alleges that the bombing was carried out as part of a massive conspiracy led by former American military and intelligence officers to use drug money to purchase weapons for the Contras. The suit, which seeks more than $20 million in damages, names twenty-nine defendants, including Owen, John Hull, Calero, Ret. Army Maj. Gen. John Singlaub, Secord and three Secord associates—Tom Clines, Albert Hakim and Raphael Quintero. All these men, who have denied the charges, were, or would become, part of North's Contra-support network.

While many of the defendants have branded the suit "an outrageous fairytale," it was filed in U.S. District Court in Miami six months before the Iran-Contra affair became public, and some credibility for the lawsuit has been generated in Congress and elsewhere.

(Though no connection has been proved between the events, on the night of the bombing Owen was in the Costa Rican capital of San José, meeting with Hull and the CIA station chief there, Joe

Fernandez. The next morning the Courier left for Honduras, feeling, as he would later testify, "somewhat saddened because anytime when reporters and Americans are killed, it's always a sad time.")

By the summer of 1984 North's three-year tour of duty at the NSC was up, and he was scheduled to return to the Marine Corps. But by this time McFarlane had come to consider North indispensable. His boundless energy and diligent staff work on a range of issues had so far done credit to the NSC, McFarlane thought, and now North had emerged as the administration's operational point-man on a cause perhaps nearer and dearer to the president than any other: the Contras. McFarlane could not afford to let him go.

So the National Security Advisor decided to approach Gen. P.X. Kelley, the Marine commandant, and ask if North could be given an extension. One Friday evening McFarlane was a guest of honor at a parade held at one of the Marine barracks in Washington. He took Kelley aside and asked if he would consider letting Ollie stay on at the NSC for another year. Kelley said a year was too long but he would permit an additional six months.

"Bud and I had discussed the merits and demerits of extending a guy like Ollie, and what that can do to his service career," recalls Kelley. "If you get away from the mainstream for too long, then you've lost the continuity of your career. You become a prima donna if you stay away too long. You taste the heady wine, and chances are, *à la* Bud McFarlane, you're not going to come back . . . You're not down in the trenches with the troops. You're up in that heady atmosphere and you start to lose your credibility with the Marines. You're now a White House guy, wearing civilian clothes, and people never see you any more. They know you're over there, and they know who you are, but you're not down in the trenches earning your pay as a Marine. You're earning it as something else . . . But that Friday night I agreed to extend him for six months."

By the summer of 1984 official CIA assistance to the Contras began running out with the officially authorized $24 million. Then in early August the House passed the second Boland Amendment, barring the agency or the Defense Department from giving any aid to the resistance. Approval in the Senate was less certain, but North began final preparations for taking on the entire Contra burden himself.

He flew off to attend strategy meetings in Dallas, where every American conservative of note had gathered for the Republican Na-

tional Convention. One meeting North had was with Owen, Adolfo
Calero and another key new player from the private sector—John
Singlaub, who was becoming increasingly active in raising private
funds for the Contras.

In 1978 Singlaub had created a storm of controversy when as
commander of U.S. forces in South Korea he had publicly criticized
President Jimmy Carter for proposing to scale back American troop
involvement there. Carter ordered Singlaub called home, and he
was subsequently allowed to resign from the military. A highly decorated veteran of three wars, the colorful, crewcutted Singlaub was
a former OSS officer who in 1944 parachuted behind Nazi lines in
France to organize Resistance forces in preparation for D-Day. He
later served as the China desk officer for the CIA and as a combat
battalion commander in the Korean War. In Vietnam Singlaub was
commander of the Joint Unconventional Warfare Task Force,
known as MACSOG, and one of the leaders of Operation Phoenix,
the controversial, U.S.-directed program designed to root out by
whatever means the Vietcong infrastructure.

On leaving the military Singlaub became increasingly active in
conservative politics. Now, as he met with North, he was ready to
embrace the Contra cause as president of the World Anti-Communist League, an international alliance of the extreme right with
some ninety branches on six continents.

Late in August North asked McFarlane for permission to travel
to Central America for another round of planning and logistical
meetings. McFarlane agreed but told North in a memo to "exercise
absolute stealth. No visible meeting. No press awareness of your
presence in the area." North met with Calero to review operational
details, and with area CIA station chiefs for a final laying on of
hands and passing of the torch.

On September 1, just after North returned to Washington, the
three Cessna planes that had been modified for combat and transferred to the Contras by the Pentagon through an accounting procedure late the previous year as part of Operation Elephant Herd
swept across the Rio Coco River from Honduras into northern Nicaragua on a mission to attack a Sandinista military-training school in
the town of Santa Clara. Just over the border the planes were
joined by an American Hughes 500MD helicopter, also outfitted for
combat.

The convoy moved in on its target, firing off rockets. The
Cessnas successfully dodged heavy ground fire and made it back to
their base in Honduras, but the helicopter was shot down and

crashed. The incident was significant since two of the three men killed in the helicopter crash were Americans—the first to die in combat during the Nicaraguan civil war. The Americans were identified as James Powell, a former helicopter pilot in Vietnam, and Dana Parker, a veteran of the Huntsville, Alabama, police department and a member of the Special Forces Unit of the Alabama National Guard. The men were affiliated with an Alabama-based soldier-of-fortune group called Civilian Military Assistance. The CIA denied that either Parker or Powell was in its employ.

Still, this was the sort of headline-generating incident that the Administration had to avoid if it held out any hope of winning back middle-of-the-road congressmen already keenly mindful of an American public that feared that Central America had Vietnam, and the specter of American boys dying, written all over it. The White House portrayed Parker and Powell as a couple of freebooting cowboys off on their own anticommunist lark. North told McFarlane in a memo that the mission had not been sponsored by the CIA, and that the Contras had launched the attack only after being "goaded" into doing so by "the nonofficial Americans."

The press began directing its attention on Civilian Military Assistance and the larger question of the relationship between the mercenaries and the CIA. But Owen and John Hull—who was rapidly emerging as an important friend of the CIA, allowing the Contras to set up camps on his ranchland in northern Costa Rica—apparently continued to have dealings with the soldiers of fortune.

Finally, in early October, Congress approved Boland II as an amendment to an omnibus appropriations bill. As signed into law by President Reagan on October 12, the measure provided: "During fiscal year 1985, no funds available to the Central Intelligence Agency, the Department of Defense, or any other agency or entity involved in intelligence activities may be obligated or expended for the purpose, or which would have the effect of supporting, directly or indirectly, military or paramilitary operations in Nicaragua by any nation, group, organization, movement or individual."

The legislation offered the administration a pinch of solace by also providing that $14 million might be appropriated to the Contra cause after February 28, 1985, if the White House could persuade Congress to rescind the restrictions. But for now, as Representative Boland put it, the amendment "clearly ends U.S. support for the war in Nicaragua."

While Boland II seemed to force the administration to walk away from the Contras, it soon became apparent that the White House action-arm—North and, increasingly, McFarlane's deputy, Admiral Poindexter—did not intend to abandon them. North and Poindexter tended to rely on the opinion that Boland II did not apply to the NSC staff because the Council was chartered as a general-policy facilitator having nothing to do with the business of intelligence. This reasoning seemed not to take into account the provisions of Executive Order 12333—signed by Reagan in 1981—which provided that the NSC "shall act as the highest executive branch entity that provides review of, guidance for and direction to the conduct of all national foreign-intelligence, counter-intelligence and special activities and attendant policies and programs."

Perhaps, the NSC had not been conceived as an organization that would have anything to do with intelligence or foreign policy operations, but if Henry Kissinger broke precedent and paved the way for a new role, or if the powers-that-be determined to not-so-transparently deputize the NSC as a mini-CIA and Pentagon, did it not follow that Boland II would cover the Council? It was like arguing that the federal park rangers were not mandated to do any cloak-and-dagger work, but if the order suddenly came in from the White House to ignore the Yellowstone grizzlies for a while so as to do intelligence work in Central America in the national interest, would not the rangers then be covered by Boland?

McFarlane's position was less clear-cut than North's or Poindexter's. He said he never had any doubt that Boland, at least in its intent, did apply to the NSC, and maintains that he instructed his subordinates to stay within the law and be especially careful not to get involved in fundraising schemes for the Contras. North and Poindexter, however, would maintain that they never heard any such warnings from McFarlane.

In any event, Boland II hardly served as a significant deterrent to the NSC. If anything, it seemed a spur. Outlining the post-Boland strategy in a memo to McFarlane, Poindexter stressed secrecy under what seemed a cover of less than serious peace talks: "Continue active negotiations but agree on no treaty, and agree to work out some way to support the Contras, either directly or indirectly. Withhold true objectives from staffs."

North said it was clear what was expected of him: "The U.S. contact with the Nicaraguan resistance was me, and I turned to others to help carry out that activity," he would later testify.

Poindexter understood this could be risky, but all believed in what they were doing. "Very frankly, we were willing to take some risks in order to keep the Contras alive... until we could eventually win the legislative battle..." the admiral would later testify. "So for all intents and purposes, Colonel North largely took over ... much of the activity that the CIA had been doing prior to their being prohibited..." Once that happened, he added, North became the "switching point that made the whole system work... the kingpin to the Central American opposition."

With the Saudi money in the pipeline, Boland II initially had no practical effect at all on the Contras' ability to sustain themselves, and so North now began to immerse himself in the logistical details of running the war. Soon his office resembled a command post. He was on the phone constantly, often juggling two receivers at one time. He would talk to Secord, Owen, Singlaub, Calero, other Contra leaders, CIA agents, Casey himself, Poindexter, McFarlane, American soldiers in Honduras, diplomats in Central America and bureaucrats throughout Washington. He was working the system, prodding it. There weren't enough hours in the day. Anything and everything to do with the Contras now passed through North.

He would constantly brainstorm, tossing out ideas, some rather far out: What about setting up the Contras as a provisional government? he had suggested to McFarlane. McFarlane wished he had thought of it himself, but when he referred the idea to the State Department, the lawyers there poured cold water on it. The Contras did not effectively control any territory.

No detail was too small or trivial for North to consider. Battles, even wars, could turn on careful attention to detail. The Sandinistas had just come up with Soviet-designed HIND–D sophisticated assault helicopters, and the Contras needed surface-to-air missiles to deal with them. Secord located the missiles in China, but there were problems in arranging the shipment. End-user certificates, attesting that the missiles would actually be used in the country receiving them, were required. But the Contras were not a country. North had to come up with a nation that would serve as a shipping way-station and issue end-user certificates, asserting that it was to be the final recipient of the missiles. He found a volunteer in Guatemala. North later proposed that Washington increase its assistance to the ruling junta there by way of thanks.

In another response to the HIND helicopter threat, North, at the suggestion of Navy Secretary John Lehman, met with a British paramilitary operations expert named David Walker. North subsequently arranged for Walker, a former SAS officer, to be retained as a consultant to Calero and the Contras in carrying out special operations designed to destroy the HINDS.

On another front North, aware that Saudi funds were pledged only through the end of 1984, approved an effort in late November by General Singlaub to approach contacts of his in South Korea and Taiwan to see if they would be interested in contributing to the Contra cause. Though Singlaub's initial efforts did not bear fruit, Taiwan did contribute $2 million to the Contras in 1985, after North asked Gaston Sigur, then the NSC's senior director of Asian affairs, to intervene and appeal to Taiwan government officials whom he knew.

McFarlane and other senior officials worried about the position Washington put itself in after soliciting money from the Saudis and the Taiwanese, believing that a quid would be expected for a quo. But ultimately that did not keep the NSC from asking and receiving. The Sigur solicitation came at a time when the administration and Congress were struggling over a bill that would have restricted textile imports from Taiwan. The bill was approved, but Reagan then vetoed it, pleasing Taipei.

Still, the Taiwan contribution did not come through until late 1985. By the end of 1984 the Saudi funds had run out and the Contra till was barren again; McFarlane returned to Prince Bandar for another round of what was perceived by critics as tin-cup diplomacy. In addition North asked Secord, who during the AWACs lobbying drive and other forays to the Middle East had established close contacts with the Saudi royal family, to follow up on the McFarlane approach.

"You can stop twisting my arm," Secord would later testify Bandar told him, "I have decided to take it up with the head of the state."

By early February of 1985 the Saudis had agreed to donate another $24 million. McFarlane again gave Reagan the good news by slipping a notecard into the president's morning briefing book. Reagan did not let on, but King Fahd had already told him about the new contribution directly. As before, Secretaries Shultz and Weinberger were left out of the loop.

Since Boland II prevented the Pentagon and the CIA from giving military-intelligence information to the Contras, North apparently decided he could remain in at least technical compliance by serving merely as a conduit of the information, so that both the Agency (the principal source) and Defense could properly be in a position to deny that they had provided it to the resistance directly. North would obtain maps and other intelligence on Sandinista positions, explaining that the material was for his own use. Then he would give the information to Owen, who would fly to Central America and relay it to the Contra command.

The extent to which North's sources, especially at the CIA, were witting partners in this would become the subject of considerable debate; five of the agents with whom North dealt would later be disciplined, and a sixth, Clair George, would choose retirement.

Alan Fiers, chief of the CIA's Central American Task Force, which headed agency operations in the region from Langley, said that in assessing a North request for information, it was a fine line differentiating between whether Ollie wanted it for the Contras or simply for his own use as the NSC staffer involved in the region. In his testimony before the congressional Iran-Contra committees, Fiers, who would eventually be reprimanded for his actions, offered numerous split-hairs in explaining why he acceded to North's requests.

"If I had delivered a map to Oliver North . . . It would have been because Oliver North said, 'I need this to brief the president,' and that is the way he dealt, bombastically and [he] would push and push and push, and the decision I had to make each time a segment came in was whether or not this was for his NSC job or something else . . ." Fiers said.

"I didn't call and pass that intelligence and say, 'Now Ollie, you can pass it to Calero and do the job,' You must remember—and I know it's difficult to understand—but you have got to remember that the key figure on policy in Central America during this period was Oliver North."

Fiers thought part of the reason for this was that North had been able to make use of a bureaucratic void that resulted from Tony Motley, the assistant secretary of state for inter-American affairs, fighting "like cats and dogs" with Constantine Menges, the NSC's man for Latin America:

"There was tension at play in the system. And essentially by default, Central American policy, in its execution and to a large degree in its formulation, fell to Oliver North," Fiers continued. "He was the person that filled the void and who dealt with these things by dint of the void and by dint of personality. And he did it. He was the person who moved and formulated and pushed and cajoled. . . . There is very little . . . that happened in Central America that I didn't talk to Ollie about . . ."

Fiers says when he asked North if everything they were doing was legal, North said it was. And Fiers seemed to take comfort in that, though he would later testify: "I never took anything he said at face value, because I knew that he was bombastic and embellished the record, and threw curves, speedballs and spitballs to get what he wanted. And I knew it and knew it well . . ."

Casey, meanwhile, though he himself was giving North off-the-record assistance at every turn, wanted to cover his bureaucratic flank and make sure that his subordinates were not drawn into trouble. In November, 1984, the director complained to McFarlane that North was conducting his operations "indiscreetly" and that too many people now knew that he was raising money and providing intelligence to the Contras.

As McFarlane noted, North had a fertile imagination, which he felt free to indulge, in his increasingly powerful position as, in effect, Contra commander-in-chief. In February of 1985, for example, North learned that a Sandinista merchant ship, the *Monimbo*, was en route back to Nicaragua from Asia carrying arms. In a memo to McFarlane, North proposed that Adolfo Calero be given this intelligence so that the ship could be either sunk or seized and its cargo diverted to the Contras.

If the seizure-option were chosen, North counseled making the move as the ship cleared the East China Sea, since no Central American country could be expected to let the *Monimbo* dock after it had been pirated. If it were to be sunk, Calero could be given the "maritime assets" to do the job before it entered the Nicaraguan port of Corinto.

In a handwritten note scrawled on North's memo, Poindexter wrote: "We need to take action to make sure ship does not arrive in Nicaragua." And in a cover note of his own to McFarlane, Poindexter added: "Except for the prohibition of the intelligence community doing anything to assist the Freedom Fighters, I would readily recommend I bring this up to CPPG [Crisis Pre-Planning Group] at 2:00 today. Of course we could discuss it from the standpoint of keeping the arms away from Nicaragua without any involvement of Calero and the Freedom Fighters. What do you think?"

The idea was never implemented, as McFarlane apparently never authorized taking it up the line. But the National Security Advisor's reaction to North's plan was mild and at least indulgent. "I don't fault him for it," he would later testify. "I think that the job, my job, the job of any responsible commander is to expect that energetic people, operating under an assignment to accomplish a

O. LAURENCE NORTH

"I AM NOT ONLY WITTY IN MYSELF
BUT THE CAUSE THAT WIT IS IN
OTHER MEN."

Track 2, 3, 4
Chorus 2, 3, 4
Chess Club 2, 3
Dramatics 4
Student Council Alternate 4
Service Squad 4
Science Club 4, President

High School graduation picture, 1961. *(Photo: Ockawamick High School via The Washington Post)*

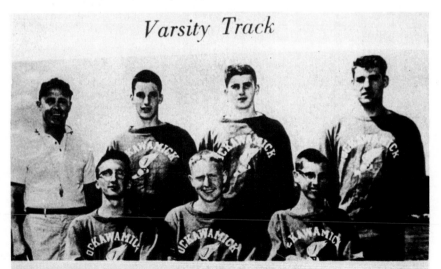

Varsity Track

BACK ROW: Russ Robertson, coach, J. Brandon, L. North, L. Tomlin. FRONT ROW: E. Van Deusen, C. Louden, K. Townsend.

North (standing second from right) on his high school track team in 1961. *(Photo: Ockawamick High School via The Washington Post)*

Annapolis graduation picture, 1968.
(Photo: U.S. Naval Academy)

Midshipman North.
(Photo: U.S. Naval Academy)

North in an Annapolis boxing team picture. *(Photo: U.S. Naval Academy via Washington Post)*

North, with Lynore White at June Week, Annapolis, 1966, just after they became "pinned." Later, however, she broke off the relationship. *(Photo: Lynore White Carnes)*

North (right) with Randall Herrod in Vietnam, 1970. Herrod saved North's life in combat in 1969; when Herrod was charged with the murders of sixteen Vietnamese civilians in 1970, North flew back to Vietnam on his own time to testify as a character witness at Herrod's court martial. Herrod was acquitted. *(Photo: Denzil Garrison)*

North (right) in Vietnam. *(Photo: Don Moore)*

North in the officers' club, Okinawa. *(Photo: Stan Ostazeski)*

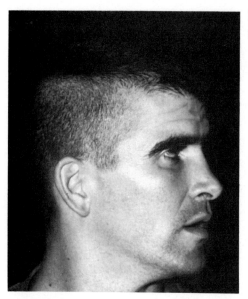

North in Okinawa.
(Photo: Stan Ostazeski)

North with members of the Kissinger Commission on the return flight from Central America to Washington in 1983. From left to right, Henry Kissinger, Senator Pete Domenici (R-New Mexico), North, and then-Representative Michael Barnes (D-Maryland). Barnes would later launch an investigation of North's role in aiding the Contras, while North assisted efforts to defeat Barnes when he quit the House to run for the Senate in 1986. *(Photo: Michael Barnes)*

Oliver North addressing Contra Donors at a January 30, 1986, dinner.
(Photo: Rebecca Hammel)

North, taking notes at a meeting with President Reagan and the hostages' families.

Mideast terrorists made North a target in 1985, so a White House photograph showing him with Contra leaders (top) was censored. A version of the same scene, without North, was issued instead (above).

North in Cyprus, October 1986, en route to Beirut where he was to pick up at least two hostages. Only one, David Jacobsen, was released. *(Photo: Associated Press)*

North and former White House chief of staff Donald T. Regan share a laugh during the Project Hope Ball in September, 1986, at the Washington Hilton. *(Photo: Neshan Naltchayan)*

Fired National Security aide Lt. Col. Oliver North on his way to his attorney's office, December 3, 1986. *(Photo: Rich Lipski, The Washington* Post)

North is besieged by newsmen as he leaves his suburban Virginia home, December 19, 1986. *(Photo: Associated Press)*

North barbecues hot dogs for his son, Stuart, sixteen, at their home in Great Falls, Virginia. *(Photo: Life Magazine/Greg E. Mathieson)*

Manucher Ghorbanifar
(Photo: The Washington Post)

Albert Hakim
(Photo: The Washington Post)

Robert McFarlane
(Photo: The Washington Post)

Amiram Nir, the Israeli Prime Minister's advisor on counter-terrorism, and Jerusalem's representative on the Iran initiative. *(Photo: AFP)*

Carl "Spitz" Channell
(Photo: The Washington Post)

Robert Owen, North's "courier."
(Photo: The Washington Post)

President Reagan and former
CIA Director William Casey.
(Photo: Rich Lipski)

Retired General Richard
Secord testifying.

Former National Security Advisor John Poindexter at the House
subcommittee hearing. *(Photo: James Kowo Atherton, The Washington* Post)

given mission, are going to try and be imaginative and to think up things that hopefully will be both prudent, viable, successful, wise, but that many times they won't. That's why you're the boss, and they're the subordinate, and so to say, 'No, don't do that.' . . . But that's my job, and I don't fault him for having been an imaginative, aggressive, committed young officer."

In the winter and spring of 1985 North decided to use some of the money being sent directly to Calero by Saudi Arabia to support other Contra leaders. The CIA had been supporting some of the leaders, but under Boland could legally no longer do so. It was also deemed necessary to broaden the Contra leadership base to make the resistance more politically acceptable. Funds were withdrawn from Calero's account in traveler's checks and hand-delivered to North by Owen. The checks came in packets of $10,000, and North began keeping over $100,000 worth in his office safe. He obtained an additional $50,000 to $75,000 in cash from Secord, for a total operational fund of $150,000 to $175,000.

North would testify that besides being used to pay various Contra leaders, the money would generally go to "support the operations that we were conducting." He said the existence of the fund was known to several people, including McFarlane, Poindexter and Casey. North said he kept meticulous records of the money flowing in and out of the account on a ledger given to him by Casey.

Many of the payments to Contra leaders were hand-carried by Owen. Sometimes he would take the funds to Central America; other times he would never have to leave Washington. On one occasion in April, 1985, Owen waited on a cold, rainy night outside the Executive Office Building on Pennsylvania Avenue and passed an envelope of cash to a Miskito Indian leader. North wanted the Miskitos to stop negotiating with the Sandinistas and join other Indian groups in a united front with the Contras.

Owen's role extended to pickups as well as deliveries. Later in the year he made three different trips to New York to retrieve money earmarked for the Contras, including one mission that netted the cause $9,500 from a Chinese grocer.

Following instructions given him by Secord, Owen showed up at the corner grocery on the Lower West Side of Manhattan and told the proprietor that "Mooey" had sent him. The man walked behind the counter and pulled out a wad of ninety-five $100 bills from his pants leg. When Owen brought the cash to Secord in the lobby of Washington's Sheraton Carlton Hotel, he told the general that the

grocer had probably taken a five-percent cut from what must have
originally been a $10,000 donation. But Secord told him the contri-
bution was intentionally less than $10,000 so as to be within the
reporting requirements of such transactions.

On the other two occasions, Owen said in his testimony, he went
to a bank, asked for a contact provided him by Secord and picked
up sealed envelopes he assumed contained cash. He then brought
them to North in his office. Secord said the money had been wired
from the Enterprise's Swiss bank account.

In the winter of 1985, the White House was hopeful that after
February 28, the deadline specified under Boland, it could persuade Congress to appropriate the $14 million. McFarlane con-
veyed to North and the rest of the NSC staff the importance that
the president attached to not "breaking faith" with the Contras, and
said that maximum effort should be put forth to win a congressional
change of heart.

North thought that the Saudi contributions guaranteed only subsistence and maintenance of the status quo. With adequate additional funding, he wrote Poindexter that "the resistance could be in
Managua by the end of 1985." But McFarlane presented him with
what amounted to a Catch–22. Unless the Contras became a credible military force and began winning some significant battles, they
would never gain political support in Congress or with the American people.

Obviously if there were to be any chance of winning any more
money from Congress, the Saudi aid had to remain an air-tight
secret. North wrote Calero: "Too much is becoming known by too
many people. We need to make sure that this new financing does
not become known. The Congress must believe that there continues to be an urgent need for funding."

Yet the Contras could not appear impoverished either. They had
to have enough wherewithal to be credible. So to those within the
administration who were out of the secrecy loop, North represented the Contras as self-sufficient. To those who knew nothing of
the Saudi assistance, the continued viability of the Contras came as
a surprise.

In March, CIA field agents whom Casey had not clued in reported to him: "Since the cutoff of official funds to the anti-Sandinistas in May of 1984, they have been able to field a viable guerrilla
fighting force, have increased their numbers, and improved their

tactical efficiency. It is estimated that to maintain the level of activity that they have, it would cost an estimated one and a half to two million dollars per month. There is, however, no intelligence on the source of this income, except that it comes from private groups, and possibly some U.S. business corporations."

As part of his continuing effort to make the Contras viable, North, in early March, engineered a media event to dramatize that the various Contra factions were now united and working in common cause. He had three principal Contra leaders—Calero, Alfonso Robelo and Arturo Cruz—gather in San José, Costa Rica, and issue what came to be known as the San José Declaration.

The document was an espousal of unity and shared goals, concluding with the wish that "love for our fatherland overcome selfishness and foreign involvement." It called on the Sandinistas to enter into peace talks and institute sweeping democratic reforms, changes which North and the Contras, it would seem, felt Managua would never agree to, but that gave the resistance a more reasonable, moderate aura. North planned stepped-up Contra attacks when the Sandinistas failed to meet the declaration's conditions.

Though North wanted to cast the three Contras as visionary founding fathers of a new Nicaragua who had toiled together in a spirit of compromise to draft the Jeffersonian declaration, it had actually been hastily written primarily by North himself several weeks before in a Miami hotel room.

The response to the San José ceremony was disappointing, Ollie felt. He had pushed for a much grander event, but other officials had insisted that it be toned down. The original North idea called for staging a Contra constitutional convention aboard a Caribbean luxury liner called the *Sea Goddess*, which reportedly was to have been chartered by Walter Annenberg, the former ambassador and old Reagan friend. The signing of the declaration would take place as the *Sea Goddess* was flanked by a ceremonial escort of navy submarines and aircraft carriers. Then the declaration could be proclaimed from Communist-liberated Grenada, or if that seemed laying it on a little thick, then from Boston or Philadelphia. But U.S. policy-makers insisted on the more mundane San José option.

Later in March, building on the San José event, North and his nominal boss, NSC political-military affairs chief Don Fortier, sponsored a multifaceted plan featuring lobbying, a media offensive and almost daily presidential speeches urging Congress to lift the Boland restrictions. The plan included a ten-page daily chronology describing each staff member's assignments.

With that plan, and his San José effort, no one could accuse North of not thinking big. But some felt his estimate that the Contras would take Managua by the end of the year was without foundation. One such observer was Army Gen. Paul Gorman, commander of the Southern Command from May of 1983 through February of 1985. To North's distress, just as Congress was readying to consider the administration's request to lift Boland and grant the $14 million, Gorman made the rounds of official Washington talking down the Contras' fighting ability:

"Oliver was terribly concerned about my attitude..." Gorman told the Iran-Contra committees. "What I was saying in those days was that I did not see in the Nicaraguan resistance a combination of forces that could lead to the overthrow of the government or the unseating of the Sandinistas... Oliver got very exercised about that and called me and said, 'Would you try and put together an op-ed piece?'... which he allegedly was going to get placed in the Washington *Post*. It never was, and I gather it's because what I wrote displeased him.... He saw me as a problem in terms of what I was saying, and I think he was just doing his damndest to get me to shut up—old general, put a cork in it."

Congress, it seemed, remained more impressed by the Gorman skepticism and the fundamental continuing question of the wisdom of U.S. policy toward Nicaragua than by North's visions of Contra success and communism's threat looming over the Rio Grande. In late April it rejected the administration's request to undo Boland and appropriate more money to the resistance.

By this time, though he had been nominally urging his staff to try to overturn Boland, McFarlane had also become deeply skeptical of the wisdom of pursuing a policy based almost solely on covert action.

"Ollie and I differed on that strongly," McFarlane would recall. "Covert action is supposed to be a marginal kind of activity to enhance a foreign policy goal, not to be its foundation. Especially when you're going to fight a war. And in my judgment, if it was important, you shouldn't go with covert action as the core of your policy... Well, I don't think Ollie wrestled with it to that level. He just looked on it as a problem of a needy society being oppressed, and we should help them.

"The president didn't hear these arguments and he had decided to go to covert action, and so North and I were to carry it out. And yet, by '85, when the Contras had been in operation for going on three years plus, I went down and met with Calero in Honduras and tried to really absorb what kind of a movement this was. Are they well-meaning, are they truly nationalists, are they of the people and supported by the people? And are they competent?

"Well, they really didn't fill the bill on competence at all. They were, yes, well-meaning, and I thought popular, because *La Prensa* and the Cardinal, and other institutions that are closer to the people than I was, said they were. I suppose it's a cynical way to look at it, but if we were going to support these people, it meant winning with the Congress.

"Now the Congress really wasn't going to provide more money to support these people unless they could demonstrate that they could win. The core—not the far left or the right, but the swing voters in the middle that you might persuade this is sensible, it is in our interest, it's important—says, 'All right, but can they win? I'll support you if they can, but I won't if they can't.'

"And that was the place where Ollie and I really disagreed, and it was really ingrained in '85 ... And I said to him, 'We might hope they win. We would like for them to win, but we cannot kid ourselves. If they cannot win, then we'd better cut their losses and our losses and recognize that we'd better take this problem on when Americans are more stirred up about it. And maybe that'll have to be Mexico, but let's not kid ourselves and get more of them killed for no good reason.'"

But North did not buy what to him had the ring of Vietnam all over again. More importantly, neither did Ronald Reagan.

While McFarlane may have differed with North on some substantive issues, he also realized that Ollie had now become virtually indispensable to the Administration's effort to hold the Contras together. He was the man through whom everything flowed.

The previous summer McFarlane had persuaded P.X. Kelley to extend North's tour of duty at the NSC by six months. That time was now expired, but McFarlane decided he still couldn't afford to let North go. He would go back to Kelley and ask for another extension.

Meanwhile North had been selected to attend the top level course for senior officers at the Naval War College, starting in the summer of 1985. He had already completed the program for junior-level officers before coming to the NSC. North sought advice from friends and colleagues about what to do.

One evening he sat around his EOB office pondering his options with Secord and Robert Lilac, an Air Force Colonel who, like North, was a member of the NSC's political-military affairs unit. As they sipped some Chinese beer that Lilac had brought along, Secord, who had graduated from the Naval War College, recommended that North take the assignment. It would be a good career move if he was seeking senior rank. But North was hesitant. He said he thought his work on Central America and terrorism was too important to leave. He also talked it over with McFarlane, and said that if it could be worked out with General Kelley he would like to stay on.

McFarlane went back to Kelley and over breakfast asked him to grant North a year's extension. They discussed the pros and cons. Kelley noted that if North let the Naval War College appointment go by he would have to be reselected if he ever wanted another chance to go. But the Commandant said he supposed North might still get a chance to command a battalion some time if that was still a goal.

"In any event, Bud's view for the country was that he wanted to keep Ollie for another year," Kelley recalls. "So I had no reason to object to it . . . If the National Security Advisor to the President of the United States asks for a Marine to be extended, he's extended."

BLUE RINSE, HAM HOCKS & DOGS

WITH the loss of another round in Congress, North found himself trying to quell panic among Contra leaders who had been counting on the additional funding. The vote was a bitter pill, a vote of no confidence in administration policy that raised serious questions about the future of the Contra movement.

They were locked into a subsistence cycle, unable to reach beyond the Saudi funds for more money that could fuel an offensive and change the dynamics of the war—both in Nicaragua and Washington. North, who believed so passionately in the Contras and their cause, couldn't understand why most of the American people did not; polls still showed a healthy majority thought that getting mixed up in the Nicaraguan civil war was folly.

But the public just did not understand, North thought. They did not know anything about Nicaragua, or realize how the Sandinistas had betrayed the revolution. They did not know anything about the Contras or the noble ideals they were fighting for. They did not know about the stakes, about the dominoes ready to fall, unless the U.S. took a stand. In *that* sense, the principle was the same as in Vietnam. But now the battle was only a stone's throw from Miami. Where was the recognition of the threat? Of the clear and present danger? If the people were not aroused, they had to be made aroused.

Closer to home, North and other Contra-boosters in the administration were coming to realize that the White House itself was not presenting a united front on the importance of the Contra issue.

Some clearly thought it more important than others. The president himself remained committed; the problem was that the "pragmatist" element of the White House staff was not as keen on the issue and was effectively preventing Reagan from expending too much political capital on Nicaragua.

The events leading up to the April vote on undoing Boland provided a good example. North, White House Communications Director Pat Buchanan and Faith Ryan Whittlesey, head of the Outreach Working Group on Central America that had been created in 1983—all had urged Reagan to push the administration position in a dramatic appearance at the Orange Bowl in Miami on the anniversary of the Bay of Pigs invasion. But Chief of Staff Donald Regan had nixed the Orange Bowl speech because Senate Republican leaders wanted the president to lobby Congress for a deficit reduction package.

Regan's priorities were astonishing, North and his allies believed. The legions of God-fearing Reagan loyalists at the grassroots could hardly be expected to get worked up over the arcane, eye-glazing deficit issue. But the Gipper at the Orange Bowl? Sending forth freedom-and-democracy rhetoric, punctuated by a little broken Spanish here and there, in front of all those flag-waving Cubans? Now that would have been a spectacle that could have gotten conservative blood flowing, headlines blaring and maybe some congressional votes changed. But it hadn't happened.

Now, North and other members of the administration's Contra group decided that what was really needed was a massive public-relations, fundraising and lobbying effort that could kill three birds with one stone: the need to raise money from wealthy benefactors at home to supplement the Contras' secret foreign assistance; the need finally to excite the public about Nicaragua, particularly those people in the districts of swing-vote congressmen; and lastly, the need to generate enough of a clamor on the far right so that Don Regan and others on the White House staff would be beaten into submission and allow the Contra issue to be given the consistently high-profile treatment it deserved.

This project would establish still another important cog in North's private-sector wheel, and propel him into conducting a range of activities that some felt bordered on violating the Hatch Amendment prohibiting active-duty military officers from engaging in partisan politics. But there was stronger suggestion that the sophisticated fundraising and propaganda network that would be erected under the aegis of North and the National Security Council did breach prohibitions against expending public funds to lobby Congress and using tax-exempt organizations to raise money to buy arms for the Contras.

The project would evolve into a scandal of money and politics that represented a dramatic extension of earlier White House efforts to blend public relations with policy on the Central American front. It was an attempt to manipulate American public opinion in what some observers would consider to be the most provocative aspect of the entire Iran-Contra affair.

North's key private-sector links for this new endeavor would be Richard Miller, head of International Business Communications (IBC), the Washington public relations firm, and Carl "Spitz" Channell, a then-obscure fundraiser who owned a network of small companies that raised money for right-wing causes.

The administration's two Contra public-relations machines—the Outreach Working Group on Central America and the Office of Public Diplomacy—had been churning along for the last two years, to some, but clearly not enough, effect. So in the spring of 1985, Public Diplomacy, the group headquartered at the State Department but effectively run by the NSC staff, decided to expand its efforts by nearly quadrupling the money it had been paying its principal contractor—IBC—to be the chief architect of spreading the good word on the administration's Nicaraguan program.

IBC had been founded in 1984 by Miller, who had served as director of broadcast services for the 1980 Reagan presidential campaign. Miller went on to do public affairs work at the Department of Transportation and the Agency for International Development before resigning to launch IBC. The company offered services in media relations, public affairs planning and political analysis, among other things. In 1984 Miller, then thirty-one years old, began working with Francis Gomez, who had recently left his job as the State Department's deputy assistant secretary for public affairs.

As soon as Gomez resigned his job at the State Department he received a contract to assist State's own Office of Public Diplomacy in its effort to buff up the Contra image. The contract was renewed in May of 1984 and then assumed by IBC later that year. In all, through the fall of 1986, Public Diplomacy would issue Gomez and IBC seven noncompetitive contracts on the Contra account worth $441,084. In 1984 IBC also began representing one of Adolfo Calero's organizations, the Nicaraguan Development Council, an as-

signment which gave the company an opportunity to make further
inroads with Calero and the Contra leadership.

In early 1985 Miller got involved in planning a major Contra
event—a fundraising dinner for the Nicaraguan Refugee Fund at
which President Reagan was scheduled to speak. Also involved in
staging the affair was Spitz Channell.

The forty-year-old Channell, a short, florid-faced man with a thin
blond mustache grew up in Elkins, West Virginia, a lumbering
town where his parents owned a thirty-two-room motel. He attended American University in Washington, served in the army
and then managed the family motel for nine years before getting
into conservative politics by working for the National Conservative
Political Action Committee. NCPAC was the attack dog of the New
Right, specializing in raising funds to defeat liberal congressmen
and senators. Channell eventually became NCPAC's first national
finance chairman, where he was known for arranging Washington
briefings for large contributors. This would become his speciality
on the Contra beat as well.

In 1982 Channell left NCPAC to form the Channell Corporation,
which offered fundraising consulting to various political campaigns.
In 1984 he began to establish other groups—first the American
Conservative Trust, a political action committee, and then the National Endowment for the Preservation of Liberty (NEPL), which
was certified as a tax-exempt, nonprofit educational foundation and
would emerge as the queen bee in Channell's conservative hive.
Other Channell organizations would include a lobbying group
called Sentinel, and another political action committee called the
Anti-Terrorism American Committee. He would also head up Western Goals and the Western Goals Foundation, two groups founded
by Larry McDonald, the late John Bircher and Democratic congressman from Georgia who was killed aboard Korean Air Lines
Flight 007, shot down by the Soviet Union.

In its application for tax-exempt status NEPL advanced the innocuous aim of "educating members of the general public on American political systems and societal institutions." And in a provision
meant to restrict it effectively from partisan politics or lobbying,
NEPL agreed that "the corporation shall not espouse policies or
positions, the accomplishment of which may only be achieved by
the passage or defeat of legislation."

Channell was particularly interested in foreign policy, and while
many Washington insiders doubted that money could be raised
purely to advance a given policy, he felt his contributors were com-

mitted enough to the Reagan agenda that they could be moved to give generously.

In January of 1985 NEPL ran a large newspaper ad congratulating Reagan on his second-term inauguration. The ad caught the eye of one Edie Fraser of the Washington public relations firm Miner & Fraser. She called Channell to compliment him on the ad and asked if he would like to help her in preparations for the Nicaraguan Refugee Fund dinner. Channell agreed, and this was his initiation into the Contra cause. Working on the dinner, he met Miller. Soon they both met North, whom they would assign the code name "Green"—as in the color of money.

Channell had told Fraser that he knew of some wealthy conservatives who might like to make large contributions if a short private meeting with the president could be arranged in return. Fraser had passed the message on to North: "Ollie," she wrote. "Very Imp. Two people want to give major contribs., i.e. 300,000 and up if they might have one 'quiet' minute with the President."

Reagan delivered the keynote address at the dinner, held on April 15 at the J.W. Marriott Hotel, and the dinner's sponsors received a briefing on Central America from McFarlane and Vice-President Bush. Also attending the gala were such conservative luminaries as Bob Hope, singer Wayne Newton and former football star Roger Staubach. The dinner raised $200,000, but after various expenses, plus nearly $100,000 in "consultant fees" were deducted, there was only about $3,000 left for the Contras themselves.

The president was in good voice that night: "I truly believe," he said, "that to do nothing in Central America is to give the first communist stronghold on the North American continent a green light to spread its poison throughout this free and increasingly democratic hemisphere." Though the president's appearance clearly was not enough to keep Congress from voting to deny the $14 million nine days later, Channell concluded that because of Reagan's attachment to the cause, Contra aid was a promising issue on which to base a fundraising and public education campaign.

He decided, therefore, to launch a joint venture with Miller. Channell needed the expertise and official contacts of Miller and IBC, which was regarded as a virtual extension of the Office of Public Diplomacy and the NSC. One of Channell's first steps, through IBC, was to have Adolfo Calero authorize him to solicit funds on the Contras' behalf.

In a "Dear Spitz" letter, Calero wrote Channell: "Please help us to achieve our dream, a free and democratic Nicaragua, not tied to

a hostile Soviet threat but to a peaceful democratic American tradition. All resources you can raise will be appreciated. We can put all
of them to good purposes."

For his first major Contra venture Channell decided to sponsor
an "event" at the White House for a select group of his prior and
potential NEPL contributors. The purpose was to raise funds and
raise the Contra consciousness of the donors. Through North, a
briefing was arranged for June 27, 1985, at the Executive Office
Building.

At the briefing North had his first substantive meeting with
Channell, then went on to give the featured presentation, showing
slides and delivering what came to be his standard speech about
Nicaragua and the Contras. He told of a Soviet and Libyan military
buildup under the Sandinista regime, religious and political repres-
sion, the needs of the Contras and the importance of the U.S. supporting their cause—warning of a wave of Nicaraguan immigrants
coming to America if the Contras did not prevail.

Afterward, as would become the Channell custom, the guests
were escorted across the street to the elegant Hay Adams Hotel for
a reception, dinner and overnight accommodations—all compli-
ments of NEPL and IBC. At the dinner Channell presented Calero
with a check for $50,000, representing money raised to date.

NEPL staged at least four other group Contra briefings for its
biggest givers through the spring of 1986. All were carefully coordinated through North and the White House.

"You are one of a small group of dedicated Americans who has
stood by President Reagan . . . in support of his agenda," went a
typical invitation sent out by Channell. "It will be a pleasure to
meet you in Washington on [date] when you attend our special
security briefing followed by a working dinner . . . Please be reminded that your accommodations at the Hay Adams Hotel are
taken care of and there is no expense to you." Guests were met at
the airport by limousine.

At the reception and dinner Channell and his associates would
try and determine which of the guests were the most promising
targets. They found that some of the wealthy donors could be in-
duced to contribute more if they knew their money would go for
specialized training, the purchase of arms and sophisticated weaponry, or perhaps the resupply of an elite Contra unit like the
"Larry McDonald Brigade," named in honor of the late John
Bircher. This tack made the contributors believe that their money
was having a special impact rather than just being lumped in with

food, clothing and the more mundane "humanitarian aid." These
were men and women of means who wished to indulge in a little
adventure capitalism, and they were pleased to have found a pipeline into the administration that effectively allowed them to purchase their own brand of foreign policy.

"I wasn't interested in [my money] going for chocolate bars or
soda pops," recalls one donor, E. Thomas Clagett, who contributed
$20,000 after a meeting with Channell and North. "I wanted some-
thing to kill the commies—direct military support for the troops—
guns and ammunition...Certainly nobody ever told me it was
going to buy toys."

North drew up a wish-list of "big ticket items" that Channell
could hold out as a carrot to particularly promising prospects.
Those who showed signs of responding were given the chance to
meet personally with North, and if they made a contribution of
more than $300,000, a brief "off the record" session could be ar-
ranged with the president himself.

But for all the work put into the group briefings, Channell's biggest scores were private sessions arranged for people whom he was
certain were ripe prospects. It was at these one-on-ones where
North did his best work, softening the prospect up for what the
folks at NEPL liked to refer to as "the call to the altar."

In September of 1985 Channell chartered a private plane and
flew North down to Dallas to meet with Nelson Bunker Hunt.
Channell had a target-list of up to $5 million worth of goodies
that he hoped North could touch Hunt for, including a light
plane and a grenade launcher. North made his pitch at a small
dinner at the Petroleum Club, attended only by Hunt, Channell
and Daniel Conrad, the executive director of NEPL. After making his usual presentation, North said he could not legally ask for
funds himself, but that contributions could be made to NEPL.
Then, rather dramatically, he left the room, leaving Channell to
collect the money in the second part of what Sen. Warren Rudman, the New Hampshire Republican, would later refer to as
"the one-two punch."

Though North was careful not to solicit funds directly, he did
write several fundraising appeals, using NSC stationery, to more
than thirty of Channell's contributors. "During 1985, the hope of
freedom and democracy in Nicaragua was kept alive with the
help of the National Endowment for the Preservation of Liberty,
and fine Americans such as you," North wrote Hunt in a letter
dated January 24, 1986. "In the weeks ahead, we will commence

a renewed effort to make our assistance to the Democratic Resistance Forces even more effective. Once again, your support will be essential."

At the September, 1985, Dallas meeting, Hunt did not come near Channell's $5 million pipedream, but he did make it worth their while. He wrote out two checks to NEPL for $237,500 each—one a contribution, the other a loan.

Another NEPL target who received red-carpet treatment was a New York businessman named William O'Boyle. After getting an invitation by Mailgram, O'Boyle flew down to Washington for the EOB and Hay Adams treatment in March of 1986. Channell told O'Boyle that there were a select group of Americans who were quietly contributing money to purchase "lethal supplies" for the Contras in support of President Reagan's policy. NEPL had had O'Boyle "checked out" to attest that he had the credentials to join this elite group. If he were interested, a breakfast meeting with North could be arranged. O'Boyle agreed.

At breakfast North read from a notebook and ticked off items the Contras needed: several million rounds of "NATO" ammunition, light Maule aircraft at $65,000 apiece and antiaircraft missiles. As was by now his custom, North noted that he "could not ask for money as a government employee." Channell held out the promise of a meeting with the president if O'Boyle contributed $300,000 or more. O'Boyle flew home to New York to think it over, and ended up giving $130,000 for the purchase of two Maule airplanes. In response to another written solicitation, he later donated another $30,000.

But Hunt and O'Boyle paled next to Channell's jewels: two very rich, elderly widows named Barbara Newington and Ellen Garwood. Both women had given generously to Channell's organizations in the past.

In preparation for a November, 1985, solicitation of Newington, Channell prepared a pitch for North in which Ollie would tell the widow that "[you are] the most secure person we know in the U.S." and "we are asking you to take on a project that requires your kind of person." The session was to focus on the need to combat the Soviet HIND helicopter. Miller prepared a file folder containing a photograph of the HIND, and another photo of a shoulder-fired surface-to-air missile that could knock the copter out of the sky.

At Newington's suite in the Hay Adams, North described in detail the capabilities of the missiles and said he knew where they could be obtained. Before long, Ollie left the room, allowing Channell to come in for the kill. Over the next four to six weeks Newington gave NEPL $1.1 million worth of stock. All told, in 1985 and 1986 Newington gave the organization $2,866,025.

Garwood, a cotton heiress from Austin whose husband had been a Texas Supreme Court justice, was almost as generous. In April of 1986 she flew to Washington to attend a round of NEPL meetings. Channell had warned her in advance he was going to ask her for more money than she had ever given before. On the evening of the last day of the meetings, Garwood met in the Hay Adams lounge with Channell and North, whom she had been briefed by on several previous occasions. North gave her an update on the Contras, told her the situation was again desperate. The resistance soldiers were badly in need of arms and ammunition. They were poorly clothed and hungry. They might not survive until Congress got around to renewing aid again—if it ever did.

Then, still in Garwood's presence but in hushed, whispered tones, North and Channell discussed several items on a list, which Channell then showed to Garwood as Ollie once again rose to leave. The list itemized such materiel as bullets, hand grenades and antiaircraft missles. Channell said these were what the Contras had to have to continue the struggle.

Garwood soon wired NEPL $470,000 in cash, and donated $1,163,506 worth of her stock. The following month, she sent in another $350,000 in cash. All told, in 1986 alone, Garwood contributed $2,518,135. The Contras honored her by naming one of their helicopters the *Lady Ellen*.

Garwood and Newington were no aberrations. Rich elderly women whom some observers came to refer to as the "blue-rinse brigade," were a favorite Channell target. His donor lists were filled with designations like "retired" or "housewife," and he would court them by doing little things he thought they might appreciate—like sending a basket of fruit around Christmas time. But he did not confine his fundraising net just to the United States. He took at least one trip to Europe "to raise money from rich German widows," according to Jane McLaughlin, a former Channell employee who said she resigned after suspecting that perhaps not all of the money he was raising was getting through to the Contras. McLaughlin took NEPL records with her and made the rounds of the press, giving interviews and speaking out against Channell: "He would say: 'I don't care if they have to mortgage their homes or sell their children. What we are doing is more important,'" McLaughlin told the New York *Times*.

Channell would speak of his clout at the White House but be very protective of his main source. "I was told by Spitz that you must never refer to Colonel North as Colonel North over the phone," McLaughlin added. "It was crucial to keep these things quiet." Channell, reportedly, would often tape his phone solicitations and play them for people around the office so that they could have a model presentation to refer to if they wanted.

Nearly overnight, it seemed, Channell had evolved from a fundraising unknown to a fundraising phenomenon. As the money rolled in he moved his labyrinth of companies from a row-house district in northeast Washington to a suite of offices on Pennsylvania Avenue near the White House. He moved into a $300,000 condominium overlooking Rock Creek Park and availed himself of a stretch limo. According to NEPL records he used his organizations to pay credit-card bills, housecleaning expenses and to give himself a loan to pay his 1985 federal income taxes.

Channell's rise to prominence coincided with the two-year period from October of 1984 to October of 1986 that the administration was barred from providing direct military aid to the Contras.

Despite the Garwood-Newington successes, Channell was ever alert for even bigger contributions. But the private Contra lobby's hope for its largest windfall ended in almost laughable cries of fraud.

In the spring of 1985, Long Island adventurer Kevin Kattke surfaced again, phoning North to say that a man purporting to be a Saudi prince was proposing to donate $14 million from the sale of his personal allotment of Saudi oil to the Contras. North, explaining that he could not make solicitations directly, referred Kattke and the prince to Miller at IBC. Soon Miller was hired to market the prince's oil in return for a $1 million slice of the profits. Miller kept North informed of his dealings with the prince, and Ollie was so excited about the prospective windfall for the Contras that, according to an FBI agent's deposition, he told McFarlane and President Reagan all about the prince.

But unknown to North, as he and Miller tried to develop their new benefactor in the ensuing months, the prince was being investigated by the FBI for bank fraud. It seemed that a $250,000 check he had tried to pass at the William Penn Bank in Philadelphia had bounced. By the time the affair played itself out, the alleged prince, who called himself Ibrahim Al-Massoudi, had been unmasked as an Iranian con man named Mousalreza Ebrahim Zadeh. But not before he had stung Miller for $370,000, convinced North and federal Drug Enforcement Administration agents that he could help rescue some of the American hostages being held in Lebanon, and generally embarrassed a host of Reagan Administration officials who had dealt with him.

Kattke had gotten the prince-ball rolling. When he was not at Macy's, he had taken to moonlighting as a commodities broker in Manhattan in an effort to finance his private foreign-policy adventures. A Lebanese acquaintance had introduced him to the prince, who wore long, gold-braided robes, diamond rings and a Rolex wristwatch.

The prince, saying he was the brother of Saudi Prince Abdullah of Jeddah, tried to interest Kattke in a deal to buy forty metric tons of gold from Saudi Arabia. Kattke signed on, and though things moved slowly the prince looked and acted his part by taking Kattke out to New York's most expensive restaurants and entertaining him at his ostentatious house in Fresno, California. Meanwhile, Kattke said he confirmed the prince's bona fides through U.S. agents and a telephone conversation with Prince Abdullah himself, who according to Kattke, attested that the man was in fact his brother.

When the prince said he was having a little problem with his visa, Kattke called Howard Teicher, the NSC staffer for Middle East affairs. The prince got on the phone with Teicher and began talking away in Arabic, at one point warning Teicher of an impending coup in the Sudan, which later, in fact, took place. When Kattke and the prince fell to talking about world affairs and worthwhile causes, the subject of the Contras came up and the prince volunteered to make his $14 million contribution. Which was when Kattke called North and the referral to Miller was made.

Kattke and the prince flew down to Washington to see Miller at his IBC office on New Hampshire Avenue, next door to the Nicaraguan embassy. According to Kattke, as they walked in Miller's Lebanese secretary remarked that it was wonderful a fellow Arab would help the Contra cause, and tears came to her eyes. Miller introduced Kattke and the prince to Frank Gomez, then made his presentation on Contra requirements—alluding to arms while stressing the need for a C–130 transport plane to act as a portable hospital.

Before long the prince had invited Miller to participate in the same gold deal he had enticed Kattke with, and also mentioned that he could be helpful in gaining the release of the American hostages in Lebanon. Miller quickly relayed the offer to North, who had the White House's Hostage Location Task Force conduct an interview with the prince. From the outset, Miller had misgivings about the prince, and undertook some research to see if he was who he claimed to be. But North later told him that the CIA had confirmed that the prince was legitimate, and that his information about the hostages was also correct.

So, with North's approval, Miller and Gomez established a Cayman Islands corporation called I.C., Inc., to receive the anticipated Contra donation from the prince. Miller later told authorities this was done to avoid federal income tax on the proceeds and to hide the transaction from public view. Although no funds would ultimately materialize from the prince, I.C., Inc.—whose name was later changed to Intel Co-Operation, Inc.—would become a key waystation in the North-Channell-Miller Contra fundraising operation.

On July 18, 1985, an FBI agent came to interview North about the bureau's investigation of the prince in connection with bank fraud. North proceeded to give the agent a crash course in the Contra movement, and said he had deemed the prince to be so important to the administration's policy that the National Security Advisor and the president himself had been informed of the prince's offer to assist the Contras. He "confided" to the agent that the NSC had remained in contact with the prince because of the Contras' dire financial straits. North also asked that the prince not be interviewed before the end of the month when Congress was scheduled to have another vote on Contra aid. An FBI grilling now could also jeopardize any donation that the prince might make, North added. As the agent left, North introduced him to Adolfo Calero, whom he described as "the George Washington of Nicaragua."

During the subsequent grand jury investigation of the prince, North called Oliver "Buck" Revell, the FBI's executive assistant director, to request that Miller not be questioned about ongoing sensitive government policies. Miller's dealings with the prince had been in his capacity as an NSC consultant, North said, asking that Revell relay his concerns to the United States attorney in Philadelphia, who was heading up the probe of the prince. Revell agreed.

The FBI's interest in the prince in a criminal investigation did not, it seemed, deter North from continuing to use him to develop leads on the hostages. In August North ordered agents from the Drug Enforcement Administration—whom he had managed to get assigned to assist him in trying to free the hostages—to go to Geneva in an effort to get new travel papers for the prince because his passport had allegedly been stolen. But even with the help of North's friend Faith Ryan Whittlesey—who had been promoted to U.S. ambassador to Switzerland after her work on the Outreach Working Group on Central America—the agents could not get a U.S. passport for the prince. They did get another country to issue him travel papers, however.

The prince and one of the DEA agents remained in Geneva for some time thereafter, but by September North evidently developed sufficient doubts to ask Secord to fly over and interview the prince. Secord reported back that he thought they had all been taken for a ride, that the prince was a fraud.

On the eve of his trial Mousalreza Ebrahim Zadeh pleaded guilty to defrauding both the Philadelphia bank and another in California. He is now serving time in a Texas federal prison.

Miller told authorities he spent about $370,000 on various ventures with Zadeh. North approved the expenditures, including $32,500 which Miller sent to Zadeh in Europe. Some $15,000 of that amount was used to finance DEA hostage operations. According to the final report of the congressional Iran-Contra committees, North told Miller he could reimburse himself for the $370,000 loss from Contra funds sent to IBC by Spitz Channell.

If the phony prince had been real and actually paid the $14 million he had originally promised, he could have had forty-six private meetings with President Reagan at the $300,000: rate such sessions were being sold by the North-Channell-Miller combine. In 1986 alone Reagan met privately with at least seven Channell-Miller contributors.

Though North had clout, Channell and Miller felt they needed even more of an insider to guarantee the presidential meetings. Accordingly they hired David Fischer—a former Reagan campaign aide who had gone on to become special assistant to the president with an office adjacent to the Oval Office—to ensure inner-sanctum access. Fischer had been special assistant from 1981 to April of 1985, during which time he had almost constant interaction with Reagan.

In December of 1985 Fischer was retained by IBC to arrange private meetings with the president for NEPL contributors, and according to the congressional report, was paid about $50,000 for each session that he set up. Between December of 1985 and February of 1987 IBC paid Fischer a total of $397,400 and another $265,000 to Martin Artiano, a Miller acquaintance who had found Fischer for the Contra lobby. Channell's NEPL reimbursed IBC the entire $662,400 it paid the two men.

The use of private Reagan meetings as fundraising bait was deemed necessary, but there was at least some White House concern that the president, in meeting and thanking people who had given money to the Contra cause, might be violating lobbying statutes prohibiting the executive branch from spending money to influence Congress, unless authorized to do so.

"Objections may be raised that the President is violating the spirit of the anti-lobbying provisions by enlisting these private groups to lobby Congress," warned presidential counsel Fred Fiedling in a January 21, 1986, memo. "Care should accordingly be taken to avoid any suggestion of White House control of these groups."

And in what would become one of his most widely quoted in-house computer messages, North expressed the same concern in a May 16, 1986, note to Admiral Poindexter: "The President obviously knows why he has been meeting with several select people to thank them for their 'support for Democracy' in Cent Am."

Reagan would assert he thought that the donors he met with were giving money for pro-Contra television advertising.

Occasionally during this period the Contras received some private money that did not originate from the Channell network.

One source was beer baron Joseph Coors, a Reagan confidante and member of the president's "kitchen cabinet" who in June of 1985 went to see his friend Bill Casey to ask what he could do to help the Contras. "Ollie North's the guy to see," replied Casey. The CIA director promptly arranged for Coors to see North, who suggested that Coors might like to purchase a light Maule airplane for $65,000. Coors agreed and was given the account number of a firm called Lake Resources Inc., a Swiss shell company formed by General Secord and his "Enterprise." At Lake Resources the $65,000 was comingled with foreign contributions to the Contras and, later, profits from the sales of arms to Iran. North told him that the plane would be used for humanitarian purposes only, Coors would later testify.

And according to the congressional report, in the fall of 1985 North and Roy Godson, an NSC consultant, were able to enlist the conservative Heritage Foundation in a plan to direct money to the Contras. Heritage gave a $100,000 "grant" to the Institute for North-South Issues (INSI), a nonprofit group controlled by Miller and Gomez. INSI kept $20,000 of the money as an "administrative fee" and sent the remaining $80,000 off to I.C., Inc., the Cayman Islands Contra-laundering post. From there the money was sent on to Lake Resources in Switzerland.

Heritage had not originated the $100,000. The money was given to it by a contributor arranged through Godson and his friend, Pittsburgh attorney Clyde Slease. Slease had met with North and McFarlane on the need to raise "humanitarian" funds for the Contras. According to the congressional report the true objective of the subsequent Heritage "grant" was disguised in correspondence between Miller and Heritage president Edwin Feulner. Miller had said the grant would be for the preparation and dissemination of educational materials on Central America.

Godson also arranged for a Philadelphia stockbroker named John Hirtle to bring two prospective Contra donors to meet North in Washington. In December, 1985, one of the contributors donated $60,000 in a check made out to INSI.

At one point North sketched a chart (see page 234) showing the network of inter-relationships of these activist conservative corporations that he referred to as his "Project Democracy companies." The chart was later discovered in North's safe after he was fired, and reprinted in the Tower Commission report.

The flow chart is a matrix of three rows and three columns featuring boxes that contain the acronymns of the various companies in the network. The top of the vertical columns are labeled "U.S.;" "MULTI (US & O/S)" or multi-nationals U.S. and overseas; and "O/S only," or overseas only. These refer to the areas in which the companies operated. In the three horizontal rows North wrote: "Resource Development," "Financial Mgt." and "OP Arms," to refer to the types of activities the companies performed.

Next to Resource Development seven corporations are listed. Two of them are under the United States column—Spitz Channell's NEPL, and ACT, or American Conservative Trust. Two are

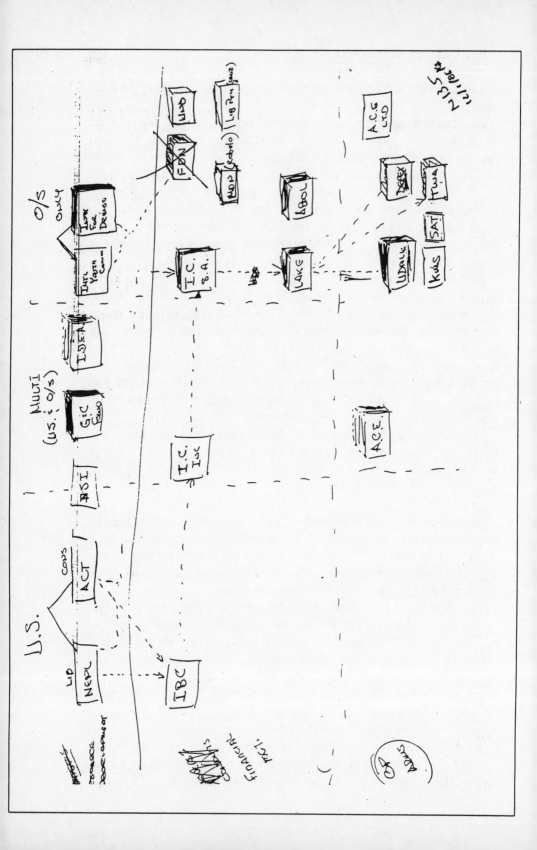

under "MULTI: G & C Found," or the Gulf and Caribbean Foundation—a pro-contra group, one of whose founders, former Congressman Dan Kuykendall, worked for Channell—and "I.D.E.A.," or the Institute for Democracy, Education and Assistance, an organization founded by North courier Robert Owen.

North put one of the companies on the U.S. and MULTI dividing line: INSI, or the Institute for North South Issues, which seemed to be merely a corporate shell for IBC, having the same personnel and doing the same work.

The last two companies in the Resource and Development line, under "Overseas only," are "INTL YOUTH COMM," an apparent reference to the International Youth Year Commission, and "INST FOR DEMOC," which has not been otherwise identified. The International Youth Year Commission was established by the United States Information Agency, and was used by USIA as a conduit for funds to the Contras. From 1981 to 1985, USIA gave the youth commission $540,000. A leader of the commission was Roy Godson.

On the second row, next to "Financial Mgt," IBC was listed under the U.S. column, Intel Corporation was listed under MULTI, and under Overseas only was "I.C.S.A.," believed to stand for Intel Corporation, *Sociedad Anónima*.

From I.C.S.A., there is a dotted line drawn down to "LAKE," a reference to Secord's Lake Resources Swiss shell company, and the repository for Contra funds. From Lake Resources North extended dotted lines down to six other companies, all of which were either subsidiaries of, or cogs in, the Secord Enterprise; Udall Research Corporation, Defex-Portugal, Trans World Arms, Southern Air Transport, and Amalgamated Commercial Enterprises. There is another box with the initials "KMS," which is not further identified.

North's use of the term Project Democracy to describe this interlocking corporate web was provocative because of the existence of President Reagan's above-aboard initiative under the same name to promote democratic institutions around the world. Reagan announced his "Project Democracy" in 1982, proposing to nurture "the fragile flower of democracy" by providing federal money to carry out the kinds of foreign policy initiatives that other government agencies seemed ill-suited to perform. Project Democracy, which later became known by its current name—the National Endowment for Democracy—attracted broad bipartisan support with the understanding that it was not in any way to function as a CIA.

But the New York *Times* reported in February, 1987, that Reagan's original Project Democracy had been perverted by Ollie North; that the original Project Democracy had actually had a covert dimension, and that the Reagan Administration's entire secret Contra supply operation and later, its sale of arms to Iran, were all part of North's Project Democracy.

The story was roundly denied by all concerned, and both the Tower Commission and the congressional Iran-Contra committees would conclude that North merely adopted the term Project Democracy to describe his activities. They said there was no evidence that North's actions were in any way connected to the public, above-board Project Democracy.

Yet the reporter who wrote the *Times* story, Joel Brinkley, says he stands by his account. Perhaps the strongest part of the article was its citing of an August, 1982, secret White House memo setting the agenda for a cabinet-level meeting on Project Democracy, which said: "We need to examine how law and executive order can be made more liberal to permit covert action on a broader scale."

One solution was apparently to vest more authority in the National Security Council so as to evade the oversight of Congress. In March of 1983 the White House hosted a meeting of billionaires with the apparent intention of raising money for Project Democracy. In many ways the Spitz Channell network would become an extension of this philosophy: turning to the can-do private sector to carry out what the Congress was unwilling to do.

At least four of the companies North listed on his chart in the "Resource Development" row—NEPL, NSI, Gulf & Caribbean Foundation, and IDEA—are linked to the National Endowment for Democracy through Prodemca, one of the endowment's main subsidiaries.

Gulf & Caribbean leader Dan Kuykendall got involved in Central American and pro-Contra lobbying through Prodemca. Owen's IDEA is an outgrowth of the Center for Democracy, Education and Assistance, which was run by a friend of contra leader Arturo Cruz. Cruz was the co-founder of Prodemca and a recipient of grants from the endowment, as well as a substantial monthly salary from North. Channell's NEPL was a key financial backer of both Prodemca and the endowment, while INSI received a half-million-dollar grant from the endowment.

These links, the 1982 memo cited in the New York *Times* story, plus the wholesale integration of intelligence and public relations at the NSC—symbolized by ex-CIA man Walter Raymond as a leader in the Office of Public Diplomacy—all suggest that the covert dimension of Project Democracy merits further investigation.

After the administration narrowly lost its April, 1985, bid to get another $14 million for the Contra war effort it adopted a fallback position of pushing for humanitarian aid. This campaign was given a fortuitous boost when Nicaraguan President Daniel Ortega made an ill-timed visit to the Soviet Union, which conservatives quickly pounced on as Exhibit A that Moscow was pulling Sandinista strings.

Channell saw the opening and quickly had one of his groups, the American Conservative Trust, produce a series of TV ads supporting the White House bid for humanitarian aid. "We all know what happened when the last vote failed," said one of the commercials. "While Sandinistas danced in the streets, Commandante Ortega celebrated in Moscow... Tell your congressman you want freedom to stay alive in Nicaragua."

On June 13, twelve Democrats changed their April vote, and Congress approved $27 million in "humanitarian aid" to be channeled through the State Department's newly created Nicaraguan Humanitarian Assistance Office. The vote was a major victory for the administration in its effort to regain momentum for the Contras.

The White House was appreciative of Channell's efforts. In an October 10, 1985, letter to Channell, President Reagan wrote: "Your organization's efforts to go to the public via television in support of this program was a significant factor in helping people to understand this issue." And in a "Dear Spitz" note of his own, North went further: "Your paid advertising and support of the President's program was critical to our success."

But the ad campaign for humanitarian aid was a mere scrimmage in preparation for what would turn into an all-out Channell television ad blitz and lobbying drive directed at swing-vote congressman in the spring of 1986, when the administration requested $100 million in new aid for the Contras and the reinstallation of the CIA to run their war effort. To power that drive, Channell launched what he called "the Central America Freedom Program."

Internal NEPL documents cited in a definitive article on the Contra lobby written by Peter Kornbluh for the *Village Voice* in the fall of 1987 leave no doubt as to NEPL's strategy: "Target Democratic swing votes in the House (sixty three total, thirty six in just eight states)." The lobbying program and the TV ad campaign (dubbed "Freedom Fighter's TV") cost about $2 million, most of which came from funds Channell and North had raised from the "blue-rinse brigade."

But mixed in with the larger Channell-Miller pot was the not insignificant $441,084 that IBC had received in contracts from the State Department's Office of Public Diplomacy—money which had been on the increase since the spring of 1985.

In March of 1985 in preparation for the April vote on the administration's request for another $14 million, IBC had been awarded a $90,000 six-month contract to perform "media services" for Public Diplomacy—a nearly fourfold increase from the $24,000 three-month contract IBC had received in October of 1984 in the aftermath of the Boland Amendment's approval. According to an April 11, 1985, memo to the federal comptroller's office from the State Department's Frank Gardner, payment on this contract was expedited "so that IBC, which finds itself temporarily in dire financial straits, may have the funds in days ahead to intensify its efforts in public diplomacy on behalf of the president's Easter peace proposal in Nicaragua."

Then in September of 1985 Otto Reich, director of the Office of Public Diplomacy, gave IBC a one-year $276,186 contract to upgrade its media program and build a computerized list of 3,300 people, along with their organizational affiliations, who could help the administration advance the Contra cause.

As Kornbluh noted, this last contract was peculiar on two counts. First, it was classified "secret." Reich's deputy, John Blacken, argued in a February 24, 1986, memo that "release of the general nature of the contract would allow elements unfriendly to the U.S. to deduce sensitive interagency operations . . . the secrecy of which is fundamental to their success." An investigation by the State Department's inspector general later found no basis for the secret designation. Secondly, the contract was unsigned, and IBC was not paid until a year after the agreement was authorized, which was curious since the State Department had asserted just five months earlier that the company was in "dire financial straits."

IBC was never in a financial pinch since its Contra operations were now totally interwoven with NEPL and Channell. IBC records show that in 1985 and 1986 Channell's tax-exempt NEPL sent IBC a total of $4.9 million, $1.14 million of which IBC kept for itself. So during the year that it waited to be paid its $276,186 from the Office of Public Diplomacy, IBC did not exactly have cash-flow problems. During those two years nearly sixty percent of its income came from NEPL.

But now, as he prepared to launch his spring, 1986, TV ad campaign targeting certain congressional districts, Channell was walking a tightrope over Federal Election Commission laws, tax exemption laws and lobbying laws. Lawyers advised him on how to cope. At a February 20 meeting NEPL lawyer Curtis Herge warned that they "would have to stay away from the words 'target' and 'congressman.'" When Channell wondered what terms they should use instead, Herge suggested the phrase "educate the general public about this crisis."

The White House urged Channell on. In another "Dear Spitz" letter written the following day, February 21, the president wrote: "Your efforts to educate the American public on the true nature of the communist regime in Nicaragua are critically important. I am confident that your work will make clear to all that we face a choice between communism on the North American continent and support for the Nicaraguan freedom fighters. There is no doubt that we must champion the cause of freedom. Your Central American Freedom Program is a vital link in the effort to forge a democratic outcome in Nicaragua . . . The Sandinista propaganda barrage . . . cannot go unanswered. In the next few weeks we will initiate a historic effort to achieve congressional support for the freedom fighters in Nicaragua. If this effort is successful, it will herald the first light of a new dawn of freedom in Nicaragua. Your Central American Freedom Program puts you on 'America's Front Line' in the battle for democracy."

Channell allocated $1.2 million for the pro-Contra TV commercials, which were produced by Baltimore's Robert Goodman Agency. "Our strategy [is] to target those congressmen who, by virtue of their record on Nicaragua, seemingly have yet to make up their mind," Goodman told Channell in one memo. "This national spot program is a pioneer attempt to effectively influence public opinion as prelude to a critical congressional debate and vote."

In February and March seven of the ads were aired 1,100 times —mostly in the home districts of thirty congressmen whom Channell deemed pivotal. Most of the thirty were southern Democrats, representing areas with a total population of about thirty-three million. Some of the footage used in the commercials featured the

Soviet HIND helicopter being used by the Sandinistas. Film of the helicopter in action was obtained from the Pentagon by North.

Channell supplemented the TV campaign with a $600,000 program that sent Contra leaders around the country on the lecture circuit. Most of the speaking engagements were in the nation's largest cities and media markets, but some were in the districts of the thirty swing congressmen. Finally records show Channell spent more than $100,000 hiring several Democratic lobbyists to lobby the congressmen directly—just in case the other two tacks had escaped their notice.

But in spite of all this, on March 20 the House voted 222 to 210 to reject the $100 million in new Contra aid being sought by the administration. Still, the vote was close enough that Channell and the White House thought they could win when the issue came up again in June. This time the swing congressmen were narrowed to eleven Democrats in Texas, North Carolina, Maryland, Kentucky and Tennessee. Channell laid plans for a final $200,000 TV-ad buy in those districts the week before the scheduled vote.

During this period the administration put on a full-court press. North issued more fundraising appeals, writing directly to wealthy donors. On May 1 he followed up on a letter sent by a Channell aide to a wealthy Philadelphian, Bruce Hooper, that had asked for funds for both humanitarian and military purposes. "Dear Bruce," North wrote on NSC letterhead. "I hope you will remain steadfast with the President as he leads this effort. I know personally that he values your help very much... Please maintain your invaluable strong support." Within a few days North met with Hooper, and on May 27 Hooper sent NEPL a check for $100,000.

Ollie was also tapped to deliver his special Contra briefing to the Council for National Policy (CNP), an eclectic grouping of some of the country's most influential conservatives, including Nelson Bunker Hunt, Joseph Coors, Jerry Falwell, Pat Robertson, Richard Viguerie, Paul Weyrich and Arnaud de Borchgrave—editor of the Washington *Times*, published by the Rev. Sun Myung Moon. The meeting took place May 31 in Nashville, which just happened to be in the home district of one of the eleven targeted congressmen, Democrat William Boner. Three other Tennessee Democrats—Ed Jones, Bart Gordon and Jim Cooper—were also on the Channell list.

CNP meetings are not open to the public or press, and North, as usual, insisted that his remarks to the group be kept off the record. But a tape recording of his speech was made, and a copy of the tape was later obtained by the Washington *Post*.

The tape was illuminating; not only did it provide a rare, verbatim record of North's Contra stump speech, but it also offered insights into how he moved a crowd and blended emotional patriotic themes to rally the faithful to an important cause. Often his voice would crack as he told stories about the Contras, and he gave his audience the sense that he was letting them in on secrets or information that the liberal press was probably suppressing.

He pressed all the right buttons, lashing out at Soviet expansionism, the godless Sandinistas and Washington for not being part of the real world. There were allusions to a spineless Congress that could not be counted upon to do the right thing.

North also raised the specter of a brown wave of immigrants pouring into the United States from Nicaragua unless democracy were restored. Jobs and American culture needed to be protected. But for real alarm there was no matching North's climactic warning that unless the United States drew the line in Nicaragua we would soon find terrorists roaming in our midst, gunning down innocent civilians in the streets. All in all, the speech was truly the world according to Ollie.

He began by telling the group where things stood in the war against terrorism, but soon made a transition to the paramount issue at hand. "It is indeed important to address the root causes of terrorism, but it is even more important that the Soviets know that they cannot indeed support this kind of activity—regardless of how covertly—and get away with it with impunity," North said. "And I would allege that the best way to do that is to prosecute individual terrorist organizations just as we have, yes, but to go after the Soviet model in the true sense of the word. Less than three hours' flight time from here [in Nicaragua], there is a Soviet model . . ."

"What do the Soviets intend? Well, if nothing more, they intend to outspend us in our own hemisphere. The Soviets are outspending us almost four to one in our own hemisphere in both economic and security aid to their friends versus our friends. This is at a time when our Congress threatens next year to reduce our assistance to the Latin American and Central American democracies by between seventeen and twenty-three percent. The Soviets next year, we estimate, will spend $6.9 billion for their friends, while we reduce ours . . .

"At Lourdes, Cuba, is the largest signals-intelligence site in the world . . . They have a direct dial-tone indicator code and a computer down there which they stole from the United States, and that computer shunts telephone messages in the Pentagon, White

House and CIA prefixes directly into the earphones of a Soviet
linguist who translates it and immediately broadcasts it back to the
Soviet Union for action. Fort George Meade, Maryland, is our facility. Fort George Meade is thousands of miles from the Soviet
Union. This facility is 123 miles from the United States.

"What we have in Cuba today is a society dedicated to one thing.
And that is the advancement of 'scientific socialism,' as the Soviets
have defined it. The youth of Cuba are brought up to become the
finest field army in the world today. I say that knowing, and as you
do, that I am indeed a Marine infantry officer in real life, and
Washington is not real life. That is the finest field army because
every single officer in it gets combat experience before he becomes
an officer. And he gets it in places that the Soviets want him to
practice his deadly trade. The Cuban military is engaged around
the world as the surrogates of the Soviets. They're the mercenaries
of the twentieth century.

"The Cubans are actively engaged throughout the world, but
there is now a place much more vital to our interests, and this time
on the mainland of this hemisphere. This is the poor tortured country of Nicaragua, which could become the next Libya. This time not
thousands of miles away in the Mediterranean, but three hours of
flight time from here.

"What we see happening in Nicaragua is widely unknown to the
American people. We have been unable, in this administration, to
communicate the real threat that Nicaragua poses to our nation. It
is indeed a national security threat of the first order. Not just because their combined military capabilities outweigh all other nations that surround them together. But because of the
extraordinary investment that the Soviets have placed inside this
country. It is the largest development of a military infrastructure
that has ever occurred in this hemisphere. And yet, just last week,
we were accused by a House subcommittee of militarizing Honduras...

"The deliveries by the Soviet Union that have occurred this year
have been remarkable, while the Congress has dithered over the
issue of whether or not we should support the democratic resistance in Nicaragua. Four Soviet—not Bulgarian or East German—
but Soviet military deliveries have occurred at Corinto. Most
recently, more helicopters...

"Every week, a Catholic school is closed in Nicaragua and replaced by a state school in which children learn to add using
AK–47s and grenades. Why is it that the people of this country flee

by the thousands? Nicaragua today is the only country in Latin America with a decreasing population. It isn't because of birth control. It's because they have opened the gates... Historically, a communist takeover will beget a flight of between ten and twenty-five percent of the population. That has already happened in Afghanistan—twenty-seven percent of the population. Cambodia, Laos, Vietnam, Cuba, and now it's happening in Nicaragua...

"The growth of the democratic resistance [the Contras] has been astounding. In 1982, there were roughly 6,000 people in the resistance. On May 9, 1984, when the Congress cut off U.S. government funding to the resistance, there were 7,900. On October 10 of 1984, when the Boland Amendment became effective and we had to withdraw our last seventy-three advisers to the resistance, there were 10,000. Since then, the resistance has grown to 27,000 young men and women who have taken up the cause of democracy against a government that is cruelly repressive.

"Some are as old as this fifty-nine-year-old farmer [*showing slide*], whose entire family was murdered: his wife and five sons laid out on his kitchen floor because they gave water to a resistance column that passed by their home. These young men and women, who have taken up this cause, have decided to fight for what they believe in. And their cause is, indeed, democracy.

"And yet the most sophisticated disinformation and active-measures campaign that we have seen in this country since Adolf Hitler has been launched against our support of these people. The government of the United States has acted in paralysis... The seventeen men that sit at this table as the inner council of the Nicaraguan Democratic Force [*showing slide*]... of those seventeen men, eleven of them fought against Somoza. And yet our media would have you believe that these are corrupt *Somocistas*.

"Why is it that these people are today denied even the basics of survival? In January, while we were still providing $27 million of humanitarian assistance, they were operating deep inside Nicaragua. Today, they've been reduced to mere small-unit operations. And less than 8,000 of them remain inside because of the effectiveness of the HIND helicopter. Small unit patrols like this are no longer equipped with good uniforms and boots. In fact, boots are the number-one item that they plead for all around the world from their previous benefactors.

"And yet, because the United States government has been unable to act—unable to take the very difficult, but very necessary, political steps—we can no longer help them. And very soon we will be back to emergency wards like this one [*showing slide*]. This was the intensive care unit prior to January, before our medical help began to arrive. Medical help that has now been cut off. And that man, second from the right, just had surgery and is recovering in a tent that doesn't even have mosquito netting. We can no longer provide medical help. We can no longer provide anything in intelligence... We can no longer provide the boots. We can no longer provide the food.

"All we offer them is a chance to die for a cause they believe in. And somehow this nation has got to do more.

"The only people in the conflict in Nicaragua that are today buried beneath a cross are those that fight for the resistance. Those that die in the EPS—the Sandinista People's Army—get buried beneath the plain stone slab at a military cemetary. But the resistance buries them beneath a cross.

"Somehow this nation has got to do more. In the next few weeks, we'll have that chance. The Congress of the United States is going to... take up the cause of the Nicaraguan aid to the resistance again. I believe it's possible for our Congress to do the right thing. There is no doubt that the Sandinistas have decided what they are going to do. The Cubans have decided, the Soviets have decided, the Bulgarians, the East Germans, the Libyans, the PLO. It is now up to the Congress to decide whether or not we are able to do something about what is going on in Nicaragua...

"Many of the members have seen this briefing and others like it. Many choose to ignore it. If we fail to provide the support that is so necessary for these people, this country [the U.S.]—which last year had twenty-three of its citizens killed by terrorism around the world—will very soon find its citizens being gunned down on its own streets.

"Last year, 1.2 million illegals entered the United States across the Mexican border. About 800,000 of them were Mexicans. This year, already over a million have crossed the border, and we're not even half way through the year. They are fleeing what they see as the takeover of Central America by surrogates of the Soviet Union. And they are terrified. And they are fleeing to what the president has called 'the last great hope of mankind on earth.'

"It is time that we realize that this is not a domestic partisan political issue. It is, indeed, a national security issue of the most profound importance. It is imperative that the United States act in its own interest to help those who want nothing more than our assistance. Not our troops, not our planes, not our Marines or our

Rangers. Just our help in bringing about a democratic outcome in that country. It is time we all stood up and asked for just that."

North sat down to a thunderous ovation.

On June 25 the Congress voted again. This time five Republicans and six Democrats switched their votes, giving the administration a 221-to-209 victory that put the CIA back in business with $100 million to work with.

But the influence of the final Channell effort was apparently negligible, since only one of the targeted congressmen, Albert Bustamante of Texas, switched his vote. Among the others a backlash against strong-arm tactics developed, and there were protests that the White House—and North—had stooped to low blows that went beyond the normal give-and-take of politics.

Yet in the more than twelve months that Channell had been involved in pressing the administration's Contra cause, there was no question that there had been a steady increase in congressional support for the White House's policy. Channell wrote Chief of Staff Donald Regan in August: "On the day in June of the historic House reversal, which resulted in a victory for Ronald Reagan on Freedom Fighter aid, it was determined that the National Endowment for the Preservation of Liberty... had carried the support program for the president successfully into thirty-two of the fifty-one Democratic districts that ultimately stood with Ronald Reagan on this issue."

Later North would present Channell with a "freedom fighter" commendation from the president.

Though Channell had success in coaxing money from old ladies, it was not so much his charm with the elderly but the imprimatur of the White House on his and Richard Miller's IBC that was the key to the success of their private Contra lobby.

IBC was widely viewed as a de facto branch of the State Department and the NSC. Channell was wired into IBC, but could also boast of several thank-you letters from Reagan on his own. He liked to refer to himself as the administration's "point man" on Contra aid, and he once told a reporter that he could raise "$40,000 before lunch" from Reagan supporters.

In August of 1986 Channell, in a bid to build an international clientele, even promised members of Mexico's conservative opposition party that he would intercede on their behalf with President Reagan if they donated money to the Contras. "I think you would agree with me that you and your people do not have the closeness with President Reagan that you so richly deserve," Channell wrote. "If the President were to know that you and your people were actively supporting his policies in Nicaragua, there is no doubt that he and the White House would be far more attentive to your plight in Mexico . . ." But Channell's entreaty was rejected.

In October Channell moved to cement his ties to the White House by entering into a contract with Nofziger Communications Inc., headed by Lyn Nofziger, the long-time Reagan advisor who had left the administration in 1982 to launch his own business. Under the agreement Channell was to pay Nofziger $240,000 over the next year for general political consulting and the use of his influence at the White House to assist Channell in his various endeavors.

Miller and IBC, meanwhile, were not resting on their Contra laurels either. Under its State Department contracts IBC had also given public relations advice to the Salvadoran military, and accompanied two defectors—former Salvadoran guerrilla Miguel Castellanos and Sandinista interior ministry official Alvaro Baldizon—on publicity tours of the United States. And in September of 1986 IBC handled logistics for the American tour of Philippine President Corazon Aquino.

Looking beyond Contra aid toward the 1988 presidential campaign and the post-Reagan era, IBC and Channell planned to stay loyal to the administration and cast their lot with George Bush. So in early 1986 they devised a plan to help Bush make inroads into the Reagan conservative base.

"The vice-president needs a vehicle which he can utilize to reach the high-dollar donors in the conservative ranks," said a section of a report from IBC to Channell: "These donors perceive him as a liberal Republican unsure of himself and without determination to lead in tough circumstances."

To help Bush IBC proposed that starting in January of 1986 they launch several "Freedom Forums" to which certain people from Channell's "Select 500" contributors' list would be invited. Bush would appear at the gatherings and discuss issues of the day. The vice-president himself was enthusiastic, writing Channell on January 16 to say that he found "the foreign policy issues you plan to discuss to be of great interest to me, as well as to the President. My personal interest is such that I hope to be able to participate." But the project apparently never got off the ground.

*　*　*

As the $100 million for the Contras kicked in, in the fall of 1986, there grew to be less of a need for Channell's Contra fundraising efforts, but a final accounting of his work shows that he and Miller, with the active assistance of North, made a significant contribution to keeping the Contras afloat financially.

According to the final report of the congressional committees investigating the Iran-Contra affair, the tax-exempt NEPL raised about $10 million for the Contra cause in 1985 and 1986—ninety percent of which came from a dozen contributors. Over half the total came from Ellen Garwood and Barbara Newington, the two elderly widows.

Of the $10 million, about $4.5 million was given to, or spent on behalf of, the Contras. The rest was kept by Channell and Miller for salaries and expenses incurred by their organizations, such as the paying of David Fischer and his associate, Martin Artiano, to arrange audiences with Reagan.

Most of the $4.5 million was disbursed by IBC's Miller at the direction of North, the report concluded. More than $1 million went for television advertising and lobbying. About $1.7 million was washed through IBC and I.C., Inc. in the Cayman Islands, and sent on to Secord's Lake Resources. Another $1 million was passed through Miller's companies to accounts controlled by Adolfo Calero, and about $500,000 was distributed to other persons and groups involved in pro-Contra activity.

Miller and Frank Gomez formed a second Cayman Islands corporation in May of 1986—World Affairs Counselors, Inc.—to receive the flow of funds from Channell. The money-laundering was evidence of an elaborate effort to conceal the true purposes and methods of operation of the private Contra fundraising network. Other indications were the practice of referring to North as "Green," and the creation of a project called "Toys" in the Channell books to disguise money earmarked for arms and ammunition.

Disguising the purchase of arms was necessary because that was not within the purview of NEPL's mandate as a tax-exempt, nonprofit, educational foundation. A cover story for the Toys account was that it was to be used to buy Christmas presents for the families of the Contras. Another nickname for the Toys project was "Patton," since its first contributor was George Patton III.

The logical extension of a television advertising campaign aimed at pressuring a wayward congressman on the Contra issue was a

campaign to further punish the congressman for his Contra malfea-
sance by working to defeat him when he came up for reelection.
Pro-Contra stalwarts, on the other hand, could be helped.

So Channell also funneled some of the money he raised through
NEPL to several of the organizations in his conservative network,
including the lobbying group Sentinel and his two registered political action committees: the Anti-Terrorism American Committee
(ATAC) and the American Conservative Trust (ACT).

ACT and ATAC reported spending $113,000 on television ads in
1986 supporting the reelection efforts of Republican senators Bob
Dole of Kansas, Paula Hawkins of Florida and Jeremiah Denton of
Alabama, as well as GOP congressmen Robert Dornan of California, Henry Hyde of Illinois and James Courter of New Jersey.
Dole, Hyde, Courter and Dornan, who were never seriously
threatened, won reelection, while Hawkins and Denton were defeated. Channell also opposed Democratic congressman Tim
Wirth's try for the Senate in Colorado, but Wirth won.

Thousands more dollars were spent to defeat Democratic congressmen who opposed the Contra policy, including Ron Coleman
of Texas, W. G. Hefner of North Carolina and House Speaker Jim
Wright, on whom NEPL produced a thirty-seven-page "action
plan" designed to "force Wright to revisit the issue of Contra aid."
Still, all three men won reelection.

But the man for whom Channell reserved most of his wrath was
Michael Barnes, the Maryland Democrat who as chairman of the
House Foreign Affairs Committee's Subcommittee on Western
Hemisphere Affairs had been one of the Congress's most vocal
Contra critics and a constant thorn in the side of the administration.
Barnes, who had come to question publicly North's role in assisting
the Contras, was leaving his House seat to run for the Senate.

Handwritten notes from NEPL records that would later be publicly released tell of Channell's determination to "destroy Barnes
[and] use him as [an] object lesson to others" who might question
North's activities in supporting the resistance. "Barnes—wants to
indict Ollie. Watergate babies—want to get at the Pres through
Ollie. Want another Watergate. Put Barnes out of politics. If we get
rid of Barnes, we get rid of the ringleader and rid of the problem."

Channell-controlled groups then poured money into commercials
and newspaper ads which depicted Barnes as a communist dupe
and/or sympathizer, implying he was under the control of Libya's
Moammar Khadafy and Iran's Ayatollah Khomeini.

Barnes was subsequently beaten in the Senate primary by a congressional colleague, Barbara Mikulski, who also opposed Contra aid.

But that did not matter to Channell, at least for the moment. Donning the hat of one of his political action committees, he claimed credit for ousting Barnes and sent a telegram to North exulting in the good news: "We have the honor to inform you that Congressman Michael Barnes, foe of the freedom fighter movement, adversary of President Reagan's foreign policy goals and opponent of the President's vision for American security in the future, has been soundly defeated in his bid to become the Democratic candidate for the U.S. Senate from Maryland. His defeat signals an end to much of the disinformation and unwise effort directed at crippling your foreign policy goals. We, at the Anti-Terrorism American Committee, feel proud to have participated in a campaign to ensure Congressman Barnes's defeat."

North, who, in the presence of NBC newsman Fred Francis, had referred to Barnes, a former Marine, as "a traitorous bastard," was pleased as well.

A stunned Barnes, now a Washington lawyer, has been trying to sort out the larger motives for his targeting. "An active-duty military officer . . . attacking a candidate for the United States Senate is highly unusual, to say the least. Here you are, you're Ollie North. You've got enormous resources at your disposal. You go after this guy Barnes, who's been after you, and who you regard as being bad for the country . . . It adds an enormously serious dimension to all this [the Iran-Contra affair].

"Ollie's very complex," Barnes continued ."He's obviously a capable guy able to exert tremendous energy and enthusiasm. But people like that need guidance and control, which he apparently didn't have."

Barnes says he believes North and his superiors gradually came to believe that by working out of the NSC and the White House, they had successfully fallen through the cracks of the Boland Amendment into a cocoon from which they could operate with impunity. "They came to the view that, 'Hey, Barnes or whoever can't get us because we're not the State Department. They can't get us because we're not the CIA. We're the White House. Nobody can get us. As long as we're willing to lie, we can do whatever we want. We can really do what we know is right for this country."

Meanwhile, in the general-election campaign, Channell decided he didn't want Mikulski, the woman who beat Barnes, elected to the Senate either. So he invested about $90,000 on commercials and advertisements tagging her as too liberal. But Mikulski's Republican opponent, Linda Chavez—who happened to be a former colleague of North at the White House, where she had been active in the Outreach Working Group on Central America—found the ads so offensive that she called North and unsuccessfully appealed to him to have Channell stop running them. Despite Channell's efforts, Mikulski was elected.

The Democrats, predictably, cried foul at all of Channell's campaign doings. The Democratic Congressional Campaign Committee filed a complaint with the Federal Election Commission charging that Channell's groups had violated federal election and income-tax laws while abusing the privileges accorded tax-exempt organizations.

In the spring of 1987 Channell himself conceded that at least some of those allegations were true. Along with Richard Miller, he pleaded guilty to criminal tax charges of conspiring to defraud the government by raising tax-deductible funds for the nondeductible purpose of supplying arms to the Contras. Announcing their intention to cooperate with Lawrence Walsh, the special prosecutor named to investigate the Iran-Contra affair, both Channell and Miller in their pleadings, reported in the press, named Oliver North as their co-conspirator.

THE SOUTHERN FRONT

CONGRESS' approval of $27 million in humanitarian assistance for the Contras in the summer of 1985 kept the troops in beans, boots and medical supplies, freeing up more of the still secret Saudi- and Spitz Channell-generated aid for purely military uses. Though by this time, various newspaper articles had appeared charging that the White House and, specifically, North were actively engaged in assisting private efforts to aid the Contras in an end run of the Boland Amendment, the NSC adopted a damn-the-torpedoes approach and got on with the business of running the war.

North, as he reviewed the needs of the suddenly-flush-with-cash Contras, concluded that there were at least two assets that they clearly lacked: an effective resupply operation, and a Costa Rican-based southern front that would force the Sandinistas to divert their attention from the northern sanctuaries based in Honduras.

Since February, North had been urging Calero to set aside $10 million of the Saudi funds to start up a resupply operation, but Calero had persisted in stockpiling arms to the point of developing a surplus. The problem was how to deliver the weaponry and other supplies to the Contras fighting deep inside Nicaragua. In order to win and hold territory, it was imperative that the Contras take up positions inside Nicaragua, not just make cross-border forays from the Honduran camps. Yet some of the positions the Contras were taking up were weeks away from the north by foot. They had to be resupplied by air.

Until now General Secord's role with the Contras had not expanded much beyond that of arms broker. But since the CIA had officially dropped out of the picture, the Contras had proved themselves unable to attend to the resupply function: the airlifting in of materiel as well as the purchase and maintenance of the planes. The Contras also plainly lacked the trained personnel needed to elude consistently Sandinista air defenses and to establish an adequate communications system—all the unglamorous but necessary functions that Secord termed the "sinews of war."

North and Secord had also heard rumors of corruption within Contra leadership ranks. Secord's man in the field, Raphael Quintero, was saying that Mario Calero, Adolfo's brother, had purchased inadequate ponchos, boots and other supplies from New Orleans. Not all the money allocated for supplies was being properly spent. The troops in the field were angry.

So North resolved to expand the Secord role beyond arms procurement to handle all the logistics of the Contra war effort as well. And dissatisfied with the Contra leadership's handling of the Saudi money, Ollie also decided that he and Secord would administer the funds directly.

These were some of the issues on the agenda as North convened a summit meeting of sorts on July 1 between the principals waging the war on behalf of the Contras. The session was held in a conference room of the Miami International Airport Hotel, inside the terminal building. Present, besides North, were Calero; Enrique Bermudez, the FDN's military leader; Secord and his two associates, Tom Clines and Raphael Quintero.

North, as usual, was running late. He did not arrive from Washington until around 9:30 that night, and it was 10:00 before the meeting got started.

North began by saying that there were numerous reports of corruption within Contra ranks, and he strongly criticized Calero in front of the group. The troops were said to be using substandard equipment. They had just bought a plane that was useless. North warned that no one would want to contribute to the Contra cause unless such problems were rectified.

"Ollie was really wire-brushing Calero," Secord recalls. "He [Calero] was nearly humiliated."

Calero denied any impropriety, but North abruptly cut him off. He said several times that unless the CIA got involved again soon, the resistance was going to go down. He, North, was holding it all together with a shoestring.

They reviewed operations and logistics, talked about their vulnerabilities and sought agreement on what to do until the CIA could reenter the picture. It was agreed that a viable air resupply operation had to be mounted and that a southern front had to be developed. The meeting lasted until 4 A.M., after which North left and flew back to Washington on his waiting government jet so that he could attend the morning NSC staff meeting.

North had not specifically mentioned that his solution to the Contra leadership disarray was to have Secord take on vastly expanded responsibilities. Secord himself had been reluctant at first to accept more duties, but ultimately agreed.

"I conceived the resupply operation and funneled money into it," Secord remembers. "I warned North it was going to cost millions, and it did. It was an emergency situation. Clines and Quintero pleaded with me not to do it. They said it was not a money-maker and we had done all we could. But it was an emergency, so I decided to go ahead."

Almost immediately after the Miami meeting, North, assuming the hat of Secretary of State George Shultz, met in his office with Lewis Tambs, the newly appointed U.S. ambassador to Costa Rica, and gave him a charge: to open up the southern front when he arrived at his post.

Tambs, a college professor of Latin American history, had gotten to know North while serving as a consultant to the NSC from 1982 to 1983. He had then been named ambassador to Colombia, where he remained until taking on his present assignment in mid-1985.

While serving in Colombia, one of Tambs's main jobs had been to try and implement a crackdown against Colombian drug-smuggling to the United States, a role which had prompted drug traffickers to threaten his life. In 1984 his embassy residence had been bombed. North had arranged for members of Delta Force, the army's elite counterterrorist unit, to be sent down to protect Tambs. After his Colombian tour there had been those on the far right who were pressuring the administration to fire Tambs because they thought he was not sufficiently doctrinaire, but North had been a voice at the White House who had spoken up for Tambs. So the ambassador had reason to feel grateful to Ollie.

On receiving the instruction from North to open up a southern front, Tambs did not raise so much as an eyebrow. Even though he did not work for North he accepted the order as if it had come from his new boss, Elliott Abrams—who had replaced Langhorne Motley as assistant secretary of state for inter-American affairs—or

Shultz himself. Tambs knew North was one of just three people who now sat on a scaled-down Restricted Interagency Group (RIG) presiding over the day-to-day formulation of administration policy in Central America—the other two being Abrams and the CIA's Alan Fiers. Also, Tambs, despite his status as an ambassador, was no stranger to taking instructions from the NSC. It had been William Clark, the National Security Advisor in 1982, who had given him his marching orders on battling the drug traffickers in Colombia.

As for the restrictions on U.S. assistance to the Contras in force at the time under the Boland Amendment, Tambs did not give them too much thought. "They have a saying in the foreign service," he would later tell the congressional Iran-Contra committees. "When you take the king's shilling, you do the king's bidding."

Besides, as long as he was facilitating the use of private funds, Tambs thought he was on solid legal ground. "Any aid in opening a southern front would come from what we casually called 'private patriotic Americans...'" he testified. "If private individuals were going to aid the freedom fighters, that certainly was their business."

Tambs said the term *private patriotic Americans* was "Ollie's term. He liked that one."

With North and Secord now controlling the money flow, Secord, after the Miami meeting, had had his business partner, Albert Hakim, establish the Swiss shell company, Lake Resources Inc. The Secord "Enterprise" would now receive all donations and make all disbursements for Contra activities via Lake Resources.

In early August North and Secord sat down to thrash out the details of establishing a resupply program that would include aircraft, spare parts, communications, full maintenance services and trained pilots. Secord elected to subcontract the entire operation out to Richard Gadd, a retired air force lieutenant colonel who, like Secord, had a background in covert operations.

Gadd had met Secord in 1980 while both were working on rescue plans for the American hostages being held in Iran. After his retirement in 1982, Gadd had established a highly successful business transporting intelligence agents and counterterrorist units on covert operations for the Pentagon, using "low and slow" flight techniques to avoid enemy detection. Most of Gadd's contracts had been with the army's top-secret Special Operations Division. It was the kind of work that the government, by all rights, should have been doing itself, but the armed services concluded that no one performing that specialized work could do it better than Gadd. Plus, in the private sector, his activities were always deniable.

Secord, in his capacity as Contra arms broker, had already called on Gadd to help arrange deliveries of arms flights to the Contras via Portugal. So Gadd seemed an ideal candidate to handle the expanded responsibility of setting up the resupply operation.

North and Secord decided that the most logical forward base for the supply flights would be El Salvador's Ilopango air base. As for the southern front, Secord concluded that to service the area it would be necessary to construct an emergency landing strip nearby in Costa Rica.

On August 10 North flew down to Costa Rica, where he met with Ambassador Tambs and Joe Fernandez, the CIA station chief in San José. They discussed the construction of a secret airbase that could serve as a refueling stop and forward base for supply flights, and also as a general supply depot for the southern front.

North returned to Washington and dispatched his courier, Rob Owen, to scout out a proposed location for the airstrip at Santa Elana—a sliver of lush, mountainous jungle terrain jutting out into the Pacific Ocean from northwest Costa Rica. Owen met with Tambs, then went out to survey and photograph the peninsula with Fernandez. It seemed that the property was owned by a group of people headed by an American named Joseph Hamilton, and managed by a colonel in the Costa Rican civil guard. Owen had an initial conversation with the colonel, then flew back to Washington and sent a memo to North, proposing a cover story so that the locals would not get suspicious about the land being used as a Contra airbase.

"The cover for the operation is a company, owned by a few 'crazy' gringos, wanting to lease the land for agricultural experimentation and for running cattle," Owen wrote. "A company is in the process of being formed. It might be a good idea to have it be a Panamanian company with bearer shares, this way no names appear as owners. The gringos will own two planes, registered to the company and duly registered in the country in question. Cattle will be purchased as will some farming equipment and some land plowed. The main house, which sits next to the Pan American highway, will be vacated and used by the gringos. It will be possible to use third-country nationals, although this was not extensively discussed. The colonel will provide a cook, the peons to work the farm, and security."

To negotiate the purchase of the land from Joseph Hamilton,

North turned to an old Marine buddy whom he had served with in Vietnam, William Haskell. Haskell, who lost an eye in the war, was now a Maryland tax consultant. Using the alias Robert Olmsted, Haskell flew to Costa Rica to meet with Tambs and Hamilton, and to negotiate with Costa Rican authorities for security at the airstrip after it was built.

Eventually Hamilton agreed to sell the land for several million dollars, and Tambs persuaded the Costa Rican government, apparently concerned about the Sandinista arms build-up, to permit the construction of an airstrip for refueling stops by planes that had already dropped supplies to Contra elements inside Nicaragua. At North's request, Gadd assumed responsibility for overseeing the construction of the airstrip, while Secord paid out more than $190,000 from Enterprise funds for local contractors and security at the facility. The money was channeled from Lake Resources through Secord's Panamanian-based Udall Research Corp.

The construction of the secret runway began under the code name "West Point." North then turned to nailing down the use of the northern supply base at Ilopango in El Salvador. In September he asked an ex-CIA operative named Feliz Rodriguez, who had a close relationship with a Salvadoran commander stationed at Ilopango, to assist in securing facilities at the base for the contras. Rodriguez agreed, and proceeded to make the necessary arrangements.

To administer the $27 million in humanitarian aid, President Reagan had created the Nicaraguan Humanitarian Assistance Office (NHAO), to be run by the State Department. Secretary of State Shultz appointed Robert Duemling, a veteran ambassador, to head NHAO.

Under the terms of the new law, the CIA was no longer barred from giving the Contras intelligence information, but neither the Agency nor the Pentagon could administer any of the humanitarian funds, and the funds could not be diverted to military use. Still, there was immediate confusion as to what precisely constituted humanitarian aid, and NHAO had difficulty deciding which items were and were not "humanitarian" within the meaning of the statute.

Unbeknownst to Duemling, North set out to merge part of his operation with NHAO by instructing Rob Owen to apply for a position with the new group. But despite North's glowing recommendation of Owen as a "can do" kind of person "who knows the scene," Duemling declined to hire him. The Contra leadership then weighed in with Duemling on Owen's behalf. The directorate of the United Nicaraguan Opposition (UNO)—Calero, Arturo Cruz and Alfonso Robelo—sent the ambassador a letter appealing for Owen's assistance. The letter was actually written by Owen, then signed by the three Contras. But Duemling still refused to hire Owen.

There were also logistical problems with some of the NHAO supply flights, and North sought to use this to his advantage with Duemling, arguing that someone like Owen could smooth the way. Finally Duemling relented and agreed to award a $50,000 grant so that Owen could serve as a liaison to UNO and the Contras. The grant was given to the Institute for Democracy, Education and Assistance (IDEA), a tax-exempt group Owen had formed in January of 1985 and had run out of his house. Owen, the soldier of the Reagan Doctrine, hoped that the corporation would serve as a vehicle to help all groups resisting communism around the world. Start-up money had been provided by Calero, but the grant from NHAO marked the first time IDEA began to function.

North—who had suggested, if not instructed, Owen to form IDEA—immediately took advantage of Owen's new job by having him continue to function as his liaison and logistician on the ground with the Contras, helping to get the resupply operation started— except that now Owen's trips to the region would be paid for by NHAO, thereby saving money for the Enterprise. Though the terms of Owen's contract with NHAO specifically barred him from performing "any service" related to lethal supplies "during the term of this grant," Owen continued to carry out his dual role. When he returned to Washington after a trip he would submit two reports: one to NHAO and one to North.

Later, North further involved himself in NHAO by again convincing the unsuspecting Duemling to hire Richard Gadd, Secord's associate, to fly humanitarian-aid missions down to the Contras.

By mid-1985, in addition to the Saudi- and Channell-generated assistance, there were a variety of private patchwork efforts in place which—with the approval and support of North and the White House—also helped sustain the Contras during the Boland prohibition.

As early as 1984, before Boland went into effect, the administration had taken care to disguise the true identity of its private support network by laying the foundation for a bogus Contra-donation campaign.

Edgar Chamorro, a former member of the Contras' FDN directorate, recalls that in June of 1984 Adolfo Calero had called the Miami FDN with "orders from the CIA" to take out a series of newspaper advertisements in such papers as The New York *Times* and the Miami *Herald* soliciting donations to Nicaraguan refugees in the name of a Panamanian-based group called the Human Development Foundation Inc.

"The victims of communist dominated Nicaragua need your help," said the ad's headline. "Two hundred thousand Nicaraguans out of a population of 2.7 million have fled their country to escape the ruthless Sandinista regime. While the able resist, children, women and the elderly live in refugee camps and city slums of neighboring Central American countries in sub-human conditions. We appeal to the generosity of the American people to help us give our brothers and sisters help for today and hope for tomorrow."

Actually, Chamorro told the Miami *Herald*, the ad was written and paid for by the CIA to create the illusion that the Contras were generating a fresh stream of cash on their own, and to disguise the agency's efforts to launder funds flowing in from foreign and private sources.

Until Secord received North's stamp of approval in the second half of 1984, and even afterward, the administration used a variety of sources to funnel arms to the Contras, including: Ronald Martin, a Miami arms dealer; and John Singlaub, the retired major general who was chairman of the World Anti-Communist League and its American affiliate, the U.S. Council for World Freedom.

Singlaub remained in frequent telephone contact with North and met with him at least once a month. The two had what amounted to a wink-wink relationship. "I say, 'This is what I'm going to do,'" Singlaub told Robert Parry of the Associated Press in June of 1985. "'If it's a dumb idea, send me a signal.' Nobody has called me and told me, 'You're screwing up.'"

The activities of the colorful Singlaub were attracting considerable notice in the press, attention which Singlaub later told Congress North encouraged. The general could serve as a lightning rod that might keep the spotlight away from what North himself was doing.

While North didn't discourage Singlaub's arms initiatives on behalf of the Contras, he did encourage Calero not to deal with any of Secord's competitors. But the prices Singlaub was quoting the Contras were considerably lower than Secord's. The difference was

that Singlaub was not taking a commission, while Secord was adding a markup of at least 20 to 30 percent. Still, North did what he
could to see that the arms flow passed through the Enterprise.

But Singlaub continued to make his presence felt. Through his
World Anti-Communist League contacts the general reached out to
friends in South Korea and Taiwan and put them in touch with the
administration about contributing to the Contras. Taiwan contributed $2 million in 1985.

Singlaub was also the unifying figure in a network of conservative
groups that established Contra fundraising programs—ostensibly
to send humanitarian aid to Nicaragua "refugees." Besides his own
U.S. Council for World Freedom, Singlaub helped coordinate pro-
Contra efforts with such groups as the Unification Church, the
Christian Broadcasting Corporation, the VFW, the Nicaraguan Patriotic Association, Citizens for America and Refugee Relief International. These organizations raised hundreds of thousand of dollars
in cash, food, medical supplies, clothing, boots, uniforms, boats,
helicopters and other items which lay on the humanitarian/lethal
cusp or, at the least, freed more of the Saudi-Channell funds for
military purposes.

Finally Singlaub also recruited mercenaries to help the Contras.
In a March, 1985, trip to Central America, the general met with
Contra leaders and promised, according to a report he gave North,
to recruit and send "a few American trainers" who could provide
"specific skills not available within this [sic] current resources." He
specified that these men would be "civilian (former military or CIA
personnel) who will do training only and not participate in combat
operations."

The Colorado-based *Soldier of Fortune* magazine adopted the
Contra cause in a major way, training both Contras and Salvadoran soldiers at its academic-sounding Institute for Regional and
International Studies. In the spring of 1985 the magazine led a
mission to the Contra camps in both northern and southern Nicaragua to train the resistance in how to cope with the Soviet
HIND helicopter threat. "Our entry into the camps was anti-helo
training we hoped would produce the smoking hulk of a HIND
on the jungle floor," read the magazine's account of the foray.
"We had nailed up posters all over southern Nicaragua offering a
$100,000 reward from *Soldier of Fortune* to the first HIND crew
to defect with its MI-24s intact. And we'd been passing out re-
prints of the CIA's manual on guerilla warfare—as a public service, of course."

Dozens of mercenaries from around the world flocked to the Contra camps seeking high adventure and, presumably, communist scalps. Called "wild geese" by the Contras, many of the mercenaries were ex-Special Forces soldiers who, while not especially significant in the war's grand scheme, nevertheless played important roles as trainers, consultants, mechanics, pilots and, occasionally, combatants. North, the NSC and the American military in the region knew about, tolerated and at least tacitly supported the presence of the mercenaries as a means of providing limited, and readily deniable, First World know-how to the Third World Contras.

The leading mercenary group was the Alabama-based Civilian Military Assistance (CMA), the organization which had had two of its members shot down and killed over Nicaragua in September of 1984 during Operation Elephant Herd. Formed in 1983 by Thomas Posey—a retired Marine sergeant, Vietnam veteran and former Ku Klux Klansman, according to Peter Kornbluh's book, *Nicaragua: The Price of Intervention* —CMA had begun raising money for the Contras by placing gallon pickle jars in hardscrabble general stores around the South. A message on the jars said: "Takes all of us to fight in order to stop the communists in their tracks and send them back to Russia. Fifty cents will buy one bullet to be used against them right now."

Posey liked to call members of his flock "missionary-mercenaries." In January of 1985, at President Reagan's second-term inaugural in Washington, Posey met with Rob Owen. Owen, saying that he was representing North, proceeded to enlist Posey in the then embryonic effort to open up a Contra southern front along the Costa Rican border. Posey agreed to get involved.

While laying plans for organizing the southern front, there was also renewed plotting to take the life of Eden Pastora, the renegade Contra leader who had refused to join forces with the Calero-led FDN. The principals in these discussions were Calero, Owen and John Hull (the American rancher in Costa Rica and friend of the CIA), according to a participant in the talks, Jack Terrell, who spoke to the author in a telephone interview.

Terrell was a former Alabama corrections officer who had gone on to dabble as both a mercenary and a businessman, including a stint as a regional sales manager for General Electric in the early 1980s. He had been involved with CMA and the Contras since September of 1984.

Terrell says Calero had asked him to meet with Hull, whom the Contra leader described as "the CIA's liaison to Costa Rica." A meeting was arranged at a Houston hotel in early January. Terrell registered under his code name, "Flaco," which is Spanish for "the thin one." Present at the meeting were Terrell, Hull, Owen and a Texan named Lanny Duyck, whom Terrell described as "our financial liaison between private contributors and CMA."

They discussed the logistics of establishing the southern front. "I was trying to find out who was going to pay for all this," Terrell recalls. "I asked Hull. Then Owen said, 'I take $10,000 a month in cash to Costa Rica to Hull. If we need more money we can get it.' I asked him where the money came from. He said the NSC. I said 'What's the NSC?' He said, 'The National Security Council. You know, Ollie. Ollie North.'

"But Owen did more listening than talking," Terrell said. "At one point he left the meeting and went to call Calero. We had talked about using 240 men to set up the southern front, including Contras from various groups, and some Americans. But Owen thought I meant all Americans. He got nervous and went to tell Calero that that was too many Americans. I knew what the little sucker was doing. I thought he was a college kid that had walked into the wrong room. He was not a [mercenary] community-type person. They definitely wanted Americans to be involved, just not that many. They even got down to telling us what kind of rifles we'd be using, but they said we'd have to train with .22s in Costa Rica to keep the Costa Rican authorities off our backs...

"It was Hull who first brought up Pastora. He asked if I knew Pastora. I didn't know who the hell he was. Then he said Pastora was a communist who flew the Sandinista flag in his camp. He said he had given him ammo and Pastora had turned around and sold it to the Sandinistas... He went on and on about how terrible this Pastora was. Then he said, 'We gotta get rid of the sonuvabitch.' I said, 'What do you mean?' He said, 'Kill him.'

"I was told to draw up a scenario how it was gonna be done, and to be ready to present it in Miami a week later at a meeting in Calero's house. My initial reaction was that if this guy's a commie, and it's part of the job, I'd do it."

Present several days later at the Miami meeting were Calero, Owen, Posey, Duyck, Joe Adams—an American serving as Calero's bodyguard—and several other Contra leaders. The agenda was the FDN's approval of the Owen-Hull-CMA initiative to open up a southern front. After some preliminary discussion, it was Terrell who raised the Pastora issue by way of preparing to lay out the plan that Hull had instructed him to draw up.

"Calero went into a tirade about Pastora," Terrell remembers. "He said Pastora had called him a homicidal *Somocista*. He said 'That sonuvabitch has got to go.'"

Terrell then presented his plan to kill Pastora, which was designed to make it appear as if the Sandinistas were responsible. The plan called for Calero to extend an olive branch to Pastora by inviting him to a meeting in the Costa Rican capital of San José. Calero would actually fly to San José to add credence to the story. But Pastora, as he left his home base to make the trip to San José, would be kidnapped, taken to Hull's ranch and, during the night, taken across the border into Nicaragua by a group dressed in Sandinista military uniforms. Early the following morning, the fake Sandinistas would go into the center of the nearby village of El Castillo, arouse the local populace, bring in Pastora and then stage a public hanging. They would stress to the people that this is what can happen if you cooperate with the Contras.

Calero and the others seemed satisfied with his plan, Terrell recalls. The meeting then continued for several more hours, during which time Terrell said he began to develop increasing doubts about the idea of killing Pastora. "I just thought we were fixing to get involved in something that had international consequences. If we participated in it I decided that the people sitting right there in that room wouldn't let us live to tell about it. So finally, during a coffee break, I took Posey, Duyck and Adams aside and told 'em I didn't think we could go through with this thing. I told 'em why, and I asked for a vote right then and there to see if they agreed with me. They did, 4 to 0."

Terrell has told essentially the same story in the libel case brought unsuccessfully by Hull against Avirgan and Honey in Costa Rica, as well as in a deposition for Avirgan and Honey's civil suit, and before a Miami federal grand jury which, at this writing, was still investigating these allegations, along with related charges.

Hull strongly denied Terrell's allegations in an interview, as did lawyers for Calero and Owen, though all confirmed that the meetings in question did take place. Duyck took the Fifth Ammendment when asked about the second plot on Pastora in a deposition for the Honey-Avirgan case. Adams and Posey, in telephone interviews with the author, confirm that there was a plot against Pastora, but deny any involvement themselves and say Terrell was spearheading it.

Terrell's entry in his journal for that day, which he says was made several hours after the meeting took place, generally supports his

account: "The 'termination' of Zero [Pastora] discussed with Adol-
pho [sic]..." the notes said, as reproduced in *La Penca*: Report of
an Investigation, an account of the bombing of Pastora's press conference by Avirgan and Honey. "Many people involved. Some look
like Cubans, some Nicaraguans, some Argentinian—A.C. [Adolfo
Calero] very upset with statements made by Pastora. Says he too
Sandinista. Must die. Big problem. Asks me to put it together and
not tell them how it will be done, just do it. Will have complete
cooperation of all Costa Rican officials. Have several safe houses in
C.R. under control of John Hull and Bruce Jones (another American rancher and neighbor of Hull's in northern Costa Rica). Seems
Rob Owens [sic] in on most of this... Am told he is private consultant and liaison man for U.S. [Company]... Must appear that Sandinistas did it. Discussion on capturing Zero and having men
dressed in captured uniforms. Am told this must be very visible hit
and people must believe the Sandinistas did it. Am told to let Hull
know when ready to move... A.C. open to anything. He desparate
[sic]. Wants and needs southern front."

Word was later passed back to Calero that Terrell and his friends
did not want to go through with the Pastora hit. Posey, after a pep
talk from North, was evidently reinvigorated about the general
Contra cause and the southern front specifically. Terrell, though he
had opted out of the Pastora assignment, did not ask out of CMA or
helping the Contras. But Owen, at least, was worried about Terrell's continued involvement in the movement.

"Would seem a good idea," Owen wrote North in a January 31,
1985, memo in which he referred to Terrell by his code name, "to
deal with Flacko [sic] as soon as possible. Probably will not be
scared off as he believes he has done nothing to violate the neutrality act. If he is held probably will still move forward after he is let
out, unless he can be locked up for a good long time. Best bet
might be to dry up his funds, have someone talk to him about
National Security and put the word out that he is not to be
touched. But, if possible it might be wise to do this in some way
that doesn't ruin whatever potential CMA has for the good of the
cause. Posey has been doing the best he can to either sit on Flacko
or deal him out, but that is not possible because right now Flacko
knows too much and it would do no one any good if he went to the
press. He has got to be finessed out."

In mid-March, Terrell says, he and a group of twelve other
Americans were rousted from their Honduran base camp by Honduran authorities and ordered to leave the country. Terrell said the

Hondurans explained they were acting under orders from Washington. North would acknowledge that he arranged to have Terrell expelled. Terrell later quit CMA and has since become an outspoken critic of administration policy toward Nicaragua. He now works for the International Center for Policy Development, a Washington-based anti-Contra group.

Meanwhile, working with the 2506 Brigade, a Cuban exile group, Posey continued to organize the southern-front operations in Costa Rica. He recruited two Englishmen—John Davies and Peter Glibbery—and a Frenchman, Claude Sheffard. Then two American adventurers—a former Florida highway patrolman named Robert Thompson, and Steven Carr, the twenty-six-year-old son of a Naples, Florida, IBM executive—showed up in Miami to help 2506 Brigade member Rene Corvo assemble a planeload of weaponry bound for Costa Rica.

Over the next several weeks Carr, Thompson and Corvo gathered together a mini-arsenal, including .50-caliber machine guns, G–3 automatic rifles, 60-mm mortars and 20-mm cannons. On March 6 Carr and Corvo loaded the weapons onto a small chartered plane at Ft. Lauderdale and flew to Ilopango, where the cargo was unloaded by Salvadoran soldiers and flown ahead to Costa Rica. On March 9 Glibbery, Davies and Sheffard flew to Costa Rica commercially, accompanied by Hull.

During the following month or so the mercenaries set up camp along the border in northern Costa Rica and launched several inconsequential forays into Nicaragua trying to help establish the southern front. Then on April 25 Carr, Glibbery, Davies, Sheffard and Thompson, along with nine Nicaraguans, were arrested on Hull's ranch by Costa Rican authorities and charged with "carrying out unauthorized activities."

Predictably the arrest of the mercenaries went nearly unnoticed, except at *Soldier of Fortune*, yet the incident proved to be a significant turning point in the Reagan Administration's secret Contra-support program: After three months' sitting behind bars in a Costa Rican jail with no immediate prospects of getting out, Carr and Glibbery began giving interviews to reporters and leveling accusations against Hull and his alleged involvement in the secret war as well as his links to Owen and the NSC. They said they had met with Owen at Hull's ranch, that Hull had asserted he was being paid $10,000 a month by the NSC to support the Contra effort, and that Hull was storing a quantity of C–4 plastic explosives so-that the Contras could carry out sabotage missions inside Nicaragua against economic targets.

The mercenaries' charges—denied by Hull—were made to dozens of reporters from various news organizations and generally served to energize the press and focus it inward toward the role of the White House—particularly North—in supporting the Contras during the Boland prohibition.

It was the first, albeit small, unraveling of the administration's program.

Glibbery also told of seeing Claymore mines on the ranch, where-upon, he said, Hull had remarked: "We may need that to do an embassy job later on." This was an apparent reference to a bizarre plot to assassinate Ambassador Tambs and blow up the Ameri can embassy in Costa Rica, then blame the attack on the Sandinistas in an attempt to build support in Washington for aiding the Contras.

The assassination plan—which was reported to have included a $1 million reward for Tambs' death put up by Colombian drug dealers still nursing a grudge over the ambassador's efforts to cramp their style while he was stationed in Bogota—was disclosed in mid-1985 by Jesus Garcia, a Florida corrections officer who had been recruited by Posey to help CMA earlier that year. Garcia spoke after being arrested for illegal possession of an automatic ma-chine gun, which he had obtained on behalf of Posey's CMA.

"In early February, 1985, I was approached by several members of the Freedom Fighters group regarding a planned operation in Costa Rica," said Garcia in a statement issued on his behalf by the Dade County Public Defender's office in Miami. "We met at the Howard Johnson's Motor Lodge in Miami, Florida, where Bruce Jones, Steven Carr, Mr. Thompson and Mr. Glibbery were all staying. The purpose of the meeting was to enlist my assistance in a conspiracy to attack the United States embassy in Costa Rica and assassinate the former United States Ambassador to Colombia. . . . The stated purpose of this conspiracy was to blame this operation on the Sandinistas, thus gaining support for the Freedom Fighters . . . We were all to fly to San José, where we were to meet and be provided back-up by Mr. John Hull and Mr. Bruce Jones. This operation was being coordinated by Mr. Tom Posey of Decatur, Alabama, who is providing support here in the United States for this operation."

Garcia also released a letter he had received from Steven Carr, written from the latter's Costa Rican jail cell: "I'm an American all the way," Carr wrote, "but I stop at killing other Americans for the sake of CIA war games."

OLLIE & FAWN

IF every scandal needs a heroine, then there had to be a Fawn Hall, North's striking blonde secretary whom the tabloids would christen the "Iranscam Beauty."

Where many found it difficult to follow the numbing, transcontinental intricacies of the Iran-Contra affair, when Fawn burst upon the scene—that was an element of the story everyone could relate to: the loyal secretary who just happened to look like Farrah Fawcett.

The reporters loved her. After all, chronicling Fawn's doings beat tracing corporate records and numbered Swiss bank accounts. The lowbrow press lumped her in with the year's other featured sex kittens—Donna Rice and Jessica Hahn—as "The Girls of Summer." But Fawn, to her credit, would reject out of hand that dubious badge of American celebrityhood—the half-million-dollar offer to pose nude for *Penthouse* magazine.

Part of Hall's allure, of course, was her very name: Fawn. It was not a nickname but her real name. As in Bambi, and fragile innocence. Her mother had preferred the name Danielle, but the father had insisted on Fawn, so Fawn it was. There was no middle name. Some wondered what turn the Iran-Contra saga might have taken had Mrs. Hall chosen to favor Fawn with her own given name: Wilma.

On one level, "Fawn" fit. Even at five-foot-nine, she was frail, a reedy skinny-minny who, though she lived at home with her mother and stepfather, was sickly and didn't eat enough. She had strong, traditional values and, at twenty-seven, was still holding out for Mr. Right.

On the other hand, Fawn was hardly a shrinking violet. She was a fun-loving, genuine chick who modeled part-time, tooled around in a red muscle-car and smoked Marlboro Lights. Ice-blue eyes and a cascading blonde Farrah Fawcett hairdo completed that part of the picture.

Fawn was also thoroughly likable, friendly and high-strung—sort of an East Coast Valley Girl who talked terribly fast and peppered her speech with the syntax of her generation: "Like, you know, I mean." She was honest, self-aware and intensely loyal to North. She was unsophisticated, but smart.

Overall, the Fawn package added to North's growing caché at the NSC. People started coming into his office just to gawk at his secretary. While they were there, maybe they'd transact a little business with Ollie, or maybe they wouldn't. One admirer was Bob Dutton, a retired air force colonel who would later coordinate air drops and other logistics for North and Richard Secord in the contra supply operation. On one particularly arduous sojourn to the Central American bush, Dutton was apparently daydreaming of Fawn. "I delivered 10K of grenades..." he cabled North in a coded message. "Will take 10K of mortars tomorrow... Send Fawn. Can't survive on milk and cookies."

Hall was aware that she had a slew of office admirers but tried to maintain a sense of balance. "I think it's very flattering to be depicted as beautiful, blonde, tall," she said in an interview. "I think I'm attractive, but I think there are people more attractive, and I think there are people less attractive. You have to put yourself in perspective."

In any case, Ollie and Fawn looked like the All-American couple. They were the Ken and Barbie of the White House.

Of course they weren't married. But since they worked closely together over long hours, and they were both attractive, rumors inevitably began circulating that they were having an affair. North was aware of the talk, and he began making it a point to tell visitors to his office that he and Fawn were not involved. He even went public with such preemptive denials, telling a reporter for the New York *Times* in August of 1985: "I have the prettiest secretary at the NSC. Everybody thinks I'm having an affair with her, but I'm not."

Some thought North doth protest too much, but those who knew him and Fawn well were convinced there was nothing between them. Ollie, they said, was born-again and a hopelessly loyal family man; Fawn was no scarlet woman.

Still, the rumors persisted and years later, after they had become famous and Fawn had been reassigned to the Pentagon, she remembers that North called her one day to say he'd heard a major newspaper was about to run a story saying that they had had an affair.

"I said, that's absurd..." Fawn recalls. "He said, 'Hall, you just remember, people are always going to think something like that, because had they been in that situation... they would not have done the same thing. They would not believe that two people could actually work together without having something like that go on....' He also said the article was going to say he had bought my red Fiero for me, and that he had bought me an island. And then we laughed hysterically. But nothing was ever written...

"I mean, it's absurd. I would never do that. He's like a father to me. I mean, I do care about him a lot. But he made a very good point. People, if they were capable of doing it, would think we were capable of doing it... You see two attractive people and people automatically think something's going on. That was never, never the case."

If North's wife, Betsy, was jealous of Fawn, she gave no indication of it, and the two women seemed to get along well enough. "She's a wonderful, wonderful woman..." Fawn says of Betsy. "She's into horses and her kids. She's real lighthearted, she's very cute and funny. You know... we'd talk about the office and this and that, and she'd go, 'Oh, who's that?' And I'd explain it to her, and she'd go, 'Oh, I just can't keep track of all these people.' She talks very fast like me. I have always thought to myself that if I were ever to have a family, I would love it to be like theirs, though I'd like my husband to be there a little more often than he was."

North had confided to Fawn that he had been through some rocky times with Betsy, but that they had decided they were deeply in love, and in fact were each other's best friend. "He many times referred to her as 'my best friend.'"

And if the Norths bickered, it was over the same mundane issues that afflicted all marriages, Fawn thought. "It was just typical stuff. You know, when Ollie's there, he always wants the kitchen cleaned up right away. And Betsy's like, 'No, no. Let it sit.'"

Betsy seemed to readily accept North's long hours—at least she never complained to Fawn. "She always laughed and said, 'Oh well... He'll be home at ten o'clock or whatever.'" But Fawn wasn't sure the kids were so forgiving.

Once Hall had sensed that the Norths' eldest daughter, Tait, resented the fact that her father was rarely home. "So one evening, I guess Tait was at the office, we were talking and I just turned to her and I said, 'Tait, you know your daddy is very special. I know there are times when he's not there. He's not there at night a lot... But he cares a great deal about you. And there are a lot of kids out there whose parents are there all the time. But they're not really there.'"

So North may hardly have been home, but when he was, it was quality time, Fawn believed. Once he had left the office at five P.M. so he could see Tait at cheerleading practice. Another time, he'd organized a scavenger hunt for her sixteenth birthday, picking out the prizes, hiding them and writing out the clues in poetry.

North had a traditional, almost courtly view of women, which seemed to show up in his relationship with Fawn. Whenever they worked late at night, and left the office together, he would always walk her to her car. Or if he stayed on after she left, he would summon a White House guard to escort her. He was solicitous, protective, unfailingly polite and rarely used off-color language in her presence. "If something slipped out in front of me, he always apologized," Hall says. "He went, 'Oops, excuse me.' And it didn't slip out very often. He was always a real gentleman."

That approach was a hit with Fawn, who was very much the traditionalist herself. But higher-ranking career women with policy-making jobs equivalent to North's seemed less enamored of his style, and he seemed rather befuddled by them.

"Women were homemakers to Ollie," says Neil Livingstone, a consultant on terrorism and friend of North's. "He had a Marine view of the world on women. He wasn't a skirt-chaser, but he'd get a gleam in his eye, and occasionally would make a mild, locker-room-type remark about someone's physique... You had the feeling all women were all good or bad in his cosmology: there were those you married and those you serviced on liberty. All women broke down that way. So professional women confused him. When someone like that came in the room, he wouldn't know how to handle it. He would stand up and be courtly."

As Fawn felt like a daughter to North, she said he often assumed the role of father-figure to her, showing, for example, a keen interest in whom she was dating. Actually, she worked such long hours she didn't date much, but it happened that most of the men she did go out with while working at the NSC were foreigners. North looked askance at that.

"He told me he was going to set me up with a good old American boy," Hall remembers. "He was always trying to introduce me to Roger Mudd's son. But I always said no, no no. No blind dates. But he was very concerned about it."

The object of North's greatest concern on the Fawn boyfriend front was thirty-three-year-old Arturo Cruz, Jr.

Cruz used to be a Sandinista and some U.S. officials were concerned that he might be a security risk. North was using Saudi donations to subsidize Arturo's father, Arturo Cruz, Sr.—leader of one of the three main Contra factions—to the tune of $7,000 a month. Arturo Jr. had been a Sandinista official until 1982 when he jumped over to become an influential Contra strategist. In connection with rebel politics, Arturo met North, Washington's principal liaison to the Contras, and in one of his 1985 visits to North's office, he also met Fawn. He became taken with her, and the two began a courtship which would last about fifteen months.

Though most Contras had once been Sandinistas, at least until the revolution of 1979, some Americans worried that 1982 was a little late to see the light, and that Arturo might still be doing business with Managua—and Havana, too. Arturo had worked in the Nicaraguan embassy in Washington after the revolution, then returned to Managua where he took a position in the Sandinista front's International Relations Directorate, a shadow foreign ministry of sorts. During that period, "Arturito," as he is often called, made several visits to Cuba, became acquainted with Cuban officials and married a Cuban. Cruz's mother-in-law was a member of the Cuban Communist party.

Young Cruz met regularly with North to discuss the rebel movement, but in 1986 they quarreled over internal rebel politics. His access to Ollie waned, but he kept seeing Fawn regularly. During this time, U.S. intelligence reportedly monitored a meeting between Cruz and two senior Sandinista officials at a regional peace conference in Guatemala. Cruz said the meeting was just social.

While it may be true many Sandinistas had joined the Contras, Cruz raised special worries because of his once-close working relationship with North and his continuing dating relationship with Hall. Cruz has told friends it was a nonpolitical romance and that the two never discussed Fawn's White House activities. No evidence ever emerged that he was a double-agent, nor was he apparently ever questioned. But some American security officials did try to persuade Hall to end the relationship on security grounds.

Fawn said she was questioned by David Major, an FBI agent assigned to the NSC staff. She said Major told her it was well

known throughout Central American political circles that she was
dating Cruz, and that U.S. ambassadors in the region were "very
concerned" about it. Fawn thought this odd since North, though he
had told her he disliked Arturo, had never objected to the relationship on security grounds. She would have thought she'd hear about
anything like that from Ollie first.

"He knew where my loyalty stood," Fawn says of North. "He
knew that I was loyal to him and loyal to my country. That I would
never divulge anything. And I was adamant about that... Had Arturo ever asked me anything... it would have been automatically
clear that he was going out with me for other reasons. I would
never do that. Absolutely not.

"I think the real reason I went out with him—not to slight Arturo, he's a very smart person, but I hadn't dated anybody in quite
a long time. And although he's a pretty nice guy... we just didn't
get along. And the relationship lasted a lot longer than it should
have. I just didn't have the heart to break it. It would have been
broken a lot sooner had I had the heart to do it."

Far from being offended by the inquiry from Major, Fawn was
pleased that her government was alert enough to ask. "Look at it
this way: thank God that they were concerned about it. If they
weren't, I'd be a little concerned. But Arturo obviously is on our
side... I didn't know at the time all that background on him. I
knew he was with the Sandinistas. But one thing Arturo told me
was that if you weren't a Sandinista when the revolution happened,
you weren't a good Nicaraguan. The revolution happened to get rid
of Somoza, who was just abusive... But that was all betrayed."

Working at the Pentagon, pre-North, Fawn had been used to
calling her bosses by their military titles. But at the civilian-domi-
nated NSC, that was out. Not even the military men were referred
to as major, colonel or whatever their rank happened to be. So
when the twenty-four-year-old Fawn first signed on with North at
the NSC in 1983 and greeted him as "Major North... people
looked at me like I had a disease," she recalls, laughing. "I mean, it
was Ollie."

But after they got acquainted, they began calling each other by
their last names. It seemed a combination of informality and affection. "He used to call me Hall, and I called him North. It was like,
'Hey, Hall, get this.' Or, 'Hey, North, get this,' you know...
Sometimes when I was really tired, I'd say I couldn't handle this
anymore, and he'd laugh and say, 'Hey, Hall, I've been through

worse. You're twenty-seven.' And I said, 'See? I've lost three years of my life with you.' I didn't mean it, you know. I mean, we had a good relationship. A good working relationship."

She got some overtime, but not all that she was entitled to. She wouldn't put in for all of it because she felt guilty. No other secretary on the NSC worked the hours she worked, and she didn't want to make waves. Plus there was a limit of ten hours of overtime per week for each secretary. None of the others came close to using their allotted ten hours, so Fawn felt as long as the overtime budget was there, she should be given her due if the other secretaries didn't work as hard. But she didn't want to show them up, so she never made an issue of it.

Fawn had been accepted by her peers after overcoming the initial obstacles of her looks and her lineage. Her mother was Wilma Hall, who in government secretarial circles is a near-legend. Mrs. Hall had been at the NSC for seventeen years, was secretary to Henry Kissinger during his reign at the council, and had been at his right hand when he made the secret overtures to China. She later became secretary to Robert McFarlane and John Poindexter when they succeeded to the post of National Security advisor.

Some say Fawn helped North by using her mother to increase Ollie's access to McFarlane and, later, Poindexter. "If Ollie wanted to see Bud or John, all he'd have to do is have Fawn call mom," says one of North's former colleagues. But Fawn denies this, saying North earned his access because he was handling some of the most sensitive issues in the White House. And anyway, she and Wilma would never discuss the substantive parts of their jobs and would often go days without any contact, she added.

North had warned Fawn when he hired her that she might have a difficult time at first. The other secretaries might think nepotism was at work because of Wilma. Then, too, Ollie had chosen Fawn over another woman who was older and had kids, and there would be those who assumed he had picked Hall solely because of her beauty.

But Fawn had persevered and distinguished herself as a first-rate secretary who was indispensable to North. She was his Della Street: not just a secretary but a right hand and a confidante. Though her looks may have been distracting to some, she was clearly qualified for what she did. She had more than six years of experience before coming to the NSC. She had taken a part-time secretarial job at the Pentagon at the age of sixteen while still in high school. Then she began working full time for the navy in 1977, where she remained until 1983 when she was detailed to the NSC and North.

Becoming a secretary had been a lifetime goal. Raised in suburban Annandale, Virginia, in placid middle-class surroundings, Fawn was always drawn more toward work than academe.

She appreciated her mother's hard work. Her parents were divorced when she was small. Then Wilma had remarried, to Ronald Hall, a photographer for the Department of Defense. Fawn recalls a happy childhood. "I wasn't a cheerleader, and I didn't go to football games...But I had a few friends and we hung out and, you know, just did the things that kids do."

She pondered modeling as a full-time career, and even went for a tryout at Barbizon, but Wilma counseled against it. She had also been a talented artist, churning out watercolors, silkscreens, pen-and-inks. But that seemed too impractical. She had thrilled to her mother's tales of working for Kissinger and taking dictation as he conversed with Chou En-Lai in China. Being a secretary seemed a heady, interesting life, if you could get the right job.

"So I went into it because I liked it," Fawn recalled. "And I was excellent at shorthand. I love shorthand. You either love it or you hate it. And I love being a secretary...A secretary is not just a typist. A secretary is a facilitator. And I think there are a lot of women out there who want the title 'executive assistant,' and all that stuff. Why? Why is it so demeaning to be a secretary if you're good? A secretary is, in fact, you know, in many ways a boss's right-hand man. If she's good. I mean a clerk-typist is a clerk-typist, a receptionist is a receptionist and a secretary is a secretary."

Fawn had wanted to go to work right away; college held no appeal. She wanted to strut her stuff in the real world. She wanted to make a statement. She bought a sporty, fire-engine red Pontiac Fiero with a license plate that read FAWN. She wore expensive clothes.

"Yeah, I wanted to have nice things. I bought a brass bed. I wanted to have an apartment with just a few nice things...I didn't want to spend fifty dollars on something when I could spend a hundred dollars and get something that was really worth something. I bought things. I bought nice things. And the money went."

Even being a GS–9 at the NSC only paid about $25,000 a year. So she took a second secretarial job for a while, until that became too much of a strain, then did some part-time modeling.

Before going to work at the White House, Fawn attended the Cappa Chell Modeling Agency and Finishing School. At the finishing school she took a variety of classes, including personality, etiquette, social graces, skin care, hand care, makeup and hairstyling. She also completed the modeling program, learning such techniques as "pivoting" and "projecting."

"I love clothes," she says. "I love to keep up with fashion. And that was one thing I had a hard time dealing with, moving to the White House . . . I came in and people were wearing blue skirts and white shirts and ties around their necks, and penny loafers. I didn't want to stick out, but I didn't want to compromise my own feeling of who I was."

She was primarily a runway model, working at fashion shows, and though she loved the work, her NSC job was so demanding she would frequently have to turn down jobs because she didn't have the time.

In early 1986, Fawn's work pace finally caught up with her and she suffered a collapsed lung, which confined her to a wheelchair for a time. The office routine just seemed a blur of activity—her fingers flying away at the word processor, answering phones, taking messages and directing traffic in and out of North's office. There always seemed to be a crisis; the atmosphere was frenetic.

But North didn't seem frazzled by the pace. Though he was pursuing the most serious business in the land, he never seemed self-absorbed or serious, Fawn thought. In fact, he had an impish smile and a twinkle in his eye that spelled wiseguy, and he had a keen sense of humor that he often used to defuse tension. Like the time after the invasion of Grenada, when he had broken her up with his report that Eugenia Charles, the sixty-five-year-old prime minister of Dominica, had leavened an otherwise dull meeting with Caribbean leaders in the Oval Office by earnestly thanking Reagan for liberating Grenada, and saying to him with great conviction: "Mr. President, you have *big* balls!"

Fawn's desk was in an anteroom outside North's small, cramped office in Room 392 of the old Executive Office Building. Nearby was a coffee machine that was always on, and tacked above the machine was a piece of right-wing pop art: a mock poster touting a film called *The Return of Walter Mondale*. The poster promised that the candidate would be "More boring than ever."

North's stuffy quarters consisted of a desk, a couch and a chair. On the walls were finger paintings and drawings done by his children; a photo of President Reagan posing with Contra leaders, and North in the background; and all manner of maps—including Nicaragua, El Salvador, Libya, Lebanon's Bekaa Valley, Beirut and various aerial photographs. An old Marine uniform hung in a corner, and on the windowsill there sat a Chinese People's Liberation Army fur hat emblazoned with the red star.

His desk was overflowing with reports, memos and other paperwork, and behind the desk were a slew of books—mostly on Central America—and a Bible. There were three telephones: one was black-and-white, for normal use; one was beige, for secure calls; and the other, known as the "gray line," was a direct link to the headquarters of the National Security Agency in suburban Maryland.

There were three computer terminals in the office: one provided instant access to the wire services and could tap into the NSC network to send and receive messages; a second linked up with secret cable traffic between Washington and American embassies around the world; and the third tied North to a counter-terrorism operations center at NSA headquarters.

Ollie's days would start at 7:30 in the morning with a senior staff meeting, which was supposed to be attended only by the directors of each section of the NSC. Though North was a deputy director, his accounts were so weighty that it was understood he would attend this meeting. He usually would not go home at night before 10:00, and often he would stay until midnight or 1:00 in the morning.

North rarely had time to read the newspapers. Fawn never did. She never even took breaks like most of the other secretaries did. He seldom went out to lunch with anyone, and then only if it was a working lunch. She would often urge him to go have a quick sandwich with some of his friends who would call the office. She had stacks of messages piled up, calls to return. She wished he wouldn't neglect his friends, no matter how busy he was, and she tired of having to put them off. But he always said there simply wasn't time. So they would just have lunch at their desks—Fawn would usually go downstairs and bring back a salad from the cafeteria.

"He'd always have a general or somebody waiting outside to see him," Fawn remembers. "And I'd buzz and go, 'Ollie are you done yet? Hurry up!' And he'd go, 'All right, all right. I'll be there in a few minutes.' And fifteen minutes would go by and I'd say, 'I'm sorry, sir, just a few more minutes.' I was always doing that. That's how I got to know the people that were out there, and now they're friends of mine."

North was a compulsive memo-writer and note-taker. He spent

hours writing notes on his word processor, sending messages to McFarlane, Poindexter or whomever—messages that would later be retrieved by the Tower Commission. He wouldn't share the substance of those messages with Fawn.

"I used to always try and get him off the word processor," she said. "I didn't know exactly what Ollie was writing there. I used to say, 'Ollie, we have other stuff to do.' And he'd say, 'I'll just finish this note.' I used to always be the whip behind him, trying to get him to move on to other things. I don't know a lot about what was in those notes."

When North wasn't using his word processor to fire off a message, he would often scribble notes in one of the small spiral notebooks he kept filling. He would write both mundane and substantive material in the pads—everything from reminders to bring home milk to notes taken at meetings, Fawn said.

Much of the time, of course, North would not be in the office at all. At a moment's notice he could be off to the Middle East, Europe or Central America. And since he had been threatened by the terrorist Abu Nidal, Fawn booked his airline tickets under the name William Goode—an alias for which the CIA had supplied North a passport. Ollie seemed to get off on the cloak-and-dagger stuff. Fawn supposed it was a bit silly that he insisted on using such code names as 'Goode,' 'Steelhammer' or 'Blood and Guts.' But boys will be boys, or perhaps security demanded it, she didn't know which. And Fawn thought it was kind of fun. She had a code name too: Sunshine.

Fawn could be territorial when she felt others were intruding on her professional relationship with North. When Robert Earl—like North, a Marine lieutenant colonel—and Craig Coy, a Coast Guard commander, were assigned to work with North on terrorism and set up shop in his outer office, it upset the routine Hall had grown accustomed to. Earl and Coy even began performing some of the tasks Fawn had been doing—such as coordinating the correspondence between President Reagan or Vice-President Bush and the hostage families. So she went to North to protest.

"I said, 'You know...I enjoy this part of my job. Please let me keep this.' And he said, 'Hey, I understand. We've got to work here together.' And he kind of straightened things out.

"I remember another time he and Bob were kind of in there bullshitting and I walked in," she continued. "You know, they were talking. And I always considered whatever bullshitting that Ollie did with those guys in the end was very productive because it was about work. But because we were working at such a fast pace, I thought that any time you were just talking, even if it was about business, it was wasting time, when I had zillions of phone calls for him to return, and I was, like, trying to get those out, so my responsibilities would be done so I could leave the office. And I guess Bob said, 'How do you let her walk in and tell you what to do? I've seen you get rid of sergeants for less than that.' And Ollie just turned to him and said, 'Listen, she's the best one I've ever had.'"

As others gave him loyalty, so North returned it, Hall said. He would tolerate no criticism of people who worked for him or of those whom he considered his friends. And by skillfully using his amiable persona, he was often able to cajole recalcitrant subordinates into being more productive.

"There was a girl in 392 who worked in our suite," Hall remembers. "There were three of us secretaries. She had a tendency to slam the phones, and for some reason if you asked her to do something she—if you weren't directly her boss—wouldn't do it. She was like, 'I work only for'... whoever. She wasn't a team player, in other words. And nobody else could ever get her to do anything. But Ollie would walk over, we'd be in a crunch, and he'd say, you know, 'Can you, Janet, would you... do this for me?' And he slowly turned her around. I mean, it was amazing...

"He was very charming, inspiring. He gave my life direction... He gave my life a lot of meaning. He was a sincere person. He was good to a lot of people, and they would follow him forever. I wouldn't say that about anybody, but I would feel pretty safe saying it about Ollie North. I've just never come across a person as honest and good-natured as him in my life. He doesn't tend to say bad things about people. He's just a fair person.

"There were times when he got frustrated, but in four years I never saw a temper. He made everyone work as a team. I mean, he was of course the boss and you respected that, but he didn't make that a point... I worked for the man for four years. I came to know him. I never saw a flaw in him. I mean, that's pretty deep to say ... But I never did. The only thing I'd see was that he was always running late... And I was always the whip trying to get him to be there. That was my job.

"I didn't ask questions because I believed in whatever he was doing. I don't believe that he was doing any of this for himself. I mean, Ollie North didn't need an extra star for his shoulder. He didn't need to be assistant Secretary of State, or he didn't need to be assistant Secretary of Defense. Colonel North has always been Colonel North... He never changed like a lot of people do when they get into the White House. They get White House-itis. They get into the hub of where the power is and they start feeling like, you know, they're bigger and better, and for some reason they inflate themselves... Ollie's always been Ollie North. He never changed."

Proof, for Fawn, that North never got White House-itis, as she put it, was the fact that he often spoke longingly of returning to the Marine Corps and assuming a command. He may have been involved in heady stuff at the NSC, but in the Corps such political work was looked upon with disdain. Many of the leathernecks thought Ollie had gone political, and it was no secret that he was losing promotion opportunities the longer he stayed at the White House.

Once, in 1985, it was decided that Ollie would be transferred to Camp Lejeune and take over a battalion, Fawn said. It had been all set. He had his orders, his house outside Washington was rented and the family had gathered their things in boxes ready for the movers. Then one day the phone rang at home, and it was the Marine commandant, P.X. Kelley. North's daughter, Sarah, answered and told her father it was the commandant calling. North took the phone and loudly said, "Sure, right!" pretending to be irritated with her. And it was, in fact, Kelley. He said McFarlane had decided that Ollie should stay in Washington; that they couldn't afford to lose him now.

As North's secretary, Fawn typed and handled some of the most sensitive documents in government. But she was still a secretary. She rarely, if ever, stepped back and thought about the larger issues she was dealing with. She would read a memo for grammar and punctuation, not for content. Still, she came to have some impressions about the operations they were involved in, and would occasionally express her thoughts to North.

On the Contras, the U.S. was supposed to be lending equal weight and support to the three main factions—headed by Adolfo Calero, Alfonso Robelo and Arturo Cruz, Sr.—while trying to bring all three together in a unified fighting force. But Fawn said it was widely known that North favored Calero. "I thought in order to make this thing work we couldn't have that perception," and so she let him know.

The Iran initiative she would see as an effort to thwart Soviet designs on Tehran, not as an arms-for-hostages deal. "Khomeini was very ill, and oftentimes when there is instability in a country, that's the time when communism or the Soviets intervene in a country—when it's weakest. And my interpretation was that there were people over [in Iran] who were concerned about it. And . . . that these people sought us out and talked about it. And we, you know, through thorough checking, responded."

As for the hostages in Lebanon, there was constant pressure to win their release. "The media was pushing—'You're not doing enough.' The families were pushing—'You're not doing enough.' They were driving it down our throats . . ."

Though she sometimes complained about the long, torturous hours she worked, Fawn wouldn't have traded her job for any other. Beyond the specifics of any given issue, what gave her a rush was simply the sense that she was right there at the cutting edge of history unfolding.

And she had the strong feeling that in working for North, she was on the side of the angels. There was a great sense of urgency about their work. A sense of life-and-death importance. There was a feeling of esprit de corps. They had access to intelligence and information that Congress and the American people did not. Those who opposed them just didn't have all the facts. She believed in the justness of their cause. There may just be times—and she knew this was problematic—when going above, or around, the law was justified. In pursuit of the greater good.

In any case, she had an unshakable confidence in North. She admired his can-do spirit. Where others might see this drive as zealotry, she saw it as energetic, positive, hardworking. He was the Puritan ethic itself. And whenever there was a crisis, Ollie would handle it. She noticed that around the White House, when things got really sticky, a "let Ollie do it" mindset seemed to develop among the powers that be. And he would always respond. He would never kiss off an assignment with a lame excuse, as others she knew did. If a job needed to be done, he'd take care of it right then and there. Hall liked and admired that.

She also liked his passionate advocacy of the causes he believed in, and she came to believe in those same causes. Especially the Contras and Central America.

"He cared passionately about the Contras and the need to support them. Congress went back on that promise. Those people are down there. Who speaks for America, the president or the Congress? We have to work together on this. It's not fair to people down there to say you're going to support them and then leave them dry. You flip back and forth. It's really hard . . . I guess Ollie thought that once we gave them our word that we shouldn't go back on that. That was unfair. He doesn't want to see American troops down there. I mean, why not support people who are willing to fight themselves? . . . Here was a man trying to do the best for his country . . . It's just sad we overlook what we're doing here—we're tearing each other apart. And we all overlook the motives behind everything. I've never seen Congress try so hard to make sure a law was abided by. I mean, there are other laws, you know? I'm just saying that we've got to put this all in perspective."

They were ideologues bent on implementing a policy they believed in intensely, though they knew the policy was on shaky legal ground at best. "I really do think he was walking a fine line," she admits. "I didn't know if he crossed that line or not. My opinion was that it was important to support the Contras. . . . I didn't see Ollie North as a dishonest person or someone that would be doing something for himself. There must have been a reason why he was doing it. And all I'm saying is, it wasn't my place to say . . . History shows that there have been tons of cases [where breaking the law has been justified]. Your wife is about to die and you have to break the law and speed; civil rights; there's all different areas where that's been proven. I believe it was important to bridge the gap in funding, and I don't know—we still don't know—if it was against the law."

Fawn fervently believed that North always acted out of the purest patriotic motives. "Ollie tried his best to do what was best. Anybody that's done his best is bound to find victory and find failure. People are sitting around criticizing Ollie when he did what he knew was best for this country. And I think people ought to stop and think about that. This is not a guy from Wall Street pocketing money . . .

"They want so much to say that this was a total failure. I don't find it that way. And I think it's wrong for people to cloak-and-dagger this whole thing and make it a sideshow. It's not a sideshow, what happened. . . . I believed in this. I still believe in it . . . The American people are impressed with the fact that we were patriotic people and that we were doing this for the country. And I don't want to cheapen that . . . I understand that the people have a right to know certain things, but for the security of the nation, there are certain things that people don't need to know."

STONEWALLING

NORTH was irritated by the press nipping at his heels.

Those doing the earliest nipping, in June of 1985, were Robert Parry of the Associated Press and Alfonso Chardy of the Miami *Herald*. In a June 3 memorandum to Poindexter, North said that he had played hardball with Chardy. He said he had instructed Adolfo Calero to warn the reporter that if he "printed any derogatory comments about the FDN or its funding sources that Chardi [sic] would never again be allowed to visit FDN bases or travel with their units."

In the same memo North had also expressed concern about rumors that Parry had a potentially damaging story in the works. A week later Parry published the first story specifically linking North to private Contra-support efforts.

Then the publicity resulting from allegations made by the jailed mercenaries in Costa Rica, Steven Carr and Peter Glibbery, had not been helpful to North's desire to remain essentially in the woodwork as a White House covert operative. Finally, in early August, there began a drumbeat of stories in major newspapers that chipped away at, and finally shattered, North's closely guarded anonymity.

On August 8 the New York *Times* published a front-page article saying that the Contras had been receiving direct military advice from White House officials on the NSC. But the *Times* acceded to White House requests that it not name North on the grounds that to do so might threaten his safety. The story said only that the operation was being run by "a military officer who is a member of the National Security Council." It quoted "a senior NSC official," believed to be McFarlane, as saying the officer in question was a

"worker bee" who had done "whatever is allowed by law" to help
the Contras, including providing advice prior to Contra attacks and
facilitating the supplying of logistical support.

The Washington *Post* prepared a story for the following day essentially restating the *Times* article, but naming North. That night,
when the White House got wind of the *Post*'s plans, Press Secretary
Larry Speakes called the *Post*'s managing editor, Leonard Downie,
at home and asked that North's name be taken out of the story.

Speakes again explained that North was concerned about his
safety. When Downie asked specifically how North stood to be
harmed, Speakes said he did not know but that McFarlane had
spoken directly with the *Times* about that and he could do the same
for the *Post*. McFarlane turned out to be traveling and unavailable,
so Speakes offered to have North call Downie. Meanwhile Downie
ordered North's name removed from the early editions.

When North called Downie he did not offer many more specifics
than Speakes. "He just said he and his family would be in danger,"
Downie recalls. Though unsatisfied with the explanation, Downie
said that out of caution he decided to have the name kept out of the
remaining morning editions. But he ordered the preparation of a
more detailed story for that Sunday—a story that, unless the White
House could offer a more compelling reason to withhold North's
identity, would go ahead and name him.

The result was an August 11 page-one profile of North, complete
with an accompanying article on the jump-page inside. Whereas
most people in government had probably not seen the earlier Parry
and Chardy pieces, circulated chiefly in the so-called provinces,
there would be no missing the two *Post* stories appearing the same
day under the byline of reporter Joanne Omang:

"In a city of largely invisible staff workers, Marine Lt. Col.
Oliver L. North of the National Security Council staff has emerged
as an influential and occasionally controversial character in the implementation of the Reagan Administration's foreign policy," the
story began. It said he had played a "pivotal" role in the White
House's Central America policy, and "in that capacity, his activities
raise questions about a gray area of government policy. At a time
when Congress had voted to outlaw direct aid to the anti-Sandinista
rebels in Nicaragua, North worked actively to assure the counter-
revolutionaries, or Contras, that the U.S. government fully supported their cause."

The story further said that while North agreed to be interviewed,
McFarlane had refused to allow it. The article quoted McFarlane

defending North: "He's not a rogue elephant but rather like a son of mine," the National Security Advisor said.

The publication of the *Post* profile stirred conservatives to the same degree of protest that might have attended the naming of a CIA agent. Downie began receiving harassing phone calls at home around 5 A.M. from a man who protested the use of North's name. The man, who refused to identify himself, "was fairly well spoken, with a crisp, military-type bearing," Downie recalls. When the caller persisted in refusing to call the newspaper during office hours and had made about five or six phone calls to Downie's house at the same early-morning hour, Downie decided to write North a letter, thinking the colonel might know something about the calls.

"The letter merely said I thought he should know someone had been harassing us in early-morning phone calls," Downie said. "I got a letter back from North saying he was investigating this and he regretted it. Then the phone calls stopped." Several months later, when Downie was meeting with CIA Director Casey on an unrelated topic, Casey asked Downie: "How are you and Ollie getting along?" The director clearly knew all about North's spat with the *Post*. Downie then told him the story about the phone calls, and, he reports, Casey chuckled.

The *Post* story created a ripple. Eleven days later even the Soviet newspaper *Izvestia* weighed in with a profile of North, calling him "the favorite of the American extremist" who "spares neither time nor effort in mobilizing the forces of reaction . . . with the aim of removing the legal obstacles in the way of escalating the war against the Nicaraguan people." Then Abu Nidal, the Palestinian terrorist, released a "hit list" which included North's name. Furious, North fretted that his ability to work covertly had been blown. He was convinced that the *Izvestia* piece and the Abu Nidal hit list had been the work of the Soviet KGB. This was precisely why he had tried to keep his name out of the *Post* and *Times* stories. Still, for all the sudden provocations from afar, the most immediate concern of North and the White House was the reaction to the articles on Capitol Hill.

In the third week of August, Representative Michael Barnes, the Maryland Democrat who was chairman of the House Subcommittee on Western Hemisphere Affairs, and Representative Lee Hamilton, the Democrat from Indiana who was chairman of the House Permanent Select Committee on Intelligence, each wrote a letter to McFarlane asking for an explanation of the NSC's actions—specifically North's—in support of the Contras. The chairman and vice-chairman of the Senate Select Committee on Intelligence—respectively David Durenberger, Republican of Minnesota and Patrick Leahy, Democrat of Vermont—also wrote McFarlane asking for an explanation, as did another congressman, Illinois Democrat Richard Durbin. But it was the Barnes and Hamilton inquiries that occupied most of McFarlane's and his staff's time.

Barnes's letter, dated August 16, said recent press reports "raise serious questions regarding the violation of the letter and spirit of U.S. law." He asked if the NSC staff had been involved in providing the Contras with tactical military advice, contacts for potential financial contributions or "otherwise organizing and coordinating rebel efforts." The letter concluded with a request for all information and documents "pertaining to any contact between Lt. Col. North and Nicaraguan rebel leaders as of enactment of the Boland Amendment in October, 1984."

Hamilton's letter, less demanding, requested "a full report on the kinds of activities regarding the Contras that the NSC carried out and what the legal justification is for such actions given the legislative prohibitions that existed last year and earlier this year."

McFarlane first responded to Hamilton, writing the congressman on September 5: "I can state with deep personal conviction that at no time did I or any member of the National Security Council staff violate the letter or spirit" of congressional restrictions on Contra aid. He added: "I am most concerned . . . there be no misgivings as to the existence of any parallel efforts to provide, directly or indirectly, support for military or paramilitary activities in Nicaragua. There has not been, nor will there be, any such activities by the NSC staff."

The same day McFarlane sent out that letter he met with Senators Durenberger and Leahy, assuring them that "no law had been broken," and that "there was no intent to circumvent restrictions Congress placed on aid to the Nicaraguan resistance." He said he was confident that no NSC staff member had either helped the Contras or solicited outside help on their behalf, adding: "I can't believe everything everyone says, but I do believe Ollie."

Five days later McFarlane met with Hamilton and other members of the House Intelligence Committee and offered them similar assurances. At the end of the session Hamilton told McFarlane: "I, for one, am willing to take you at your word."

The September 5 letter to Hamilton would serve as the model for five others North would prepare and send out over McFarlane's signature in response to the congressional inquiries. Replying later to charges that he had lied to Congress, McFarlane, testifying before the congressional Iran-Contra committees, would concede only that his responses had been "too categorical . . . I did not give as full an answer as I should have." But North, testifying before the same committees, would go further, conceding that the statements were "false . . . erroneous, misleading, evasive and wrong."

When Barnes's letter arrived at the White House, Admiral Poindexter assigned North to draft a reply, noting on a memo that "Barnes is really a troublemaker. We have good answers to all of this." Poindexter would later acknowledge in his Iran-Contra testimony that his intent at that time was to "withhold information" from Barnes.

The search for documents to comply with Barnes' request was conducted narrowly, excluding a search of the files in North's office. Within a few days about fifty relevant documents were assembled, ten to twenty of which were considered worthy of review by the NSC's general counsel, Paul Thompson. Thompson passed on the documents to McFarlane and raised the possibility of asserting executive privilege in declining to turn them over.

McFarlane selected six memorandums, all from North to himself, which "seemed to me to raise legitimate questions about compliance with the law," he would later testify. "An objective reading would have taken passages in each of these memorandums to be either reflective of a past act that was not within the law or a recommendation that a future act be carried out that wouldn't be."

The first memo, dated December 4, 1984, described a meeting between North and a Chinese government official in which North tried to persuade the Chinese to sell weaponry to the Contras via Guatemala, which had agreed to cooperate in the end-user certificate scam. This showed that North, less than two months after the adoption of the most restrictive version of the Boland Amendment in October, was trying to obtain antiaircraft missiles and launchers for the Contras. The memo also recounted a North meeting with General Singlaub in which the general detailed his efforts to solicit funds for the Contras from South Korea and Taiwan—as well as the proposal by David Walker, the former British Special Air Services officer, offering to conduct sabotage operations for the Contras.

The second memo, dated February 6, 1985, was North's proposal either to sink or seize the Sandinista merchant ship *Monimbo*. The third memo, dated March 5, 1985, was North's request that more aid be funneled to Guatemala in return for its agreeing to participate in the end-user certificate dodge. The fourth document, dated March 16, 1985, was North's "fallback plan" to help the Contras if Congress did not vote more aid. His recommendations included: the president publicly urging Americans to contribute funds for humanitarian aid to the Contras; creating a tax-exempt corporation to receive donations; and going back to Saudi Arabia with a request for another $25 million to $30 million.

In the fifth memo—April 11, 1985—North described how the Contras had spent the $24.5 million that had been given them since "USG (United States government) funding expired." Most of the money, he said, had gone for "arms, ammunition and other ordnance items." Finally, in the sixth memo, dated May 31, 1985, North outlined the "near-term outlook" for the Contras, describing a continued close U.S. involvement with the resistance during the Boland prohibition.

These memos, though they represented only a fraction of the correspondence between North and McFarlane, could not be handed over to Barnes, inasmuch as they revealed what seemed an ongoing attempt to subvert Boland. Accordingly McFarlane and North held a series of meetings between August 28 and September 12 to fashion a strategy to deal with Barnes. What they discussed, according to the final report of the congressional Iran-Contra committees, was altering the memos, but North and McFarlane now differ as to what their purpose was in doing this.

According to McFarlane's testimony, as they reviewed the documents North said that his memos were being misinterpreted. For example, North had written that the Contra leadership in the FDN "has responded well to guidance on how to build a staff." But North actually meant that the guidance had come from retired military officers, not from him. "Well, as we went through them," McFarlane testified, "he pointed out where my own interpretation was just not accurate . . . and he just said, 'You are misreading my intent, and I can make it reflect what I have said if this is ambiguous to you,' and I said, 'All right. Do that.'"

North soon returned with a sample change on his April 11, 1985 memo. Where he had originally recommended "that the current donors be approached to provide $15–20M additional between now and June 1, 1985," that was now replaced with the more innocuous recommendation that "an effort must be made to persuade the Congress to support the Contras." McFarlane acknowledged in his testimony that this change left the new document "grossly at variance with the original text." But he said he never replaced the original documents with North's alterations and later destroyed the pages on which North had made changes.

But North's testimony would differ sharply on what occurred at these meetings. After bringing the documents to his attention McFarlane "indicated that there were problems with them and told me to fix them," North testified. This meant he was to "remove references to certain activities, certain undertakings on my behalf or his, and basically clean up the record... The documents, after all, demonstrated his knowledge and cognizance over what I was doing, and he didn't want that. He was cleaning up the historical record. He was trying to preserve the president from political damage. I don't blame him for that."

North testified he did not actually get around to making the requested alterations on all the memos for more than a year. In the meantime McFarlane decided not to provide Barnes with any documents at all.

In a September 12 letter to the congressman, McFarlane offered broad assurances that the NSC had complied with both the letter and spirit of Boland, and added, "None of us has solicited funds, [or] facilitated contacts for prospective potential donors..."

And though he himself had facilitated, if not solicited, the two main donations to the Contras from Saudi Arabia amounting to $32 million, McFarlane, in an October 7 reply to another query from Congressman Hamilton, denied that he knew where the Contras had obtained millions of dollars in financing. He also denied in the letter that North had been a focal point for private fundraising groups, that North had used his influence to facilitate the movement of supplies to the Contras, or that the colonel had given them tactical advice. North testified that the latter three assertions were false.

Barnes did not accept the letter McFarlane sent him. In a September 30 reply the congressmen wrote that neither he nor his colleagues could assess if the NSC had acted legally unless they were given the documentary evidence. The two agreed to a meeting at the White House on October 17. The day before the meeting Thompson, the NSC general counsel, advised McFarlane in a memo that he should tell Barnes that the National Security Advisor had no legal authority to turn over the documents in question.

The North memorandums had been written at McFarlane's instructions "in furtherance of the president's initiatives," Thompson wrote. As such they were "internal and deliberative in nature and are furthermore not NSC agency documents. As presidential advisory papers, they fall under the dominion of the president, and are no longer subject to your disposition."

At their meeting McFarlane showed Barnes a stack of documents piled on his desk. Those were the relevant documents. Barnes was free to examine them there in McFarlane's office but they could not leave the room. McFarlane later acknowledged he made this offer knowing Barnes would likely refuse it. Indeed, Barnes considered the proposal frivolous and argued that he needed the benefit of staff expertise to examine the memos. Several days later Barnes made a compromise proposal that the documents be given to the House Intelligence Committee to satisfy McFarlane's security concerns. But at that point McFarlane just let the issue drop.

The increasing press scrutiny of North's and the NSC's activities also triggered a cursory investigation by the Intelligence Oversight Board, a White House panel charged with monitoring the nation's intelligence agencies. The probe, such as it was, was conducted by Bretton Sciaroni, a former Hoover Institute fellow who had joined the board in 1984 and begun working as its counsel without having passed the bar exam. He finally passed the exam several months later on his fifth attempt.

Sciaroni's investigation consisted of a forty-minute interview with Thompson, who turned over an inch-thick stack of documents, minus the six "troubling" memos from North to McFarlane. Thompson offered assurances that North had provided only moral, not military, support to the Contras. Sciaroni then interviewed North for five minutes, and the colonel flatly denied that he had been involved in helping the Contras. Sciaroni concluded that North was telling the truth and the matter was ended.

Asked about the Sciaroni interview two years later in his testimony at the Iran-Contra hearings, North said: "I'm sure if he asked me . . . I denied it, because after all, we viewed this to be a covert operation, and he had absolutely no need to know the details of what I was doing."

ACHILLE LAURO

IF anything could serve to divert the attention of prying congressmen and journalists it was the life-and-death drama of an international terrorist incident involving the taking of American hostages—with Ollie North wearing the white hat on behalf of the good guys.

On Monday morning, October 7, 1985, four Palestinian terrorists, guns blazing, burst into the dining room of the Italian cruise ship *Achille Lauro* as it was sailing in the Mediterranean off the coast of Egypt. They wounded two passengers, gained control of the ship and soon demanded the release of fifty Palestinians being held in Israel.

The boat had been on its way from Alexandria to Port Said, near the Suez Canal, when the hijacking occurred. Most of the 680 passengers had disembarked in Alexandria for a day of sightseeing and planned to reboard the ship in Port Said. There were still 350 crew members and 70 to 80 passengers—including 14 Americans—on board the vessel when it was seized.

North, as chairman of the Terrorist Incident Working Group, the interagency panel formed in 1984 to cope with such incidents, was monitoring from the Situation Room events in the Mediterranean as they unfolded. This was the second major hijacking in four months—in June, TWA's Flight 847 had been hijacked by Shiite gunmen over Greece beginning a seventeen-day ordeal that ultimately saw all but one of the 145 passengers released safely. One, American Navy diver Robert Stehem, was shot and killed, his body shoved out of the plane and dumped onto the airport tarmac in Beirut. Now the White House was fairly aching somehow to "win" one of these jousts, to fire up the national psyche and to get even for past humiliations inflicted on a proud giant by distant, amorphous fanatics.

A military rescue option was planned from the outset. By the beginning of the second day a team of Navy SEALS—commando frogmen trained on land, in the air and in the sea and considered perhaps the best special operations unit in the United States—was in place at Akrotiri, the British air force base at the southern tip of Cyprus. As added American counterterrorist elements arrived in supporting roles, plans were laid for a mid-sea rescue attempt. The plan called for the SEALS to fly over the *Achille Lauro* under cover of darkness and execute a precision parachute jump that would enable them to land quietly on the ship's deck and eventually regain control of the vessel. The operation was set for the night of Wednesday, October 9.

Meanwhile it seemed apparent that diplomatic efforts to end the hijacking were going nowhere, and on board ship matters were quickly moving from bad to worse. The terrorists, members of the Palestinian Liberation Front, a radical splinter faction of the more well-known Palestinian Liberation Organization (PLO), had checked the nationalities of the passengers and separated the fourteen Americans, six Britons and two Austrians whom they mistakenly thought were Jewish.

These twenty-two passengers were ordered to sit in a room below deck near cans of gasoline, and the terrorists proceeded to taunt them by firing bullets in the air and playing with hand grenades. Occasionally one of the captors would spout a little political rhetoric in broken English: "Reagan no good, Arafat good."

By Tuesday afternoon the ship was nearing the Syrian port of Tartus, where the terrorists had demanded that an international team of diplomats gather to hear their demands about the release of the fifty Palestinians in Israel. They were also demanding that they be allowed to leave the ship in Tartus and be granted political asylum in Syria. When the response to these requests was too slow in coming, the terrorists warned that they would soon begin killing the passengers if their demands were not met.

At that point the group of twenty-two was ordered to move upstairs, but as they filed out of the room one of them, sixty-nine-year-old Leon Klinghoffer, a retired appliance dealer from New York who was confined to a wheelchair after suffering a stroke that had left him partially paralyzed, was told to remain behind. "You stay," one of the gunmen said. Nodding at Klinghoffer's wife, Marilyn, he added: "She goes." Mrs. Klinghoffer was escorted upstairs with the rest of the passengers, never to see her husband alive again.

The terrorists then wheeled Klinghoffer to the ship's rail, where one of them trained his Kalashnikov rifle at Klinghoffer's head and opened fire. Shortly afterward, the New Yorker's body, followed by his wheelchair, was thrown overboard into the sea.

One of the terrorists walked up to the bridge to deliver the news to the *Achille Lauro*'s captain, Gerardo deRosa. "We have killed a man," he announced. The terrorist, after having deRosa record the exact time of 3:05 P.M., then picked up the ship's radio and told Syrian authorities in Tartus of the murder. He warned that unless they were allowed to get off the boat and given asylum a second passenger would be killed within minutes. But the Syrians refused to give in to the demands, and the *Achille Lauro* turned south, back toward Egypt.

In Washington, North was stunned to learn that U.S. intelligence had lost track of the ship. Without having the precise location of the vessel at all times, any rescue operation was impossible. He turned to the Israelis for assistance. Following the TWA hijacking, in which the U.S. and Israel had worked hand-in-glove, the two nations had agreed to formalize a secret channel of communication through which they could plan joint covert operations or grapple with terrorist incidents such as the one now unfolding before them.

North, who had been named as the lead American player in this new secret pipeline to Jerusalem, called his friend at the Israeli embassy in Washington, Maj. Gen. Uri Simhoni, the military attaché. The two men met regularly in North's office to discuss terrorism and other topics of mutual interest, and had grown fond of one another.

Actually North had developed great admiration for the Israelis in general. He liked their brass and *chutzpah*, their can-do orientation in approaching a mission. They were doers, not handwringers. And the Israelis, for their part, had come to view North as a fulcrum in the White House, a man of action in a system often paralyzed by checks and balances who had made a significant contribution in energizing Washington to move against terrorists.

"For me, Oliver was a friend and one of the few people in this city that was able to make things happen," Simhoni, now out of government, recalls. "To move a bureaucracy, you have to be able to cut red tape, to cut corners. Otherwise people will just push paper and nothing will get done...In being active, the risk factor is high. If you do nothing, nobody will criticize you, but you will achieve nothing."

Now North asked Simhoni for help in locating the *Achille Lauro*. The Israelis were constantly watching for terrorists penetrating their coastline by boat and had a number of sophisticated tracking devices to help in locating the vessel. Simhoni got on the phone to Israel and within minutes called North back with the exact location, which North, in turn, passed on to the National Security Agency. But early Wednesday—the day the rescue operation was planned —the U.S., incredibly, lost track of the ship a second time, and again North had to call on Simhoni, who again patiently supplied the ship's exact coordinates after checking with military intelligence headquarters in Israel. From that point on Simhoni maintained an open secure line from his office in Washington to his headquarters at home.

Early Wednesday diplomatic activity began kicking into high gear. With the ship anchored about fifteen miles off Port Said, the hijackers established radio contact with Egyptian officials. Soon Abul Abbas, the leader of the Palestinian Liberation Front, arrived in Egypt to join the talks and deal directly with the terrorists. Though Abbas' role in planning the hijacking is uncertain, he clearly exercised considerable influence with the terrorists; as *Time* reported, when he reached them on the radio they responded, "Commander, we are happy to hear your voice."

Abbas told the hijackers that Egypt was prepared to guarantee them safe passage out of the country in his custody, if they surrendered. The Egyptians wanted the ambassadors of the United States, Great Britain, Italy and West Germany to sign an agreement approving the release plan in advance. The U.S. envoy, Nicholas Veliotes, refused, but that was not enough to stop the deal from going forward. At dusk Wednesday a tugboat sailed out to the *Achille Lauro*, picked up the hijackers and took them ashore into the custody of Egyptian authorities.

The need for a rescue over, the SEAL team, which had been planning its move for that night, was ordered to stand down and pack up for home. Diplomatic efforts now concentrated on trying to persuade the Egyptians to turn the terrorists over to either Italy or the United States. Ambassador Veliotes tried to deliver a cable to that effect from President Reagan to Egyptian President Hosni Mubarak, and Secretary of State Shultz attempted to phone Mu-

barak, but the Egyptian leader was refusing to listen to any overtures from the U.S. or Italy.

The deal with the hijackers was cut before the murder of Klinghoffer had become known, Mubarak said, and now Egypt would
fulfill its end of the bargain and give them safe passage out of the
country.

In Washington the early-morning staff meeting Thursday at the
NSC was interrupted with a message from Mubarak to McFarlane
saying that the hijackers had left Egypt. Veliotes was passed the
same message, and Mubarak even made the announcement publicly. The mood at the White House was bleak. It looked as though
the terrorists had won yet another round.

McFarlane asked North where the SEAL team was. In Gibraltar,
en route back to the States, North replied. Not fully trusting the
Egyptians, McFarlane ordered North to try and confirm that the
hijackers had left Egypt and if so, to pinpoint their location.

North made a quick sweep through the U.S. intelligence network, but failing to come up with anything definitive, again rang up
General Simhoni at the Israeli embassy.

"Uri, where are the four thugs?" North asked. Promising an answer within half an hour, Simhoni called back at 8:45 A.M. and told
North the terrorists were definitely still in Egypt. Israeli operatives
on the ground in Cairo were keeping a close watch on preparations
to fly the Palestinians out. They were definitely still in the country.
Mubarak had put out a phony story.

At once stunned and elated, North sought corroboration. He
asked Charles Allen, the CIA's national intelligence officer for
counterterrorism, to try and confirm the Israeli report. The CIA
put out orders for stepped-up intelligence collection in Egypt, particularly by the NSA, which proceeded to hone in its satellites on
Mubarak's office in Cairo.

Soon the NSA intercepted a telephone conversation between
Mubarak and his foreign minister in which Mubarak made reference to the hijackers still being in Egypt. Over the next few hours,
in a prodigious display of high-tech electronic wizardry, the NSA
weighed in with no fewer than eleven additional intercepts in
which Mubarak supplied the tail number of the Egypt Air Boeing
737 that would fly the hijackers from al-Maza airbase, as well as the
flight number and a flight plan for Algiers. It was as good as being
inside the Egyptian president's office.

The transcripts were also revealing for the insights they provided into Mubarak's distress. At first he had not known of Klinghoffer's murder and had screamed at aides when he learned of it, knowing this would likely force Washington to act. Yet he had also talked sympathetically of the PLO as Arab brethren. Politically the *Achille Lauro* affair had placed Mubarak in a vise. He certainly had no interest in alienating the United States, which gave him more foreign aid than it did any other country except Israel. But he was also under continued challenge from Moslem fundamentalists at home and could not be seen to be turning his back on the PLO.

Armed with the confirmation he needed, North raced upstairs from the White House Situation Room to McFarlane's office and quickly briefed McFarlane and Poindexter on what he knew: the four hijackers were definitely still in Cairo; they were preparing to leave for Algiers within a few hours, and the U.S. now had not only the tail number of the Egypt Air 737 that was going to fly them out but the flight number and the flight plan as well.

"We have to do something," North said.

"What can we do?" asked Poindexter.

North had an idea. "Remember Yamamoto?" he said, referring to the Japanese admiral whose plane was intercepted by American fighter jets and shot down over the South Pacific during World War II.

Poindexter, the Navy man, knew the incident well but immediately became uneasy. "You don't want to shoot it down, do you?"

"No, just intercept it and force it to land," said North.

"Where?" Poindexter asked.

"Sigonella, Sicily." replied North. There was a joint Italian-NATO base there.

McFarlane, who was on his way with Reagan to Chicago, where the president was going to lobby for his tax-reform initiative, ordered North to get moving and come up with a plan.

North called Vice-Admiral Arthur Moreau, the Joint Chiefs of Staff's representative on the interagency terrorism group, and asked for his guidance. Moreau called back within ten minutes and said that F-14 Tomcat jets aboard the USS *Saratoga* in the Mediterranean-based Sixth Fleet could scramble and do the job. Moreau had a team of officers begin working out the details of a mid-air intercept. The Navy SEAL team, still on Gibraltar, would be sent to Sigonella to try and take custody of the terrorists when they landed there. Then, if all went well, they could be flown back to the United States to stand trial for the murder of Leon Klinghoffer.

North presented the broad outline of the plan to Poindexter, who approved it. North then briefed McFarlane in Chicago via a secure data-communications link. McFarlane took the president aside in the private office of a Sara Lee bakery in Deerfield, Illinois, where Reagan approved the plan in principle but asked for more operational details about the rules of engagement and more about what the risk of casualties would be.

Moreau and his team worked up the precise rules of engagement and what they would do if the Egyptian pilot resisted orders to land. American pilots were to radio for further instructions if that happened, but it is unlikely Reagan would then have ordered the plane shot down, since the Egyptian crew and perhaps other innocent lives would have been lost. But that, as the president later put it, was something the terrorists could "go to bed wondering about."

Some officials had grave doubts about North's plan, particularly Secretary of Defense Weinberger, who warned that it could destroy U.S. relations with Egypt. Weinberger was traveling to his summer home in Maine and talking with Reagan aboard Air Force One on an open line. At one point a ham radio enthusiast monitored the conversation, raising the possibility that the security of the operation had been compromised.

But shortly after 4 P.M. Eastern time, after receiving word that the Egyptian plane carrying the terrorists had left Cairo, Reagan, while still aboard Air Force One en route back to Washington, gave his final approval for the operation to proceed. Word was flashed to the carrier *Saratoga*, which then dispatched the F–14s, and the chase was on.

To maximize chances that there would be no leaks the U.S. had decided not to clue in the Italians of their intent to use Sigonella until the last moment. But in case the Italians balked and for some reason refused to allow the forced landing in their territory, North again turned to Israel. He and Simhoni quickly came up with a contingency plan that called for the landing to take place at an Israeli military base. Simhoni arranged for Israeli jets to be sent airborne in the event they were needed. He also agreed that the terrorists could be turned over to U.S. custody.

The F–14s, meanwhile, had set up an air gate near the Greek island of Crete and were sifting traffic, waiting for the Egypt Air flight. Despite the flight plan filed for Algiers, U.S. intelligence had now determined that the plane was actually heading for Tunis. Reagan sent a cable to Tunisian President Habib Bourguiba requesting that the terrorists not be allowed to land. Similar requests were passed to Greece and Lebanon in case the plane tried to divert to these nations.

About forty-five minutes after it took off, the Egypt Air flight arrived at the F–14 air gate, flying at 34,000 feet and a speed of 400 knots. The F–14s fell in behind the plane, flying with darkened cockpits. Then at a prearranged point, the Tomcats made their move, turning on their lights and flying along either side of the Egyptian plane. The pilot was radioed instructions to follow the American jets to Sigonella. When he frantically began radioing Cairo for instructions, an American EA–6B flying nearby jammed the signals so all the Egyptian could hear on any frequency was garble. Finally the pilot capitulated and signaled that he would follow the Americans to Sicily.

Only as the air convoy was preparing to enter Italian airspace was Rome informed of the operation and asked to let the Egyptian plane land. But the Italians reacted angrily and at first refused to grant landing rights. Not until the Egyptian plane declared a fuel emergency did the Italians agree to let it land.

Waiting on the ground for the terrorists were both the Navy SEAL team and the Italian *carabinieri* in what shaped up to be a potentially dangerous jurisdictional dispute.

As the plane taxied to a stop on a runway the SEALS, dressed in black and toting Uzi submachine guns, surrounded the plane. Their commander, Maj. Gen. Carl Steiner, lay down his weapon and climbed the stairway that had been rolled up to the plane. When the door opened he found himself staring at two Egyptian commandos pointing their Soviet AK–47s at him. But after seeing the forces on the ground mobilized against them, the terrorists decided to lay down their guns and surrender. Then, as they filed down the ramp and Steiner began to escort them toward an American plane waiting with engines running, the *carabinieri* moved in on both the terrorists and the SEALS and, in effect, asserted eminent domain.

As this dramatic scene unfolded Steiner was describing the events on an open line to North and others listening in the White House Situation Room. But when the *carabinieri* made their intentions clear it was apparent to Steiner and the others in Washington that the United States was not about to engage in a shootout with an ally. They would have to stand down and hope Italy did the right thing by bringing the hijackers to trial.

Also on the plane accompanying the hijackers, to the astonishment of North and other officials involved in counterterrorism, was

Abul Abbas, whom the U.S. was already convinced had master-
minded the *Achille Lauro* seizure. Abbas was one of the founders of
the Palestine Liberation Front and was considered by many in the
West to be one of the world's foremost terrorists. His presence on
the plane was a bonus and stroke of good luck. If he could be tried
and imprisoned it would, at the least, prove disruptive to the Palestinian terrorist network, U.S. officials believed.

Diplomatic fur began flying over questions of jurisdiction. The
U.S. hoped to finesse the issue by arguing that it was an American
who had been killed and that U.S. military forces could legitimately
assert themselves at a NATO base. But the Italians noted that the
murder had occurred on board an Italian ship after it was hijacked,
and the terrorists had been captured in Italian territory on an Italian—albeit joint-NATO—base.

The Italians quickly assured Washington that they would arrest
the four hijackers and try them for murder. They offered, however,
no assurances on Abbas. The U.S. moved to have Abbas extradited,
and Reagan wrote Italian Prime Minister Bettino Craxi, arguing
that a mutual assistance treaty between the two nations required
Rome to hold Abbas for forty-five days so as to give the U.S. a
chance to build a case against him.

Within a few days, while Washington tried to serve Abbas with
an arrest warrant, he quietly slipped out of Rome aboard a chartered Yugoslav plane while wearing an airline uniform. The Italians, heavily dependent on Middle East oil and generally friendly
with the PLO, evidently decided they were taking enough of a risk
trying the hijackers without further alienating Palestinians by putting one of their leaders on trial as well.

Still, in the scheme of things, the Abbas escape had put only a
tiny damper on a stunningly successful operation. "WE BAG THE
BUMS," blared the New York *Daily News* in a headline that North
would frame and hang on his wall, and that seemed to sum up the
nation's emotional thirst for a clear-cut victory over the sinister
forces of terrorism. Even normally staid liberals like Senator Daniel
Moynihan of New York got carried away in the patriotic euphoria.
"Thank God!" he exclaimed. "We've finally won one."

Reagan, for his part, was ecstatic, and the public was ecstatic for
him as his approval ratings soared to nearly seventy percent. The
Achille Lauro affair was the second term's Grenada—only somehow better, bolder, more filled with imaginative derring-do—
which again served to redeem the Reagan promise to bring
America back. It was the kind of patriotic theater that brought out

the best in Ronald Reagan—commiserating with the widow
Klinghoffer as the embodiment of Uncle Sam, or spinning such
parables for the benefit of the terrorists as: "The message: You can
run, but you can't hide."

Needless to say it hardly went unnoticed inside the White House
that the man who had made it possible for the Gipper to enjoy this
great wave of adulation from the grass roots was Lt. Col. Oliver
North. Actually even the public knew about it if they had read the
Newsweek cover story on the *Achille Lauro* affair. It was the kind of
riveting reconstruction of a major event that reporters and editors
love to produce—filled with juicy, exclusive details which no one
but a highly placed insider could have known. *Newsweek*'s source:
North himself.

Ollie was riding high, approaching the zenith of his power and
influence. Subtly used, it was an almost blank-check sort of power
at the heart of the national security apparatus. With North perceived to have the Midas touch, McFarlane and Poindexter's already well-developed "Let Ollie Do It" mindset blossomed to even
fuller flower. Ignoring his then overflowing plate of responsibilities,
they decided to assign him his most sensitive mission yet.

IRAN

O N the night of November 17, the phone rang in North's office. It was Israel's minister of defense, Yitzhak Rabin. Even with the increasingly rarified air North was breathing these days, he was surprised to hear directly from an Israeli official of Rabin's rank. It seemed McFarlane, who was in Geneva with the president for the first Reagan-Gorbachev summit, had told Rabin that North was the man who could help him with a problem he was having.

Rabin was in New York meeting with Israeli defense procurement officials based there. On an open line to North, Rabin was circumspect. But a major snafu had developed in connection with a shipment of sensitive cargo—part of an operation which he understood North was generally familiar with. Israel urgently needed U.S. assistance in facilitating the shipment and also wanted assurances that Washington would replenish Jerusalem with not only the materiel being transported now but also with what had been sent to date. North agreed to fly up to New York immediately to discuss the matter.

No sooner did he hang up the phone than McFarlane called from Geneva telling him to expect a call from Rabin. He had just spoken with him, North said. Take care of the problem, McFarlane instructed, refraining from details since he too was speaking on an unsecure line but making it clear that North had a broad mandate to get the job done.

Arms to Iran. Israel was now making its third shipment of American-made missiles to Iran, each of which had been authorized by the United States. The shipment at hand consisted of 80 HAWK antiaircraft missiles—a step up the weapon-sophistication ladder from the 504 TOW antitank missiles that had been flown to Tehran in two earlier consignments.

Given the officially poor relations between Israel and Iran, it was now deemed too risky to fly the missiles directly from country to country. The plan called for the weapons to be flown circuitously to Portugal, transferred to another plane and then sent on to Tehran. But now, Rabin told North, Lisbon was refusing to grant the clearances required so that the HAWK shipment could go through. Could the U.S. help?

North again turned to General Secord, his private-sector Contra confederate and all-purpose logistician. For North it was a logical choice. Secord had been using Portugal as a way station for arms bound for the Contras and had good contacts in government and in the arms industry there. He was also an expert on Iran, having lived and worked there for years.

"Your discrete [sic] assistance is again required in support of our national interests," North wrote Secord in a letter that went out over McFarlane's signature on White House stationery. "At the earliest opportunity, please proceed to [Lisbon] and other locations as necessary in order to arrange the transfer of sensitive materiel being shipped from Israel. As in the past, you should exercise great caution that this activity does not become public knowledge. You should insure that only those whose discretion is guaranteed are involved."

Secord, though hardly wild about the idea, agreed to go. In for a nickel, in for a dime, he thought. He had long been urging a new U.S. approach to Iran in any case, and maybe if all went well he could get in on a commercial ground floor. Besides, North had said it was in the national interest. He had spoken for McFarlane, who spoke for the president.

With the North-Secord plunge into the HAWK transaction, they entered a murky world of international arms dealers, intelligence agents, knaves and rogues, adding to the Contra cause a second, overlapping front in what North, at least, would come to view as another national-security crusade.

The HAWK shipment was pivotal, mushrooming U.S. involvement in a heretofore deniable dalliance with Tehran. It effectively ousted Israel from the role of American surrogate and put Washington back eyeball-to-eyeball with a nation that had been its nemesis since the Ayatollah Khomeini ousted the shah in the Islamic coup of 1979. In the Iran arms initiative the underlying currency and American motivation would always be the freeing of

the hostages in Beirut. And over the next year, through innumer-
able twists, turns, failures and dashed hopes—at points where
cooler heads and more seasoned minds threatened to prevail and
scrap the operation—North was always there as the chief prod
who kept the issue alive by effectively steamrolling the malleable
McFarlane and Poindexter, using to full advantage his symbiotic
relationship with CIA Director Casey, and exploiting the emotion
that President Reagan clearly felt about the hostages.

With the HAWK shipment the U.S. started down an arms-for-
hostages road that violated its own arms embargo against Iran, its
policy of not providing arms to countries that support terrorism,
and the no-concessions-to-terrorists credo that was the heart of the
recommendations then about to be presented by the Reagan Administration's own task force on terrorism headed by Vice-President George Bush.

Iran, which had humiliated Jimmy Carter and created the conditions for his defeat in 1980, was about to prove its nonpartisanship
by stinging Reagan as well—not mortally but seriously enough to
create the gravest crisis of his presidency and puncture much of the
sunny allure that had held a majority of the American public for
five years.

The United States had officially embargoed arms shipments to
Iran since November of 1979—first in response to the dreaded
seizure of sixty-six hostages at the American embassy in Tehran,
and later because of the Iran-Iraq war. Then, in December of 1983,
in the face of widespread evidence that the embargo was having
little effect on Tehran's ability to purchase arms elsewhere and that
Iran was in fact surging in its war against Iraq, Washington
launched "Operation Staunch." This was an effort to pressure allied
governments to stop selling arms to Iran in hopes of bringing about
an early end to the war.

In January of 1984, just a month later, Secretary of State
Shultz designated Iran as a sponsor of terrorism, thereby placing
further restrictions on U.S. exports to Iran. The Shultz announcement followed conclusions by U.S. intelligence officials
that Tehran was actively supporting Lebanese Shiite groups such
as Islamic Jihad and Hizballah, which found religious inspiration
in Khomeini and were thought to have played key roles in a
series of highly publicized 1983 attacks against American interests
in the Middle East: the April bombing of the embassy in Beirut,
killing 63 persons; the October bombing of the Marine barracks

in Beirut, killing 241; and the December bombing of the embassy in Kuwait. Islamic Jihad and Hizballah had supposedly been provoked by Washington's support of the Israeli invasion of Lebanon in 1982.

But the Shultz announcement seemed only to precipitate a different tack by Shiite extremists: the kidnapping of Americans living in Beirut. There were four kidnappings in 1984: first Jeremy Levin, Beirut bureau chief for the Cable News Network on March 7; then William Buckley, the CIA station chief a week later; on May 8 Rev. Benjamin Weir, a Presbyterian minister who had lived in Beirut for thirty years; and on December 3 Peter Kilburn, a sixty-year-old librarian at the American University of Beirut.

In Washington, 1984 had been marked by the North-prodded efforts to stake out a more activist response to terrorism—at least rhetorically. In October of 1984 Shultz said: "We cannot allow ourselves to become the Hamlet of nations, worrying endlessly over whether and how to respond." But the kidnappings continued in 1985: Fr. Lawrence Martin Jenco, director of Catholic Relief Services, in Beirut on January 8; Terry Anderson, Middle East correspondent for the Associated Press, on March 16; David Jacobsen, director of the American University Hospital, on May 28; and Thomas Southerland, director of the American University's School of Agriculture, on June 9.

The U.S. cause in Beirut could not have been helped by a disastrous car bombing on March 8, 1985. In late 1984, President Reagan had authorized the CIA to create and train a counter-terrorist force in Lebanon composed of Lebanese, Palestinians and various other nationalities. But the Washington *Post* disclosed that renegade members of the group mounted an unauthorized attempt to kill Hizballah leader Mohammed Hussein Fadlallah by planting a bomb in his car. Fadlallah survived, but more than eighty people were killed.

By mid 1985, only Levin had been freed—on February 13, after nearly eleven months in captivity. Precisely how Levin attained his freedom—whether he escaped or whether his captors looked the other way and allowed him to leave—has been a mystery.

Levin initially told reporters he had escaped by wriggling out of "carelessly" fastened chains, then using a makeshift rope of tied blankets to lower himself from a second floor balcony. After a two hour walk down a mountainside in Eastern Lebanon's Bekaa Valley, he came to a Syrian Army post. Syrian soldiers took him to Damascus, where he was turned over to the United States. Despite Levin's insistence that he escaped, there was immediate unofficial speculation from a senior State Department official that he may have been allowed to escape as a result of intervention by the Syrian government.

But according to H. Ross Perot, the Texas billionaire who had long been active officially and unofficialy in helping secure the release of American hostages, Levin was actually freed as a result of a heretofore undisclosed diplomatic initiative undertaken by Rev. Jesse Jackson with the approval of the White House, and financed with $30,000 donated by Perot.

Charged with responsibility for the hostages, North had stayed in touch with Perot, and they exchanged ideas on how the Americans in Lebanon might be freed. They had first done business during the kidnapping of General James Dozier in 1982. Perot had a track record at this sort of thing. In addition to pulling off the sensational commondo raid to rescue two of his employees taken hostage in Tehran in 1979, he had worked behind the scenes trying to help Washington win the release of the Americans seized at the embassy there.

Early in 1985, in a conversation Perot was having with North, the subject turned to another man who had a track record in the hostage department: Jackson. A year earlier Jackson had gone to Syria and won the release of Lieutenant Robert Goodman, the navy flier who had been captured after his plane was shot down over Lebanon.

In an interview Perot said he could not remember if he or North first raised the idea of using Jackson, "but in any case, it was agreed I would contact him. It was awkward for the White House to approach him since he was viewed as a political opponent." Embarrassed by Jackson's Goodman coup, the Reagan Administration had actually, Perot thought, been "rude and impolite" to the civil rights leader on his return from Syria with Goodman.

So with North's knowledge and support, Perot phoned Jackson, who said he would be willing to undertake the effort. They then met in Atlanta to discuss planning and logistics. The purpose of the mission, Perot said, was simply to try and move the hostage logjam and make a humanitarian appeal for the release of as many of the five hostages then being held as possible. Though it was impossible to assign a priority to a human life, Jackson understood that if Washington was given its choice of just one hostage to be released, it wanted the CIA agent, Buckley.

Perot said Jackson made the trip in early 1985, then returned home and told him, "'We'll get somebody in a few days. It should be the man we want, but I can't promise that because the situation is so convoluted over there.'

"In a few days, it was Levin who came out. Jesse Jackson got him out, supported by me," Perot says. "In a world where everyone wrings their hands and talks about problems, Jesse went. There was no ransom. I just paid for the expenses of the operation, and that was $30,000. Jesse Jackson leaned on them to turn somebody loose. Jesse's got the contacts over there. He went over and did it. Then he walked away. He didn't grandstand . . . To Jackson's credit, he's never taken credit for this. He just went over, did the job, and came home."

Perot said he got irritated when he heard that Levin was telling reporters he had escaped. "I called the lawyer for the little son-uva-bitch and told him to have Levin call Jackson and thank him within twenty-four hours or I'd send him a bill," Perot recalls, chuckling. "He made the call."

Jackson basically confirms the Perot account. He said he did not actually go to Lebanon or Syria, but conferred with his Middle East sources in London and Rome. Jackson said that while he did not "have the same grip" on the situation as he did in freeing Goodman from Syria, he had "reason to believe that Levin's dash to freedom was made possible in part because of my efforts." But he noted that Levin's wife, Lucille, had spent several weeks in Syria in late 1984 making contacts and working for her husband's release, and that her efforts may have also played a significant role.

"Everybody's swinging in the dark and hoping that they hit a flat object," Jackson said, adding that he had consulted with the State Department before he left, but had had no contact with North or the White House. Asked why he had never taken credit or spoken publicly of his role in the Levin matter, Jackson said, "It didn't really matter, frankly. It was a team effort."

Mrs. Levin, while stressing that she was thankful for the Perot-Jackson initiative, said she believes her efforts and that of a colleague in Syria over several weeks were ultimately more significant in her husband gaining his freedom.

In marked contrast to the almost constant hue and cry that had attended the seizure of the hostages at the American embassy in Tehran for 444 days, there was little public outrage over the picking off, one by one, of the Americans in Beirut. One largely unspoken sentiment held by many was that the hostages were at fault to have been living there at all in the face of repeated warnings to flee anarchic Beirut. But the families kept up a quiet drumbeat of pressure on behalf of the "forgotten hostages," and they had two important allies. One was North, the other Reagan himself.

On June 14, five days after the Southerland kidnapping, TWA Flight 847 was hijacked by Shiite terrorists and Navy diver Robert Stetham was murdered. The incident prompted more strong words from Reagan that would come back to haunt him. "The United States gives terrorists no rewards and no guarantees," he said. "We make no concessions. We make no deals."

A few weeks later the president, following his first meeting with the hostage families in which he was visibly moved by their plight, authorized Israel to sell the first shipment of TOW missiles to Iran.

The roots of Washington's flirtation with Khomeini's Iran went back at least to 1984. Early that year McFarlane and members of his staff became concerned that the United States lacked any long-term plan to deal with strategically vital Iran. Khomeini was rumored to be ill. His death would presumably touch off a massive power struggle. Since 1979 the U.S. had lacked on-the-ground intelligence in Tehran and still basically hadn't a clue as to what was happening inside the country. The Soviet Union seemed far better positioned to exploit the turmoil of a post-Khomeini Iran than was the U.S. Washington, it was felt, should have a strategy to deal with all this. On August 31, McFarlane asked for an interagency study of U.S. relations with Iran. But the study produced nothing new and reinforced the pessimistic conventional wisdom that the United States had no intelligence or influence on what was happening in Iran. In addition the State Department and the Pentagon opposed any overtures to Iran. The CIA, desperately worried about Buckley, was supportive of a new initiative but said the issue of the hostages in Beirut had to be resolved first.

Meanwhile the Iranian who would become the pivotal figure in drawing the U.S. into the arms-for-hostages quagmire had been diligently plying his wares. Manucher Ghorbanifar was a former SAVAK informant now living in comfortable Parisian exile as a resourceful merchant *cum* arms dealer. Since the ouster of the shah, Ghorbanifar had been offering himself to various western governments, including Israel, as a pipeline into the Ayatollah's Iran.

In January of 1984 Ghorbanifar had contacted U.S. Army intelligence in West Germany, offering to discuss Iranian terrorist activities. In March he met with the CIA and told of an Iranian plot to assassinate American presidential candidates. He also hinted that he had information about William Buckley and identified an Iranian official that he said was responsible for the Buckley kidnapping. This same official would later play a key role in the arms-for-hostages dealings.

The CIA gave Ghorbanifar a polygraph test and concluded he was lying. Undeterred, Ghorbanifar contacted the Agency again in June, this time trying to arrange a meeting with another Iranian official he said was open to a dialogue with Washington. But again Ghorbanifar was given a lie-detector exam and judged to be lying, prompting the CIA to put out a "burn notice" on him, meaning that he should be regarded as an unreliable pest and one not to be dealt with.

But Ghorbanifar, convinced that the American hostages were ultimately the route to Washington's heart—and potentially millions of dollars for himself—persisted. In November he met in Hamburg, West Germany, with Theodore Shackley, the former CIA associate deputy director for clandestine operations, who had opted for early retirement in 1978 amid reports of his ties to Edwin Wilson, the rogue CIA agent now in federal prison for selling arms and explosives to Libya. Known as "the blond ghost," Shackley was something of a legend in spy circles dating back to his days running anti-Castro agents out of Miami and fighting communists as the CIA's station chief in Laos and Saigon at the height of U.S. involvement in Southeast Asia.

One of Shackley's Iranian contacts, former SAVAK counterespionage chief Manucher Hashemi, had facilitated the Hamburg meeting. Ghorbanifar bluntly told Shackley that he could arrange for the release of the American hostages in Lebanon for a straight ransom. He said that he needed a response by December 7 and that he would not work with the CIA. Shackley returned home and wrote up a memorandum on the Ghorbanifar proposal for Vernon Walters, a former CIA deputy director who was then ambassador at large at the State Department. Walters passed the Shackley memo around, but State sent back word it was not interested in pursuing the idea.

Rejected, even scorned, at every turn, Ghorbanifar nevertheless kept trying to open a channel to the United States, this time through Israel. In January of 1985 he had discussions with Roy Furmark, a New York businessman and friend of Bill Casey's who was interested in commercial ventures with Iran. Furmark introduced Ghorbanifar to Adnan Khashoggi, the Saudi Arabian billionaire. It was Khashoggi who suggested the Israelis as an intermediary and later set up a meeting for Ghorbanifar with Al Schwimmer, the founder of Israeli Aircraft Industries and an adviser to then-Prime Minister Shimon Peres, and Ya'acov Nimrodi, a major London-based arms dealer and former Israeli military attaché in Tehran.

Iran had a constant need for arms and spare parts—especially of the American variety, since the shah had bought virtually his entire arsenal from the U.S.—to meet its requirements for the war with Iraq. Though in Tehran's official pronouncements Israel was perhaps second only to the American Great Satan on the pecking order of evil states, Iran's thirst for weapons was such that it had been quietly buying up millions of dollars' worth of arms from Israel for several years.

Jerusalem's interest in dealing with Tehran—different from Washington's—was threefold. First was the enemy-of-my-enemy-is-my-friend theory: Israel felt that any way it could hurt archenemy Iraq was a good thing. Second was its desire to secure permission for any Jews living in Iran to leave the country and emigrate to Israel. Third was the economic motivation of wanting to bolster its burgeoning domestic arms industry. Israel did not want to rely on other countries to give it arms to cope with the constant Arab threat, so it had been trying to develop one of the world's most competitive and sophisticated arms industries—and become an exporter in the process to earn valuable foreign exchange. By selling arms to Iran, Israel also hoped to cultivate intelligence contacts and influence with any moderate elements that might be in the running to succeed Khomeini.

Accordingly Israel had been selling arms to Iran since before the outbreak of the war with Iraq. In 1980, with the U.S. hos-

tages still being held in Tehran, Israel had angered Washington
by selling Iran tires for American-made F-4 Phantom jets. Following Reagan's election some administration officials protested
Israel's continuing sales of arms to Iran, but others equivocated,
and Jerusalem interpreted that as a green light not only to proceed but to expand. Some of the hardware sent to Iran was weaponry captured in the 1982 invasion of Lebanon; some were
American arms. In 1983 alone Israel reportedly did $100 million
worth of arms business with Iran. But in 1984, following the rash
of terrorist incidents against the United States, Secretary Shultz
demanded that Israel stop selling American-made arms to Iran,
and Israel had apparently honored the request until now.

Which was where things stood as Ghorbanifar sat down with
Nimrodi and Schwimmer for a series of meetings in London,
Geneva and Israel during the spring of 1985. Ghorbanifar asserted that if Israel would sell Iran U.S.-made TOW antitank
missiles, he could obtain the release of the CIA's Buckley.

At this point Michael Ledeen—a former aide to Secretary of
State Alexander Haig in the early Reagan years and an expert on
terrorism who had been hired by McFarlane to work as a consultant to the NSC—entered the picture on behalf of the United
States. Ledeen, a rather mysterious neoconservative intellectual,
was also a scholar on the subject of fascism who had lived and
worked as a college professor in Rome during the 1970s and had
co-authored a book on the fall of the shah of Iran. In addition he
had widespread political contacts in Europe and Israel. In March
of 1985 Ledeen had met with a senior Western European intelligence official who, having just returned from Iran, said that he
felt the political situation there was fluid and ripe for exploiting
by the United States—through Israel, which the official said had
the best intelligence network inside Iran of any western country.

Upon returning home in April, Ledeen asked McFarlane for
permission to meet with Israeli Prime Minister Shimon Peres to
discuss possible U.S.-Israeli cooperation on Iran. McFarlane
agreed, and in May Ledeen flew to Israel, where he met with
Peres and other Israeli officials. Peres expressed interest in working with the U.S. on Iran. He also said Jerusalem wanted to resume selling arms to Tehran but would do so only with
Washington's approval.

When Ledeen came back to Washington the CIA was in the

A 1986 bathing suit shot for Raleighs from Fawn Hall's modeling portfolio.
(Photo: Ray Brown) Inset: Fawn Hall testifying *(Photo: James K. W. Atherton/*
The Washington Post)

Lt. Col. Oliver North, (far left, standing) is sworn in by Senator Daniel Inouye (far right), chairman of the Senate-House select committee investigating the Iran-Contra affair.

A copy of a snapshot of North taken by his attorney, Brendan Sullivan. Sullivan had North stand next to a stack of documents supplied by the congressional Iran-Contra committees, by way of arguing that there were too many papers to study before North's appearance at the hearings.

Lt. Col. Oliver North testifying. *(Photo: James K. W. Atherton/The Washington Post)*

North, playing the Abu Nidal card, testifying. *(Photo: The Washington Post)*

North and his wife Betsy wave to supporters from the balcony of the Russell Office Building on Capitol Hill during a break in the Iran-Contra hearings. *(Photo: Dennis Cook)*

Senate Iran-Contra counsel Arthur Liman (left) and House counsel John Nields. *(Photo: The Washington Post)*

As his attorney Brendan Sullivan reviews notes, Lt. Col. Oliver North responds to questions while testifying before the joint House-Senate panel investigating the Iran-Contra affair on Capitol Hill. *(Photo: Lana Harris)*

Two views of Oliver North: In Minneapolis (above) a protester holds a sign at an "Ollie North Is Not a Hero" demonstration at an armed forces recruiting station; in El Centro, California (below) a billboard reflects the sentiments of a citizen impressed with North's "integrity." *(Photo: (top) Bill Pugliano, (bottom) Associated Press)*

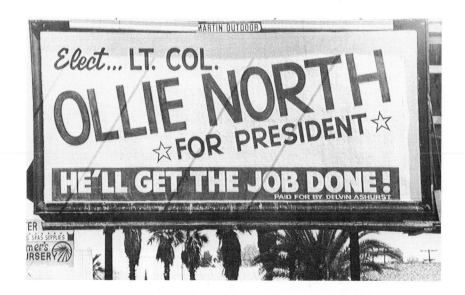

March 24, 1988. Lt. Col. Oliver North leaves the U.S. District Court after his arraignment. *(Photo: Gary A. Cameron/The Washington* Post)

midst of preparing a Special National Intelligence Estimate on
Iran, representing the American intelligence community's assessment of the situation in Tehran vis-a-vis U.S. interests. The Agency
favored an opening to Iran. The intelligence estimate, which had
been requested by McFarlane, concluded that one option in pursuing such an opening would be to sell Iran arms through an ally as a
means of gaining more influence.

The NSC thought Israel should be that ally. In June two NSC
staffers—Don Fortier and Howard Teicher—prepared a draft
National Security Decision Directive (NSDD) that if signed by
the president would establish U.S. policy. The draft NSDD
warned of a Soviet threat to Iran, recommended that anti-Kho-
meini factions be supported by the United States and urged that
U.S. allies be authorized to provide "selected military equipment" to Iran.

As the NSDD was circulated for comment only Casey liked the
idea. Secretary of Defense Weinberger wrote on a note accompanying the proposal: "This is almost too absurd to comment on . . . It's
like asking Khadafy to Washington for a cozy chat." Secretary
Shultz also disapproved, on the grounds that it would undermine
the U.S. arms embargo already in force, that strengthening Iran
was a bad idea and that Iran was actually in no danger of falling into
the Soviet orbit. Reagan, meanwhile, was keeping up the rhetorical
pressure on Iran. In a July 8 speech he declared that Iran was part
of a "confederation of terrorist states . . . A new international version
of Murder Incorporated . . . Let me make it plain to the assassins in
Beirut and their accomplices that America will never make concessions to terrorists."

Despite the presidential rhetoric, relations between the United
States and Iran had just warmed slightly as a result of Tehran's
intervention in the June TWA hijacking. The diplomatic efforts of
President Hafez al-Assad of Syria had not been enough to secure a
commitment from the Shiite terrorists who had hijacked the plane
to release all thirty-nine hostages. Four Jewish hostages were held
back. It was not until an emissary sent by Iranian parliament
speaker Hashemi Rafsanjani arrived in Damascus that the hijackers
agreed to release the final four hostages as well. Though this did
not keep him from making his July 8 "Murder Incorporated" remarks, an appreciative Ronald Reagan had sent Rafsanjani a personal letter of thanks via Japanese Prime Minister Yasuhiro
Nakasone. Rafsanjani sent a reply suggesting that Reagan might

demonstrate his appreciation by releasing millions of dollars worth of embargoed U.S. weapons purchased by Iran before the death of the shah.

According to Ledeen, he was authorized by McFarlane to tell Prime Minister Peres that Israel could go ahead and make a one-time sale of artillery shells or pieces, though "just that and nothing else." But an Israeli participant recalls that the authorization conveyed by Ledeen from McFarlane was in fact for the TOW missiles.

On July 8, the same day Reagan was likening Iranians to assassins, the Israeli team of Schwimmer and Nimrodi—bolstered now by David Kimche, the director general of the Israeli Foreign Minister—was meeting in Hamburg with Ghorbanifar, Khashoggi and an Iranian official. Ghorbanifar asked Israel to sell Iran 100 TOWs through him, promising that the sale would be followed by the release of the seven American hostages in Beirut.

Three days later Schwimmer flew to Washington to brief Ledeen on Ghorbanifar's proposal. Ledeen, delighted with what seemed to be emerging, then enthusiastically briefed McFarlane, who concluded that the U.S. should move ahead with the proposal. But in a cable to Shultz, McFarlane demurred: "Then one has to consider where this might lead in terms of our being asked to up the ante on more and more arms, and where that could conceivably lead." Schultz responded by saying that "we should make a tentative show of interest without commitment."

At this point McFarlane decided to bring the issue to the president, who was in the hospital recuperating from surgery. The meeting occurred in the presence of White House Chief of Staff Donald Regan, who had replaced Jim Baker in February, and though recollections of what happened differ, McFarlane later wrote in a note to Poindexter that the president "was all for letting the Israelis do anything they wanted at the very first meeting in the hospital." And Ledeen said that in accordance with McFarlane's instructions, he told the Israelis that the president had approved the TOW transaction "in principle," pending review of the actual details.

On July 25 the Israelis met again with Ghorbanifar, who began vacillating and making additional requests. Besides the 100 TOWs he cited the need for other weapons and spare parts for antiaircraft missiles. He said that within two to three weeks of delivery of the TOWs the hostages would be released, though he warned that his government might want to hold back a few of the captives for leverage. Though that was considerably less certain a proposition than the July 8 assurance that all seven hostages would be released in a flat trade for 100 TOWs, Kimche flew to Washington on August 2 to meet with McFarlane and obtain a final U.S. reply. Israel, fearing that the deal could become public, wanted specific assurances that Shultz knew of the plan and that the president unequivocally approved before it agreed to sell Iran the missiles.

At a meeting on August 6 McFarlane formally presented the Iran proposal, as described by Kimche, to the president, Vice-President Bush, Weinberger, Shultz and Don Regan. The deal had been revised again and was now 100 Israeli TOWs in exchange for the release of four, not seven, hostages. Shultz and Weinberger made strong objections, while no one can recall what, if anything, Bush said. The meeting ended without the president making any decision, but several days later he phoned McFarlane and authorized the Israelis to proceed with the sale of modest quantities of "TOW missiles or other military spares" which would be replenished by the U.S.

Since neither Israel nor Iran trusted each other to make good on the bargain until the missiles or the money for them was in hand, Khashoggi agreed to provide bridge financing. After much haggling Ghorbanifar agreed to pay the Israelis $10,000 per missile. Iran was paying him $12,000 for each TOW.

On August 19 Ghorbanifar appeared in Israel to make the final logistical arrangements. Iran had received the Khashoggi advance, but Ghorbanifar was unsure how many hostages would be released. Buckley, he said, would not be among those freed. Iran recognized his "special value," and he would be held back. The morning of August 20 the Israelis loaded a chartered DC–8 transport plane with 96, not 100, TOWs and the plane took off for Iran with Ghorbanifar, ever vigilant over his missiles, on board.

But no hostages were released. Ghorbanifar's rather lame explanation was that the Iranian Revolutionary Guards had taken custody of the missiles, rather than the more moderate political faction they had been intended for. Still, he said, he was hopeful hostages would be released soon. Ledeen, authorized by McFarlane to stay on the case, met with Kimche in London to consider what to do next.

Hoping that a hostage release was imminent, McFarlane ordered North to go to Europe to stand by as the operational officer for the hostage project. North was issued a passport under the alias of William P. Goode. At this point extra steps were also taken to make sure communications to and from North were secure. Poindexter established a secret channel to North, called "Private Blank Check," on the NSC's interoffice computer system.

On September 4 and 5 Ledeen and the Israelis held acrimonious meetings with Ghorbanifar in Paris. Why hadn't even one hostage been released so far despite the delivery of 96 TOW missiles? they demanded. Ghorbanifar had no satisfactory explanation, but he had a new offer: if Israel would sell Iran 400 more TOWs, one hostage would be released.

Despite the failure of the first delivery and the drastically scaled-down representations of what a second would bring, President Reagan, increasingly anxious to demonstrate at least some progress on the hostage front, gave his approval for a second shipment.

Preparing for the release of at least one hostage, North contacted Casey on September 12 and asked him for help in obtaining additional intelligence on Ghorbanifar and another Iranian official who was involved in the operation. Casey had North deal with Charles Allen, the CIA's national intelligence officer for counterterrorism. On McFarlane's orders North then asked Allen to distribute the intelligence only to Casey, McFarlane, Vice-Admiral Arthur Moreau of the Joint Chiefs of Staff and to North himself. Pointedly excluded were Shultz and Weinberger, though the latter would learn of the slight and demand to be included. But the State Department, left out of the loop, was not informed of Reagan's approval of the second Israeli shipment or of its direct linkage to the release of one hostage.

North left Washington for overseas on September 13 to await a hostage release, encountering television evangelist Pat Robertson at the airport before he left. Robertson, who calls North a friend, said later that Ollie told him that day he was on his way to Iran to negotiate the release of some of the hostages. "Would you please pray for me?" Robertson said North asked him. North later denied he had told Robertson he was going to Iran.

On September 14 another DC–8 transport was loaded in Israel, this time with 408 TOWs. Early the next morning the plane took off for Iran, again with Ghorbanifar on board to watch over his precious cargo. This time the plane landed in the city of Tabriz, not Tehran, presumably to bypass the Revolutionary

Guards. The Iranians had made it clear that the hostage to be released would not be Buckley, this time saying that he was too ill to be moved.

Hours after the missiles arrived safely in Iran, the Reverend Benjamin Weir was freed near the U.S. embassy in Beirut. Shortly afterward, North, carrying a letter for Weir from President Reagan, met with the minister and debriefed him.

Despite the one-sided nature of this triangular relationship, with Iran now having clearly bested both Israel and the United States in two major arms transactions, the initiative continued. The ubiquitous Ledeen, who worked out of North's office when he was at the NSC, was authorized to hold further discussions with the Israelis and Ghorbanifar later that month in Paris and the following month in Geneva. Now on the agenda were HAWK and other antiaircraft missiles, while Ledeen and the Israelis were still demanding the release of the remaining six hostages. Actually, it was later learned, there were then only five left alive. Buckley had died in June after being subjected to prolonged torture.

At this stage the consultant Ledeen was a key driving force keeping the initiative alive in the face of skepticism from McFarlane. Ledeen argued that improved U.S.-Iranian relations would surely result if Washington permitted Israel to send more arms to bolster the clout of moderate elements in Iran, and to remove the hostages as the lingering issue preventing an American-Iranian detente. McFarlane doubted there were any Iranian moderates, so to bolster what he felt was the National Security Advisor's flagging enthusiasm for the project, Ledeen asked Israel's David Kimche to come to Washington in early November to give McFarlane a pep talk.

"I asked Kimche to talk to McFarlane because I was convinced that McFarlane was getting ready to resign and was in a bad psychological state and was planning to abandon the entire Iran initiative," Ledeen told the congressional Iran-Contra committees.

On a parallel track North was having talks in Washington with Amiram Nir, the Israeli prime minister's advisor on counterterrorism. North and Nir were further cementing the close operational ties that had developed between the two nations in dealing with the TWA and *Achille Lauro* hijackings. In an effort to capitalize on the *Achille Lauro* mandate to deal aggressively, even preemptively, with terrorists, the two were discussing joint U.S.-Israeli operations against Palestinian and other terrorists.

North's notebooks reveal that in two meetings on November 14 and 19 he and Nir talked about two covert operations code-named "TH1" and "TH2." North had doubts about how the operations would be funded and whether they should be actual joint-ventures or Israeli missions supported by the U.S. But within a few months they would have solved the problem of from where at least part of the funding for the operations would come: from the profits of the arms sales to Iran. That would give Nir all the hook he needed to emerge as a key player in the arms initiative on the Israeli side.

Before going ahead with the third shipment to Iran, Defense Minister Rabin sought and received assurances from McFarlane that the United States was still committed to the initiative, and to replenishing Israel with the U.S. arms it was sending Tehran. Before leaving for the Geneva summit McFarlane told President Reagan about the impending HAWK shipment and Reagan's reaction was "cross your fingers . . . and keep me informed," according to McFarlane's statement to the Tower Commission.

By the third week in November the Americans and Israelis believed they had reached a deal with Ghorbanifar that would result in the release of the remaining hostages by Thanksgiving. But as the date for the proposed arms shipment drew near, it was apparent that many details, particularly the number and type of missiles that Israel would send to Iran, remained unresolved. What was certain was that both sides still fundamentally distrusted one another, so it was agreed that the weapons would be delivered incrementally, with one or more hostages being released after each delivery. The first shipment was to consist of 80 HAWKs sent through Portugal. In Geneva, McFarlane told Shultz of the latest arms-for-hostages swap, and the secretary of state exploded in anger at not having been informed earlier.

It was when the Portuguese refused to grant the necessary clearances so that the HAWKs could fly on to Iran that Rabin asked North for help in convincing Lisbon to get with the program, and North called on Secord. On November 18, the day Secord became involved, North arranged for the Israelis to transfer $1 million to Secord's Lake Resources account in Switzerland.

This $1 million, apparently to cover airplane charter expenses,
marked the first time that funds from the Iran initiative over-
lapped with funds for the Contra operation. But only $150,000
was used to pay for the charters. The remaining $850,000 was
allocated to Secord and his associates and—in the first of the
Iran-Contra affair's so-called diversions—for support of the Contras. North did not tell the Israelis of the Contra diversion until
early 1986, but they raised no objections and did not ask for their
money back.

Secord and his associate, former CIA operative Tom Clines,
along with the officer of a European arms company, arrived in Lisbon to try to pry loose the HAWK shipment but were able to make
little headway. The Portuguese were annoyed that they were being
approached through a back door, outside established diplomatic
channels, and it was apparent that the shipment flew in the face of
stated U.S. policy not to deal with Iran or with states that supported terrorism. The Secord mediation efforts were also complicated by the European businessman's reported attempt to bribe a
Portuguese official to look the other way and allow the shipment to
go through. When the government asked the U.S. embassy to clar-
ify the situation the embassy, unaware that the shipment had been
authorized, disclaimed any knowledge of it and confirmed that such
a shipment would be contrary to U.S. policy opposing arms sales to
Iran.

Despite the chaos in Lisbon, North wrote Poindexter in an interoffice memo dated November 20 that all was well. North said that
in return for the eighty HAWKs, followed by a shipment of forty
more, the five American hostages and possibly a French hostage
would be released at the U.S. embassy in Beirut, but that no aircraft would land in Iran until the hostages had been released. "All
transfer arrangements have been made by Dick Secord, who deserves a medal for his extraordinary short-notice efforts," North
wrote.

But by the next day North had to admit that the situation in
Portugal was a mess, and he called on McFarlane, the State Department and the CIA for help. On the case for the CIA was old
friend Dewey Clarridge, now head of the agency's European division.

Clarridge ordered his Lisbon station chief to get in touch with
Secord, who was calling himself "Richard Copp." Asked for an alias
by North before leaving for Portugal, Secord had looked into his

bookshelf and seen a book he had been reading at the time by
Dewitt S. Copp entitled *A Few Great Captains*, an account of army
and air force fliers during World War II. Secord thought the best
way to come up with a convincing alias was to choose a name at
random.

On the morning of November 22, though the Portuguese still
had not given their approval, an El Al 747 carrying the 80 HAWK
missiles took off from Tel Aviv for Portugal. But when the plane
reached its "go or no-go" point Lisbon was still refusing clearance.
The aircraft was sent back to Israel.

Due to the delays the El Al plane the Israelis had chartered had
to be redeployed elsewhere, and North and Clarridge decided to
use a CIA proprietary airline. The agency's associate deputy director for operations, Edward Juchniewicz, gave Clarridge the name
of the proprietary—St. Lucia Airways—and said it also was available for commercial charters. For quickly locating and procuring
the services of St. Lucia, North told Poindexter in an interoffice
message that Clarridge "deserves a medal—so does Copp." From
North, that was now two medals in two days for Secord, one for
Clarridge.

Simultaneously North also explored the possibility of diverting a
plane then in Lisbon that had been chartered by Secord's Lake
Resources to fly a load of ammunition to the Contras and have it
carry the HAWKs to Iran instead. North told Poindexter of this in a
PROF note on the evening of November 22, saying the plane could
be repainted and put into service by noon the following day. "So
help me, I have never seen anything so screwed up in my life . . ."
North wrote. "More as it becomes available. One hell of an operation." As it turned out, the Lake Resources plane was not available,
but the willingness to divert a plane from the Contra's cause to the
Iran initiative was another early example of comingling the two
operations.

During the planning for the HAWK shipment the Americans
and the Israelis involved had agreed to keep the contents of the
cargo a secret and adopt the cover story that it consisted of oil-
drilling equipment. President Reagan and his chief of staff were
told the actual contents, but the CIA, at least initially, was not.
North invoked the cover story when he first brought Clarridge
and the agency's counterterrorism chief, Charles Allen, into the
operation. "I lied to the CIA because that was the convention
that we had worked out with the Israelis, that no one else was to

know," North would later testify before Congress. But Secord
blew the cover story by giving the CIA station chief in Lisbon a
full briefing on what actually was going on.

On November 23, after a direct appeal from McFarlane to the
Portuguese foreign minister failed to bring results, the plan to
ship the HAWKs through Lisbon was finally abandoned. Under
the new plan the St. Lucia Airways charter would make a series
of flights from Tel Aviv to Iran via Turkey. Clarridge had his
station chief in Ankara get the necessary clearances from the
Turkish government, using the oil-drilling-equipment cover story.
It was decided that at least the first flight would stop in Cyprus
to disguise that the point of origin was Israel. Finally, on November 24, the first load of eighteen HAWKs arrived in Tehran.
The St. Lucia crew stayed overnight in the capital at the old
Sheraton hotel and the next day was given a non-Islamic sendoff
that included caviar.

Back in Washington on Monday morning, November 25, Poindexter informed the president that the first shipment of HAWKs
had just been made. Over at the CIA, meanwhile, Ed Juchniewicz told Deputy Director John McMahon that the agency's St.
Lucia proprietary had been used by the NSC to ferry some oil
supplies to Iran. McMahon hit the roof. Though NSC involvement in shipping oil supplies did not exactly ring true, McMahon
was not focusing on the content of the shipment so much as the
fact that the CIA could not legally permit the use of one of its
proprietaries in an operation without being authorized to do so
by a presidential finding.

Juchniewicz tried to split hairs and argue that the agency was not
involved. North had asked for help and had been given the name of
St. Lucia, which was then hired in a straight commercial deal. But
McMahon wasn't buying that. There were dozens of cable messages between Clarridge and the station chief in Lisbon, document-
ing that the agency was up to its ears in the operation. McMahon
had Stanley Sporkin, the CIA's general counsel, draw up a finding
for the president that would retroactively authorize the agency's
activities. Sporkin was briefed on the operation. It was made clear
to him that the shipment had contained missiles and that more
flights were in the works.

Sporkin and his deputies met the morning of November 26 and
drafted a finding that described the Iran initiative as a strict arms-
for-hostages transaction, making no mention of any larger strategic

objective of opening up a dialogue with Iran. It also pointedly excluded Congress from being informed and contained the rare, if not
unique, retroactive clause.

In signing the document the president would attest that he had
been "briefed on the efforts being made by private parties to
obtain the release of Americans held hostage in the Middle East,
and hereby find that the following operations in foreign countries
(including all support necessary to such operations) are important
to the national security of the United States. Because of the extreme sensitivity of these operations...I direct the Director of
Central Intelligence not to brief the Congress of the United
States...until such time as I may direct otherwise." The finding
went on to say that as part of this CIA assistance "certain foreign
materiel and munitions may be provided to the government of
Iran, which is taking steps to facilitate the release of the American hostages. All prior actions taken by U.S. government officials
in furtherance of this effort are hereby ratified."

The finding was sent to Casey, who approved it being forwarded on to Reagan for signature. That same day the president
authorized the continuation of the arms shipments to Iran but
did not actually get around to signing Sporkin's one-page finding
as drafted until December 5. Poindexter took the only signed
copy and had it locked in the safe of the NSC counsel, Paul
Thompson.

In Iran, meanwhile, the Iranians were furious to discover that
the Israelis had apparently sent them the wrong model of HAWK.
Further, the missiles had Israeli markings on them, which Tehran
considered a "provocation." A frantic Ghorbanifar sent Michael Ledeen an urgent message from the prime minister of Iran to President Reagan: "We have done everything we said we were going to
do, and you are now cheating us, and you must act quickly to rem-
edy this situation."

North sent Secord from Lisbon on to Israel, where it didn't take
the general long to diagnose the problem. Schwimmer and
Nimrodi had promised Ghorbanifar that the missiles would be able
to shoot down high-altitude Soviet reconnaissance aircraft and Iraqi
bombers, but the HAWK missiles had no such capability. The
Israeli military had not been consulted before the cargo was sent,
and Schwimmer and Nimrodi had sent the wrong missiles out of
ignorance, not deceit, Secord said.

North asked Secord to fly to Paris with David Kimche, Schwimmer and Nimrodi to meet with Ghorbanifar and explain the mistake

to him. Secord recalls that he essentially acted as a fresh-face intermediary between the Israelis and Ghorbanifar at this meeting. An
angry Ghorbanifar kept calling the HAWK transaction a "cheating
game," but seemed far more upset about the possibility of his losing
millions of dollars in commissions than he did about the state of his
country's military arsenal.

Abandoning the HAWKs, Ghorbanifar proposed a new plan calling for a phased exchange of 3,200 TOW missiles for the remaining
five hostages. They all agreed to discuss the issue further several
days later at a meeting in London that would include the principals
from the United States as well.

In Washington, the first ten days of December would prove to
be an eventful period in the history of the Iran initiative.

The week began with Richard Armitage, the assistant secretary
of defense for international security affairs, phoning North and asking him to come over to his office at the Pentagon for lunch. Armitage and North both had entered Annapolis together in 1967 as
classmates, but North had been injured in the car accident and
dropped back to the class of 1968. They had lost touch over the
years but had become reacquainted in government. Armitage liked
and respected North as a hard worker and recalls with amusement
that Ollie did not hesitate to play the Annapolis card to ask for
favors or to expedite a request.

"He'd say, 'Classmate? How's it going?' And I'd say, 'Well, let me
sit down and think,' because we weren't graduating classmates, but
classmates in the Naval Academy share a very strong bond. You're
taught from day one that classmates stand together. And he'd say,
'Classmate? . . . We want to do x, y and z . . . I really need you . . .' I
knew that when Ollie said, 'Classmate,' that's when he wanted to
put the arm on me for something . . . Ollie was known in this building as prone to hyperbole. If something was good, it was very good,
and if something was bad, it was an absolute disaster. Everything
was magnified. And I happen to believe that in Ollie's mind it
wasn't magnified—whatever he was working on was just as he was
thinking or saying. But in reality, it was less than that. I think this
extended to some of his usage of the names of his superiors, which
we subsequently learned wasn't exactly true. We used to occasionally smile to each other about how Ollie and the president had had
another conversation."

Armitage said North would often overplay his hand and invoke
Reagan's name when it wasn't necessary. "There was no disagree-

ment about the course of action or about what the right thing was to do. But the president's name would somehow come into the conversation. It was somewhat inappropriate."

Now Armitage had heard rumors that North was dealing directly with Iran in ways that could be unauthorized, and he wanted to confront him, classmate to classmate. When North told him what he had been doing, Armitage reacted strongly and told him he was off the reservation. "I said, 'Weinberger is going to think you're an idiot.' And that shocked him. He is a Marine. And for the secretary of defense to think he's a fool is not something he takes lightly. And I said, 'You've got your ass way out on a limb in my view. I think my boss doesn't know anything about it and neither does Shultz, and you better get everybody together.'"

If North was alarmed by the Armitage warning, it didn't show. On December 4, in a long memo to Poindexter composed on the NSC's interoffice computer, North summarized where the Iran initiative stood at the moment and laid out the basis for the next step in achieving what he defined as the U.S.'s three objectives: "Support for a pragmatic, army-oriented faction which could take over in a change of government; return of the five... hostages; no more terrorism directed against U.S. personnel or interests."

North said there was "extraordinary distrust" of the Americans and Israelis by the Iranians as a result of the HAWK shipment, but he also ventured that based on the state of Iranian military equipment, their incompetent management and their inability to use effectively what materiel they did have, Iran's military was "near collapse." Based on this rose-tinted scenario, North implied that the U.S. had at least some leverage with the Iranians, whom he called "primitive, unsophisticated," and he dramatically invoked the specter of the hostages' death unless Washington kept on selling arms.

While conceding the "high degree of risk in pursuing the course we have started," North said, "we are now so far down the road that stopping what has been started could have even more serious repercussions... If we do not make at least one more try at this point, we stand a good chance of condemning some or all [of the hostages] to death and a renewed wave of Islamic Jihad terrorism. While the risks of proceeding are significant, the risks of not trying one last time are even greater."

He went on to lay out the latest Iranian offer to be discussed at the meeting in London scheduled three days later: the Israelis would deliver 3,300 TOW missiles and 50 improved I-HAWK missiles incrementally to Iran in return for $41 million already on deposit and the phased release of the five American hostages plus one French hostage.

That same day, December 4, McFarlane—physically and emotionally exhausted—officially submitted his resignation as National Security Advisor. He was burned out and tired of turf battles with Don Regan, who since becoming White House chief of staff in February had insisted on sitting in on McFarlane's previously one-on-one morning briefings for the president, thereby weakening McFarlane's clout. Perhaps the recently concluded summit in Geneva, where Regan had constantly been at Reagan's elbow while McFarlane was relegated to the background, had been the last straw. Then too, McFarlane had wearied of mediating numerous disputes between Shultz and Weinberger.

Named to succeed McFarlane, in a surprise to many, was Admiral Poindexter, the career navy officer with a Ph.D. in nuclear physics. Some critics derided Poindexter as a technocrat with totally inadequate foreign-policy experience. But he was also regarded as a compromise candidate who wouldn't rock the boat and who had, after all, been the Deputy National Security Advisor for two years. Finally, perhaps significantly, Poindexter was fully up to speed and involved in the administration's two most sensitive foreign-policy operations: the Iran and Contra initiatives.

McFarlane took a job with the Center for Strategic and International Studies, the conservative think tank in Washington, but it was agreed that he would finish his work on the Iran initiative, and beyond that generally serve as a consultant to the NSC. He retained an NSC computer and a secure phone in his home, but the National Security Agency also retained its ability to monitor McFarlane's conversations on the secure phone.

On December 5, North recast his long memo of the previous day as an unsigned, unaddressed proposal which repeated the terms of the arms-for-hostages trade, but also specified that Congress would not be notified of the operation. This could be legally done, he wrote, because the requirements of reporting to Congress under

the Arms Export Control Act could be avoided as long as each of
the transactions was under $14.9 million (actually it was $14 million). So while the presidential finding signed by Reagan contemplated only delayed congressional notification, North was now
proposing not bringing in Congress at all. Finally, to allay suspicion
at the Pentagon and elsewhere as to why Israel would need to have
such large quantities of missiles replenished by the United States,
North proposed a cover story: its weapons had been damaged in
storage.

On December 6 North flew to New York to meet with Israeli
officials on the replenishment issue. It was at this meeting, according to notes taken by one of the Israelis present, that North
first said the United States planned to use profits from the upcoming arms sales to Iran to support the Contras in Nicaragua.
North would testify that he had no recollection of this, and that it
was Ghorbanifar who would raise the idea of a diversion to the
Contras at a meeting in Europe the following month.

After the New York meeting North flew off to London for the
session with Ghorbanifar and the Israelis scheduled for the following day. McFarlane, though he had officially resigned as National
Security Advisor, was due to join them on December 8 to preside
as the senior American representative.

On the morning of December 7 in Washington President Reagan convened an informal meeting in the White House residence
to review the status of the Iran initiative. Present were Shultz,
Weinberger, McFarlane, Poindexter, Don Regan and John
McMahon, sitting in for Casey, who was out of town. Shultz,
Weinberger, Regan and McMahon all spoke out against the
project. Shultz again argued that carrying out the initiative would
undermine Washington's stated policy of not dealing with terrorists, that it would probably not win the U.S. influence with any
moderates in Iran—if any existed; that news of the arms sales
would surely leak and infuriate America's moderate Arab allies,
and that all allies whom the U.S. had asked not to sell arms to
Iran in connection with Operation Staunch would be outraged to
learn that Washington itself had been doing just the reverse.

But the president, McFarlane and Poindexter spoke in favor of
continuing the initiative. Shultz would testify: "The president, I
felt, was somewhat on the fence, but rather annoyed at me and
Secretary Weinberger because I felt that he sort of—he was very
concerned about the hostages, as well as very much interested in
the Iran initiative." When Weinberger raised legal objections,

Shultz said Reagan responded, "'Well, the American people will never forgive me if I fail to get these hostages out over this legal question.'"

Interestingly, neither the failed HAWKs shipment nor the finding signed two days earlier by the president were discussed. The meeting broke up without any clear decision, but Reagan instructed McFarlane to go to London and meet with Ghorbanifar and the others, then report back to him. McFarlane was to try and break out of the unseemly arms-for-hostages cycle, or at least try to work out a way to free the remaining hostages without providing any more arms deliveries in the short term.

When McFarlane arrived in London at Nimrodi's Hyde Park flat, where the talks were in progress, he tried to pursue the high-road strategy of renewed dialogue between Washington and Tehran, areas of common interests where a political breakthrough might take place. But this tactic was soon exposed as wishful thinking since there was, after all, no official of the Iranian government in the room. The only Iranian present was Ghorbanifar, and it was clear that he was interested only in the continued viability of his commissions. Each time McFarlane tried to discuss politics, Ghorbanifar would return the conversation to the number of TOW missiles that would have to be produced to secure the freedom of each hostage.

The two men sat across from each other at a table as Secord, North (who was taking notes for the Americans) and the Israelis looked on from the side. They could see McFarlane take an instant dislike to Ghorbanifar as he railed on about the dastardly HAWK shipment and insisted on reducing everything to arms-for-hostages, thereby leaving McFarlane little maneuvering room to save face. McFarlane would later testify that he was "revolted" by Ghorbanifar, considered him to be a "borderline moron" and at one point told him to "go pound sand."

North, Secord and McFarlane flew back to Washington together on an Air Force jet. McFarlane seemed totally disgusted with Ghorbanifar and wanted the United States to cut its losses and wash its hands of the whole initiative. But North and Secord urged him not to do anything too drastic.

North, ever the optimist, was of the view that Ghorbanifar had at least delivered Reverend Weir, that there had been no more kidnappings of U.S. citizens in Lebanon since the Iran initiative began, and that Tehran's anti-American rhetoric had also cooled.

Secord said he had been arguing since 1982, when he was still in the Pentagon, that the U.S. should take another look at Iran. "We had no intelligence in Iran," he says. "We had no eyes. We didn't know which mullah was doing what to whom." So he urged McFarlane not to abandon the initiative but to reframe it somehow. "I was trying to broaden Bud's perspective. Since we were already pregnant, since we had already tried to penetrate Iran, why not try and regroup and do it right?"

North, for his part, again raised the prospect of hostage deaths if the U.S. quit now. On December 9 he wrote a memo to McFarlane and Poindexter in which he argued that "all it would take for the hostages to be killed is for Tehran to 'stop saying no' [to the kidnappers]." He said that Terry Waite, the archbishop of Canterbury's special envoy who had been trying to mediate with Hizballah in Beirut, "shares our belief that the hostages are increasingly endangered and that one or more of them could well be executed before the end of the week." North at first proposed four options: carrying out the plan as discussed in London; having Israel deliver 400 to 500 TOWs as a show of good faith following the HAWK snafu; attempting a rescue of the hostages; or doing nothing. But at the end of the memo North suggested a "fifth option": cutting out Israel and having the U.S. sell arms to Iran directly using Secord as the middleman.

McFarlane briefed the president on the London trip at a December 10 Oval Office meeting attended by North, Casey, Poindexter and Don Regan. McFarlane could not disguise his contempt for Ghorbanifar and said that the initiative was unlikely to succeed as long as he remained the leading spokesman for Iran. But McFarlane and/or North also said that pulling back now could risk the lives of the hostages. That view seemed to have a strong effect on Reagan, who wondered why they shouldn't just let the Israelis keep shipping the TOWs and call Iran's bluff.

It was clear that the president was increasingly moved by the plight of the hostages and that he was willing to take risks to free them. Politically, of course, no one wanted to see yellow ribbons popping up around the countryside again. North told one colleague that Reagan was pressuring him to free the hostages in time for them to come home by Christmas. Or, failing that, one entry in North's notebook said, "Try to get results by State of the Union"—the presidential speech traditionally delivered in January.

Still, as was the case in so many meetings with Reagan, the December 10 session ended with no clear decision or consensus on what to do next. Those in the meeting, with the exception of Chief of Staff Regan, were all predisposed toward plunging back into the initiative and seemed to read the president's emotional sympathy for the hostages as a mandate to proceed.

But elsewhere in government, those who opposed the arms sales thought the project had been stopped. Weinberger, for example, had emerged from the December 7 meeting telling aides that he and Shultz thought they had "strangled the baby in the cradle." And after returning from London, McFarlane had told Under Secretary of State Michael Armacost that the initiative should be scrapped. So Armacost cabled Shultz, who was in Europe: "Bud's recommendation, upon returning from his latest discussions, was to drop the enterprise. That has now been agreed."

But in the absence of any clear presidential decision one way or the other, those inside the White House—those at the NSC sitting at the confluence of power—decided to fill the leadership void and, as though by osmosis, interpret the presidential feeling as a wink and a nod to continue on.

Still, Poindexter wanted to reorganize the operation. Ledeen would now be dealt out, on the stated grounds that he lacked "technical expertise." So would the Israeli arms dealers, Schwimmer and Nimrodi. The Israeli liasion between the Americans and Ghorbanifar would now be Amiram Nir, the advisor to the prime minister who had successfully urged Peres to put him on the case and who had already been meeting with North on joint counterterrorism operations. Nimrodi, for one, was not pleased at being shoved out of this lucrative picture, telling an Israeli newspaper: "The starling Nir went to the raven North and told him, in the American phrase, 'Whatever they can do, we can do better,'" Nimrodi said.

Poindexter also wanted to have a broader, more comprehensive presidential finding than the straight arms-for-hostage authorization then in force, and also to have North work closely with the CIA and the Justice Department to develop a more sound legal basis for selling arms to Iran.

What was emerging was a variation of the "fifth option" North had described in his December 9 memo, a plan that would place Washington one-on-one with Tehran, using Secord's Enterprise as the operational conduit, thereby facilitating the diversion of funds to the contras that North had already broached.

About this same time Poindexter, as reported in the Washington *Post*, told two senior aides—Director of Intelligence Programs Ken deGraffenried and Senior Director Rodney McDaniel —that only he and North would be handling the "Iran account."

As he prepared to leave the White House for the last time McFarlane mentioned to Poindexter that he thought North should soon be rotated back to the Marine Corps. Ollie was approaching burnout, had already been extended at the NSC twice and it would not be good for his Marine career to be away much longer. McFarlane also told his successor he wanted to recommend North for the Distinguished Service Medal. Only one other Marine lieutenant colonel had ever won that medal—McFarlane himself when he left the White House in 1977.

Though Ghorbanifar had done precious little to date to inspire confidence in his ability to deliver on his end of a bargain, Michael Ledeen liked the Iranian. In one of his last acts before bowing out, Ledeen, with North's approval, urged the CIA to give Ghorbanifar another chance and reestablish an intelligence relationship with him. Ledeen met with the agency's counterterrorism man, Charles Allen, and later Casey himself, praising Ghorbanifar to the hilt. Casey agreed to order a new evaluation.

Ghorbanifar flew to Washington and checked into the Madison Hotel under the alias Nicholas Kralis. On December 22 he was interviewed by the chief of the CIA's Iran branch at Ledeen's home. Ledeen continued to be effusive, telling the agency man that Ghorbanifar was "a wonderful man...almost too good to be true." Allen was also there, and North showed up at the end of the interview, which focused on terrorism and Iranian political figures.

Among the things Ghorbanifar proposed during the meeting was a sting operation against Moammar Khadafy, the Libyan leader, in which Khadafy would pay $10 million to have one of his leading opponents murdered. Ghorbanifar would take the money but do nothing, and the opponent would resurface to Khadafy's embarrassment. Ghorbanifar also told of a three-man Iranian hit team that had arrived in Hamburg as part of a plan to kill Iranian exiles.

Afterward the CIA Iran specialist reported that he was "only further convinced of the...lack of trust that we could put in Mr. Ghorbanifar." A polygraph was scheduled, but in the meantime

Casey seemed to conclude that Ghorbanifar was the only game in town. The next day the CIA director wrote the president an eyes-only letter telling him that one of the ongoing initiatives the agency was exploring to free the hostages remained the plan involving Ghorbanifar.

A few days before Christmas, Casey, who that fall had been diagnosed as having prostate cancer, called Secord. He was acting on North's suggestion. As Secord answered the phone Casey's secretary said the "director" wanted to speak with him. Secord agreed, thinking to himself, "The director of what?" Casey then came on the phone with his distinctive gruff voice and Secord snapped out of his fog. Could the general come over to Langley around 4:15 that afternoon? Casey said he would leave word at the front gate to wave him right through.

Secord's car was in the shop, so he had to borrow his son's pickup truck. The roads were icy and he was about fifteen minutes late. Casey had forgotten to send word to the guards at the front gate, and Secord, in the pickup, hardly looked like a visiting statesman.

When he finally got up to Casey's office they began talking at cross purposes. Secord thought they were discussing Central America but finally realized that Casey was talking about Iran. He asked if Secord knew Michael Ledeen. Casey said he thought Ledeen was bright. Then they abruptly turned away from Iran and the subject never came up again. Casey began asking about the Contras.

Secord admitted to Casey that he still did not know enough about the resistance. Central America was not his area of expertise, but based on what he had seen of the Contras he was concerned about the quality of their leadership. And he warned that without air support they would go down; without adequate air resupply the troops would have to retreat, and he doubted they would ever get back into the field again. They also needed better intelligence and a special-operations capability. But air supply was the most pressing need.

Casey seemed to agree and thanked Secord for his efforts. He said the president was aware of his contributions and was also grateful. Secord was appreciative but stressed again that he and the Contras needed CIA support. Not trying to disguise his contempt for the Boland Amendment, Secord said that the measure was worded loosely enough that agency intelligence could be given directly to him if not to the Contras. There was certainly nothing illegal about private support. What Secord needed was the Sandinistas' electronic order of battle, air order of battle and ground order of battle.

"Casey said he would look into it," Secord recalls of the meeting. "He knew he was walking on the edge... I thought he was very bright. He was a wily old man who knew how the bureaucracy worked."

When the CIA could legally get back in the game Secord offered to turn over to the Agency all the assets that the Enterprise had generated. "Mr. Director," he said, "if and when you get your hunting license back, whatever assets we are creating right now are yours."

"Thank you very much" replied Casey.

Casey took notes during the session, which Secord thought was a sign that he had made progress. Casey had also mentioned that he spoke with North all the time. "He liked North because he was tough, smart and could get things done. There are very few people in this government who can get anything done. It's gridlock, and it's gonna stay that way until we get a strong chief executive who can take names and numbers."

A short time later Secord got another indication of the close North-Casey relationship when he attended a seminar on special operations at Fort McNair outside Washington. Secord was supposed to meet North after a dinner at the Officers' Club to talk business, but Casey collared Ollie alone in a small room for at least an hour. Whereupon Secord got tired of waiting and went home.

On January 2, 1986, Amiram Nir flew to Washington from Tel Aviv to meet with North and Poindexter. Nir had an idea on how the Iran initiative could be strengthened: getting the Southern Lebanon army to free twenty or thirty Shiite Hizballah prisoners "who didn't have blood on their hands" as an added inducement for the Hizballah terrorists to release the American hostages. Under the Nir plan, Israel would ship Iran 4,000 TOW missiles. After the delivery of the first 500, the five American hostages would be released, along with the Hizballah prisoners. If the U.S. hostages were all released, then Israel would deliver the remaining 3,500 TOWs. Nir also stressed Israel's need to receive prompt replenishment of the additional TOW missiles it would send Iran, and he renewed the proposal he had discussed earlier with North to use profits from the arms sales to fund joint U.S.-Israeli covert operations.

The same day, North contacted Stanley Sporkin, the CIA general counsel, to have him begin drafting a new and broader presidential finding that would authorize the Iran initiative in a more all-inclusive fashion. North knew that unless there was an expanded finding, the U.S. could not allow a third country, in this case Israel, to transfer American-made arms to the embargoed Iran without violating the Arms Export Control Act. North would devote much of his time over the next two weeks to prodding the CIA and others to come up with an acceptable finding that the president could sign so that the arms sales might get underway again.

When Sporkin did not work fast enough to suit North, Ollie, doubling as a lawyer, came up with his own draft finding. On Sunday, January 5 North and Sporkin met with Casey at the director's home to discuss the Nir plan as incorporated into the new draft finding. Casey read it and approved. Sporkin would testify that he felt uncomfortable omitting the hostage-release objective. North said the State Department did not want this included because it would create the appearance of a "hostage-for-arms shipment" and therefore not "look right." But Casey overruled him and said the reference should be included.

The next day North hand-carried the draft finding to Attorney General Meese, who approved it. At that morning's national security briefing, Poindexter told Reagan about the Nir plan and showed him the draft finding, intending that he examine it for informational purposes only. But Reagan not only read the document but signed it.

On January 7 the senior members of the NSC met to consider the Nir plan and the draft finding. Present in addition to Reagan were Vice-President Bush, Shultz, Weinberger, Meese, Casey, Poindexter and Regan. No one mentioned that Reagan had signed a finding the day before and the now-familiar players reiterated their now-familiar arguments for and against the initiative.

Meese said that in his opinion the arms sales through Israel were legal if they were accompanied by a finding. But as before, there was no record or recollection of Bush expressing a view. Bush's silence seemed strange. As head of a blue-ribbon task force on terrorism charged with fashioning a definitive policy on the issue for the Administration, Bush had just submitted to the president a classified report whose central conclusion—"the U.S. government will make no concessions to terrorists; it will not pay ransoms, release prisoners, change policies or agree to other acts that might encourage additional terrorism"—flew directly in the face of trading arms to Iran to win the release of the American hostages.

After the meeting, though no clear green light had been given, North called Nir in Israel and told him that the president was prepared to go ahead. North gave Nir the following coded message: "1) Joshua [Reagan] has approved proceeding as we had hoped. 2) Joshua and Samuel [Secretary Weinberger] have also agreed on method one [replenishment]. 3) Following additional conditions apply to Albert [the code name for the operation]: A) Resupply should be as routine as possible to prevent disclosure on our side. May take longer than two months. However Albert says if crisis arises Joshua promises that we will deliver all required . . . in less than eighteen hours. B) Joshua also wants both your government and ours to stay with no comment if operation is disclosed. 4) If these conditions are acceptable to the Banana [Israel] then Oranges [the United States] are ready to proceed."

But within days CIA lawyers on Sporkin's staff were raising legal objections. They concluded that both the Arms Export Control Act and the Foreign Assistance Act prohibited the arms transfer without three factors being present: U.S. consent, notification of Congress and the eligibility of the receiving country. The administration did not want to notify Congress, and there was no question that Iran was still on the embargoed list. But the lawyers said the operation could be carried out if the Pentagon sold the TOWs to the CIA under the Economy Act, after which the agency, with a presidential finding, could then sell the weapons to either Israel or Iran.

So in mid-January the deal was restructured along the lines of North's earlier "fifth option." The missiles would come directly from the United States, not Israel, and—at the suggestion of Casey, North and Poindexter—Secord would be brought into the operation as a "commercial cutout" who would receive the money for the missiles from Iran and then pay the United States. This way there would be no congressional reporting requirements.

But Weinberger was still raising objections to the plan and to the new idea of bringing in Secord. North and Casey talked about the need for the president to take charge and steamroll Weinberger by the act of implementing the operation. "Casey believes that Cap [Weinberger] will continue to create roadblocks until he is told by you that the President wants this to move NOW and that Cap will have to make it work," North wrote Poindexter in a computer message on January 15.

A new finding was drawn up, along with a cover memorandum outlining the plan to make direct sales from the CIA to Iran via Secord, who was referred to as the "authorized agent." After meeting with Poindexter and agreeing to the expanded role, Secord recalls that he was called in to the White House Situation Room to examine the finding, which made passing reference to him, and to be introduced to the relevant CIA personnel. He was then excused.

On January 17 President Reagan signed the finding. Weinberger would testify he was unaware it had been signed, while Shultz said he was not even aware of Reagan's decision to embark on another initiative with Iran—this time with the United States selling the arms directly.

To sweeten the pot for Iran, Casey and Poindexter had also authorized North to provide Tehran with some U.S. intelligence about Iraqi troop deployments. It was a cynical gesture—the CIA already had an operation in place giving Iraq intelligence on Iran.

Meanwhile the lead player for Iran remained Ghorbanifar, despite his flunking of yet another CIA lie-detector test shortly before Reagan signed the finding. Ghorbanifar failed thirteen of fifteen questions, scoring correctly only on his name and nationality. An agency officer concluded in a memo to Casey: "Ghorbanifar is a fabricator who has deliberately deceived the U.S. government concerning his information and activities. It is recommended that the Agency have no dealing whatsoever with Ghorbanifar."

Ghorbanifar showed up at his friend Ledeen's house after the test, furious that the examiner had asked questions that went far beyond what he thought were the agreed-upon parameters, and he claimed to be physically in pain from the instruments used in the exam. The test result angered Ledeen and North. Ollie had even told Ledeen before the test that the CIA would make sure Ghorbanifar flunked because it didn't want to deal with him.

North, like Casey, was of the view that while Ghorbanifar may have been a sordid character, he was the only player available and therefore worth the risk. "I knew him to be a liar, I knew him to be a cheat, and I knew him to be a man making enormous sums of money," North would later state before the congressional Iran-Contra committees. "We knew what the man was, but it was difficult to get other people involved in these kinds of activities. I mean, one can't go to Mother Theresa and ask her to go to Tehran."

Clair George, the CIA's deputy director for operations, instructed the chief of the agency's Iran branch to have nothing further to do with Ghorbanifar, and he declared to Casey that the entire operations directorate was also through with the Iranian. And, wary of Secord because of his past links with Edwin Wilson— the jailed former CIA operative—George also recommended that the Agency have nothing to do with the retired Air Force Major General.

But as he had done earlier, Casey decided to ignore the advice of his subordinates and keep dealing with both men. He liked Secord and thought Ghorbanifar, however much a rogue, could be used for whatever he could offer. Casey ordered Charles Allen, the counter-terrorism analyst, to "just take another look at this individual."

On January 13 Allen spent five hours with Ghorbanifar at Ledeen's house, discussing terrorism and Iranian government leaders. Ghorbanifar told Allen there were several projects he hoped he could work on with the United States, including the stopping of Iranian, Libyan and Syrian-sponsored terrorism; the overthrowing of Libya's Khadafy; and the ongoing arms sales to Iran to gain the release of the American hostages.

The profits from these ventures, Ghorbanifar suggested to Allen, seemingly out of the blue, could well be used for "Ollie's boys in Central America."

IRAN-CONTRA

O N January 22, five days after President Reagan signed a new finding authorizing the United States to send arms directly to Iran, North and Secord flew to London to meet with Nir and Ghorbanifar on the details of the next shipment.

North arrived at the meeting knowing how he would like the transaction structured. He had been told by the Pentagon that the base price of each TOW missile, including freight costs, was about $3,400. He had originally been quoted a price of $6,000 per missile and rejected it as too high, saying he wanted the oldest model in stock and that it didn't matter if the missiles worked well. This was not an attitude calculated to inspire trust and confidence in the Iranians, or Ghorbanifar, who was prepared to pay $10,000 for each TOW. But by then, the name of the game appeared to be generating as much profits as possible for Secord's Enterprise.

Like the rest of the meetings with Ghorbanifar and other Iranians that would ensue in Europe over the coming months, this London session took place in a hotel suite that had been bugged by the CIA so that the conversation could be recorded.

The meeting was significant, since it was here that the idea of diverting the profits from the Iranian arms sales to the Contras gathered momentum. At one point in the discussion, Ghorbanifar asked for a private tête-à-tête with North. Nir and Secord left the room, and Ghorbanifar and North then walked into the suite's bathroom. The Iranian apparently sensed that the crassness and political danger of selling arms for hostages were grating on North to the point at which Ollie's enthusiasm for the initiative might be waning. Ghorbanifar wanted to suggest some incentives to close the deal—particularly the notion of providing some extra money to help Ollie's favorite charity: the Contras. As North would later testify of the encounter:

"... The attractive incentive for me was the one he made that residuals could flow to support the Nicaraguan resistance. He made it point blank and he made it, by my understanding, with the full knowledge and acquiescence and support, if not the original idea of, the Israeli intelligence services...

"For the very first time, in January, the whole idea of using U.S. weapons ... was made more palatable. I must confess to you that I thought using the Ayatollah's money to support the Nicaraguan resistance was the right idea ... a neat idea."

Ghorbanifar's other incentive for North, also offered in the privacy of the bathroom, was a $1 million bribe, Ollie would testify, almost as an afterthought. He said he quickly told the Iranian such a thing was "out of the question," and that if bribe attempts persisted Ghorbanifar "would be out of the picture very quickly." North said he never reported this to his superiors, dismissing it as an insignificant aberation in the tradition of Iranian *baksheesh*.

North would later maintain that the first time he either heard of or considered the diversion proposal was when Ghorbanifar raised it in the London bathroom confab, but the record shows that the idea had been broached at least twice before that: first in the meeting with Israeli defense procurement officials December 6 in New York, and again by Ghorbanifar himself at his January 13 polygraph exam in Washington. North had also met with Nir in November and again on January 2 to discuss using the profits from the arms sales to fund other covert operations, though it is not certain whether the Contras were among the operations talked about.

In any event, there is no question that at the least the diversion concept came out of London energized. North came back to Washington and told Poindexter and Casey about the idea; both were enthusiastic. Poindexter said he approved the plan after only a few minutes' consideration, while Casey apparently saw it as the consummate sting.

"Director Casey used several words to describe how he felt about it, all of which were effusive," North would testify. "He referred to it as the ultimate irony, the ultimate covert operation ... and was very enthusiastic about it."

Casey immediately saw the implications of such a slush fund. It was covert capitalism—a business venture that could generate a steady stream of cash that could be used for other adventures besides aiding the Contras. Eventually Congress would probably come around and meet the needs of the resistance. But there would always be other worthwhile causes that could be nurtured— the wars of the Reagan Doctrine, counterterrorist operations with the Israelis, whatever. Such a fund could be a spymaster's dream. Full service, one-stop shopping. Sort of a 7–11 account: always open, quick and handy. The funds would be under the control of a private corporation but run under the direction of the U.S. government and used for national security imperatives. Off lines, but official enough. Only a handful would know. The director of Central Intelligence, North and Secord, perhaps. No hassles with congressional notification.

"Director Casey and I talked at length on a variety of occasions about the use of those monies to support other operations besides the Nicaragua operation..." North would testify. "We always assumed... that there would come a time... where the Congress would make available the monies necessary to support the Nicaraguan freedom fighters. And at various times, he and I talked about the fact that it might be necessary at some point in the future to have something, as he would put it, to pull off the shelf, and to help support other activities like that."

Though the diversion concept was now codified, the Contras were still very much on North's mind and taking up much of his time—despite the flurry of activity on Iran over the past several months. He had been constantly shuttling from the Iran initiative to the Contras and from the Contras back to Iran. Now, the diversion decision lent a certain unifying symmetry to both operations.

By January, the Contra-supply network was starting to gear up, albeit in sputtering fashion. Secord's man, Richard Gadd, had hired flight crews and recruited Southern Air Transport, a Miami-based firm that did contract work for the CIA, to handle aircraft maintenance. The first plane, a C–7 Caribou, had been purchased, and the construction of the secret Santa Elena airstrip to service a southern front was well underway in Costa Rica.

North had also arranged for his Contra operatives to be able to communicate securely with one another. The National Security Agency had given him fifteen top-secret KL–43 encryption devices that sent coded messages. The people using the machines loaded in a fresh cassette tape each day containing a new code. On January 15, North gave KL–43s to Secord, Gadd, Raphael Quintero, the Secord liaison in Central America; Col. James Steele, then the chief U.S. military adviser in El Savador; Joe Fernandez, the CIA station chief in Costa Rica; and William Langton, the president of Southern Air Transport. North kept a machine in his office. Every month, new codes were distributed to each member of the group to insure continued secret communications.

KL–43s in the hands of Steele and Fernandez were Exhibit A of broadening official U.S. involvement in North's covert Contra plan, in violation, it would seem, of the Boland Amendment. But during that same period, North also conferred closely with Gen. John Galvin, commander of the U.S. Southern Command, discussing the resupply operation and the southern front as well as overall strategy, planning and support.

Though it was Secord and Gadd's job to preside over the nuts and bolts of the Contra war effort, particularly the resupply operation, North decided that no detail was too small for him to be immersed in. The progress of the Santa Elena airstrip was especially worrisome. He involved himself with obtaining fuel storage facilities at the site, security arrangements, even instructions for the bulldozer operator. North also knew all the details of each weapons supply run—its contents, who was flying, and the coordinates and quadrant it was bound for.

Despite his hands-on involvement, there were continued problems. The C–7 Caribou, proud and sole symbol of the fledgling Contra air force, developed mechanical problems on a supply run and crashed. North was again forced to turn to his courier, Rob Owen, and divert charters of the State Department's Nicaraguan Humanitarian Assistance Office for delivery of lethal supplies.

And for all the talk of opening a southern front, there simply was no such thing yet. The airstrip was not finished, and the only planes available at the Ilopango Air Force Base in El Savador did not have the range to make it to southern Nicaragua and back. Further, in-fighting among Contra factions continued to mitigate against the emergence of a strong Contra presence in the south. The leading faction, the FDN, was unwilling to dedicate its precious northern-based resources to help southern-based Contra leaders.

Owen warned North in a memo that "our credibility will once

again be zero in the south" if deliveries didn't start up soon. "They have been promised they will get what they need. Who is to be the contact for these goods and who is to see that they are delivered? A critical stage is being entered in the southern front and we have to deliver."

Back on the Iran front, the decision to divert arms sales profits to the Contras had now created conflicting goals. While the stated purpose of the presidential finding was to sell arms to Iran for the release of the hostages and a larger strategic opening to Tehran, the concept behind the diversion was to overcharge the Iranians to generate maximum profits for the Enterprise and the Contras. Overcharging Iran while supplying poor-quality missiles ran counter to creating the trust and confidence necessary to secure both the release of the hostages and better relations government-to-government. Not to mention the fact that the finding which authorized the arms sales to Iran made no mention of applying the proceeds to the Contras or any other covert operation.

Meanwhile, on January 24, North prepared a memo for Poindexter called "Operation Recovery" that outlined his hopes for what was to happen next. Four thousand TOW missiles were to be shipped to Iran in increments of 1,000 each. On February 8, after delivery of the first 1,000 missiles, the Southern Lebanon Army was to release twenty-five Hizballah prisoners. The following day, all the American hostages would be freed in Beirut. On February 10, as the second shipment of missiles was delivered, selected hostages from other countries would be released. And in return for the final two shipments, the remaining foreign hostages would be turned over, along with the remains of William Buckley. On February 11, North added, in what was either whimsy or incredible political naïvete, Ayatollah Khomeini would step down.

What actually happened, not surprisingly, was quite different from the sunny North scenario. On February 15 and 16, Khomeini still very much in power, 1,000 TOW missiles were flown from Kelly Air Force Base in Texas to Israel. On February 17, an Israeli charter, stripped of its markings and flown by a Southern Air Transport crew, delivered 500 of the missiles to Bandar Abbas, Iran. To avoid flying over other countries' airspace, Secord mapped out a circuitous route that had the plane fly south down the Red Sea, around the Saudi Arabian peninsula into the Sea of Oman and the port city of Bandar Abbas. Secord monitored the flight from a command post in Israel.

North wrote Poindexter that day that the Iranians had requested delivery of the second batch of 500 missiles six days later on February 23. "They say they will release all hostages if, repeat if, intelligence is good . . . They want focus on current fighting."

Meanwhile the Iranians wanted a meeting with the U.S. in Frankfurt, West Germany, on February 19 before the delivery of the next shipment of TOWs, at which there would be a delegation of six Iranian officials, headed by a junior deputy prime minister. The Frankfurt meeting was to be Washington's first chance to meet with any official of the Iranian government in five years. But when the appointed time came, the deputy prime minister didn't appear, so North decided to fly home in a calculated display of diplomatic pique.

Distrusting Ghorbanifar, North had summoned Secord's Iranian-born business partner, Albert Hakim, to act as a translator at the Frankfurt session. The CIA objected to the use of Hakim, since it represented a further privatizing of a sensitive covert operation, but North reasserted his trust and confidence in both Hakim and Secord.

Hakim had been a friend and associate of Secord's since they met in the mid-seventies when Secord was stationed in Tehran as head of all U.S. Air Force programs in Iran. Hakim represented a variety of American firms doing business with Iran, specializing in the sales of advanced technology and military hardware. One of the first coups of Hakim's Swiss-based company, Stanford Technology, was the winning of a large contract to supply the Shah's air force with a computerized telephone monitoring system capable of eavesdropping on thousands of phone calls at one time.

Hakim quickly developed a specialty in international finance, moving money quickly and efficiently around the world, and creating holding companies to facilitate—and sometimes disguise—the movement of those funds. To promote his business, Hakim has admitted that he routinely paid off officials close to the Shah, but he saw the handwriting on the wall for the Shah and fled Iran long before the revolution. In 1980, he was tapped by Secord to play an important role in the failed attempt to rescue the American hostages in Tehran. He had returned to Tehran to help obtain vehicles and other transportation for the aborted rescue, working with U.S. Air Force intelligence.

So that was a security chit on Hakim's side as he returned to Frankfurt for the meeting with Iranian officials, which finally occurred on February 25. Ghorbanifar, when he was informed that Hakim was to sit in as a translator, had strongly objected, calling Hakim an "enemy of the state." Coming from Ghorbanifar, the former SAVAK operative, the protest was amusing, but he was working for the Ayatollah now, so the Americans supposed that such rhetoric was to be expected.

The CIA had only a few Farsi speakers available, and the only one it could provide on short notice was a woman. It was thought that the Ayatollah's men, who prefer their women cloaked in veil, would not be enamored with that idea. So Hakim was the man, though he warned that Ghorbanifar would surely recognize him. Still, the Americans concluded they could not go into the meeting relying on Ghorbanifar's translation, so Secord ordered Hakim to come up with a disguise.

With the Iranians due in just a few hours, Hakim went to the concierge of the Sheraton Hotel where they were meeting in Frankfurt and explained he wanted to buy a wig for his father. The concierge provided the addresses of a few shops, and Hakim jumped in a cab and raced to the first address given him. The saleswoman wanted to press for more detail about the wig's intended use—would Hakim be swimming in it?—than he had time for. He quickly bought a gray wig, put it atop his balding head, slipped on a pair of glasses and returned to the hotel, entering the meeting as "Ibrahim Ibrahim," an American of Turkish descent acting as a "special interpreter" at President Reagan's request.

"He looked like a totally different man," Secord recalled. "It was just amazing. Even I couldn't recognize him."

Also attending the meeting were North, Secord, Tom Twetten —the deputy chief of the CIA's Near East Division—and Amiran Nir, who was passed off as an American. North was using his William Goode alias, while Secord was "Major General Adams," whose assignment was to present the intelligence it had been agreed the Iranians would receive. The lead Iranian was the deputy prime minister. With him were an aide, two colonels introduced as being military intelligence officers, and of course Ghorbanifar.

Two meetings—which, like the earlier London session, were secretly tape-recorded—were scheduled. The first was a "political meeting" at which North was to give his high-road speech about the

Soviet threat and the goal of better U.S.-Iranian relations, together with the need to resolve the hostage problem. Secord, who did not attend the meeting, would then deliver the intelligence briefing at the second session.

Soon after the first meeting began, Hakim would testify, it became apparent to him that there was a "culture gap," and that the two sides were "absolutely on two different frequencies." The Iranians showed little interest in improving relations, focusing almost exclusively on the purchase of weapons. Hakim also saw that Ghorbanifar was distorting his translation to benefit the Iranians, so Hakim stepped in and assumed the translating duties.

If there was a culture gap, there was also a substance gap. The deputy prime minister said Ghorbanifar had assured him that the U.S. was prepared to sell Iran air-to-air Phoenix missiles. North insisted the subject had never come up until now. To the Americans, the Phoenix demand made it clear that Ghorbanifar had been telling the Iranians something totally different from what he had been telling Washington. "Essentially, Ghorbanifar, as a negotiating technique, lied to both sides to get them to the table, and then sat back and watched us fight it out," the CIA's Twetten later told the Tower Commission. "It was a real slugging match. It was awful."

Secord and Twetten briefed the two colonels in a separate meeting. They disclosed the Iraqi order-of-battle on a small section of the border with Iran, and also showed the Iranians an annotated high-altitude photograph, as an example of what the United States was capable of providing if a broader agreement could be reached.

The delegations met again the following day in the Iranians' hotel suite, where the deputy prime minister pressed his argument for the Phoenix missiles. But North and the U.S. side made it clear that the Phoenix was out of the question, at least for now. It was finally agreed that after the second 500 TOWs were shipped "a couple of hostages" would be released. The remainder would be freed after a meeting between more senior officials from each side on Kish Island off the coast of Iran. After that meeting, the United States would send on the remaining 3,000 TOWS.

As the delegations were preparing to go home, the deputy prime minister took Hakim aside in the hotel lobby and, in the presence of Secord, asked Hakim to relay a bribe offer to President Reagan.

The deputy, trying to bypass his delegation and cut a deal of his own, asked Hakim to tell Reagan that "money was no problem" if the weapons could be sold through him. Hakim and Secord were amused by the offer and took it as further evidence of the culture gap.

Back in Washington, on February 27, North recorded his impressions of the Frankfurt meetings in a computer message sent to McFarlane, who, despite his status as a private citizen, was scheduled to lead the American side at Kish Island. North seemed to conclude that the Iranians had paid more attention to larger strategic issues than Hakim said they had.

"The government of Iran is terrified of a new Soviet threat," North wrote. "They are seeking a rapprochement, but are filled with fear and mistrust... They are less interested in the Iran-Iraq war than we originally believed. They want technical advice more than arms or intelligence. The advice should be on commercial and military maintenance, not military tactics. They committed to end anti-U.S. terrorism... [and] stressed that there were new Soviet moves that we were unaware of. While all of this could be so much smoke, I believe that we may well be on the verge of a major breakthrough—not only on the hostages/terrorism, but on the relationship as a whole. We need only to go to this meeting, which has no agenda, other than to listen to each other, to release the hostages and start the process... Believe that you should be chartered to go early next week or maybe this weekend, but don't know how to make this happen. Have not told JMP [Poindexter] that this note is being sent. Help. Please call on secure [line at] your earliest convenience. Warm, but fatigued regards, North."

McFarlane sent his reply several hours later:

"Roger Ollie. Well done. If the world only knew how many times you have kept a semblance of integrity and gumption to U.S. policy, they would make you Secretary of State. But they can't know and would complain if they did—such is the state of democracy in the late 20th century..."

Though the agreement reached through Ghorbanifar before Frankfurt had called for the release of all the American hostages after the delivery of the first 1,000 TOW missiles, the U.S. side had acceded in Frankfurt to a new Iranian demand to deliver the second 500 TOWs in return only for the vague promise of the release of "a couple of hostages." So that same day, February 27, the second shipment of 500 TOWs was flown from Israel to Iran.

But no hostages were released.

The night of February 27, North, apparently unfazed, dashed off another cheery message to McFarlane, forging ahead with plans for Kish Island. He said he had just met with Casey and Poindexter and that they were in agreement on the need to proceed with the initiative. North said indications were that McFarlane's counterpart at the meeting would be Parliament Speaker Rafsanjani.

"Nice crowd you run with!" Ollie exclaimed. "God willing, Shultz will buy into this tomorrow when JMP briefs him. With the grace of the Good Lord and a little more hard work, we will very soon have five AMCITs [American citizens] home and be on our way to a much more positive relationship than the one which barters TOWs for lives." Poindexter, North added gratuitously, was "under tremendous pressure on this matter and very concerned that it go according to plan. My part in this was easy compared to his. I had only to deal with our enemies. He had to deal with the cabinet."

If the results of this latest round of U.S.-Iran talks had been dismal to date, they had been highly successful for Secord and Hakim, the merchant-diplomats whose involvement in the negotiations seemed a clear conflict of interest, especially when they believed that the profits from the arms sales belonged to them, not to the United States.

The profits were huge. Ghorbanifar paid Secord $10 million for the 1,000 TOW missiles. Secord paid the U.S. $3.7 million, thereby turning a paper profit of $6.3 million. Out of this, he would testify, he had to pay $850,000 in expenses and $2 million had to be set aside to insure the plane chartered from Israel. This left $3.4 million in working capital for the Enterprise.

Who was rightfully entitled to the arms-sales profits would become a matter of great dispute in the years ahead, with the Congress and most of American officialdom arguing that the money belonged to the United States government since it had provided the missiles. But Secord argued that the money was his and Hakim's since they did much of the engineering, negotiating and brokering of the deals and took the corporate risks.

But that was a question for the future. For the time being North and Secord were working on a very loose understanding. Still in effect during the Iran initiative, though apparently not discussed, was their 1984 agreement regarding the Contra operation that Secord would be entitled to an undefined "just compensation." Secord had agreed in principle to divert some of the proceeds of the arms sales to the Contras, but it had never been spelled out precisely how much, or what percentage of the profits, would go to the Contras. And it was Secord and Hakim who actually controlled the money in the Enterprises' Lake Resources account.

Soon after Secord received the first $10 million payment North began pressuring him to send money on to the Contras. "In February and later he wanted me to use all available surpluses to support the Contra project..." Secord would testify before the Iran-Contra committees. "There was always a certain amount of tension on this subject because North wasn't running this operation—I was, along with Hakim... We had to keep sufficient revenues in these accounts to stay fluid so that we could go on to the next operation. And remember, not one dime of U.S. money went into this operation. So we had to be very, very careful on this... I was perfectly willing to send funds to the Contras from the surpluses... But never was I able to send as much as Ollie North thought we should."

Poindexter, for his part, did not press North on how much money was actually getting through to the Contras. Having approved the diversion in principle, it was not his style to "micromanage" the operation, he said.

Ghorbanifar sent word that the Iranians wanted another preliminary meeting, this time in Paris, before the Kish Island session could take place. This request triggered a fresh wave of doubt among the handful of CIA careerists privy to the Iran initiative that either Ghorbanifar or the deputy prime minister could deliver on their promises. It had now been six months since Benjamin Weir was released, and Iran had reneged on numerous pledges in the interim.

The CIA was also growing increasingly wary of Nir since Israel's interest in the Iran arms sales remained fundamentally different from Washington's. The U.S. was now shipping its own arms directly to Iran. Israel was still being used as a way station, but that didn't seem reason enough to have Nir sit in as a principal in the negotiations with Tehran. Furthermore, the CIA suspected that Israel was unilaterally continuing to send arms to Iran as an added inducement to keep Tehran on the road to Kish Island.

Nir, sensing there was a move afoot to exclude him, had Prime Minister Peres weigh in with a letter to Reagan a few days after the Frankfurt meeting. The letter discussed the steps that needed to be taken in the days ahead, and continued to frame the initiative as a joint Israeli-American venture.

By early March the CIA had persuaded North and Secord to replace Hakim as the translator with George Cave, a retired CIA agent who had served in Tehran and spoke Farsi. Cave, who would also eventually replace Twetten as the Agency's point man on the Iran operation, had had experience dealing with Ghorbanifar and was appalled that the U.S. was doing business with him. But Cave nonetheless came out of retirement to accept the assignment.

On March 7, North, Cave and Twetten flew to Paris for the meeting Ghorbanifar said he needed before Kish Island. Nir was also present. Ghorbanifar had nothing but discouraging news: the meetings in Frankfurt had done nothing to enhance the internal political position of the deputy prime minister; the Iranians had reviewed their military requirements and concluded that in lieu of more TOWs, they needed 240 kinds of spare parts to repair the HAWK missiles in their arsenal. Finally, Ghorbanifar said that Kish Island was now unacceptable as the site for the meeting between the senior delegations. It would have to be in Tehran itself.

Like Nir, Ghorbanifar was also worried that the Americans were trying to cut him out as their channel to Iran. After the Frankfurt meeting Hakim had called the deputy prime minister and proposed that Ghorbanifar be dropped now that government officials were involved. But Ghorbanifar stressed in Paris that he was an essential link to the deputy, an essential link in the whole process. He delivered a pep talk on the need to continue on, reminding the Americans that they could apply some or all of the proceeds of the arms sales to the Contras. The other threatened party, Nir, also piped in on the need to forge ahead.

This was the first Cave had heard of the diversion proposal, and he duly noted it in a memo on the Paris meeting written for Casey. North, for his part, was discouraged by the meeting and conceded in his notes that the Ghorbanifar channel to Iran might be flawed. "We cannot verify that there is anyone else in the government of Iran aware, or even interested, in talking to the U.S. government," he wrote to himself.

As he had done after the Frankfurt meeting, North sent McFar-

lane a computer message at home, this time expressing his growing
frustration with Ghorbanifar. McFarlane wrote back commiserating: "Gorba is basically a self-serving mischief-maker. Of course the
trouble is that as far as we know, so is the entire lot of those we are
dealing with... But it is going to take some time to get a feel for
just who the players are on the contemporary scene in Tehran. So
the sooner we get started the better."

After Paris, Twetten concluded that Ghorbanifar could not be
trusted and that it was North who was deftly keeping the initiative alive by playing off the president's emotional attachment to
the hostages and the growing political potency of the issue.

"We had delivered our missiles and the shoe was on their
foot," Twetten told the Tower Commission, "but they were acting
like the shoe was still on our foot... North, who you must have
sensed by now is a man of a lot of energy and a lot of determination, essentially kept it alive because of the president's personal
and emotional interest in getting the hostages out—in my view.
The political reality of this thing was it would be very nice if you
could get a strategic thing done... But the real thing that was
driving this was that there was... a lot of pressure from the hostage families to meet with the president, and there were articles
in the magazines about the forgotten hostages, and there were a
lot of things being said about the U.S. government [not] doing
anything... And there is a lot of fear about the yellow ribbons
going back up, and that this president would have the same
problems that the last president had with the Iranian hostages
... We learned as time went on that the Iranians didn't fully
control these hostages, but as it was being portrayed... there
wasn't any question that we could get all these hostages out
through the Iranians."

At this juncture, perhaps sensing that he had finally gotten in
over his head, North asked McFarlane for advice on how and
when he should return to the Marine Corps. McFarlane replied
in a March 19 message that they should discuss it, but then went
on to suggest that North come work with him at the Center for
Strategic and International Studies, where the two could continue
doing covert operations together but from the security of the
private sector.

"Frankly, I would expect the heat from the Hill to become im-
mense on you by summer," McFarlane wrote. "Consequently, it
strikes me as wise that you leave the White House. At the same
time, there will be no one to do all (or even a small part of what)

you have done. And if it isn't done, virtually all of the investment of the past five years will go down the drain. How's this for a self-serving scenario: 1. North leaves the White House in May and takes 39 days leave. 2. July 1, North is assigned as a fellow at the CSIS and (lo and behold) is assigned to McFarlane's office. 3. McFarlane/North continue to work the Iran account as well as to build other clandestine capabilities so much in demand here and there. Just a knee-jerk musing."

North pressed on, placating the nervous Ghorbanifar by inviting him to Washington for a meeting on April 3, where they discussed the availability of the HAWK spare parts Iran was now requesting.

The following day, North wrote a long report, "Release of American Hostages in Beruit," that was to become one of the most significant documents in the entire Iran-Contra affair, if not the proverbial "smoking gun." It was a summary of the Iran initiative from its inception to date, an outline of the next shipment of weaponry and a breakdown of how the profits from the next delivery would be spent, including $12 million for the Contras. This was the document that would become known as the "Diversion Memo."

According to the plan, on April 7, Iran would transfer $17 million to an Israeli account in Switzerland. Israel would keep $2 million to buy 508 new TOW missiles as replacements for the ones which had won the release of Reverend Weir. Secord's Enterprise would get the remaining $15 million, of which $3.6 million would be paid to the U.S. for the HAWK spare parts. North then wrote that "$12 million will be used to purchase critically needed supplies for the Nicaraguan Democratic Resistance Forces. This materiel is essential to cover shortages in resistance inventories resulting from their current offensives and Sandinista counterattacks, and to 'bridge' the period between now and when congressionally approved lethal assistance . . . can be delivered."

Three days later North messaged McFarlane that he had prepared the April 4 memo at Poindexter's request for "our boss." Ollie would later testify that by "our boss," he had meant President Reagan.

At this point in early April, as North and the NSC continued the policy of trading arms with one avowed supporter of terrorism—Iran—they were actively trying to cripple another: Libya.

On April 5, terrorists exploded a bomb at the La Belle disco in

West Berlin, a frequent hangout for American GI's. One U.S. Soldier, and a Turkish woman were killed while 230 others—including about 50 American military personnel—were injured.

Stepped-up electronic intelligence-gathering through the repositioning of NSA satellites over Libya had produced what the White House considered irrefutable evidence that Tripoli was behind the bombing. On April 4, a message to Tripoli from the Libyan People's Bureau in East Berlin had been intercepted. It said: "Tripoli will be happy when you see the headlines tomorrow." In the early morning hours of April 5 came another message from East Berlin to Tripoli saying that an operation was "happening now" which could not be linked to the East Berlin Libyans. About ten minutes later, the bomb exploded at the disco.

This was the smoking gun that the White House had long been waiting for as a pretext to squash Kadafy. Since 1981, the Administration had been obsessed by Libya, and had made little secret of its desire to overthrow Khadafy and/or assassinate him. He was an acknowledged world menace who was relentlessly anti-American, anti-Israel and anti-moderate Arab. He aided and abetted terrorism, he aspired to build a nuclear bomb, he had invaded Chad and was threatening to form a federation of Moslem states in North Africa.

For years the CIA had been encouraging and supporting Libyan exile groups, as well as certain countries, notably France and Egypt, in attempts to stage a coup in Libya. But Khadafy seemed to have nine lives and had escaped several attempts on both his power and his life. Still, Washington passed up few opportunities to poke its stick into Khadafy's cage in an effort to prod, provoke and embarrass him. Libya was an easy and convenient target for the Mediterranean-based Sixth Fleet, and in August of 1981 Reagan approved a series of war games inside Libya's "line of death"—the 120-mile limit that Tripoli claimed as its territorial waters in defiance of the internationally recognized 12 miles. Khadafy rose to the bait and attacked, and the U.S. shot down two Libyan jets.

Then came the "hit team" scare—reports circulated by Administration officials of supposed evidence that five Libyan-trained terrorists had arrived in the United States to assassinate Reagan and some of his top aides. White House gates were fortified with concrete barriers. The image was that of an embattled president hunkered down in the war against terrorism, but no facts to substantiate the hit-team claims ever materialized. It appears, rather,

to have been the first volley in a sophisticated campaign of disinformation that would be bared five years later—an NSCinspired
effort to plant false stories about Libya in the press in an effort to
keep Khadafy off balance, to embolden his political opponents
and build public support for taking him out.

The TWA hijacking in June of 1985 produced another wave of
anti-Libyan sentiment at the White House. After so much tough
talk about terrorism, the U.S. simply had to retaliate. But attacks
against Iran and Syria—by all indications the more forceful propo-
nents of state-sponsored terrorism—were deemed too risky. Libya,
though there was no evidence it had had anything to do with the
hijacking, was an easier and more politically palatable target for the
testosterone-swelled Reagan White House, still looking for post-
Grenada targets to show that America Was Back, especially vis-à-vis
terrorism. A raid on Libya that killed or toppled Khadafy would be
worth three or four Grenadas.

In July McFarlane opened a high-level White House meeting
with Reagan and other top foreign-policy advisors by saying that
economic and diplomatic pressure against Libya had failed. There
was a need for stronger action. Casey, Shultz and Weinberger spoke
up in rare agreement that plans against Khadafy should be developed.

Two anti-Khadafy contingency plans were drawn up under the
code name "Flower." One was "Tulip," another effort to support
anti-Khadafy Libyan exiles. The other was called "Rose," a more
dramatic military strike against Libya that would be carried out by
the U.S. and its allies, especially Egypt. Washington would provide
air support, and one of the targets would be Khadafy's living
quarters, on the grounds that it was a terrorist hub. Though this
again raised the delicate issue of assassination, Reagan himself reportedly brushed the issue aside, saying he would take the heat if
Khadafy was killed in the raid.

Poindexter traveled to Cairo over the Labor Day weekend to
press the plan with Egyptian President Hosni Mubarak, but it
quickly became apparent that there was far more enthusiasm for
the idea in Washington than there was in Cairo, and Mubarak
plainly didn't like being pushed. "Look, Admiral," he is said to
have told Poindexter curtly, "when we decide to attack Libya, it
will be our decision and on our timetable."

Then, two days after Christmas, came the terrorist bombings of
the Rome and Vienna airports in which nineteen people were

killed, including five Americans, among them an eleven-year-old girl. The American press was quickly told that the CIA had found a Libyan connection to the bombings, but the Israelis said the Palestinian Abu Nidal was responsible. Still, the newspapers were filled with reports of NSC contingency planning for B–52 bomber strikes against Libya as well as for raids by F–111s from their base in England.

On January 6, 1986 Reagan convened a meeting of the National Security Planning Group. There was discussion of an idea proposed by North and two other NSC aides to use the navy's submarine-launched Tomahawk missile, which had a range of 500 miles and was accurate to within 100 feet, to make surgical attacks on targets inside Libya. The president made it clear he still wanted contingency planning to continue but said he was reluctant to launch an attack against Libya in the absence of clear evidence linking Tripoli to the airport bombings. Instead it was decided to stage another naval exercise off the Libyan coast, hoping to provoke an attack that could be used as justification for an all-out "retaliatory" raid. In the meantime Reagan would announce the intermediate step of economic sanctions to get that largely symbolic step out of the way so that the fist could be quickly deployed later.

On March 23, a massive American armada of 45 ships, 200 planes and the nuclear-powered attack submarine *Los Angeles* sailed inside Khadafy's 120–mile Line of Death in the show-of-force exercise code-named Prairie Fire. Libya again obliged by firing several missiles at U.S. reconnaissance planes from a land base, all of which missed. The U.S. responded by bombing a Libyan radar installation and sinking two Libyan patrol boats. There were no U.S. casualties, while some seventy-two Libyans were killed. North monitored the exercises closely at the White House, even having Casey paged at a golf course so that the CIA director could be kept informed.

On March 25, in the midst of Prairie Fire, an NSA satellite intercepted a three-line message from the head of the Libyan Intelligence Service in Tripoli to eight Libyan People's Bureaus instructing them to stand by to attack American targets and to execute "the plan." That had been followed by the April 4 and 5 messages from East Berlin to Tripoli, then the disco bombing, and the White House finally had its smoking gun.

American intelligence also learned around this time that another way Khadafy intended to hurt the United States was by offering to

pay the Shiite terrorists who were holding the American hostages
in Lebanon up to $100 million if they would turn the hostages over
to Libya. A fear that Khadafy was close to obtaining the hostages
may have been a factor in strengthening the resolve of North,
Poindexter, Casey and others to pursue the Iran initiative in hopes
that another arms shipment would win the release of the Americans
before they could be given to Khadafy.

Reagan, spending Easter in California, immediately approved
an attack on Libya when told of the NSA intercepts linking Tripoli to the West Berlin bombing, and the planners back at the
White House got down to work. North was one of those who
developed the plans and option papers for the proposed bombing.

North, again, was well positioned to make a substantial contribution in another of the Reagan Administration's major foreign-policy
adventures. The general subject was terrorism, Khadafy was perceived as one of the world's leading terrorists, and North saw himself as America's leading terror-cop. Since the presentation of the
report of Vice-President Bush's task force on terrorism three
months earlier, North had assumed a far more powerful—though
technically unauthorized—role in counterterrorism. While the task
force had adopted a policy of "swift and effective retribution"
against terrorists, it had been unable to resolve the central dispute
that had been plaguing the Administration for years about precisely
how that policy would be implemented, and who would have the
command and control authority.

Terrorism was nominally the bailiwick of the State Department, but State was not part of the national command authority
and could not make the kinds of instant operational decisions on
how best to deploy U.S. commandos during a breaking terrorist
crisis. In post-mortem analyses of how the U.S. performed in the
TWA hijacking and other terrorist incidents, most experts argued
that the command center should be located in the White House,
at the center of government. The White House could task other
agencies; State could not. But Shultz had mounted great resistance to this proposal, so the Bush task force had decided to
table the issue.

One group that was created by the task force was something
called the Emergency Survey Team (EST), which was charged with
the responsibility of positioning forces during a terror incident. Included in this group were North; Noel Koch, assistant secretary of

defense for international security affairs and the Pentagon's counterterrorism chief; Oliver "Buck" Revell, executive assistant director of the FBI; Robert Oakley, director of the State Department's office of counterterrorism and emergency planning; and the ubiquitous Dewey Clarridge, who had surfaced as head of the CIA's new counterterrorism center and who retained a knack for staying in touch with North.

Despite the Bush task force's decision to duck the command and control issue, the members of EST thought there should be a centralized operational command located in the White House. So in time they unofficially assumed that very function, calling themselves the Operations Sub-Group (OSG).

"The task force's crazy solution to the command issue was to put it in the appendix of the report and decide it later so as not to offend George Bush's *amour propre*," recalls Noel Koch. "These guys were all playing for the footnotes. But having done that we went ahead and created this damn thing in the White House quietly. We called it the OSG, but it didn't matter what you called it. . . . There had to be a cell established that had to exist in the White House, that had the ability to direct other agencies to do things, and part of what it was going to do was to plan and execute operations . . . But it was never blessed . . . because that would have required some expression as to why it existed and who ran it. What was the authority? You do that and you make George Shultz mad, so you don't do anything."

OSG was later codified by the issuance of National Security Decision Directive 207, and by North's drafting of a secret annex to the Bush task force report. Through these means North expanded his counter-terrorist powers and was given charge of the new Office to Combat Terrorism, whose existence was apparently a closely guarded secret even from other members of the NSC staff. It was from the Bush task force that North picked up his two aides, Robert Earl and Craig Coy, who would work closely with him on the Iran arms sales and other projects while still remaining officially attached to the Crisis Management Center, where North had worked earlier.

In June of 1986, as part of implementing the recommendations of the Bush report, an "Alien Border Control Committee" was established to preside over "the control and removal of terrorist aliens in the U.S. These contingency plans, seemingly a variation on the FEMA planning that North had been associated with earlier, anticipated that the Immigration and Naturalization Service might be charged with apprehending and removing a sizeable group of aliens, and suggested housing "up to 5,000 aliens in temporary [tents] quarters" at a camp in Oakdale, Louisiana. These contingency plans, apparently never implemented, generally fell under North's expanded powers.

North had frequent contact with the Vice President and his office around the time of the terrorism task force, but the Bush-North relationship dated to at least 1982 when North was the NSC staff coordinator for crisis management, when Bush had been charged with overall responsibility for crisis management at the White House. Later North had traveled with Bush to El Salvador on the death-squad issue. Bush had been only one of three government officials to express condolences to North on the death of his father in 1984, and would later second the opinion of Ronald Reagan that North was a hero. In 1987 North was invited to Bush's Christmas party.

In any event, North's expanded powers in a new counter-terrorism apparatus also created a new vehicle for exluding those who did not agree with his goals. Meeting at least weekly at the White House, OSG became, de facto, an unauthorized super-group composed of action-oriented senior members of the national security establishment who were frustrated with the system's inability to move quickly and effectively in a crisis—men who had their hands on the levers of power at their respective agencies, and who were willing to use that power to short-circuit the bureaucracy to get things done. As the only member of the group who worked in the White House, North emerged as its chairman.

"People keep saying, 'Jesus, you outrank North. How come he took on this coordinating function?'" says Koch. "But if you're at the nexus of all that power and influence, it doesn't matter who the hell you are. You're going to fire seriously. So people like Bob Oakley and others of equal stature were all effectively reporting to Ollie."

One of OSG's first accomplishments was the generating of a controversial secret finding signed by Reagan in January of 1986 authorizing the CIA to kidnap terrorists believed to have killed American citizens or to have attacked American interests and bring them to the United States for trial. The broadly drafted finding was meant to apply to the lawless environment of Beirut, where there was no central authority and anarchy was the rule, but it could apply elsewhere as well. It also authorized preemptive strikes against terrorists if an attack against Americans was thought to be imminent, as well as sabotage operations to harrass and immobilize terrorists.

North did not inform OSG members of the ongoing Iran initiative, but the group continually collected and monitored intelligence from Beirut, trying to pinpoint the location of the hostages, and drew up contingency rescue plans. North and Clarridge reportedly favored recruiting an anti-Hizballah Lebanese clan that might seize suspected terrorists from rival groups, but there was resistance to this because a similar idea had been tried with disastrous results in the March 1985 attempted car-bombing of Hizballah leader Mohammed Hussein Fadlallah. The OSG was also said to have been involved in several covert operations with the Pentagon's secret intelligence support activity, and it played a leading role in fashioning the Administration's escalating responses to Libya and Colonel Khadafy.

Planning the April Libyan bombing, North told associates that only he and a few others had worked on pinpointing Khadafy, and that they had left no written record. "There was no executive order to kill and no administrative directive to go after Khadafy," one former NSC staffer quoted North as saying at the time. "They've covered their tracks beautifully." With Reagan having signed off the previous July on the notion of targeting Khadafy, it was accepted as a given that that was the goal of the mission as planning went forward.

The Joint Chiefs of Staff decided on a two-pronged attack that would use navy jets based on the Sixth Fleet, and the faster England-based F–111s which had superior electronic defense-mechanisms to warn of enemy attack. But when France refused to permit the F–111s to fly over its airspace, their mission was complicated. The round trip would now be longer, and they would face strong headwinds over the Bay of Biscay off France.

North doubted the wisdom of using the F–111s, particularly after the French overflight refusal. He favored instead a surgical strike against Khadafy's living quarters using bombs launched offshore, thereby lowering the risks of antiaircraft fire shooting an American plane down. According to the North plan, a navy SEAL team that he had already placed in the Mediterranean region would land secretly in Libya and, relying on the latest intelligence supplied by Israeli agents on the ground tracking Khadafy's precise location, plant a homing device capable of guiding in "smart" bombs fired offshore. But Adm. William Crowe, chairman of the Joint Chiefs, is said to have rejected the idea on the grounds that it was too risky for the SEALS.

At a high-level planning meeting just before the raid was launched, North had told colleagues that he urged several other alternatives on Crowe, including using the super-secret Stealth bomber, which is able to avoid enemy radar, or a coventionally armed Tomahawk cruise missile fired from a submarine. But according to the North account, Crowe rejected both of those ideas as well, saying the Stealth was too valuable to risk, and that there were too few conventionally armed Tomahawks. The president sided with Crowe.

As North told this story to some of his associates, they could understand how Crowe must have been infuriated by the specter of the young, aggressive but very junior-ranking North calmly posing a series of reasoned, well-thought-out alternatives to the chairman of the Joint Chiefs of Staff, who seemed plodding and unimaginative by comparison. Indeed, after the meeting North said Crowe confronted him out of earshot of the president and, nose to nose, said: "Young man, you'd better watch your step." But Crowe denies the encounter ever took place, or that North even offered the series of suggestions.

Planning for the mission was finalized by April 10, but Casey reportedly favored postponing the raid for a few days to make sure American agents had time to leave Libya safely. North also wanted the extra time to obtain more intelligence on Khadafy's exact whereabouts.

Meanwhile the planned raid was the worst-kept secret in the world. The press was full of White House-planted stories about an impending strike. Then, so Khadafy might let his guard down again, stories were floated that an attack was now less likely. Which was when the raid occurred. In the predawn hours of April 14, Navy A–6 and A–7 jets attacked two Libyan bases near the port city of Benghazi 450 miles east of Tripoli, while the F–111s streaked in over Tripoli itself and hit three targets, including the el-Azziziya military barracks where Khadafy was sleeping in a Bedouin-style tent erected in a courtyard.

Although the White House officially called the raid a great success, privately most officials associated with its planning considered it an unqualified disaster. First and foremost, Khadafy had survived the attack. His wife and eight children were all hospitalized, suffering from injuries or shock, and a fifteen-month-old adopted daughter was killed—not exactly a public relations windfall for

Washington. Furthermore, some of the F–111s had had to turn back on the trip from England. The laser-guidance systems on four of the nine F–111s that did attack Khadafy's compound had malfunctioned, thereby preventing the firing of at least a dozen bombs; five of the jets failed even to engage their target; one was missing and presumed shot down; while a mistake by another of the pilots resulted in the bombing of a nearby residential area, killing more than one hundred civilians.

Nonetheless, to Reagan what counted was sending a message that the United States was willing to strike preemptively against terrorism. "Today we have done what we had to do," he said in a nationally televised address the night of the bombing. "If necessary, we shall do it again."

Two days later one of the American hostages, librarian Peter Kilburn, was found murdered in West Beirut along with two British hostages. A note found with the bodies indicated that they had been killed in retaliation for the Libyan bombing.

For North, the murder of Kilburn was particularly wrenching, in as much as he had thought he was on the verge of winning the hostage's release through an elaborate Mission Impossible scheme whereby Kilburn would have been freed in return for millions of dollars in chemically treated counterfeit designed to disintegrate into confetti in the hands of the kidnappers seventy-two hours after they received the money.

A Canadian claiming to represent Kilburn's captors—evidently not Hizballah—had contacted U.S. officials, producing one of Kilburn's identification cards as evidence of his bona fides. Negotiations on a ransom had ensued, finally settling at more than $3 million in small bills. An early attempt to make the ransom had failed after the first batch of chemicals had caused the cash to disintegrate within twenty-four hours. North blamed the CIA and the FBI, who were involved in the ransom effort with him, for taking too long to come up with the right formula. By the time they did, the Libyan raid had taken place and Kilburn was killed.

The experience reinforced North's notion that the most efficient way to conduct a covert operation was to work outside official channels. "North was very frustrated," one administration official told the New York Times: "The CIA didn't work it fast enough, and it led him to believe they were hopeless."

Indeed, just a month after the Libyan bombing North wanted to pursue an unofficial channel offered by Ghorbanifar to a ranking Libyan who was supposedly dissatisfied with Khadafy and wanted to reach out to Washington. The Libyan wanted to meet North in Europe, saying that Tripoli was willing to stop attacking the U.S., stop training terrorists and begin conducting more commerce with the West. Poindexter authorized North to explore the overture. "The CIA are really bunglers," he wrote North. "You had better pass most of this to Casey directly. I would not pass it to anybody else. Leave me out of it."

As North tended to Libya and the Iran initiative, he had not forgotten the Contras. His priority remained patching together a viable air supply operation, particularly for troops fighting in southern Nicaragua. CIA field officers were giving him off-the-record help—preparing flight plans, briefing crews on Sandinista antiaircraft positions and providing mechanical supplies. But the southern front was still not being serviced consistently, making it impossible to keep troops in the field for extended periods.

On April 20, North and Secord flew down to El Salvador and met with FDN Contra leaders, Colonel Steele and Felix Rodriguez, the former CIA operative who was coordinating the Contra resupply effort with local authorities at Ilopango. North and Secord said that the southern front was not the strategic force that it should be, and complained that the FDN was still not freeing up enough of its stock for use in the south. For their part, the FDN leaders complained about the condition of the airplanes. Though the C–7 that had crashed was back in service and they had since purchased a second C–7, along with a twin engine C–123 and a Maule single-engine, propeller-driven light plane, they were all too old to be effective, the Contras said. North told them they would have to make do.

Two days after this meeting Rodriguez decided he wanted to quit. He was growing increasingly uncomfortable with the people who were running the Contra operation. In February, he had called North with a complaint that one of the mechanics involved in the airlift program was constantly drunk and had admitted to being involved in drug-running. North put Secord on the phone to deal with the complaint, and that was the first Rodriguez learned that Secord was involved in the supply effort. Rodriguez knew Secord had been associated with Edwin Wilson, the renegade ex-CIA agent Rodriguez himself had worked with in anti-Castro operations during the sixties. Rodriguez considered Wilson a traitor for having been convicted of selling arms and explosives to Libya, and distrusted those who had become involved with Wilson later in his career.

Then Rodriguez learned that another Wilson associate, Tom Clines, was also involved in the operation, and that he was reportedly buying hand grenades for $3 apiece and selling them to the Contras for $9. Rodriguez, who was a volunteer, thought that was too much profiteering and concluded that the Wilson crowd would taint the entire operation.

If Rodriguez had a rabbi in government it was Donald Gregg, his old CIA case officer in Vietnam who now served as Vice-President George Bush's national security advisor. Before starting work as the Contra liaison at Ilopango in the fall of 1985, Rodriguez for six months had been advising the Salvadorans in their war with the leftist insurgents, and before beginning that assignment he had briefed Gregg and Bush on his mission.

Now on May 1, eleven days after the North-Secord meeting, Rodriguez flew to Washington for a meeting with Bush that he had arranged through Gregg. According to a scheduling memo in Bush's office the purpose of the meeting was "to brief the vice-president on the status of the war in [El Salvador] and resupply of the Contras." But aides to Bush, whose knowledge of the nature and extent of the Contra supply effort would become the hottest of political topics in the presidential campaign of 1988, assert that only Salvador was discussed, not the Contras — an account confirmed by Rodriguez.

On the way to Bush's office Rodriguez stopped by to see North and told him he was quitting. North was not particularly satisfied with the job Rodriguez had been doing but feared that without the Cuban's close contacts with Gen. Juan Rafael Bustillo, the Ilopango commander, the entire Contra supply network could be thrown off base. North urged Rodriguez to take a vacation and stay on, but Rodriguez said he was firm about leaving, then went to his appointment with Bush.

Ollie proceeded to preempt Rodriguez' plans. Before he could tell the vice-president that he planned to leave Central America, North slipped into the meeting and told Bush what a great job Rodriguez had been doing. As he was being praised to the hilt Rodriguez felt it too awkward to follow through with his plan to quit. So he returned to Ilopango, though still disgruntled.

Secord, meanwhile, had concluded that Richard Gadd was not getting the job done. "There was poor leadership, poor supervision and it was being run too expensively," Secord recalls. "North was on my back all the time during this period asking where this aircraft operation was. 'They're dying down there,' he'd say. I was embarrassed. I kept making excuses. But those same excuses weren't even washing with me. But what can you say? I was doing the best I could."

Secord decided to fire Gadd and hire Robert Dutton, an air-force colonel with a covert-operations background whom Secord had known and been friendly with for years. They had served together in Iran and worked on the second hostage rescue mission, which was never launched. Secord, Dutton and their families usually took an annual ski trip together in Aspen. That March, riding up a chairlift together, Secord had asked Dutton to take over the Contra air supply operation. Secord explained that the program was being conducted "at the behest of the White House." Dutton asked no further questions. He decided he had no further "need to know." Dutton skied down to the bottom of the mountain, rode up again with his wife and talked the idea over with her. Then he told Secord he would retire from the Air Force and be ready to start by May 1.

Dutton flew down to El Salvador to assess the facilities and the assets. There were about nineteen pilots, loadmasters and mechanics based at Ilopango. A warehouse on the base maintained an array of munitions and supplies for the Contras, including assault rifles, light machine guns, ammunition, C–4 explosives, parachute rigging, uniforms and other material. The flight crews and mechanics lived in three safehouses on the west side of San Salvador. The headquarters, home of chief pilot William Cooper—a veteran CIA pilot who had flown thousands of hours for the agency's Air America proprietary in Southeast Asia—was referred to as "House Number Three." Dutton would have preferred to have the headquarters located at the base, but they couldn't get the use of a phone there so Cooper's house, which did have a phone, became the nerve center.

Cooper had recruited several other Air America graduates, many of them now over fifty years old. They were nominally employed by a Pennsylvania air-services firm acting as a commercial cutout, but they knew their orders came from Secord's Stanford Technology Trading Group International, Inc. Periodically they would fly up to a Southern Air Transport office in Miami and pick up their pay—envelopes stuffed with $100 bills, usually about $10,000 at a time.

Dutton found that the planes were, in fact, in terrible shape, with maintenance the same. They had no backup spare parts. If something broke down they had to send off to Miami and the aircraft was out of action for at least five days. The pilots weren't filling out flight plans or routine maintenance forms. There was no organization. But Secord's instructions for Dutton were that the air program could receive little additional funding. He had to manage with what he had, but manage better and tighter and put in strict cost controls.

Despite the hope that things would run more smoothly now that Dutton was on board, the demands of the Iran and Contra initiatives were taking their toll on North. He was clearly tiring. On May 16 he wrote Poindexter warning that unless Congress soon authorized the CIA to come back and run the Contra operation "we will run increasing risks of trying to manage this program from here with the attendant physical and political liabilities. I am not complaining, and you know that I love the work, but we have to lift some of this onto the CIA so that I can get more than 2–3 hours of sleep a night." A few weeks later, North sounded even more overwhelmed, stressing in another note to Poindexter the need to get the CIA reengaged so that the operation could be "better managed than it now is by one slightly confused Marine lieutenant colonel."

On May 16 President Reagan convened a meeting of the National Security Planning Group (NSPG) to discuss the question of soliciting foreign assistance to the Contras. The Administration was continuing to seek congressional authorization for the CIA to resume officially its program of covert aid, but in early May, Poindexter wrote North that the president had said: "If we can't move the Contra package before June 9, I want to figure out a way to take action unilaterally to provide assistance." Reagan seemed ready to confront Congress on the constitutional question of who controlled foreign policy.

When he heard this, North came up with an action-option for the president: the Contras could seize some territory inside Nicaragua and set up a provisional government. Reagan would then recognize the Contras as the true government of Nicaragua and openly provide them with assistance. North told Poindexter that Casey liked the idea.

And in a memo for the NSPG meeting North had other ideas on how to raise some quick money: $15 million could be "reprogrammed" from the Pentagon to the CIA and sent on to the Contras as humanitarian aid; the president could make a public appeal for private donations to the Contras by U.S. citizens; or there might be a "direct and very private presidential overture to certain heads of state."

Among those attending the meeting in addition to Reagan were Bush, Shultz, Weinberger, Casey, Poindexter and North. Shultz spoke up in favor of certain countries being approached for help, and North noted that such approaches were legal under the Intelligence Authorization Act of 1986.

No one at the meeting mentioned the fact that Saudi Arabia had already donated $32 million to the contras, $24 million of which had been committed personally to Reagan. Nor was it noted that Far Eastern countries had been approached, or that Taiwan had given $2 million just six months before. Shultz, who had never been informed of the Saudi or Taiwan contributions, was instructed to draw up a list of countries that might now be asked to help.

Later that day North got word that Secord had sent in $5 million of the $15 million due the Enterprise from the pending shipment of arms to Iran. That gave the Contras $6 million on hand and North could write a message to Poindexter saying, "This reduces the need to go to third countries for help."

Poindexter, apparently not wanting to tell Reagan of the diversion, did not inform the president of the fresh $5 million. But North worried that more money would lead to a higher profile for the operation. "The more money there is (and we will have a considerable amount in a few more days) the more visible the program becomes (airplanes, pilots, weapons, deliveries etc.) and the more inquisitive will become people like Kerry, Barnes, Harkins [sic] et al.," North wrote. He was referring to Sen. John Kerry (D-Mass.), Rep. Michael Barnes (D-Md.), and Sen. Tom Harkin (D-Iowa). "While I care not a whit what they may say about me, it could well become a political embarrassment for the president and you."

But with Shultz preparing to approach other countries for Contra aid, North obviously wanted to avoid the diplomatic contretemps that could result if the Secretary of State hit up the Saudis and Taiwanese, not knowing they had already contributed.

"At this point I'm not sure who on our side knows what..." North wrote Poindexter. "I need your help... I have no idea what Shultz knows or doesn't know, but he could prove to be very unhappy if he learns of the [Saudi Arabia and Taiwan] aid that has been given in the past, from someone other than you. Did RCM [McFarlane] ever tell Shultz?"

Poindexter replied: "To my knowledge Shultz knows nothing about the prior financing. I think it should stay that way."

But McFarlane later did tell Shultz. Then Elliott Abrams, the assistant secretary of state for inter-American affairs, suggested that the oil-rich Indonesian state of Brunei might be a candidate for a donation to the Contras. North told Fawn Hall to type the number of Secord's Lake Resources Swiss Bank account on an index card, and Abrams took the card with him to a meeting in London with an official from Brunei.

Traveling under an alias, Abrams met the official at a hotel, and as they went walking in a nearby park Abrams asked for $10 million in "bridge financing" for the Contras. Asked what Brunei would get in return, Abrams would testify that he responded: "Well . . . the president will know of this, and you will have the gratitude of the secretary and of the president for helping us out in this jam."

"What concrete do we get out of this," the man from Brunei persisted.

"You don't get anything concrete out of it," said Abrams, handing over the note card with the account number typed on it.

The sultan of Brunei later wired $10 million to the account number Abrams had supplied, but the money was never received because either North or Hall had transposed one of the numbers on the account, and so it was accidentally sent to someone else.

Despite the Brunei snafu, the infusion of Enterprise cash representing the first diversion of profits from the arms sales to Iran had removed some of the financial pressure on the Contra war effort, at least in the short term. A planeload of munitions paid for by the Enterprise and earmarked for the southern front arrived at Ilopango in late May. Dutton got permission from General Bustillo to enlarge the warehouse to accommodate the new materiel, and the Enterprise assumed control over all the supplies so that FDN leaders would not try to hold any of it back from the south.

Dutton also drew up a reorganization plan approved by North and Secord whose purpose was to try and disguise the role of Ollie and the general. The plan said that "B.C. Washington has operational control of all assets in support of Project Democracy." Project Democracy was North's term for the broad Contra support effort while B.C. Washington was a nonexistent company made up by Dutton and meant to refer to North and Secord.

Secord had been named as one of the defendants in the massive civil lawsuit filed in May by freelance journalists Martha Honey and

Tony Avirgan arising out of the 1984 bombing of Eden Pastora's press conference in Costa Rica, and the lawsuit was attracting publicity. North had also been in the newspapers, and there was a need to take extra precautions. In addition, North and Secord both suspected that the disaffected Felix Rodriguez was supplying Avirgan and Honey with information.

Finally, North summoned Rodriguez to Washington and confronted him, claiming that he had NSA intercepts showing that Rodriguez had been compromising the security of the operation by speaking over unsecure phone lines. Rodriguez, who considered himself something of a Cuban John Wayne, was furious that North would impugn his behavior in that way and challenged him to produce the intercepts. According to Rodriguez and Dutton, North in effect backed down, saying something about Rodriguez not being authorized to see such sensitive data and having to go through the Freedom of Information Act.

North let the tensions in the room simmer, then said he still wanted Rodriguez to stay on the job. Though he didn't say so, North continued to fear that the Contras were vulnerable at Ilopango without Rodriguez's pipeline to the Commandante, General Bustillo. North could offer $3,000 a month. Rodriguez accepted.

On his way out Rodriguez looked up at a television that had been droning on in the background as they were talking. A congressional debate on aid to the Contras was in progress. As Rodriguez would later testify at the congressional hearings, North gestured to the congressmen and said: "Those people want me, but they cannot touch me because the old man loves my ass."

In mid-April Ghorbanifar sent word that the Iranians now had new demands. They wanted a phased release of the hostages following the arrival of the American delegation in Tehran, and the delivery of the HAWK spare parts.

This represented at least the fifth major change in the Iranians' position since February when they had first agreed to release all the American hostages after the first 1,000 TOW missiles were delivered. At the Frankfurt meeting that position had been modified to a pledge to only release a "couple" of the hostages after the second batch of 500 TOWs was delivered. The rest of the hostages would be freed after a meeting of senior American and Iranian officials on Kish Island. Based on those assurances, the U.S. had delivered the second load of 500 TOWs, but no hostages had been released. Then at another preliminary meeting in Paris the Iranians had said they wanted HAWK spare parts in lieu of the 3,000 remaining TOWS, and that the senior-level meeting would have to be in Tehran, not Kish Island. Now the U.S. was being told that there would be a phased release of the hostages based on the *delivery* of the HAWK spare parts, not just the arrival of the Americans in Tehran.

Poindexter was furious, and in an April 16 computer messsage to North, claimed to be communicating the president's frustrations with the operation as well. "There are not to be any parts delivered until all the hostages are free in accordance with the plan that you have laid out for me before. None of this half-ship-ment-before-any-are-released crap. It is either all or nothing. Also, you may tell them that the president is getting very annoyed at their continual stalling. He will not agree to any more changes in the plan. Either they agree finally on the arrangements that have been discussed, or we are going to permanently cut off all contact. If they really want to save their asses from the Soviets, they should get on board."

Meanwhile Secretary of State Shultz had heard from his ambassador in London, Charles Price, that the NSC was selling arms to Iran and that the State Department had been deliberately cut out. Shultz, who still thought the Iran initiative had been blocked and was unaware that Reagan had signed the January 17 finding authorizing the arms sales, confronted Poindexter on May 3 in Tokyo, where the president was attending an economic summit meeting. Poindexter told Shultz that there was no official U.S. involvement, and he made no mention of McFarlane and North's pending secret mission to Tehran.

Annoyed that word of the initiative had somehow leaked, Poindexter wrote North: "We really can't trust those SOBs."

"We cannot trust anyone in this game," agreed North, concluding that this episode underlined "the need to proceed urgently to conclude this phase of the operation before there are further revelations. We all know that this has gone on too long and we do not seem to have any means of expediting the process short of going to Iran."

On May 6, North and George Cave flew to London to meet with Nir and Ghorbanifar for another meeting to fix the prices of the HAWK spare parts. Poindexter had instructed North not to tell anyone he was going to London and to have no dealings with the nosy U.S. embassy there. In discussing the upcoming meetings in Tehran, Ghorbanifar said that the Iranians would be represented by Rafsanjani, President Khameni, Prime Minister Musavi and possibly the Ayatollah's son, Ahmed Khomeini.

In London, Cave telephoned the Iranian deputy prime minister who was still arguing that all the spare parts should be delivered at the same time the Americans arrived in Tehran. According to Cave, after some haggling, it was agreed that the Americans would bring some of the spare parts with them, and that as the talks were held an Iranian team would be dispatched to Beirut to bargain for the release of the hostages. When the hostages were released, the rest of the spare parts would be delivered.

This represented still more erosion in the U.S. position and violated Poindexter's instructions that no parts should be delivered without the release of the hostages. Also, the Iranians "bargaining" with the kidnappers implied that Tehran lacked the clout to deliver on its end of the bargain. North, it would seem, was either unaware of the understanding Cave reached or concealed it from Poindexter when he wrote the National Security Advisor that same day, May 6: "I believe we have succeeded... Release of hostages set for 19 May in sequence you have specified. Specific date to be determined by how quickly we can assemble requisite parts. Thank God—he answers prayers."

Back in Washington North and McFarlane made their final preparations for the trip to Tehran. North urged Poindexter to arrange a meeting with Casey, Shultz, Weinberger and the president to review the final arrangements for the trip. But Poindexter, wary of broadening the inner covert circle, nixed the idea. "I don't want a meeting with RR, Shultz and Weinberger," he wrote North.

And though North, Secord and Cave had all argued strongly that the U.S. side should have insisted on a preliminary meeting with Iranian officials to set a specific agenda for the Tehran meeting, Poindexter rejected that idea as well, on the grounds that one trip to Tehran for Americans was dangerous enough without adding a second. He also thought the presence of someone as senior as McFarlane would reduce the risks that the Americans might be harmed or taken hostage.

Actually, North was increasingly worried about his own security and that of his family. In late April, in the aftermath of the Libyan bombing, North's life had been threatened when his name appeared on a hit list released by Abu Nidal, the Palestinian terrorist. North told colleagues that this followed other incidents in which his tires had been slashed, sugar had been poured into the gas tank of his car, threatening phone calls had been placed to his home, and lights had been shone into the house from the road at night. Once someone had placed a package in his mailbox and inside the package was a piece of paper with the word "Bang" written on it. He didn't mind, but Betsy and the kids were getting scared, Ollie said.

On May 9, the FBI came to interview North about the alleged threats. He told them of a few additional incidents, saying that he had been followed, that his dog had been poisoned and that a fake bomb had been left in his mailbox. He hadn't kept the device, so the agents couldn't analyze it. He had written down the license number of the car that had followed him, but despite several requests from the FBI for the number, he failed to turn it over.

North would testify that the FBI told him it could not offer him any protection, and that his superiors had come up with no solution to the threats except a reassignment to Camp Lejeune, which, given the raft of national security exigencies on his plate at the moment, was clearly out of the question.

He tried to get a secure phone installed at his house to justify the installation of a government security system around his property, but that couldn't be worked out either. Then he called several private security firms but was told it would be several weeks before they could even come out for an estimate, and several weeks after that before they could install a system. North wanted action now, so he mentioned his problem to Secord, who said he thought he could help.

Secord sent Glenn Robinette over to see North. Robinette was a retired CIA agent who had spent twenty years with the agency as an electronics specialist and now worked as a security consultant. Secord, increasingly worried about the Honey-Avirgan lawsuit pending in Miami, had hired Robinette in March to try and come up with some damaging information against the two freelance journalists. Actually Secord had no idea who Honey and Avirgan really were and told Robinette to find out, though he assumed they were communist dupes of some sort. He needed to put this lawsuit in the proper perspective.

Robinette came over to survey the North house on April 30 and met with Betsy, whom he found to be a "lovely lady." She told him that Ollie traveled a lot, came home late at night when he was in town and that she was feeling uneasy. Robinette met with North several days later in Ollie's office and assured him that he was trying to design a security system that would blend nicely around his country/suburban home, which Robinette said he understood was "not a SAC [Strategic Air Command] base." The two met again May 10 at Secord's office, and Robinette said he thought the system would cost about $8,000 to $8,500. Ollie urged him to try to keep the costs down, saying, "Remember, I'm a poor lieutenant colonel."

Robinette selected a contractor for the job and paid out $6,000 as a down payment. But he didn't send North a bill. Rather, he went to Secord, who had hired him, and asked for $7,000–$6,000 to be reimbursed and $1,000 as a commission for himself. Secord reached into a briefcase or desk drawer in his office and handed Robinette $7,000 in cash.

Meanwhile, Secord's partner, Hakim, had also been moving to take care of North. Hakim thought the trip to Tehran was a dangerous one. He had, after all, fled from the Revolution. He knew that the Ayatollah's minions were a crazy, unpredictable lot. The hostage-taking at the American embassy had not surprised him. Now, a high-level American delegation was traveling to Tehran for the first time in seven years. Who knew what could happen? So Hakim had told North that if anything did happen and he did not come back, his family would be taken care of.

"Mr. Hakim said to me, 'If you don't come back, I will do something for your family...'" North would testify. "Now by that point in time, I had come to know that Mr. Hakim was a wealthy man in his own right. I was grateful for the assistance that he had been providing in translating over several very difficult days of discussions with the Iranians. And several days thereafter, when he suggested that my wife meet with his lawyer in Philadelphia, I agreed that my wife should do so. The purpose, as I understood it, of that meeting was that my wife would be in touch with the person who would, if I didn't return, do something for my family. My wife went to the meeting in Philadelphia several days thereafter... There was no money mentioned, no account mentioned, no amount mentioned, no will mentioned, no arrangement. The meeting focused on how many children I had, their ages, and a general description of my family. A brief meeting in the offices, as I remember, of Touche Ross, a respectable firm in Philadelphia..."

As the Tehran trip drew near, Hakim moved to set aside funds from the Iranian arms sales profits and create a "death benefit" account for North. Hakim thought $500,000 was appropriate, but Secord said that was too much. When Hakim suggested $200,000 instead, the general didn't seem enthusiastic but didn't raise any objections either, so Hakim took the silence as approval and, on May 20, opened the account in that amount.

It was Hakim's habit to assign names to the various bank accounts he presided over, and North's he called "Button"—a reference whose meaning would become the source of endless speculation among students of Iran-Contra trivia. Hakim said during his testimony that it was short for "belly button," but did not otherwise explain the name other than to say it was an inside joke that he and his American attorney, William Zucker, had shared. According to Secord the expression grew out of Zucker's comment, after he met Betsy North in Philadelphia, that she was "cute as a button." Secord thinks Hakim, not totally familiar with American slang, somehow added "belly."

Hakim also wrote North into a will in a way that Ollie could gain control of $2 million of the arms-sales profits if both Hakim and Secord died. If all three died the money would be split equally among their heirs.

Hakim would testify that by this time he had become "extremely fond of Lieutenant Colonel North. To me he's an amazing person . . . I really love this man." Hakim appeared outraged when it was suggested that perhaps this was a case of "love at first sight," since he had only known North for three months and met with him just once before establishing the so-called death-benefit account and drawing up the $2 million will.

The more cynical members of the Iran-Contra committee were suggesting, of course, that Hakim and Secord were trying to ingratiate themselves with North—their government godfather, the man in a position to continue funneling them millions of dollars worth of Iran-Contra business. And intentionally or not, by establishing a death-benefit account and giving him a security system, they were also, in effect, compromising North, since it is illegal for federal employees to accept gratuities.

But these were all legal niceties that would not arise for months. For now, as he prepared to go to Tehran, North was comforted to know that a security system was being built to protect his home and his family, and that Hakim had taken steps to insure that his family would be taken care of if he did not come home.

Casey had also impressed on him the dangers of the Tehran trip. The director had told him the United States might disavow the mission if anything went awry, and warned that he had to be prepared to deal with the prospect of being tortured. "We knew by then that Bill Buckley, a man who I knew, was probably dead, and that he had been tortured," North would testify. "We knew that he had given as much as a four-hundred-page confession under torture that we were making every effort to recover. And Director Casey told me that he would not concur in my going ... unless I took with me the means by which I could take my own life."

North did not seem to be going out of his way to disguise the drama and danger attached to his trip. He told one of his deputies, Robert Earl, that if he did not come back from Tehran Earl should destroy the contents of the bottom drawer of one of the office safes.

Hakim, for his part, thought Ollie was ready, willing and able to die in Tehran. "The biggest satisfaction that can be given to him [is] if he would enter into an environment that he could get killed for his country," Hakim testified. "I sensed that so many times."

TEHRAN

THE unmarked Israeli cargo plane began its final approach through the brown smog blanketing Tehran. It was about 8:30 A.M., Sunday, May 25, 1986.

On board the jet were 208 boxes of spare parts for HAWK, antitank missiles, and several human beings shoehorned in amidst the weaponry.

The American delegation, led by McFarlane and North, was tense. Their visit marked the first time since 1979, when the U.S. embassy in Tehran was sacked and hostages taken, that there had been any high-level contact between the two countries in Iran.

The personal and political risks attending the trip were enormous. In Iran, anti-American sentiment was perhaps not at the fever pitch that it had been at the height of the hostage crisis, but the Ayatollah Khomeini and his followers still dined out on trashing Washington at every opportunity. Culturally, philosophically and politically they remained at fundamental odds with the United States, intent on embarrassing or slighting her whenever possible. Tehran's behavior was unpredictable at best.

Poindexter had given McFarlane four pages of instructions in a "terms of reference" document that would form the basis for his talks in Iran: no additional spare parts other than those carried aboard the plane were to be delivered until all four remaining American hostages were released in Lebanon. That was the core agreement that had to be reached before there could be any further discussions. Once the hostage question was resolved, then McFarlane should lay out Washington's views on the Middle

East, Iranian terrorism and the expansion of fundamentalism, and the situation in Afghanistan, as well as Soviet designs in the region.

On a more personal level, McFarlane wanted to get rid of the sense of disquiet that his resignation had left him with. Having been at Kissinger's right hand in the great opening to China, he still yearned for his own diplomatic home run. Reopening the door to Iran, and freeing the remaining American hostages en route, would be a bold stroke.

So, like North, McFarlane was willing to take the chance of visiting enemy territory, and was carrying with him the means to take his own life. But he was still apprehensive about the mission. Since there had been ongoing U.S.-Iranian meetings in the safety of Europe, McFarlane was puzzled as to why they had to go to Tehran at all. He had been told that Iranian leaders couldn't risk leaving the country, given the political sensitivities of breaking bread with the Great Satan. Thus this would be McFarlane's last attempt to salvage an initiative whose wisdom he had come to doubt as it ebbed and flowed through months of stealth and deceit. Several times he had recommended that Washington simply walk away from the negotiations, but they had always resurfaced under North's prodding.

"Looking back, I think Ollie was in a near-desperate situation at this point," McFarlane would recall in an interview. "He had taken quite a lot of the burden for whether this succeeded or failed onto his own shoulders, when really it should have remained a matter of judging what was the confidence in these people to deliver. And Ollie, like everybody else, could see that it was quite low. And he didn't want to accept that, so he began to put a spin on what he was reporting, saying, 'We're almost there, one more try,' wanting to be hopeful about it, when he himself didn't have any basis for hope."

But North thought there was always hope. And to make a strong first impression, he had come bearing gifts for the Iranians: a cake and several antique, nickel-plated pistols.

After one of the last negotiating sessions in Europe with Manucher Ghorbanifar—the principal Iranian intermediary—North and his Israeli counterpart, Amiram Nir, had thought it would be nice to offer the Iranians a cake, perhaps with a key on top, to symbolize the opening up of a new era in relations between Washington and Tehran. So before leaving Israel on the last leg of the trip to Iran, North had gone to a bakery in Tel Aviv and ordered a chocolate cake with a key on top. The Americans had all chuckled at the prospect of the fiercely anti-Zionist Iranians munching on a kosher cake. As for the guns, Ghorbanifar had said the Iranians would be greatly impressed by the presentation of some finely crafted sidearms. So Secord had had one of his assistants buy them in Europe.

These items were to help get the talks off on the right note, but North believed negotiations would succeed on their own merits. After all, both sides needed the other. When all was said and done, it always seemed to come down to something as crass as arms for hostages, though North was ready to argue the geostrategic high road as well.

In North's view of the world, the globe was carved up into spheres of superpower influence, and he firmly believed that to attain its historic goal of a warm-water port in the Persian Gulf, Moscow had plans to take over Iran, just as it had Afghanistan. The U.S. had intelligence that North felt indicated the Soviets were manipulating events inside Iran in order to set up a pretext for its allies inside the revolutionary government to "invite" Russia to step in when the right conditions arose.

To that end, Moscow was trying to peddle false intelligence estimates showing Iraqi armed forces to be in dire straits, primed for an Iranian "final offensive" which could effectively end the six-year-old war and bring a glorious victory to Tehran. Actually, Baghdad had plenty of air and land forces left, and could also use nerve gas and other chemical agents, unavailable to Iran, to defend itself. So Iran was being lured into a trap that could in fact leave it exposed to an Iraqi "final offensive." It would be at that point, North thought, that Moscow's allies in Tehran would invite it to send forces into the country to prevent an Iraq victory—the same scenario that was played out in 1979 when Afghanistan had "invited" Moscow in to quell the anti-Communist insurgency there. North felt the Soviets were convinced Washington was so estranged from Iran that there was nothing it could do to block the Russian plan from succeeding.

Despite widespread skepticism throughout Washington, North genuinely believed there was a faction of moderate Iranians in power who wished to tilt toward the West and do business with the United States. The first evidence of this had been the TWA hijacking in June of 1985 when Iran intervened to help free the remaining Jewish hostages. And he saw evidence of a sharp decline in Iranian-sponsored terrorism from mid-1985 to mid-1986.

So as far as North was concerned, the fledgling U.S.-Iranian relationship had already borne some fruit, and the moderates were
not just a figment of his fertile imagination. He wasn't just whistling
Dixie here. He had every hope—no, expectation—that the trip to
Tehran would result in the freeing of the hostages and the turning
of a new page in U.S.-Iranian relations, thereby propelling the
president into a prime position for the 1986 congressional elections
coming up in the fall.

Yet just three days before, so as not to place all his eggs in this
basket, North had adopted a parallel track. He had asked H. Ross
Perot, the Texas billionaire, to send $1 million in cash to Cyprus as
part of an attempt to ransom the hostages in Lebanon. Perot had
dutifully dispatched a courier to bring the funds to Cyprus, where
the man rendezvoused with two federal Drug Enforcement Agency
agents whom North had arranged to have work with the National
Security Council on the hostage-release project.

It didn't occur to North that one operation might undermine the
other—he just wanted to maximize his chances of gaining the release of some or all of the hostages. Nor was he concerned that
paying ransom flew directly in the face of U.S. policy against terrorism. Less than three weeks before, in a lengthy statement on the
issue, the State Department had said: "The policy of the U.S. government is ... to reject categorically demands for ransoms, prisoner
exchanges and deals with terrorists in exchange for hostage release."

The plane carrying the American delegation and its cargo of
spare parts landed at Tehran's Mehrabad Airport and taxied slowly
to the terminal. North and the others peered outside their windows, taking a hard look around. Heat was shimmering off the tarmac. The airport was surrounded by drab concrete apartment
buildings, many of them left half-finished since the fall of the shah
and now populated by squatters. And hanging outside the terminal,
prominently displayed for arriving passengers to see, was a huge
banner, in English and in Farsi, that was a sign of the times:
"America Cannot Do a Damn Thing," it said.

The plane stopped, dropped its stairway and the passengers
began filling out—first McFarlane, then North and the other
members of the delegation: George Cave, Howard Teicher, who
was head of the political-military affairs section and a Middle East
expert; and Amiram Nir, the Israeli who had been intimately

involved in the arms-for-hostages negotiations from the outset. The U.S. had initially nixed Nir from the trip, but Prime Minister Peres had appealed. The decision was left to McFarlane, who relented. Nir was to be presented as an American.

The group, dressed in business suits, filed inside the terminal. They expected to be greeted by Ghorbanifar, at the least, but there was no one. No one at all. Finally, Cave began conversing with an Iranian functionary. The man walked to a nearby phone, placed a call, and returned to say that officials had been dispatched to fetch them. Meanwhile, they could sit in the terminal and wait.

The Americans thought this reception was bizarre, to say the least. Here they were, the first official U.S. delegation to come to Tehran in seven years, supposedly ticketed to see the president, prime minister and speaker of the Parliament, and no one was there to greet them. They had all heard of snubs, but this was ridiculous. Then something happened that made them all think their airport welcome, or lack thereof, was being carefully orchestrated. A series of F-4 fighter jets began taking off down the runway and screaming into the skies, one after the other. The Americans stared out through the terminal windows with fascination at Tehran's own version of the Paris Air Show.

"It was an obviously contrived show," recalls McFarlane. "The takeoff of F-4 after F-4 in a way that made no sense at all except to impress us... There were no attacks against Iraq during that time. It was simply a mustering of every available airplane and getting them airborne to impress us that they were secure and not vulnerable, and that any leverage we might have felt we had because of their decrepit state of maintenance was unwarranted."

Finally Ghorbanifar and several Iranian officials showed up. Ghorbanifar apologized profusely, saying he'd thought the Americans were due to arrive two hours later than they had. Making genial small talk, Ghorbanifar assumed the role of host, leading his guests briskly past customs—thereby obviating the need for the Americans to display the false Irish passports they had brought.

They climbed into three cars and, with no other security evident, headed off on the twenty-five minute ride to the old Tehran Hilton, now known as the Independence Hotel, which would be their quarters.

Tehran is an ugly city, set on a sloping plain, plagued by both mud and dust, and as they drove across the city McFarlane recalled "an air of subdued torpor." The streets were quiet during Ramazan, the month of fasting. There was the occasional pack animal. Women were all in their post-shah garb of *chadors*, no Western dress allowed.

The Americans were shown to their rooms on the top floor of the hotel. They had the run of the whole floor, which consisted of about a dozen rooms with a suite on the end. McFarlane was given the suite, and the others each took rooms nearby. One room they used solely for their communications gear, which included secure voice radio or teletype. A CIA technician manned the equipment at all times. Assuming all the rooms were bugged, the Americans decided to discuss policy only on a balcony outside, or in the communications room—in each instance using a noise machine as a backdrop.

It was agreed that the Americans would sleep for a few hours to try and ease their jet lag, then both sides would convene the first meeting in the late afternoon.

The first meeting began at 5:15 P.M. in the living room of McFarlane's suite. North and Cave were wearing concealed transmitters so as to secretly tape-record the proceedings.

On the Iranian side, there were five men, including Ghorbanifar. The lead Iranian was a junior deputy prime minister who spoke English haltingly and quickly lapsed into his native Farsi. As George Cave translated, the deputy allowed as to how he was very happy to welcome the U.S. delegation to Tehran. He regretted the inconvenience at the airport, and said he hoped this meeting could prepare an agenda for other political talks.

McFarlane replied that President Reagan also hoped these initial contacts could signal a new chapter in relations between the two countries. He then made the following opening statement:

"In these talks, on bilateral matters, we would hope to make clear that the U.S. accepts the Iranian revolution and has no wish or presumption of influencing it in any fashion . . . I'd like to stress something at the beginning. Obviously we've had disagreements over the past eight years. But the U.S. recognizes that Iran is a sovereign power, and we should deal on the basis of mutual respect, not intimidation. That's why before we begin high-level talks, we put behind us hostage-taking which has occurred in the past. We are pleased that informal talks resulted in agreement on release of American hostages. Once that is completed, we can begin serious talks. I want to stress our appreciation for your hospitality, especially during Ramazan. All of us are pleased to be here. This can lead to an historic new beginning."

The deputy smiled politely and decided to take the opportunity to lecture the Americans on the facts of life of the revolution and the general Iranian state of mind.

"This revolution was totally depending on God, independent Iranian power and unique ideology," he said. "These factors allowed this revolution to come into being. This revolution came to power because for years this nation was under dictatorial pressures. These pressures contributed to the revolution's success. I am sure you can feel how the nation and people think after so many years under pressure. Iran can now act freely. What do you expect from them now that they are free? I want to express a very important point. This revolution cost much blood. After so much blood, the people don't want hostility directed against them. The leader and the people expressed their will to look forward, not to the past...

"We have a famous saying: 'Past is a mirror for the future.' It is not the time to discuss what went wrong over past five years, but I want to emphasize a few points. We don't want to align with East or West, but that doesn't mean we don't want relations. Iran had relations with the U.S. at first. But refuge for the shah and interference in our internal affairs damaged relations... To rebuild a bridge of confidence will take time. We are moving toward this goal. Best proof and reason we are moving is informal meetings and your presence here in Iran."

McFarlane would later recall that his first and last impression of his opposite number on the Iranian side was that of a young and nervous "fourth-rate functionary" who was considerably out of his depth. He seemed not to be fully briefed on what had transpired earlier, and unable to carry out the responsibility of the negotiation. But McFarlane rejected an initial impulse to order the deputy to bring in someone more senior.

The talk turned toward working up an agreeable agenda—something which at least North felt should have been hammered out beforehand in preliminary talks at the staff level. Of course, this was still the staff level, as far as Iran was concerned.

"The first item should be U.S. goals in the area," the Iranian said. "The basic priority is to build a bridge of confidence. Both

Iran and the U.S. must build confidence and trust. Once a bridge of confidence is established, then other priorities can be addressed and solved. We expect from you that the U.S. will supply physical support to Iran. U.S. support will be with us. This is the best way to build confidence. For the U.S. to demonstrate that it is with Iran."

That didn't sound like Washington's stated policy of neutrality in the Iran-Iraq war, so McFarlane took a diplomatic detour. "Regarding the commitment of the U.S. to turn a page, that is expressed by my presence on behalf of the president. The corresponding commitment on the part of your government to put the past behind us is to use your influence to secure the release of captive Americans. They are not held by Iran, but the captors are also subject to Iranian influence. Finally, as an earnest showing of our good faith, we are prepared to transfer certain items which may be of assistance. We have brought some of these with us. In virtually all cases, we could handle via aircraft. If not, other items will follow as this sequence evolves. Perhaps we could start discussions tomorrow morning on goals. At the conclusion of this session, we could have specialized sessions on the Soviet Union and Middle East situation."

Besides Russia and the Middle East, the Iranian said his side would also like to discuss Afghanistan, Lebanese affairs, Kurdistan, the Iran-Iraq war and Washington's view of the Iraqi regime. McFarlane said that was fine and proposed writing out the agenda that night.

Then the Iranian abruptly changed subjects, casually telling the Americans that "for humanitarian reasons we have acted on your hostages. But we expected more than what came on the aircraft." The HAWK spares, he might have said, but everyone in the room understood. McFarlane said all the parts couldn't be carried on one plane. The rest could be readily summoned.

The Iranian again stressed his country's humanitarian motives and sought to distance Tehran from the kidnappers. "Iran did not take these people captive," he said.

North, making his first contribution, indulgently said how grateful the U.S. was for Iran's humanitarian intervention, then, in a flight of wishful thinking, leaped to the question of whether Tehran wished to be publicly thanked for its efforts with a statement issued in Washington after the hostages were released. "We hope this will happen in the next few hours," he added.

The Iranian quickly brought North back to reality. Things weren't so easy in the Middle East. "We started the process, but cannot forecast when it will happen," he said. "We can discuss this affair later. We expect, anyhow, to receive more items from you so that we will be in a better position with our leaders. I want to make this point very clear. Iran has been at war for six years . . . We are expecting more equipment."

It was becoming increasingly apparent that each side had a different understanding of the terms that had led to this meeting. But rather than confront Ghorbanifar, the middleman, then and there, the question was finessed for the moment.

McFarlane said the agreement that was concluded earlier would be honored to the letter. "A bridge of confidence is a useful metaphor," he added. "I have come as an expression of good will. In addition to my own presence, we put items on the aircraft which can be brought forward. The corresponding act on your side, a humanitarian gesture, involves the release of our people. While separate and not related, these acts do contribute to mutual confidence . . ."

"Everything depends on good will and restored confidence," the Iranian agreed. "But there are some things which cause doubt. We were told that one half of the equipment would be brought with McFarlane. You did not bring one half. This behavior raises doubts about what can be accomplished."

"Let's be clear," McFarlane snapped. "I have come. There should be an act of good will by Iran. I brought some things along as a special gesture. So far nothing has happened on your side . . ."

The Iranian apologized, sensing he had gone too far. He said he and his colleagues weren't decision-makers, just messengers, but they had told their leaders that half the parts would be delivered.

North tried to offer a technical reason for the deficiency rather than a political reason. He said the plane had weight and fuel limitations.

The Iranian, now almost whining, said that some of the spare parts were used.

McFarlane had heard enough. Angrily, he shouted: "I have come from the U.S. You are not dealing with Iraq. I did not have to bring anything. We can leave now!"

The Iranian persisted that his side now had serious internal political problems, having promised half the spare parts up front. If the plane could only hold one quarter, why couldn't the U.S. have said so? Still, the problems could be worked out with patience. An Iranian team was in Beirut to deal with the hostage issue. "We have done all that we should do. We respect our guests' need."

The meeting broke up at 7:00 p.m. and the Americans went off to bed—exhausted and generally depressed by the day's events. No one had greeted them, and they had so far dealt only with functionaries. This was hardly the stuff of Chou En-Lai and the opening to China.

But the normally stolid and dour McFarlane summoned up some humor in later cabling Poindexter his account of the first session: "It may be best for us to try to picture what it would be like if after nuclear attack a surviving Tatar became vice-president, a recent grad student became Secretary of State and a bookie became the interlocutor for all discourse with foreign countries."

George Cave would later remark that the fact the deputy's breath "could curl rhino hide" was of no help either.

The Americans awoke the next day to more confusion. It was the airport scene revisited: nothing was happening. Finally the junior Iranian deputy who had led his side the day before turned up late in the morning and McFarlane told him he expected to meet with his minister. The deputy said he hoped his minister would come later, but for now he had instructions to carry on the negotiations. McFarlane said the deputy could meet with his staff—he would boycott the talks until a more senior Iranian appeared.

It was not until 3:30 Monday afternoon that the second meeting convened—minus McFarlane who stayed in his room, hoping to send a signal of U.S. upset. The deputy prime minister and an assistant to the prime minister appeared for the Iranians.

North blurted out that the U.S. was "confused and concerned. We have tried for months to come to a point where we could talk government-to-government. Some in our government opposed. McFarlane favored. I was convinced that necessary arrangements had been made. We received President Reagan's permission to proceed. We have now been here for over a day and no one will talk with us. Where are we going? Nothing is happening."

The deputy wondered why North was so upset. "We were both happy last night," he said. "Why are you now confused? We are

working to make things happen. We have similar problems with our
people, but don't see any insurmountable problems."

This interchange underscored a cultural chasm now evident for
both sides to see. The Iranians couldn't fathom the Americans' demand for instant action and instant results, while North and his
confreres couldn't abide the Iranian snail's pace. The U.S. side was
more ready to chalk it up to incompetence than any Middle Eastern mystique.

The deputy asked to see McFarlane, whereupon North walked
next door and prevailed on his leader to join the meeting.

The deputy was effusively apologetic, telling McFarlane he was
at his beck and call. "I want to remove obstacles. Sorry, I want to
solve problems, misunderstandings, so they won't be repeated."

McFarlane said he was glad to hear that, but repeated that before coming to Iran, he had understood that preliminary problems
affecting mutual trust had been resolved—freeing the hostages on
the Iranian side and delivering some weaponry on the U.S. side.
"But upon arriving, I learned that the steps had not been taken by
your government. That is disappointing. The more important purpose is to share with your ministers how to restore a basis of trust
between us. There are crucial matters related to the Soviet Union,
Afghanistan and Iraq that we should discuss. But we cannot begin
to address these problems until preliminary problems are solved.
Perhaps your government is not ready to deal with these larger
issues. Maybe we should wait for another day. But I must depart
tomorrow night. I would like to meet with your ministers. But I
cannot if preliminary problems have not been solved. I have nothing more to say."

At 9:30 that night the two sides met again, still without McFarlane. But the Iranians were now led by a new and ranking official,
Naja Fabadi, a leading member of the Iranian parliament who was
senior foreign affairs advisor to Speaker Rafsanjani. Fabadi was a
short, solidly built man in his sixties with graying hair. Speaking
good, only slightly accented English, Fabadi proceeded to extend
his own welcome to the American delegation.

North, hoping to avert a return to square one, took the offensive
before the advisor could break out of his greeting mode.

"We have a great opportunity to establish a relationship between
our two countries," he said passionately. "There is a long history of
unfortunate relations which cannot be forgotten in a minute. Men
of good will have a chance to build a bridge of confidence. We may

be able to work toward a common goal. I hope you've seen the proposed agenda. It provides a basis of discussion between our leaders. There is a technical agenda as well. All contribute to this great opportunity. I explained our respective commitments and the process to the president. Perhaps we came prematurely, with our hopes too high. Our hope was to remove certain hurdles to a better relationship. We understand it is hard for both our countries. But we have acted in good faith. The key is in your hands. It is not easy to turn that key. Misunderstandings have occurred. We have put them aside."

Fabadi seemed impressed by North's remarks. "You did a great job coming here, given the state of relations between us," he said. "I would be surprised if little problems did not come up. There is a Persian saying: 'Patience will bring you victory.' They are old friends. Without patience, we won't reach anything. Politicians must understand this."

There's great value in simply talking, North agreed. "There are factions in our governments that don't want something like this to succeed. This is why McFarlane grew angry when things didn't take place as I suggested they would. He took a risk urging our president to do this. There is great opposition to this project. We have to be able to show progress, not for personal reasons, but for the future. This is not a deal of weapons for release of the hostages. It has to do with what we see regarding Soviet intentions in the region. We accept the Iranian revolution and respect your sovereignty. Some people want to ensure that our countries find a common foundation for the future . . . What we had hoped was to agree on the direction for a dialogue between Iran and the U.S. Political decisions will be required. We may not agree this week or year. But this process must begin. It can begin in total secrecy, with certain nonpolitical actions."

Fabadi wondered whether the U.S. could keep a secret.

"We will try," said North, "but one of the greatest liabilities is a lack of secure communications." North offered to show the Iranians a device that would ensure secret communications. "We can secretly put someone here," he said. "We know the Soviets are trying to find out what we are up to. We know the Soviets know a little bit about this and are trying to find out more. They will make a major effort to expose us. Our major hope is to pacify this opposition through technical measures. If your government can cause the release of the Americans held in Beirut, ten hours after they are released aircraft will arrive with HAWK missile parts. Within ten days of deposit, two radars will be delivered. After that delivery, we would like to have our logistics and technical experts sit down with your experts and make a good determination of what is needed. We need a technical survey. It must be done very secretly. However, if we go home without setting aside obstacles, there will be new obstacles."

Then Fabadi asked to hear the U.S. view on the Soviet threat to Iran. Howard Teicher weighed in with a summary of the Russian military posture around the country. Moscow had twenty-six divisions, he said. Deployment in the Trans-Caucasus has been improved, and military readiness had generally been stepped up. The Soviets were also increasing crossborder forays into Pakistan, and occasionally Iran, as part of a terror campaign against Islamabad for its support of the Afghan *Mujhadeen.*

"There are training camps for Mujhadeen in Iran," Fabadi said. "Weapons and logistics support are provided. We are ready to send troops into Afghanistan. The Russians already complain about Iranian bullets killing Russians."

North, ever ready to up the weapons ante, asked if it would help to give the *Mujhadeen* TOWs as well.

Fabadi thought not, saying the greatest difficulty the Afghan rebels faced was gas and napalm. "We need help curing wounded. Many die due to lack of first aid. Do you have anything more to say about Russians?"

George Cave said the U.S. had eight hours' worth of briefing materials.

Fabadi said he would like to hear the intelligence briefing and agreed to the other agenda items proposed by the Americans. "We are ready to listen in all areas." But first Fabadi wanted to deliver his own lecture on the Iranian revolution.

"We have to bring up some subjects from the past around the revolution," he said. "We don't need to discuss what came before. We believe that the United States from nineteen seventy-eight made mistakes against all peoples. Our own belief is that our revolution is greater than the French or Russian revolutions. There have been more changes. Today we feel many in the Third World are thinking as revolutionaries, like us.

"You see many pictures of Khomeini in the Afghan trenches. He is their leader. We see the Imam's picture in South Africa, Lebanon and West Africa. There are protests in Marrakech. We didn't send this picture in the mail. We have no relations with Morocco that would allow us to give them the Imam's picture. The influence of this revolution has passed to many Moslems. Islamic countries express themselves honestly. But there is bad propaganda against us in America and Europe . . .

"We are against kidnapping. What happened here," he continued, referring to the seizure of the American embassy in 1979, "was exceptional. Because of one exceptional act, we should not be considered terrorists. When we turn to the subject of our relations, there are many serious things to say. We saw past U.S. leadership trying to destroy all the bridges of confidence. We did not start confronting you. This was not the clergy, army or party. It was the people. In such a revolution, there is no law and order. Not one drop of American blood was spilled one year after the revolution . . . But the U.S. supported Bakhtiar, who confronted us harshly. We do not accept that. We did not see you sitting alone doing nothing. If there is only one other country in the world against the Soviets, it is Iran. We have a famous saying: 'Enemy of your enemy is your friend.' You don't see it this way. Because we are neither East nor West, you are both pulling us. Neither the U.S. nor the Soviet Union likes independent states.

"I'm sorry to be so harsh. But I need to be frank and candid to overcome differences. We have the same problem that you have. Some here oppose relations with the U.S. I am happy to hear you believe in an independent sovereign Iran. We are hopeful that all American moves will be to support this dialogue. But we feel the whole world is trying to weaken us. We feel and see the Russian danger much more than you. You see the threat with high technology. We feel it, touch it, see it. It is not easy to sleep next to an elephant that you have wounded. To weaken Iran does not mean the Soviets want Iran. It means they want to reach the warm waters of the gulf. Our gulf neighbors know this. We share thousands of kilometers of land and a water border. If we are weakened, you can forecast what will happen."

Fabadi paused to let his words sink in. The Americans were sitting at rapt attention, listening carefully. While on a totally different philosophical wavelength, they had to admit Fabadi was an eloquent spokesman for his cause.

"When we accepted your team with McFarlane it symbolized a new political development here. But there has been a misunder-

standing. When we accepted his visit it did not mean a direct dialogue would occur on the spot. It is too early at this stage . . . Our
relations are dark. They are very bad. Maybe you don't like to hear
it, but I must be outspoken. The Iranians are very bitter. Many
Iranians call America the Great Satan. The first revolutionary government fell because of one meeting with Brzezinski.

"As a government, we don't want to be crushed tomorrow. We
want to stay in power and solve these problems between us. We
should not insist on special issues or a ministerial meeting. There
was no agreement that when McFarlane led the team it would
lead to ministerial meetings. Let us turn the key in a way that
will work. We don't see the release of the hostages as the key.
You all must know that establishing this dialogue is the greatest
challenge. China, Russia, Lebanon are easy. If you wanted formal
meetings, McFarlane would have been received differently."

But North said he had told McFarlane he would meet Speaker
Rafsanjani, Prime Minister Mousavi and President Khomeini. "I
was told this would happen," North insisted. To underscore the
stature of his superior, he reminded Fabadi that McFarlane had
been at the right hand of Kissinger in preparing the opening to
China.

Fabadi asked who had promised that McFarlane would have
ministerial level meetings. North quickly said it was Ghorbanifar.

It was increasingly apparent that Ghorbanifar had lied to both
sides to get them to come to the same table. So Fabadi moved on.
"Iran does not just want to discuss spare parts," he said. "I want to
state clearly, we do not encourage terror. Even the Imam officially
condemned skyjacking. We accept that we have influence in Lebanon. Many Islamic groups in Lebanon respect the revolution. We
sent a man to Lebanon. We are very hopeful that we can help you
and solve this problem. By solving this problem we strengthen you
in the White House. We are waiting for an answer. As we promised, we will make every effort. We are working right now. We
hope to get you news about the situation tomorrow. We will finish
the job without waiting for the other parts. Regarding the agenda,
we are willing to discuss all the items you proposed, especially the
items where we have mutual interest. Afghanistan, the Soviets,
Iran-Iraq war, Lebanon. We are ready to discuss. We have some
objections to your positions on some of these issues. I have been
appointed to represent Iran in this dialogue. I hope this will be a
good start."

North asked what the chances of gaining the release of the hostages really were.

"I answered you," the advisor said. "They're difficult to deal with. But anything we start, we are hopeful about." He wanted to get off the hostage issue and began discussing his country's concern about the Russians.

"They have missiles that can reach Tehran, as well as high-altitude jets. You can't compare quality and quantity of our weapons. But the will of the Iranian people is greater than the Soviet people. I myself have a sister with two sons who were martyred in the war. One body was not even found. Two others are handicapped. All four were volunteers. I have a younger brother who was not accepted as a volunteer. He took his older brother's I.D. when he returned from Ahwaz.

"Martyrdom is great. We congratulate the family of martyrs with congratulations and sorrow. During Ramazan, we ask God to let us be a martyr if we are to die. Ramazan is the night of fate and power. Russians sell their rifles and prisoners for cash. Such a Russian can't fight an Iranian. But if we try to get such technology to fight them, they will not fight. Millions of Soviet Moslems listen to our influence. Many of them believe the Imam is their leader, not Gorbachev. They are real Moslems. Secret groups in the Soviet Union print the Koran and distribute it. Their heart is on this side of the border. If we put aside nuclear power, we don't think Russians will take advantage of Iran. Of course, everything is possible with these people."

Fabadi paused for a few moments, then continued. "We appreciate and want to discuss everything with you . . . Rafsanjani said officially Iran is ready to buy weapons from America. This was a very positive statement. We really find more confidence and trust in our discussions. We hope in this way we can have a general dialogue before we come to the technical level. We want TOWs, especially with technicians. We would appreciate your advice on F–14 / Phoenix and Harpoon missiles.

"You know how our people face you in public. When the spare parts come on a large scale, the public will naturally know where they come from. The air force, land forces, Pasdarans will see. But they don't need to know about the dialogue. Naturally, after some of this movement, our leaders could meet and accept this change officially. We rule on the basis of the people. We respect our people's will. This is our policy. The people hear the Parliament—

three sessions a week. We have to prepare the people for such a change. Step by step. We need to prepare the nation. Meetings between U.S. and Iranian leaders will take place publicly in this context. If you are serious about solving problems, I am sure official trips and high-level meetings will take place. The Imam has said we are ready to establish relations with all the world except Israel. But you have to remove the obstacles. This is why we are ready to discuss the agenda as you gave it, with some changes. Speed up what has been agreed. You are a real superpower. I hope you don't mind being a superpower. You have much more capability. A few 747s can carry a lot in one day. We would be very pleased to discuss our specific needs."

Despite these fascinating excursions into the postrevolutionary Iranian psyche, the Americans still didn't understand why there couldn't be high-level talks. They had waltzed throughout Europe with Ghorbanifar. Now they were in Tehran, ready to go. "Rafsanjani has acted and spoken in a way that indicates Iran could benefit from a dialogue," said Teicher. "You just stated that the Imam said Iran is ready to establish relations with all the world except Israel. What is the problem?"

Fabadi retreated into the Iranian dialectic. He explained that the leadership is both affected and influenced by the people. It was an interactive relationship. "It's not whatever the Imam says. His word is accepted because he talks from the heart of the people. This is why the leadership of Iran is not something dogmatic. It is not a dictatorship, religious or otherwise. The leadership depends on the wisdom of public opinion. After the death of Brezhnev, Iran sent a delegation. The leadership was attacked by the nation for this act. No one went out to Chernenko's funeral. If you are serious, everything can be solved."

It was now 1:50 A.M., and the two sides had been talking for more than four hours. They decided to call it a night, while North promising that he would urge McFarlane to rejoin the discussions. "He doesn't always take my advice—such is the fate of all advisors," North offered good-naturedly.

After the Iranians left, the Americans filed down to McFarlane's room to give their leader a briefing. Fabadi had been impressive, they agreed. He wasn't a minister, but he was knowledgeable and clearly spoke with authority. There seemed to be movement in Beirut, but they could only wait to see what was delivered. In the meantime, there seemed little chance of higher-level meetings. This wasn't perfect, but Fabadi was several cuts above the deputy who had greeted them in the opening session. While it wasn't protocol, McFarlane should meet with Fabadi and make the most of the limited time they had in Tehran, North and the others recommended. McFarlane agreed to meet them halfway. The staff would resume talks with the Iranians in the morning, then he would meet one-on-one with Fabadi later, McFarlane said.

Negotiations resumed again at 10:00 the morning of May 27 with North leading the U.S. delegation. Fabadi said he had news from Beirut.

"We heard early, but I felt you were sleeping," he said. "There is a development which requires a decision. Our messenger in Beirut is in touch with those holding the hostages by special means. They made heavy conditions. They asked for Israel to withdraw from the Golan Heights and South Lebanon. Lahad must return to East Beirut, the prisoners in Kuwait must be freed, and all expenses paid for hostage-taking. They do not want money from the U.S. Iran must pay this money. We told them these conditions must be reduced. We can't make this work. We are negotiating. We are ready to pay for humanitarian reasons. We are negotiating other conditions. We are hopeful these negotiations will succeed."

North and the other Americans could not believe the *chutzpah* of the kidnappers, asking to be reimbursed for taking hostages. The other demands were almost as ludicrous. But before the session had a chance to deteriorate further, McFarlane sent word that he would see Fabadi in his suite. As the foreign affairs advisor got up to leave, the session broke up into individual talks in the corridor.

In their discussion, McFarlane and Fabadi plowed over much of the rhetorical high ground that the others had covered in earlier meetings. Then McFarlane recounted the history of U.S.-Iranian dealings over the past year, mindful that Fabadi had probably only heard the Ghorbanifar version. He said there had been several agreements negotiated in the past twelve months that the Iranians had either sought to alter at the last minute or delay, and that President Reagan had been greatly frustrated by this. The president had only reluctantly agreed to this meeting, and with strict conditions: that the U.S. side would bring with it a portion of the

spare parts; that on the Americans' arrival, the Iranians would obtain the release of all the hostages, and that after their release, the
remaining munitions that had been paid for would be flown to
Tehran. Those not yet paid for would be sent on receipt of payment.

At hearing this, Fabadi grew quite agitated, according to McFarlane's account, and asked to know precisely who had agreed to such
terms. McFarlane again fingered Ghorbanifar. Fabadi soon asked
for a break to caucus with his colleagues.

At that point, McFarlane cabled Poindexter: "My judgment is
that they are in a state of great upset—schizophrenic over their
wish to get more from the deal, but sobered to the fact that their
interlocutors may have misled them. We are staying entirely at
arms' length while this plays out."

Another meeting convened at 5:00 P.M., this time with all the
principals in attendance. Again, Fabadi had an update from
Beirut.

"The last contact with our man in Lebanon reported that he
was able to eliminate three demands: the withdrawal of Israel
from the Golan, South Lebanon and the transfer of Lahad to East
Beirut. We will solve the money problem. The only remaining
problem is Kuwait. We agreed to try to get a promise from you
that they would be released in the future. The only problem is
that the men here are not in agreement. These documents are in
Ghorbanifar's handwriting. This is what I told you about this
morning. If there has been a mistake in our agreement, it is not
our fault. Maybe Ghorbanifar made a mistake. The problem is
very simple. The only thing to discuss is what comes first and
what comes later. The intentions of the two groups, based on
what's written here, leads me to believe that agreement should
be possible."

Fabadi pointedly addressed McFarlane: "I think we can come
to a final agreement since you are an important person in your
country. We, like you, want to solve this problem and get on
with it."

McFarlane said he appreciated the effort and spirit which the
Iranians were now bringing to solving the problem. But he said his
instructions were firm: without results, meaning a freeing of all the
hostages, the talks were to end. "These are very firm instructions,"

he stressed. "All the items that have been paid for are loaded and poised for release the minute the hostages are in our custody. Their prompt delivery within ten hours is our solemn commitment." As for the Da'Wa prisoners held by Kuwait, McFarlane said it was U.S. policy not to interfere with any other country's judicial policies.

The advisor then proposed a slight change of position. "Since the plane is loaded," he said, "why not let it come? You would leave happy. The president would be happy. We have no guilt based on our understanding of the agreement. We are surprised now that it has been changed. Let the agreement be carried out. The hostages will be freed very quickly. Your president's word will be honored. If the plane arrives before tomorrow morning, the hostages will be free by noon. We do not wish to see our agreement fail at this final stage."

McFarlane wondered if the hostage and weapons issues couldn't be separated. "As a humanitarian gesture? We delivered hundreds of weapons. You can release the hostages, advise us and we'll deliver the weapons."

Fabadi said "Okay." But he added that his superior would like the staffs to draw up a formal accord as to what had already been agreed to, so as to eliminate any misunderstandings stemming from the Ghorbanifar-mediated discussions. "Something is apparent in our letters. I am not blaming the staffs. We want to reach a new understanding."

McFarlane agreed, whereupon the Americans returned to their quarters and began work on a final draft agreement.

At 9:30 the two sides, minus McFarlane, reconvened. North handed over a copy of the draft agreement, along with a Farsi translation prepared by Cave and Ghorbanifar.

The six-point agreement provided that:

1) The U.S. would launch a 707 jet from a neutral site at 1:00 A.M., or 3½ hours from then. The jet, containing the remainder of the HAWK spare parts paid for by Iran, would land in Tehran at 10:00 A.M., May 28.

2) Iran would arrange the release of the hostages and return the body of William Buckley, the kidnapped CIA agent who had been tortured in Iran, both to occur no later than 4:00 A.M., Tehran time, on the 28th.

3) If the hostages were not released by 4:00 A.M. the aircraft

carrying the HAWK missile parts would turn around and not land in Tehran, and the U.S. delegation would leave Iran immediately. But if the hostages were released by 4:00 A.M. as planned, the American group would stay in Tehran until noon on the 28th.

4) The U.S. would deliver to Bandar Abbas, Iran, two phase-one IHIPIR radar jets compatible with the HAWK missile system already in possession of Iran. The delivery would take place after release of the hostages, and within ten days of receipt of payment for the radar systems.

5) Both governments would continue a political dialogue in secret until both agreed to make it public. The dialogue would include "consideration of further defense needs of Iran."

6) To enhance communications between the two countries, the U.S. would place a satellite communications team, with appropriate equipment, secretly in Tehran. Iran agrees that the U.S. communicators would be accorded normal diplomatic privileges.

The Iranians studied the proposal anxiously. They conversed among themselves in Farsi, asking about spare parts and the timing of deliveries.

"How are we supposed to free the hostages by 0400?" asked Fabadi.

North said he didn't understand the timing problem. "With McFarlane earlier today you told us they would be free by noon."

He had said that, Fabadi conceded. "But it is now late. Our dispute is over the lack of complete agreement. What can you say about the [prisoners] held in Kuwait?"

North proposed the following statement: "The U.S. will make every effort through and with international organizations, private individuals, religious organizations and other third parties in a humanitarian effort to achieve the release and just and fair treatment for Shiites held in confinement, as soon as possible." But North warned that to ensure the continued well-being of the prisoners, there could not be any more terrorist activity directed at the royal family in Kuwait.

The Iranians asked to caucus and think about the proposal, and shortly afterwards, Fabadi and McFarlane met again privately. The two haggled for a few more hours until finally, around 11:30 P.M., McFarlane concluded that he was being strung along and ordered the U.S. team to pack and depart. But fifteen minutes earlier, the

American delegation had learned that its plane had not yet been refueled, leaving it semistranded. The Iranians had bought at least a few more hours.

According to a memorandum written at the time by Cave, the Iranians spent the next two hours quarreling among themselves, with each saying he would hold the others responsible if nothing came of the negotiations. Then, at 2:00 A.M., Wednesday, May 28, the Iranians asked McFarlane for assurances that the U.S. would deliver the remaining spare parts two hours after the hostages were released, instead of the six-hour differential now proposed. McFarlane agreed, saying if he was given a precise time when the release would occur, he would arrange for the aircraft to arrive in Tehran two hours later. He gave the Iranians until 6:30 A.M. to give him a time for the release.

At this point, Cave recorded that the Americans retired to grab a few hours of sleep, "knowing that we had at least out-frazzled them."

Only North did not sleep. Determined not to let the talks dissolve at the last minute because of what he viewed as McFarlane's stubborn bravado, North desperately wanted to salvage something. They couldn't have come all this way for nothing. He went out to the corridor and sought out Ghorbanifar. The two who had the most riding on the outcome of the talks then walked over to a corner and began talking in earnest. Ghorbanifar argued that the logistics of getting all four hostages released in the short time imposed were simply too formidable. Two hostages they could manage, but not four. Why not call the second plane in and settle for two hostages now, and the second two as soon as Iran could arrange their release? It was just a matter of time, Ghorbanifar stressed. North thought it over, then agreed. The two struck a private deal.

North quickly went to the U.S. team's communications room and radioed Secord in Tel Aviv to launch the second plane. Time was of the essence and North felt justified in giving the order to launch without consulting McFarlane. He would let the aircraft get more than halfway, then, just before it reached its final checkpoint before crossing into Iranian airspace, he would awaken McFarlane, tell him of the agreement, and give him a chance to turn the plane around if he disapproved. Under the circumstances, this was a reasonable concession to the chain of command, North thought.

At the appointed hour, North roused McFarlane and told him what he had done. Disbelieving at first, McFarlane then grew enraged and lashed out at North, accusing him of insubordination. It was all the hostages or none at all, he said, ordering the plane turned back to Israel. North at first tried to argue mildly with McFarlane but soon gave up when he saw his boss' jaw was set.

"Ollie had such a high personal stake in this—perhaps even to the point of misleading Poindexter and me about what had been agreed on," McFarlane would recall. ". . . From the time we got on the ground until the time we left, he was almost frantic in trying to talk to, console, coerce the Iranians, particularly Ghorbanifar... His strategy was to be accommodating, instead of telling them to stuff it rather than be diddled with."

At 7:50 A.M., nearly ninety minutes after McFarlane's appointed deadline, the deputy prime minister appeared and essentially reiterated the North-Ghorbanifar proposal. "They think they can get two out now, but it will require joint action on the other two," he reported.

But McFarlane would have none of it. "It's too late," he said. "We're leaving."

Ten minutes later, Fabadi arrived and repeated the same proposal: two hostages freed now and two later around a coordinated arms delivery, but McFarlane told him it wouldn't work. "You are not keeping the agreement. We are leaving."

There was considerable confusion and tumult as the Iranians tried to slow the Americans down, but McFarlane was determined to leave. Shortly after 8:00, they were on their way to the airport.

The Iranians escorted them to their plane, begging them to the last minute not to leave so precipitously.

"Why are you leaving?" the deputy shouted as the Americans boarded their aircraft.

McFarlane told him to tell his superiors that this was the "fourth time they had failed to honor an agreement. The lack of trust will endure for a long time. An important opportunity was lost."

The door closed behind him and the plane revved up its engines preparing to depart. It was 8:55 A.M.

As the Americans started the long flight back to Tel Aviv, the sense of frustration, loss and disappointment inside the plane was palpable. Tension lingered from the drama surrounding the departure, and few words were spoken. McFarlane felt that some members of the team, particularly North and Nir, were angry at him for resisting the Iranian entreaties. But so be it. McFarlane felt comfortable with his decisions, then and now.

"I was committed to staying three days," he recalls. "But at the end of the three days, when we hadn't gotten beyond where we were—not on the hostages or a higher level of official—I said, 'This is ridiculous. We are being made fools of... Let's got out of here.' Looking back, had I known going in that we didn't expect to get anybody out—which I think is the truth—or that we didn't have a hard commitment, then getting two might have seemed like a moral victory. But believing you were going to get four, plus remains, then getting two, was a breach. Plus it puts you on a track of continually negotiating arms for bodies, and it's just outrageous."

By the time they landed in Israel, McFarlane's sense of outrage had turned more towards depression. The long reach to Tehran had ended ignominiously with nothing in hand. Far from making history for fashioning a new opening in Iran, they may have gained a spot in infamy if all the seamy details of this episode were revealed. Meanwhile, they were back to square one. He would have to prepare his briefing for the president, and recommend—yet again— that the entire initiative be scrapped.

There was a swirl of activity on the tarmac at Ben Gurion Airport outside Tel Aviv. North was coordinating the removal of the gear from the plane and searching for a way to communicate to his agents in Cyprus to get a status report on the Ross Perot ransom effort. McFarlane was waiting for the CIA communicator to get a satellite link so that he could report in to Poindexter.

North ventured over to McFarlane, hoping to cheer him up. In so doing, North decided to unburden himself of a secret that apparently only he, Casey and Poindexter, in government, were privy to. As explosive as the revelation that the U.S. had been selling arms to Iran was to become, what North was about to tell McFarlane was akin to a political earthquake.

"Well, boss, don't think this has been a total loss," North said cheerily but matter-of-factly. "We've been marking up our military sales to Iran, then using some of the Ayatollah's money to help the Contras down in Nicaragua."

McFarlane seemed unfazed, accepting this screaming headline with equanimity, betraying no emotion on his face, as usual. He would later recall assuming that North's diversion had been approved by higher authority. It was probably a compartmentalized intelligence operation and North had just indiscreetly told someone who had no "need to know," McFarlane thought. So he would simply keep what North later called "the deepest, darkest secret of the whole activity" under his hat. Briefing President Reagan on the Tehran trip a few days later, McFarlane did not raise the matter of the diversion.

RANSOM

As if Tehran had not been bad enough, North soon learned that his parallel effort to ransom the hostages with $1 million supplied by Ross Perot had also gone down the tubes.

In early June Perot dispatched one of his aides to Cyprus carrying the $1 million in cash in a suitcase. This time the money was real, not the chemically treated counterfeit North had used in the botched attempt to free the late Peter Kilburn.

The Perot aide met up with Secord operative Tom Clines and two federal agents from the Drug Enforcement Administration who had been assigned to work with North in trying to free the hostages.

According to the plan, sources developed by the DEA agents were to have arranged for the release of at least two of the Americans in return for a ransom of $1 million per hostage. The hostages were to have been placed in speedboats and taken to a spot off the coast of Lebanon, where they would rendezvous with the *Erria*, a Danish-flagged ship recently purchased by Secord's Enterprise for $312,000. But the deal collapsed when the intermediaries insisted that the $1 million be paid in advance and the DEA agents refused.

That was the final chapter in a bizarre, seventeen-month effort overseen by North to ransom the hostages, even as he was pursuing their release through the sale of arms to Iran. The DEA operation, as it came to be referred to in light of that agency's involvement, again showed that the United States was willing to go to almost any lengths to get its hostages released, and it represented something of a case study of North's penchant to privatize covert operations and bypass the federal agencies which normally would have been

responsible for such initiatives. And in its use of private funds to
pay both ransom money and the expenses of government agents; in
its ignoring of congressional reporting requirements; and its flaunt-
ing of U.S. policy against paying ransom for the release of hostages,
the DEA operation not only violated the law but was, in many
respects, the larger Iran initiative in microcosm.

In January of 1985, Edward Hickey, then an assistant to President Reagan, casually asked his friend and neighbor in the Virginia
suburbs, DEA agent "Kevin Innes," if he thought DEA could help
locate the American hostages in Lebanon. Lebanon was a prime
area for drug trafficking, and Hickey had a personal interest in the
hostages since he was a friend of William Buckley. Innes told
Hickey that another DEA agent, "Philip Burlage," had widespread
contacts in the Middle East who might be helpful. (The names of
these two agents are fictitious.)

Shortly thereafter, Hickey and his military aide, Gen. Matthew
Caulfield, met with both Innes and Burlage, and Burlage confirmed he had a source who was well-wired throughout Lebanon.
Hickey then approached Admiral Poindexter and encouraged him
to include the DEA on the White House's Hostage Location Task
Force. Poindexter agreed, and the DEA assigned Abraham Azzam,
an Arabic-speaking agent of Lebanese heritage, as its representative on the task force.

The DEA authorized $20,000 for Innes and Burlage to use in
travel expenses and payments to sources to try and develop information on the location of the hostages. If the sources were productive they were to be turned over to the CIA for operational
handling because by law, DEA agents were only supposed to be
involved in operations relating to drug enforcement.

In February, Azzam, Innes and Burlage met with Burlage's
source in Geneva and again in New York. The source claimed to
have contacts who could secure the release of the hostages from
their captors. He said $50,000 would be needed to start the opera-
tion, and that the hostages could be released if the U.S. were prepared to sell military hardware directly to the captors. North,
several months before Washington became involved with Tehran,
told the agents the U.S. could not sell weapons.

In early March North met with Innes and Burlage along with
Hickey and Caulfield. The DEA agents gave North a full briefing
on their plan but said the CIA was reluctant to pay out the $50,000
necessary to get started without proof that Burlage's source was

legitimate. In a follow-up telephone call Caulfield gave North more details, acknowledging, according to the Iran-Contra committees' report, that the DEA effort was "not very sophisticated." He said the plan now called for the release of four hostages for $1 million each, once the $50,000 was paid to the source.

North's notes reflected his initial dilemma: "Fundamental decision: Do we pay ransom?" But he didn't agonize long. Soon Ollie would become the leader of the DEA project, even pulling off the bureaucratic sleight-of-hand of getting Innes and Burlage detached from DEA and assigned directly to him.

Meanwhile Innes and Burlage arranged for two CIA agents to meet Burlage's source in New York. The CIA men came away sufficiently convinced of the source's bona fides to authorize paying out the $50,000. So the cash was passed to the source in two installments. But soon the ante was upped. On May 2 the source told the DEA agents he now needed $200,000 to give to his contact, who could locate Buckley and obtain proof that he was still alive. After that payment, the source said, the $1-million-per-hostage plan could unfold.

Azzam, the DEA man on the hostage task force whom Innes and Burlage were supposed to be reporting to, became concerned when he learned that the source's contact, who was demanding the $200,000, was a known thief and drug-trafficker. Azzam told CIA officials of his fears and they agreed that the money should not be paid in the absence of indisputable proof that Buckley was alive. This proof was to consist of a photo of Buckley holding current newspapers with the date visible, or something equally convincing.

In early May Burlage's source went back to Lebanon to try to get the proof while Innes and Burlage waited offshore in Cyprus. The source returned with less than convincing evidence: a Beirut newspaper with Buckley's initials scrawled on it. The CIA and FBI judged the handwriting not to be Buckley's—also, the middle initial was wrong. At that point Clair George, CIA deputy director for operations declared the entire DEA plan "a scam, a fake," nothing more than "hocus-pocus."

Judging North to be far more sympathetic to their plan than either Azzam or the CIA, the two DEA agents began working the back-channel to Ollie. Azzam first noticed this when Innes and Burlage took the newspaper with Buckley's purported initials to North before showing it to him or the CIA. Friction developed between North and Azzam. When Azzam asked North how he intended to raise the $1-million-per-hostage ransom, given that public funds were out of the question since ransoming was against policy, Ollie told him not to ask.

But Azzam guessed correctly that the benefactor was Ross Perot. Earlier Perot had offered to donate a plane to the DEA, which Azzam had refused, and he was fully aware of the colorful Texan's penchant for helping the government conduct sensitive, deniable covert operations. When Azzam told the CIA of his suspicions regarding Perot and North learned of it, he was furious with Azzam for having compromised Perot. Azzam couldn't understand North's reaction, since the CIA, not DEA, was to have the operational role.

Meanwhile Innes and Burlage urged North on. Presenting a slightly modified plan, they assured him that their source could deliver if given $200,000 to spread around Lebanon in various bribes, and $2 million for the release of two hostages. They also, North recorded in his notebooks, told him they would like to begin reporting directly to him so as to get the DEA "off their backs."

North met their source in Washington and was satisfied he was legitimate. On June 7 he wrote a memorandum to McFarlane, then still the National Security Advisor, outlining the DEA operation and saying that $2,200,000 would be provided by a "donor." Revealing still another diversion, North also wrote in the memo that the DEA agents' expenses, and other costs of the operation, were being paid from funds allocated to support the Contras. He asked McFarlane to approve the plan and have Attorney General Edwin Meese detail the DEA agents to the NSC for thirty days. McFarlane approved.

On June 10, North prepared a memo for Meese describing how the DEA agents would deposit the $200,000 and open a bank account for the remaining $2 million, which he said would be given by the "donor to bribe those in control of the hostages." North also asked Meese to assign Innes and Burlage to the NSC for no more than a month. Meese agreed.

In late May Jay Coburn, Perot's courier, delivered $200,000 in cash to North without obtaining a receipt. North stored the cash in his office safe but told Innes that federal employees could not handle the money. So for that job Innes suggested his brother, who as a family member would be trustworthy and who he said also had experience in security issues.

North readily gave Innes' brother the $200,000 in cash, plus $11,000 in traveler's checks from the Contra account for expenses. Innes and his brother then flew to Cyprus, where they met the

DEA source and gave him the $200,000 to take to Lebanon.

As North and his people waited for the payment to bear fruit, other events intervened: the hijacking of the TWA flight on June 14 by Lebanese terrorists, as well as the supposed death of one of the DEA source's contacts in Lebanon. Under the circumstances the source claimed to be leery about approaching those in control of the hostages. He returned to tell the DEA agents that he now thought the hostages could best be freed in return for arms.

Despite these lame excuses, the loss of the $200,000 and the introduction of the new demand for arms, the DEA agents remained on the case. And though their thirty days under North were up they would continue to report directly to him for the next year. They wrote, according to the Innes deposition, no reports on their activities and destroyed all their notes after reporting verbally to North.

In October, removing all doubts about the status of Buckley, the CIA agent's captors announced that they had killed him. The man whose release the DEA source had been chasing for $200,000 was now officially gone.

On another track in January of 1986 North, the CIA and the FBI were developing their plan to win the release of hostage Peter Kilburn through the production of the chemically treated counterfeit. To support the expenses for this operation North returned to the apparently bottomless Perot well and brought forth another $100,000.

Meanwhile the CIA's Charles Allen, who was already involved in the Iran initiative, took over the Hostage Location Task Force. North also recruited an army major from the Defense Intelligence Agency who had experience in the Middle East. Innes and Burlage did not sit on the task force but North advised the members that the two agents would be useful resources.

The major, who was selected to play a lead role on the task force, did not care much for Innes or Burlage. He characterized them to the congressional Iran-Contra committees as "street toughs in camelhair coats" who were "street-smart but not very knowledgeable of other federal agencies . . . outside their own, nor knowledgeable certainly in any way, shape or form, about Middle East or international relations, or politics or the military."

Yet Innes and Burlage continued to be well-stoked with *chutzpah*. At their first meeting with Allen and the major they said they did not want to deal with the CIA Operations Directorate. Allen told them they could report to the major.

In January of 1986 Innes and the major went to New York to

evaluate a new DEA source who, if accepted, would be paid from CIA funds. After the meeting the major told North he had reservations not only about the source but about the entire DEA operation, based as it was on paying ransom to win the release of the hostages. But North said he liked Innes and Burlage because they were "action-oriented."

When the major also told Charles Allen of his reservations about the DEA plan, Allen replied that North had told him that President Reagan had said he would "go to Leavenworth if necessary" to free the hostages. The major interpreted this to mean that Reagan would be willing to act illegally, but he dismissed the remark as North bluster.

In late April the major submitted a paper to North presenting a range of options for obtaining the release of the hostages. The paper urged that any efforts to win their freedom through the sale of arms to Iran be rejected. North, now some eight months into a program that was doing just that, agreed and told the major that selling arms to Iran "was against official U.S. policy... [and] encouraged terrorism." In May the major left the hostage task force.

But North continued to place some of his chips on the DEA operation while pursuing the broader Iran initiative at the same time. So Innes returned to Cyprus to work on another hostage rescue plan, using the new DEA source that the major had found unreliable. Innes called Burlage in the U.S. and asked for $30,000 —$20,000 for the source and $10,000 for expenses. Burlage turned to North, who this time asked Secord and the Enterprise to provide the money. Secord agreed, whereupon a third DEA agent flew to Switzerland and obtained $30,000 in cash from Albert Hakim, the Enterprise's chief financier.

The new hostage-release plan supposedly called not for bribery but for a rescue. Certain elements in Lebanon were to be paid $1 million to rescue each hostage, then once they were freed they would be ferried in speedboats to the Enterprise ship *Erria* waiting off the Lebanon coast.

Just after North and McFarlane returned empty-handed from Tehran, Perot's courier flew to Cyprus, $1 million in tow. He spent several days waiting for the deal to be consummated, but it never was. Secord, whose man Clines was on the scene, says the negotiations turned into a "Chinese fire drill... flakier than normal."

A final DEA-related project that was flirted with in June consisted of an effort by Secord and Amiram Nir to use one of the DEA sources to help develop a forty-man paramilitary force in Beirut that would be used to try and rescue the hostages. "Dick rates the possibility of success on this operation as thirty percent," North wrote Poindexter, "but that's better than nothing." However, North later told the Iran-Contra committees in secret testimony that although "a fairly significant amount of money" was spent developing this option, no rescue attempt was ever mounted.

Perot, now fed up with the ineptitude of the hostage release efforts—and out $300,000—told North that he should have been kept more closely informed. Citizen McFarlane, asked by North to try and pacify Perot, called the Texan and asked him "not to be too hard on Ollie." In addition President Reagan dashed off a letter to Perot on June 11 saying: "I have been briefed on your effort over the past several weeks on behalf of our Americans abducted in Beirut. On behalf of the American people I want to thank you for your discreet assistance in this regard. My hope is that we may yet succeed in reuniting these men with their families and loved ones. Thanks again and God bless you."

Perot didn't stay mad long. In fact, five months later, after North's world came crashing down and he had been banished from the White House, Perot would rally to his defense and make it clear to the world that Ollie was his kind of guy:

"The fact you need to know today is that under this Administration Colonel Oliver North was the man that had the key job," Perot told reporters, "and it offends my sense of fairness that that's the man the whole world has put in the barrel and is beating up on beyond recognition . . . I knew when and where every penny was being used. My people handled all the money. Oliver made sure of that. He went the extra mile to make sure of that. He was that type of guy—100 percent integrity."

Defending his willingness to pay millions of dollars for the release of the hostages, as well as his 1982 offering of $500,000 to win the release of Gen. James Dozier—kidnapped by the Italian Red Brigade—Perot said that since 1969, through four presidencies, he had quietly been involved in "helping Americans in distress around the world . . . Presidents always say we don't pay ransom. Presidents always say what they have to say . . . But you've got two choices: you do something unconventional like getting private funds to take care of it, or you let them kill the hostages."

As long as the private sector put up the money, the government could maintain the fig-leaf denial that it was not violating its own policy of paying ransom to terrorists. "As I understand the government's policy," Perot said, "it is they don't want to use U.S. money, but if and when they can find a willing citizen to help in matters like this, then they can go to great efforts to save the person's life."

Perot was the more-than-willing patriot, doing his duty as he saw it with the resource available to him—money. He disarmed questioners with a quip—"Why didn't they call before 1969? Hell, I didn't have any money before 1969"—and offered real-world advice on how to deal with terrorists: "Forget the Marquess of Queensberry Rules," he said. "Forget what would work in Lima, Ohio. Forget our three branches of government. You're over in an eye-for-an-eye, tooth-for-a-tooth country; you're over where people never got the word, and you've got to deal with them in their culture, and their way, and their mentality. But you never give them anything in advance.... You swap. You don't go to the bazaar, pay for the rug and hope it gets delivered to the hotel... I mean, it's hard-ball, straight-up negotiation. You don't give them anything 'til you get what you want."

Though he didn't mention he'd been snookered for $300,000, that little speech expressed the no-bullshit, damn-the-torpedoes, do-what-you-have-to-do, play-the-hand-you're-dealt, bureaucracy-busting, can-do spirit that was Perot's trademark.

North couldn't have said it better himself.

GUNS DOWN, DRUGS UP

WITH the need for funds seemingly always desperate, some leading Contra supporters used profits from the sale of drugs to buy weapons and supplies for the resistance, according to those involved, and to testimony before the Senate Subcommittee on Terrorism, Narcotics and International Operations.

"I'm not proud of it, but we didn't have any choice," one Contra leader, Octaviano Cesar, told the subcommittee in April of 1988. "I mean, the U.S. Congress didn't give us any choice" when it adopted the Boland Ammendment in late 1984 cutting off further funding. Cesar said he himself was not a dealer, but he had been aware that some of the Contras' support was coming from drug dealers.

One of those dealers, convicted drug smuggler George Morales, a Colombian serving a sixteen-year federal-prison sentence, told the committee that several U.S. government agencies, including the CIA, were aware that he was channeling "millions of dollars" in drug profits to the Contras and approved of it.

Cesar, the brother of Alfredo Cesar, a member of the Contra directorate, told the committee that he had told a CIA officer about the group's involvement with Morales, and he said the CIA man replied that this would be acceptable as long as the Contras "didn't deal in the powder," meaning cocaine. The CIA denied this testimony and reiterated earlier statements that none of its agents has ever condoned drug trafficking by the Contras.

Morales and others described a "guns-down, drugs-up" operation whereby weapons would be flown to the Contras and the planes would then be loaded with drugs for the return flight to the United

States. Morales and one of his pilots, Gary Betzner, who is also in prison after being convicted of drug trafficking charges, told the committee that they arranged to send weapons to the Costa Rican farm of American expatriot John Hull. After unloading the weapons, Morales and Betzner asserted, they took back duffel bags of cocaine that were stored at or near Hull's farm.

Cesar and two other Nicaraguan exiles active in the Contra movement, Karol Prado and Marcos Arguado, also told the committee that the flights carrying drugs left from Hull's ranch.

This gave added weight to testimony given Kerry's committee in October 1987 by Bill Crone, a former business partner of Hull. Crone testified then that Costa Rican officials "on the level of U.S. congressmen" warned him that he should stay clear of Contra drug-running occurring on Hull's ranch. Kerry had called a hearing to investigate why Hull had been awarded $375,000 by a U.S. government overseas development agency for the stated purpose of re-opening a wood-processing factory near Quesada, Costa Rica. But documents showed the money was not used for the purposes intended.

Hull has consistently denied that his ranch was used as a drug-trafficking way-station.

Arguado helped arrange Contra arms shipments for North's White House network and was close to Hull. Prado was a former lieutenant of Contra commander Eden Pastora, and it has been those affiliated with Pastora who have been the main suspected drug traffickers. The rival, and largest, Contra faction, the Nicaraguan Democratic Force, headed by Adolfo Calero, has vigorously denied any connection with drugs—as has Pastora himself, though the congressional Iran-Contra committees released a CIA document dated April 1986 that said the agency found it difficult to believe that senior Pastora aides could be "so involved" without his knowledge.

But by mid-1986 Pastora was no longer a force in Contra leadership ranks, and North had recruited others in an effort to organize the Southern Front. In this effort some of North's operatives enlisted the help of another Contra leader, Popo Chamorro. Prado alleged before the Senate subcommittee in April, 1988, that Chamorro was directly involved in drug smuggling on Pastora's behalf.

Morales, who was the Miami distributor for the Colombian drug cartel, said he had bought three airplanes for the Contras and donated $4 million to $5 million in cash from drug profits to their cause, adding that the Colombian cartel was also involved in helping the Contras. His motive, he said, was to try and get protection from U.S. authorities for his drug-trafficking operation. He said he was upset that he had not received a lighter prison sentence after his work in supporting the Contras.

Betzner told the committee that the first Contra flight that Morales asked him to make was in 1983 when he flew from Opa Lacka, Florida, with a load of grenade launchers, stopped at a U.S. Naval air station in the Florida Keys to pick up some ship mines, then flew on to the Ilopango air base in El Salvador where the U.S. Contra support operation was headquartered. He then flew to Colombia, picked up 6,000 pounds of marijuana and flew back to the U.S. In July of 1984 Betzner said he flew a quantity of machine guns and small arms to Hull's ranch, where he loaded seventeen duffel bags and three boxes of cocaine for the return trip home. He said he made a similar run to Hull's ranch and back—delivering guns and returning with cocaine—ten days later.

The testimony of the five men prompted the subcommittee chairman, Senator John Kerry, the Massachusetts Democrat, to say that there was now proof "beyond a reasonable doubt" that there was a connection between the Contras and drug trafficking. The testimony culminated a two-year investigation into the Contra-drug issue by Kerry and his staff.

"When you have five witnesses in a row corroborating the same thing, I think we now have an inescapable conclusion about what is going on—that the clandestine Contra supply effort got mixed up with drugs," Kerry said. "And it happened because some people in the Reagan Administration were willing to look the other way. Politics got into it. That's my conclusion."

Other pilots who have said they delivered weapons for the Contras and flew drugs back to the United States include Michael Tolliver and Werner Lotz.

Tolliver, a pilot now serving a forty-month sentence for conspiring to import marijuana, has said that on one return flight, after ferrying weapons to the Contras in Honduras, he flew more than twelve tons of marijuana to Homestead Air Base in Miami. He says he was paid $75,000 and left the Contraband in custody of the Air Force. A Homestead spokesman said he had no knowledge of the story.

Lotz, who is serving a federal prison sentence for drug trafficking, has told the Kerry subcommittee that he flew weapons to Central America and picked up cocaine at Hull's ranch on the way home.

Steven Carr and Jesus Garcia—the two Florida mercenaries who worked for the Contra cause, have told reporters that they saw cocaine stored alongside weapons waiting to be shipped to the Contras. Carr later died of an apparent drug overdose.

North, it would seem, was at least aware that some Contra leaders were apparently dealing with drug traffickers although there is no suggestion or evidence that he in any way sanctioned or encouraged it. Lawrence Spivey, an American filmmaker who worked closely with the Contras and knew North, has said that in early 1985 he saw Miami-based FBI reports on the Contra drug charges in North's office.

Courier Rob Owen wrote North in April 1985 that some Contra leaders "are questionable because of past indiscretions" involving "drug running." Owen named one leader as a suspect and said flatly that another was then engaged in drug running out of Panama. Owen wrote North another memo in February of 1986 in which he said a Contra plane had been used to transport drugs.

Several passages in North's notebooks contain cryptic allusions to drug money providing arms for the Contras, including one reference which said: "$14 million to finance Supermarket came from drugs." The "Supermarket" was apparently a warehouse in Honduras where a weapons dealer stored arms that Contras purchased.

Another North notebook entry contained an allegation from a Contra leader "A.C."—Adolfo Calero—that "Pastora revealed his drug dealing." In still another entry North wrote: "DC-6 which is being used for runs out of New Orleans is probably being used for drug runs into the United States."

Owen was never asked about the Contra drug running in his testimony before the congressional Iran-Contra committees. The committees decided not to investigate the issue, though they did ask North a few questions about it in an executive session held July 9, 1987. According to North's since declassified testimony at that session, he said he had no knowledge of drug money being used to buy weapons for the Contras. However, he said he did know of two former Pastora lieutenants who were "potentially implicated in the movement of drugs."

Explaining his notebook references, North said he and Casey were wary of buying arms for the Contras from the Honduran supermarket because of concerns that it was financed by drug money. He said the statement from "A.C." regarding Pastora was "probably an allegation." As for the entry about the DC-6 runing drugs, North said the plane did not belong to the U.S. government, and that when he received the report, he turned it over to the federal Drug Enforcement Administration.

The New York *Times* reported in January of 1987 that federal drug investigators had uncovered evidence in the fall of 1986 that American pilots flying arms to Central America for the Contras were smuggling drugs back to the United States on their return flights.

When the crew members, many of whom were based in El Salvador, learned that they were being investigated by U.S. authorities, one of them warned that they had White House protection and used North's name, the *Times* reported. But the officials were said to have concluded that the crew member's warning was probably a bluff and that the smuggling was a freelance effort done for the pilots' personal gain rather than on behalf of the Contras. Though North had intervened in other federal investigations that touched on the Contras' activities, the *Times* said officials believed there was no evidence that North or anyone else had done so in this case.

The Kerry subcommittee was also told in June of 1987 by Ramon Milian-Rodriguez, a former Panamanian lawyer now serving a thirty-five-year prison sentence on racketeering and drug-related charges, that he had given $10 million on behalf of the Colombian drug cartel to Felix Rodriguez, the former CIA operative who was North's Contra liaison at the Ilopango base in El Salvador.

"The cartel figured it was buying a little friendship," Milian-Rodriguez (no relation to Felix) is reported to have testified before Kerry's subcommittee. "What the hell is ten million bucks? They thought they were going to buy some good will and take a little heat off of them. They figured maybe the CIA and DEA will not screw around so much." Milian-Rodriguez testified that Rodriguez had approached leaders of the Colombian Medellin cartel for money and that the drug kingpins believed Rodriguez was working for the CIA.

The CIA called Milian-Rodriguez's allegation "absurd." Kerry's committee met behind closed doors with Felix Rodriguez in August of 1987, and Rodriguez denied having either received or solicited the $10 million.

Another target of the Kerry investigation was one Michael B. Palmer, a forty-one-year-old Florida native who in early 1988 walked away from what authorities considered an air-tight case of marijuana smuggling after a federal prosecutor in Detroit dropped the charges "in the interest of justice."

In 1985 and 1986, the period in which Palmer had allegedly been involved in smuggling marijuana, he was flying "humanitarian aid" to the Contras under a State Department Contract. According to his indictment, Palmer regularly flew marijuana from Colombia to the United States from 1977 to 1986. He was making so much money, the question arises why he needed to bother working for the State Department. One of Palmer's associates, Leigh Ritch, suggested in testimony the reason was that through his Contra connections Palmer was given access to classified information from law enforcement that served to protect the drug-running operation.

Ritch testified that Palmer was "the top man of our organization," and that the group grossed billions of dollars in marijuana smuggling. "Palmer, having his connections through the U.S. Coast Guard and stuff, was tipping us about certain times that shipments should come up," Ritch testified.

The Boston *Globe* quoted a U.S. Customs official in February of 1988 as saying that Customs, at the request of the CIA, did not search planes used in the Contra supply operation. Questions about Palmer were raised in March of 1987 when a plane registered to the Miami-based Vortex, Inc., was delayed in Miami for a full inspection by a Customs official. No drugs were found on the flight, but when Palmer, then a Vortex vice-president, showed up to claim the plane, a computer check turned up his pending marijuana smuggling charges. Palmer told the Customs official that he and Vortex were working for the CIA, and after checking with the agency, the inspector, according to the *Globe*, was told that Palmer was telling the truth.

In late 1985 and early 1986 Vortex was paid $97,000 by the State Department to fly several DC-6 planeloads of humanitarian aid for the Contras from the U.S. to Central America. It is unknown if there was any relationship between North and Vortex, though the company's phone number was in North's notebooks, without further explanation. (The State Department also paid $231,587 to a Miami-based shrimp-importing firm called Ocean Hunter for its services as a "broker" in the dispensing of humanitarian aid to the Contras. The payments were made during the first six months of 1986, at the same time that Ocean Hunter was under investigation by the FBI and the DEA for alleged drug-smuggling activity. Robert Owen, under his Contract with the State Department's Nicaraguan Humanitarian Assistance Office, was in charge of the Ocean Hunter account.)

Further information about Palmer's ties to law enforcement were contained in a January, 1988, affidavit given by another alleged drug smuggler, Alejandro Cerna Sanchez, who was awaiting trial in Detroit on charges that he attempted to smuggle 25,000 pounds of marijuana into the United States. Sanchez said Palmer told him in 1986 that because of his activities on behalf of the Contras, he knew the times and places of Coast Guard patrols. Sanchez said in the affidavit that Palmer "stated that he had been smuggling weapons and ammunition in cargo vessels from Argentina to Honduras for the Nicaraguan Contras and that he was given a code or password that changed every week and would ensure a safe and undisturbed passage."

Palmer told Senator Kerry's subcommittee in April, 1988, that he had become a federal informant in early 1986, and that all his activities since that time had been sanctioned by various government agencies.

One of the most controversial cases involving drugs and the Contras has to do with Julio Zavala, a Nicaraguan lawyer and Contra activist who maintained a residence in San Francisco. In 1983 federal agents raided Zavala's house and seized a quantity of cocaine, a U.S. military rifle, a grenade and about $36,000 in apparent drug profits.

But when the case came to trial, Zavala, who was convicted and is now serving a jail sentence on the drug offense, produced two letters from Contra leaders in Costa Rica saying that the money had been sent to him to purchase humanitarian aid for the Contras. The Justice Department agreed to return the money and subsequently gave Zavala a check for $36,020.

Officials from the Justice Department—notably the U.S. Attorney's office in Miami—were told repeatedly that the Contras were involved in drug running, but in most cases failed to launch prosecutions, though some of the drug dealers involved were charged.

"We've had all these questions come to us over the past year-and-a-half of our investigation, and the only thing the Justice Department tells us is that they are coincidences or unsubstantiated allegations," said Kerry. "I think there's a lot more than just coincidences."

At issue is the credibility of the Reagan administration's ballyhooed "Just Say No" to drugs campaign, and whether the administration was willing to condone lawbreaking by those who were helping the Contras to advance the White House's foreign-policy interests.

While there is now little question that U.S. agents helped finance the war in Indochina through heroin trafficking, no evidence has emerged to suggest that the CIA or any other agency of the U.S. government systematically financed the Contra war with drug money, or that most Contra leaders were actively engaged in such activity. Rather, the evidence suggests that some Contra leaders and supporters saw drug trafficking as a quick and easy way to raise funds for the cash-starved resistance, and that various U.S. officials, when they came to have knowledge of such activity, looked the other way.

Nowhere was this look-the-other way ethos more clearly demonstarted than in North's and the administration's dealings with Panamanian strongman Manuel Noriega, who was indicted in Florida in February of 1988 on charges of racketeering, cocaine trafficking and money laundering.

Washington had known for at least fifteen years that Noriega was heavily involved in the international drug trade and other crimes, but because he was regarded as a rabid anti-communist his illegal activities were tolerated.

North met with Noriega at least twice in Panama in 1985 to elicit the dictator's help in training the Contras, pledging in return that ths U.S. would help Panama ease its foreign debt crisis, according to testimony given Kerry's subcommittee by José Blandon, a former Panamanian intelligence officer and Consul-General in New York.

Blandon said he attended both meetings. The first occurred in June of 1985 aboard a yacht near the Panamanian city of Balboa. North said he needed Contra training areas, since direct American support was banned under the Boland Ammendment. Noriega agreed to help and the Contras were trained at two Panamanian bases.

At a second North-Noriega meeting in October, 1985, Blandon said, Noriega complained that Panama was in dire financial straits and he requested U.S. help in easing its $3.8 billion foreign debt. North offered to do what he could, and over the next year Panama received more than $200 million in private and international development bank loans.

North continued to maintain contact with Noriega in 1986 over the matter of Panamanian assistance to the Contras. In one internal computer message, North reported that Noriega was willing to continue helping the Contras if the White House would help him improve his public image. To that end, International Business Communications (IBC), the Washington public relations firm that

North and Spitz Channell used to funnel money to the Contras, was given a $35,000 monthly retainer from September 1, 1986, to December 31, 1987, by a Panamanian group identified by Blandon as a front for Noriega.

Noriega used the group to send messages to North, while North would use IBC to send messages to Noriega, Blandon told Kerry's subcommittee.

Also in 1986, according to both Blandon and the congressional Iran-Contra committees' final report, Noriega offered to send Panamanian soldiers inside Nicaragua to engage in assassinations and sabotage missions. Admiral Poindexter "approved the sabotage plan but instructed North not to become involved in conspiracy or assassination," the report said. But the sabotage plan was apparently never carried out either.

Blandon also said that North and Noriega plotted for Panama to seize an East Bloc arms shipment off El Salvador and claim that it had been sent by Nicaragua to help the Salvadoran rebels in their civil war. This would have helped prove the Reagan Administration's thesis that the Sandinistas were trying to export revolution in the hemisphere.

But the plan went awry when the New York *Times* published an article in June of 1986 detailing Noriega's illegal activities. Angered by the story, Noriega had Panama seize the arms shipment two days after the article appeared, but he ordered the cargo kept, declining to go through with the plot against the Sandinistas. Secord then reportedly tried to buy the arms cargo on behalf of the Contras but Noriega refused.

At Senator Kerry's hearings in April, 1988, Francis J. McNeil, former Deputy Assistant Secretary of State for Intelligence and Research, said that by mid 1986 the Administration had faced up to the fact that Noriega was trafficking in drugs, but opted to do nothing because it still considered him a vital Contra supporter. "A decision was made to put Noriega on the shelf until Nicaragua was settled," testified McNeil, who resigned in 1987.

GOD & COUNTRY

As the summer of 1986 began, North looked more and more exhausted. Often he would be so busy during the day that he would not have time to talk with Secord, the man he had to remain in almost constant contact with in order to manage the two-front, Iran-Contra monster. So on his way home late at night North would often stop at Secord's home in McLean, Virginia, for midnight meetings.

They would sit in Secord's kitchen and talk as North had a beer or two. Sometimes Secord's wife would fix North something to eat. He usually hadn't had dinner.

"He looked like hell," Secord recalls. "I spoke to him. As I got to know him, I came to have affection for him. He's very likable and a good man. I was worried about his health and his effectiveness. We were in a very hot project and your mind doesn't function well if you're exhausted. Too often he'd schedule himself for ancillary activities like interagency meetings. I urged him many times to delegate so he could focus on the flashpoints. But he said nothing would get done if he didn't do it.

"When they find a good horse, they ride him, because there aren't any that actually do anything in this gridlocked bureaucracy of ours... I've characterized Ollie as an Army mule: they load 'em and load 'em 'til they finally break their backs, and then they eat 'em."

Bob Dutton, Secord's sidekick on the Contra-supply operation, also found North to be near the breaking point. "The guy was darn near killing himself," Dutton says. "They talk about Secord having to go to the fat farm. He did go. Hakim sent him because his blood pressure was 180 over 145. I mentioned to Ollie that it was a good thing Dick was taking a week's break to try to get himself under control. Ollie said, 'Why, what's the matter with him?' And I told him his blood pressure, and he says, 'That's not so bad. Mine's 205 over 180.' And I looked in his eyes and the blood vessels were nearly breaking from the pressure. It was just off the scales."

McFarlane also saw the pressure building in North, and on June 10, showing his still-active hand, he sent Poindexter a message suggesting that perhaps the time had come for North to leave the NSC. "It seems increasingly clear that the Democratic left is coming after [North] with a vengeance in the election year," McFarlane wrote, "and that eventually they will get him—too many people are talking to reporters from the [Contra] donor community and within the Administration. I don't know what you do about it, but in Ollie's interest I would get him transferred, or sent to Bethesda for disability review board... That would present a major loss to the staff and Contra effort, but I think we can probably find a way to continue those things. In the end, it may be better anyway."

Given North's 1974 assignment to Bethesda for emotional distress, this message would later be widely interpreted as another effort to have North's psyche attended to. But McFarlane denied any such intent, saying, in an interview, that he meant only to suggest that North retire on a physical disability. In light of the mounting political storm brewing on the Contra front, and because North had probably already become too controversial and been away too long ever to have a viable career in the Marine Corps again, McFarlane apparently thought Ollie should cash in his disability chit.

"When he came out of Vietnam he was reviewed by disability review board for combat wounds—back and legs," McFarlane recalls. "He was almost put out of the Marine Corps for combat-related wounds. He argued and complained and lobbied... and was able to get out of being surveyed. However, the rules are that you can ask to be reevaluated if you decide that your injuries get worse, and so it was in that context that I was urging that maybe if the Marine Corps was not going to treat him well, that he retire, based upon a physical evaluation.

"And then in June after I got back from Tehran with him, that trip was the first extended period of time I'd had with Ollie since I left government six months before. I learned that kind of a rush of things had occurred since I left. Astonishing things had happened, not the least of which was the diversion of money, and the fact that they had allowed these negotiations to go on and on and on, and they obviously didn't get the hostages out. And Ollie seemed to be . . . doing things that weren't really authorized. I didn't know those things—as a civilian probably I didn't want to know, nor probably did I have the authority. But I thought that at least I ought to tell John that in my judgment, Ollie was in over his head and ought to be sent back."

In times of stress, North could find at least some refuge and comfort in the realm of the Lord. Since his born-again experience at Camp Lejeune in 1978 when Gen. John Grinalds had convinced him first-hand of the power of prayer, North had become an increasingly committed charismatic Christian. He and his wife attended prayer groups, went on religious retreats and were active in a charismatic church.

That August North took his son Stuart out to California's Yosemite National Park for several days on a wilderness trek called "Adventures in Fathering." The program was sponsored by a Christian group and was designed to strengthen father-son relationships. North had been largely an absentee parent the previous five years, and this was an opportunity for some quality time with his son.

There were about fifty fathers and sons on the trip. They were divided into four groups and would go off on day-long excursions through the High Sierras after being given a question to contemplate—such as, what could they do at home to become closer, and what could they build on together from this trip? North relaxed and seemed to blend easily wisecracking with the seriousness of the trip's religious-family agenda. He charmed and kidded his group leader, Mary Jane Breedveld, with a little cornball Marine humor, telling her she had shamed him by leading them effortlessly up steep trails, proving only that he was never too old to learn how to take a hill.

At night all four groups would come together to "share" and give testimony about their relationship with God and how religion could be integrated into their everyday lives. Ollie talked about his spiritual life, and he included something of life at the White House.

"I was deeply impressed with Colonel North . . . ," recalls Tim Hansel, director of Summit Expeditions, which conducted the trip. "He shared his life story in an interesting way. He told his story in the third person. He started telling a story about a young boy, and you didn't catch on for a while that he was talking about himself. He talked about harrowing experiences. He said God had gotten his attention through some near-death experiences. He said he had had several close calls with death where he had come out un

scathed. After those experiences he said it came to him. He said
God had wanted to break in, and at first he had been resistant and
hard-headed, but God had finally gotten his attention, and he
talked about the incredible transformation it made in his life."

Breedveld remembers being most struck by something else that
North told the group. "He said he prayed with President Reagan
behind closed doors," she recalls. "He just wanted to let us know that
was something that was part of life at the White House. He said they
had prayed together over different situations. He was just letting us
know that that did go on at the White House. He didn't say it was just
he and Reagan. I had the impression it was just a small group of two or
three. He wasn't saying this to brag. The context was that this
administration thought prayer was important. That was important to
Oliver North. Having the Lord in Oliver North's daily life was important. He didn't say he initiated it, but he said that it went on . . . I
found it comforting to know that the president prayed. But it was a
surprise, too, because I didn't expect to hear that."

Hansel says North made "a strong impression on the group with
his candidness, humor, openness and receptivity. He was so ap-
proachable, not the least bit standoffish. I was also impressed with
the kind of dad that he was. He spent a lot of quality time with his
son . . . It was a strong but tender relationship . . . The day he left I
remember he said he had to be somewhere at six the following
morning. He was under incredible pressure, yet it didn't show the
least bit during the course. You wouldn't have thought this guy was
anything but a salesman. He had great poise."

Back in Washington, North was active in a weekly prayer and
Bible-study group under the auspices of Officers' Christian Fellowship, an organization designed to promote faith and family stability
among military officers. The prayer group consisted of about eight
to twelve people, husbands and wives, who usually met at a different house for about two-and-a-half hours in the evening.

The time was fairly rigidly structured: socializing for the first
fifteen minutes, thirty minutes for "sharing," or talking about problems that the members wanted to pray about; about forty-five minutes for Bible study and discussion of certain passages of scripture
that the host family would be charged with selecting. Then they
would have dessert and more "fellowship."

"North and I had something in common in the sense that we
were both very proud Marine officers who thought we could do no
wrong," recalls Marine Maj. Michael Lundblad, who had been a

student under North at the Basic School in Quantico. "At one point
we realized we were not perfect. For me, it was losing a friend in a
scuba-diving accident. I then realized God was a real person and
was trying to get my attention.

"Sometimes the discussions at prayer group would get into military issues. If there was a major issue that God could have a hand
in—the Persian Gulf, for example—we'd pray for the safety of the
sailors. We in the military are peacemakers, contrary to popular
belief, and we'd pray for peace. Sometimes we'd pray for specifics
—more money for the defense budget. And of course we'd pray for
Christian issues . . .

"In the sessions Ollie was well-grounded in the Scriptures and
was filled with the spirit . . . He had a big-picture view and brought
another dimension to the study groups. Ollie was willing to speak
out. He never cared about his own personal gain. He was mission-
oriented.

"Toward the end Ollie got so busy his attendance at the groups
whittled down to nothing. But we'd still meet with Betsy. She took
his absence in stride and we prayed for Ollie when he wasn't there.
She enjoyed the Bible study because it gave her support. Support
for the family is critical in Officers' Christian Fellowship because of
how much officers move around and the lack of stability. She's a
human being. There were points when she wished she could have
had Ollie around more, but she knew God had a plan. And the
Lord was in charge with Ollie."

Another close Christian friend of North's said Betsy was "as
strong a believer as Ollie. She's been a tower of strength throughout their marriage. Through Vietnam and Okinawa she held the
family together and made it work. It's a healthy, vibrant unit, not
something one usually sees in the military. It was definitely accomplished through religious faith."

Lundblad said he found North "very warm and outgoing and
'other-concerned.' That's why he's so devoted to the Contra cause.
He had the greatest ability to see the world. He knew the person-
alities of the people in the Middle East because he had been there.
He had a sense of the Israelis' struggle. In the Old Testament the
Israelis were exiled and the Lord said they'd be back together . . .

"At North's home we'd talk sometimes about how to bring people
into the movement. We'd sing songs, and sometimes in those spiritual times you'd get a 'fuzzy feeling inside'—which, translated,
means a warm feeling from the spiritual Scripture songs."

Lundblad said he wasn't sure how North integrated religion with the workplace, but for him it went like this: "Every morning I would pray to walk with God that day, to be given a sense of vision, that God would give me the ability to face every day. I try to portray that in my personal example—that I walk the walk of a good Christian and people would notice that and say I'm different. I have blended the two successfully."

Another member of the prayer group, Navy Commander Don Frahler, said the participants didn't consider themselves "holy rollers," but certainly to the right of the Christian mainstream.

"The group became close," he remembers. "If a person discussed a problem at Bible study we might call during the week to see how everything was going... People would make 'requests'—requests to pray for a certain problem that a member of the group was having. Ollie's requests were mostly family-related, but also work-related. He'd say he was working on a big problem and would ask us to pray for him so he could come up with a proper solution that would glorify God and be proper for the country. He was as active a participant as I. Very open about his Christianity... I think Ollie felt comfortable about spreading the word because he was extremely dynamic and he was very good at talking about Christ."

Retired Col. Orville Lippold recalls that North approached prayer group meetings with as much energy and dedication as he did his job. "Whenever Ollie had the group over to his house you could count on a typed outline of the chapter and Ollie would be one hundred percent ready to teach. You felt he had read the book and written his own on it! He inspired participation by his knowledge of what he was teaching... He spoke with confidence. He didn't treat it like a lecture—more like a discussion. Ollie didn't have time to really socialize outside of Bible study. He was working so hard, but he didn't appear to be exhausted. He had the durability of an elephant. He realized that we knew the importance of his job, so we understood why he was gone a lot."

Around Christmas in 1984 North took his family to a Pennsylvania retreat run by Officers' Christian Fellowship for several days of outdoor activities such as skiing during the day, followed by Bible study, singing, praying and sharing at night. His daughter, Tait, later returned to work at the center as a summer volunteer.

"I remember seeing North conduct evening sessions," says the director of the center, Ret. Maj. Clay Buckingham. "I remember him talking about his life at the NSC. He talked about the people he worked with. He was very articulate and engaging and intelli gent. He talked of the opportunity of Christian witness—telling other people about Jesus Christ. He said there was a good opportunity at the NSC to spread the word."

They grappled with issues like the relevance of Christianity to everyday life and tried to resolve the conflicts between being a good soldier and a good Christian, or lying while doing intelligence work and still maintaining integrity. "He struggled with his relationship with Christ," continued Buckingham. "Like all people in high positions he struggled with what he was doing. Who are you loyal to, God or your commander-in-chief?"

Outside the prayer group setting North could feel comfortable talking about his religious life in everyday conversation—particularly with fellow Christians. Almost every week, for example, he would get a haircut and invariably discuss matters of the spirit with his barber, Issa Saliba.

"We'd talk about religion—not much about politics," says Saliba. "We never had real deep discussions, but he felt we believed in the same thing. Some charismatics believe that if you don't speak in tongues you're worthless, or not a good Christian. Ollie wasn't like that. He was very kind with his beliefs. He didn't try to convert you into his church. Most of the time we would talk about our born-again experiences. I used to call him Brother North, and he called me Brother too. When he left or finished a discussion with someone he would say, 'God bless you.' He never pushed his faith on anyone. He's a good Christian, and he's good for his country. He trusts the Lord for everything. You never feel he's down. Especially after the Iran scandal, he'd say that he's relying on prayer and he needs my prayers too."

One day Saliba's pastor, the Reverend Stephen King of Cherrydale Baptist Church in Arlington, Virginia, came in to get a haircut and struck up a conversation with North after he heard Ollie telling Saliba that he had stopped to help some people whose car had gotten stuck in a ditch.

"Literally, their car had gotten stuck in a ditch and he used his four-wheel drive to help them out," King recalls. "In conversation he learned that they were brothers and sisters in Christ... He was talking about helping the people out of the ditch, and how his back had been healed through prayer, and it was obvious that he had a very close relationship with Christ.... He didn't mention any names. He just said that a brother put his hands on him and prayed for him. I thought it was wonderful, and it really seemed to strengthen his faith and motivate him spiritually. Our whole con-

versation was about Christ and the healing process. What stood out
was his personality, his winsomeness and his sincerity.... Six to
eight months later I was at a briefing on the Contras he gave at the
White House for the National Association of Evangelical Ministers.
I told my wife, 'That's the man I told you about in the barber shop.'
He was superb. He was extremely convincing and persuasive.
Honestly, all the ministers were equally impressed."

North belonged to the Church of the Apostles, a charismatic
Episcopal church in Fairfax, Virginia, outside Washington that has
become one of the fastest growing parishes in the country. Ten
years ago the congregation numbered only about eighty people;
today more than two thousand turn up on Sundays at the auditorium of Fairfax High School, where the church holds its services to
accommodate the large crowds.

The Apostles' growth reflects inroads that the charismatic movement has made among historically staid Episcopalians since 1960
when Father Dennis Bennett, rector of St. Mark's Episcopal
Church in Van Nuys, California, made headlines nationally by in-
forming his incredulous congregation that he had prayed in
tongues. "We are Episcopalians, not a bunch of wild-eyed hillbil-
lies!" shouted one church member at Bennett.

But since then the Episcopal diocese has opened its doors to the
charismatics in measured tolerance, to the point where today about
ten percent of the country's 7,800-odd Episcopal parishes are charismatic. While membership in the mainstream Episcopal church
has been declining for years, charismatic ranks are growing.

Compared to the traditionalists, the charismatics exhibit a far
greater sense of urgency and zeal while actively blending morality,
patriotism and the family with their religion. Charismatics feel a
sense of mission, of being standard-bearers for a social morality that
has its roots in the gospel. Born-again, they feel they are special
and on a path of righteousness in a world roiling with turmoil and
sin. The traditionalists are generally more content with their lot,
have less of a sense that they have divined The Way, and do not
believe that Armageddon is necessarily at hand.

On Sunday mornings at North's Church of the Apostles the atmosphere is decidedly informal, even fun. Some members of the over-
whelmingly white congregation are dressed up, others are not.
Kids roam about the aisles while the service is in progress. The
music is upbeat—Up-With-People-style—mostly from guitars and
pianos. There's a good deal of hugging, even among the men.

Words to hymns and prayers are flashed on a huge overhead slide projector, and an American flag is prominently displayed on stage nearby. When songs are played the congregation claps along in rhythm and many people extend both arms skyward in classic charismatic pose. After a song is finished there is much murmuring to "Praise the Lord."

At one point in the service members of the congregation are asked to pray with their neighbors. People join hands and ask each other if there is anything they would like to pray about. Visitors are welcomed enthusiastically. Afterward ministers fan out to different sections of the auditorium and offer communion.

At one typical Sunday service attended by North and his family in July of 1987 Rev. Brian Cox delivered a sermon on the theme of destiny. The implication was that the congregants did not shape their own lives. Rather, they were living a life preordained for them by God.

"What do you understand to be God's plan for your life now, and what are you doing about it?" Cox asked them. "All of us live in families, all of us live in some kind of neighborhood, most of us work, some of us go to school, some of us . . . are homemakers, but wherever we are, the Lord has put us there to make the difference for Him. To bring glory to the Kingdom. . . . The places where you are . . . that's no accident. That is part of God's plan. That is part of what He wants you to glorify for His kingdom. Ministry is not just what we do here at the church . . . I believe that most ministry is meant to be out there in the world."

Cox also told his assembled that to get closer to God, they should consider, "the gift of tongues."

"I've discovered a very interesting thing," he said. "I have found myself praying less and less . . . in English and more and more in the spirit. Because what happens when you pray in the spirit is that you are turning over control of prayer to the holy spirit. Because it says here in Verse 27 that the spirit intercedes for the saints in accordance with God's will. . . . Now I don't want to suggest that someone who lacks the prayer language, that they're somehow deficient. I don't want to suggest that prayer language is a sign that someone is definitely saved and other people are not. Prayer language is one manifestation of the holy spirit . . . If you find that this is something that you've been resisting in your life, if you've said, 'I don't want to speak in tongues,' or, 'The Lord hasn't seen fit to give me that gift,' I would ask you to reconsider that thought. Perhaps this is a gift God wants to give you."

Cox closed by saying that not only did God have an individual destiny for each of them, he also had a "corporate destiny" for the Church of the Apostles. "There is no other church like Church of the Apostles... There never has been. There never will be. God has not called Church of the Apostles to do everything, but I believe that God has a destiny for this congregation... I believe that the destiny is in the process of unfolding, and I believe that the most exciting days of being a part of this family lie ahead of us."

At the White House North networked with and gave briefings on Central America to, all the leaders of the Christian Right, including Jerry Falwell of Moral Majority, the Christian Broadcasting Network's Pat Robertson, who would soon become a Republican presidential candidate, and Tim LeHaye, head of the American Coalition of Traditional Values—a group of about two hundred fifty leading evangelical ministers. North shared the pastors' vision of God and country, and to the preachers Ollie was a shining example of American righteousness.

"He struck me, as he struck the American people, as a man of integrity, and as a man with a willingness to pay any price to get a job done," says LeHaye, whose wife Beverly runs a conservative group called Concerned Women for America that North addressed twice. "The ministers were extremely impressed. Most of us had the feeling that when the Marine Corps can produce men like this, there's still hope for America."

Robertson enlisted North to help him in obtaining military records in support of the $10-million libel suit he filed in 1986 against former congressman Paul (Pete) McCloskey, the California Democrat, who had claimed that Robertson used his father's political influence in the early fifties to avoid combat in the Korean War. North agreed to help and put Robertson in touch with a Marine general in the Pentagon who provided copies of the service records. After North was fired Robertson called to tell him he thought he was getting "a raw deal" and publicly said he thought North was being offered up as a "sacrificial lamb."

On at least one occasion North used his born-again associations to help divert aid to the Contras, according to Rev. Phil Derstine, of the Florida-based Gospel Crusade, Inc. Derstine says North provided him with contacts among Contra leaders which facilitated the delivery by his group of humanitarian aid to the resistance. North's efforts also helped Derstine's group produce a documentary film extolling the Contra cause called *Studies in Faith and Freedom.*

"We had been in Honduras and Central America for twenty years," says Derstine. "After the war in Nicaragua heated up we learned that refugees were pouring into our missions, but we hadn't known much about the problem. There were a lot of stories about churches being burned down and pastors being harassed, so we figured we'd go down and investigate . . . It was definitely a Christian issue because Christians were being persecuted."

North heard about Derstine's trip and called to offer his help. "Oliver North called and told me that he was a born-again believer and he hoped we had a successful trip and said he'd help us in any way possible . . . I think Ollie was excited that a religious group was looking into the matter. No one else from the Christian standpoint was interested . . . It was interesting that he introduced himself as a born-again believer. I was pleased, not skeptical. He said 'Praise the Lord' a few times, and was talking like a good Christian."

Derstine and his group had planned only to go to Honduras and speak with Contras based there, but when they arrived they learned that North had arranged for a private American plane to fly them to a Contra camp thirty miles inside Nicaragua. They got film footage of Contras praying at the front, and established useful contacts with the resistance. When they returned to Honduras they were debriefed by the State Department. Derstine met North again in February of 1986 at the convention of the National Religious Broadcasters when Ollie gave the group his special Contra briefing and slide presentation.

North knew his Bible. He kept a copy in his office and occasionally he could be seen reading the Bible walking to work in the morning after parking his gray station wagon that sported the pro-life bumper sticker, GOD IS PRO-LIFIC. He liked to quote from psalms—"The Lord is my shepherd," or "The Lord is my ever-present strength."

Even with people he did not know to be religious North would not hesitate to use Christian phrases during everyday conversation.

"Ollie would say, 'Godspeed and God bless,' instead of 'See you later,'" says Neil Livingstone, the author and consultant on terrorism who is a friend of North. "There's a mystical side to Ollie. To Ollie, religion, flag and family are all part of the same makeup . . . I think he started to feel destined—that he was going to move and shake and transcend. He thought he could get down-and-dirty in the trenches and none of it would rub off on him."

Robert McFarlane agrees. Religion, he said, was "a very strong part of North's makeup. He had kind of a metaphysical orientation to things . . . Ollie did often make clear to me in conversation, as well as to peers on the staff, that prayer, and confidence in the fact that he was being led by the Holy Spirit, was very matter-of-fact with him. He always felt that what he was doing was justified because he was accountable to a higher authority."

When Don Fortier, who had been North's nominal boss in the NSC's political-military affairs unit and later Poindexter's deputy, contracted liver cancer, North read the Bible to him in the hospital and gave him spiritual counseling. When Fortier died, North accepted it as God's will.

One former NSC colleague recalls that once, when he was having difficulty getting North to comply with a request, Ken deGraffenried, the NSC's intelligence director, suggested that he go into North's office and read to him from the New Testament. Partly as a joke and partly out of curiosity to see what would happen, the official did so.

"Ollie glowered at me at first, but soon he turned into a pussy-cat," the official recalls. "He became placid and cooperative—and said he was going to do whatever it was I was asking for . . . On another occasion I heard him say that he had been wounded in battle and he felt that he had been spared by God in order to do something important, and this was it . . . He made it very clear he believed in God's will and that what he was doing was something extremely important and that it was a mission. And that if somebody was not cooperative he not only was hurting the country, he was not doing God's will . . . I don't think there's any question he thought he was doing God's work at the NSC."

CULMINATIONS

AFTER returning from Tehran, McFarlane, North and Howard Teicher discussed their trip at a meeting with President Reagan, Vice-President Bush, Donald Regan and Poindexter.

McFarlane did most of the talking and argued that there should be no further arms sales to Iran and probably no more meetings until all the hostages were freed. "The president didn't comment, really," McFarlane told the Tower Commission, "but that was not untypical. He would often hear reports [and] say that he would think about it . . ."

At this point it had been nearly a year since the NSC staff first floated the idea of renewed contacts with Iran, and during that time Iran had been sold 1,508 TOW missiles, 18 HAWK missiles and some HAWK spare parts. Tehran had also been given sensitive U.S. intelligence information on Iraqi orders of battle. Although all this had netted the release of only one hostage, and William Buckley had died in captivity, Reagan, through his silence and inaction at the McFarlane debriefing, implicitly allowed the initiative to continue.

All concerned had incentives to go on. Iran was still desperate for weapons, the U.S. still wanted its hostages back, Israel wanted better relations with Tehran, and Ghorbanifar wanted his money.

To finance the HAWK parts shipment, Ghorbanifar had borrowed $15 million from Adnan Khashoggi, but McFarlane and North had brought only one pallet of spare parts to Tehran, and Iran had refused to pay—leaving Ghorbanifar unable to repay Khashoggi.

The Israelis and Ghorbanifar knew that Washington had to be placated by the release of at least one hostage in order to be credibly led on. Israel therefore urged Ghorbanifar to pull off a release in time for the July 4 Independence Day celebration and the Statue of Liberty's 100th anniversary. On July 2 Ghorbanifar sent word to Jerusalem that he could deliver, and Amiram Nir excitedly called North, telling him to prepare for the release of one hostage in time for the July 4 bash. North immediately sent a hostage-debriefing team to the U.S. base at Weisbaden, Germany. But there was no release.

Poindexter chewed North out for raising hopes falsely, while North, feeling betrayed, sent word that he didn't want to talk to Nir again until further notice.

Meanwhile on the Contra front North's name was popping up in the press again with increasing frequency, notably in the Miami *Herald*, which published several articles spotlighting North as the focal point of a systematic White House effort to sustain the Contras militarily in apparent violation of the Boland Amendment. The publicity prompted Congress to launch another investigation into whether the Administration was complying with Boland.

Representative Ronald Coleman, a Texas Democrat, introduced a resolution of inquiry on June 4 that plainly had North as its target. "My resolution of inquiry seeks answers and information on two central questions," Coleman said. "Did Lieutenant Colonel North develop and implement a plan for Contra funding in the event that Congress did adopt the Boland Amendment? . . . Second, what was the degree of [his] involvement with the Contra high command before, during and after the Boland Amendment became the law of this land? Did he assure the Contra generals the Administration would find a way to ensure continued funding and assistance, even in the event of a congressional ban? Did he, as alleged, provide regular tactical and logistical assistance to the Contra high command on a regular basis? Did Lieutenant Colonel North then implement a sham network of intermediaries to filter his continued advice to the Contra generals, in direct violation of at least the spirit of the Boland language?"

Coleman said he was introducing the resolution "very reluctantly," but added: "No one can be allowed to operate above the law of this great country—least of all those officials obligated to defend our Constitution."

Poindexter worried about North's increasingly high profile. "I am afraid you are letting your operational role become too public," he wrote North in a computer message. "From now on I don't want you to talk to anybody else, including Casey, except me about any of your operational roles. In fact, you need to quietly generate a cover story that I have insisted that you stop."

This admonition was in response not only to the publicity North had been receiving, but to Poindexter's learning that Ollie had discussed selling the Enterprise's ship *Erria* to the CIA for use in a covert operation to beam anti-Khadafy, pro-West radio programming into Libya. But the CIA declined, and the operation was never conducted. Despite Poindexter's directions, North testified that he continued to keep Casey informed about everything.

On June 25, the Coleman inquiry notwithstanding, the House voted to approve the Administration's request for $100 million in Contra aid—marking the first time in more than two years that it had voted to supply lethal aid to the Contras. With Senate support for the Administration a given, the House vote was a triumph for the White House and was received euphorically by the NSC—North in particular. Though the measure would not become law for another three months, the CIA would soon be back in business running the Contra war, and for the increasingly beleaguered North, the end of his Contra responsibilities was at least now in sight.

North felt a sense of great accomplishment. In the face of congressional determination to destroy the Contras, he had kept them alive for more than two years. He had made sure they received guns, beans and bullets to prosecute the war. He had kept faith with the resistance as he had pledged he would. And despite a few storm clouds on the horizon, in the form of a handful of pesky reporters and the new congressional inquiry, he had basically been able to keep the details of his operation a secret.

Meanwhile the press attention North was receiving, together with the House vote allowing the CIA to reenter the game, emboldened some North critics within the NSC to complain to Poindexter that it was time to remove the shroud of secrecy from the Contra account and take it away from Ollie.

The CIA's Vincent Cannistraro, who served as the NSC's senior director for intelligence programs, told staff counsel Paul Thompson that now that the program was going to be publicly funded again it should go through his, Cannistraro's, intelligence office and be administered in the usual way rather than in the mysterious North manner. What North had been doing with the Contras had been closely held, but rumors that he had been engaged in illegal activities were rife among NSC staffers—particularly North's critics.

One of the most vocal critics was Jackie Tillman, an ultra-

conservative former aide to United Nations Ambassador Jeane Kirkpatrick who spoke fluent Spanish and now worked in the Latin
American affairs section of the NSC. She had her own contacts among
the Contra leadership who had told her stories about North. She, in
turn, had shared some of her concerns with Cannistraro—notably
that North kept large amounts of cash in his office and was passing
some of it to Contra leaders. She warned that if this ever came out, the
Contra movement could be compromised and seriously damaged.

Though Cannistraro felt that some of what motivated Tillman was
bureaucratic jealousy because North had effectively cut her out of
the Contra action, he shared her worries. In addition, the FBI's
man on the NSC, David Major, had told him that North was trying
to interfere with a Bureau investigation into allegations that the
Contras were involved in running drugs. So Cannistraro laid out
these complaints to Thompson, together with his request that the
Contra program be brought officially onto the reservation again.

Thompson conferred with Poindexter and returned to tell Cannistraro not to worry, that all of North's activities had been approved by Attorney General Edwin Meese. Several days after that,
North came to Cannistraro and complained that Poindexter had
stripped him of much of his portfolio and was getting ready to
transfer him to London to serve in a Marine detachment there.

But nothing changed: North stayed on at the NSC and kept his
assigned responsibilities. Months later, when the Tower Commission made public the treasure-trove of internal computer messages
between the Iran-Contra principals, Cannistraro concluded—after
reading the Poindexter warning to North to lower his profile and
develop a cover story that he was doing other things—that Ollie
had been acting out a charade in complaining that the admiral had
stripped him of his duties.

North was upset at the internal sniping directed at him and blamed
much of it on Tillman, complaining to Cannistraro that she was
disruptive, incompetent and a threat to the Contras. She should be
fired, he said. When Cannistraro defended Tillman, North blew up.

Poindexter would testify that he "wanted to provide a significant
amount of cover for Colonel North and his activities." He directed
North to stop writing about his activities, so Ollie no longer wrote
"logged" memos that would be kept in NSC files. He confined most
of his writings to internal computer messages, which he believed—
incorrectly, as it turned out—were erased from the computer's
memory after they had been sent.

Poindexter also kept North's title downgraded to deputy director of political-military affairs instead of the grander special assistant to the president, for example, which could have focused more attention on Ollie. But Poindexter also saw the bureaucratic tension over North as a way of putting up another smokescreen to ease the pressure on Ollie. So in mid-July the admiral apparently leaked a story to the Washington *Times*, which reported July 15 that North's position on the NSC staff was "precarious" and that NSC "soft-liners" were conspiring to "edge him out."

When North, after reading the story, sent Poindexter an emotional note offering to resign, the admiral fired off a reassuring note in reply, virtually confessing that he was the leaker. "Now you are getting emotional again," Poindexter wrote North. "It would help if you would call Roger Fontaine [the former NSC aide who had joined the Washington *Times*] and Jerry O'Leary [another reporter for the paper] and tell them to call off the dogs. Tell them on deep background, off the record, not to be published, that I just wanted to lower your visibility so you wouldn't be such a good target for the libs... I do not want you to leave and to be honest, cannot afford to let you go."

Though Ollie was safe, he did not pass the word to his conservative pals in the press, who were now primed to weigh in with ringing defenses of him. Suzanne Garment of the *Wall Street Journal* ran a column July 18 asking: "What should you do about the NSC staffer who served as liaison to the Contras through these years? (a) Shower him with glory (b) take him to lunch (c) give him a big, fat demotion. The answer is (c), of course, which means that Lt. Col. Oliver North is in trouble.... For senior officials to turn their back on a man with Colonel North's record at a time when he is under outside attack is simply not decent behavior." Evans and Novak followed three days later with another ode to Ollie, concluding that the threat against him symbolized the gradual transformation of the NSC under Poindexter from "arbiter of interagency struggles and control point for operations to a bland paper machine that makes President Reagan victim rather than master of the bureaucracy."

Finally on July 26 a hostage was released in Beirut—Father Lawrence Jenco. But amid the joy in Washington there was also confusion, because no more weaponry had been sent and it was unclear what Ghorbanifar had unilaterally promised Tehran to win Jenco's release.

North and George Cave flew to Frankfurt the next day to meet with Ghorbanifar and Nir. Ghorbanifar said he had told Tehran that the

U.S. would deliver the remainder of the HAWK spare parts and two HAWK radar systems in return for a phased release of the hostages. In addition, the Iranians were complaining that they had been over-charged by $10 million for the HAWK spare parts, and Ghorbanifar had told them that if this could be proved, the U.S. would make amends by providing 1,000 TOW missiles free of charge.

Ghorbanifar's excursion as a lone diplomat bargaining on behalf of the United States left the Americans in an awkward position since McFarlane, in Tehran, had rejected any phased release of the hos-tages in return for the delivery of the rest of the HAWK spares. And even though Washington had not offered the concessions Ghorbanifar had just made on its behalf, if the U.S. did nothing in light of the Jenco release, Ghorbanifar would likely tell Iran that the Americans were reneging on a deal.

North and Casey were marching in lockstep on what to do next. Accede to the new Ghorbanifar demands, they advised Poindexter, or the three remaining hostages could be killed. The plan proposed by North envisioned the phased release of the three hostages in return for the phased delivery of the rest of the Hawk spares, the two radar units and 1,000 more TOW missiles. Poindexter agreed, and on July 30 he obtained President Reagan's approval to proceed.

McFarlane and Poindexter's earlier decision to hold to all-or-noth-ing terms had thus been reversed.

Though the first step of North's phased plan called for the release of another hostage before the HAWK parts were delivered, that part of the plan was quickly glossed over by the U.S. side, which decided to go ahead and deliver the spares on August 4 — despite the fact that no hostage had been released. Iran promptly complained about the quality of the August 4 delivery, saying that 177 items that it had ordered were not included in the shipment and that 63 of the items sent were defective.

On August 6 the Iranians sent Israel a 1985 price list for HAWK spare parts, proving that they had in fact been overcharged by 600 percent. Though the Enterprise had plenty of cash on hand to give the Iranians at least a partial refund, North instructed his aide, Robert Earl, to mark up future shipments by a multiple of 3.7. North's solution to the overcharge complaint was to have the CIA prepare a price list that could justify the prices. But the agency's Office of Technical Services was unable to come up with a credible-looking made-up list.

So the deal stalled, with Ghorbanifar claiming to be still $10 million in hock to his creditors and growing increasingly restive. The Americans, for their part, were fed up with Ghorbanifar's money problems and double-dealing and decided to seek another intermediary to the Iranian government—a "second channel," as it came to be called.

North was bobbing, weaving and covering up, stamping out small brush fires breaking out around him that individually and collectively threatened to pry the lid of secrecy off the Contra operation.

In this regard North tried to use his contacts with the FBI to initiate or speed up investigations of people and groups he considered a threat. According to the final report of the congressional Iran-Contra committees, at one meeting with FBI agents in June, he complained that the Bureau had not: contacted an NSC staffer who North thought was the source of rumors linking him to allegations of Contra drug trafficking; investigated Daniel Sheehan, lawyer for the Christic Institute representing Tony Avirgan and Martha Honey in their civil suit against Secord et al.; interviewed a reporter who had claimed that North had threatened him; examined the basis and sources of allegations made against North by Senator John Kerry of Massachusetts, Senator David Durenberger of Minnesota and Representative Lee Hamilton, chairman of the House Intelligence Committee. But since none of North's complaints could be traced to foreign intelligence sources, the FBI dropped its investigation of these issues.

But North soon interested the FBI in another burr in his saddle: Jack Terrell, the former mercenary who had become disenchanted with the Contras and was now working to support the Christie Institute in its lawsuit. Secord's private eye, former CIA agent Glenn Robinette, had been trying to gather some derogatory information on Terrell. In mid–1986, the FBI, having been tipped that pro-Sandinista agents might be planning to assassinate President Reagan, had suspected that Terrell might be involved in this plot.

North heard about this and on July 15, called FBI executive assistant director Oliver "Buck" Revell, and told him he had a contact that might be helpful in the investigation of Terrell. It was Robinette, whom North promptly made available that night to meet Revell's agents. Robinette had met Terrell four days earlier while posing as a lawyer interested in collaborating with Terrell on a book-and-movie deal. Robinette said he was in daily contact with Terrell and offered to help the FBI in its investigation.

Terrell had been quoted in the press as a source for allegations that some of those involved in the Contra-support operation were engaged in gunrunning, assassination plots and drug-running, and that North

and Owen were using John Hull's ranch in Costa Rica as a base for
Contra southern front operations. Terrell seemed willing to tell his
story to whomever wanted to hear it. He talked to the FBI, the U.S.
Attorney's office in Miami, and he was also working with the staff of
Senator John Kerry, the Massachusetts Democrat. Then, after Terrell
appeared on the CBS television program "West 57th" in late June,
North and Secord decided to put Robinette on the case to try and
determine precisely how much Terrell knew of their operations.

In a July 17 memo, apparently written for Secord, Robinette
concluded that "Terrell may actually possess enough information—
either from first-hand personal knowledge or from other sources—
to be dangerous to our objectives. A review of my notes made from
meetings with Terrell appear that what he knows . . . could be embarrassing to RS [Richard Secord] and whoever . . ."

Robinette went on to suggest that the Enterprise invest in a helicopter service that Terrell wanted to start in Costa Rica, with the
understanding that "the 'investors' would require that he reduce or
stop his 'political talking' as it would 'affect our investment.'"

The same day North wrote Poindexter a memo about Terrell,
saying that several months earlier he had become "an active participant in the disinformation/active measures campaign" against the
Contras and was now a "terrorist threat." North told Poindexter
that the FBI would be meeting that night with "the Project Democracy security officer." He did not name Robinette, but explained
that after the West 57th story, "Project Democracy officials decided
to use its security apparatus to attempt to determine how much
Terrell actually knows about their operations."

North added that the FBI was "preparing a counter-intelligence/
counter-terrorism operations plan for review by OSG-TIWG tomorrow." The acronymns stood for the Operations Sub Group—the
interagency group on terrorism that North had been the driving force
in creating in the aftermath of the Vice-President's task force report in
January—under the Terrorist Incident Working Group.

In a memo to Poindexter on July 25 North reported that the
Operations Sub Group, which he chaired, had "made available to
the FBI all information on Mr. Terrell from other U.S. Government
agencies." North added that the FBI and the Secret Service had
put Terrell under "active surveillance."

But the Robinette memo of July 17 suggests that North's interest
in Terrell had less to do with counter-terrorism than how much Terrell knew about the Enterprise and the White House connection to
the Contra-supply operation. Terrell's voluntary statement to Jef-

frey Feldman, an assistant U.S. Attorney in Miami, had already prompted Feldman to begin an investigation into Hull, Owen, North and the Contra-supply operation—a development that triggered at least one concerned memorandum from Owen to North.

So North responded to the threat in two ways: first through Robinette in the private sector and second, while chairman of OSG, launching an investigation of Terrell.

On July 22 the FBI interviewed North, who, according to the congressional report, said he had heard of Terrell eithteen months earlier after a Contra-intelligence officer complained of Terrell's alleged brutality. North also said he had heard that Terrell had tried to import guns into a Central American country and had claimed to be a former Special Forces soldier and a CIA agent.

Asked about Secord, North said Secord ran an import-export business and consulted for the Pentagon, but he stressed that Secord did not work for him. According to the report, North also added that neither he nor his staff was responsible for supporting, funding or administering Contra programs, and he denied that he was involved in any covert operations run from the U.S.

The FBI followed Terrell for a time, but concluded he was no threat to assassinate the president and dropped its investigation. There are indications the Bureau suspected it had been used by North to try and harm Terrell. Buck Revell later told the *Wall Street Journal* that he and other FBI agents were concerned that North might be using Secord and Robinette to run a "plumber's unit" from the White House aimed at gathering intelligence to discredit political opponents.

One former Contra activist who worked with North, Philip Mabry of Texas, says that he monitored leftist groups in the Fort Worth area that opposed the Administration's policies in Central America. Mabry said he took photographs of demonstrators and collected their literature, then sent the material to North at the White House.

Mabry says North also asked him to write the FBI to urge it to investigate these opposition groups. Mabry did so, in November of 1984, naming such groups as the National Network in Solidarity with the Nicaraguan People and the Inter-Religious Task Force on Central America—as well as such individuals as former U.S. Ambassador to El Salvador Robert White, actress Jane Fonda, singer Jackson Browne and Raymond Bonner, a former New York *Times* reporter. Mabry received a letter in reply from Revell saying, "Your concerns and comments will be carefully reviewed."

Apparently the FBI was engaged in this sort of activity anyway. In January of 1988, the Center for Constitutional Rights, a New Yorklawyers' group, revealed that it had obtained 1200 pages of files under the Freedom of Information Act showing that from 1981 to 1985 the FBI had conducted surveillance of hundreds of individuals and groups who opposed the Administration's policies in Central America.

On August 6 North met with eleven members of the House Intelligence Committee, which was pursuing Representative Coleman's resolution of inquiry. Significantly, the meeting took place not on the committee's turf but on North's—in the White House Situation Room.

Adhering closely to the script Robert McFarlane had given Congressman Barnes a year earlier, North used the broadest of brush strokes, explaining that his job was to coordinate contacts with the Contras and assess their viability as a democratic unit. He assured the committee that he "did not in any way, nor at any time, violate the spirit, principles or legal requirements of the Boland Amendment." He denied he had raised money for the Contras or given them military advice. He said he had only a "casual" relationship with Robert Owen and had never given him any guidance. And he had had no contacts with Gen. John Singlaub in 1985 or 1986.

Though North would later testify he did not tell the truth to the intelligence committee, Chairman Lee Hamilton, the Indiana Democrat, had no inkling of that at the time. He said that he appreciated Poindexter's "good-faith effort" in arranging the meeting, and that he was satisfied with North's answers. Hamilton told Representative Coleman the inquiry was finished. "Based on our discussions and review of the evidence provided, it is my belief that the published press allegations cannot be proven," Hamilton wrote in a letter to Coleman.

North, having dodged another bullet, sent Poindexter a message telling him things had gone swimmingly.

"Well done," Poindexter responded.

Then there was the case of the Honduran general, José Bueso Rosa, who had been convicted in the United States of plotting to assassinate the president of Honduras in 1984, and sentenced in July of 1986 to serve five years in a federal prison. North considered Rosa a "friend" of Washington who had been helpful in providing Honduran bases as well as training and support for the Contras. Fearing that if Rosa had to serve a prolonged federal prison term he might reveal what he knew about the official U.S.

role in aiding the Contras while Boland was in effect, North intervened with the Justice Department to ask for leniency for Rosa.

In a September 17 message to Poindexter, North wrote that Rosa had been under the impression he would only have to serve a matter of days or a few weeks at a minimum security institution before being released. North fretted that if Rosa had to serve five years "he will break his long-standing silence about the Nicaraguan resistance and other sensitive operations." He said he had scheduled a meeting for the following morning with Associate Attorney General Stephen Trott, the FBI's Revell, and Assistant Secretary of State Elliott Abrams to explore the possibility of getting Rosa a pardon, clemency, a sentence reduction or simply deportation. The purpose, said North, was to try to keep Rosa from "feeling like he was lied to in [the] legal process and start spilling the beans."

Poindexter replied: "You may advise all concerned that the president will want to be as helpful as possible to settle this matter."

North enlisted the aid of Gen. Paul Gorman, former commander of the U.S. military group in Central America, and the CIA's Dewey Clarridge, in his meetings with various officials and in making the case that Rosa had only been peripherally involved in the plot to assassinate President Roberto Suazo Cordova. The Justice Department initially resisted, saying that Rosa was a terrorist, and pointing out that the plot was to have been financed through the sale of more than $10 million worth of cocaine in the U.S. Rosa and his co-conspirators had planned to mount a coup during the civil unrest they expected to follow the murder of Cordova.

North persisted in arguing that Rosa was a "friend of the government" who had been "always ready to assist us" and "helpful in accommodating our military." Finally the Justice Department agreed to have Rosa transferred to the minimum security federal prison at Elgin Air Force Base in Florida.

There was still another threat of exposure that September, this time from Costa Rica, where the newly elected president, Oscar Arias, was planning to reveal the existence of the secret airstrip for the Contra southern front at Santa Elena. The CIA station chief in San José, Joe Fernandez, called North and said Arias was planning a press conference to say that the airstrip had been built with the assistance of several U.S. government officials including North, Fernandez and Ambassador Lewis Tambs as part of an American operation to resupply the Contras—in violation of Costa Rican law.

North immediately called Elliott Abrams and told him the Arias press conference had to be stopped. North, Abrams and Tambs conducted a conference call and thrashed out a plan. Arias was soon scheduled to make a state visit to Washington. Tambs would call Arias and tell him his visit would be at risk if the press conference went forward. Tambs made the call and was able to persuade Arias-not to make the announcement—at least for the time being.

In his report to Poindexter, North tended to exaggerate his own role in averting this latest crisis, saying he had personally called Arias: "I recognize that I was well beyond my charter in dealing with a head of state this way, and in making threats/offers that may be impossible to deliver."

Replied the admiral: "Thanks, Ollie. You did the right thing, but let's try to keep it quiet."

But on September 25 Arias decided to go forward with at least part of the story, though not accusing the United States directly. He had his interior minister announce the discovery of "a secret airstrip in Costa Rica that was over a mile long and which had been built and used by a company called Udall Services for supporting the Contras." Robert Olmstead, the alias used by North's Marine buddy William Haskell, was named as the man who set up the airfield as a "training base for U.S. military advisers."

North went into action, assuring Poindexter that "all appropriate damage-control measures . . . to keep USG [United States government] fingerprints off this" were being undertaken. Udall Resources, one of Secord's Panamanian shell companies, would "cease to exist by noon today," North told Poindexter. "The office is now gone, as are all files and paperwork." He added that "Olmstead is not the name of the agent—Olmstead does not exist."

The New York *Times* picked up the press conference story, and North quickly drafted press "guidance" for the administration if there were any follow-up inquiries. The guidance, approved by Poindexter, said that the airstrip had been offered to Costa Rica "by the owners of the property who had apparently decided to abandon plans for a tourism project . . . No U.S. government funds were allocated or used in connection with this site, nor were any U.S. government personnel involved in its construction. Any further inquiries should be referred to the government of Costa Rica."

Though North had again concealed the U.S. hand, he recommended to Poindexter that Arias be "punished" for making even the more limited disclosure.

Secord's business partner, Albert Hakim, took the lead in developing the Iranian second channel. This placed Hakim, who estimated a reopened trade market between the United States and Iran to be worth $15 billion, in an apparent conflict-of-interest position trying to promote his own business interests while at the same time doing a diplomatic turn for his adopted country.

Hakim contacted an Iranian expatriate whom he had once employed, and this man, after making it clear he expected *baksheesh* for his services, produced a new candidate to deal with Washington. This official was a leading young member of the Iranian Revolutionary Guard and a nephew of Parliament Speaker Rafsanjani. The Americans quickly began calling him "the Relative."

The Relative flew to Brussels for a debut meeting with Secord and Hakim on August 25. Secord came away impressed. In a message to North he grandly described the discussions as a "comprehensive tour de force," and said that "my judgment is that we have opened up a new and probably much better channel into Iran."

The U.S. learned that the Relative's meeting with Secord and Hakim had gained support in Tehran. The deputy prime minister, who had met with the McFarlane delegation in May, called George Cave to say that his boss approved of the Relative's contacts with Washington.

On September 9 Poindexter met with President Reagan to give him an update on the Iran initiative and the tentative emergence of the second channel. But North worried that ominous news that same day might scuttle the entire program: another American, fifty-three-year-old Frank Reed, director of the Lebanon International School, was kidnapped in Beirut.

But the new kidnapping evidently gave Reagan no pause. Poindexter emerged from the meeting with instructions for North to continue developing the second channel while, if possible, dropping Ghorbanifar. However, if the second channel did not produce, Ghorbanifar could still be used.

Three days later, on September 12, another American—Joseph Ciccipio, age fifty-six, acting comptroller of the American University in Beirut—was abducted. North suspected that the deputy prime minister—edged out by the Relative as Iran's new channel to the United States—was responsible for the Ciccipio kidnapping, but blamed Reed's seizure on another group.

And so the two hostages whose release Washington had gained in more than a year's dealing with Iran—Weir and Jenco—had been canceled out in four days with the kidnapping of two more. If there was worry or outrage among those in-the-know in Washington that

Tehran was merely replenishing its hostage supply to maximize its leverage with the U.S., the concern was muted. Preparations went forward to test the Relative's bona fides by flying him to Washington for a look-see.

North wanted the CIA to handle the arrangements for flying the Relative and his aides to Washington, but as usual the agency did not move fast enough to suit Ollie. He complained in a note to Poindexter: "Why Dick [Secord] can do something in five minutes that the CIA cannot do in two days is beyond me—but he does." Secord eventually made the arrangements, and the Relative, along with an aide and a security guard, arrived in Washington on September 19. Secord booked them into the Sheraton Hotel in Tyson's Corner near his office.

The first meeting took place in North's office at the EOB adjacent to the White House, while the second session was at Secord's Stanford Technology Trading Group International in suburban Vienna, Virginia. Both meetings were secretly recorded by the CIA.

The Relative was carrying a wish-list of arms, including offensive weapons to be used in the war against Iraq, and he requested technical assistance in the use of some of the weapons. North said that in principle he saw no problem with most of the items on the list, but he said Iran would have to pay market rates for the arms—at least until the hostage issue was resolved. North urged the Relative to pay Ghorbanifar the money owed him so that he and his financiers could be kept quiet.

Ollie then gave a dissertation on the need to solve the hostage problem before U.S.-Iranian relations could be normalized. It was an interesting variation on the speech North had made to the Iranians numerous times before. As if to convey the impression that the United States was not obsessed with the issue, North said that while the hostages were important, thousands of Americans died every year from car accidents and lung cancer—a seeming non sequitur unless viewed as an attempt to put hostage deaths into some larger perspective more attractive to the Iranians:

"The issue of hostages and terrorism must be dealt with since it is a political obstacle," North told the Relative. "On the other hand, you should realize that fifty-two thousand people in the United States died last year in automobile accidents and one hundred thirty-thousand died from lung cancer. Five United States hostages rarely make the newspapers or the television. But because this is a democracy, if the president is found to be helping Iran with this obstacle still in the way, it would be very difficult to explain to our people."

While the Relative said he was confident the hostage impasse could be resolved, he displayed what some of the Americans thought was a refreshing burst of candor when he acknowledged that Iran's influence over the Hizballah captors was limited. Tehran could probably get some of the hostages freed, but not all, he said.

The Relative took up the issue of the Da'wa prisoners—the Shiite terrorists who were being held in Kuwait. North said the U.S. could not interfere in Kuwait's affairs but predicted that if Iran renounced terrorism, Kuwait would free the prisoners in phases. For the moment, at least, this issue seemed finessed.

The Relative also sought American help in overthrowing Iraqi President Saddam Hussein (North said the U.S. could make no such commitments), and in raising the price of oil (Ollie said Washington had "similar interests with respect to oil"). Pending the development of more formal relations, the Relative also suggested forming a joint U.S.-Iranian commission to nurture the ties between the two countries. North agreed and promptly appointed himself, Secord and George Cave as the American representatives.

Finally, the Relative asked for a public signal from Washington that relations were indeed improving, so that his superiors in Tehran might be reassured. North agreed to insert a phrase in an upcoming Voice of America Farsi broadcast thanking Iran for its assistance in resolving the recent hijacking of a Pan American Airways plane.

Late the night of September 19, at the end of the first day's talks, North and Hakim took the Relative on a tour of the White House.

North was feeling upbeat about the direction the discussions were taking with the second channel. He wanted to impress the Relative with the grandeur of the White House mansion and show off his own bona fides so that the Iranian might be assured he was dealing with the highest reaches of American government. North wanted to make sure this trip stood out in marked contrast to the disastrous Tehran visit the Americans had made in May—maybe give the Relative something to talk to the Revolutionary Guard about back home.

They looked in at the cordoned-off Oval Office and paused for a minute or two so that the Relative could contemplate the locale and the mystique attached to the most powerful political position in the world. What did the Ayatollah have to match this?

Then they strolled through the White House corridors, North the enthusiastic tour guide, pointing out this room and that, noting various objets d'art and discoursing expansively on American history as Hakim translated.

North paused before a painting of Theodore Roosevelt and told the Relative how Roosevelt had helped negotiate the end of the Russo-Japanese War of 1904–05, thereby winning the Nobel Peace Prize. Ronald Reagan and the Untied States would be willing to lend their good offices to help end the war between Iran and Iraq, North said.

Ollie also tried to keep the mood light. Stopping before an odd painting showing a group of dogs sitting around a conference table, with one of the dogs asleep, North told the Relative that the picture showed the Reagan cabinet at work, and that the sleeping dog was Bill Casey. The Relative roared with laughter.

"That broke the ice," Hakim recalls.

Secord, North and the rest of the Americans were amused to learn that the Relative and his small retinue could not allow the rare opportunity of visiting the land of the Great Satan to go by without partaking in the delights of the flesh. Free, however briefly, from Tehran and all its sexually repressed clerics, the Iranians repaired to their Virginia hotel room and waited to be serviced by some American ladies of the night.

But it took a while. According to Secord, the Iranians' CIA handlers had to place forty-four calls to local escort services before they could turn up some girls willing to make the trek over to the Tyson's Corner Sheraton. The CIA bugged the Iranians' rooms, of course, and Secord later reviewed the sometimes titillating transcripts of the tapes.

If the Relative and his friends had just proved that all boys will be boys, the next day and throughout the talks they still persisted in trying to claim the religious and moral high ground. There was a constant effort to invoke God's name and support, to try to show that Tehran was on the side of the angels.

Once, during the first day of talks in North's office, the Relative had insisted on taking a break so that he could pray. But he didn't have his customary prayer rug. So one of North's aides, Craig Coy, offered his gym towel. The Relative took the towel, went into Robert Earl's office to pray, then resumed the talks with North.

"When you talk to Iranians from this revolutionary government you're subjected to all kinds of religious boilerplate: Ali Akbar, etc.," says Secord. "We used to call it 'Page Number One.' They always try to establish that God is on their side. It's hard to deal with someone if they have God on their side."

So North, no slouch in the God department himself, quickly moved to play his own religion card with the second channel in an effort at least to neutralize the holier-than-thou tack. He kept a Bible prominently displayed on the negotiating table and stressed that President Reagan was a man of God who believed deeply in the Holy Book. North even cited some of Reagan's alleged favorite passages in Genesis and Galatians.

"Ollie was quite dramatic about it, and gave them a little lesson," remembers Secord, chuckling. "He talked about the God of Abraham, and he returned to that theme again toward the end of the talks . . . When you're in this kind of game there's a lot of bullshit flowing back and forth. You can't just sit there and take it. We were in a cold-blooded business there. We were trying to make some headway."

Finally, both sides began kidding each other about the religious war and implicitly agreed to a truce. "During a coffee break," says Secord, "the head of the second channel said to George Cave and I: 'What in the name of God is this guy North up to? We just left a country full of *mullahs*. We come here and what do we find but another goddamn *mullah*.' He said to me, 'General, we have only one trump card, and you have taken it from us.'"

The two days of talks ended amiably but with no hard agreements. Still, the Relative had requested another meeting and agreed to stay in touch through Secord and Hakim, so North dashed off a note to Poindexter on September 22: "Talks going extremely well. They and we want to move quickly beyond the 'obstacle' of the hostages. Sincerely believe that RR can be instrumental in bringing about an end to Iran/Iraq war—à la Roosevelt w/Russo-Japanese War in 1904. Anybody for RR [Ronald Reagan] getting the same prize?"

On September 26, after the VOA item was aired, the Relative wired $7 million to the Enterprise's Swiss bank account as a deposit toward the next arms purchase, and soon sent word that Iran would like another meeting with the Americans in Frankfurt on October 6.

On October 2 North wrote Poindexter a long memo saying that the Relative had just returned to Tehran from Beirut and was promising good news about the hostages at the Frankfurt meeting. The Relative was placing a high priority on the U.S. providing a "definitive sampling of intelligence" vis-à-vis Iraq. North said he and Casey agreed that the U.S. could give Iran some information without tipping the balance of the war toward them, and that in any case, such intelligence was "highly perishable, given the dynamic nature of the conflict." Still, North suggested providing "a mix of factual and bogus information."

He said he and George Cave were being besieged with calls from Amiram Nir and the Iranian deputy prime minister, anxious about the status of the earlier agreements reached with them and worried about being ditched in favor of the second channel. North suggested that Secord be sent to Israel to "ameliorate Nir's angst over his 'new status.'"

On the religious front North also noted that the Relative would be bringing a Koran to Frankfurt as a gift, and the Americans could not afford to be one-upped. He said he had purchased a Bible that he would like President Reagan to inscribe personally with a passage from Galatians 3:8. "This particular excerpt is important in that it is a New Testament reference to Abraham, who is viewed by Moslems, Jews and Christians as the progenitor of all the world's nations," North wrote. "It would be most effective if the President hand-wrote the inscription and initialed/signed it without addressing the note to any particular person."

North also recommended that only he, Cave and Secord be permitted to deal with the Iranian intermediaries from now on—everyone else should be cut out. He concluded: "A memo from you to the President has not been prepared for obvious reasons. It is hoped that between now and 3:00 P.M. Friday you will have an opportunity to privately discuss this with the President and obtain his approvals/signatures on the steps indicated above."

The "obvious reasons" for not preparing a memo for Reagan were presumably to give the president deniability, though a signed Bible from Reagan would be Exhibit A of presidential involvement. Nonetheless, Poindexter agreed to have Reagan inscribe the Bible, and he approved the trip to Frankfurt.

Poindexter was enthusiastic about the second channel and the prospects of the Frankfurt meeting. He wrote McFarlane: "Your trip to Tehran paid off. You did get through to the top. They are playing our line back to us. They are worried about the Soviets, Afghanistan and their economy. They realize hostages are obstacle to any productive relationship with us. They want to remove the obstacle. [The Relative] has been in Beirut, says he has good news for Frankfurt. We shall see. Still insisting on group release. If this comes off, may ask you to do second round after hostages are back. Keep your fingers crossed."

McFarlane was still ready and willing on the sidelines. "If you think it would be of any value, I might be able to take a couple of months off and work on the problem," he responded to Poindexter.

"No guarantees . . . but I might be able to turn something up. Think about it."

The Frankfurt meetings were notable for the further dramatic erosion of the U.S. negotiating stance and the violation of its policies against terrorism, flights of fancy by North and the further codifying of privatization through the elevation of Hakim to the position of "Secretary of State for a Day."

North, Secord, Cave and Hakim represented the U.S. while Iran was represented by the Relative and a Revolutionary Guard intelligence official. This official had been present at the February 25–26 meetings in Frankfurt with Ghorbanifar and the deputy prime minister, and had received the U.S. intelligence briefing given then by Secord. The official had also been in evidence in Tehran during the McFarlane visit. Because he took consistently negative positions and always insisted on further concessions to Iran, some of the Americans called him "the Monster." But in the Frankfurt session he would dominate the Relative, and Hakim, considering him the key to reaching an agreement, began calling the intelligence official "the Engine."

Thus the second channel now consisted of two leading members of the Revolutionary Guard—the military arm of the most radical elements in Iran. The decision to deal with these men further undermined the original stated objectives of the U.S. in undertaking the Iran initiative: to establish ties with moderates.

The Engine described himself grandly as the "extraordinary representative of the coopertative assigned to deal with the relationship with the United States." But he made clear there was no unity in Tehran on forging better relations with Washington.

Secord began by telling the Iranians that President Reagan had approved the sale of more HAWK parts, radar units, 500 TOW missiles and three pallets of free medical supplies. North went further and said there were no longer any restrictions on the sale of offensive weapons, except that the weapons could not be the sort that would "allow and encourage" Iran to seize Baghdad.

The Relative had asked for howitzers and 500 howitzer barrels in Washington. The only "problem" North said he saw with that was that the quantities demanded would force the U.S. to open up a new production line. Secord suggested that Iran approach a friendly third country, and Washington would "look the other way." North assured the Iranians that "all of this and more can be done, but we need to fireproof our president by removing the obstacle—

meaning the hostages. Ollie then turned over the "very sensitive" real and bogus intelligence, warning that "if it ever became known that we have done this we would be finished in terms of credibility as long as President Reagan is president."

North and Secord gave their boilerplate hostage speech, promising that if only this thorny issue could be resolved, relations between the U.S. and Iran could flourish. They even raised the possibility of a new Marshall Plan—massive American financial support for Iran in rebuilding its war-torn economy.

The Engine continued the Relative's more realistic stance on the hostage issue, stressing that they did not hold the Americans and could not guarantee that the Lebanese who did would listen to Tehran "one hundred percent." Nor was there any agreement in Tehran on how the hostage question should be resolved, he said. North seemed to accept this retreat, charitably remarking that the American side sympathized with the Iranians' problems in winning the hostages' release.

On the matter of Saddam Hussein, North adopted a completely different tack from the one in Washington. He agreed that Iran was no threat to other countries in the region and said it had become apparent that it was Hussein who was preventing peace.

"Do you really believe this?" the Engine asked North.

Ollie said he did and that the "inner circle of our government knows that." Claiming to convey President Reagan's view of the Iraqi leader, North used a coarse expletive that the congressional Iran-Contra committees, in describing this exchange in their final report, deleted. When Hakim balked at making such a literal translation, North told him, "Go ahead. That's his [Reagan's] word, not mine." Reagan later told the Tower Commission that the statements quoted by North on Hussein were "pure fiction."

When the Engine at one point asked North for ideas on how to resolve the hostage impasse, North first said: "Let me give you some ammunition for your guns." He then began talking about the Da'wa prisoners. Ollie said he recognized the desire of the Hizballah Shiites holding the American hostages to win the freedom of their "brethren who are held in Kuwait as convicted terrorists." He offered assurances to the Iranians that although the U.S. had told Kuwait the prisoners were its business, Washington would not be critical if the prisoners were released. He asserted that Kuwait would release the terrorists in time if Iran promised that there "would be no more attacks on the amir of Kuwait."

By way of impressing on the Iranians the risks the U.S. was

taking in dealing with Tehran, North said that in a meeting before they left Washington to discuss whether or not to go ahead with the arms sales, Secretary of Defense Weinberger had told the president: "I don't think we should send one more screw until we have our Americans back from Beirut, because when the American people find out that this has happened, they'll impeach you."

But North also again told of Reagan's desire to play peace-broker in the Iran-Iraq war, even creating an imaginary meeting between himself and the president at Camp David in which North had presented the Relative's wish-list of arms for the chief executive's consideration. But he said Reagan ordered him to "stop coming in and looking like a gun merchant." North said the president then pounded his fist on the table and said: "I want to end the war!"

When he presented Reagan's signed Bible to the Iranians, North said: "We inside our government had an enormous debate, a very angry debate . . . over whether or not my president should authorize me to say, 'We accept the Islamic revolution of Iran as a fact . . .' He went off one whole weekend and prayed about what the answer should be, and he came back almost a year ago with that passage he wrote in front of the Bible I gave you. And he said to me, 'This is a promise that God gave to Abraham. Who am I to say that we should not do this?'"

After letting that bit of drama sink in for a moment or two, North presented a handwritten seven-point program that he said Reagan had authorized him to present as a blueprint for how the two sides should now proceed:

First, Iran would pay for 500 TOWs and the remainder of the HAWK spare parts. Second, within nine days the U.S. would deliver those items, plus the free medical supplies. Then, third, all the American hostages would be released. Fourth, Iran would pay for 1,500 more TOWs. Fifth, within nine days the U.S. would deliver the 1,500 TOWs plus technical support for the HAWKs, updated intelligence on Iraq and an American communications team that would be based in Tehran. Sixth, Iran would then release John Pattis—an American engineer who worked for a U.S. firm in Tehran and had recently been arrested and held as an alleged spy—and turn over the body of William Buckley, along with a copy of Buckley's confession. Seventh, the U.S. would then identify sources for other items on the Relative's arms list, and Iran would work to release the hostages of other nationalities also being held in Beirut.

The next day the Engine countered with his own seven-point program, which proposed a phased arms-for-hostages exchange. According to the Engine's plan the U.S. would lay out a timetable for supplying the arms on the Relative's list and commit itself to providing both offensive and defensive weaponry. Second, one hostage would be released. Third, more intelligence would be provided and the U.S. and Iran would jointly evaluate the Russian, Afghan and Iraqi situations. Fourth, Iran would "only promise" to seek the release of the remaining two hostages, but this would be linked to progress with the Da'wa prisoner issue. Fifth, shipment of the arms on the Relative's list would begin while Iran would try—but not promise—to win the release of the other two hostages. Sixth, the U.S. would work with Kuwait on the release of the Da'wa prisoners. And seventh, the U.S. and Iran would agree to work within the framework of the Hague settlement to provide Tehran with the arms it had paid for under the shah but which Washington had embargoed since the seizure of the U.S. embassy in 1979.

But the Engine presented his counterproposals to an increasingly distracted U.S. side. North had received word from home that an Enterprise plane carrying three Americans on a Contra supply flight had been shot down over Nicaragua by a SAM-7 missile. Pilot William Cooper, co-pilot Wallace "Buzz" Sawyer and a seventeen-year-old Contra radio operator were dead. The third American—ex-Marine Eugene Hasenfus—the "kicker" who tossed supplies from the plane to waiting forces below—parachuted out and survived the crash but had been captured by the Sandinistas.

The plane crash was already creating a major stir in the American press, and it would clearly take all of North's ingenuity to keep this latest bombshell from revealing the U.S. hand in the Contra operation. He decided to return to Washington immediately and tend to the crisis, but before he left Frankfurt North told the Iranians that based on the Engine's proposal, the differences between the two sides were so great they would "pass each other like ships in the night."

He said dramatically that his seven-point list had been "given to me by the president of the United States of America. And there's no way on God's green earth that I'm going to violate my instructions...That's the president's authorized list. That's all he authorized...In fact, he told me, 'Don't give away more than you have to.' That is everything he authorized me to talk about."

But North didn't want to give up either. "Why don't you guys hold this discussion after I'm gone, okay?" he suggested to the group. But he warned that if there was no acceptable proposal by the time he arrived home in Washington he would tell Poindexter there was no agreement and the second channel would have to be closed.

And then North was gone. Secord and Cave also departed. Left behind with the Iranians to represent the interests of the United States was the Iranian-born Albert Hakim—private citizen and entrepreneur.

The Contra supply flight had left Ilopango airbase in El Salvador the morning of October 5 carrying ten thousand pounds of ammunition to be dropped to Contra forces fighting in northern Nicaragua. The C–123K cargo plane flew a southern route to avoid Sandinista antiaircraft positions in the north.

When the plane did not return, the CIA station chief in Costa Rica, Joe Fernandez, mobilized Contra forces in southern Nicaragua to begin searching. Secord's man, Bob Dutton, notified North's office, and Robert Earl tried to arrange for a U.S. military search-and-rescue operation. The night of the crash Felix Rodriguez, the Contra liaison at Ilopango, called Col. Samuel Watson, an aide to Vice-President Bush, and reported that the plane could not be found. Bush's national security advisor, Donald Gregg, had learned in August from the still-restive Rodriguez that North was involved in the Contra supply operation, but Gregg says he did not inform Bush.

Then on the afternoon of October 6 the Sandinistas announced that the plane had been shot down near the Costa Rican border. Scouring the wreckage, the Sandinistas produced for reporters a card issued to Hasenfus by authorities at Ilopango identifying him as an "advisor" working with the base's "*Grupo USA.*" There were similar cards linking Cooper and Sawyer to the base. The Nicaraguans also found business cards belonging to North courier Robert Owen; P. J. Buechler, an official at the Nicaraguan Humanitarian Assistance Office (NHAO) in Washington; and an I.D. card given to pilot William Cooper by Southern Air Transport of Miami.

The Sandinistas charged that the flight was part of an operation run by the CIA—a charge soon supported by Hasenfus, who was marched off to jail and began holding press conferences and giving interviews in which he said the supply flights had been supported by CIA agents in El Salvador.

North, of course, was the linchpin of the Contra supply operation, but in addition to him, at least Fernandez, Ambassador Tambs and James Steele, the U.S. military group commander in Central America, were all government officials then involved in assisting the Contras. North would also testify that Elliott Abrams knew that the Hasenfus flight was part of the Contra supply operation that the U.S. was overseeing, though Abrams would later assert the narrow view that he was unaware of North's link to the Hasenfus flight.

Despite the official U.S. involvement in both the flight and the larger Contra operation, the administration categorically denied that it had any connection to the downed plane.

Secretary of State Shultz said the Hasenfus plane had been "hired by private people" who "had no connection with the U.S. Government at all."

There is no evidence that President Reagan knew of the specific details of the Hasenfus flight, though Poindexter and other NSC staff officials did know, and members of Bush's staff, at least, knew. Yet they permitted Reagan to make strong denials. Asked by reporters if the government had any connection to the Hasenfus flight, Reagan responded: "Absolutely none . . . There is no government connection to that at all . . . We've been aware that there are private groups and private citizens that have been trying to help the Contras—to that extent—but we did not know the exact particulars of what they're doing."

But behind the scenes, North and others were hard into a protective mode.

Before the crash was even announced Fernandez sent Dutton a secure KL–43 message worrying that the tail number of the plane could be traced: "Situation requires we do necessary damage control. Did this [aircraft] have tail number? . . . Please advise ASAP. If so, we will have to try and cover quickly as record of tail number could lead to a very serious implication."

Two days later, before North had returned from Frankfurt, plans were made at a Restricted Interagency Group (RIG) meeting attended by Abrams and the CIA's Alan Fiers, among others, to safeguard the official connection. The CIA's Vincent Cannistraro wrote Poindexter about the decisions taken at the meeting, saying that the Contras would be "asked to assume responsibility for flights and to assist families of Americans involved." The group also decided to develop press guidance, saying that there was "no USG involvement or connection but that we are generally aware of such support contracted by the Contras."

A week after the crash the Contras dutifully came forward to say it was their flight and that the U.S. government was not involved.

At the same time Abrams, North and Nestor Sanchez, the Pentagon's top Central American expert, developed a different variation of that cover story, which was that Gen. John Singlaub had been the man in the private sector who had organized the Hasenfus flight. But they didn't have a chance to consult with Singlaub before this version was passed to the press and widely reported. When Singlaub heard about it he angrily denied that he had had anything to do with the operation.

North also testified that Abrams asked him to raise some private-sector funds to arrange for the retrieval of Cooper's and Sawyer's bodies to the United States.

Meanwhile, both the FBI and federal Customs agents had appeared at the offices of Southern Air Transport in Miami. North promptly called both agencies, raised the specter of national security and tried to get the investigations delayed, limited or quashed altogether.

He told Buck Revell at the FBI that he was concerned agents investigating the crash might discover that Southern Air Transport was also involved in supporting sensitive, ongoing efforts to free the hostages in Lebanon. Ollie claimed not to know anything about the plane that was shot down.

As for Customs, North told Assistant Commissioner William Rosenblatt that his agents were investigating "good guys" who had committed "no crimes." Customs—which had recently entertained another North request to limit an investigation into allegations that Maule Aircraft Corporation of Georgia had illegally shipped four light planes into Central America to support the Contras—soon agreed to narrow its probe to the activity of the C–123 itself rather than the activities of Southern Air.

Shortly afterward Poindexter weighed in by calling Attorney General Meese to ask that he delay the FBI and Customs investigation of Southern Air, explaining that some of the airline's employees were involved in the Iran initiative. Meese passed word to then FBI Director William Webster, who agreed to stop his investigation for ten days.

Then North met with Casey. There was nothing but bad news— things were starting to unravel on both the Contra and Iran fronts. Not only were serious questions being raised about the role of the government in the Hasenfus flight, but Casey said that a friend and former legal client, Roy Furmark, had just told him that two Canadian investors Adnan Khashoggi had used to provide $10 million in bridge financing for Ghorbanifar were threatening to disclose the U.S. role in the Iranian arms transactions as well as North's role in the diversion of profits to the Contras—unless they were paid the money owed them. North and Casey considered several options in dealing with the problem, including raising still higher prices charged the second channel to generate enough cash to pay off Ghorbanifar and thus the investors, or simply taking a hard line with Khashoggi and his Canadians—telling them that if they disclosed the operations they would never get paid. In the meantime Casey ordered North to "clean up the files." Poindexter, too, urged him to destroy all his Contra files, according to North's and Poindexter's testimony.

On October 12, following several days of statements by Hasenfus to the press, North wrote McFarlane telling him of the need to get Hasenfus a lawyer and saying that he had raised $100,000 for Hasenfus—a reference that some investigators would later interpret as so-called hush money. "We urgently need to find a high-powered lawyer and benefactor who can raise a legal defense for Hasenfus in Managua," North wrote. "If we can find such persons we can. . . . hold Gene and Sally Hasenfus together (i.e., on our side). By Tuesday a Swiss lawyer should be in Managua. We should not rely on this person to represent the whole case since he is supported by covert means . . . Have also located approx. $100K from a donor who does not care if his contribution becomes known. Can you help?"

McFarlane could sense the pressure North was under. He decided to write Poindexter again: "At some point I would like to raise Ollie's situation with you. I really think he has become every Democrat's best target and as hard as it would be to lose him, it will serve your and his long term interest to send him back to the Corps."

Trying to maximize their options, North, his aide Robert Earl, and Dutton met in a bar to discuss the possibility of mounting a rescue operation to free Hasenfus, according to Earl, but nothing ever came of the idea.

The Hasenfus affair was gradually eroding the increasingly implausible Reagan Administration insistence that it not only had had nothing to do with the flight in question but was above reproach in its conduct for two years under the Boland Amendment. And within two weeks the Sandinistas turned up a provocative new paper trail that was grist for a fresh round of skeptical and negative press: phone records from the American pilots' safe house in San Salvador showing numerous calls to Secord's and North's offices.

Back in Frankfurt, Ambassador *extraordinaire* Hakim had been doing some extraordinary work. He would later testify that he felt under intense pressure from North to produce an agreement. Ollie had stressed that the president wanted at least one hostage back home in time for the midterm elections. So within twenty-four hours Hakim had hammered out what would later become widely known as "the Hakim Accords."

Hakim's nine-point plan differed substantially from North's

seven-point program and contained a number of concessions. These included: the release of only one and a half hostages (defined as one definitely and a second "with all effective possible effort"); the delivery of 500 TOWs before any hostage was released and a promise to supply 1,000 more later; providing technical support for the HAWKS, updated intelligence and an unspecified plan for the release of the 17 Da'wa prisoners in Kuwait; a reduction in the price of the TOWs by $2,400 per missile and the abandonment of the demand that William Buckley's remains be returned along with a transcript of his confession. The question of the two recently kidnapped American hostages was not addressed.

Secord returned to Frankfurt from a quick business trip to Brussels and transmitted the Hakim Accords to North by way of a KL–43 secure communications device.

Overall, the plan represented not only significant slippage in the U.S. bargaining position but another undermining of the country's policy against terrorism. In addition to continuing to sell weaponry on generous terms, the program provided for the release of only one hostage—not all three—and seemed to offer unilateral concessions on the Da'wa prisoners, though Washington had criticized countries that freed terrorists out of fear of reprisals.

In fact, on October 14 the State Department, unaware of the work concluded by Hakim just days earlier, released the following statement in response to press speculation that the Da'wa prisoners might be released in exchange for the U.S. hostages in Lebanon: "We will not negotiate the exchange of innocent Americans for the release from prison of tried and convicted murderers held in a third country, nor will we pressure other nations to do so. To make such concessions would jeopardize the safety of other American citizens and would only encourage more terrorism."

Shultz would later say of the plan negotiated by Hakim: "Our guys . . . they got taken to the cleaners."

But Shultz, as before, had been kept out of the loop. North, commending the plan to Poindexter, reported that his "donkey act" in Frankfurt had had "quite an effect" on the Iranians. The Engine had confided to Secord that if he returned to Tehran "without the hope of further help he would be sent back to the front." North minimized the concessions in the new plan and asserted that the Da'wa release could be pulled off "without any great complications." There was a need to move ahead quickly because "the situation in Lebanon is getting much worse and we may be getting close to the end of the line for any further movement," he added.

Poindexter routinely got President Reagan's approval, and North passed the good word to Ambassador Hakim.

Hakim, meanwhile, was still concerned with North's financial wherewithal. Whereas before the Tehran trip he had referred to the $200,000 "Button" account primarily as a death benefit in case Ollie met his demise among the *mullahs*, now Hakim and his Geneva-based American lawyer, William Zucker, were pondering a way to get at least some of the money to North—perhaps to help out down the road with his children's education.

The problem was it was illegal to give money to a government employee. Before the trip to Tehran Zucker had met with Betsy North in Philadelphia and gathered information about the North family with a view to channeling money through relatives. But Zucker had ultimately deemed that approach not feasible. Then, according to Hakim, Zucker had suggested the possibility of creating a job for Mrs. North by paying someone to employ her— maybe through a real estate developer, or by giving Mrs. North the commission on the sale of a piece of property.

On October 10, over lunch in Geneva, Zucker asked Washington lawyer David Lewis for his advice on the possibility of transferring $70,000 to someone in the U.S. through a real estate deal.

"We got into a discussion of the real estate transaction," Lewis testified before the Iran-Contra committees. "I guess I was asking some questions about the nature of the property or what was involved. And Mr. Zucker indicated to me that there wasn't a specific property involved . . . I guess I got the impression . . . that he had a wealthy client who wanted to . . . reward someone here in the U.S. and was looking for a business transaction to do it in. And we discussed ways that that might be done.

"But then as we went on, he began to indicate to me that, in fact, it was not necessary that there even be a real business transaction. He essentially was looking for a cover for someone to merely pay money to a certain person here in the U.S. I then asked him who the person was, and he said the person was the wife of someone in the White House . . . The money was earned by the person in the White House in some unrelated matter, but they did not want to pay the money to the person in the White House because of his sensitive position. I then asked him who the person in the White House was, and to the best of my recollection he said it was Lieutenant Colonel Oliver North."

Hakim would testify that in all his dealings with North after the

Zucker-Betsy North meeting in Philadelphia before the trip to Tehran, Ollie did not protest the attempt to pass money to him, or otherwise discuss the subject. "Basically what I did was I put a wheel in motion, and then if the North family wanted to open the door to my notion, they could," Hakim said. "If they wanted to close the door to it, they could also do that."

But apparently the real estate caper was never attempted, and North testified that no money was ever transferred to him or members of his family.

Hakim said temptation had been offered to North on other occasions, but he had resisted. In one of the negotiating sessions with Tehran, the Iranians had presented North with an expensive Persian rug as a gift, along with some pistachio nuts. He declined the rug, saying that as a government official he could not accept any gifts. But then he took a handful of the pistachios and said, "However, I will accept this."

North set about implementing the Hakim Accords—despite the fact that on October 21 another American, Edward Tracy, was kidnapped in Beirut—the third kidnapping in six weeks.

On October 28 500 TOW missiles were delivered to Iran. The following day North, Secord, Hakim and Cave met with the Relative and the Engine in Mainz, Germany, south of Frankfurt, to discuss the promised release of one or two U.S. hostages now that the TOWs had been delivered and to implement the rest of the nine-point agreement.

The meeting began ominously with an announcement by the Relative that dissension in Tehran over dealing with the Americans had prompted opponents of the initiative to publish five million pamphlets revealing the McFarlane visit in May. In addition, a faction of Hizballah radicals had published an account of the ongoing negotiations between Iran and the United States for distribution in Lebanon. These events had created such a stir in Tehran that the Relative and the Engine said they had almost been prevented from coming to Germany for the meeting at hand.

Worried about dissent in his country, the Relative asked North precisely who in the U.S. government supported the initiative. North said Reagan, Bush, Casey, Poindexter and Donald Regan were all in favor, while Shultz and Weinberger were opposed. "No one else counts," Ollie said, adding that Congress would not be informed until the hostages were released.

Speaking of the hostages, North said he couldn't understand why

the Iranians did not just "exercise every possible amount of leverage they've got to get those people out." He said this was puzzling
because "we agree that as soon as they're out we can do all kinds of
good things . . . The big problem I've got is the whole damn appearance of bartering over . . . bodies." Trying to move the process
along, North then divulged some sensitive intelligence information
designed to help Iran in its war with Iraq.

The prospect of the U.S. giving Iran long-term military assistance if more hostages were released dominated the agenda. The
Relative said Iranian Parliament Speaker Rafsanjani had taken a
personal interest in getting the country's inoperable Phoenix missiles battle-ready. Iran needed technical help.

"I'll tell you what I'll do," said the Relative. "You send that technician to help us with the Phoenixes, I will personally get the third
[hostage] out, and I could tell you where the rest of the guys are. I
will learn where they are."

The option of having the second channel simply disclose where
the hostages were located and then have the U.S. mount a rescue
operation was the approach that Secord favored. Beirut had flat
terrain. Helicopters could land easily at night, and the Sixth Fleet
could be stationed offshore to support the operation. What had
always held Washington back was its inability to pinpoint the location of the hostages. Secord found this maddening.

"In Beirut it always mystified me why we couldn't pin down the
location of these hostages," Secord says. "It's a small place. I told
Ollie many times: 'If I were the director [of the CIA], I would
assure you I'd find them.' I'd find them by issuing the necessary
orders and tasking the necessary resources. . . . I made no secret of
my continuing disdain for the Agency. That was shared by Bill
Casey all the time. Why have them if they're going to be scared all
the time? Why not just hire CNN? You could get real-time reporting from every place on earth, couldn't you? I was quite sarcastic
about their continued failure [to] locate the hostages . . .

"The second channel asked if it was an option—giving us the
location of the hostages—if they couldn't deliver . . . They didn't
have the kind of control over Hizballah that many believed . . . This
was my preferred option all along. I urged North to consider this.
It seemed to me it would be a great thing for the United States.
North was enthusiastic about it. But he knew that the bureaucratic
mumbo jumbo that goes on in counterterrorism back here in Washington is deadening. Why do you think they've never launched a
successful hostage rescue? There have been a lot of movies about

the 'A Team' or some team bursting in. But that's movies only. We haven't got around to doing it in real life."

North told the Relative he feared that if the U.S. sent technicians to Tehran to service the Phoenix missiles, the Americans might be discovered. "If there is a visible effort made by the United States government when there's a long list of hostages being held in Lebanon, this president is going to get stoned" by U.S. allies, North said.

"And by his own people," Secord piped in, adding that if an Iranian leader would just get three American hostages out of Lebanon "We'll go back in an rebuild his goddamn air force. I built it once. I'll go back in and build it again. That was my baby. I built that air force—four and a half years on it."

Secord also estimated that with his technical help the Iranians could find in their own supply stocks "a billion dollars' worth of stuff they don't know they've got—in two weeks."

Continuing this sky's-the-limit tack, North added that if the Iranians would only get the hostages out the U.S. would send them "a million" TOWS and open up a foreign military sales account so that Tehran could get better prices. And on the Da'wa prisoner front, North tended to sound like Indiana Jones when he told the Iranians that he had "already met with the Kuwaiti foreign minister, secretly, in my spare time between blowing up Nicaragua."

As for toppling Saddam Hussein in Iraq, Secord finessed the issue by promising that "we" would talk to another country in the region, but that "it's going to take a lot of talk, a lot of talk."

After the Mainz meeting North wrote Poindexter that the Relative had offered assurances that two of the original three hostages being demanded would be released by Hizballah in the next few days. He proposed that he and Secord travel directly to Beirut to coordinate the release and urged that the president announce the release as soon as the hostages were in American hands "before CNN knows it has happened." This way, North said, Reagan would be "seen to have influenced the action," while the Syrians would not.

He added: "This is the damnedest operation I have ever seen. Please let me go on to other things. Would very much like to give RR two hostages so he can take credit and stop worrying about these other things."

North and Secord flew to Cyprus to begin making arrangements for the release of the hostages. North briefed John Kelly, the U.S. ambassador in Beirut, and instructed Kelly not to notify the State Department of the pending release, implying thereby that this was President Reagan's wish.

On the night of October 31 a U.S. Army helicopter flew North and Secord from Cyprus to Beirut. They were on the ground from about midnight to 3 A.M, briefing the people at the American embassy on the intelligence they had been given by the second channel about where the hostages would be released. They weren't sure whether the release would occur in West Beirut or the Bekaa Valley. The Iranians had asked Hizballah to make the release in West Beirut, per North and Secord's instructions, but they weren't sure the request would be honored so both locations would have to be covered.

The White House was so certain the hostage release was imminent that on November 1 it alerted House Democratic Leader Jim Wright. Nothing happened that day, but on Sunday, November 2, two days before the U.S. midterm elections, one hostage was released: David Jacobsen.

There was no second hostage as had been promised.

Secord and his Contra aide Robert Dutton, who had joined the group in Cyprus, flew back into Beirut to debrief Jacobsen. North, incredulous that only one hostage had been released, planned to join them that night, but had weather forced him to postpone his arrival until the next day. North met with Jacobsen at the embassy for a short time, then escorted him to Wiesbaden, Germany, where he was reunited with his family.

That same day, November 3, came the bombshell revealing the entire U.S.-Iranian initiative. The Lebanese weekly *Al-Shiraa*, picking up on the Hizballah tirades that the Relative had warned were being circulated around Beirut, exposed the McFarlane trip to Tehran as part of ongoing negotiations between the two countries. On November 4 Rafsanjani went before the Iranian Parliament and confirmed the story.

But after that speech the Relative sent word to North that Iran still wanted to continue the initiative. And in Washington the action-oriented NSC was certainly ready to charge ahead. Howard Teicher, the Middle East staffer who had accompanied the Americans to Tehran, read the diplomatic tea leaves with blinders on. He declared in a memo to Poindexter that the *Al-Shiraa* story and the visit to Syria by a high-level Iranian delegation together were "the clearest possible signals we could receive that the succession struggle is underway, and United States-Iranian relations are likely to play an important role in the struggle."

North, for his part, was visibly agitated over the *Al-Shiraa* revelations. As he saw the entire operation beginning to unravel, he seemed to react with denial and unreality. Though the world now

knew, North was still going to keep up the facade with his colleagues on the NSC. To one, the FBI's David Major, he poured out
a bizarre tale.

Bursting into Major's office, North angrily called the *Al-Shiraa*
report "disinformation," and said the United States had not been
trading arms for hostages at all. It had been trading hostages for
hostages. What really happened, North said, was that he had ordered the relatives of Iranian government officials kidnapped and
held in cages in various locations throughout Europe. Each time an
American was freed in Beirut, North had then ordered an Iranian
freed. North claimed that the Lebanese report had originated from
leaks in the NSC, and he demanded that Major conduct an investigation to see who was responsible.

Stunned, Major had not known whether to believe what North
was telling him about kidnappings or not. Later he sent North a
computer message asking if he had been telling the truth; Ollie
did not respond. Major sent him another message; again North
ignored it. Finally after receiving a third query demanding to
know if he had been telling the truth, North sent back his reply:
"Yes."

The story, of course, was fantasy— an apparent effort to cover what
North wanted to see as enemy disinformation with disinformation of
his own. But as Major told the tale to equally incredulous colleagues, it
mostly served to underscore questions among some NSC staffers
about North's judgment and his flair for blending fact with fiction.

On Casey's instructions, North would testify that at this point he
began destroying key files, including the operations ledger that the
director had given him to keep a detailed accounting of the money
flowing in to support the Contras and other activities.

On the other hand Ollie was still desperate to keep things alive and
couldn't entirely let go. So he mounted a final flurry of activity— flying
off to Geneva for a meeting with the Engine, offering further concessions on the Da'wa prisoners and even drafting a statement for
Rafsanjani suggesting how the Iranian leader might put the best spin
on their joint project. In North's proposed statement Iran would
proclaim "the enduring reality of its Islamic Revolution" and "His
Holiness the Imam's gracious command that acts of terrorism are not
acceptable to advance the aims of the Islamic Revolution." North
asked the Engine to "carry this message for me as a personal favor for
the cause we both believe in."

But the tenor of North's writing in his notebooks through these days suggested that in his heart of hearts he knew it was over; he began speculating on how history would judge his efforts. He said he felt the goal of releasing the hostages had been worth it, and that the public would approve once all the facts came out. At that point, he wrote, the U.S. would be seen as being on the side of the angels.

COVERUPS

NORTH, Poindexter and Casey knew that the *Al-Shiraa* story was only the proverbial tip of the iceberg, so their instincts were to contain, conceal and cover up.

Appealing to the president's concern for the safety of the hostages, North and others were initially able to persuade Reagan to follow a no-comment strategy in an effort to ride out the storm of press interest that was developing. But some important members of the Administration—notably Secretary of State Shultz —regarded the coverup mode as untenable.

Shultz would testify that the *Al-Shiraa* report had been news to him. He said he did not know prior to November of 1986 that the U.S. had made direct arms sales to Iran that year, or that the president had signed a finding permitting the sales. He had learned about the McFarlane mission to Tehran after it occurred, but had not known that the Americans had carried spare parts with them, and he had been advised that the trip marked the end of the Iran initiative.

Shultz had been in Europe when the *Al-Shiraa* story broke and immediately found himself bombarded with questions from reporters. "The big story the press is after is to establish that the U.S. violated its own policy by cutting a big secret arms deal with Iran in order to get our hostages released," Shultz cabled Poindexter. While he said he had been racking his brains to think how Washington might put the best spin on this, he advised Poindexter that the best course was simply to make the facts public as soon as possible.

But the admiral resisted. "I do not believe that now is the time to give the facts to the public," he responded, but asserted that "when we do lay out the facts it will be well received since it is a good story."

Reagan briefly broke the no-comment posture on November 6 in an aside to reporters at a bill-signing ceremony. In response to a question, the president allowed that "the speculation, the commenting and all, on the [Al-Shiraa] story" had "no foundation." Though this stopped short of a flat denial, Reagan went on to complain that the press speculation "is making it more difficult for us to get our other hostages free."

But the pressure from the press and public for the Administration to give a full accounting steadily grew to the point where it soon became apparent that the North-Poindexter-Casey stonewalling tack would no longer work. The president would have to say something substantive, and so on November 10 he convened a meeting of his top advisors to discuss what kind of statement he should issue.

Attending the meeting were Bush, Shultz, Weinberger, Poindexter, Casey, Meese, Regan and Alton Keel, Poindexter's new deputy national security advisor. Poindexter dominated the discussion, purported to be a review of the facts surrounding the Iran initiative, but according to notes taken by several of those in attendance his comments were marked by important omissions and false or misleading statements, including the following:

Poindexter talked only of the January 17, 1986, finding and did not mention the December 5, 1985, finding or the one which superseded it on January 6, 1986. He said, inaccurately, that the initiative had begun when U.S. officials happened upon an Israeli arms warehouse in Portugal while attempting to learn if Jerusalem was sending arms to Iran. He said that the first shipment of 500–odd TOW missiles from Israel to Iran in August and September of 1985 had been made without U.S. approval; in fact, Washington had approved the shipment. And he said the total number of TOW missiles purchased by Iran had been 1,000, when actually it was 2,004.

Despite the mounting pressure, Poindexter continued to argue that "no statement [is] needed. News has peaked." There would be no hearings until January "so [we] should not say anything." But Shultz, expressing amazement that he had not been informed of the January finding until November, said the whole initiative boiled down to "ransom . . . [We] must not gild [the] lily." He said he was worried that the Administration would put out "technically correct statements that are not fully descriptive."

President Reagan said he wanted to make a limited statement, the general thrust of which would be that there had been no ransom and no dealing with terrorists. Some things simply could not be discussed out of ongoing concern for the safety of the hostages, as well as those in Iran with whom the U.S. had been secretly dealing. In any case the main purpose of the initiative had been to win a strategic opening to Iran. Winning the release of the hostages was only a collateral benefit.

Various advisors began helping gather material for a speech that Reagan would deliver in a televised address to the nation on November 13. North wrote the original draft, and Poindexter reviewed and approved key sections of the speech that other White House staffers questioned. On the twelfth the president presided at a briefing for congressional leaders on the arms sales. Poindexter actually gave the briefing, and again, either omitted key facts or made inaccurate statements.

In his speech to the country, Reagan said the Iran initiative had been underway for about eighteen months. He said the United States had been trying to achieve a new relationship with Iran, help end the Iran-Iraq war, end Tehran's support for terrorism and, incidentally, win the release of the American hostages in Lebanon.

Reagan said he had authorized only that "defensive weapons" and spare parts be provided, and that the overall quantities were so small they could "easily fit into a single cargo plane." The weaponry had not been enough to tip the balance in favor of Tehran in its war with Iraq, Reagan said, and he asserted, without mentioning the three Americans kidnapped since September, that since the initiative started, there had been no evidence of any Iranian complicity in acts of terrorism directed at the U.S.

Attacking as "wildly speculative" and "false" stories in the press that suggested Washington had been engaged in an arms-for-hostages operation, Reagan said he had complied fully with the law and that the country "did not—repeat, did not—trade weapons or anything else for hostages, nor will we." Reagan made this statement despite having signed the secret December 5, 1985, finding, which explicitly authorized a trade of arms for hostages.

North, Poindexter and others then turned in earnest to tailoring the facts to support Reagan's claims.

The medium for this tailoring was a series of chronologies written from November 7 to November 20. What began as a one- or two-page exercise in providing a brief outline of the Iran initiative for those not in the know evolved into a seventeen-page, single-spaced, detailed exposition of the various events that had occurred over the previous eighteen months, including rationales for taking the steps. Although several people had a hand in preparing the NSC chronologies, only North, Poindexter and McFarlane falsified the facts. North would testify that he and the two others intentionally misrepresented key events in the chronologies.

Poindexter tasked North with presiding over the nitty-gritty formulation of a "definitive" chronology, making it clear he was to omit
any references to the diversion of funds to the Contras.

It soon became apparent that the controversial issues to contend
with would be the shipments of arms that had occurred prior to
Reagan's January 17, 1986, finding; whether the early Israeli arms
shipments were legal; and whether there had been a violation of the
Arms Export Control Act. The act prohibited a foreign recipient of
advanced U.S. weaponry from sending the arms to a third country
unless Congress was notified. The third country also had to certify in
writing that it would use the weaponry only for self-defense—obviously something Tehran would not have been ready to do.

Commenting on North's first chronology—dated November 7,
which accurately noted the August and September, 1985, shipments
of 504 TOW missiles and the November 1985 shipment of eighteen
HAWK missiles from Israel to Iran—McFarlane wrote Poindexter
suggesting that it "might be useful to review what the truth is." The
truth, he said falsely, was that the August and September shipments
occurred when the Israelis "went ahead on their own," after he had
disapproved. He did not mention the November HAWK shipment.

Subsequent versions of the chronology then picked up on
McFarlane's theme of no prior U.S. approval for the August and
September shipments while making no reference to the November
shipment or to discussions between Israel and the U.S. on Iran
from June to September of 1985. Then a November 17 version of
the chronology incorrectly asserted that Washington was not aware
of the August and September shipments at the time they were
made. This version did note the November HAWK shipment, but
said nothing about U.S. knowledge or approval.

The untruths in the chronologies did not extend just to the pivotal 1985 shipments. The documents also said that "all appropriate"
or "relevant" cabinet officers had been consulted throughout the
initiative, and that all the ams sales had been "within the limits of
established policy and in compliance with all U.S. law." Nor was
there any mention of the December, 1985, finding that had retroactively authorized the November shipment and framed the
issue as purely an arms-for-hostages deal.

Over the next two days further erroneous drafts were prepared
as the Administration struggled to come up with an operative set of
facts in time for a presidential news conference scheduled for the
nineteenth. The speech to the nation on the thirteenth had not

deflected the widespread skepticism, and now the president would
have to submit to questioning. It was agreed that two of the questions Reagan was likely to face were: Did the Israeli shipments
made on behalf of the U.S. break the law? And had the Arms Export Control Act been violated?

The night of the eighteenth North convened another session to
continue tailoring the chronology. "Let's get our little nipper in
here and find out WTF is going on," North wrote one of his assistants, Robert Earl. McFarlane also came down to the Old Executive Office Building at North's request to help in preparations for
the press conference and to examine the latest draft of the chronology. When he arrived, North and several others were working fe-
verishly, reorganizing, rewriting, cutting-and-pasting and making
new entries in the ever changing chronology.

McFarlane suggested a number of revisions in Reagan's proposed
opening statement, then began reviewing the chronology. He recommended that the chronology say that Reagan, after authorizing a
"dialogue" with Tehran in July 1985, rejected two Israeli efforts to
send arms to Iran, but the U.S. had subsequently learned in late
August that Israel had transferred more than 500 TOW missiles to
Iran. North incorporated the change immediately and, according to
McFarlane, said: "It looks to me like what we're putting together
here will assure that the president isn't hurt by this, and there
won't be a problem."

Later, Secord came in to check out the chronology, but didn't
like what he saw. "I got down several pages into the document,"
Secord recalls. "Ollie was looking right at me. I came to this part
about the November HAWK shipment, and it had been completely
altered to say that U.S. officials didn't know about it. It was wrong.
I stopped and Ollie knew I was going to stop. He was looking right
at me. I said, 'This is bullshit. This has been changed.' And Ollie
said McFarlane went through it, and he was in charge, and he
knows what the true story is. I said, 'I guess you guys don't need
me anymore,' and I got up and left."

Reagan's November 19 press conference was perhaps the most
discombobulated of his presidency. Intentionally or not, he made
numerous mistakes and misstatements, among the most prominent
of which were: his denial of any involvement of third countries in
the arms sales; his insistence that the only shipments the United
States was involved in were those made after his January 17 finding; his assertion that only 1,000 TOWs were sold to Iran; and his
repeated claim that "everything that we sold [to Iran] could be put

on one cargo plane and there would be plenty of room left over."

The White House quickly put out a "clarification" on just one of the mistakes—on third-country involvement. In what would become a famous explanation of Reagan's uneven performance that night, White House Chief of Staff Regan would later suggest that the NSC had offered up so many conflicting versions of what had happened in the days preceding the press conference that "this sort of confused the presidential mind . . ."

By creating false chronologies, those who had participated were "committing the president of the United States to a false story," North would later concede in his testimony.

Shultz had watched the press conference and was appalled. The next day he met with the president. For openers, Shultz said, Reagan had told him the day of the press conference that he had known of Israel's November, 1985, HAWK shipment to Iran, yet he had proceeded to deny both third-country involvement or any U.S. involvement prior to the January 17 finding. In Shultz' view, Poindexter and North were using the president's vaunted skills as a communicator to try and pass off their misstatements on the public.

Shultz testified that he reviewed the factual errors with Reagan and that the president acknowledged U.S. involvement in various shipments—including the November 1985 HAWK delivery. But Reagan said "what he expected to have carried out was an effort to get an opening of a different kind to Iran, and the arms and the hostages were ancillary to that—that was not his objective," Shultz testified.

The secretary of state said he replied: "Well, I recognize that, Mr. President, and that is a good objective, but that isn't the way it worked." He also told Reagan that he was being given misinformation by his own staff.

On November 20 North, Poindexter, Casey, Meese and others met to prepare and coordinate testimony that both Poindexter and Casey were scheduled to give the congressional intelligence committees on the Iran affair the following day.

Casey's immediate problem was that it had been a CIA proprietary airline that had actually delivered the HAWK missiles to Iran in November of 1985, but the president had just denied any U.S. involvement in the shipment at his press conference. The NSC's solution was again to advance the cover story it had initially agreed to use with the Israelis: that the plane did not contain HAWKs, just oil-drilling equipment.

This lie was inserted into an updated November 20 version of the chronology that afternoon, shortly before the meeting was convened to coordinate Casey and Poindexter's testimony. The November 20 chronology, which was to form the basis for both men's congressional briefings, contained the following four misstatements:

—In mid-November of 1985 the Israelis said they were close to a breakthrough with Iran and asked if Washington could provide an airline that would secretly fly some passengers and unspecified "cargo" to Iran.

—The Israelis' assured the U.S., which was upset over the earlier TOW shipments, that the cargo was actually oil-drilling equipment, and only then did Washington agree to provide the CIA proprietary airline.

—Not until January of 1986 did the U.S. learn that the real cargo had been HAWK missiles.

—Washington's "belated awareness" of this "raised serious concerns that these deliveries were jeopardizing our objective of arranging a direct meeting with high-level Iranian officials." So Poindexter had registered "our stringent objections to the HAWK missile shipment" to Jerusalem and said that the U.S. would have to see that the HAWK missiles were returned, which they were in February.

North said at the meeting that "no one in the U.S. government" knew before the fact that the November shipment contained arms (untrue). He wanted that phrase inserted in place of "no one in the CIA" to eliminate the inference that if the Agency did not know, someone else in the government did. North also said the U.S. had had to force Iran to return the HAWKs. He had "jawboned" Tehran into returning the missiles, Ollie added.

Actually, of course, it had been the Iranians themselves who insisted on sending the HAWKs back because Israel had sent them the wrong model. But North's version of events was accepted. All the senior officials present at the meeting deferred to North's version of the facts.

Later that evening, however, in the face of strong objections from Shultz, who specifically recalled facts to the contrary, references to the oil-drilling equipment were dropped from the chronology. The secretary of state had warned Reagan that the testimony Casey was about to deliver was a lie, and the State Department's legal advisor, Abraham Sofaer, had threatened to resign if Casey delivered the testimony as prepared. But the U.S. authorization of the November, 1985, shipment was still denied in the chronology.

On November 21, in his closed testimony before the House and Senate Intelligence Committees, Poindexter claimed that: the U.S. had learned about the August-September, 1985, shipments only after the fact; the U.S. did not learn until January of 1986 that Israel had sent eighteen HAWK missiles in the November 1985 shipment; and the U.S. had persuaded the Iranians to return the missiles in February; he said he had only learned the day before, November 20, that there may have been prior U.S. knowledge about the HAWK shipment.

Casey, albeit indirectly, continued to assert the oil-drilling equipment cover story. The director told the congressmen that the CIA had been asked in November of 1985 to have one of its proprietaries transport "bulky cargo." The crew had been told that the cargo contained oil-drilling spare parts, he said, giving no hint that the NSC and some of his own CIA staff knew that the plane was carrying arms.

That morning Attorney General Meese had convened his top advisors to discuss all the conflicting versions that the Administration had developed internally in an attempt to explain the Iran initiative. There seemed to be total confusion and numerous discrepancies in the recollections of the key players. Meese decided that he would ask the president to authorize him to gather the facts so that the Administration could begin speaking with one voice.

Meese met with the president later the morning of the twenty-first, along with Poindexter and Don Regan. Meese said because the Iran initiative had been so compartmentalized it had been difficult to develop a clear overall picture of what happened. He suggested that he be authorized to interview the principals and gather the facts in order to develop a coherent understanding of what had occurred. Reagan gave his approval, and it was agreed that Meese would conduct his inquiry over the weekend and try to report back to the president in time for a scheduled meeting of the National Security Planning Group on the afternoon of Monday, November 24.

Meese would testify that when he began this fact-finding inquiry he was acting not so much as attorney general of the United States but as "legal advisor to the president."

While Meese was meeting with President Reagan, Robert McFarlane was meeting with Michael Ledeen, the former NSC consultant who had been the key American intermediary with Israel in 1985 when the Iran initiative was born. They met at Ledeen's Washington house. Ledeen was frustrated by how the reaching-out to Iran that he had helped create was in fact playing out. North had advised him to get a lawyer, but Ledeen didn't see that any laws had been broken. He was frustrated that the Administration was not putting its best foot forward and explaining itself better.

Trying to forge ties with Tehran had been a good and noble under-taking, Ledeen felt. He wanted to talk publicly about his role in the affair. He had direct, first-hand knowledge on the origins of the initiative and could speak to that. He had been cut out later, and could truthfully say he had no idea what had happened in 1986. But when he suggested that he be allowed to speak out, North had said no.

Now Ledeen wanted to take the matter up with McFarlane, dis-cuss the unfolding investigation and have McFarlane comment on Ledeen's recollection of various events.

Ledeen told the Iran-Contra committees in a deposition that McFarlane said he thought Ledeen could talk to some reporters on background to help them better understand what had happened, but it was not yet time to go on the record. When he did talk about it, McFarlane advised, he should not say that he had been on an official mission representing the NSC when he met with Prime Minister Peres in 1985. Ledeen could not understand the rationale for this, unless McFarlane thought Ledeen should not expose his own role.

"Look, Bud, you can't protect me in this," Ledeen said. "There's no way, because my name is already out and it's all over the place, and all the people who were in those meetings will eventually make that point, and people can add."

Soon North appeared, apparently unannounced, and "in some distress," as McFarlane recalls it. He began talking with McFarlane about various meetings that were scheduled that afternoon. Accord-ing to Ledeen, McFarlane said he was to meet with Meese in a few hours, and was trying to get the sequence of all the events that had occurred over the past two years clear in his mind. McFarlane told North he thought he had everything straight, except for the No-vember, 1985, HAWK shipment, which he said he could not recall.

McFarlane got up to leave and offered to drop North downtown. North turned to Ledeen. "We have to get together. Please call Fawn and get yourself signed in for this afternoon. Come and see me."

Driving back to the Executive Office Building, McFarlane and North at first made small talk about their families. McFarlane re-members that Ollie told a story about one of his kids, then turned pensive and said: "I think it's time I had a shredding party."

McFarlane wanted to make it clear to North that North was under no obligation to protect him. "I said, 'Listen, I have no reser-vations about what I have done, and I don't think there's anything wrong to it," McFarlane recalled in an interview. "'So don't feel like you've got any obligations like that . . . Get the truth out and the Lord will take care of it. Don't worry about that.' And he said,

'Yes, I know that.' And he digressed for a moment on the peace that had come over him since he had begun to pray about these things."

North later denied having used the term "shredding party," saying he told McFarlane that all important documents had already been destroyed. But the evidence shows that much of the key shredding would occur later that very day.

North conferred with Poindexter in two separate early-afternoon meetings. At one of the sessions North brought along a notebook from 1985 that contained contemporaneous references to his involvement in the November, 1985, HAWK shipment, which Poindexter had told Congress that morning the U.S. had not known about until January of 1986. When North said he intended to destroy the notebook, Poindexter did not object.

That afternoon the admiral had been asked by Meese to produce all relevant NSC documents on the Iran initiative for examination by the Justice Department's fact-finding team. Poindexter told North about the Meese call and said investigators wanted to examine documents the next day. North assured his boss that all the documents relating to the diversion had already been destroyed.

"Does the president know that we used this money to support the resistance?" asked North.

"No," said Poindexter.

Alerted by Poindexter that Meese's men were coming, Ollie shredded more documents later that afternoon. Robert Earl in his deposition said North asked him to turn over his Iran file to him, remarking: "It's time for North to be a scapegoat."

He then ordered Fawn Hall to alter four memoranda that he had written McFarlane in 1985—memos showing he had been active in raising funds and providing the Contras with military assistance during the Boland ban. These were the memos that McFarlane had isolated as potential problems during the 1985 congressional investigation.

After getting the original memos, North made handwritten changes on each to eliminate the Boland-related problems. Then he gave the memos to Hall and ordered her to prepare new "originals" containing the changes he had just made. This gave Hall pause, but she assumed Ollie had his reasons, so she didn't question the order. After making the changes, she destroyed the originals and was preparing to file the new versions away when she became distracted by North shredding large quantities of documents. She put down the memos she had finished doctoring and offered to help North and Earl with the shredding.

Hall ran the shredder as North and Earl carted documents to and from their offices. The documents included phone logs, computer and KL–43 messages. Hall estimated that a one-and-one-half-foot pile of papers was destroyed—so many that the shredder jammed and she had to call the Crisis Management Center for assistance in fixing the machine.

Poindexter also destroyed evidence. After Meese called him and requested that he produce all the relevant Iran documents, NSC Counsel Paul Thompson produced a batch of papers from a secure safe, including the only signed copy of the president's December, 1985, finding that had retroactively authorized U.S. participation in the November HAWK shipment.

Poindexter proceeded to rip it up, along with certain computer messages that he had stored with the finding in the safe.

Poindexter would later acknowledge at the Iran-Contra hearings that he destroyed the finding to spare the president political embarrassment since the document had characterized the initiative as a straight arms-for-hostages proposition. But since Reagan was presumably aware of what he was signing, Poindexter could not explain how his destruction of the finding could have negated its existence. And in solving the political problem, Poindexter created a legal one: by ripping up the only copy of the December 5 finding, he had destroyed the only legal authorization for the November HAWK shipment.

At mid-afternoon North took time out from his shredding to meet with Ledeen. There was one key question on Ollie's mind.

"What would you say if you were asked if you knew anything about a shipment of HAWK missiles to Iran in November of 1985?" he asked Ledeen, as Ledeen later recounted the conversation for congressional investigators.

"I would tell the truth . . . which is that I was aware of it, and I knew about it," Ledeen replied. "But I did not, and do not, know who authorized it, or how and why the authorization took place."

That was fine, North said. They chatted for a while about the unfortunate turn of events. North said there were some things he had been hoping to save for his grandchildren, but now he was going to have to shred them. Ledeen, not sure what to make of that, said he hoped North's job was secure despite the rumors circulating that he was going to be fired.

"I serve at the pleasure of the president," North said rather grandly, "and any time the president thinks I'm becoming a burden, I'll be happy to leave."

Indeed, North had gone so far as to tell several friends, colleagues and superiors that if the Iran initiative or the Contra operation, or both, were ever exposed, he was to be the designated "fall guy."

North would testify that as early as the spring of 1984 he had discussed the "fall-guy plan" with Casey. The context, he said, was Congress' pending adoption of the Boland Amendment and the Administration's secret decision to obtain funding for the Contras from foreign governments. "It was seen that there would need to be someone who could . . . take the fall" if the official U.S. role in violating Boland was discussed, North said. Then, as his operational role expanded to include Iran as well, North volunteered to take the rap for both programs. "I'm not sure Director Casey ever said, 'It has to be you, Ollie.' It was probably Ollie saying, 'Well, when [disclosure] happens, it will be me,'" North added.

Part of him seemed to relish the prospect of taking the spear in his chest—tragically, perhaps, but heroically. All part of his guts-and-glory ethos. Hakim had sensed it when he said of North: "The biggest satisfaction that can be given to him [is] if he would enter into an environment that he could get killed for his country."

Even among friends who might have thought he was laying it on a little thick, North would often strike a high-drama posture:

"He said quite early on, 'Someday I'll have to resign in disgrace,'" recalls friend and admirer Neil Livingstone, the terrorism consultant. "He said, 'They're going to get me, but I'm prepared to walk in front of bullets for the president of the United States.'"

Rather than looking inward to contemplate the cause of his demise, North always looked outward. His us-versus-them orientation apparently prompted him to conclude that his most visible political antagonists in Congress—people like Sen. John Kerry of Massachusetts and Rep. Michael Barnes of Maryland—were Sandinista/KGB dupes.

"He thought there was a KGB plot to discredit him, publicize him and ruin him," says Livingstone. "He said he had evidence of the east bloc wanting to win the war in Washington, not Nicaragua. He thought his enemies were trying to get him by feeding Kerry and Barnes . . . He'd say, 'It may be true we're doing all this, but is it right that the eastern bloc should use a senator to make their case?'"

In any event, disclosure of the Iranian arms sales in November of 1986 prompted talk of implementing the fall-guy plan—but with a wrinkle. According to North, Casey told him shortly after the *Al-*

Shiraa revelations that North might not be "big enough" to take the hit. Casey thought, "It's probably going to go higher," North testified, and suggested that "Poindexter might have to be a fall guy."

Also on the afternoon of November 21 Meese had selected three aides to help him in his investigation: William Bradford Reynolds, assistant attorney general for the Civil Rights Division; Charles Cooper, assistant attorney general for the Office of Legal Counsel; and John Richardson, Meese's chief of staff. They began their interviews immediately.

McFarlane told Meese and Cooper that he believed the November 1985 HAWK shipment contained oil-drilling equipment—until he learned otherwise in May of 1986. But the attorney general knew that George Shultz had a coterminous note saying McFarlane had told him about the HAWK shipment before it occurred. McFarlane volunteered nothing to Meese about the diversion of profits from the Iran arms sales to the Contras, nor did he mention North's comment made just a few hours before about holding a "shredding party."

After the interview McFarlane asked for a private word with Meese. The former national security advisor said that although he had accepted public responsibility for the Iran overture in a speech the previous night so as to "protect the president," he wanted the attorney general to know that Reagan had been "four square" behind the arms sales to Tehran. Still, according to Cooper's testimony, McFarlane said he was doing his best to "keep the president's interests uppermost in this. I'm trying to protect the president." Meese remarked it was better for the Administration legally if the president had approved the early arms shipments.

As soon as the attorney general left, McFarlane went to a pay phone and called North to fill him in on the Meese meeting. North's notes of the conversation indicate McFarlane said the Arms Export Control Act was not a concern, and that Reagan might say he made a "mental finding." McFarlane elaborated in a computer message to Poindexter: "It appears that the matter of not notifying [Congress] about the Israeli transfers can be covered if the President made a 'mental finding' before the transfers took place. Well, in that sense we ought to be okay because he was all for letting the Israelis do anything they wanted at the very first briefing in the hospital. Ed [Meese] seemed relieved at that."

It wasn't until late the following morning, Saturday, November

22—more than twenty-four hours after the Meese investigation
began—that Reynolds and Richardson came over to North's office
to examine documents. No steps had been taken to seal the office
to retain evidence, and no such action would be taken for another
three days.

Robert Earl took out a batch of accordion-style brown folders
from the shelves behind North's desk, and the men from Justice
began perusing them. North was not there.

After about an hour Reynolds came to a white folder with a red
White House label on it containing what appeared to be another
version of a memorandum he had already read. He flipped through the
undated memo but noted on page five something he had not seen in
the other two versions he had read: a paragraph saying that $12 million
in profits from the Iranian arms sales would be used to buy supplies for
"the Nicaraguan Resistance Forces." The memo said the materiel was
needed to "bridge" the gap until "congressionally approved lethal
assistance . . . can be delivered." Reynolds was stunned. He quickly
gave the memo to Richardson, who also was shocked.

Around 1:45 P.M. they decided to break for lunch, and on their
way out bumped into North, who was just arriving. They introduced themselves and mentioned that they had not yet seen the
1985 files. Ollie promised to produce them.

Reynolds and Richardson walked to the Old Ebbitt Grill, where
they met Meese and Cooper for lunch. When he was told about the
discovery of the diversion memo, the attorney general's usually
cherub face turned deadly serious, and he said simply: "Oh, shit."

After Reynolds and Richardson left, North reviewed more documents and selected some additional candidates for the shredder. But
the shredder in North's office was jammed, and since it was Saturday,
other shredding locales in the EOB were closed. North would later
cause a sensation by his testimony that when Reynolds and Richardson
returned after lunch he continued shredding in their presence. But
the two Justice Department officials strongly denied this, and Earl
confirmed that the office shredder was down at the time.

As Meese's men continued reading what was left of North's files,
North himself worked nearby at his desk and talked on the telephone. Richardson took notes as North spoke. Once Ollie appeared
to have been talking to an Israeli while using the code name
"Beethoven" to refer to Poindexter. According to a Richardson deposition, North told the caller that while a lot of information on the
Iran initiative had already come out, the most sensitive part of the
operation had not yet been revealed.

At one point North told Reynolds and Richardson he was ready to answer their questions, but they told him they were just reviewing documents and that he would be interviewed by Meese later. Ollie remarked that he "would not be long for this job," and that he had retained a lawyer. Reynolds and Richardson had the impression North was trying to crack a joke.

At mid-afternoon North went over to Poindexter's office, where the admiral and Casey were finishing up a two-hour lunch. Among other things, the three men discussed the Iranian second channel and the status of hostage-release efforts. Despite everything that had happened in the past three weeks, they had not given up. Nothing would help take the steam out of an emerging scandal like the release of another hostage or two, they thought.

Back in his office, North called Meese to arrange his interview. The attorney general asked to see him the following morning, but Ollie said he wanted to go to church and take his family to lunch afterward, as was his habit. So Meese agreed to two P.M. Sunday.

Exactly six minutes after the North-Meese call, Casey phoned the attorney general and requested a meeting. The two agreed to meet at Casey's house at six o'clock that evening.

Though by then Meese had every reason to believe that the CIA director was a central figure in the Iran initiative and—given the diversion memo—possibly the Contra operation as well, he chose to see Casey alone, and to take no notes.

This became a pattern with Meese. Whereas prior to the discovery of the diversion memo he had made a habit of interviewing witnesses with at least one aide present who took notes and served as a witness, after the memo was found in North's files, every witness the attorney general interviewed—with the exception of North himself—he saw one-on-one and took no notes. These included sessions with Casey, Poindexter, McFarlane, Don Regan and Vice-President Bush.

According to Meese's testimony Casey told him on that Saturday evening that he had been visited in October by a former business associate, Roy Furmark, who had said that certain Canadians who had helped finance the Iranian arms sales had not been paid and were therefore threatening to expose the operation. It was blackmail. Furmark said the Canadians claimed to have known that some of the proceeds from the arms sales had been used for Israeli or U.S. government operations. Asked by Meese why he had not mentioned this earlier, Casey reportedly said he had seen no reason to come forward prior to this inquiry.

Though he admittedly recognized the discovery of the diversion memo as a bombshell, Meese says he never asked Casey about it—despite the Director's reference to Furmark saying that proceeds had been diverted for official U.S. projects—because he had not yet had an opportunity to interview North. "I felt" he would testify, "It was not appropriate to discuss this with anyone, even as good a friend as Mr. Casey, until I found out what it was all about."

Sunday morning, November 23, North, who had told Meese he was unavailable in the morning because he wanted to go to church, called McFarlane at home and asked if he could come see him. McFarlane really *was* leaving for church at the time, so he suggested North come to his office at the Center for Strategic and International Studies around noon. Ollie said he would bring his lawyer with him.

McFarlane got to his office at noon and put on a pot of coffee. North arrived about twelve-thirty, saying his attorney, Thomas Green, would be along shortly. According to McFarlane, North, after accepting a cup of coffee, began talking about the rapidly unfolding events of the past week.

"It's been a rocky three or four days, but I think everything's going to be all right," McFarlane recalls North told him. "But there's still one problem which is going to be hard to explain—the diversion."

"Well, it was approved, wasn't it?" McFarlane asked.

"Yes, it was approved. You know I wouldn't do anything that wasn't approved. The trouble is that it's a matter of record. I put it on a memo to the admiral."

"Well, just lay it all out," McFarlane advised. "You've always acted under someone else's direction, and I don't think it's a thing you can be held accountable for."

"I hope so."

North did not explain why he thought the diversion memo could be a problem since he did not know at that point that the Justice Department had discovered it, and he believed he had already destroyed all incriminating documents. But he would testify that he could not recall telling McFarlane of the troublesome diversion memo at this meeting.

Presently, Green arrived. Green was actually General Secord's lawyer, and for the time being was doing double duty representing North. At first North had been reluctant to consult a lawyer, but Secord had insisted that he talk with Green. Green and McFarlane had not previously met, so they engaged in some small talk, with the lawyer discoursing on his background as an assistant U.S. attorney. He said he had been involved in cases like this before and advised both North and McFarlane to testify fully and truthfully about their involvement and let the chips fall where they may.

Soon the former national security advisor had to leave for another appointment and told North and Green they could continue using his office but to turn the lights out when they left. As McFarlane left, Secord appeared. The two commiserated briefly about the great unraveling, and McFarlane departed. Secord had come to pick up some tickets to that afternoon's Redskins football game that Green was not going to use.

Meanwhile Meese and his fact-finding team were meeting to prepare for their interviews with North, reviewing the evidence they had amassed so far and considering what questions they would ask the lieutenant colonel.

North appeared at Meese's office alone at 2:15. The attorney general, Cooper, Reynolds and Richardson were waiting. Meese stressed that he wanted a full accounting and did not want North to hold back any details to protect either himself or the president. But over the next three hours and forty minutes North would tell a tale that blended some fact with some fiction.

Meese sat at his desk while North and the others gathered their chairs around one end of the desk. Reynolds and Richardson took notes and Meese did most of the questioning. At one point Meese's secretary interrupted to say that she was going out for food and drinks and North asked for a hamburger. When the secretary returned, North ate his hamburger as he fielded questions from the attorney general.

North "was not nervous," recalls Cooper. "He was very matter-of-fact. Very calm. Very much one of the guys. He tried to pal around. I had only met him three days before, but at one point he called me 'Coop.' It was an aggressive effort to be friendly. But it didn't seem to be inconsistent with his personality. If he was aware of the trouble he was in, he masked it very well. He's a very cool customer."

North said he had not known of the first shipment of 504 TOW missiles in 1985 until after it occurred. As for the November HAWK shipment, North claimed he had been told by Israeli Defense Minister Rabin that the cargo was oil-drilling equipment and hadn't learned otherwise until Secord inspected the contents in Israel. That was untrue.

North said when he learned from Secord that there were

HAWKS on the plane he notified the CIA. He also asserted that
Poindexter had known nothing of the November shipment. Both
those statements were untrue.

North conceded that he had not told the truth about the HAWK
shipment when he, Meese, Cooper, and others had met just three
days earlier to prepare for Casey and Poindexter's testimony before
Congress. He admitted that he had not "jawboned" the Iranians
into returning the HAWKS, but that Iran had been dissatisfied with
the missiles and returned them itself.

Describing how the money flowed, North continued to spin a
tale. Iranians had paid the Israelis, who had paid the CIA, which
reimbursed the Army for the weapons. But he made no mention of
the middleman Secord and the Enterprise's Lake Resources account through which the money had passed.

The attorney general then handed North the diversion memo.
Ollie had written the document the previous April, and it was basically a long summary of the Iran initiative up to that point. It was
not until page five that North had written that $12 million from the
proceeds of the next arms shipment would be sent to the Contras.
Meese started at the beginning of the memo and asked North if the
entire program was not essentially an arms-for-hostages deal.

North claimed that while he had tried to stress the strategic component of the initiative to the president, as far as Reagan was concerned "it always came back to the hostages." It was a mistake to
conclude that the president had been interested in the strategic
dimension because he simply wanted the hostages out, North said.

The strategy of the attorney general and his men was to discuss
casually the more innocuous sections of the memo before asking
about the diversion itself. But finally Meese directed North's attention to the page in question and asked how much money had gone
to the Contras. North paused for a moment and was "visibly surprised," as Cooper recalled it.

North said only two shipments of arms had produced funds that
were diverted to the Contras, though he claimed not to know precisely how much money had been sent. He said only three people in
government had known of the diversion: Poindexter, McFarlane, and
himself. He did not think the CIA knew. If North's testimony at the
Iran-Contra hearings was to be believed, however, that last statement
would seem to be questionable, since he would describe Casey as
being a virtual soulmate privy to all his secrets from 1984 on.

Meese asked if he had discussed the diversion with the president, and North said he had not. Poindexter had been his point of contact with Reagan. Meese, wondering if Reagan had ever seen the memo or approved the diversion, asked if there would not be a record if that were true, since the NSC kept records of all the paperwork that was forwarded to the president. North agreed. It was in that context that Ollie then asked:

"Why, was there a cover memo on this or something?"

"No," said Reynolds.

"Should we have found a cover memo?" asked Meese.

"No, I just wondered," North replied. Then he volunteered to check his files to see if he could uncover any document that might indicate the memo had been sent to Reagan, or if there had been presidential approval. The attorney general and his men weren't holding their breath for Ollie to get back to them on that one.

North claimed that the idea for the diversion had come from Israel—probably Amiram Nir—but this was inconsistent with notes from Israeli officials taken in December of 1985 indicating that North raised the idea.

Meese asked if there was anything else he had not told them, and North said there was not. Then North expressed the hope that the diversion would never have to be revealed publicly. If it were not, he said, then the only other "problem" would be the November, 1985, HAWK shipment, which had been made without a presidential finding. To those present, North's hope could seem an indirect appeal for a coverup; according to Cooper, the statement hung in the air like a lead balloon.

"He was explicit in his statement that he hoped this would not be made public," Cooper says. "It was to that which no one replied because everyone else in that room knew good-and-damn well that this was going to be blurted out."

At that point Meese said he had to leave to go pick up his wife at the airport, and Cooper questioned North about his authority for participating in the November, 1985, HAWK shipment. Asked again if he really believed the shipment contained oil-drilling equipment, Ollie said he didn't, but then remarked with a laugh that he'd bet he could pass a lie-detector test saying he did think the cargo was drilling equipment.

The interview concluded just before six P.M. with none of the Justice Department officials asking if North had engaged in any shredding, and again without them taking any steps to secure his office. Cooper later defended their actions, saying that there was no reason at that point to think that any crime had taken place. He admitted that the thought of North destroying evidence simply never occurred to them.

"Call me naive," he said in an interview, "but it never entered my mind that North or anybody else would be shredding documents. Keep in mind that we were conducting our investigation on the instructions of the president. North was not lying to Congress when he lied to us. He was lying to the president... An effort to deceive me and Meese was tantamount to an effort to deceive the commander-in-chief. I never fully appreciated the possibility that he would be shredding documents or trying to spirit them away...I found him highly believable both in the November 23 interview and in the one before that. He is one helluva good liar."

After the interview North called both McFarlane and Poindexter and told them the diversion had been discovered. He also called Nir in Israel and told him. When North asked if Jerusalem would accept responsibility for the plan, Nir said no. "I cannot back this story," North's notes quote Nir as saying.

Alarmed by the discovery of the diversion memo, which he apparently thought he had destroyed, North then proceeded to make sure that neither the Justice Department nor any other agency would find another incriminating document. He stayed in his office through the night, shredding papers until at least 4:30 A.M.

The following afternoon, Monday, November 24, Meese came to see Poindexter in the national security advisor's office.

"I assume you're aware of the memo that we found in Ollie's files," Meese said.

"Yes," said Poindexter.

"Were you aware of this?"

The admiral said he had been "generally aware," and was prepared to resign. He would rely on Meese to tell him when.

Meese did not ask if Poindexter had told the president of the diversion, and Poindexter volunteered nothing.

The attorney general then walked to the Oval Office for a meeting with Reagan, where he proceeded to lay out the details of his three-day investigation. The key element was the diversion of Iranian arms-sales funds to the Contras, which had been carried out by North, Meese said. Poindexter had had general knowledge and was offering to resign.

Don Regan, who was also attending the meeting, took charge. He said they would have to get the story out quickly. The president

would make a general announcement at a press conference and
then let Meese brief reporters on the details. They would appoint
an independent commission to conduct an investigation. Poindexter's resignation would be accepted and North would be sent
back to the Marine Corps. The president, in despair, suggested
they sleep on it overnight and take action the next day.

Back in his office as revealed in NSC computer transmissions,
Poindexter had a message waiting for him in his computer from
North: "There is that old line about you can't fire me, I quit . . . I
am prepared to depart at the time you and the President decide
. . . We nearly succeeded. Semper Fidelis. Oliver North."

Poindexter sent back a wistful reply that seemed to hold out a thin
hope that their action wasn't over yet. "Thanks, Ollie," Poindexter
wrote. "I have talked to Ed twice today on this and he is still trying to
figure out what to do. I have told him I am prepared to resign. I told
him I would take the cue from him. He is one of the few besides the
President that I can trust. If we don't leave, what would you think
about going out to the CIA and being a special assistant to Bill? This
would put you in the operational world officially. Don't say anything
to Bill yet. I just want to get your reaction."

DRUMROLL

PRESIDENT Reagan faced the press at noon on November 25 and did what he had to do, no more.

Leaving the details to Meese, Reagan conceded that "serious questions of propriety" had been raised in the implementation of his policy toward Iran. Poindexter was resigning and North would be "relieved of his duties," the president announced before departing the White House press room.

North retreated to the suburban Virginia hotel room Secord had rented and took his now celebrated phone calls—first from Bush and then from Reagan. The president, far from being angry, gave Ollie his "national hero" blessing and authoritatively predicted that the Marine's story would one day be a Hollywood smash.

But North did not bask long in the glow of the Gipper's call. He responded to the urgent entreaties of Fawn Hall: they were securing his office and she had discovered those unshredded, troublesome documents. With lawyer Tom Green in tow, North returned to his office and escorted the frightened Fawn—documents bulging from her person—past a checkpoint and out into the cool night air. She passed the papers to Ollie in Green's car, and when the lawyer asked what she would say when asked about shredding, Fawn replied she would say shredding was done daily.

Hall was put to the test just two days later, on Thanksgiving, when Jay Stephens, an attorney in the White House counsel's office, called her at home and asked her to respond to published reports that had already appeared saying quantities of documents had been shredded in the days leading up to the president's press conference. "We shred every day," Fawn told Stephens, as rehearsed.

As the breadth of the emerging scandal became apparent, and as press attention reached—and maintained—a fever pitch, events unfolded quickly:

—Meese announced that he was launching a criminal investigation on the question of the diversion, then six days later said there was sufficient evidence of wrongdoing to warrant the appointment of an independent counsel. A three-judge panel later selected Lawrence Walsh, a former federal judge and president of the American Bar Association, as the Iran-Contra special prosecutor.

—Former Senator John Tower of Texas was named to head the presidential commission that would investigate the NSC, along with former Maine Senator and Secretary of State Edmund Muskie, and Brent Scowcroft, President Gerald Ford's national security advisor.

—North, Poindexter, Secord and a number of lesser lights made their initial rounds of Capitol Hill, responding to the subpoenas of various congressional committees, and all took the Fifth Amendment. McFarlane testified openly.

—Casey was hospitalized after suffering a seizure in his office, and later underwent surgery to remove a cancerous tumor from his brain.

—The House and Senate announced the formation of committees to investigate the Iran-Contra affair. Daniel Inouye, the Hawaii Democrat of Watergate note, was named chairman of the eleven-member Senate Committee, and Sen. Warren Rudman, the New Hampshire Republican, was named vice-chairman. Representative Lee Hamilton, Democrat of Indiana, was selected to head the fifteen-member House committee, and Richard Cheney of Wyoming was named the ranking Republican. Both committees began their work separately, but soon pooled their efforts and announced they would hold joint public hearings in the spring.

Meanwhile, incredibly, the Iran initiative sputtered forward. In early December, George Cave asked Hakim to set up another meeting with the second channel. Representing the United States in the meeting, which took place on December 13 in Frankfurt, were Cave and the State Department's Charles Dunbar, who spoke Farsi. State, at Shultz' insistence, had been at least nominally put back in charge of U.S.-Iranian relations. Hakim would agree to attend only if his lawyer were present, but when Cave refused, Hakim walked out. Representing Tehran was the Engine.

The Engine said that despite the press revelations, Iran hoped the initiative could proceed within the "already established framework." This meant the nine-point Hakim Accords, but as they went

over the nine points it was the first that Dunbar or the State Department had heard of such an agreement.

Then Dunbar broke the new rules of the game to the Engine:
arms could no longer be a part of the U.S.-Iranian relationship. The
Engine, disbelieving, quietly told Dunbar that that "would bring us
back to ground zero." He said Dunbar had to be mistaken, and
suggested that he return to Washington to be brought up to speed
on the North-Secord-Hakim program.

When Dunbar came home and told Shultz of the nine-point
Hakim Accords, Shultz immediately sought a meeting with the
president. Though Poindexter insisted that Reagan had approved
the Hakim Accords—at least those points which involved the government directly—Shultz would testify that when he briefed the
president on the nine-point plan, Reagan was "astonished, and I
have never seen him so mad. He is a very genial, pleasant man . . .
But his jaws set and his eyes flashed and both of us, I think, felt the
same way about it. And I think in that meeting I finally felt that the
president understood that something is radically wrong here."

With that Shultz-Reagan meeting, the Iran initiative was officially put to rest.

On January 26, 1987, Reagan gave a seventy-six-minute interview to the Tower Commission in which he said he approved the
August, 1985, shipment of arms from Israel to Iran. But in a second
interview, Reagan denied having approved the shipment; then, in a
final session, said he couldn't remember what he had done. The
president also asserted to the commissioners that he had not realized that his NSC staff was helping the Contras.

On February 26 the Tower Commission released its final report,
blaming the Iran-Contra debacle on key White House aides and
Reagan himself, who, the commission concluded, had failed to control his staff or grasp the import of what they were doing.

The report was surprisingly tough on the Administration. What
had originally been conceived as a systemic look at how the NSC had
strayed from its traditional role of arbiter of interagency differences to
operational leader had evolved into an investigation of precisely what
happened in the Iran-Contra affair. Through the diligence of a young
computer wizard named Kenneth Kreig, a Pentagon intern, the
commission had been able to uncover a treasure trove of documents: a
four-foot stack of internal NSC messages raised from the memory of a
White House computer—messages that North apparently thought
he had permanently erased.

The messages—including key communications from North to

McFarlane and North to Poindexter—were all dated. If they were strung together in a chronological time line, it was possible to reconstruct the chain of events that had led to Iran-Contra and get inside the minds of the key players to see what was driving their actions at a given time. It was raw history. The total reservoir of documents would be greatly expanded by the congressional Iran-Contra committees, but the White House computer messages were a key element in the enormous paper trail which, for all North's shredding, would enable investigators and historians to crack the essence of the case.

Ollie, for his part, was now toiling away anonymously at a desk job at Marine headquarters, compiling reports on the use of Marine personnel and resources, just passing the time until his twenty years would be up in May of 1988 and he could put in for retirement.

But North was hardly out of the public eye. In the aftermath of his firing from the White House he had crossed the great divide into enduring fame. Television tracked his every move, while newspapers and magazines churned out a flood of profiles. The press— and America, so it seemed—simply couldn't get enough of Ollie North. They were fascinated to know how a junior-level NSC official, a Marine lieutenant colonel, could have amassed such astonishing power and influence. He had mystery and star quality, and in a few short weeks had clearly made the enormous leap from faceless career Marine to matinee idol.

North was not giving any interviews, but he was always good for a wink, a wave and a puckish smile for the throngs of reporters who had virtually taken up residence at the base of his driveway in suburban Virginia in one of the longest-running media stakeouts ever. Even in his no-comment mode he was a fixture on the evening news, driving to work in the predawn darkness, then pausing briefly for a word or two under the white glare of television floodlights.

The White House, meanwhile, had been busily backing away from the president's characterization of North as a "national hero." What emerged in its stead was an effort to portray Ollie as a man who had essentially strayed off the reservation, given the president erroneous or misleading information and thereby steered an unwitting White House into two of the biggest scandals in years.

White House aides leaked stories depicting Ollie as walking the thin line between reality and fantasy, as someone who exaggerated his influence and relationship with the president. Logs were released showing that North had had nineteen meetings with Reagan over the

years, none ever alone. Other stories materialized to show North's
tendency toward hype: while he told the FBI the previous spring that
those threatening him had poisoned his dog, evidently the dog had
just died of old age. And when the story leaked about North telling
NSC colleague David Major that he had authorized the kidnappings
of Iranians, then White House Press Secretary Larry Speakes took
the unusual step of confirming it. Speakes said of North: "I sometimes
felt that he was playing some kind of role, that he was watching a
movie on the screen with himself the star in it."

The trouble with hanging North out to dry was that it was essentially an incompetence defense—an admission that Reagan had lost
control of his own staff and had little idea what was going on around
him. But the Administration continued to be critical. Some—including Nancy Reagan, Secretary of Defense Weinberger and Don
Regan—lobbed grenades at North for hiding behind the Fifth
Amendment and publicly urged him to come forward to tell his
story so as to spare the president further embarrassment.

Asked by a CBS radio reporter early one morning how he might
reply to critics like Mrs. Reagan who were urging him to come
forward, North paused at the wheel of his car and delivered his
most substantive comment to date:

"There have been a number of people who have suggested that I
abandon my individual rights under the Constitution of the United
States. The president has not asked me to do that. I don't believe the
president really wants me to abandon my individual rights under the
Constitution. People have died face down in the mud all over the
world defending those individual rights. It's the thing that makes this
country so much different than any other country in the world.

"And I don't think you guys," North told the throng of reporters,
"even though you keep asking the question, really consider the
implication of a person being forced to abandon his rights under the
Constitution. How many of you guys are going willingly to give up
your First Amendment rights?

"Let me tell you something. I have, over the past twenty-three
days, found myself abandoned by former friends and so-called
friends and colleagues. I continue to place my trust in the Lord. I
would refer you to Psalm 7, Verse 1. I continue to place my trust in
the family I just left behind me, and I will continue to take the
advice of my counsel, and I'm grateful for the support of my Lord
and my Christian friends."

Then North drove off. The reporters, finding North almost serene, raced to look up Psalm 7, Verse 1. It read: "O Lord my God, in thee do I put my trust; Save me from all of them that persecute me, and deliver me."

If Ollie was trusting in the Lord, he was also clearly trusting in his lawyer, Brendan Sullivan, a senior partner in the powerhouse Washington firm of Williams & Connolly, headed by one of the country's leading trial lawyers, Edward Bennett Williams. Sullivan was of the scorched-earth school of law—attack on all fronts.

Accordingly, on February 24, two days before the Tower Report was to be released, Sullivan filed a federal lawsuit on North's behalf seeking to nullify the law under which Walsh was named independent counsel. Sullivan argued that only a presidential appointee had the power to prosecute cases against the United States, not Walsh, who had been appointed by a panel of judges. Sullivan claimed this was an unconstitutional violation of the separation-of-powers doctrine.

Ten days later, seeking to resolve the issue raised by the North suit, Attorney General Meese gave Walsh a parallel presidential appointment. Sullivan then promptly filed another suit challenging the Meese move, charging, among other things, that the attorney general could not appoint Walsh without the advice and consent of the Senate.

At a hearing to argue the merits of the lawsuits, North's celebrity was never more evident. The Justice Department lawyer serving as the nominal opposition walked over to introduce himself to Ollie, as did George MacKinnon, one of the three federal judges who had appointed Walsh. "I just wanted to meet him," Judge MacKinnon explained to incredulous reporters after shaking North's hand and telling him a story about World War II.

At the hearing North's attorneys argued that Walsh was a "vigilante" operating under broad, loosely defined powers; both challenges against Walsh were dismissed. Still, Sullivan kept fighting at every turn, later even going so far as to refuse Walsh's request to obtain a sample of North's handwriting.

The release of the Tower Report was cause for another deluge of Ollie stories, since he was the report's protagonist. The report—with its blizzard of detail and primary-source memoranda and computer messages—showed the world that North, in overseeing the Iran initiative and Contra supply operation, had presided over a vast international network of ships, planes, intelligence agents, corporate shells and Swiss bank accounts. He was a manager of both the macro and the micro, impervious to bureaucratic niceties, thriving on crisis, and obsessed with gaining the release of the hostages at all costs.

But if the Tower Report showed anything, it was that North had, in fact, kept his superiors exhaustively informed at every turn. He had been a prolific memo writer whose energy, drive and determination had often steamrolled his superiors into giving him approval for his actions. But approval was approval.

The day the report was released, North again referred reporters —waiting at the base of his driveway for any tidbit he cared to drop them—to the Bible. Today's lesson was the Eighth Beatitude of Matthew 5: "Blessed are they which are persecuted for righteousness' sake: for theirs is the kingdom of heaven."

But if North, in his impromptu minipress conferences at Scapegoat Central—as some of the reporters on stakeout duty referred to his house—was trying to position himself as a fall guy and martyr, his press was steadily growing worse.

There had been a string of damaging revelations since he was fired, including accounts of his flair for exaggeration; his hospitalization for emotional distress at Bethesda in 1974; his intervening in various federal investigations; his acceptance of the security system from Secord, in apparent violation of laws prohibiting a federal employee from accepting gratuities; and his having not told the truth to Congressman Hamilton's intelligence committee in the summer of 1986. Then had come the Tower Report.

"The choices on Marine Lt. Col. Oliver North seem to be narrowing swiftly and drastically," wrote Raymond Coffey in the Chicago *Tribune* after release of the Tower Report. "He clearly is not, by any stretch of imagination or goodwill, the 'national hero' that President Reagan proclaimed him to be immediately after firing him late last year. And what we are left with now is a choice, it would seem, among North being (a) an ideological cowboy run amuck (b) an habitual and determined liar (c) a calamitously ignorant, naive and delusional operative with approximately the same qualifications for working at the National Security Council as Walter Mitty or (d) all of the above."

Things did not get any better. In late April and early May, Walsh cut the first two notches in his belt. First, Carl "Spitz" Channell, the Contra fundraising wizard, pleaded guilty to conspiring to defraud the government by soliciting money for military aid to the Contras while claiming that the money was going to his tax-exempt group, the National Endowment for the Preservation of Liberty. A

week later International Business Communications President Richard Miller pled guilty to the same charge. Both men named North
as their co-conspirator.

After Channell's guilty plea, North seemed stunned but still firm
in his own resolve to fight any charges brought against him: "I have
no way of imagining what kind of pressures there might have been
that were brought to bear on Mr. Channell to make that kind of a
plea advisable," Ollie told reporters. "But I can tell you this.
Everything that I did was done in the best interests of the United
States of America, and this Marine is never going to plead guilty to
anything."

Whereas many public-relations-conscious Washington lawyers
would have immediately trotted North out on a television program
such as "Nightline" to try and stem the tide of bad press and offer
up at least a partial defense, Sullivan did not believe in that. There
was no percentage in playing ball with the press, he felt. You could
not control what would happen. He would wait and have North tell
his story at the proper time and in the proper form.

Sullivan also came under criticism from some quarters for his
attacks against Walsh. But the lawyer remained convinced that a
multifront battle against the independent counsel gave him the
best chance of ultimately winning the battle where it counted: in
court rather than in the court of public opinion.

But the immediate battle to be fought was in Congress, where
the Iran-Contra committees were ready to begin their public hearings. Sullivan got on with the business of preparing his client to
face the nation.

The hearings convened on May 5 with more than two hours of
opening statements by members of the Senate and House committees all seizing their moment in the sun. The opening statements
clearly displayed the committees' partisan and ideological fault-
lines, with Democrats attacking the Administration and Republicans defending the president and criticizing Congress for following
a "schizophrenic" policy on Nicaragua and the Contras.

All the members tried to hit their best rhetorical high-notes.
Senate Chairman Daniel Inouye said: "These hearings will examine
what happens when the trust, which is the lubricant of our system, is
breached by high officials of our government. The story is one not of
covert activity alone but of covert foreign policy. It is a tale of working
outside the system and of utilizing irregular channels and private
parties—accountable to no one—on matters of national security,

while ignoring the Congress and even the traditional agencies of foreign-policy-making. The story is both sad and sordid. People of great character and ability, holding positions of trust and authority in our government, were drawn into a web of deception and despair."

Senator William Cohen, the moderate Republican from Maine, said: "I should point out that a portion of Congress' house is constructed of glass. While a majority of Congress' members wanted to be on record in opposition to the Contras, they were unwilling to accept responsibility for terminating all assistance. As a result, the Administration aggressively searched through the shifting restrictive funding conditions set by Congress and exploited every ambiguity in the law to carry on its policy of military and paramilitary support."

There were sharper ideological splits on the House committee than on the Senate panel, which was generally more moderate to conservative in cast. On the crucial question of aid to the Contras, for example, eight of the eleven Senate committee members— three of the six Democrats and all five Republicans—had voted to provide $100 million in military and humanitarian support for the resistance in the key March, 1986, vote. On the House side six of the nine Democrats on the committee voted against Contra aid in June of 1986, while the remaining three, and all six Republicans, voted to support the president.

But as is true of all congressional committees, the final work-product of the Iran-Contra panels would be mostly shaped not by their members but by their staffs, which in turn were a reflection of the chief counsels—Arthur Liman for the Senate and John Nields for the House.

Liman, fifty-four, was a senior partner in the New York firm of Paul Weiss Rifkind Wharton & Garrison. A specialist in securities law and white-collar crime, Liman had defended such people as real estate developer John Zaccaro (husband of former Democratic vice-presidential candidate Geraldine Ferraro), corporate raider Carl Icahn and fugitive financier Robert Vesco. In 1971 he served as chief counsel of the New York state commission on the Attica prison riot and oversaw the production of a report that was so compelling and well written that it received a nomination for a National Book Award. Viewed as a moderate Democrat, Liman also supervised the disbarment proceedings of Richard Nixon in New York and, in 1985, accepted an appointment by New York Mayor Ed Koch to investigate allegations that the city medical examiner had covered up cases of police brutality. There Liman found serious mismanagement but no evidence of criminal culpability or coverup.

Nields, forty-four, was a former Justice Department lawyer and defense attorney who now was a partner at the Washington law firm of Howrey and Simon, where he handled criminal and commercial litigation. Nields, who had longish hair and cut a WASPy swath, had been chief counsel to the 1977–1978 House investigation of Korean influence-peddling on Capitol Hill.

The first witness was Secord, appearing voluntarily and without immunity. In four days of testimony Secord sat ramrod-straight and came across as feisty, proud and self-assured. He provided the first clear accounting of the Enterprise's finances, revealing that of the $14 million in profits from the Iranian arms sales in 1986 only about $3.5 million had gone to the Contras—a far cry from the $10 million to $30 million that Meese at his initial press conference in November of 1986 had said was diverted. A total of $8 million remained in the Swiss bank accounts controlled by him and Hakim, Secord said.

Besides North, the former general testified, McFarlane, Poindexter and Casey all had knowledge of what his private-aid network was doing. Many considered the reference to Casey revealing. But there would be no opportunity to question the CIA director, for on May 6—the second day of Secord's testimony—Casey died of pneumonia and cancer at age seventy-four.

Liman cast doubt on Secord's assertions that he had not made and used profits from the arms sales, and succeeded in eliciting from the general the sense that he regarded the CIA as rank amateurs, and that the nation's stake in the Iran-Contra operations had been safer in his own hands.

Secord said he had assumed all along that President Reagan was aware of his activities but had no direct knowledge. He testified that North once remarked that he had told the president that "it was very ironic that some of the Ayatollah's money was being used to support the Contras." North could have been joking, but Secord said he didn't think so. He depicted Ollie as his main government contact and the central figure in both the Iran initiative and the Contra operation.

Following Secord was Robert McFarlane, who was testifying just three months after he had attempted suicide by taking an overdose of Valium and who evoked considerable sympathy. McFarlane, who also appeared without immunity, still seemed overcome with guilt. He told of Reagan's charge to keep the Contras together "body and soul," but was quick to try and absolve the president of any blame, saying Reagan's motives and direction to his subordinates were always "in keeping with the law and national values. I don't think he is at fault here, and if anyone is, I am."

But most members of the committees were not buying that. "I appreciate your willingness to shoulder great responsibilities," said Hamilton. "I admire you for it, but I cannot accept that answer. You spoke for the president, and the responsibility must rest with him as well as with you."

McFarlane, speaking in a near-robotic monotone, went on to tell of Reagan's efforts to solicit foreign donations for the Contras and said the president had personally approved the 1985 effort to ransom two of the American hostages being held in Beirut for $2 million (provided by Ross Perot). McFarlane admitted to misleading Congress into believing North had done nothing wrong, and conceded he had made changes in the White House chronology in November of 1986 so as to "minimize the President's role." He told of North's intention to hold a "shredding party," and said he believed the Boland Amendment did apply to the NSC staff.

Robert Owen, the thirty-four-year-old, self-styled courier and "foot soldier" in the secret Contra war, provided colorful and often riveting testimony of forays to the Central American bush for North, as well as bagman drops in front of the White House and cash pickups at Chinese groceries in the bowels of New York City. And when Owen testified that Johnathan Miller, a mid-level White House aide serving as deputy assistant to the president for administration and management, had helped him hand out cash to Contra leaders on occasion, Miller promptly resigned.

Owen sketched a portrait of himself as an earnest true-believer and follower of Ollie North, whom he called his covert "godfather" and whom he said he loved "like a brother." At no time was Owen's adoration of North more on display than when, as a closing statement, he read the following ode to Ollie that had been written by John Hull, the American Contra-booster in Costa Rica:

"Today on the fertile plains of Central America, cattle graze peacefully. On the wooded hills and green valleys, monkeys play, parrots fly and songbirds send forth their music that echoes over a troubled land. In this far corner of the Third World, we have known darkness and despair that at times seemed almost too much to bear. We have stood by the charred remains of our fallen airmen; with head bowed and eyes wet with tears, have felt the hardships and the sorrow that must now be borne by their loved ones.

"We've held the hands of our gallant fighters and prayed with them as their life's blood seeps slowly into the dark, damp earth of the jungle. We've held in our arms children no more than four years of age who have been shot while trying to flee Nicaragua to a safe haven. We have a burning desire to strike back at those whose intent is to enslave us, to try and stem the Red Tide that threatens to overwhelm us. We have known indifference, even betrayal, from political and religious leaders of America.

"Fear, anguish, and despair are with us daily, yet in our darkest hours we have three things that sustain us: our faith in God Almighty, the love and support of our families, [and] the knowledge that on this troubled earth there still walk men like Ollie North. Men that have shown bravery in their youth, wisdom in their adulthood and patriotism throughout their life.

"Ollie, your enemies are more clever and treacherous than ours, yet you have given all you had to give. We have so very little to give you in return, yet we want you to know that in our hearts and in our prayers, you are with us daily. Not only in elegant churches, but at crude altars in the jungle candles burn for you. In our lifetime you have given us the legend. To the future, you are giving our children a chance to live as free individuals. And for those things, we say, 'Thank you, Ollie North.'"

Owen was followed by Contra leader Adolfo Calero, who confirmed what most of the world already knew: that North had provided the Contras with supplies and military advice during the Boland ban. He said he had given North $90,000 in traveler's checks between March and July of 1985 to assist in a hostage-rescue operation. Congressional investigators determined that $25,300 of this was used by Drug Enforcement Agency agents in their hostage-recovery attempts, while $2,440 of the checks were cashed by North to make miscellaneous purchases at drug stores, grocery stores, gas stations, restaurants, hotels, and in one case to buy hosiery.

This last revelation seemed especially to tarnish North's hero image. No explanation was forthcoming from Brendan Sullivan and Ollie, still waiting in the wings, but even some of North's staunchest defenders on the Iran-Contra panels, people such as Senator Orrin Hatch of Utah, were apparently given pause by this and forced on the defensive. It had always been a given that Ollie was operating above the fray on principle. Hosiery? The wiseguys, unkindly and without any proof, buzzed that it had to be for Fawn.

A parade of lesser players followed Calero to the witness stand, including: former General John Singlaub; wealthy Contra supporters Ellen Garwood, Joseph Coors and William O'Boyle; Secord operative Bob Dutton; Felix Rodriguez; Ambassador Lewis Tambs; the CIA's Costa Rica station chief Joe Fernandez (appearing in closed session); and Assistant Secretary of State Eliott Abrams, who admitted to misleading Congress about Administration involvement in providing aid to the Contras.

Hakim, cast in the role of Unscrupulous Persian Rug Merchant, told of his $200,000 "Button" account, initially intended as a death benefit for North if he were killed in Tehran. He then tried, without much success, to give a satisfactory explanation of his efforts, and those of his lawyer William Zucker (who, as a resident of Switzerland fell out of reach of the committees' subpoena power), to direct part of that money to Mrs. Betsy North in payment, unsolicited, for a future job. The notion of North or his heirs coming into this kind of money, even though Hakim said none of it had been paid, served to detract further from Ollie's luster.

Testifying about his negotiations with the second channel, Hakim played willingly into Arthur Liman's efforts to sound grave warnings about the danger of entrusting diplomacy to private citizens—especially the likes of Hakim and Secord, who had a direct financial interest in the agreements they were propounding. Hakim testified that in negotiating the nine-point "Hakim Accords" and, through North and Poindexter, getting President Reagan to approve them, he felt he had done a better job than Secretary of State Shultz could have done. In addition to his commitment pledging the U.S. to seek the release of the seventeen Da'Wa prisoners held in Kuwait, Hakim said Secord also assured the second channel that the United States would "fight Russians in Iran" if the Soviet Union ever invaded.

The appearance of Fawn Hall provided the glamor highlight of the hearings to date—for the first time since opening day the networks went live. As she walked into the hearing room, there was an explosion of clicking cameras.

Fawn Hall had become something of a media sensation since February, when it was revealed that she had helped North shred documents and that she would be granted immunity in return for her testimony. Until photos were published alongside reports of her shredding, the public had been unaware of her beauty. With this awareness the scandal acquired its missing ingredient—Fawn was a bombshell, a loyal and adoring secretary, as it were, to James Bond as Ollie North.

Demands for fresh pictures were so great that Fawn's lawyer, Plato Cacheris, agreed to make her available for a photo-opportunity. With her aquamarine eyes and her windswept Farrah-do, Fawn Hall appeared on the steps outside Cacheris' office dressed in black boots and a boxy tweed coat. Pirouetting for the cameras, she took no questions, but smiled and delivered herself of Andy Warhol's line about everybody being famous for fifteen minutes. Then she dropped out of sight again—until it was her turn at the hearings.

Now, wearing a black-and-white jungle-print blouse, she seated herself at the witness table as the photographers clicked madly and spectators scrambled to fill every last seat. Senator Inouye, who had been wearing sunglasses against the glare of the TV lights, now held up a piece of paper above his eyes—the better to see.

Taking care to distance herself from other blonde secretaries like Elizabeth Ray who had become tangled in Washington scandals, and showing herself to have a nice sense of humor as well as timing, Hall declared in her opening statement: "I can type." And then, seriously: "My hours were long and arduous, but I found my job to be most fulfilling. I was a dedicated and loyal secretary, and performed my duties in an exemplary manner."

Though she said she was privy to no substantive details, she offered this defense of her boss: "I strongly believed then as I do now that the efforts made to support the Contras, obtain the release of the American citizens being held hostage, and respond to moderates in a country as strategically important as Iran were carried out with only the best of intentions in the interests of this country, the United States. I admire Lieutenant Colonel North for his professional integrity and beliefs, his personal commitment to this country, and his ability to be a friend when one is needed." This was followed by: "[I would] also like at this time to recognize his wife Betsy and their four children for their commitment and their sacrifices."

She then recounted her dramatic tale of shredding and taking documents out of the White House. And though she later retracted the statement, she gave what many considered a revealing reply when asked if she had realized that altering documents was wrong. "Sometimes," she said, "you have to go above the written law." Liman and most members of the committees seized on this as perfectly in keeping with the ethos of the North-Casey-Poindexter-Secord-Hakim network.

Next, Glenn Robinette, the former CIA operative whom Secord had hired to dig up damaging evidence against Tony Avirgan and Martha Honey—the free-lance journalists who had filed the sweeping civil suit in Miami—gave testimony damaging to North about the security fence he had installed at Ollie's Great Falls, Virginia, home.

Robinette revealed that in December of 1986, just after North had been fired from the NSC, Ollie had asked him to provide invoices for the $14,000 security system that Secord had paid for. Since North had never offered to pay for the fence before, and Secord had already paid, Robinette said he was surprised when North asked him to send a bill for work that had been finished the previous July. Feeling sorry for North after his firing, Robinette said he sent him two invoices totalling $8,000—one dated July 2, the other September 22.

North then responded with two back-dated letters of his own. The first was dated May 18 and was apparently intended as an authorization for Robinette to go ahead and install the security system. Ollie wrote that he understood he had two options: pay the $8000 over two years, or have free use of the fence until 1988 when he would retire from the Marine Corps, at which time he would make his house available for a "commercial endorsement" of Robinette's company. That was a somewhat puzzling offer, since in May of 1986—the supposed date of the letter—Ollie had not attained celebrity.

North's second letter, dated October 1, was even more curious. It was chatty in tone, and said he hoped Robinette would agree to the commercial-endorsement option in lieu of payment. "We just don't have $8,000 without borrowing it..." North wrote. "I don't want you to be caught short, but I don't want to have to resort to holding up gas stations on my way home from work at night either."

While some of the North partisans on the committees tried to defend him by saying the government had failed in its duty to protect the Marine against threats, others said he could have gotten adequate protection if he had wanted it. Senator Rudman later produced letters from the Secretary of the Navy and the legal counsel for the Marine Corps saying that North would have been entitled to protection from either the Navy or the Marines had he asked for it, but he had not asked.

Two months earlier, in April, North had been given round-the-clock protection by the Naval Investigative Service because of fears he had been targeted for assassination as the one-year anniversary of the April 14 Libyan bombing approached. From April 13 to 17 North and his family actually moved to Camp Lejeune, North Carolina. Afterward he returned home and fifteen to twenty agents were assigned to guard him daily—five or six per eight-hour shift.

When Noel Koch, the former deputy assistant secretary of defense for international security affairs, testified, Ollie's world of secret code words was illuminated. Koch said North had given him the name Aaron, while an Israeli arms purchasing agent in New York was known as "the bookkeeper." North called himself Paul. Under consideration was a proposal to sell TOW missiles ("dogs") to Iran ("apple") by the U.S. ("orange") with the assistance of Israel ("banana"). Iran was then to try and help win the release of the American hostages ("zebras"). To talk about this plan, Koch met with his Israeli counterpart at Washington's National Airport ("the swimming pool").

"I take it there never came a time when Colonel North said that Paul was sending Aaron and the bookkeeper to the swimming pool to get a price so that orange could send some dogs through banana to apple for some zebras," Senate Committee Counsel John Saxon asked Koch.

"In all truth," Koch admitted sheepishly, "you would sort of start down that road and get so self-conscious that you couldn't do it. This is not the way this kind of thing is normally done." But North apparently liked the codes.

Finally Assistant Attorney General Charles Cooper testified about the November 20 meeting at which North had spearheaded the effort to have Casey give false testimony to Congress. He also told of North's interview in Meese's office the day after the discovery of the diversion memo. Asked if he would believe North's testimony under oath, Cooper said he would not.

Over the previous two months North, though absent, had seemed a constant presence at the hearings. His role and his actions had been the central thread in the testimony of virtually every witness. And though North had landed all these witnesses in varying degrees of trouble, they all still seemed to like him and spoke fondly of him.

Earlier in June, the Iran-Contra committees, over the objections of Independent Counsel Walsh, had voted to grant North limited immunity from prosecution so as to compel his testimony at the hearings. Under the agreement anything North said publicly could not be used against him, but Walsh was, of course, free to prosecute North based on any evidence he could gather independently of the hearings. And he had been doing just that for months, sealing material with the court to prove that it was gathered before any appearance by North.

The hearings greatly complicated Walsh's job with respect to North, and in deference to that, the committees had postponed taking Ollie's testimony as long as possible to give Walsh more time to gather evidence. This had given North a considerable advantage for the hearings, since he now had the benefit of having heard the testimony of every key witness, with the exception of Poindexter.

Still, Brendan Sullivan, wanted every edge he could get. On June 17, the eve of North's first scheduled interview by congressional investigators, Sullivan sent word that North would refuse to give the committees a private deposition, as other witnesses had done, before his public testimony the first week in July. The lawyer did not want to give them a roadmap on Ollie.

Though this was a rebuff of Congress, the committees were faced with a choice: either accept Sullivan's terms, or institute contempt proceedings and risk a month long delay that could prevent them from keeping to their timetable of finishing the hearings in August and producing a final report by late fall. Inouye and Hamilton came back with a counterproposal that Ollie testify in a closed executive session of the committees, but Sullivan rejected this.

Now even some of the Administration's staunchest defenders were annoyed. Representative Cheney warned that if North refused to testify he "would move in the eyes of many of us from the posture of having been a man trying to serve his country and his president to a figure with a serious legal problem and obviously not the pillar of patriotism that he would like to have portrayed."

A compromise was finally reached whereby North agreed to give limited private testimony solely on the question of whether Reagan had known of the diversion. Under the accord Ollie also agreed to deliver all the documents the committee had subpoenaed from him, including his notebooks.

There were about 3,000 pages of notes in North's notebooks, many of which were a gold mine of leads. The notes chronicled North's daily actions and thoughts between 1984 and late 1986, but under terms of the agreement that the committees hastily reached with Sullivan, he and North were allowed to black out all portions of the notes that they deemed "irrelevant" to the panels' work. No one from Congress oversaw the deletions, and as a result a sizeable portion of the notes—perhaps as much as thirty to forty percent—was blacked out and never reviewed by congressional investigators. This was a major gap in obtaining a full accounting of North's activities, and that Sullivan was able to cut such a deal was a measure of how anxious the committees were to hear from Ollie. Sullivan retains control of the original notebooks, and at this writing it is believed that the Special Prosecutor's office has not gained access to them.

All in all, the negotiations with Congress were a clear victory for North. Not knowing what the witness' testimony was going to be, John Nields, Liman and other questioners would be at a decided disadvantage. North, would come on stage without a formal dress-rehearsal, but criminal-law experts familiar with Brendan Sullivan knew that North would hardly be unrehearsed. Down at Williams & Connolly, they were drilling him with every imaginable question, and they had taken the time to study the tendencies of Liman, Nields and each member of the committee. By post time, they were thoroughly conversant with the enemy.

So the stage was finally set for Ollie and a week of midsummer-day dramas for which the television networks announced they would preempt their regularly scheduled soap operas. There was the promise of the real thing on Capitol Hill.

But offstage, one of the country's leading experts in drama— Ronald Reagan—was not worried. "There ain't no smoking gun," the Gipper told reporters, doing his best screen gangster for them.

"THE GOOD, THE BAD & THE UGLY"

A FEW minutes after nine o'clock on the sweltering morning of Tuesday, July, 7, 1987, North strode into the packed Senate Caucus Room behind a flying wedge of security men.

His Navy guard detail had been boosted to thirty five agents a day for the hearings. The security presence created the sense of a head-of-state arriving, not a Marine lieutenant colonel, though as the entire country knew by now, this was no ordinary Marine lieutenant colonel.

An explosion of clicking cameras recorded the scene. At five foot nine, North seemed shorter and slighter than he looked on TV. He had a fresh, prickly haircut that revealed considerable gray. The familiar gap-toothed grin anchored a pug nose and wrinkly eyes. And of course, he was wearing his uniform, with six rows of medals.

Since he had worn it for his two Fifth Amendment appearances on Capitol Hill the previous December, there had never really been any doubt that he would wear it at the hearings, but his use of the uniform had emerged as an issue among some Marines who thought he had served the Corps poorly.

These critics noted that he had never worn the uniform in five years at the NSC, so why should he wear it now? Was it not self-serving to, in effect, drape himself in the flag? After all, Poindexter, who was still in the Navy, wore civvies for his appearances on the Hill. But North was on active duty and therefore entitled to appear in uniform if he wanted to, the Marine Corps said. He did want to, and perhaps as importantly, Brendan Sullivan would not have had it otherwise.

For in trying to accomplish their goals at the hearings—talking over the heads of the committees, communing directly with the people of the country through television, and presenting North as the persecuted patriot being scapegoated for merely carrying out the orders of his superiors in furtherance of the national interest—the uniform was essential.

The camera angles and the physical lay of the land inside the August Caucus Room where the McCarthy and Watergate hearings had unfolded were favorable to North. The Senate and House committees—twenty-six members plus assorted staff—were seated on raised platforms looking down at North in what gave the appearance of an unfair fight. This, plus Sullivan's skillful stacking of briefing books and other documents on top of each other around North, created the image of Ollie in the bunker.

In case anyone missed this latter point, Sullivan displayed a picture of North back at Williams & Connolly standing next to all the relevant documents that the committees had amassed. The documents, when piled on top of each other, were taller than North. The papers were so voluminous that he had not had time to read them all, Sullivan complained.

There was more skirmishing over North's request to make an opening statement. Under the rules of the hearings, opening statements by witnesses had to be delivered to the committees forteight hours before the witness' appearance. But North had turned his in just forty-five minutes earlier.

"Here once again the witness is asking us to bend the law and to suggest that he might be above the law," Senator Inouye told Sullivan in denying the request. If North wanted to make an opening statement, he could do so forty-eight hours from then—on Thursday morning. Inouye, known for his fairness and even temper, would give North latitude but would not cede him the floor—or the flag. The senator, who had lost his right arm fighting in World War II, was wearing his Distinguished Service Cross, the nation's second highest medal of valor—higher than any of North's.

Since the committees, in dividing up responsibilities for witnesses, had designated North as a House witness, John Nields, the chief House counsel, began the questioning. He had no deposition to guide him. He would just have to start.

"Colonel North," Nields said, "were you involved in the use of the proceeds of sales of weapons to Iran for the purpose of assisting the Contras in Nicaragua?"

North took the Fifth.

There were a few gasps among the spectators at the mere thought that after seven months of silence, and before a nationally televised audience, he would plead the Fifth Amendment again. But Brendan Sullivan was just protecting the record. The committees were prepared for this ritual first step. Inouye routinely reminded North that he was there pursuant to a committee subpoena, and under court order, he could not take the Fifth. He had been granted immunity from prosecution based on testimony he provided. Ollie would now finally talk.

To Nields, the most important issue raised by the Iran-Contra case was the abuse of secrecy, and the question of how the government could best balance the need occasionally to conduct covert operations with the principles of an open, democratic society. So he moved immediately to what for him was the heart of the matter. He asked North if the Iran initiative and the Contra resupply program were covert operations.

"Yes, they were," said North.

"And covert operations are designed to keep secrets from our enemies?"

"That is correct."

"But these operations were designed to be secrets from the American people?"

"I think what is important, Mr. Nields, is that we somehow arrive at some kind of understanding right here and now as to what a covert operation is," North said. If Nields—whose thinning light brown hair worn over his ears and collar made him look as if he might have been a hippie in the sixties—didn't know what a covert op was, then, by God, Ollie would tell him. "If we could find a way to insulate with a bubble over these hearings, that are being broadcast in Moscow, and talk about covert operations to the American people without it getting into the hands of our adversaries, I'm sure we would do that. But we haven't found the way to do it."

"But you put it somewhat differently to the Iranians with whom you were negotiating on the eighth and ninth of October in Frankfurt, Germany, didn't you?" countered Nields. "You said to them that Secretary of Defense Weinberger in his last session with the president said, 'I don't think we should send one more screw . . . until we have our Americans back from Beirut, because when the American people find out that this has happened, they'll impeach you'—referring to the president."

Sullivan objected, but North didn't mind answering. "That is a bald-faced lie told to the Iranians," he conceded, "and I will tell

you right now, I'd have offered the Iranians a free trip to Disneyland if we could have gotten Americans home for it . . ."

"And when the Hasenfus plane went down in Nicaragua, the
United States government told the American people that the
United States government had no connection whatsoever with that
airplane," continued Nields. "Is that also true?"

"No, it was not true. I had an indirect connection with that
flight . . ."

Now Nields would try and lecture North: "In certain communist
countries the government's activities are kept secret from the people. But that's not the way we do things in America, is it?"

But North responded with what would be the first of dozens of
speeches that he would make over the next week. Nields, Arthur
Liman and the committees were conflicted about how to respond to
these tangents. In a court of law a judge would have cut North off
and stricken the remarks from the record. But the hearings had a
different agenda. They were a morality play *cum* civics lesson for
the masses about what had gone wrong in two American foreign
policy initiatives, and what lessons could be learned so that the
mistakes would not be repeated. North's speeches—though they
would have the short-term effect of extolling his own virtues and
turning members of the committees into ogres—were also revealing. They spoke to his rationale and what motivated him, and they
helped build a record. So most of the time co-chairs Inouye and
Hamilton decided to let Ollie run.

"Counsel," said North, "I would like to go back to what I just said a
few moments ago. I think it is very important for the American
people to understand that this is a dangerous world; that we live at
risk and that this nation is at risk in a dangerous world. And that they
ought not to be led to believe, as a consequence of these hearings,
that this nation cannot or should not conduct covert operations. By
their very nature, covert operations . . . are a lie. There is great deceit, deception practiced in the conduct of covert operations. They
are, at essence, a lie . . . The American people ought not to be led to
believe by the way you're asking that question that we intentionally
deceived the American people, or had that intent to begin with. The
effort to conduct these covert operations was made in such a way that
our adversaries would not have knowledge of them, or that we could
deny American association with it, or the association of this government with those activities. And that is not wrong."

Nields was not making the headway on the secrecy issue that he
had hoped for, so he decided to drop the line of questioning. He

recalls being "floored" by Inouye's decision not to let North give his opening statement. If the colonel had read the statement, Nields felt, it might have allowed to him to take out some of his initial aggressions against Congress for its failure to provide enough sup- port for the Contras, and he might have been more relaxed. But now North was being combative and flip. Not having had the op- portunity to question him beforehand was already having its effect.

"It made a significant difference in the way he was questioned and the way he was perceived," Nields recalls. "I was unable to avoid areas that I needed to question him about but which it turned out that he had nothing particularly significant to say on . . . And if he had been questioned in advance, I would have known what kinds of answers he would give and could have made a much more informed judgment on how to structure the questioning. For exam- ple, I could have begun by confronting him with every false state- ment to which he had admitted in executive session."

But as it was, Nields was largely groping in the dark. So he decided he would get to the question the whole country was wait- ing to have answered: whether Reagan had known of the diversion. "Various people had advised me to smash his credibility first, but I decided not," says Nields.

So he asked North: "One question the American people would like to know the answer to is what did the president know about the diversion of the proceeds of Iranian arms sales to the Contras. Can you tell us what you know about that, sir?"

"You just took a long leap from Mr. Hasenfus' airplane . . ." cracked North, warming up for speech number two. "I never personally discussed the use of the residuals [North did not like the term *diversion*] or profits . . . with the president. I never raised it with him and he never raised it with me during my entire tenure at the National Security Council staff. . . I assumed that the president was aware of what I was doing and had, through my superiors, approved it.

"I sought approval of my superiors for every one of my actions, and it is well documented. I assumed when I had approval to pro- ceed from either Judge Clark, Bud McFarlane or Admiral Poin- dexter, that they had indeed solicited and obtained the approval of the president. To my recollection, Admiral Poindexter never told me that he met with the president on the issue of using residuals from the Iranian arms sales to support the Nicaraguan resistance, or that he discussed the residuals or profits for use by the Contras with the president, or that he got the president's specific approval. Nor did he tell me that the president had approved such a transaction. But again, I wish to reiterate that throughout, I believed that the president had indeed authorized such activity.

"No other person with whom I was in contact during my tenure at the White House told me that he or she ever discussed the issue of the residuals or profits with the president. In late November two other things occurred which relate to this issue. On or about Friday, November 21, I asked Admiral Poindexter directly, 'Does the president know?' He told me he did not. And on November 25, the day I was reassigned back to the United States Marine Corps for service, the president of the United States called me. In the course of that call the president said to me words to the effect that, 'I just didn't know.'

"Those are the facts as I know them, Mr. Nields. I was glad that when you introduced this, you said that you wanted to hear the truth. I came here to tell you the truth—the good, the bad and the ugly. I am here to tell it all, pleasant and unpleasant, and I am here to accept responsibility for that which I did. I will not accept responsibility for that which I did not do."

North had just said a mouthful: he assumed Reagan had known of the diversion but had no direct proof; he had received approval for everything he had done; and he would take responsibility for his own actions but not others'. North had been glancing down at the table in front of him as he made this speech, which was so well delivered that Inouye thought Ollie might have gotten in a portion of the banned opening statement.

"May I make an inquiry of the witness?" the senator interrupted. "Was that response from a written text?"

"Those are from notes that I made in preparation for this session, sir," replied North.

"It is not a verbatim written text?"

"No sir, it is not."

Nields pressed on to elicit the answer that would round out the leads of the morning news stories. In the executive session that had been held on the question of Reagan's knowledge of the diversion, North had revealed to the committees that he had written not just the diversion memo that had been found in his safe, but at least four other diversion memos.. They had been written each time there was a proposed sale of arms to the Iranians that was in final enough form to warrant approval by the president.

"And you sent these memoranda up the line?" Nields asked.

"It is my recollection that I sent each one up the line," replied North, "and that on the three where I had approval to proceed, I thought that I had received authority from the president. I want to make it very clear that no memorandum ever came back to me with the president's initials on it, or the president's name on it, or a note from the president on it—none of these memoranda."

This was a bombshell. There had been not one, but at least five diversion memos—four of which North apparently shredded. So while he had no direct knowledge that Reagan had known of the diversion, there were now at least five opportunities for Reagan to have known—*if* Poindexter had forwarded the memos on to the Oval Office.

For someone who had told numerous colleagues that he would be the one who would inevitably "take the fall" for the Iran-Contra affair, North's first day of testimony was notable for his decided reluctance to take that fall alone. By the end of the day he had accused several cabinet-level officials of conspiring to give false information to the president and to Congress, or of being aware of elements of the Iran or Contra operations.

Ollie spoke contemptuously of "heroes" who had come forward in November of 1986 to blow the whistle on false cover stories that he and others were putting out. "I didn't make a lot of the decisions I am accused of making," he said, adding later that there had been "a whole cadence of people" who had "wittingly" participated in coverups. "I didn't consider myself to be the lone wolf out here creating paper that nobody else knew about . . ."

"By putting out this false version of the facts, you were committing, were you not, the entire Administration to telling a false story?" asked Nields.

"Well . . . I'm not trying to pass the buck here, okay?" said a visibly irritated North. "I did a lot of things, and I want to stand up and say that I'm proud of them. I don't want you to think, Counsel, that I went about this all on my own. I realize there's a lot of folks around that think there's a loose cannon on the gundeck of state at the NSC. That wasn't what I heard while I worked there. I've only heard it since I left. People used to walk up to me and tell me what a great job I was doing, and the fact is there were many, many people—to include the former assistant to the president for national security affairs, the current national security advisor, the attorney general of the United States of America, the director of central intelligence, all of whom knew that to be wrong."

It had been McFarlane, North said, who had charged him with keeping the Contras together "body and soul," and the job had expanded after funds dried up in 1984. "I guess it just fell to me by default," he said.

Without being prompted, North said that it was Casey, who after the Iran-Contra operations began to unravel in the fall of 1986 told him to destroy documents. "Director Casey and I had a lengthy discussion about the fact that this whole thing was coming unraveled, and that things ought to be cleaned up, and I started cleaning things up," North said. He also named Assistant Secretary of State Elliott Abrams, Assistant Secretary of Defense Richard Armitage and the CIA's Alan Fiers and Dewey Clarridge as having been aware of some or all of his covert operations.

North tried to pass off his shredding as routine, but acknowledged that after learning of Meese's inquiry on November 21 he began shredding with "increased intensity." That got a laugh.

But when he tried to be funny, North tended to bomb. "My memory has been shredded," he responded during one exchange about shredding documents. And when Nields asked him about the number of memos that he sent Poindexter or President Reagan, North replied: "Judging by the pile of paper you just gave me, I sent too many."

He made clear his disgust with Congress: "There were other countries in the world and other people in this country who were more willing to help the Nicaraguan resistance survive and cause democracy to prosper in Central America than this body here." And after acknowledging that he cut back on his memo-writing after Congress began showing an interest in his Central American activities, he said defiantly: "I didn't want to show Congress a single word on this whole thing."

By the end of the day, though he had acknowledged a catalog of sins—including not telling the truth to Congress, destroying evidence and covering up to protect the president—North's dramatic sense of time and place had clearly succeeded in papering over his admissions, throwing the committees on the defensive and casting himself as the well-meaning patriotic prince.

He did this, in part, by using a kaleidoscope of facial expressions and emotions—smirks, winks, frowns, arched eyebrows, cocked chin, lumpy throat, and moist eyes—that reinforced his preferred image of strong, noble, ideologue struggling to do what was best for the country in the face of efforts by a vacillating, hand-wringing, process-obsessed, weak-kneed Congress to derail him. He was handsome, articulate, unrepentant, proud, defiant and flip, and the uniform served to underline all the best of these qualities. He was the can-do guy. "This kid," he said of himself, was the person people came to when they wanted action. When they wanted something done.

All around the country, they were watching North on television, fascinated and intrigued. The nation's leading TV critic, the Washington *Post's* Tom Shales, wrote a string of authoritative essays chronicling North's appearances at the hearings daily—as seen on television. The Shales pieces were a window into the birth of Olliemania. Shales pronounced Day One boffo television and gave the first round to Ollie on dramatic points alone:

"Somebody really ought to boil the tape down and submit it to PBS for 'Great Performances...'" Shales wrote. "House Counsel John W. Nields, Jr., the guy with the Ichabod Crane haircut... was no match for North, who acted like someone who'd studied a dozen old movies to prepare for the appearance. Burt Lancaster in 'Seven Days in May' and Jimmy Stewart in 'Mr. Smith Goes to Washington' might have been two of them. When it comes time to make 'Oliver's Story,' the TV mini-series, however, North would seem the only one for the role. He would have to play himself, like he did yesterday. He's got the role down pat. The eyebrow work is masterful.

"North so early and so clearly put the committee on the defensive, made the committee look churlish and small, that his tour de force brought to mind some of the great screen bamboozlers of all time—say, Groucho Marx as Rufus T. Firefly in 'Duck Soup,' making a mockery of an inquisition into the whereabouts of the Fredonia war plans that he had hidden in Mrs. Teasdale's safe... Whether it continues to be a merry chase, with the fox outsmarting and outcharming the hounds, remains to be seen. Arthur Liman, the Senate counsel, is usually more hard-nosed and aggressive than Nields. Can it be that the more Congress puts the screws to North, the more victimized and saintly he will look in the eyes of the viewing nation?...

"At the moment, like they say in pro wrestling, Ollie North is the 'television champion.'... Some day my prince will come? Oh, but he's already here. Or at least he thinks he is... His appearance isn't just a chance for everyone watching to play political analyst. It's a chance for everyone watching to play psychiatrist. Oliver North returns to the national couch today."

If Day One had been the day that North seized the patriotic high ground, Day Two would be the day that he set out to solve the image problems that had been created by the "Button" account, his acceptance of the security system from Secord, and his cashing of thousands of dollars of Contra traveler's checks for what appeared to be personal use. These were nettlesome issues that had to be dealt with.

So if there were any questions that North was ready for, these were the ones. He would just wait for Nields to lob them in, then knock them out of the park. He would give three variations on the Checkers speech Richard Nixon had made thirty-five years earlier.

"There's been testimony, as I'm sure you're aware, that a death benefit account was set up by Mr. Hakim with the name Button, for the benefit of your family in the event of your death," Nields said. "Were you aware of any such account?"

"No," replied North firmly. "Totally unaware of it. First I heard of it was through these hearings... And it was a shock. An absolute shock." But he conceded later that prior to his trip to Tehran in May of 1986, when Casey had told him that he should take with him the means to take his own life ("I did not tell my wife and children that, and they may be hearing it for the first time right now"), Hakim had offered to "do something" for his family if Ollie did not return. North said he was grateful and agreed to have his wife meet with Hakim's lawyer in Philadelphia so that she would know whom to contact if he did not return from Tehran. There was no money discussed at the meeting, and the lawyer merely gathered information about the number of children he had and who else was in his family, North said.

"I then went and, thank God, returned safely from Iran," Ollie testified. "After that trip there was one more call to my wife from the lawyer... [He] asked for the name of an adult executor for our family, in the event, I suppose, that neither my wife nor I were around. I told my wife, 'Don't call him back. It is unnecessary.' She never did. She never heard from him again, and she has never made contact with him again. No money was ever transferred to my possession, control, account—or that of my wife, or that of my children. I never heard about 'belly buttons' until these hearings began. Does that answer your question, Counsel?"

Nields asked if North was testifying to what he had been told by his wife.

"On the advice of counsel," Ollie replied, not about to involve Mrs. North, "I have not revealed any of our privileged marital communications. I have given you a surmise, based on what I know the facts to be."

"In other words, Counsel, don't call his wife," snapped Brendan Sullivan.

Nields moved on to the fence: "Were you aware that that security system was paid for by General Secord?"

North now played his Abu Nidal card. "The issue of the security system was first broached immediately after a threat on my life by Abu Nidal. Abu Nidal is, as I'm sure you and the intelligence committees know, the principal, foremost assassin in the world today. He is a brutal murderer...

"He targeted me for assassination. We then made an effort over the course of several days to have the story killed and not run on the U.S. media. Nonetheless, it ran, and I believe the date was the twenty-eighth of April. The initial assessment was that this was a response to the attack on Libya... [in] which I had a small role to play."

North said he asked for FBI protection and was refused. His superiors told him the only thing they could do to assure his security was to transfer him to Camp Lejeune. He called private security companies to get estimates on a system, and was told it would be several weeks before they could come out to even survey the job. He needed help now. So Secord sent over Glenn Robinette.

"Now, I want you to know..." North said, throwing down the gauntlet, "I'll be glad to meet Abu Nidal on equal terms anywhere in the world, okay? There's an even deal for him. But I'm not willing to have my wife and four children meet Abu Nidal and his organization on his terms. And I want you to know what was going through my mind. I was about to leave for Tehran. I had already been told by Director Casey that I should be prepared to take my own life. I had already been told that the government of the United States... might even disavow the fact that I have gone on the trip... If there is a law that prevents the protection of American government employees and their families from people like Abu Nidal, then, gentlemen, please fix it, because this kid won't be around much longer, as I'm sure you know. But there will be others, if they take activist steps to address the problem of terrorism, who will be threatened."

Then, revealing the degree to which he had been prepared for this line of questioning, North, in the event anyone still doubted the evil nature of Abu Nidal, proceeded to quote from various newspaper and magazine descriptions of the terrorist. Ollie, concluding that "Abu Nidal makes the infamous terrorist Carlos look like a Boy Scout," then brought out the *coup de grace*: a huge blowup, mounted on cardboard, of a *Newsweek* article describing Abu Nidal's role in the December 27, 1985, attacks on the Rome and Vienna airports that killed twenty people, including five Americans. An aide leaned the exhibit on the table in front of North so the committees—and the photographers—could get a good view.

After an appropriate pause North said: "One of the people killed in the Christmas massacre, and I do not wish to overdramatize this, but the Abu Nidal terrorist in Rome who blasted the eleven-year-old American Natasha Simpson to her knees deliberately zeroed in and fired an extra burst at her head, just in case. Gentlemen, I have an eleven-year-old daughter, not perhaps a whole lot different than Natasha Simpson, and so when Mr. Robinette told me on or about the tenth of May that he could immediately install a security system, I said: 'Please try to keep it to the eight thousand to eighty-five hundred dollars. I am, after all, a Marine lieutenant colonel, and I live on my salary.' And he installed that system."

Nields tried to break in at this point to stem the dramatic flow, but North would not be denied. He had to finish his answer. He had to explain his attempt not to divulge the fact that Secord had paid for the system. Better not even to wait to be asked about this. Just stage, in effect, a preemptive strike and address it on his own terms: he admitted to backdating and writing two letters to Robinette to try and disguise the Secord payment.

"As I told you yesterday, I was going to tell you the truth—the good, the bad and the ugly. This is the truth. I did probably the grossest misjudgment that I have made in my life. I then tried to paper over that whole thing . . . It was not an exercise in good judgment." But he did not want to concede too much: "I'm also suggesting to you, gentlemen, that if it was General Secord who paid the bill . . . you guys ought to write him a check because the government should have done it to begin with. Thank you, sir."

It was a ten-strike which touched and exploited almost every emotional button that there was to press. Who, indeed, could fault a low-paid Marine lieutenant colonel for taking steps to protect his family against the threats of a certifiable terrorist by accepting help from a friend after the hapless government could not get its bureaucratic act together to help one of its own?

In this speech North had also: reminded the committees and the public of his "small" (translated: *large*) role in the Libyan bombing; made it clear that he had risked his life for his country in going to Tehran; attacked everyone's favorite target—Congress—for a security breach in making public his address and for somehow being at fault for his having accepted a private security system; attacked the dreaded media for irresponsibly publicizing that he had been threatened by Abu Nidal; and positioned himself squarely on the side of good and righteousness in his *mano à mano* holy war against Abu Nidal.

"It was a wonderful speech," recalls one House committee member, Rep. Ed Jenkins, Democrat of Georgia. "It took away that whole issue. How do you attack that? Even though it was a non-

answer, all of that was just a great show. And I loved it as a spectator. I respected the obvious preparation that went into it."

Nields seemed in no mood to buck Ollie's surging tide. He would
just lob up the third broad subject area—ask no specific questions
—and let Ollie do his thing. "There's been testimony about use of
traveler's checks. I'd like to give you an opportunity to answer or
explain that testimony," Nields said. "I take it you have it in mind."

"I do have it it mind, Counsel. I appreciate the opportunity.
Again, you'll have to indulge me a bit." North then launched into a
long explanation of the facts of financial life in running the Contra
operation. The operational account, he said, consisted of about
$150,000 to $175,000—$100,000 of which was in traveler's checks
from Adolfo Calero, and the rest in cash from Secord. The money
went to support Contra leaders and Contra activities, and also the
DEA hostage recovery effort. But there were times when the balance in the account dwindled down to zero, and to meet operational needs, North said, he would often have to use money from
his own pocket. He would then reimburse himself with the traveler's checks. Casey had urged him to keep meticulous records and
even provided an operational ledger that North had used. But Ollie
said he had destroyed the ledger, on Casey's orders.

It was, some might say, the classic dead man's defense, but North
made it ring true: "Every single one of those traveler's checks which
bore my name were used by me to defray an actual operational
expense as it happened. I'd cash a check, for example, at Miami
Airport, and hand the money to a resistance person who I met with
there. Or I flew myself off to someplace; because we were trying to
avoid the use of appropriated funds. We used this account to live
within Boland and to hide the fact that NSC travel was being conducted . . .

"We had one dickens of a time trying to protect my travel. And as
you undoubtedly know, gentlemen, I made an enormous amount of
travel. The schedule was brutal. Much of it was paid for out of that
operational account. There were times when that account was
down to zero, no money in it. . . . Under those circumstances, I
would use my own money, Lieutenant Colonel Oliver North's pay-
check money, his own money that he had earned, and I would use
it for an operational expense. I would therefore make a notation in
the ledger: 'spent $250 on going to Atlanta to meet with somebody.'
And the next time I got cash or traveler's checks, I would use those
checks to reimburse myself . . .

"I never took a penny that didn't belong to me . . . And I want to

make it very clear that when you put up things like Parklane Hosiery, and you all snicker at it, and you know that I've got a beautiful secretary, and the good Lord gave her the gift of beauty, and the
people snicker that Ollie North might have been doing a little
hanky-panky with his secretary. Ollie North has been loyal to his
wife since the day he married her. And the fact is, I went to my
best friend, and I asked her, 'Did I ever go to Parklane Hosiery?'
And you know what she told me? 'Of course you did, you old buf-
foon,' you went there to buy leotards for our two little girls.' And
the reason I wrote the check to Parklane Hosiery, just like the
checks to Giant, is because I was owed my money for what I had
spent in pursuing that covert operation.

"You gentlemen may not have agreed that we should have been
pursuing covert operations at the NSC, but we were. We had an
operational account, and we used the money for legitimate purposes
within that covert operation. Does that answer your question, sir?"

"Yes," said Nields, practically running up a white flag.

"Thank you," said North. Ollie, when he knew he had hit a home
run, was in the habit of concluding with the polite, if somewhat
condescending, flourish: "Does that answer your question, sir?"

Nields was surprised how effective North's answers about his
personal finances had been, given the facts. He decided to give
North the benefit of the doubt and leave well enough alone. The
committees could not risk becoming the heavy on what, in the final
analysis, were petty financial issues that were more appropriately
in the special prosecutor's domain. The committees' agenda was to
explore the larger governmental issues. So Nields decided not even
to press North about the $1,000 in traveler's checks he had given
Rob Owen as a wedding present, or about the letters from the
Secretary of the Navy and the Marine counsel saying they had
never received requests from North for protection in 1986, following the Abu Nidal threat.

"I also did not think it was in the cards to prevent this fellow
from telling history the way he wanted to," recalls Nields. "I think
it had something to do with the beating he had taken previously—a
month and a half of negative testimony which he couldn't respond
to, and it didn't feel right to rein him in. Also, when he would run,
he'd usually run into a few cabinet officials on the way. So it was
revealing, if at the same time annoying.

"A lot of people felt you had to hurt North in order to hurt his
testimony. You had to make people dislike the person to make them
dislike his conduct. I was philosophically opposed to that, but I'm

aware that there's truth to it. I don't know if I chose the right way of skating through it or not."

In any case, Nields skated on, getting North to say he thought the diversion was a "neat idea," and getting him to concede his role in altering and destroying documents and not telling the truth to Congress. North tried to argue that if he had told the truth, people —presumably hostages or cooperative Iranians—could have been killed. In one of his most memorable statements of the hearings, he said: "I want you to know lying does not come easy to me. I want you to know it doesn't come easy to anybody. But I think we all had to weigh, in the balance, the difference between lives and lies."

. He had lied to Congress in the past, but he was telling the truth now, North asserted. Still, his disregard for Congress shone through clearly when he accused it of making "incredible leaks" when "American lives were at stake." He cited the Nicaraguan harbor mining as an example, adding: "These kinds of leaks are devastating. They are devastating to the national security of the United States." This apparently got Senator Inouye's back up, and he lectured North that the FBI and the CIA had found no leaks during the two years he had chaired the Senate Intelligence Committee.

Expanding on his reluctance to be the fall guy for everyone, North said it was the prospect of criminal charges being brought that had changed everything. "I was supposed to be dropped like a hot rock when it all came down and I was willing to serve in that capacity," he insisted. But he said he "was not willing to become the victim of a criminal prosecution."

North also discussed his relationship with Casey in some detail, depicting the late Director as his intelligence godfather. He painted a portrait of Casey as his personal case-officer, saying that the CIA director had "almost drawn up" the Contra supply operation, and had suggested that Secord be brought in. He said Casey had been an enthusiastic supporter of the diversion, calling it "the ultimate irony, the ultimate covert operation," which could generate monies that might be used for other projects. When Congress restored Contra funding, Casey thought "it might be necessary at some point in the future to have something, as he would put it, to pull off the shelf, and to help support other activities like that."

Ollie still found the occasion to inject a one-liner or two. He had gone by a variety of code names, one of which was William Goode. Nields seemed confused and at one point asked: "Are you Goode?"

"I was very good," replied North, not missing a beat.

Tom Shales, continuing to watch The Ollie Show, found the second day even more riveting than the first.

North's Day Two, Shales wrote, was "a new classic in the annals of melodramatic political rhetoric," on a par with Nixon's Checkers speech and FDR's "complaint that the Republicans had stooped to attacking even 'my little dog, Fala.' North stopped short only of taking out family photos of his wife and kiddies or getting down on one knee for a chorus of 'Swanee.' It was bravura, it was electric, it was vaguely deplorable, but it was fascinating to behold. It will be studied for years in universities, political forums and, perhaps, medical laboratories."

When North took on Abu Nidal, Shales said, it was as if Ollie was "swaggering sitting down... On the stand, North continued to stretch more emotive and rhetorical muscles than all the Barrymores put together. Now contrite, now accusative, now coy, now disingenuous, now proud, now sheepish, now feisty, now weary, he was a whole season of Broadway theater rolled into one rollercoaster morning."

Shales noted that at one point late in the morning, while North was still speaking, all three networks cut away and showed pictures of President Reagan leaving the White House to board a helicopter for a trip to Connecticut. "The juxtaposition was eerie and incriminating," he wrote. "The little guy, the lieutenant colonel, was sweating it out on the hot seat, practically a sacrificial functionary, while the top man in the chain of command could be seen waving and smiling and larking about, looking coldly and unfeelingly oblivious to North's plight. It was one of the ugliest images of Ronald Reagan's presidential career...

"Ollie, Ollie, Ollie. Is it actually possible you will ever be prosecuted for your errors and sent off to prison? Would the American people stand for it after watching this Herculean performance on television?" According to an ABC News poll, 58 percent of Americans watching found North believable, while 70 percent said he was "performing well."

"Performing well?" queried Shales. "If the Emmy were a medal and there were any more room on Ollie's chest, he would be a shoo-in. . . . He has materialized at these hearings like some ghost from the past—a straight-arrow, duty-honor-country, loyal-to-his-wife type who one might have thought now only existed in movies. He is John Wayne in 'They Were Expendable.' He is John Garfield in 'They Made Me a Criminal.' He is Errol Flynn in 'The Charge of the Light Brigade.'"

By Day Three, the senators and congressmen on the Iran-Contra committees were openly nervous. Their offices were being flooded with pro-Ollie calls, telegrams and letters. The thrust of the sentiment was that North was a patriot doing his duty at others' direction, and the committees were unfairly attacking him. Nields had finished his questioning, but the House minority counsel, George Van Cleve, had the floor this morning, followed by chief Senate Counsel Arthur Liman in the afternoon. The press was playing up the Liman-North encounter as a showdown. The politicians were being criticized, yet they weren't even in the game. The lawyers had all the action.

Sen. David Boren, Democrat of Oklahoma, was the first committee member to speak out in frustration. He said that he and other members were fed up with sitting by like "potted palms" while Ollie rolled the lawyers. In a departure from decorum that reflected the mounting home-state political pressures the committee members were feeling, Boren was particularly critical of Nields and said that the members could have done a better job of questioning North. Liman would extend into Friday, and it would not be until then that the members got their chance—by which time the public would have concluded that the committees had kept "that poor man" at the witness table long enough, Boren complained.

Recalls one of the Senate committee's associate counsels: "I don't think the members had really focused on how persuasive North was going to be or how the medium of television was going to play to his strengths. He would talk about encroaching communism in this hemisphere, or about how Congress vacillated or supposedly leaked like a sieve. These were all things that Joe Lunchbox could really understand, while our response was more abstract—a discussion of whether the ends justified the means, or relations between the executive and legislative branches... One senator was beginning to hear from the folks back home that he should get off the committee. 'You guys gotta stop harassing Ollie,' he told us. The imagery was Ollie, the All-American shining knight, against ... Nields the hippie."

Senator Rudman of New Hampshire, who was sniped at by his home-state Manchester *Union Leader* during the hearings for being too harsh on the Administration, heard the pro-North outcries but was confident the committees could turn the sentiment around over the long haul.

"Our phones were ringing," Rudman remembers. "It strengthened my belief that the American people can be influenced by television, by heroes and perceived heroes, and that the people who devote themselves to unpopular causes, which we were doing in the hearings, simply have to have patience to be vindicated. But I wasn't panicked by it all. Some of my colleagues were nervous. They thought they were being made fools of, and that they were being made to look inept, and that they were going to get criticism at home for having this fellow before them so long, and so forth... Had I had my druthers, John Nields would not have done the direct questioning. I think that would have changed the whole week."

But Nields, despite the criticism directed his way, was feeling okay about himself. "I didn't feel badly about the way it had gone," he recalls. "I thought his testimony was extremely revealing. I didn't think I'd been a star. I felt medium-to-good about it... On North, I went as far as I wanted to go. I thought it was my responsibility to cover the waterfront of bringing out the facts. I wanted to touch all the significant areas. I wasn't aware of the effect he was having on the viewers until after I had completed my questioning on the second day. I was surprised at the reaction. I didn't understand it very well... I think what I didn't realize, and now fault myself for, was that the viewing public for North was new. I was proceeding on the assumption that whoever I was doing this for had seen the previous month and a half... And they would have developed a lot of facts about North. But a whole new audience tuned in."

North began his third day on the stand by reading his opening statement that had been ruled out of order on the first day. He praised his "best friend"—his wife, Betsy, who was making her first appearance at the hearings dressed in a blue-and-white polka-dot dress, with white collar and white cuffs and a string of pearls around her neck—and he praised Ronald Reagan as a great president. North said he had harbored no "fantasy" that he was actually the president, but told of a let-Ollie-do-it mindset that developed on the White House staff.

"I readily admit that I was action-oriented, that I took pride in the fact that I was counted upon as a man who got the job done," he said. "And I don't mean by way of criticism, but there were occasions when my superiors, confronted with accomplishing goals or difficult tasks, would simply say, 'Fix it, Ollie,' or 'Take care of it.'"

North made it plain that he regarded the hearings as a stacked deck. "Apparently the president has chosen not to assert his preroga- tives, and you have been permitted to make the rules..." he told the committees. "You put the testimony which you think is helpful to your goals up before the people and leave others out. It's sort of like a baseball game in which you are both the player and the umpire... I believe it is inevitable that the Congress will in the end blame the executive branch, but I suggest to you that it is the Congress which must accept at least part of the blame in the Nicaraguan freedom- fighters' matter. Plain and simple, the Congress is to blame because of the fickle, vacillating, unpredictable, on-again-off-again policy to- ward the Nicaraguan democratic resistance... In my opinion, these hearings have caused serious damage to our national interests. Our adversaries laugh at us, and our friends recoil in horror."

But Ollie said he had nothing to apologize for. "I am going to walk from here with my head held high and my shoulders straight because I am proud of what we accomplished. I am proud of the efforts that we made, and I am proud of the fight that we fought." Then, in the event the committees had missed which way the polit- ical winds were blowing, North added: "I would just simply like to thank the tens of thousands of Americans who have communicated their support, encouragement and prayers for me and my family in this difficult time."

Attorney Van Cleve, representing the House committee Repub- licans, then led North on a sympathetic recounting of the highlights of his military career, starting in Vietnam, noting his medals for valor, and letting Ollie say: "I would also point out that we didn't lose the war in Vietnam. We lost the war right here in this city."

At one point Van Cleve's questioning was interrupted when two men suddenly jumped up from the spectator section shouting and holding up a banner that read: "Ask About Cocaine Smuggling"—a reference to the allegations that the Contras had been involved in drug smuggling to finance their war effort. At the first sounds of noise, North ducked, as if a gun had been fired and the likes of Abu Nidal had somehow pierced the inner sanctum of the Senate.

Van Cleve also had North tell of his dramatic involvement in the TWA hijacking crisis, the *Achille Lauro* affair, and the trip to Tehran, and offered him the unchallenged opportunity to make the case for supporting the Contras during the Boland ban.

Then it was Arthur Liman's turn.

Where Nields had been uninterested in learning about North the man in preparing for his examination of the witness, Liman had devoted considerable time to learning as much as he could about the Marine's character and persona. Liman sought to understand what made North tick. He had approached Ollie's friends and asked them to tell him about Ollie. He had talked to Fawn Hall informally about her impressions of her former boss. He had even tried to chat up Brendan Sullivan; Sullivan did not bite. He did not want any kind of a relationship with Liman, formal or informal, that might have given the Senate counsel the opportunity to better know—and therefore best—North.

Liman was curious about the Annapolis connection that bound the key Iran-Contra players: North, McFarlane and Poindexter. He wondered to what extent they would feel they had to go down with the ship rather than come clean. Was taking the fall a natural reflex for all of them?

And he wondered, too, about the effect of Vietnam on North—his frustration and anger at what had happened, and how that had motivated him: Congress and the press had lost the war. Now, perhaps, when Ollie's turn came to be in power, he would feel he had to rectify past wrongs and show the world how to fight a war right.

Finally there was North's unabashed zeal, his strong conviction—along with Secord—that he, rather than Congress, the press or anyone else, knew best what was in the national interest. Liman was a firm believer in Justice Brandeis' credo that the people who had done the most damage historically were people who thought they had discovered the truth and were prepared to pursue it at all costs.

"I think I understood Oliver North as well as a stranger can know another person," Liman says. "And I was not surprised at all. I knew that he was charismatic. I knew that he was an extraordinarily persuasive person."

He said that until Nields finished with North, he didn't really know what he was going to ask. He had known generally what areas Nields was going to explore, but he had not known what North's answers were going to be. "I didn't know whether, when John finished, I was going to ask him any questions, questions for an hour or questions for a day. And also, I made it a practice, since I was counsel for the Senate committee, to get a sense of what the members want me to do, and I can't get that sense until the witness is finished testifying.

"I saw no reason to be confrontational with North. North got on the stand and said, 'I lied, I cheated, I deceived and I did it all for my country and on orders.' And to me, therefore, it became important to try and bring out the implications of what he was saying . . . He has a great sense of place and time, Oliver North . . . He saw himself as playing on the stage of the country. He understood that he would damage his credibility not just with the committee but with the nation if he minced words, and so he got up there and the first words out of his mouth were: 'I lied, I deceived, I shredded, I altered, and how many times do you want to humiliate me by making me repeat it?' That's a very tough kind of tesimony to deal with."

Liman rated North's performance as "almost flawless," and didn't consider the Marine's emotion affected: "I don't think he has to put some kind of vinegar in his eyes to make him cry. I think he summons up those emotions. When he delivers a speech on the Contras, and he gets to the grave of the Contra, he cries. Some people cry at funerals. It's not fake. It's their personality, but Oliver North is a very emotional person, and I think that anyone who doesn't realize that is missing the person."

So on the afternoon of July 9 Liman began a sympathetic dissection of North, intending to tie together thematically what the witness had laid out in the raw to Nields. America's hearts were still no doubt with the Ollie on view at the witness table. Liman was jowly, with a double chin, fettucine hair and a decided New York accent. "It was apple pie versus bagels and cream cheese," wrote the Los Angeles *Times'* Howard Rosenberg.

"Colonel," Liman asked, "is it fair to say that November 25, 1986, was one of the worst days in your life?"

North, suspecting some kind of curve ball, conferred with Sullivan.

"I wasn't asking if it was one of the worst days in Mr. Sullivan's life," said Liman, drawing laughter from the audience.

North came back to the microphone and took the high road: "I will tell you honestly, Counsel, that I have had many worse days than that. Most of those were days when young Marines died, and there have been days since then that are worse in some respects. I would not recount the last three days that I have been here as being particularly pleasant. It was a difficult day."

Liman moved toward an exploration of the fall-guy plan, seemingly more than willing to buy North's belief that he was a scapegoat—that November 25 was a day when his life changed forever, and he became the subject of a criminal investigation.

North, at one point referring to his role as that of a "Roman centurion," said that the fall-guy plan assumed that "this was not going to be a matter of criminal behavior, but rather one of denia-

bility for the White House . . . for political purposes. And when I
say 'political purposes,' I'm speaking not only domestic, but international ramifications. That is one of the essences of plausible deniability in a covert operation."

"Are you saying, Colonel, that you were prepared to take the rap
for political purposes, but not for criminal purposes?"

"Precisely . . . There was probably not another person on the planet
Earth as shocked as I was to hear that someone thought it was
criminal," North said. "And I can tell you that that shock was compounded when I heard later that there was to be an independent
counsel, and further compounded when I was the only name in the
appointment order for that independent counsel — the only person on
the planet Earth named in that appointment order, Counsel."

North wanted to have it both ways on the fall-guy issue: he
wanted the credit for being the one who was ready, willing and able
to stand up and take the heat, yet he was also bringing just about
everyone but the president into the soup with him. In seeking to
make the distinction between taking a political hit and a criminal
hit, he was attempting to create the impression that he was willing
to be the fall guy, but not the patsy.

Whatever, Liman seemed sympathetic to North for having taken
an unanticipated fall. But while presumably disarming North with
this tactic, he was also drawing from the witness repeated acknowl-
edgments that his behavior in lying and deceiving was in violation
of the Naval Academy's values of honor and trustworthiness that he
had sworn to uphold as a midshipman.

Where North had owned the morning, now Liman's silky, seemingly sympathetic line of questioning seemed to throw Ollie off
balance. He was hesitant at times, and Sullivan was moved to in-
terject angrily and repeatedly in an attempt to redirect Liman to
other subjects. Once he said Liman was "in Dreamland," and another time said fairness was "out the window" in Congress.

But even when moving to related areas, such as the basis for
North's assumption that Reagan had approved the diversion, Liman
sketched a portrait of Ollie as a blind, unquestioning loyalist. There
was this telling exchange:

North: "I had assumed from the day I took my post at the National Security Council that those things which required the approval of the president — and I sent forward memoranda soliciting
that approval, and I got the authority to proceed on various initiatives — had indeed received the approval of the president. I've testified to that."

Liman: "And it wasn't until Admiral Poindexter answered your question that that assumption was shaken."

"It wasn't shaken. He simple denied that the president knew."

"Did you ask him: 'Admiral Poindexter, why did you not discuss this with the president?'"

"No."

"Why not?"

"First of all," said North, "I'm not in the habit of questioning my superiors. If he deemed it not to be necessary to ask the president, I saluted smartly and charged up the hill. That's what lieutenant colonels are supposed to do. I have no problem with that. I don't believe that what we did, even under those circumstances, is wrong or illegal. . . . I've told you I thought it was a good idea to begin with . . . I still think it was a good idea, Counsel."

"And have you wondered why, if it was a good idea, that the president of the United States dismissed you because of it?"

"Let me—let me just make one thing perfectly clear, Counsel. This lieutenant colonel is not going to challenge a decision of the commander-in-chief, for whom I still work. And I am proud to work for that commander-in-chief. And if the commander-in-chief tells this lieutenant colonel to go stand in the corner and stand on his head, I will do so. And if the commander-in-chief decides to dismiss me from the NSC staff, this lieutenant colonel will proudly salute and say: 'Thank you for the opportunity to have served,' and go. And I am not going to criticize his decision, no matter how he relieves me, sir."

If that was the most revealing testimony of the day, the most sensational came when North claimed that while Attorney General Meese's aides were reading the files in his office on November 22, he continued to shred documents in their presence. This provoked incredulous laughter from the audience, but a strong denial from the alleged Inspector Clouseaux at the Justice Department that the incident had ever occurred.

Though apparently somewhat unnerved by Liman, North emerged from Day Three still very much in control of the political winds. He was pulling much higher TV ratings than the soap operas did, and the crowds outside on Capitol Hill were big. So North walked out onto a Senate balcony with his wife at his side and waved to his admirers in the street below.

Monitoring North's evolving TV image, Shales concluded that Liman "really didn't leave much of a scratch on The Little Colonel. The Little Colonel that could. And did."

Shales marveled that Ollie's patriotic pieties rang true, not hollow or hopelessly cornball. "North delivers these gollywhompers with a radiant sort of righteousness that's infectious, if slightly creepy. You want to believe, like you want to believe Superman can fly and that Tinkerbell won't croak from drinking the poison meant for Peter Pan... Beholding this performance in all its holy fervor, studying that fastidious innocent glow on North's face... one could sense a quality that has helped make North such an irresistible television character this week. We love watching him partly because, let's face it, he loves being here.

"He loves talking about how hard all this has been on himself and his family, he loves getting indignant over real or imagined slurs from the committee, he loves brandishing the lingo of espionage and secrecy..." All in all, concluded Shales, The Ollie Show was "bona fide, certified, total-immersion television. It's almost impossible to tear yourself away."

At the dawning of Day Four, Olliemania had reached overdrive.

A New York *Times*—CBS poll reported that an overwhelming majority of Americans believed that North was telling the truth about the Iran-Contra affair and most felt President Reagan was lying. As North and Brendan Sullivan had hoped, the public viewed the colonel as a patriot and believed he was following orders from the president. Yet there were indications that the audience was responding more to his personality than to his message— listening to the music, but not the words. The poll found that only 18 percent of those surveyed considered North a national hero, and a majority said he had been wrong if he broke the law.

The White House, hoping Olliemania would translate into a groundswell of support for its Contra policy, announced it had been innundated by expressions of support for North—4,961 in favor and only 220 opposed. "Obviously the Administration is pleased that much of the story of our support for the Contras and the freedom fighters in Central America is being portrayed by Colonel North to audiences that are appreciative and understanding," said White House spokesman Marlin Fitzwater. But while the people loved Ollie, they still seemed to want nothing to do with the Nicaraguan situation. According to a National Public Radio poll, 72 percent still rejected giving military aid to the Contras. Help for its Contra policy was the best the White House could hope for from North, since otherwise his testimony had brought devastating new disclosures about high-level involvement in various coverups and lies.

There were pro-North crowds outside Capitol Hill chanting that he should run for office, not go to jail. Some people were actually passing folded-up money to police guards at the Senate building and saying with a wink, "Pass it on to Ollie."

Sullivan thought it time to give the press first-hand evidence of how North was being received in the heartland. He brought in two tall piles of telegrams and placed them on the witness table in front of his client—the better for the committee members to see Exhibit A of the rising popular tide and how it would be foolish to trifle with the object of that adoration. It was a menacing display. During recesses, Sullivan let the press read some of the telegrams:

"Next male child will be named Oliver," promised one fan in Morristown, New Jersey.

"Give 'em hell, Ollie."—Pasadena, Texas.

"Don't let the bastards get you down."—Orange Park, Florida.

"God love you, son. Keep well. Money to follow."—Spring Valley, California.

"Never mind the liberal lynch mob. We are proud of what you did."—Littleton, Colorado.

"You're doing wonderfully. Chin up. Kiss your wife, children. Pet your dog. I'm 81. Friends here believe you."—Hemet, California.

"Colonel, I congratulate you on your decorum in the face of those illbred hyenas putting you through this hell," concluded a note from Michigan.

But if Liman noticed any of these missives as he resumed his questioning on Friday morning, he gave no clue. Asking North about the process by which the diversion was approved, Liman got North to testify that Poindexter had warned: "This should never come out."

Taking North through a recounting of his freewheeling negotiations with the Iranian second channel, Liman drew from the colonel that he had not been given State Department authority to commit the United States to agreeing to the removal of Iraqi President Saddam Hussein, or to support a plan to release the seventeen Da'wa prisoners—nor had he received "specific authorization" from Casey or Poindexter.

And North did not seem bothered by having entrusted private-citizen Hakim to negotiate alone on behalf of the United States, even though Hakim had a direct financial stake in the outcome of those negotiations. Actually, said North, Hakim's financial interest "offered a greater chance for ultimate success" in securing an agreement.

North continued to exhibit his feelings about Congress, insisting that to have informed even the intelligence committees about the secret Contra supply operation "would have caused it to be terminated." When Liman suggested there had to be a better way than for the White House to lie to Congress, North replied: "I have suggested one of those better ways: divulge nothing."

But the chief news of the day came from Liman's boring-in on North's Wednesday reference to Casey's intention of using the profits from the Iran arms sales to establish an "off the shelf" intelligence operation. The secret-government theme needed amplification, Liman felt. He asked if this concept did not amount to having a CIA outside the CIA.

North said he didn't think so.

"Well," pressed Liman, "wasn't this an organization that would be able to do covert policy to advance U.S. foreign policy interests?"

"Well, not necessarily all covert," replied North. "The director was interested in the ability to go [to] an existing—as he put it— off-the-shelf, self-sustaining, stand-alone entity that could perform certain activities on behalf of the United States . . . Several of those activities were discussed with both Director Casey and with Admiral Poindexter. Some of those were to be conducted jointly by other friendly intelligence services, but they needed money."

"Colonel?" asked Liman quietly, pausing for dramatic effect.

"Yes, Counsel?" said North, not averse to a dramatic moment.

"You understood that the CIA is funded by the United States government, correct?"

"That is correct."

"You understood that the United States government put certain limitations on what the CIA could do, correct?"

"That is correct."

"And I ask you today, after all you've gone through, are you not shocked that the director of Central Intelligence is proposing to you the creation of an organization to do these kinds of things outside of his own organization?"

North said he wasn't shocked. It all seemed logical to him. "I don't see that it was necessarily inconsistent with the laws, regulations, statutes and all that obtain. I don't see that it would necessarily be unconstitutional. I don't see that it would necessarily be in any way a violation of anything that I know of . . . You know, maybe I'm overly naive, but I don't see what would be wrong with that."

Then, without naming the ship *Erria*, or the nature of its originally conceived mission to beam pro-Western propaganda into

Libya, North told how he and Secord had quickly purchased a ship using Enterprise funds because Casey had requested it and complained that his own CIA couldn't do the job.

"This organization produced it practically overnight..." said North. "It didn't cost the taxpayers of the United States a cent."

Liman, wanting to make it clear that this was an unaccountable rogue operation, wondered if President Reagan had signed a finding authorizing the purchase of the ship.

"No, but there was nothing that prohibited the purchase of the ship by the private commerical companies that were supporting that activity..." said North, seeming to miss, or perhaps choosing to ignore, the point. "And the ship was there to serve the foreign-policy goals of the United States. The fact that we were—the whole operation was terminated before it could do so was unfortunate, in my humble opinion."

"Was the president of the United States told about the fact that that ship had been purchased?"

"I do not know."

"The Congress wasn't told. Correct?"

"They certainly know now."

"They weren't told at the time."

"I don't believe they were, sir."

Toward the end of Liman's questioning on the Casey off-the-shelf operation, Rep. Bill McCollum, Jr., a House committee Republican from Florida, decided to raise a "point of order."

"I think Mr. Liman is out of line in asking questions that prejudge opinion of this committee," he complained. "He is phrasing his questions to make an argument to slant it as though the entire committee thinks that this is a horrible thing. He doesn't speak for everybody."

McCollum's statement reflected the increasing political tensions making themselves felt on the committee as North's testimony continued, as his popularity soared and as the members remained on the sidelines. It was an extension of the frustration first voiced by Senator Boren. Some members were chomping at the bit to mollify home-state pressure by climbing aboard Ollie's bandwagon when it came their turn to ask "questions."

Rep. Henry Hyde, conservative Republican of Illinois, publicly defended the lawyers but later—en route to presenting Betsy North with a bouquet of roses—told reporters he agreed that the lawyers were getting too much air time. "We're the spear carriers in this opera," Hyde said. "The New York lawyer and the Washington lawyer are staging this summer stock. We talk when they let us, and fear the bell." Hyde said North's performance was the most stirring and patriotic display "since the first time I saw Jimmy Cagney singing 'Yankee Doodle Dandy.' A man comes in who was the hunted and turns out to be the impresario."

About McCollum's defense of North, Sen. Paul Sarbanes, Democrat of Maryland, publicly noted that McCollum had said only two weeks earlier at the hearings that the failure of North, McFarlane and Poindexter to tell all to Attorney General Meese about their roles "... may well be a crime. If it is not a crime, it is certainly one of the highest acts of insubordination and one of the most treacherous things that has occurred to a president, it seems to me, in our history."

Sen. William Cohen, the Maine Republican, later defended Liman's right to ask questions as he saw fit, and called the Casey-North off-the-shelf scheme "perhaps the most serious revelation to have taken place during the course of these proceedings... If members of Congress are not disturbed about that revelation, then I think the American people should be."

The first committee member to question North, Georgia's Representative Jenkins, picked up Liman's off-the-shelf line of questioning and got North to acknowledge that while the United States had nothing to do with financing the operation, it was to have directed it. Still, no elected official in the country had had knowledge of the plan, he conceded, thereby making it unaccountable.

North offered that if it were up to him, he would channel as much of the $8 million left in Iran arms-sales profits—from which the Casey off-the-shelf operation was to have been funded—to the Contras. Jenkins, a supporter of Contra aid, noted that Hakim had already refused to turn over the money to the United States.

"Give me ten minutes with Mr. Hakim," Ollie suggested, bringing down the house with laughter.

"You think if you have ten minutes that you can get Mr. Hakim to turn over that $8 million?" obliged Jenkins.

"If I could meet with anybody without a bunch of lawyers around, I reckon I could, sir," North said, laughing.

Jenkins, a former county prosecutor who liked to project a country-lawyer image, saw an opening to ask a serious question. "Really, you are a very articulate person and very persuasive. And looking back on this, do you think that sometimes you may have persuaded your superior to take certain action, even when cabinet members were opposed? Simply because of your eloquence and very sincere beliefs?"

North was not about to disagree with that. If you can do it, it isn't bragging. He was a communicator. He could persuade people. He had. "I have no doubt about that..." Ollie said. "The good Lord gives us all certain gifts."

Sometimes North brimmed so full of confidence—even cockiness—that he rather overplayed his hand, going for a home run in response to virtually every question. This seemed to be one of those sequences.

Jenkins, being helpful, said it was not so much North's own jurisdiction over the pool of money that would be used to fund the off-the-shelf operations that concerned him, but any "future Ollies" who might come along and decide to, say, give some of the money to the Sandinistas.

"They better look out for me if they did," said Ollie.

Later, fielding softballs tossed to him by Representative Cheney, North described the *Achille Lauro* operation, concluding: "And it all worked like clockwork, and everybody smelled good when it was done."

And so it went, until Ollie was moved to close out the day and his week's testimony with a dramatic appeal for Contra aid. "Hang whatever you want around the neck of Oliver North..." he said. "But for the love of God and for the love of this nation don't hang around Ollie North's neck the cutoff of funds to the Nicaraguan resistance again. This country cannot stand that..."

By the end of the day on Friday—after all the defense he had to play against Liman and occasionally against Jenkins, and after exchanges in which his ego appeared to have strayed from its leash— some, it seemed, were beginning to feel that Ollie's pieties of the first three days were finally beginning to sound slightly unctuous.

"Suddenly, North didn't seem like Jimmy Stewart so much any more," concluded Tom Shales in his Day Four Olliewatch. "He seemed more like Charlton Heston."

But this was still a blip-on-the-screen, minority view—perhaps just a hint of trouble for Ollie on the horizon. All in all North's four days on the witness stand thus far had been off the charts of success by any standard. He had quenched the country's thirst for a hero, for someone who believed passionately in what he did, and was willing to stand up and give the powers-that-be what for. Dan Rather of CBS called the North testimony "a tour de force," and actually talked seriously about the Marine making a run for public office. *Newsweek*'s cover proclaimed "Ollie Takes The Hill: The Fall Guy Becomes a Folk Hero."

But North still had two days to go and there would be the weekend for the white heat he had generated to cool down—for people to pause and contemplate what he said rather than *how* he said it and how he *looked* saying it; for the Iran-Contra committees to contemplate the public-relations beating they had taken; and for some members to return and give their own speeches to North. They would try to get the public to grapple with the contradictions in the emerging portrait of North: how his professed expressions of duty, honor and truthfulness could be reconciled with his admitted record of lying and deception, even if in a cause he obviously believed in.

Liman tried a little spin-control on reporters as they left for the weekend, telling them that North was essentially offering "the Nuremberg defense—everything he did he did on orders." The fundamental question, he said, was whether the country was going to allow policy to be made in secret without elected officials being consulted. He suggested that the public, after the initial emotional response to North had passed, would conclude that unaccountable secrecy was no way to do business. "Americans can respect somebody as a hero and still say they want their elected representatives to run the government," Liman said.

If the first four days had been dominated by North's speechmaking, he would be forced to cede the microphone for most of the final two days. The committee members, rather than just continuing to grill North, finally got their mugs on the tube while offering up their own theories on the implications of the colonel's words and deeds in a democracy, and the effect he was having on the country.

Perhaps the most quoted statement was made by Sen. George Mitchell, the Democrat from Maine, since it was Mitchell who confronted North on the assumptions which seemed to underlie much of his passionate rhetoric: the implication that he had a corner on the God-and-country market, and that people who disagreed with his strongly held political views were somehow less patriotic or less favored in the eyes of God.

Mitchell, the first questioner on Monday morning, July 13, began by eliciting agreement from North that every American should obey the law, whether he or she agreed with that law or not. Mitchell, a former federal judge, had in mind at least the Boland Amendment and the requirement that Congress be notified of intelligence operations.

He reminded North that in the American form of democracy public policy is the product of open debate, because the public has a right to know what its government is doing and why, and because

of the benefit of hearing opposing points of view in reaching a reasoned decision. When covert action is necessary, the president is
deprived of the benefits of open debate, Mitchell continued, but
the law tried to compensate for that by requiring the chief executive to notify either the congressional intelligence committees or
eight of the Congress's top leaders—four from each party. The reason for the law was to give the president the benefit of different
points of view.

"You've talked here often and eloquently about the need for a
democratic outcome in Nicaragua," Mitchell said to North. "There's
no disagreement on that. There is disagreement over how best to
achieve that objective. Many Americans agree with the president's
policy. Many do not. Many patriotic Americans, strongly anti-communist, believe there's a better way to contain the Sandinistas, to
bring about a democratic outcome in Nicaragua and to bring peace
to Central America. And many patriotic Americans are concerned
that in the pursuit of democracy abroad we not compromise it in
any way here at home.

"You and others have urged consistency in our policies. You've
said repeatedly that if we are not consistent, our allies and other
nations will question our reliability. That's a real concern. But if it's
bad to change policies, it's worse to have two different policies at
the same time: one public policy and an opposite policy in private.
It's difficult to conceive of a greater inconsistency than that. It's
hard to imagine anything that would give our allies more cause to
consider us unreliable than that we say one thing in public and
secretly do the opposite. And that's exactly what was done when
arms were sold to Iran and arms were swapped for hostages."

Mitchell, whose mother was an immigrant and his father the or-
phaned son of an immigrant, went on to say that the most exciting
thing he had done in his life was preside at citizen swearing-in
ceremonies as a federal judge. He said he loved to talk with the
new Americans after they had taken their oath of allegiance to the
United States, and to hear their stories about why they had come
here. One of the main reasons expressed, particularly by those
from totalitarian states, he added, was the freedom to disagree with
the government.

"Now you've addressed several pleas to this committee . . . none
more eloquent than last Friday, when in a response to a question
from Representative Cheney you asked that Congress not cut off
aid to the Contras, 'For the love of God and for the love of country.'

"I now address a plea to you. Of all the qualities which the American people find compelling in you, none is more impressing than your obvious deep devotion to this country. Please remember that others share that devotion, and recognize that it is possible for an American to disagree with you on aid to the Contras, and still love God, and still love his country just as much as you do.

"Although He's regularly asked to do so, God does not take sides in American politics, and in America, disagreement with the policies of government is not evidence of lack of patriotism. I want to repeat that: in America, disagreement with the policies of government is not evidence of lack of patriotism. Indeed, it's the very fact that Americans can criticize their government openly and without fear of reprisal that is the essence of our freedom and that will keep us free.

"Now I have one final plea. Debate this issue forcefully and vigorously, as you have and as you surely will, but please do it in a way that respects the patriotism and the motives of those who disagree with you, as you would have them respect yours. Thank you very much, Colonel."

Though he had been the object of that lesson, North was clearly moved. Tears welled in his eyes.

Two Republicans—Senator Rudman of New Hampshire and Senator Cohen of Maine—also addressed themselves to the policy ramifications of North's testimony.

Responding to North's statement that Congress was to blame for the Contras' difficulties because it had been fickle and vacillating in its support for the resistance, Rudman cited polls indicating that Americans had consistently opposed the Administration's Contra policy, and that it was difficult for the White House to pursue the policy under such circumstances. "The American people have the constitutional right to be wrong," Rudman said. "And what Ronald Reagan thinks or what Oliver North thinks, or what I think, or what anybody else thinks makes not a whit if the American people say 'enough.' And that's why this Congress has been 'fickle' and has vacillated."

Cohen said there were several lingering questions from North's and the Administration's actions in the Iran-Contra affair which there needed to be a consensus on, including: whether any administration could avoid compliance with a law by conducting a covert operation; whether Congress could be lied to about a covert operation; whether, as in the North-Casey off-the-shelf plan, U.S. assets could be sold at a profit to generate money to fund other operations not known or authorized by Congress; whether private entrepreneurs could be used to conduct a government covert action; and whether foreign countries could be solicited to fund programs not authorized, or rejected, by Congress.

"Long after the sheer force of your personality has faded from this room," Cohen told North, "and that may be a very long time indeed, and long after these cameras that are here today are clicked off, I think the American people are going to be left to deal with the policy implications of what has occurred and what's been said in this room . . . We have to ask what it means to reject not the voice of the loyal opposition but the voice of the majority in Congress and the country . . . A democracy demands not only that the rights of the minority be protected, but that the rules of the majority be respected. And that's true even if you and I believe the majority is wrong. We have to respect the rule of law until we can change the law itself. Because otherwise, the rule of law will be reduced to the law of rule."

But North's defenders remained fervent in their support of the colonel. The leader of the pro-Ollie block, Sen. Orrin Hatch, the Utah Republican, looked at North and said: "I don't want you prosecuted. I don't. I don't think many people in America do. And I think there's going to be one lot of hell raised if you are."

Representative Hyde said North personified "the old morality— loyalty, fidelity, honor and, worst of all, obedience." He defended North's and the Administration's penchant for secrecy, noting that secrecy had been used to good advantage in the Constitutional Congress of 1787 and the Israeli-Egyptian meetings which produced the Camp David accords in 1978. He seemed to suggest that it was the political makeup of the Administration and the Congress that had forced the White House underground. "When you have a liberal Democratic Congress," Hyde said, "God bless them all, the people elected them and that's democracy and all that good stuff, and you have a conservative Republican president, you've got a recipe for gridlock. Nothing will happen. And that is the problem we have to deal with in our Central American policy."

Democratic Rep. Jack Brooks, the crusty, cigar-chomping ex-Marine from Texas, injected a little spice into the civics-lesson tone that the hearings had taken on by tweaking North for testifying under immunity. "As you know, I didn't vote to grant you immunity from prosecution because of the general principle," Brooks told North. "I think government officials should be fully accountable for their actions. You've stated numerous times during the past few days that you didn't think you'd broken any laws . . . If you felt so strongly that you hadn't, I had a little difficulty understanding your reluctance to testify without immunity."

Brendan Sullivan was incredulous. "Do you know anything about the Fifth Amendment and its purpose?" he asked Brooks.

Brooks, who seemed fed up with Sullivan's attack-dog objections on North's behalf, cut the lawyer off. "Mr. Chairman, I've had quite enough listening to Mr. Sullivan..." he said. "We didn't hire him as our lawyer, and I don't need him to advise me."

North fenced with Brooks, and advised Rep. Thomas Foley, Democrat of Washington, what was and was not "in the purview of the legislative branch." On the final day, after a lengthy skirmish among members of the committee, North was able to present his famous Contra slide-show that he had so effectively used to help raise money for the resistance. But since turning out the lights was deemed a security risk, the slides could not be projected on the screen. So North was left to hold them up to the light and deliver his narration without anyone being able to see the slide. It was audio, but no video. Still, it was a twenty-minute Contra commercial shown live on all three networks, and the White House was delighted.

But mostly North sat, listened and nodded respectfully on Monday and on Tuesday, his last day, when he was lectured by the Senate chairman, Inouye, and the House chairman, Lee Hamilton.

Before Hamilton addressed North, Rep. Louis Stokes, Democrat of Ohio, also reached rarified rhetorical air. He commended North for keeping the promise he delivered at the outset of his testimony.

"I think it has been good, I think it has been bad, and I think it has been ugly," said Stokes. "I suppose that what has been most disturbing to me about your testimony is the ugly part. In fact, it has been more than ugly. It has been chilling, and in fact frightening.

"I'm not talking just about your part in this, but the entire scenario—about government officials who plotted and conspired, who set up a straw man, a fall guy. Officials who lied, misrepresented and deceived. Officials who planned to superimpose upon our government a layer outside of our government, shrouded in secrecy and only accountable to the conspirators."

Stokes noted that North had said many times that he worried about the damage these hearings were causing the United States around the world. Stokes said he worried more about the hearings having shaken the faith of children in America in their government. "This is not our democracy's finest hour," he said.

Then, recalling Senator Mitchell's remarks about immigrants, Stokes, who is black, said that minorities had not always enjoyed justice and equality under the law. "We had to abide by the slow and arduous process of abiding by law until we could change the law through the judicial process. In fact, Colonel, as I sit here looking at you in your uniform, I cannot help but remember that I wore the uniform of this country in World War II in a segregated army. I wore it as proudly as you do, even though our government required black and white soldiers in the same army to live, sleep, eat and travel separate and apart, while fighting and dying for our country. But because of the rule of law, today's servicemen in America suffer no such indignity.

"Similar to Senator Mitchell's humble beginnings, my mother, a widow, raised two boys. She had an eighth-grade education. She was a domestic worker who scrubbed floors. One son became the first black mayor of a major American city. The other sits today as chairman of a House intelligence committee. Only in America, Colonel North. Only in America. And while I admire your love for America, I hope that you will never forget that others too love America, just as much as you do, and that others too will die for America, just as quick as you will."

Before the two chairmen gave their closing remarks, Senator Rudman took the microphone and announced that "something has occurred that . . . has been so disturbing to me that I wanted to say what I'm going to say, probably over the chairman's objections." He said that over the past three days the Iran-Contra committees had received calls from people who made "ugly ethnic slurs" against Senator Inouye, who is of Japanese descent, and that the calls were "extraordinarily insulting to the members of this committee.

"The chairman was recommended for the Congressional Medal of Honor for assaulting two German machine-gun nests in northern Italy, and then falling on the third one which was destroying his company, when he lost his arm which he left on that battlefield in Italy . . . He is one of the greatest men I have ever known, and the country ought to know the kind of leadership the Senate chairman exerts—and for all Americans to condemn the kind of ethnic slurs that have no place in America."

North said softly, "I fully agree, Mr. Rudman."

Then, asked by Inouye if he would like to make a closing statement, North replied: "I would simply like to thank the American people who have responded with their good wishes, their support, their prayers through what has been for me and my family a long and difficult ordeal. I thank them for that, and I salute them. That is my statement, sir."

Hamilton then told North he had a few "impressions" he wanted to share.

"What strikes me is that despite your very good intentions, you were a participant in actions which catapulted a president into the most serious crisis of his presidency, drove the Congress of the United States to launch an unprecedented investigation, and I think probably damaged the cause, or the causes that you sought to promote . . .

"In your opening statement you said that these hearings have caused serious damage to our national interests. But I wonder whether the damage has been caused by these hearings, or by the acts which prompted these hearings? I wonder whether you would have the Congress do nothing after it has been lied to, misled and ignored? . . .

"Now let me tell you what bothers me. I want to talk about two things: first policy and then process . . . I am very troubled by your defense of our secret arms sales to Iran . . . Selling arms to Iran in secret was, to put it simply, bad policy. The policy contradicted and undermined long-held, often articulated, widely supported public policies in the United States. It repudiated U.S. policy to make no concessions to terrorists . . . and to stop arms sales to Iran. We sold arms to a nation officially designated by our government as a terrorist state. This secret policy of selling arms to Iran has damaged U.S. credibility . . . The policy achieved none of the goals it sought. The Ayatollah got his arms, more Americans are held hostage today than when this policy began, subversion of U.S. interests throughout the region by Iran continues. Moderates in Iran, if any there were, did not come forward."

Regarding process, Hamilton told North that while covert actions in a democracy may be necessary, they must have checks and balances, and in this instance those procedures were ignored. "The intelligence committees of the Congress were not informed and they were lied to. Foreign policies were created and carried out by a tiny circle of persons, apparently without the involvement of even some of the highest officials of our government. The Administration tried to do secretly what the Congress sought to prevent it from doing. The Administration did secretly what it claimed to all the world it was not doing. Covert action should always be used to supplement, not to contradict, our foreign policy . . . It should not be used to impose a foreign policy on the American people which they do not support."

The Iran-Contra policies were also marked by unaccountability and deceit, Hamilton said. "I am impressed that policy was driven by a series of lies—lies to the Iranians, lies to the Central Intelligence Agency, lies to the attorney general, lies to our friends and allies, lies to Congress and lies to the American people." Hamilton also reminded North that Congress was intended to be a partner, not an adversary, to the executive branch in charting foreign policy.

"As I understand your testimony, you did what you did because those were your orders, and because you believed it was for a good cause. I cannot agree that the ends has justified these means—that the threat in Central America was so great that we had to do something, even if it meant disregarding constitutional processes, deceiving the Congress and the American people. The means employed were a profound threat to the democratic process... Methods and means are what this country [is] all about. We subvert our democratic process to bring about a desired end—no matter how strongly we believe in that end—we've weakened our country, and we have not strengthened it. A few do not know what is better for Americans than Americans know themselves. If I understand our government correctly, no small group of people, no matter how important, no matter how well-intentioned they may be, should be trusted to determine policy."

Hamilton concluded: "I don't have any doubt at all, Colonel North, that you are a patriot. There are many patriots, fortunately, and many forms of patriotism. For you, perhaps, patriotism rested in the conduct of deeds, some requiring great personal courage, to free hostages and fight communism. And those of us who pursue public service with less risk to our physical well-being admire such courage. But there's another form of patriotism which is unique to democracy. It resides in those who have a deep respect for the rule of law and faith in America's democratic traditions. To uphold our constitution requires not just the exceptional efforts of the few, but the confidence and the trust and the work of the many. Democracy has its frustrations. You've experienced some of them, but we, you and I, know of no better system of government. And when that democratic process is subverted, we risk all that we cherish. I thank you, sir, for your testimony, and I wish you and I wish your family well."

Inouye began his closing remarks by delivering a strong rebuttal to North's claim, made earlier that day, that security leaks by two U.S. senators had warned Libya of the pending U.S. air raid in April of 1986 and therefore contributed to or caused the deaths of two American pilots on the mission. Inouye cited a series of news stories beginning a week before the April 14 attack which quoted

Reagan Administration sources as saying that a raid against Libya was imminent.

North had also said that in the aftermath of the *Achille Lauro* affair in 1985 "a number of members of Congress" made statements "that very seriously compromised our intelligence activities." But *Newsweek* magazine, which first published details of the *Achille Lauro* interception, took the unusual step of reporting, in its edition following North's appearance at the hearings, that its source for the *Achille Lauro* story had been none other than North himself.

The *Newsweek* story about North seemed a classic case of biting the hand that fed you, but editors of the magazine evidently found what they considered North's holier-than-thou attitude about leaking information too much to tolerate, and decided to break the confidential-source relationship. They knew the colonel well at *Newsweek*. On one occasion, North had come up to New York for a power lunch with *Newsweek* editors, and though everyone knew who he was North had insisted on being introduced around the room under an assumed name.

Actually North had done business with a handful of Washington reporters and was an important source for them—notably David Halevy of *Time* magazine; John Walcott, then of *Newsweek* and now of the Wall Street *Journal*; Shirley Christian of the New York *Times* and the Evans-and-Novak column.

Halevy, a friend and admirer of North, says he used to meet with Ollie an average of once a week, and that they often would have lunch at the McDonald's at 17th Street and Pennsylvania Avenue, half a block from the Executive Office Building. North, he said, would have a Big Mac and fries and discourse on the Contras or other world hot-spots. "Ollie tried, through me, to get the American public informed, and he did a very good job in trying to do it. I think the word 'leak' is a pejorative."

North, on several occasions, tried to get stories about him or his operations killed, and Robert Parry and Brian Barger—two reporters who then worked for the Associated Press and did some of the important early reporting on North's involvement with the Contras—believe that their stories would have run sooner had not North been meeting simultaneously with Associated Press executives over the fate of hostage—and AP correspondent—Terry Anderson. Associated Press editors deny being influenced by North.

In any event, after countering North's claims about congressional leaks in the Libyan bombing, Inouye resumed his closing remarks.

He said that society needed and nurtured heroes because they served as a unifying force.

"I believe during the past week we have participated in creating and developing very likely a new American hero..." Inouye told North with some apparent irony. "I'm certain the life and the burdens of a hero will be difficult and heavy. And so, with all sincerity, I wish you well as you begin your journey into a new life... As a result of your very gallant presence and your articulate statements, your life, I'm certain, will be emulated by many, many young Americans. I'm certain we will... receive an abundance of requests from young citizens throughout the land for entrance into the privileged ranks of cadets of the military services. These young citizens, having been imbued with the passion of patriotism, will do so. And to these young men and women, I wish to address a few words.

"In 1964, when Colonel North was a cadet, he took an oath of office, like... hundreds throughout the service academies. And he also said that he will abide by the regulations which set forth the cadet honor concept. The first honor concept... is a very simple one: a member of the brigade does not lie, cheat or steal...

"And when the colonel put on his uniform and the bars of a second lieutenant, he was well aware that he was subject to the Uniform Code of Military Justice.... And that code makes it abundantly clear that orders of a superior officer must by obeyed by subordinate members—but it is lawful orders... In fact, it says members of the military have an obligation to disobey unlawful orders. This principle was considered so important that we—we the government of the United States—proposed that it be internationally applied in the Nuremberg trials. And so, in the Nuremberg trials, we said that the fact that the defendant—"

"Mr. Chairman, may I please register an objection?" interrupted Sullivan. He had heard enough. He wasn't about to have his client likened to a Nazi.

"May I continue my statement?" said Inouye.

"I find this offensive," declared Sullivan, in one last confrontation, which seemed only fitting as North's own Six Day War drew to a close. "I find you engaging in a personal attack on Colonel North, and you're far removed from the issues of this case. To make reference to the Nuremberg trials I find personally and professionally distasteful, and I can no longer sit here and listen to this."

"You will have to sit here, if you want to listen," said Inouye.

"Mr. Chairman, please don't conclude these hearings on this unfair note," said Sullivan. "I have strong objections to many things in these hearings, and you up there speak about listening to the American people. Why don't you listen to the American people and what they've said as a result—"

Inouye banged his gavel.

"—of the last week. There are twenty thousand telegrams in our room outside the corridor here that came in this morning. The American people—"

"I'm sure that there are," said Inouye.

"The American people have spoken, and please stop this personal attack against Colonel North . . ."

"I'm not attacking him personally."

"That's the way I hear it, sir."

The Sullivan outburst evidently had its effect, for when Inouye resumed, he chose not to finish his Nuremberg thought. Instead, the senator wearily reiterated some of the points that had been made by his colleagues: that North's testimony admitting he had lied had been painful to listen to; that the ends did not justify the means; that this was a government of laws, not men; that airing of differences in public was a sign of strength, not weakness; and that democracy, while frustrating, should be given a chance to run its course.

"This has been a long day," Inouye concluded. "I know that all of us are desirous of a rest. Colonel North, with all sincerity, I thank you for your assistance these past six days. You have been most cordial and your presence should make your fellow officers very proud of the way you have presented yourself. And to your lady, I wish her the best. She has sat here throughout these days with patience and grace. You have a fine lady."

With that, wearing the hero's mantle which Inouye, along with a large segment of the country, had just bestowed on him, North left the hearing room for an uncertain future: a Marine long gone from the White House, but not about to fade away.

OLLIE'S WORLD

WHEN North finished testifying he was followed minutes later by Robert McFarlane, who had requested permission to make a return appearance to rebut parts of Ollie's testimony.

Speaking in his somnolent monotone that was all the more noticeable after the electricity that had attended North, the former national security advisor proceeded to deny a number of points that his close friend and one-time aide had made, including the fundamental assertion that everything North did had been authorized by his superiors.

"I did not authorize many of [North's] activities," McFarlane testified, saying there were times when Ollie crossed over the line to "... an operational role and that was not authorized ... Our basic disagreement involves a clear implication from his testimony that I permitted ... the creation of a separate, clandestine and far-reaching network of private operations that involved private profits, and which was to be concealed even from other members of the executive branch. This is untrue, because it is unthinkable."

McFarlane painted a picture of North as an independent operative who kept him informed only generally about what he was doing, perhaps, he suggested, so as to protect him and give him deniability. Mostly McFarlane repeated what he had already testified to in May, and, trying to walk the fine line between defending himself and not hurting North, took care to say that Ollie had not acted out of "malice or deception."

Next was Admiral Poindexter, who took the spear that North had dodged. He said he never informed President Reagan that proceeds from the Iranian arms sales had been diverted to help the

Contras, but added that he was confident Reagan would have approved the idea if he had been told about it.

Improbably casting himself in the role of Harry Truman, Poindexter, in between puffs on his constantly lit pipe, declared: "I made the decision. I felt that I had the authority to do it. I thought it was a good idea. I was convinced that the president would, in the end, think it was a good idea. But I did not want him to be associated with the decision . . . On this whole issue, you know, the buck stops here with me."

Poindexter also acknowledged that he watched Reagan sign the December, 1985, finding authorizing a direct arms-for-hostages swap, and said he later ripped up the finding to protect the president from political embarrassment.

The following day the White House denied that Reagan would have approved the diversion, as Poindexter claimed. Asked at the hearings to comment on this, the admiral said: "I understand that he said that. I would have expected him to say that. That's the whole idea of deniability."

Poindexter's testimony was received with considerable skepticism. Some members of the committees said they simply didn't believe him, and a Washington *Post*–ABC poll indicated that a majority of Americans thought Poindexter was withholding information and covering up for Reagan. Polls also showed most people believed the president knew of and approved the diversion.

The admiral's testimony was laced with "I don't recalls," which many regarded as inconsistent with someone who had been praised in fitness reports for having a photographic memory. Many also felt that for a career military bureaucrat with a reputation for keeping his superiors informed of even the smallest details to have not told Reagan about something as important as the diversion was implausible.

Like North, Poindexter was unrepentant and at times defiant, blaming Congress and the press for exaggerating the importance of the Iran-Contra affair and openly admitting to keeping Congress in the dark. "My objective all along," he said, "was to withhold from the Congress exactly what the NSC staff was doing in carrying out the president's policy."

With Poindexter's testimony that he did not tell Reagan about the diversion, there was no more suspense, and much of the air was let out of the rest of the hearings. The aftermath to the drama of North's six days of testimony overshadowed the rest of Poindexter's.

Merchants around the country developed a cottage industry catering to "Olliemania." There were Ollie T-shirts, Ollie bumper stickers, Ollie dolls, Ollie haircuts, Ollieburgers (shredded beef topped with shredded American cheese and shredded lettuce), Ollie recipes, and even Ollie-for-President boomlets.

Not since 1951, when Gen. Douglas MacArthur was fired by Harry Truman for insubordination and returned to take Congress and the country by storm, had any American soldier made such a dramatic appearance on Capitol Hill.

"I've seen every hearing they've held in the last forty years— McCarthy, Kefauver, Watergate," Washington restauranteur Duke Ziebert, whose place is a hangout for politicians, athletes, journalists and lawyers, told the Chicago *Tribune*. "But no one has captured the American public like Ollie North. Even when he's not telling the truth he's beautiful. The guy is so charming."

If North had seized the nation's attention by the throat, the paradox of Olliemania was that there was little support for North's goals. The public has consistently opposed U.S. involvement in Nicaragua. Most Americans never bought Ollie's, or the Administration's, view that what this conflict really represented was Gorbachev's shadow along the Rio Grande. And there was little or no support for trading arms to Iran for the release of hostages.

But that people didn't support the goals did not seem to matter. As in Vietnam, North could be the good soldier in a bad war. His appeal was not so much left or right as populist.

In an astonishing role reversal, North succeeded in transforming the pre-hearings public perception of him as mysterious cowboy run amok—a lone ranger whose horse jumped the fence for a romp through Indian Country without authorization—to persecuted patriotic victim, just following orders.

He was the scapegoat whom everyone could identify with—an eager beaver who did anything his bosses told him to, then was called to task by those same bosses. He was the God-fearing, lean-and-mean fighting machine, whose frequent invoking of God's name had fused religion and patriotism putting him on the side of the angels. He was the Marlboro Man without the Marlboro. The Rebel With a Cause.

He was also the man who, after being caught, donned his uniform and defied anyone to question his good and sincere intentions.

North at times seemed not to understand why he was even at the hearings at all; why he had been called to account for doing his duty for God and country. He was standing where the liberals had stood in the fifties. There had been a giant flip-flop in America. The liberals now had the institutional power and were persecuting conservative anti-communists. The liberals had replaced Joe McCarthy as the inquisitors. But North challenged the committees by suggesting that they were the ones who should be investigated, not him. He was the right-wing's fantasy come to life, whose clarion-call performance gave at least a short-lived fifteen percent boost to the Contra cause in the polls.

Ollie resisted all efforts by the committees to housebreak him— much to the delight of the public, it seemed. North did not just admit that he had lied to members of Congress; he told them that the hearings had brought disgrace upon the country, and they took it. Though some members politely scolded him for his special view of the constitution, no one rose up to tell him that it was perhaps *his* behavior, not Congress's, that had brought disgrace upon the country.

He had testified on his own terms. Attorney Brendan Sullivan had given the members a good mugging. Many thought the committees should have taken a harder line with North. It was their hearing, after all. They were the senators and the congressmen. North was a Marine lieutenant colonel. Yet he had acted like he owned the place.

North had dazzled, deftly manipulating the focus of the hearings away from the rule of law to whether Congress should even be a player in foreign policy. A country thirsting for heroes had been bewitched by a uniformed Peter Pan who embodied the myth and images of lost innocence and lost youth in a world where all is good and green. Ollie was greeting-card platitudes, county fairs and lemonade stands.

He had great adventures to tell and people always loved to listen to a good thriller. It didn't seem to matter that he had failed at most of what he set out to do. He had worked Herculean hours and fought the good fight. That he was running in place the public saw as irrelevant.

His celebrity overwhelmed his transgressions. He proved once again that a great actor can save even a lousy script. As long as the performance is first rate, the sins can be forgiven.

People attending the hearings generally found North far less compelling than those watching on TV. The cameras had softened his hard, bony features and warmed to his moist eyes.

Indeed, Olliemania was a case study in the astonishing power of television to elevate style over substance, hearts over minds, sentiment over facts. That North projected the *image* of truth and righteousness was far more powerful than the fact that he had admitted to lies and other misconduct.

When North was finished, so was television. The networks stopped gavel-to-gavel coverage of the hearings and began rotating. The Iran-Contra committees could get back to pondering the policy ramifications of the scandal in the relative seclusion of being attended to by the printed press and radio.

Olliemania was really Marshall McLuhan 101. The medium—and how North looked saying what he said, how he handled himself, what values he radiated, how charismatic he was, and how well he entertained—was the message. Not what he said. It was a primer on how drama can take over political life. Ollie had dropped into the nation's living room, up close and personal, and stayed for a week. People got to know him. They liked him. He was passionate and sincere. When the pollsters called, people would say they liked Ollie but weren't so sure they approved of what he had done. In any case, they could forgive him.

On one level the North hoopla said as much about contemporary American society as it did about Ollie himself. It evoked a culture clash of sorts between the old and the new morality, between small-town values and big-city values, between Peoria and the Eastern Establishment, between "squares"—the military, Main Street Rotarians, and other God-fearing folk on the one hand, and the now-sullied "best and the brightest" on the other; between passionate evangelism and mainstream religion, agnosticism or atheism.

"What we saw was genuine drama: a patriotic son of the republic who, confronted with a grave moral dilemma—whether to betray his comrades and cause, or to deceive members of Congress—chose the lesser of two evils, the path of honor," wrote Patrick Buchanan, the former Nixon speechwriter and Reagan communications director, in his syndicated column. "It was magnificent. The American people watched daily the anguish and pain of a genuinely moral man, and Contrasted that with the stuffy self-righteousness of the Pharisees putting him through his ordeal."

When some reporters and commentators expressed bewilderment that North would be accorded hero treatment, Buchanan wrote that this "exposed not only how far the national media is out of touch with America, but how far apart we, as a people, have become—and not simply on the issue of Central America. Americans of Left and Right no longer share the same religion, values or codes of morality; we only inhabit the same piece of land."

This kind of rhetoric amounted to a declaration of passive civil war.

Underlying North's disdain for Congress was the belief that in taking on the committees, he was finally fighting the "real enemy" —the ones who had "lost" Vietnam and later prevented the Reagan Administration from doing the right thing on behalf of the Contras.

Those who know North well say Vietnam still burned within him. Though he served heroically there, and professed at the hearings to believe that no soldier who has seen war wants to see another, he spent most of his time on the NSC fanning the flames in Nicaragua in defiance of the law. North never swallowed Nixon's hollow "peace with honor" refrain. He wanted, it would seem, to recoup in Central America the honor that the United States lost in Vietnam. He wanted to refight the war.

". . . I came back from a war that we fought in Vietnam to a public that did not understand, in my humble opinion, that they had been lied to," he testified. "The American public did not know what we suffered, what we endured, or what we tried to achieve. And I think the same thing prevails for the Nicaraguan resistance today . . . The Congress of the United States left soldiers in the field unsupported and vulnerable to their communist enemies . . . You then hold this investigation to blame the problem on the executive branch."

Nicaragua was Vietnam redux—the real battlefront was in Washington.

North had a premonition of what would happen if the U.S. failed the Contras, as it had South Vietnam. "Ollie told me about a dream he had, a horrible nightmare," says Reagan Doctrine visionary and New Right adventurer Jack Wheeler. "Ollie said: 'I dreamed that our support of the Contras failed. The Democrats had frustrated everything. We were left with a second Cuba. That has to go. One way or the other the Sandinistas have to go. So the president made the decision to invade. I was called back to the Marines. And I landed on the beach in Nicaragua. There facing me on the beach, with a rifle in his hands, was Adolfo Calero. He didn't want an American invasion. He wanted Nicaraguans to save their own country.'"

North was a warrior ill equipped to negotiate the subtleties of diplomacy and politics. His was a black-and-white world, not gray. Many presidents have resisted placing military men in positions of power since civilian control is so central to the constitution. But Reagan loved the military and actively integrated it into his government—particularly at the NSC, where he was the first president ever to have more than one national security advisor who was a military man. McFarlane, like North, had been a Marine lieutenant colonel and Poindexter was an active navy rear admiral. In 1986 military officers made up more than one third of the NSC staff—a much higher percentage than in any other previous administration.

The NSC has been a breeding ground for military aides who ingratiate themselves with their superiors, work killer hours and then rise to attain enormous authority. Alexander Haig and Brent Scowcroft are two examples from earlier administrations, though they did not abuse their power.

Some scholars have divided the military archetypes into two groups: the "Ikes," after President Dwight D. Eisenhower, and the "Macs," after General MacArthur. The Ikes are men who were brilliant military officers but who clearly believed in, and willingly submitted to, the concept of civilian rule. Besides Eisenhower, they included Gen. George C. Marshall, architect of the Marshall Plan, and originally George Washington. Other Macs in addition to MacArthur include Gen. George Armstrong Custer, Gen. George Patton; Curtis ("Bombs Away") LeMay, one time head of the Strategic Air Command, who was George Wallace's running mate on a third-party ticket in 1968; North acquaintance Gen. John Singlaub, relieved of his Korean command by Jimmy Carter; and finally, Ollie himself.

Whether a military officer turns into an Ike or a Mac might have something to do with family background. Marshall and Eisenhower came from nonmilitary families while MacArthur's father was a general who quarreled with President Taft. North's father was a decorated veteran of World War II.

Some Macs have had political ambitions, others have not. But most, in their lust for guts and glory, have expressed antipathy toward, or frustration with, the constraints of democracy.

North was a war hero in over his head at the White House in the delicate political and diplomatic missions he was assigned. He is the kind of guy you would want in the foxhole next to you during a firefight, but not running the country. He needed close supervision and never received it.

His was not to think, it was to charge and take the hill. It was to do, not to question. Nowhere was this better illustrated than in his memorable statement at the hearings, when he said to Arthur Liman: "I'm not in the habit of questioning my superiors. If he [Poindexter] deemed it not to be necessary to ask the president, I saluted smartly and charged up the hill. That's what lieutenant colonels are supposed to do... And if the commander-in-chief tells this lieutenant colonel to go stand in the corner and stand on his head, I will do so." Precisely the qualities that made North a great soldier made him a bad statesman.

North's world was a world of secrecy, where the shredder was as common an office fixture as a desk or a chair. It was a world of distrust: Congress, the State Department, the Pentagon, the bureaucracy, the press were all to be shunned, if not regarded as the enemy.

North's world was, as he testified, a "dangerous world" where the cult of the covert reigned supreme. It was a running ideological crusade wherein a small core-group of patriots—himself, Casey, Secord, Poindexter and, to a lesser extent, McFarlane—was forced by a spineless Congress, a cumbersome bureaucracy and a hostile press to drift off-lines to do what they knew to be in the national interest. National security, in whose name all manner of sins have been carried out, demanded it, and they were the ones best equipped, best qualified and best positioned to act.

In North's zealous world he and those of his ilk were the patriots, while those who disagreed with him, as Senator Mitchell implied, were seen not only as unpatriotic but as likely communist dupes.

North saw himself in pitched battle against the evil Ayatollah and communism everywhere. In talking of these struggles he would sometimes refer to himself in the third person—showing both a healthy ego and a fantasy quality that suggested he sometimes saw himself as a character in a story, or as Larry Speakes said, the star of his own movie.

In North's world, fact seemed to mix easily with fiction, and many have asked how he managed to attain the position of responsibility that he did, given certain aspects of his record.

In the scheme of things, his having been admitted to Bethesda Naval Hospital in 1974 for emotional distress after he and his wife were having marital problems is insignificant, though former National Security Advisor Richard Allen has said that if he had known of the incident, he would not have approved North's coming to the NSC in 1981. But the brief stint at Bethesda said nothing about North's ability to be an effective Marine.

More relevant, perhaps, was his apparent failure to disclose the hospitalization in the DD–398 Statement of Personal History form that every Marine seeking a top-secret clearance must complete. Plenty of North's colleagues and superiors in the Marine Corps were aware of his hospitalization, but people at the NSC, when they were considering his application, were not.

In preparing his resumé for the NSC, North misstated his record at least twice. The resumé said North had served as a "platoon and company commander in combat and participated in both conventional and unconventional warfare operations in Southeast Asia." But he was never a company commander in Vietnam, and the Marine Corps says there is no record of his ever having been involved in unconventional warfare.

He seemed to embroider his background when there was no need to. In 1985, testifying as a character witness in the trial of Frank Reed, an NSC colleague who had been charged with securities fraud, North said that before attending the Naval Academy he had been a pre-med student "at Rochester"—rather clearly implying the University of Rochester. Actually he had been an English major at the State University of New York at Brockport, which is outside Rochester. He then testified that in Vietnam he had been an "infantry platoon and company commander in the Special Operations Force, team commander." But Marine officials say they know of no such unit, and again, there is no record of North serving in any classified or covert assignments. North had been a regular infantry platoon commander, period. He also testified at the Reed trial that he had served in Vietnam "from 1968 through the early part of 1970, and then again in 1971." Records show he served only from December 1968 to November 1969. He returned briefly in August of 1970, on his own, to testify for Randy Herrod at the latter's court-martial.

Aside from North's admitted lying to Congress about the Contras, his admitted lying to the Iranians, his admitted falsifying of the Iran initiative chronology, his admitted shredding of documents and his admitted lying to various Administration officials as the Iran-Contra affair unraveled in November of 1986, there are stories, statements or claims that he has made to various people while at the NSC that are either untrue, strongly denied, or unconfirmable and thought to be untrue. These include:

—His relationship and access to Reagan. North would often tell his colleagues he had just come from a meeting with "the boss," implying it was alone with the boss. He told a United Methodist Church group in 1986 that he briefed the president twice a week: once on terrorism and once on Central America. But according to the White House, North had only nineteen meetings with Reagan, always in a group, never alone.

—The widely recounted story North told to several friends and colleagues of his solo meeting with Reagan in the aftermath of the

invasion of Grenada. North, worried that the returning students had
not been briefed about the U.S. invasion, was said to have gone into
the White House residence to apologize to Reagan personally for
what might be a public-relations nightmare. Reagan told him to calm
down and watch on TV as the students got off the plane in South
Carolina. When the first student kissed the ground, North told
several friends and colleagues that the president put his arms around
him and said: "You see, Ollie, I told you not to worry. You can trust
Americans." But White House spokesman Marlin Fitzwater, after
checking with Reagan, says the incident never occurred.

—North told former *Time* magazine reporter David Halevy that
in the aftermath of the raid on Libya in April of 1986 he learned
just before President Reagan was scheduled to address the nation at
9:00 P.M. that one of the American planes had been shot down off
the Libyan coast. Reagan's speech as written reportedly said that all
the planes had returned safely to their base. Seconds before air
time North was said to have burst into the Oval Office and made
the proper correction on the Teleprompter. Halevy reported the
anecdote in a lenghty profile he wrote of North with Neil Livingstone in the July, 1987, issue of *Washingtonian* magazine. Fitzwater
said this too never happened.

—North's statement to a Christian group while on a wilderness
trip with his son in August of 1986 that he prayed behind closed
doors with Reagan. Fitzwater says this is also fiction.

—North's tale of derring-do told to friend and conservative activist Andy Messing about his flying a plane over El Salvador in the
spring of 1983 and rescuing some wounded government soldiers.
According to Messing, North told him he was flying a small plane
with navy Lieutenant Commander Albert Schaufelberger, deputy
chief of the fifty-five-member American military group in El Salvador, at his side when they heard a radio call for help from Salvadoran troops who had come under fire by leftist guerrillas. When
the call went unanswered North responded, landed the plane on a
dirt strip and loaded two wounded men on the plane. As they prepared to take off again a Salvadoran guerrilla popped out of the
jungle and strafed the plane with machine-gun fire, puncturing the
fuel tank and blowing out the windshield. North took off anyway,
barely clearing the trees at the end of the runaway, and not getting
full power because of loss of fuel spurting from the tank. He glided
the plane back safely to Ilopango, making a dead-stick landing. The
two Salvadorans later died.

When North became famous this story, anonymously sourced but

originating from Messing, was widely reported, and only added to
Ollie's legend. Schaufelberger was later shot and killed, but his
commander at the time, John Waghelstein, and then U.S. Ambassador Dean Hinton, said they never heard about the incident and
believe they would have. No one knew that North could fly. Messing admits he can offer no confirmation.

—North's claim to NSC colleague David Major the day the Iran
initiative was revealed that he had ordered the kidnapping of relatives of Iranian officials. This was clearly not so.

—North told Poindexter he had forestalled Costa Rican President Oscar Arias's threat to blow the whistle on the secret airstrip
at Santa Elena in September of 1986 by personally calling Arias and
threatening to cut off U.S. aid. Actually, it was Ambassador Lewis
Tambs who called Arias.

—He told colleagues he had served in Angola, but there is no
record of this, and it has never been confirmed.

—In another anecdote published in the *Washingtonian* article,
North told Halevy that he had handled the sharing of intelligence
with the British during the Falklands war and had traveled to Argentina with then Secretary of State Alexander Haig. But Haig
denies this.

—Another North story told to several colleagues has him accompanying special Middle East Envoy Philip Habib on a mission to
Israel in June of 1982, just before the Israeli invasion of Lebanon.
As reported by Halevy in the *Washingtonian* article, while Habib
was dining with Prime Minister Menachem Begin, North was invited by Defense Minister Ariel Sharon to join him for dinner at his
desert ranch. Sharon supposedly briefed North on Israel's invasion
plans, then floated a diplomatic stratagem: Israel planned to encircle two Syrian tank divisions that were positioned at the northern
section of the Bekaa Valley around the Beirut–Damascus Highway.
Sharon proposed that Washington then rescue the Syrian divisions
—so as to draw Damascus into the American bloc of moderate Arab
states. North then supposedly rushed back to the American embassy in Tel Aviv and flashed the proposal to then National Security
Advisor William Clark, who was with President Reagan in Versailles. But no one ever took the Sharon proposal seriously, and it
never went anywhere, the article said.

The anecdote is roundly denied by all sides. Clark says he never got
any such cable from North. Habib dismissed the story as "a bunch of
shit, to put it mildly . . . It's sheer fantasy." He said not only had North
not accompanied him on the trip, but he had never even met North.

According to the Middle East staffers on the NSC who monitored the Habib mission, North had never left Washington, and they dismiss out of hand the notion that a staff officer then that junior would have been chosen to go on such a sensitive diplomatic mission.

Still, North told NSC colleagues that when he returned from the Habib mission, and word of his back-door diplomatic efforts reached Secretary of State Shultz, a furious Shultz took North aside and told him: "Son, I'm the only Marine in this administration who makes foreign policy." But Shultz flatly denied, through a spokesman, that he ever had such an encounter with North.

—The story of North's dog. Ollie told numerous people, including the FBI, that the dog had been poisoned—presumably by those whom he said had been threatening his life. But one of North's neighbors told the Los Angeles *Times* that the dog had actually just died of cancer. "It got old and died," the neighbor said. "Ollie told everybody it died for effect."

—His testimony that he shredded documents in front of Justice Department officials on November 22, 1986. This is strongly denied by the two officials.

One former NSC colleague and friend of North's tried to draw a distinction between Ollie as a "bullshitter" and Ollie as a liar. He said North's friends all knew he had a propensity for exaggeration, and suggested it was up to people on the receiving end of North's statements to try and separate the harmless yarn from the more serious lie. "There's a bit of the charlatan in Ollie," says this friend, who is still in government and asked not to be quoted by name. "He's a bullshit artist. It's one of the endearing aspects of the guy, but it can cause heartburn for those who don't know him well. It's his persona... That was no act [at the hearings]. He's a real character. That's his charm."

To justify some of his more serious untruths North might have quoted Churchill, who said that truth was sometimes so important it had to be protected by "a bodyguard of lies." As it was, at the hearings, he coined his own phrase, saying that he had had to make choices between "lives and lies."

North's justifications for lying stirred debate among military ethicists, but left one of his old Annapolis mentors, William Corson, disappointed. "It comes down to clichés," Corson, a decorated former Marine Corps officer, told one interviewer. "Honesty is not the best policy. It's the only policy... Oliver North got everything I was trying to teach him wrong."

Like Reagan, whom people liked even if they disagreed with him

on any manner of issues, North was Teflon-coated. The printed
press had gone to some length to detail North's transgressions, but
the image of Ollie strutting his stuff at the hearings overwhelmed
all that. It had been the same with Reagan early in his presidency.
At first reporters aggressively revealed all the mistakes and misstatements the president made at news conferences and elsewhere.
But it didn't matter. Reagan's style and manner were so engaging
that the people loved him anyway. So the press stopped reporting
the Reagan bumbling. Similarly, in the aftermath of North's bravura
performance, most reporters, faced with the outpouring of Olliemania, seemed inhibited from writing further about the North
record.

In many other respects, North seemed to be Ronald Reagan in
miniature.

They were both cold-warrior soulmates, but whereas Reagan had
only played some of North's roles in the movies, Ollie was the
genuine article. Psychohistorians will have a field day speculating
about the desire for the aging Gipper to latch on to a surrogate son
like Ollie who could actually play out his dreams. Ron Reagan, Jr.,
cavorting about in his underpants on "Saturday Night Live" was
perhaps not quite the Halls-of-Montezuma stuff that the president
had had in mind. And Ollie, ever in search of father figures—his
college boxing coach Emerson Smith, McFarlane, Secord to a degree and Casey all filled at least part of the bill—must have been
receptive to the notion of hitching his wagon to the president of the
United States, the man who had brought America back.

Reagan and North were both essentially simple, uncomplicated
men who were far more comfortable contemplating a placid, nostalgic
vision of the past than facing an uncertain future. They were both
handsome, terribly sincere, jaunty, nonintellectual, naive and unsophisticated, exalters of the military and extollers of old-fashioned,
God-and-country values. They both reached their respective heights
in large measure through their charm and ability to persuade. Their
view of the world was based more on moral, anti-communist imperatives than on actual knowledge of that world. They both saw the
Contras as the equivalent of Founding Fathers, and saw winning in
Nicaragua as America's ticket back from the trauma of Vietnam.

They both, in pursuing the Iran and Contra polices, showed
remarkably poor judgment. Both saw Congress and the press as
nettlesome nuisances rather than essential components of the democracy. They both loved covert action, and had contempt for bu-

reaucrats and government generally. They were both casual about rules and the rule of law. Both seemed fundamentally opposed to peace and accommodation with the Soviet Union, preferring instead the proxy war strategy of the Reagan Doctrine. They both loved a good story, and were not above juicing it up into a yarn.

Reagan could teach North nothing about television, however. Ollie had proved at the hearings that he was every bit as good as the Great Communicator himself. Both had a silky tenor voice and could call up a perfectly timed catch in the throat at will. North's eyes were probably more moist than Reagan's, but so much the better, for as producer Norman Lear said during Ollie's testimony: "TV loves moist."

Some explained Olliemania as a reaching out for a younger, stronger version of the aging, increasingly detached Reagan—an extension of the country's affection for the president as his luster faded.

Fading luster or not, Reagan still enjoyed an enormous reservoir of public goodwill, and that, in the final analysis, probably explains why only the president's prestige was hurt by the Iran-Contra affair. There was no outrage, because the scandal lacked a villain.

Watergate, at its heart, was a sordid political dirty trick that became serious when Nixon and his aides covered it up, but it had ncne of the constitutional ramifications that the Iran-Contra affair did. If Richard Nixon had been found guilty of selling arms to a terrorist state and using part of the proceeds to fund a war that Congress had banned, and then tried to set up the unaccountable North-Casey mini-CIA, he very likely would have been impeached by Congress.

Watergate cut deep because Nixon was a villain. Reagan was not. In fact, he was beloved, so his possible impeachment was never even seriously contemplated. Plus, he was a lame duck, anyway.

Reagan—with the help of the press, which remained obsessed with the Watergate-legacy question of what-did-he-know-and-when-did-he-know-it—succeeded in framing the issue of his culpability or lack thereof solely on the narrow question of whether he had known of the diversion. So when "President Poindexter" stood up at the hearings and said the buck stopped with him and Reagan had not been told of the diversion, the real president was taken off the hook.

The larger and more fundamental issues—lying to and ignoring Congress, disregarding the rule of law and running what amounted to a secret government—were never really addressed. Reagan was never called to account for anything so basic as presiding over an outlaw presidency. He tossed it all off with a wink, a smile and an "I don't recall." Like North at the hearings, Reagan's response to the scandal was a case of personality overwhelming sins. He proved that a popular president can break the laws and flout the will of Congress and the people, and get away with it.

The publication of the final report of the congressional Iran-Contra committees in November of 1987 was an anticlimax that reinforced this notion. The report's central recommendation was decidely "unsexy": the president should keep the Congress better informed next time. The press quickly agreed, and put the scandal to bed. After all, Gorbachev was coming to Washington. There was life for Reagan after Iran-Contra.

Given the political reality of no impeachment, and since all the operative legislation had already been passed in the aftermath of the Church Committee hearings in the mid-seventies, the Iran-Contra committees were left with nothing more to do than chide the president for ignoring the laws that were on the books.

Still, the report was a meticulously researched, well-written overview of the scandal that strongly criticized Reagan. Arthur Liman says that the criticism contained in the final report meant that if America had a parliamentary system of government, Reagan would have faced a vote of no-confidence.

Where the Tower Commission saw the problem as Reagan's detached style of management, the committees saw the problem as Reagan's casual attitude toward the law. Where the commission painted a portrait of a distracted, disengaged president who let his NSC aides run amok, evidence gathered by the congressional committees suggested that Reagan was far more active and informed about both the Iran and the Contra operations, with the probable exception of the diversion.

The report found that the government had been run by a "cabal of zealots," which reflected Reagan's mistrust of government and his preference for action-oriented private-sector types, and ultimately created an unaccountable mini-CIA that was about to be institutionalized when everything started to unravel. The requirement to issue presidential findings was circumvented. When findings were issued they were drafted so broadly as essentially to give the CIA a blank check, and they were sometimes used to avoid complying with other laws—such as appropriations measures and statutes governing the export of arms. Never has a finding contained a provision requiring that the finding itself should not be disclosed to Congress.

Fundamentally, Reagan failed to heed the constitution's admonition to take care that the laws be faithfully executed, and he failed to instill a respect for the law among his subordinates. Secrecy, deception and disdain for government and the rule of law were the common threads running through the Iran-Contra affair.

For seven years Reagan lacked public consensus in his Central America policy. Generally the public saw neither the Sandinistas as a threat nor the Contras as the solution. But choosing ideological purity over consensus was, after all, what the Reagan Revolution was all about, so he opted for covert operations. But covert operations is actually the wrong term. It suggests a series of forays with limited objectives. This was actually a prolonged covert war, and a covert foreign policy.

Oliver North's actions were a reflection of Reagan's own disdain for government and its balky checks and balances. Government, Reagan has often said, is not the solution but part of the problem. This anti-Washington, anti-government attitude that Reagan continued to champion even while residing in the White House and running the government helped to create the atmosphere that spawned North and Iran-Contra.

And Regan's landslide reelection win over Walter Mondale in the 1984 general election may have contributed to a sense that he and others at the White House had the mandate to do essentially whatever they pleased. Recalls Allan Myer, the former army officer who entered the NSC with North in 1981: "What made the NSC go operational? That's the wrong question. It had more to do with success begetting success. In November of 1984, forty-nine states went to Reagan. He was pissed he didn't get Minnesota . . . There was a sense of 'Maybe let's double the bet . . . Let's get bolder.'"

North's appreciation of the Reagan view of government had already been underscored by his Vietnam experience. This was also the case with Secord and some of his other private operatives. Privatization was actually an extension of the Reagan Administration philosophy that government is fundamentally ill equipped to do most things, and that the private sector is the hub of competence and efficiency.

Further, North's outside-the-system ethos reflected a popular cultural notion—exemplified in movies and various television crime shows—that legitimate authority is not always up to the job, and therefore it is necessary to turn to private patriots to kick ass. While the Iran-Contra committees may have preached that the ends don't justify the means, popular myth caters to a different premise.

North and the White House, using funds raised by American conservatives and foreign sultans, effectively charted and implemented a foreign policy they knew Congress would have shut down if it had known about it. That is why they kept it secret—not because they feared leaks. Perhaps no administration since JFK's worked the press harder and manipulated it more effectively than Ronald Reagan's, so North's and others' complaints about leaks never rang true. The issue of leaks was a red herring to deflect attention from the more fundamental issue of who should have the power to conduct foreign policy.

North essentially argued that when it came to covert operations, presidents should be permitted to waive compliance with laws requiring them to keep Congress informed. "Part of a covert operation," he testified at the hearings, "is to offer plausible deniability of the association of the government of the United States with the activity. Part of it is to deceive our adversaries. Part of it is to ensure that those people who are at great peril carrying out those activities are not further endangered. All of these are good and sufficient reasons to destroy documents." This was a pragmatic rationale for breaking the law.

Reagan's strong ideological bent, together with his *laissez-faire* style and his clear disinterest in substantive detail, fostered an environment where military men could flourish, fill vacuums and implement what Reagan either said he wanted done or signaled was his will. This created the operational, rather than the traditionally deliberative, NSC.

Poindexter's consistent testimony was that he knew the president well enough to feel confident Reagan would have approved of his actions, while North said he always assumed the president had approved his actions. Since Reagan has never condemned the actions of either man, and in fact still believes North is a national hero—even if he has qualified that characterization somewhat so as to apply mostly to his military record—there is ample reason to believe that Poindexter and North were correct in the assumptions they testified to.

While Reagan once admitted, probably under pressure from his advisors, that the "sale of arms got tangled up with the hostages," he has since insisted that it was never an arms-for-hostages trade. Reagan's memory may be selective. While he told three different stories to the Tower Commission and has been foggy on other aspects of the Iran-Contra affair, he is sharp as a tack when it comes to recalling his halcyon Hollywood days.

The *New Republic* reported in October of 1987 that when showed a picture of himself making a B-movie fifty years earlier, the Gipper immediately named the movie, *Sergeant Murphy,* supplied the plot and even remembered being tricked into riding a wayward horse one afternoon after filming was through for the day. When it came to Iran-Contra, he could not recall much of anything, but again denied that the Iran initiative was an arms-for-hostages trade.

The taking of control by North, Casey and Poindexter of two foreign policy initiatives as vital as the Iran and Contra programs, together with the systematic exclusion of Congress and even key cabinet members like Shultz and Weinberger, had all the elements of a junta or a *de facto* palace coup. Two Democrats on the Iran-Contra committees, Sen. Paul Sarbanes of Maryland and Sen. Sam Nunn of Georgia, have observed this, as have others, notably Theodore Draper, in a series of articles for the *New York Review of Books.*

"This junta was not a fully premeditated plot worked out by practiced conspirators," wrote Draper. "It arose by degrees because some high officials were so possessed by a determination to impose their own beliefs and policies on the country that they were willing to violate its most fundamental principles of government and to form a band of true believers bonded together against all those who did not agree with them. We usually think of a junta as planning to overthrow a president; this junta came into being to overthrow an established constitutional rule of law, with the help of a president."

The NSC, the chosen instrument of the junta, was given increased power in December of 1981 by Reagan's signing of Executive Order 12333, which made the NSC responsible for all intelligence activities. That order, ironically, rendered moot the argument that the Boland Ammendment did not apply to the NSC, and instead formed a basis for its activism.

Reagan's failure to step in and clearly resolve the fundamental differences of opinion over Iran-Contra between the North-Casey-McFarlane-Poindexter wing of his government and the pragmatic Shultz-Weinberger wing no doubt emboldened the action wing to step into the breach. Whether Reagan was ignorant of this, winked at it or actively aided and abetted it is, in the end, irrelevant. It happened, and it happened on his watch. If he didn't tilt or appear to tilt toward the junta, he nevertheless squelched any opposition to it.

North, as if he didn't already have a full enough plate with the Contras, was also given charge of the Iran initiative by McFarlane —thereby creating the opportunity to merge the two operations. Poindexter approved the merger.

Poindexter, like North, was unsuited to become national security advisor. He was a nuclear physics Ph.D. and career bureaucrat with little or no experience in foreign affairs. His primary qualifications were that he was deeply involved in both the Iran and Contra operations. So there was continuity. And where McFarlane had exhibited some uncertainty and qualms about his role, Poindexter showed none. His willingness to rip up the key December, 1985, finding and take the diversion hit for Reagan—together with his utter lack of regret or remorse at the hearings—all certified that.

Like any member of a junta, North often seemed to be more concerned with the enemy within than without. There was Ollie's January 14, 1986, message to Poindexter on Casey's seeing Weinberger as a threat: "Casey's view is that Cap will continue to create roadblocks until he is told by you that the President wants this to move NOW and that Cap will have to make it work." And North's February 27, 1986, message to McFarlane expressed sympathy for Poindexter: "My part in this was easy compared to his. I had only to deal with our enemies. He had to deal with the cabinet."

North's tragic flaw was that in his sincere zeal to promote democracy, he helped subvert it; in his desire to protect and defend the Constitution he swore to uphold, he trampled some of its most fundamental precepts.

The same might be said of Casey, who was North's kindred spirit and the soul of the junta. Their relationship seemed a perfect fit: Casey had a strong vision of what he wanted to do. He regarded Congress and much of his own CIA with contempt. North—ready for action in the NSC—was a means for Casey to work around the system. Though it never got geared up, the Casey-North, off-the-shelf, mini-CIA was the sheltered eye of the hurricane from which they could do battle against communism and the forces of evil in the world they both saw as so dangerous. It was to have been an unaccountable cocoon of righteousness, out of reach of prying bureaucrats, congressmen and reporters. And as North said, missing the point, it would not cost the taxpayers a cent.

North idolized Casey. Casey was much older, the product of a different war—a demonstrated winner—and a confidante of and direct link to Reagan. North, impressionable and always respectful of his elders, was willing and honored to do anything Casey asked of him. And in an NSC where there had been almost constant upheaval—four national security advisors in five years—North had as much loyalty to Casey as he did to any of his nominal bosses.

Casey and North together made a formidable team with more than enough clout to either roll over McFarlane and Poindexter or elicit passive—and occasionally active—cooperation from them. If Reagan were to make a cameo appearance, he could easily be manipulated.

North, it seemed, did not distinguish between lying to foreigners as part of an intelligence operation, and lying to Congress to prevent democratic accountability. That an operation was covert was reason enough for its existence. To justify the operation, or to try and reconcile it with the other needs of a democracy, seemed beyond North's realm of consideration or even comprehension.

It is true, or at least can be argued, that the stronger the democracy the less efficent a foreign policy is likely to be, the less likely that America will reassume her former role as Free World *gendarme*. But was the judgment of the cowboy clique—in deciding to sell arms to Iran, in pursuing war at all costs with the Sandinistas, and in substituting secrecy for foreign policy—better than that of the democratic purists who said no? Has the U.S. position in the world been weakened or strengthened as a result of Iran-Contra?

Clearly, most of what North did has to be judged a colossal failure.

Arms-for-hostages—in addition to being contrary to announced American policy to begin with—was always an uneven trade, because while the U.S. had the arms, the Iranians did not have the hostages: Hizballah did, and Tehran's influence over the terrorists was uncertain. And at this writing, there are more hostages in Beirut than when the initiative began. If anything, U.S.-Iranian relations are more strained now than before.

While North undeniably helped keep the Contras alive during the Boland prohibition, in the long run one wonders if he did not hurt their cause more than he helped it. And by the spring of 1988, despite North's and Reagan's best efforts, peace was threatening to break out in Central America. The Contras, tired of fighting, opted to sign a cease-fire agreement with the Sandinistas in March and enter into negotiations with their sworn enemies. As for the famous diversion, it actually provided only $3.5 million for the Contras, while at this writing another $8 million still languishes in Hakim and Secord's Swiss bank account.

More fundamentally, North seriously damaged the president he professed to love.

For in Ollie's world, not only the Congress, the press and the people were out of the loop, but the secretaries of state and defense were excluded as well. North and his people consistently ignored the democractic will of the majority.

"Before the vote, zeal may convince," wrote Leon Wieseltier, in a January, 1987, essay for the *New Republic* entitled "Democracy and Colonel North." "After the vote, zeal may corrupt. Of course the proudly procedural charter of the American system has its special frustrations. But it offers protection against precisely that thrilling sense of rightness, which over the centuries has caused more crimes and more abuses of power than parliamentarianism . . . To be sure, the colonel did not develop a theory for modifying the American way. He merely modified it. Now Rambo, now Gomer Pyle, he insulted the principle of law that constitutes the distinction between democracy and the lesser forms of public life . . . North's patriotism is plain, but it is hard to get too choked up about a man who would give his life for a country he cannot understand."

The Church Committee hearings produced four main tests to ensure that covert actions are compatible with democratic principles: first, that they should be consistent with open policies. (Would Reagan have been willing to declare publicly that he was selling arms to Iran?). Second, the Administration must itself have established procedures to review covert operations to ensure that a whole range of people are not cut out, as they were in Iran-Contra. Third, that the President cannot have "deniability"—thus the reason for signed "findings." Fourth is congressional review. All four tests were violated in the Iran-Contra affair.

"In a democracy, if you carry this to its logical extreme, you don't have a democracy anymore . . ." Senator Rudman told a television interviewer during the hearings. "Those are the important lessons that history will write about this entire event."

On March 16, 1988, North and Poindexter were indicted by a federal grand jury in the most sweeping criminal action taken against former White House officials since Watergate. Also charged were Secord and Hakim.

Only hours after his two former aides were indicted, President Reagan, in effect staging a diversion of his own, ordered 3,200 U.S. troops to Honduras to respond to a cross-border foray by Sandinistas against Contra base camps on Honduran soil. The American boys were back within ten days, after conducting their exercises some 100 miles from the border. But on the day it was announced, Reagan's dramatic statement had its no-doubt-intended effect of stealing some of Special Prosecutor Lawrence Walsh's thunder.

Of the twenty-three counts charged in the indictment, sixteen were against North. They alleged that he:

—conspired to defraud the United States by diverting profits from the Iranian arms sales to help arm the Contras, despite a ban on military aid at the time;

—stole government property (the proceeds of the arms sales);

—engaged in wire fraud in connection with the diversion;

—made false statements on four different occasions: three times to Congress and once to the attorney general;

—obstructed a congressional inquiry (three counts);

—obstructed a presidential inquiry;

—concealed, falsified or destroyed official documents;

—received an illegal gratuity (the security system from Secord);

—obstructed justice in trying to conceal receipt of the security system;

—converted for his personal use at least $4,300 of the more than $90,000 in traveler's checks obtained from Adolfo Calero;

—conspired to defraud the United States of tax revenue in the Spitz Channell Contra-fundraising operation.

Five days earlier McFarlane had pled guilty to four misdemeanor counts of withholding information from Congress, and agreed to serve as a prosecution witness against North and the three others.

If found guilty on all counts, North could face up to eighty-five years in prison and $4 million in fines.

The day of his indictment, North, dressed in uniform, held an emotional press conference at which he reasserted his innocence, noted that the Sandinistas were on the march again and cast himself as a constitutional martyr in the executive-legislative clash over control of foreign policy.

"It is a sad irony," he said, "that the decision to indict me should occur today, a day in which the communists in Nicaragua invaded their democratic neighbor, a day which is the fourth anniversary of the abduction of William Buckley, and the third anniversary of the kidnapping of Terry Anderson, two of the American hostages we tried so hard to rescue...

"The indictment is also sad for our country, for all the men and women who work to protect it and to make our government work. It is a particularly painful thing to my wife Betsy, our four children and me. Throughout my service as a Marine officer, I have always done my very best, often working night and day to get the job done, and to do so honorably. I am proud of my service to our country and those with whom I served, both in the Marine Corps and on the National Security Council.

"Unfortunately, I have now been caught in a bitter dispute between the Congress and the president to deter communism in Central America, and the president's duty to protect our citizens against terrorist acts abroad. It is a shame that the new battleground for such a fight will be the courtroom. I did not commit any crime. I intend to fight any allegations of wrongdoing for as long as necessary... I will never give up. We will win."

Just two days later, North, this time dressed in a business suit, called another press conference, and announced that he was retiring from the Marine Corps. The retirement had been expected since he would have twenty years in as of May, and in light of the Iran-Contra affair his prospects in the Corps seemed less than bright. Accumulated leave gave him full credit for his twenty years of service so that he could retire immediately.

In light of his indictment, North said it was inappropriate to remain in the Marines any longer because he would likely have to subpoena "the highest ranking officials" in the Reagan Administration in preparation for his defense. "That strikes me as a course of action incompatible with my continued service as a Marine officer," North said, his voice cracking with emotion as he stood next to an American flag in his lawyer's office.

"Accordingly, with great sadness, I have tendered my request to retire from the Marine Corps. I thank you, God bless you and *Semper Fidelis*. I love the United States Marine Corps and the courageous brothers in arms that I have served with."

Lawyers for North and the others promised to file a barrage of motions challenging the prosecution on numerous fronts—motions which threatened to delay the trial until after the November, 1988, election, if not derail it altogether. The two key legal issues to be resolved before a trial could get under way were North's challenge to the constitutionality of special prosecutor Walsh's appointment, and the issue of taint—whether Walsh gathered his evidence outside of the congressional hearings, as required, since all four men indicted had testified at the hearings under immunity. Named to preside over the trial was U.S. District Judge Gerhard Gesell, age seventy-seven, who more than a decade ago was the judge in the so-called plumbers portion of the Watergate case.

And, of course, looming in the background was the possibility that President Reagan might pardon some or all of the defendants. A New York *Times*–CBS poll taken after the indictment showed that 64 percent of Americans opposed a pardon for North before a trial. There was an even split—43 percent for and 43 percent against—on the question of whether North should be pardoned if he was convicted after a trial.

Many believed Reagan telegraphed his intentions on March 25 —nine days after the indictment—when, in highly unusual public comments regarding a pending trial, he said he did not think any of the four were guilty of a crime. Of his favorite Marine, the president added: "I still think Ollie North is a hero."

CHAPTER NOTES

PHILMONT

—On page 19, the quote from the man wearing the VFW hat appeared in the Philadelphia *Inquirer,* August 16, 1987.

—On page 25, North at the Brigitte Bardot film comes from Rolling Stone, July 16–30, 1987.

ANNAPOLIS

—On page 40, the ritual of "getting the brick" is described in *A Sense of Honor* by James Webb, Bantam Books, 1982, pp. 220–222.

On page 44, the account of President Kennedy speaking at the Naval Academy is based on the New York *Times,* August 2, 1963.

—On page 59, the quote from Rev. Laboon first appeared in the Chicago *Tribune,* March 8, 1987.

—On page 64, the quote from Jeffrey Dumas, appeared in the Baltimore *Sun,* May 15, 1983.

THE CORPS

—On page 97, the quote from the former Quantico instructor who disliked North comes from the Washington *Post,* December 24, 1986.

—On page 109, Michael Hedges of the Washington *Times* also contributed to the Hugh Aynesworth story.

THE WHITE HOUSE

—On page 132, the Miami *Herald*'s story about North's work at FEMA appeared on July 5, 1987. North denied at the Iran-Contra hearings that he had helped draft a plan that would suspend the constitution. Senate Chairman Daniel Inouye (D-Hawaii), cut off an attempt by Rep. Jack Brooks (D-Texas) to delve further into North's FEMA work, saying it was classified.

CENTRAL AMERICA

—On page 140, the quote from one of Casey's CIA colleagues—"It was like he was hydroplaning on the way to the nursing home"—comes from *With the Contras: A Reporter in the Wilds of Nicaragua* by Christopher Dickey, Simon and Schuster Inc., New York, 1987. Page 101.

—Page 158. Jefferson Morley, writing in the New Republic on May 25, 1987, first discussed the role of the conference with respect to North and the Iran-contra affair.

GRENADA

—On page 174, Casey's quote—"Hey, fuck it. Let's dump the bastards"—comes from *Veil*, by Bob Woodward, Simon and Schuster Inc., New York, 1987, page 289.

BODY & SOUL

—On page 193, some of the detail of McFarlane's session with Bandar comes from Woodward, page 353.

BLUE RINSE, HAM HOCKS & DOGS

—On page 225, the quote from E. Thomas Clagett comes from the Washington *Post*, March 12, 1987.

—On page 235, the author was assisted in deciphering North's flow chart by a special issue of Executive Intelligence Review, April 1987, pp. 8–10.

—On page 237, the text of the Channel commercial is quoted from "The Contra Lobby," by Peter Kornbluh, *Village Voice*, October 13, 1987.

THE SOUTHERN FRONT

—Page 259. According to the report of the congressional Iran-Contra committees, Secord's commission averaged thirty-eight percent.

ACHILLE LAURO

—Page 292. North's dealings with Simhoni were first reported in "The Ollie We Knew," by David Halevy and Neil Livingstone in *The Washingtonian*, July, 1987. This article broke new ground on the Israeli role in the Achille Lauro affair. Simhoni, in an interview with the author, confirmed most details cited by the article on his and Israel's role.

—Page 293. North's quote—"Uri, where are the four thugs?"—comes from *The Washingtonian*.

—Page 293. Details of the NSA intercepts come from Woodward, page 415.

—Page 296. Details of the plane interception come from *Newsweek*, October 21, 1985.

IRAN-CONTRA

—Page 348. Reagan saying he would take the heat if Khadafy was killed comes from Woodward, page 412.

—Page 348. Mubarak's quote to Poindexter was reported in the Washington *Post*, February 20, 1987.

—Page 349. NSA satellite intercept comes from Woodward, page 444.

—Page 352. The quote attributed to North from a former NSC staffer comes from "Target Khadafy," by Seymour Hersh, New York *Times Magazine*, February 22, 1987.

—Page 353. The supposed confrontation between North and Admiral Crowe comes from Hersh in the Times magazine article, February 22, 1987.

OLLIE'S WORLD

—Pages 541 and 542. The quote from Jack Wheeler comes from the Washington *Post*, December 26, 1986.

INDEX